Fusion of Cu

GW01034820

Cross / Cultures

Readings in the Post/Colonial Literatures in English

26

Series Editors:

Gordon
Collier
(Giessen)

Hena
Maes-Jelinek
(Liège)

Geoffrey
Davis
(Aachen)

Amsterdam - Atlanta, GA 1996

FUSION OF CULTURES?

Edited by

Peter O. Stummer

and

Christopher Balme

ASNEL Papers 2

Typography and layout: Gordon Collier

∞ The paper on which this book is printed meets the requirements of "ISO 9706:1994, Information and documentation - Paper for documents - Requirements for permanence".

CIP-GEGEVENS KONINKLIJKE BIBLIOTHEEK, DEN HAAG

Fusion of cultures?

Fusion of cultures? (ASNEL papers 2) /
ed. by Peter O. Stummer and Christopher Balme. — Amsterdam - Atlanta, GA 1996 : Rodopi. — (Cross/Cultures, 26 ; ISSN 0924-1426 ; ASNEL papers 2)
Teksten in het Engels.
ISBN: 90-420-0044-9 (bound)
ISBN: 90-420-0043-0 (paper)
NUGI 951
Trefw.: post-koloniale engelstalige letterkunde ; tekstanalyse.

ASNEL Papers are produced under the auspices of
the Association for the Study of the New Literatures in English
in German-Speaking Countries
(GNEL — Gesellschaft für die Neuen Englischsprachigen Literaturen e.V.)

©Editions Rodopi B.V., Amsterdam - Atlanta, GA 1996
Printed in The Netherlands

TABLE OF CONTENTS

vi

ACKNOWLEDGEMENTS

"I Don't Care if Your Nanny Was Black," first published in *Possibilities: Literary Arts Magazine* 1.3 (1993): 54. by permission of the author.

"Epitaph," first published in *Native Song* (Laurencetown Beach, Nova Scotia: Pottersfield Press, 1990): 71-72. by permission of the author.

Frontispiece: *Between the Tree and the Moon* (1993) by the Nigerian artist Rufus Ogundele, in the possession of Peter O. Stummer; by permission of the artist.

All the photographs by Peter O. Stummer.

ILLUSTRATIONS

*R*ufus Ogundele, *Between the Tree and the Moon* (1993; collection of Peter O. Stummer). Photo: Peter O. Stummer.

INTRODUCTION

T HE MAJORITY OF THE ESSAYS collected in this volume originated in the
sixteenth conference of the Association for the Study of the New Literatures
in English on the "Fusion of Cultures?" held at the University of Munich in
September 1993.

The intention in organising the event had indeed been to transgress the received
wisdom of recently established post-colonial orthodoxy with its emphasis on difference and alterity, on subversion and counter-discourse. Writers such as Ama Ata
Aidoo and Festus Iyayi, though belonging to two different generations, will equally
insist that they are not for the life of them able to perceive where the "post-" in
"post-colonial" should at present come from. Of course, we did not want to return to
notions of "World Fiction"[1] and be landed again with some kind of blue-eyed cosmopolitan global harmony. On the contrary, with Sivanandan's IMFundamentalism
very much in mind, we suggested the investigation of diaspora and the historicity of
homogeneity-constructions. We were interested in the politics of terminology, and
advocated a reconsideration of syncretism, cross-fertilisation, and creolisation, as
well as of comparative studies.

The alleged end of the Enlightenment project with its concomitant abandonment
of the concept of progress had, to all appearances, nonetheless left the
developed/underdeveloped divide unaffected.[2] Nor was this restricted to the
economic sphere only, as incidents connected with the editing of an anthology of
South Pacific writing seemed no doubt to indicate.[3] Nor had the political climate in
the West changed for the better – far from it; it had significantly deteriorated, with a
considerable increase in racially motivated violence, arson and murder. If the
travelling academic happened to be black, the probability of him or her being taken
for just another unwanted asylum-seeker tended to be very high at the German
border. It became apparent that postmodernism in its exaggerated relativism had
subliminally taken a lot of civilised behaviour for granted and was shocked to find
that this was far from being the case. In such a context a continuous emphasis on
difference can easily become a grievous fault when the spirit of equality and the
renunciation of hegemony cannot be guaranteed to accompany it.

Hans Magnus Enzenberger's attack on the "hollowness of human-rights
universalism" could perhaps be seen as a symptom of resigned retreat, if not as

---

[1] *TIME* (8 February 1993): 50–55.

[2] Cf B. McGrance, *Beyond Anthropology: Society and the Other* (New York: Columbia UP, 1989).

[3] The controversy between Albert Wendt and C.K. Stead, or, more accurately Faber's insensitivity about
latent eurocentric criteria for the selection of contemporary stories, which led to the withdrawal of writers
such as Grace, Hulme, Ihimaera. For a more detailed discussion of the issue, see Rod Edmond, *Wasafiri* 20
(Autumn 1994): 73–76.

cynicism, but others have actually used progressive jargon to hide their cultural combativeness, as was the case with Alain de Benoît, who has wilfully subscribed to the idea of difference, only to promote the old idea of French cultural nationalism,[4] or as with Samuel Huntington in the United States, who has belligerently proclaimed a renewal of the Cold War,[5] but with other players, and along purely cultural lines.

Yet the practice of what Edouard Glissant preaches as "cross-culture identity" instead of "single-root identity"[6] can be seen in many instances. In Great Britain, for instance, we have a writer such as Robert Crawford, who stresses the multilinguistic and multicultural nature of Scottish writing, in that it combines English, Scots and Gaelic;[7] we have Barry Anderson and his EKOME dance company from Bristol, where British elements are intertwined with traditions trom the Caribbean and from Ghana; or, similarly, the Bhangra group NACHDA SANSAAR from Birmingham, where Indian rural traditions are widely used and modified; or, for that matter, the theatre of Alex Mukulu and his group IMPACT INT. in Uganda, who use music, dance and folklore for a theatre that entertains but also comments on political life. This is very much akin to what Bode Sowande does with his ODU THEMES in Nigeria or Merle Collins, together with AFRICAN DAWN, in Great Britain.

Writers like Shirley Lim, Smaro Kamboureli, Witi Ihimaera, Bode Sowande, Merle Collins and John Figueroa – all present at the Fusion of Cultures? conference – demonstrate in their writing what it is like to operate from a multiple background, although they do not go in for any extra label of self-characterisation as does the African–Canadian George Elliot Clarke from Nova Scotia, who quite explicitly calls himself an Africadian.[8]

To keep in mind Henry Louis Gates, Jr.'s dictum that all cultural purity is nothing but a myth seems to be more difficult than one would have thought. So one can only try and heed the timely warning that difference needs always to be defined against common experience,[9] that some recent insistence on difference comes dangerously close to nineteenth-century colonial rationalisation,[10] and that the recent rage in the United States for "diversity facilitators" has not only been widely counterproductive, in adding "yet another coating of mandatory sanctimony to a society that already has trouble talking about things frankly and honestly,"[11] but has

---

4 Richard Herzinger, "Der neue Kulturnationalismus," *Die Zeit* 34 (20 August 1993): 40.

5 Herzinger, "Der neue Kulturnationalismus," 40.

6 In an interview with Michael Dash, *Caribbean Review of Books* 5 (August 1992): 17–19; 19.

7 *Literature Matters* 11 (September 1992): 4.

8 *Possibilities: Literary Arts Magazine* 1.3 (1993).

9 Observation made by Tony Dunn at Warwick University in May 1994 on the occasion of the 4th British Studies Colloquium.

10 As argued in Robert J.C. Young, *Colonial Desire: Hybridity in Theory, Culture and Race* (London: Routledge, 1994).

11 Richard Bernstein, in *Dictatorship of Virtue: Multiculturalism and the Battle for America's Future* [1994], as quoted by Richard Rorty in "A Leg-up for Oliver North," *London Review of Books* (20 October 1994): 13, 15.

also provided a sideshow of sorts for the likes of William Bennett and Alan Bloom to camouflage their real concerns behind the smoke-screens of multiculturalism and political-correctness criticism.

The contributors to this volume, then, do not aim so much to deconstruct various kinds of serviceable Other (although this often occurs, too), as attempt to walk the tightrope between unduly muting and excessively highlighting difference.[12]

Not surprisingly, a conference-title of this interrogative nature attracted a heterogenous range of contributions. Nevertheless, clear focal points of dialogue formed, which the editors have tried to re-focus under a set of thematic headings.

An important topic of discussion was the terminological framework within which to speak of cultural fusion. Among a number of competing terms such as fusion, hybridity, and cross-fertilisation, syncretism attracted a wide variety of applications. Christopher Balme delves into the history of the term, elucidating its heritage in religious studies and cultural anthropology, and examining more recent applications in literary criticism and theatre studies. He concludes that syncretism today, as a concept in modern scholarly discourse, has undergone complete revalorisation from its pejorative overtones of cultural impurity in the nineteenth century to a positive term denoting inventiveness, creativity and balanced inter-cultural transfer. Applications of the term to specific fields of artistic endeavour can be found in Bode Sowande's discussion of what he calls the "syncretic aesthetics" of modern Nigerian theatre, which encompasses the popular Yoruba Travelling theatre of Herbert Ogunde as well as the "high-brow" texts of Wole Soyinka, Ola Rotimi, Femi Osofisan and Sowande himself. Flora Veit–Wild surveys syncretism in Southern African writing and the performing arts, including in her discussion popular forms such as dub poetry. Inspired by Wilson Harris, Uwe Schäfer identifies syncretism as the central poetological principle underlying both Harris's own novels and those of Bessie Head, defining its fundamental dynamic of negotiating between disparate elements as "a prerequisite for poetic imagination and creativity." Peter Stummer concentrates on the fate of both cultural products and writers as they attempt to negotiate and cross cultural boundaries. He looks at the fate of Australian films in Germany; Black American writers in Africa and, finally, examples of successful artistic fusion in the field of music.

The second section focuses on questions of diasporic identities and on writers possessing or negotiating between these. A striking feature of post-colonial writing is the ever-increasing number of "hyphenated" identities mediating between two or even more cultures. West Indians in New York or Toronto, Hong-Kong Chinese in London, Indians living in America: the biographies of Salman Rushdie, Paule Marshall, Timothy Mo, Maxine Hong Kingston, and Bharati Mukherjee – all these are living interrogations of definitional categories based on national identity.

---

12 This metaphor is also employed by Edward E. Sampson in *Celebrating the Other: A Dialogic Account of Human Nature* (New York: Harvester Wheatsheaf, 1993): 147; Sampson, on the whole, somewhat optimistically advocates "[undistorted] dialogism" (my addition).

Consequently, it is not surprising that these writers attracted considerable attention. The novels of Paule Marshall, a first-generation American born of Barbadian immigrants, are read by Bernard Melchior and by Margaret Keulen against the background of her mediative cross-cultural project. Shirley Geok–lin Lim reads Timothy Mo's novels (himself a Hong-Kong Chinese, educated and now resident in Britain) as reconfigurations of the diasporic subject under the adverse conditions of enforced diasporic collectivity. Transcultural identities also form the central focus of studies by Sämi Ludwig and Walter Göbel, who deal with the writing of Bharati Mukherjee. Born and raised in Calcutta, Mukherjee moved to Canada in her early adult life and has now settled in the USA. Ludwig also draws parallels with the work of Maxine Hong Kingston, a Chinese–American author.

Given its past colonial history and present post-colonial predicament, it is not surprising that Africa and writing from and about it should form a major contribution to the topic of cultural fusion. As a "dark" continent which was literary "mapped out" by European imperial powers in the late nineteenth century in a Berlin conference room, it is apposite that Africa should figure at the start of this section in a study of Western writing from that period. Detlev Gohrbandt reads the popular novels of R.M. Ballantyne, author of juvenile fiction for impressionable young Victorian and early-twentieth-century males. Gohrbandt shows how the iconographic and linguistic maps of the dark continent created in Ballantyne's novels were basically reflexive, referring more to home than abroad. Moving forward to the 1930s, Tobias Döring re-evaluates the textual strategies at work in the semi-autobiographical novel *Africa Answers Back* by the Ugandan scholar Akiki Nyabongo. Döring shows how this hitherto underrated work not only reverses but also, in Homi Bhabha's sense of colonial mimicry, "rehearses" patterns of colonial discourse. Thomas Brückner devotes his attention to fusions of oral forms in the African novel. When one thinks of Amos Tuotola and Chinua Achebe, then this is certainly one of the earliest and privileged fields of formal syncretism in europhone African writing. Less formal innovation seems to be evident in the particular thematic genre of Zimbabwean war-fiction. Although represented by protagonists from both sides of the conflict, these novels reveal few typically post-colonial traits; Wolfgang Hochbruck ascertains instead, in contemporary Zimbabwean literature as a whole and war-fiction in particular, a "continuing colonialism of the mind."

A genre which is attracting an increasing amount of critical attention is that of autobiography and life-history among Native peoples. Often written in collaboration with white authors, these texts reveal a typical post-colonial hybridity, as the authorial subject is no longer monolithic but plural. Intercultural authorship has been accepted as a genre characteristic and is reflective of new creative tensions. This issue becomes even more complex when the life-histories are of and by Canadian Métis, an ethnic group issuing from intermarriage between European explorers, trappers, settlers and Cree or Ojibway women. Armando E. Jannetta discovers in the life-histories of Métis people a double consciousness and double-voiced discourse moving along a continuum of racial identities and relationships. Autobiography of a different kind is treated by Werner Sedlak in his discussion of prison memoirs by African writers (Ngugi wa Thiong'o, Molefe Pheto and Wole Soyinka). But, even in this highly focused genre, Sedlak finds a link with the conference-theme, for all three writers reflect on a culture of resistance which is syncretic in nature, appropriating as they do, for their critical social and political analyses, Greek, Christian and African elements.

Prison-memoirs make it clear that cultural fusion is not just a question of formal and aesthetic play but is frequently linked to concrete political issues and agendas. Perhaps the most international of political discussions issuing from a post-colonial text is the aftermath of the *fatwa* placed on Salman Rushdie because of his novel *The Satanic Verses*. Rather than re-stating the diplomatic responses to this act, Frank Schulze–Engler undertakes a searching re-evaluation of the theoretical premises underpinning the ambivalent reaction of some prominent post-colonial critics to Rushdie, the crisis, and his novel. He uncovers a set of "crypto-normative" (Jürgen Habermas) values underlying not just the specific critique by Gayatri Spivak, Tim Brennan and others of Rushdie but of their post-colonial theory in general, which re-introduces new essentialisms while combatting old ones. While the discussion of multiculturalism in the USA may not have the spectacular international re-percussions of the Rushdie case, it nevertheless places questions of cultural fusion, coexistence or dysfunction in a political arena. Berndt Ostendorf points out that the multiculturalism debate is one that first emerged at universities, where it was recognised that a hiatus had emerged between educational theory and social practice. Ostendorf argues that this site of debate was not just by chance, but was a logical result of the fact that higher education is today the sole path to high-paying positions in US society. Multiculturalism is thus a question of political praxis, of the inequitable distribution of educational resources, and not one of arcane theoretical (re)positioning. Whether primarily through immigration, as in the USA, or through conquest or slavery, New-World societies are all characterised by varying degrees of cultural fusion. Petronella Breinburg discusses the creolised forms in Surinam as an extreme case in point. With reference to Winti culture and the Sranan language, she demonstrates the simultaneity of cultural fusion and the existence of two parallel cultures.

As in most Caribbean societies, the cultural fusion or heterogeneity of Surinam is the result of waves of European conquest, slavery, indentured labour and changing linguistic power-struggles. Derek Walcott is perhaps the Caribbean writer who has given most articulate expression to this ambivalent heritage, in poems, plays and essays. In his opening address to the conference, reprinted here, John Figueroa follows the weft and woof of Walcott's *Omeros* against the backdrop of a many-cultured St Lucia, looking into the interdependence between going places and being displaced, of combining the heroic of epic tradition with the fortune and misfortune of ordinary people. After reviewing literary treatments of the Haitian revolution within and beyond the Caribbean, Gordon Collier re-reads Walcott's creative preoccupation with this historical moment, arguing for a re-evaluation of his early verse-play *Henri Christophe* in terms of its intertextual strategies and its crucial position in the development of Walcott's dramatic voice and oeuvre, and setting it against shifts of linguistic and dramaturgical revealed in the playwright's later commissioned approaches to Caribbean history.

The link between gender studies and post-colonial criticism has received a good deal of attention in recent years, so it was interesting that gender issues did not loom so large in our discussions as might have been expected. One writer, however, who explicitly links issues of gender and culture, particularly the tensions between different intracultural models, is the Zimbabwean writer Tsitsi Dangarembga, whose novel *Nervous Conditions* was the subject of two papers. Heike Härting compares this novel with Margaret Atwood's *The Edible Woman* and finds common ground, in that both provide "medical histories of colonialism," insofar as womens' bodies can be seen as a space of colonisation, whatever the political order. The scholarly team of Torti/Kilb/Stein likewise applies gender theory to Dangarembga's novel, interrogating issues of identity against the background of the post-structuralist discussion of the concept of identity.

Conference participant Cliff Watego maintained that the question-mark was the most important element in the conference-title, because, from an Aboriginal Australian point of view, what mattered was really how to respond to "cultural white-out." Watego's remark focused attention on the major difficulty inherent in the post-colonial critical project, which is to find any kind of common ground for the enormous diversities of cultures and historical experiences subsumed under this designation. Although forms of cultural fusion, creolisation and syncretism were generally treated by contributors in a positive sense, the conference-topic was seldom questioned in a fundamental way. Nevertheless, Watego's comment should be borne in mind, in the sense that cultural fusion can very quickly turn into cultural effacement. It is the difficult balancing-act of combining cultural difference and tension as a source of creativity without reintroducing new cultural hegemonies that writers and scholars have to address.

PETER STUMMER

❧ ❖ ❧

W iti Ihimaera
(Munich, September 1993; photo Peter Stummer)

S maro Kamboureli
(Munich, September 1993; photo Peter Stummer)

CHRISTOPHER BALME

Inventive Syncretism
The Concept of the Syncretic
in Intercultural Discourse

With expanded communication and intercultural influence, people interpret others, and themselves, in a bewildering diversity of idioms – a global condition of what Mikhail Bakhtin called "heteroglossia." This ambiguous, multivocal world makes it increasingly hard to conceive of human diversity as inscribed in bounded independent, cultures. Difference is an effect of inventive syncretism.[1]

I N THIS STATEMENT THE HISTORIAN, anthropologist and cultural critic James Clifford articulates the essence of what he terms the "predicament of culture." Clear lines of demarcation between cultures, which existed when the discipline of ethnography came into existence in the nineteenth century, are becoming increasingly difficult to distinguish in an internationalised world of mass communication and information exchange. Significant for the present observations is the final sentence, which expresses the notion of "inventive syncretism." Clifford is undertaking in this formulation a reassessment and revalorisation of a hitherto perjorative term. In the conceptual world of the nineteenth and early twentieth century, clear cultural boundaries were essential for cementing identity, and expressed notions of difference and even superiority vis-à-vis other nations and cultures. In this world-view, which encapsulates the essence of colonialism in both its paternalistic and aggressive, exploitive manifestations, any suggestion of mingling and interchange was synonymous with dilution, deracination and breakdown.[2] *Inventive syncretism,* on the other hand, assumes a view of cultural change that is fundamentally dynamic, that presupposes openness and a creative utilisation of disparate, heterogeneous cultural products. Syncretism can thus be reinterpreted as one of the positive results of what has been the fundamentally destructive process of direct or indirect colonisation and cultural imposition.

In the following comments I wish to provide a sketch of the way in which this paradigmatic shift has come about in several disciplines that use the concept of

---

[1] James Clifford, *The Predicament of Culture: Twentieth Century Ethnography, Literature, and Art* (Cambridge MA: Harvard UP, 1988): 22–23.

[2] For a discussion of nineteenth-century English attitudes to cultural and racial mixing, and in particular the concept of hybridity as it shifts from a biological to a cultural paradigm, see Robert J.C. Young, *Colonial Desire: Hybridity in Theory, Culture and Race* (London: Methuen, 1995).

syncretism. Through this necessarily brief piece of intellectual history I also hope to show why the term syncretism is applicable to the processes of cultural mixing that pertain in the field of literary studies.

Syncretism: etymology and application

The etymology of the term syncretism is uncertain. It probably goes back to a coinage introduced by Plutarch: *sugkretismos*, meaning union of the Cretans.[3] The term reappears in the writings of Erasmus, particularly in *Corpus reformatorum*, in which he urges the Humanists to abandon their internal disputes and to form a common front against the danger posed by the antihumanist movements. In this sense, syncretism came to mean in the sixteenth and seventeenth centuries the fusing of philosophical or religious doctrine and took on the connotation of doctrinal confusion. The term retained this somewhat pejorative taint into the nineteenth century, when it was adopted by the emerging discipline of religious historiography to describe various manifestations of religious fusion, particularly in the Hellenistic period, when Greek and Roman belief-systems merged. From the nineteenth century onwards, historians of religion used the term more or less consciously in this pejorative sense to designate "hybrid," "impure" religious phenomena deriving from a combination of religions, which corresponded therefore to a state of decadence and reflected the inability of certain religions to exist "dans la rigueur de leurs formes constitutives."[4] The following definition by the religious historian James Moffatt, which appeared in 1921, provides a succinct summary of this usage, although free here of pejorative undertones:

> "Syncretism" denotes generally an unconscious, wide-spread tendency, due to or fostered by some re-adjustment of political relationships or by some clash of civilisations. There is a blending of religious ideas or practices, by means of which either one set adopts more or less thoroughly the principles of another or both are amalgamated in a more cosmopolitan and less polytheistic shape.[5]

Moffatt limits his investigation of the term to the ancient world and the rise of Christianity in the first centuries AD and to the influence of other religions and cults on its development. There is, however, no mention in his article of the syncretic cults and religions of the New World.

With the establishment in the Twenties and Thirties of the new discipline of comparative religion and a phenomenological approach to religious studies, the term "syncretism" was expanded to cover such phenomena as Voodoo, the popular

---

[3] Cf Plutarch, *De fraterno amore* XIX: "for, although the Cretans were frequently at faction and feud with one another, they became reconciled and united whenever a foreign foe attacked them. This they called 'syncretism'." Cited in: *Encyclopaedia of Religions and Ethics* (Edinburgh, 1921), vol. 12: 155.

[4] *Encyclopaedia Universalis 17* (Paris: Encyclopaedia Universalis, 1985): 539. The religious historian Carsten Colpe has documented the pejorative use of "syncretism": "The first application of the term to a situation in the history of religions probably occurred in an anonymous review (of an edition of Minucius Felix) that appeared in *Fraser's Magazine for Town and Country* (London, 1853) vol. 47: 294." *The Encyclopedia of Religion*, ed. Mircea Eliade (New York: Macmillan, 1987), vol. 14: 218.

[5] James Moffatt, "Syncretism," *Encyclopaedia of Religions and Ethics* (Edinburgh, 1921), vol. 12: 156.

religion of Haiti, as well as many other cult-practices in the Caribbean which were beginning to attract the interest of ethnographers. Syncretism was compared and contrasted with "conversion" as one of the centrally dynamic forms of religious contact, but, unlike conversion, which in its apostolic and missionary zeal tends to downgrade the values of the belief-systems encountered, syncretism is based on mutual respect and reciprocal exchange of values and beliefs.[6]

Since the Sixties there has been a considerable surge of interest in syncretism among scholars of comparative and historical religion. A series of symposia with accompanying proceedings have all recognised the terminological imprecision with which the concept is applied. The most systematic attempt to date to provide a broadly based theoretical model for syncretism in both historical and systematic religious studies has been made by Ulrich Berner.[7] Berner's point of departure is Luhmann's theory of systems:

> Syncretism can be comprehended as one of the possible reactions to a situation of uncertainty caused by the encounter of different systems: it is a reaction which pursues the goal of suspending this uncertainty by removing the borders of the systems and thereby removing the situation of competition between the systems.[8]

Concepts such as "uncertainty" and religions as competing systems have application to wider situations of culture-contact which the processes of colonialism and missionisation brought with them. However, Berner shows hardly even passing interest in such examples of syncretism, illustrating his model instead with a case-study from the early period of Christianity.[9]

Despite Berner's attempts at systematisation, it is clear that even in the area of religious studies, where the term has long been established and has gained a certain currency, syncretism is used to designate a very broad range of phenomena. In a recent review and discussion of the subject, the religious historian Carsten Colpe comes to the conclusion that without a specific context a precise definition is not possible. It is possible, however, "to use the concept of syncretism as a category of historico-genetic explanation."[10] At the end of his wide-ranging survey of various applications, Colpe re-states the fundamentally positive valorisation of syncretism, especially in its reflection of tolerance and intellectual vigour:

---

[6] This is the thesis of R. Pettazoni, "Sincretismo e conversione," *Saggi di storia delle religioni e mitologia* (Rome, 1946): 143–51. A similar thesis is advanced by the Dutch scholar G. van der Leeuw, *Phänomenologie der Religion* (Tübingen, 1933), paragraph 25.

[7] See Ulrich Berner, "Heuristisches Modell der Synkretismus-Forschung," in *Synkretismusforschung: Theorie und Praxis*, ed. Gernot Wiesner (Göttinger Orientforschungen 1; Wiesbaden: Harrassowitz, 1978) and Ulrich Berner, *Untersuchungen zur Verwendung des Synkretismus-Begriffes* (Göttinger Orientforschungen 2; Wiesbaden: Harrassowitz, 1982). The latter contains a detailed survey of research and discussion of the various symposia.

[8] Berner, "Heuristisches Modell," 12.

[9] Berner analyses the syncretistic elements in the teachings of the Greek theologian Origenes (185–253 AD); cf Berner, *Untersuchungen zur Verwendung des Synkretismus-Begriffes*.

[10] Colpe, "Syncretism," 219.

> A tolerant attitude to all that is of value in the world is thus a basic condition for the rise of any syncretism, as well as a basic virtue of the human being who is shaped by syncretism and in turn supports it. In addition, however, an enormous intellectual power is required in order to cement all the elements together into a new type of tradition and, further, to maintain the combination of the erudite and the popular.[11]

Syncretism and cultural reinterpretation

Colpe's notion of syncretism as intellectual reshaping shows that the term has application far beyond the borders of comparative religion. Indeed, it has also found use by cultural anthropologists in very much the same way to characterise a specific form of cultural reinterpretation.

> Reinterpretation marks all aspects of cultural change. It is the process by which old meanings are ascribed to new elements or by which new values change the cultural significance of old forms. It operates internally, from generation to generation, no less than in integrating a borrowed element into a receiving culture. Syncretism is one form of reinterpretation.[12]

This observation by the American anthropologist Melville J. Herskovits, published in 1956, marks an important step in the process of methodological reassessment among cultural anthropologists. Hitherto their interest had been focused primarily on societies which were still more or less "untouched" or strongly resistant to westernisation. The great studies in functionalist anthropology by Bronislaw Malinowski and E. Evans–Pritchard were preoccupied with apparently static social systems, and placed emphasis on "systems in balance, on social homeostasis, and on timeless structural pictures," as the anthropologist Clifford Geertz has observed.[13] It is little wonder, then, that Herskovits, who carried out extensive field work in Haiti, should begin to question such homeostatic, functionalist models and find them inadequate to explain what had happened, and was still happening, in a syncretic society such as Haiti. The examples of syncretic reinterpretation that Herskovits cites are drawn almost entirely from the realm of religious practices: the New World cults such as Voodoo in Haiti, *candomblé* in Brazil, and Shango in Trinidad.

The revalorisation and expanded application of the term syncretism in ethnographic discourse goes hand in hand with a fundamental reassessment of the precepts underpinning the discipline. Most importantly, the very notion of cultural anthropology as a science with immutable laws has been radically questioned over the past two decades. An articulate exponent of such methodological self-interrogation is Clifford Geertz, who has proposed a semiotic, interpretative view of cultural analysis.[14]

---

11 Colpe, "Syncretism," 226–27.

12 Melville J. Herskovits, *Man and his Works: The Science of Cultural Anthropology* (New York: Alfred A. Knopf, 1956): 553.

13 Clifford Geertz, *The Interpretation of Cultures: Selected Essays* (New York: Basic Books, 1973): 143.

14 "believing with Max Weber, that man is an animal suspended in webs of significance he himself has spun, I take culture to be those webs, and the analysis of it to be therefore not an experimental science in search of a law but an interpretative one in search of meaning." Clifford Geertz, *Interpretation of Cultures:*, 5.

Instead of globalising, functionalist accounts of cultures, Geertz proposes a micro-perspective – what he terms "thick description."[15] In an essay on ritual and social change in Java, Geertz is able to demonstrate on the basis of a case-study the destabilisation of an intact, functioning syncretic religious system under the influence of westernisation, Islamic fundamentalism and other ideological pressures. In this example, a situation of "balanced syncretism," as he terms it, provides the basis for "cultural homogeneity," which is in the process of being undermined by rapid social and ideological changes.[16] Important here is the positive valorisation that Geertz attributes to the term "syncretism" – it is used in conjunction with expressions such as "balanced" and "homogeneity" – and that a functioning syncretic society is in fact the point of departure and the end product of social upheaval. Geertz describes the mini-crisis of a funeral where no one knew precisely which rite should be performed and who should oversee it. The crisis resulted in an intense religious debate among the participants and reflection on the very precepts behind the belief-systems of the community. The image Geertz creates is one of a patchwork quilt which literally begins to come apart at the seams.

By analogy, one could extrapolate that, in general, cultures which find themselves in a process of rapid change, crisis, and acculturation are continually involved, consciously or unconsciously, in similar processes of reinterpretation; there is constant re-evaluation of cultural practices, in the course of which "webs of significance" are re-formed and redefined. In the realm of literature and art, writers and artists involved in creating and working in syncretic processes are having to refashion meanings from diverse cultural sources to create a new quilt in which the seams have varying degrees of visibility.

The process of radical reassessment which ethnography is undergoing at present is to a large extent due to demographic and cultural changes. Particularly the large, multicultural centres of the Third World are producing new cultural forms which pose very special problems for ethnographic methodology and practice. In order to describe this phenomenon, which is a product first of urbanisation and then of the "global flow of meaning," anthropologists such as James Clifford and Ulf Hannerz operate with the synonymous terms "syncretism" and "creolisation." Hannerz points, for example, to polyglot urban centres in Third-World countries and their involvement in what he calls "an intercontinental traffic in meaning."[17] Here disparate ethnicities and cultures have been drawn together and have produced new "creolised" cultural forms. These in turn are exported around the world, be they in the form of books, music, fashion, or theatre. Clifford links syncretism with a notion

---

15 "The aim is to draw large large conclusions from small, but densely textured facts; to support broad assertions about the role of culture in the construction of collective life by engaging them exactly with complex specifics." Geertz, *Interpretation of Cultures*:, 28.

16 Geertz, *Interpretation of Cultures*:, ch. 6: "Ritual and Social Change: A Javanese Example," 147–48.

17 Ulf Hannerz, "The World in Creolization," *Africa* 57.4 (1987): 547. Hannerz stresses the movement from a centre to the periphery, from international metropolitan centres via "bridgeheads" (national metropolitan centres) to remote rural villages.

of "postculturalism" which questions the very idea of firm, homogeneous cultural identities:

> In a world with too many voices speaking all at once, a world where syncretism and parodic invention are becoming the rule, not the exception, an urban, multinational world of institutional intransigence – where American clothes made in Korea are worn by young people in Russia, where everyone's "roots" are in some degree cut – in such a world it becomes increasingly difficult to attach human identity and meaning to a coherent "culture" or "language."[18]

The emergence of post-colonial syncretic literature is thus a natural response to situations of cultural multivocalism. The beginnings of the movement in the Thirties through the Fifties resulted from the predicament of binary cultural encounter: the interaction between an indigenous and a Western tradition.

Post-colonial literary theory

Analogous to the new anthropologists, literary theorists working in the area of post-colonial literature have begun operating with the terms "syncretism" and "hybridism" in order to provide a comprehensive theoretical model for certain developments in the New Literatures in English, previously known as Commonwealth literature. In the study *The Empire Writes Back: Theory and Practice in Post-Colonial Literatures*, which is the first attempt both to provide a synthesis of developments and to formulate a body of theory to account for this relatively recent phenomenon, the authors propose four theoretical models. They justify their undertaking by claiming that European theory has been unable to deal adequately with "the complexities and varied cultural provenance of post-colonial writing."[19] In roughly chronological order, the following structures are identified: national or regional models; race-based models; comparative studies of two or more post-colonial literatures; and, fourthly, "more comprehensive comparative models which argue for features such as hybridity or syncreticity as constitutive elements of all post-colonial literatures."[20] Of the four models proposed, the syncretic one appears to be the one flexible enough to account for the polycultural nature of the literatures to be studied. As in the new anthropology, the term syncretism takes on a positive valorisation: "the strength in post-colonial theory may well lie in its inherently comparative methodology and the hybridised and syncretic view of the modern world which this implies."[21] It has been particularly West Indian writers, the study argues, such as Wilson Harris and Edward Kamau Brathwaite who have propounded a view of "creative syncretism" in opposition to monocultural Western theory. They perceive in their own creole societies capacities for renewal and creative regeneration, a potential Harris terms the "paradox of cultural heterogeneity, or cross-cultural capacity, [which] lies in the evolutionary thrust it restores

---

18 Clifford, *Predicament of Culture*, 95.

19 Bill Ashcroft, Gareth Griffiths & Helen Tiffin, *The Empire Writes Back: Theory and Practice in Post-Colonial Literatures* (London: Routledge, 1989): 11.

20 Ashcroft et al., *The Empire Writes Back*, 15.

21 Ashcroft et al., *The Empire Writes Back*, 37–38.

to orders of the imagination, the ceaseless dialogue it inserts between hardened conventions."[22]

When one actually considers the cultural provenance of some of the major writers in the post-colonial literary tradition, such as V.S. Naipaul, Salman Rushdie, and Michael Ondaatje, then categories of race and "national" literatures are of little relevance. Similarly, new categories such as Black-British writing ask more questions than they provide adequate theoretical or conceptual demarcation-lines. Many representatives of this latter group of writers hail from the Caribbean, but the epithet also includes writers of African, Indian and Pakistani origin. Their homogeneity in this case is *ex negativo* – the experience of exclusion from white British society. In the light of such biographies, of which there are an ever-increasing number, it is little wonder that theoretical models utilising some notion of syncreticity, hybridity or creolisation (the terms seem to be used interchangeably) are gaining increasing support in post-colonial literary criticism.

Syncretic theatre and performance

The concrete application of the term "syncretic" to theatre, drama or the performing arts is a very recent phenomenon and in most cases no more than an epithet to designate some form of polycultural performance-style. The performance theorist Richard Schechner discerns in the ritual performances of the Yaqui Indians of Arizona and Mexico a "syncretic mixture of Catholic, Hispanic and Yaqui pre-contact elements."[23] Schechner is using the term here in its anthropological sense of cultural redefinition. A concrete application of the concept to theatrical products, thus closer to the present investigation, is suggested by Colin Taylor in a brief article on Wole Soyinka:

> In his visionary projection of this [Yoruba] society, Soyinka has adopted a syncretic style – fusing the disparate elements of Yoruba song and dance, proverbs and mythology, elements from an ancient tradition of mask and folk-operatic drama, interaction with an anthropomorphic pantheon of gods – in the service of a central controlling viewpoint, aimed at shedding light on the dynamics of a society in transition.[24]

Although Taylor enunciates here some of the central tenets of syncretic theatre – fusion of performance styles, incorporation of ritual and mythic elements to find a new way of presenting in theatrical terms a post-colonial society in the process of change – he unfortunately does not elaborate this insight, being principally concerned to explain why Soyinka's plays have been neglected in North America.

The most comprehensive attempts to apply the concept of "syncretism" to the performing arts have come, perhaps not surprisingly, from two studies dealing with

---

22 Wilson Harris, *The Womb of Space: The Cross-Cultural Imagination* (Westport CT: Greenwood, 1983): xviii. Cited in Ashcroft et al., *The Empire Writes Back*, 152.

23 Richard Schechner, "Intercultural Performance," *Drama Review* (T94) 26.2 (Summer 1982): 3. In this editorial Schechner tries to establish links between interculturalism and postmodernism, although syncretic practices, borrowing, and "the making of new cultural stuff," are, he argues, "the norm of human activity."

24 Colin Taylor, "Seeing Soyinka," *Theatrum: A Theatre Journal* 10 (Summer 1988): 35–38; 36.

black South African music and theatre. In his study of South African township
music and performance, David Coplan, an ethnomusicologist, takes the anthropological concept of syncretism and applies it systematically to aesthetic products. He
defines "syncretic" as the "acculturative blending of performance materials and
practices from two or more cultural traditions, producing qualitatively new
forms."[25] In this study of township "performance culture," a concept embracing
music, dance and drama as well as the contexts and occasions of performance,
Coplan provides a detailed analysis of the disparate elements which have gone into
the formation of this performance culture over the past hundred years. The social
prerequisite for the new forms, Coplan argues, was urbanisation, the coming
together of different ethnicities, combined with a multitude of Western influences
via education, church and the mass media. He argues forcibly that the openness of
Township artists, musicians and performers to these "outside" influences
(especially, since the Sixties, to Black American culture) should be seen neither as
"slavish imitation" nor as the rejection of "a subjugated but precious African
heritage":

> It is rather the result of a creative syncretism in which innovative performers combine
> materials from cultures in contact into qualitatively new forms in response to changing
> conditions, needs, self-images, and aspirations.[26]

In a recent article on South African theatre,[27] the theatre-scholar Temple
Hauptfleisch has elaborated a detailed set of categories to describe the
heterogeneous performance-culture of the country. His six categories distinguish
between indigenous–traditional forms, indigenous–contemporary (to which belong
such disparate elements as gumboot dances, funerals, church services); three
different categories of "Western theatre" (Hauptfleisch is critical of the simple
Western/African distinction); and, finally, indigenous "hybrid" theatre incorporating
elements from the other five categories. "Hybrid theatre" corresponds roughly to
Coplan's concept of syncretic performance. When Hauptfleisch writes "theatre," he
means in fact a concept of "performance" as defined by Richard Schechner, which
can encompass initiation ceremonies, gumboot dances, funerals, as well as the
whole gamut of imported Western forms such as drama, ballet, and opera.
Following Coplan, he detects already in the indigenous communal forms (the
second category – church and funeral services, with their links to political protest) a
process of "hybridisation":

> The primary factor in all this is the process of hybridisation, the mingling and borrowing
> which created something not quite African, not quite Western, but somewhere in the middle.
> Church services utilising African dance and music, traditional communal dancing utilising
> American jazz music and Western clothing. And part of the hybridisation lies in the radically

---

25 David Coplan, *In Township Tonight: South Africa's Black City Music and Theatre* (London: Longman, 1985): vii.

26 In Coplan, *Township*, 236–37.

27 Temple Hauptfleisch, "Beyond Street Theatre and Festival: The Forms of South African Theatre," *Maske und Kothurn* 33.1–2 (1987): 175–88.

redefined sociocultural functions of these new forms, which at times forcefully dictates not only the form but also the content of the performance.[28]

The main focus of his article is directed, however, towards indigenous, hybrid theatre, known internationally as Township Theatre, where "all the varied strands of convention, tradition and experimentation somehow seem to get tied together in a hybrid form of performance which is uniquely South African."[29] The final product is certainly uniquely South African, but the syncretic process underlying the creation of Township Theatre is an international phenomenon.

This brief survey has indicated how the concept of syncretism has undergone a complete reversal of meaning. When one compares the connotations of "impurity" and "degeneration" involved in its use by historians of religion in the nineteenth century with the suggestions of tolerance, reinterpretation and invention in contemporary ethnographic discourse, it can be seen that the semantic change undergone by the term reflects a fundamental shift in Western thinking about other cultures. The pejorative usage in the nineteenth century mirrors very much that century's concern with national identity and difference, both within European cultures and in contradistinction to the non-European cultures that the European powers were in the process of colonising. The increase in syncretic phenomena which commentators such as Hannerz and Clifford point to is certainly a reflection of the historical processes of decolonisation and post-coloniality which have become most marked since the Second World War. The interest in syncretism also reflects a change in thinking and in the way cultural phenomena are apprehended. Cultural homogeneity – the notion of it and the search for it, particularly by pre-war anthropologists – appears to be a peculiarly Western conceptual construct, and has seldom, if ever, existed. As Richard Schechner has observed: "There is no culture uninfluenced by foreigners – invaders, evangelists (Moslem, Christian, Buddhist), traders, colonisers."[30] In this sense, then, syncretism as a category in literary criticism is a necessary but ultimately transitional concept for describing cultural interaction – necessary, because the processes of mixing and recombination are indeed striking; transitional, because in the context of the globalisation of culture it will ultimately be superfluous to define the norm of cultural process.

⋙ ❖ ⋘

---

[28] Hauptfleisch, "Beyond Street Theatre," 181.

[29] Hauptfleisch, "Beyond Street Theatre," 184.

[30] Richard Schechner, "Introduction: Towards a Field Theory of Performance," *The Drama Review* 23.2 (June 1979): 2.

WORKS CITED

BERNER, Ulrich. "Heuristisches Modell der Synkretismus-Forschung," in *Synkretismus-Forschung: Theorie und Praxis*, ed. Gernot Wiesner (Göttinger Orientforschungen 1; Wiesbaden: Harrassowitz, 1978).

————. *Untersuchungen zur Verwendung des Synkretismus-Begriffes* (Göttinger Orientforschungen 2; Wiesbaden: Harrassowitz, 1982).

CLIFFORD, James. *The Predicament of Culture: Twentieth Century Ethnography, Literature, and Art* (Cambridge MA: Harvard UP, 1988): 22–23.

COLPE, Carsten. "Syncretism," in *The Encyclopedia of Religion*, ed. Mircea Eliade (New York: Macmillan, 1987), vol. 14.

COPLAN, David. *In Township Tonight: South Africa's Black City Music and Theatre* (London: Longman, 1985).

Encyclopaedia Universalis (Paris: Encyclopaedia Universalis, 1985), vol. 17.

GEERTZ, Clifford. *The Interpretation of Cultures: Selected Essays* (New York: Basic Books, 1973).

HANNERZ, Ulf. "The World in Creolisation," *Africa* 57.4 (1987): 546–59.

HAUPTFLEISCH, Temple. "Beyond Street Theatre and Festival: The Forms of South African Theatre," *Maske und Kothurn* 33.1–2 (1987): 175–88.

HERSKOVITS, Melville J. *Man and his Works: The Science of Cultural Anthropology* (New York: Alfred A. Knopf, 1956).

MOFFATT, James. "Syncretism," in *Encyclopaedia of Religions and Ethics* (Edinburgh, 1921), vol. 12.

SCHECHNER, Richard. "Introduction: Towards a Field Theory of Intercultural Performance," *Drama Review* 23.2 (June 1979): 2.

————. "Intercultural Performance," *Drama Review* 26.2 (T94; Summer 1982): 3.

TAYLOR, Colin. "Seeing Soyinka," *Theatrum: A Theatre Journal* 10 (Summer 1988): 35–38.

YOUNG, Robert J.C. *Colonial Desire: Hybridity in Theory, Culture and Race* (London: Methuen, 1995).

❧ ❖ ❧

BODE SOWANDE

Syncretic Aesthetics
in Modern Nigerian Theatre

W HEN TWO OR MORE ELEMENTS OF CULTURE are mixed dynamically, the end product is basically different from the respective original components; this is the simplest analysis of syncretism. My focus is on the end product, which is the result of a willing marriage or shotgun wedding between forces that are necessarily distinct, often to the point of non-recognition, from the individual marrying elements. This end product may be a child from whose complexion we can intuit the original marrying pigmentations.

Syncretism is a stage of derivation from the history of any two or more cultures coming into contact via either the productive routes of trade, the coercive means of conquest, or the vagaries of human migration. It is therefore one of the dynamics of cultural evolution, by force or by pastoral means.

As a starting-point we recognise in examples from Africa both passive and dominant cultural elements. There are among African peoples the post-colonial realities of two traditions, Arabo-Islamic and Christian–Western. These two forceful historical legacies facilitate our understanding of the centrifugal origins of today's cultural experiences in rural and urban Africa, both on the African continent and in the African diaspora.

In the diaspora, the pains of conquest and alienation have led to therapy in the form of syncretism, along with the force of moral resistance, because the African soul needed to assert itself against traumatic domination and the pains of cultural genocide. Consequently, the dominated culture countered with an active creolisation of the aggressor's language.

In Brazil, Cuba, and Trinidad, to cite three examples, the African slaves healed their spirit through the incarnation of African gods in a new cosmology which had a place for Christianity. The Yoruba god of thunder, lightning and storms, Sango, became Xango, asserting an approximation in the syncretic church of present-day Brazil.

The change of orthography – from Sango to Xango – is significant, but on the level of daily existence: by a more mundane means, the creole vernacular or pidgin has evolved to free the tongue and linguistically recapture the African spirit from relentless colonial assault. This creolisation retains the non-written traditions of oral Africa. Creole or pidgin is a self-creative verbal means of communication, and is resistant to the limitations of any fixed orthography.[1] Creole is a recent creation of African orature. Our time-scale extends to antiquity.

Therefore it is both in the experience of practical religion and in existential communication that we encounter syncretism most strongly in the colonial and post-colonial history of Africa. From these levels it becomes easier to trace and to feel the aesthetic vibrations which must later be found in the form and content of African creative arts, my present examples for which are drawn from the aesthetics of contemporary Nigerian theatre.

But before proceeding beyond definitions I must refer briefly to the Arabo-Islamic experience. This is because it is often assumed that Arabo-Islamic African culture is thoroughly African rather than being a colonial or post-colonial phe-nomenon. In modern Nigerian theatre, for example, the performing-arts tradition in the North places greater emphasis on poetry and music than on the dramatic arts, mainly because of the strict bias of Islam. The cultural *tabula rasa* that the Islamic conquest enforced in inscribing or constructing an Arabo-Islamic replacement has created the present-day notion that there never was any indigenous culture. The assertion of a syncretic dynamic is here not as strong as in the Southern animist religions. The northern Nigerian accepts or insists that the concept of the creator God must be Allah. Allah is an Arabic name for God. By now the totalitarian colonial incursion of Arab culture has succeeded in establishing itself over a largely animist African society.... In Nigeria one colonial experience thus conceals its coercive origin through a thorough cultural assimilation that was not without the force of genocide in the interest of religious faith; this is the Arabo-Islamic legacy in the city-states which became Northern Nigeria.

The other colonial experience is more recent, and its violence will engender a high degree of cultural symbiosis; this is the Christian–Western legacy of the south of Nigeria. The performing-arts tradition of the missionary churches, which was cultivated to promote Christianity in an animist society, met with a rich tradition of popular dramatic art among the colonised. This encounter initiated an inevitable process of aesthetic syncretism, which has been the hallmark of major works for the theatre ever since.[2] What we experience is a robust interaction of two mature traditions. One comes from the shrines of classical Greece and Rome, the other from

---

[1] "Orature" is a recent coinage in the African experience; the term is intended to give to oral literature the kind of integrity that is implicit in written literature, when the two are compared. It may be argued that orature, through its inbuilt memory-book, has a more adaptive and imaginative line of communication from one time-scale to another. Since it is a non-written archival system that we experience, passing information from one person to another or from one time-scale to the other demands a more rigorous use of the creative imagination than we may find through the written word. The best African writers today, it may be concluded, stand on the shoulders of orature masters of ages past. This legacy is very often underestimated or plain forgotten. In this context even the violent contacts of African languages with European languages resulted in *creole*, a valid wellspring of orature.

[2] Wole Soyinka's essay "The Fourth Stage" shows the respective integrity in the original cultural references for a theatre poetics, a tradition which has its modern continuities. See "The Fourth Stage," in *Myth, Literature and the African World* (Cambridge: Cambridge UP, 1976).

the ashes of an African civilisation[3] that once gave light to the civilisation of Greece, Rome's elder brother, which conquered a Europe whose eclectic civilisation is not without the benefit of sciences born of Islamic scholarship.

In colonial Lagos the Nigerian élite was made up of "Creoles" from Sierra Leone with established family branches in Abeokuta and racial memories extending to the ancient Oyo empire of the Guinea coast, whose old appellation was the "slave coast." The same applies to the African–Brazilians and African–Caribbeans as to the Nigerian Creoles: they all spoke the colonial language well and worked in the colonial civil-service cadres or as emerging professionals in law, medicine, teaching and the clergy. The earliest artisans and civil engineers in the construction industry also came from this class, particularly among the African–Brazilians. Their Christianity might have been ramrod-straight, but their dialect at home was strongly syncretised. The church had two powerful major denominations, Roman Catholic and Anglican. The African–Brazilians were Catholics, while the Sierra Leone Creoles and the African–Caribbeans were largely Methodist or Anglican.

After the end of the Second World War the upsurge of African nationalism stimulated africanisation movements within the churches. Both the Roman Catholic and the Anglican Church resisted this process of africanisation, but those who wanted African drums, spontaneous dancing and holy-spirit possession in religious services soon broke off to establish various types of African churches, which have gained in numerical strength since that time. These African churches, with appellations like the Cherubim and Seraphim Church, developed a liturgy which allowed for trance and its interpretation, prophesy, live drum-music and dance, belief in demons and their inferiority in strength to the Holy Ghost, belief in witchcraft, and public confession. This liturgy catered adequately to the African psyche, and its methodology was thoroughly syncretic. Today the original Cherubim and Seraphim Church has given birth to other types with different names, either by mutations through "Holy Christ revelations" of new founders or through the schisms typical of conflict-situations.

Some of the war-veterans introduced cabaret as popular entertainment, and, when the nationalists rebelled with a new genre of church-music, the Yoruba dramatist Hubert Ogunde was inspired to establish the first professional Yoruba theatre in Lagos. Ogunde drew on the use of this new church music and employed it in his dramatisation of biblical stories and themes from Yoruba mythology.[4] The instant

---

3 Cheikh Anta Diop, in *The African Origin of Civilization*, articulates an empirical analysis of an African origination of civilisation. It counters effectively the denigration of African history which was necessarily propagated to justify the barbarism of the slave trade, and the "civilising" credo of Christianity. This denigration of Africa aimed at perpetually asserting that the culture of Africans was inferior to that of the Europeans; Diop explodes this myth.

4 See Ebun Clark & Hubert Ogunde: *The Making of Nigerian Theatre* (Oxford: Oxford UP, 1979). While Duro Ladipo and his contemporary Kola Ogunmola received the attention of university research in Nigeria,

popularity of this theatre cannot be appreciated without an insight into the use of story-telling in indigenous culture and the integration of song and dance in the dramatic enactment of these stories. Ulli Beier defined this theatre-aesthetic as "folk opera," but the musicologist Akin Euba has redefined it as "music drama," while a more contemporary definition is "total theatre." Total theatre is a well-integrated craft of dialogue, song, dance, narration and movement typical of Yoruba dramatic art. The same idiom may be identified in other cultures, but on the Nigerian stage it constitutes an instance of syncretised aesthetics.

The Yoruba of South-West Nigeria celebrated this total-theatre experience, while performances by Duro Ladipo, whose masterpiece is *Oba ko so*, attained international acclaim, and Hubert Ogunde remained the doyen of this movement until his death in 1991. The canon of plays in this genre numbers in the hundreds, both minor and major creations, from the post-war period of the Forties to the present, when live theatre in the Yoruba dramatic tradition has, sadly, suffered a battering from an inclement economic climate.

The English-language theatre being largely literary, it has enjoyed greater longevity through textbook studies of well-known playwrights. One such genre of dramatic literature is total theatre, with syncretic aesthetics at its core. Plays by Wole Soyinka in this genre include *Kongi's Harvest*, *Death and the King's Horseman*, *From Zia with Love*, as well as such early pieces as *Dance of the Forests*, while *The Lion and The Jewel* presents the style in a very accessible idiom.

Again, the canon of such plays is numerically quite large, major examples being Ola Rotimi's history play *Kurunmi*, Wale Ogunyemi's *Langbodo*, Sowande's *Farewell to Babylon*, and Femi Osofisan's *The Chattering and the Song*. Zulu Sofola has the same kind of total-theatre dramaturgy in her chief work, *King Emene*.

In the respective indigenous languages of these Nigerian playwrights and dramatists we encounter a rich orality – from which, in the case of Soyinka, one may conclude that the Yoruba language had more to offer the English language than the English language to the Yoruba. This is the result of the effective creative syncretism of language that we find in Soyinka's plays.[5]

---

the theatre of Hubert Ogunde was largely snubbed due to the "pop" culture of his music-theatre. This academic snobbery began to change in the early Seventies. Ogunde also cultivated a bias against "academics" of the theatre.

[5] Of all plays by Soyinka which have a total-theatre structure, *Opera Wonyosi* (1981) constitutes a special case. Here we have total theatre à la Yoruba fitting easily into the music-drama of Brecht's *Threepenny Opera*. The hallmark of syncretic aesthetics even presents itself in Soyinka's pun in the title *Opera Wonyosi* – "Opera wonyosi" is Yoruba for "the mindless fool buys himself a wonyosi lace fabric as garment." Wonyosi is a Yoruba coinage meaning "sweetened with salt." This is slang for the most expensive lace fabric of the time. In his boundless vanity, the ostentatious person boasts that he has a most exquisite lace fabric for his garments. In this case he is a mindless fool, because "wonyosi" lace does not survive its first laundering. Its multicoloured patchwork of petals pales into the bargain. *Opera Wonyosi* is a double pun for a Nigerian audience which understands the two languages of English and Yoruba. In this case the Yoruba language has enriched the English language.

Experience has shown that, unless a director, irrespective of cultural background, is familiar with the indigenous aesthetics of Yoruba theatre, the confrontation with music arts, dance arts and mimetic arts may prove a daunting task on the professional stage. The dramatist in this "strange" field may, for an easy escape or a richer experience, choose a relevant creative adaptation. When Topher Campbell directed *Flamingo* by Bode Sowande at the Gate Theatre, London, in 1992 he shifted the emphasis to the "word"-base of the play, avoiding completely the dance and song expressions in order to adapt to the director's strength and the audience's access to the play within the confines of the Gate. Reviews in the London press reacted positively to Campbell's work.[6]

The primary challenge facing any director of total theatre is how to assume sensitively the directorial roles required for dance, music, and other expressive elements therein; but it would be reductionist to assume that total theatre becomes impossible on a "foreign" stage because of such challenges. Where total theatre is achieved, the syncretic aesthetic governing performance shows that the end product is richer than the original cultural components; and that is its strength.

What the Nigerian playwright Ola Rotimi has done in his own dramatic writing is to yorubanise his English dialogue and to emphasise the use of spectacle in performance. Spectacle is at the core of the entertainment often enacted in the Oba's palace, and that palace is the focal stage of the Yoruba community – as in Ola Rotimi's *The Gods Are Not To Blame*, where it resembles the concentration on the Oba's palace in most of the Yoruba plays of the early total-theatre era. The "Yorubanglish" in the Rotimi text sounds prosaic on the page, but leaps into fluid performance on stage.

It is tempting to postulate the thesis that the closer a play is to oral–literary performance the easier it is for a Nigerian audience to identify a "syncretised" theatrical experience, while the closer a play is to a strictly literary tradition the easier it is to discover the enrichment of the English language resulting from the integration of two cultures. Ola Rotimi, through the Yorubanglish of his epic tragedies, typifies the first category, while Wole Soyinka is a poet of the second; these two types remain generally valid, though there are several others in-between.

However, a warning should be issued against restricting the Nigerian dramatic tradition to the "total-theatre" pigeonhole, despite the latter's dominance on the Nigerian stage. The wealth of Nigerian theatre is such that playwrights and dramatists are not restricted in practice to the types cited above. Total theatre is not

---

6 Press reviews of *Flamingo* (1986) by Bode Sowande, produced at the Gate theatre, London, in 1992: Jeremy Kingston in the London *Times* (17 April 1992, reviews section: "Dramatic Coup succeeds"); Michael Aritti in the London *Evening Standard* (21 April 1992, "Bribe Talking"): 44; Sarah Hemming in theLondon *Independent* (28 April 1992).

a dogma but a live example of an indigenous dramatic art-form, exemplified here by the Yoruba of Nigeria.

For us, "total theatre" is a branch of contemporary theatre, and it cannot be the definitive Nigerian theatre-form. Its syncretic nature is an "enrichment," but this aesthetic will lead us to other forms of theatre without songs or dance, and these forms will retain cultural authenticity and contemporary validity. We must always anticipate an eclectic ideal in this African theatre-movement.

WORKS CITED

ARITTI, Michael. "Bribe Talking," *Evening Standard* (London), 21 April 1992: 44.

CLARK, Ebun & Hubert OGUNDE. *The Making of Nigerian Theatre* (Oxford: Oxford UP, 1979).

DIOP, Cheikh Anta. *The African Origin of Civilization: Myth or Reality,* tr., ed. & intro. Mercer Cook (Westport CT: Lawrence Hill, 1974).

HEMMING, Sarah. Review of Bode Sowande's *Flamingo, Independent* (London), 28 April 1992.

KINGSTON, Jeremy. "Dramatic Coup Succeeds," *Times* (London), 17 April 1992: Reviews section.

LADIPO, Duro. *Oba Kò So: Opera* (Ibadan: University of Ibadan, Institute of African Studies, 1987).

OSOFISAN, Femi. *The Chattering and the Song* (Three Crowns series; Ibadan: Ibadan UP/ Oxford UP, 1977).

ROTIMI, Ola. *Kurunmi: An Historical Tragedy* (Three Crowns series; Ibadan: Ibadan UP/ Oxford UP, 1972).
———. *The Gods Are Not To Blame* (Three Crowns series; Ibadan: Ibadan UP/Oxford UP, 1974).

SOFOLA, Zulu. *King Emene: Tragedy of a Rebellion* (Ibadan/London: Heinemann Educational, 1974).

SOWANDE, Bode. *Flamingo and Other Plays* (African Writers series; London: Longman, 1987).

SOYINKA, Wole. "The Fourth Stage," in Soyinka, *Myth, Literature and the African World* (Cambridge: Cambridge UP, 1976).
———. *Opera Wonyosi* (London: Rex Collings, 1981).

❧ ❖ ❧

$\mathcal{B}$ ode Sowande
(Munich, September 1993; photo Peter Stummer)

L esego Rampolokeng
(Munich, September 1993; photo Peter Stummer)

FLORA VEIT–WILD

Festivals of Laughter
Syncretism in Southern Africa

That i rhyme is not a crime
i only shoot the british
with the bullets that are english
(Lesego Rampolokeng)

I N JANUARY 1994, the South African National Arts Coalition (NAC) announced a campaign for freedom of expression under the banner "Festivals of
Laughter" to coincide with the election campaign in South Africa in April
1994. The NAC hoped to stimulate "on-the-edge" arts activities in order to "assert
the right to freedom of expression by encouraging [...] provocative, yet innovative
and original forms."[1] Proposed activities included:

> The Braai[2]-the-sacred-cow-monument sculpture exhibition
> The Not-approved-by-the-Publications Board Short Story competition
> The Completely Politically Incorrect Stand Up Comedy Festival
> The Riotous Assembly Street Theatre and Dance Festival
> The Anything-but-the-anthem Best Original Song Competition
> The Oh-shucks-no-subsidy-bucks short film festival
> The Have-you-slugged-a-politician-today Poster Competition.

The subversive character of the NAC campaign is intrinsically linked with the
development of syncretic forms of art in South Africa; at the same time it is a
magnificent illustration of the carnivalesque quality of this development.

In the history of art, syncretism has traditionally been seen as the impure, the
deviation from the canon, the anti-hierarchal, close to bastardisation; it thus implies
being outcast, marginalised. In that sense, it can be connected with the Bakhtinian
carnival tradition in literature[3] which mobilises all "abnormal" and fantastic human
instincts and desires in order to ridicule and subvert dominant cultures and
discourses. Carnivalesque laughter, says Bakhtin, is festive laughter. "The entire
world is seen in its droll aspect, in its gay relativity [...] This laughter is ambivalent:
it is gay, triumphant, and at the same time mocking, deriding. It asserts and denies,
it buries and revives. Such is the laughter of the carnival."[4] The Festivals of
Laughter are a splendid example of this: "The new South African culture will draw

---

[1] National Arts Coalition, Media Release, Johannesburg, 24 January 1994.

[2] Afrikaans word for barbecue.

[3] "Carnival is presented by Bakhtin as a world of topsy-turvy, of heteroglot exuberance, of ceaseless
overrunning and excess where all is mixed, hybrid, ritually degraded and defiled" (Peter Stallybrass &
Allon White, *The Politics and Poetics of Transgression*, London: Methuen, 1986: 8).

[4] Mikhail Bakhtin, *Rabelais and his World*, tr. H. Iswolsky (Cambridge MA: MIT Press, 1968): 11–12.

27

unashamedly from all the diverse elements of its constituent cultures – it will disdain purity and embrace contamination. This is a bastard culture. This will be a truly South African culture."[5]

The following analysis of literary syncretism in South Africa and Zimbabwe is based on a recognition of its subversive, counter-discursive qualities. While the terms syncretism and hybridity are often used synonymously,[6] I distinguish between syncretism as applying to the literary product (which represents a fusion of elements of different yet still recognisable origins) and hybridity as a completely new subject-position and consciousness arising out of such fusion.[7] Here I follow Homi Bhabha's concept of the "Third Space," which he defines as the hybrid moment in history where people, in times of transition, "are now free to negotiate and translate their cultural identities in a discontinuous intertextual temporality of cultural difference."[8] "The process of cultural hybridity gives rise to something different, something new and unrecognisable, a new area of negotiation of meaning and representation."[9]

In South Africa, we are in the middle of experiencing this hybrid moment of history. Especially since February 1990,[10] the syncretic character of South African culture – polyglot and multi-ethnic – is reflected in a multiplicity of literary styles which explore cultural difference as well as the hybridity arising from uncertain identities. This move to free culture from the restrictions of anti-apartheid protest and ANC politics is spearheaded by NAC, which emerged in 1993 from a broad alliance of arts practitioners in South Africa. NAC aims to promote democratic, anti-discriminatory and non-aligned cultural politics in the future South Africa. NAC members are united by a "shared horror at the prospect that the practices of the ANC's Department of Arts and Culture could be dignified into policy."[11]

Unsafe issues

Possibly the most daring recent publication of writing "on the edge" and the first of its kind to have come out of Africa is the anthology *The Invisible Ghetto: Lesbian and Gay Writing from South Africa*.[12] It reflects very vividly the opening of the cultural

---

5 Ian Barnard, review of *Out of Exile: South African Writers Speak*, ed. Kevin Goddard & Charles Wessels (1992), *Research in African Literatures* 24.3 (Fall 1993): 132.

6 See Christopher Balme in the present volume, and Bernd Schulte, *Die Dynamik des Interkulturellen in den postkolonialen Literaturen englischer Sprache* (Heidelberg: Winter, 1993): 76 and passim.

7 While Bill Ashcroft, Gareth Griffiths and Helen Tiffin in *The Empire Writes Back* (London: Routledge, 1989) seem to suggest a similar usage, they never define a clear distinction.

8 Homi Bhabha, "The Commitment to Theory," *New Formations* 5 (Summer 1988): 22.

9 Homi Bhabha, "The Third Space," in *Identity: Community, Culture, Difference*, ed. Jonathan Rutherford (London: Lawrence & Wishart, 1990): 211.

10 February 1990 marks the official beginning of political liberalisation in South Africa: President de Klerk announced the unbanning of oppositional political parties, the lifting of restriction orders and the release of political prisoners, including Nelson Mandela. This prepared negotiations between the government and the ANC towards general and free elections and the end of apartheid.

11 Ivor Powell, "The Shape of the Arts to Come," *Weekly Mail* (December 10–16 1993): 41.

12 Ed. Matthew Krouse (Johannesburg: COSAW, 1993).

sphere I have mentioned. In short stories and poems, gays and lesbians write about their very private stories, loves, desires and rejections. In interviews and biographical accounts, such "closed books" as the very frequent homosexuality among South African mine-workers or the lives of male sex-workers are investigated without any false moral restrictions. Joaquim from Mozambique, who works as a hooker in Johannesburg, says: "It's nice to be gay. But for the black people, it's something funny to them, if you don't sleep with women. They don't understand what kind of a person you are. They call you a moffie, *stabane*.[13] [...] It's nice to have sex with a black guy, but as I'm black they don't really turn me on. I prefer the white men because they got soft skin, nice hair, nice faces, nice eyes. And a nice body."[14]

Voices from a variety of languages, ethnicities and social backgrounds are brought together and blended into in a truly hybrid consciousness; this hybridity emanates from the liminality of transgressing into areas which have been prohibited for a long time, both by the South African state and by official anti-apartheid politics. A moving example is the story "Stalwart" by Shaun De Waal. Russell Blair, a veteran of the South African Communist Party who returns home after thirty years of exile, recognises, full of sadness, that he joined the party because "he had failed in love."[15] Individual feelings such as love, personal inclinations and desires were for a long time disregarded and suppressed by anti-apartheid politics. Blair's admission of failure in the personal field implies the (re)discovery of the individual voice set against a collective consciousness; it has a vigorous anti-discursive potential. Such entering into the terrain of "unsafe issues" and breaking of long-guarded taboos ("sacred cows") stands fully in the carnival tradition of denuding, unmasking and uprooting power structures. *The Invisible Ghetto* is an important contribution to this process.

Mixing languages

A precursor of new syncretic tendencies in poetry is the little-known Wopko Jensma. In his 1977 collection *i must show you my clippings*[16] Jensma blends poetry with photographs and woodcuts and uses a variety and mix of languages: English, Afrikaans, and street slang. His poems, inspired by Dadaists like Hans Arp, play with words, letters and graphic patterns, and in an anarchistic way try to explode the shell of white-dominated South Africa:

> yes, open the sluices, suck me into the crowd!
> it's long been time – time's long overdue
> i jensma, i have come to blow all that boodle
> i jensma, i the incarnate of vincent van gogh

---

13 Township slang for queer, literally meaning "hermaphrodite."

14 "Joaquim and Bester. Two Sex-Workers," recorded by Matthew Krouse, in *The Invisible Ghetto*, ed. Krouse, 109.

15 *The Invisible Ghetto*, ed. Krouse, 168.

16 Johannesburg: Ravan, 1977.

> i jensma, i am also a socalled real artist[17]

In this anaphoric incantation, Jensma conjures up the almost magic power of the "i," the individual voice, which he directs as a weapon against the system of oppression. His "clippings" reflect a fragmented perception of reality and his refusal to accept a ready-made version. The syncretic use of language is an integral part of this. Thus Sheila Roberts observes on the back cover of Jensma's book: "as it is impossible even from a close examination of his poetry and woodcuts to determine the colour of his skin [...] and as he writes in various 'voices,' from English and Afrikaans to Tsotsi and Gammattaal,[18] he does indeed appear to be the first wholly integrated South African."

The creolisation of language as language variance is generally seen as an important feature of post-colonial writing.[19] It is a strong, dynamic element in recent trends in South African literature. In the Cape area, the "Kaaps" poets have re-appropriated Afrikaans as their literary language. The sociolect "Kaaps" is a Cape patois, a working class variety of Afrikaans which is socially despised by white South Africans. Now several coloured writers "have turned the insult around and advocated the distinctive use of patois in literature."[20]

Similarly, black poets in Johannesburg have started to use the street language Tsotsitaal. In a "Jo'burg Poems Project" during the Arts Alive Festival in Johannesburg in September 1993, poets of all colours expressed the pulse of the big city through the rhythms of many languages.[21] The following example, which mixes English and Afrikaans, reflects some of the tensions in the rapidly changing climate of Johannesburg:

> Northwards...
> Smog,
> N3, M2 West, M1 North
> [...]
> "Kom '94 dan sal ít net soos Bosnia wees";
> Dis 'ie vrees van Jo'burg.[22]
> "Go to town, are you nuts?"
> (Smog. Grey. Black).
>
> Metamorphosis. The place,
> en sy mense ook.[23]
> Most unaware of its passing;
> some the same –
> ('48).[24]

---

[17] End of the poem "the ceiling just caved in today," in Jensma, *i must show you my clippings*, 71.

[18] Urban slang forms that mix several European and African languages.

[19] Cf Ashcroft et al., *The Empire Writes Back*, ch. 2.

[20] Hein Willemse, "Black Afrikaans 'Soubesie' Poesie,'" *Southern African Review of Books* (February–May 1990): 27–29; see also Willemse, "Die Skrille Sombesies: Emergent Black Afrikaans Poets in Search of Authority," in *Rendering Things Visible*, ed. Martin Trump (Johannesburg: Ravan, 1990): 367–401.

[21] Cf Fiona Lloyd, "Images of the Changing City: Painting Pain, Memory and Music with the words of Six Languages," *Africa South and East* (November, 1993): 36.

[22] "By '94 it'll be just like Bosnia; / That's your fear of Jo'burg."

[23] "and also its people."

Words and music

Syncretic use of the polyglossic situation in South Africa is also made by poets who use deconstructed "english" from the Rasta culture and mix it with bits of Afrikaans.[25] Whether reggae- or jazz-like, many such poems are close to music. The mixing of genres and media through language, song, painting, photography, collage techniques in print, performance or sound is another important feature of the multi-voiced new South African culture.[26] This fusion of forms is also beginning in Zimbabwe through performances by the Tumbuka Dance Company, a multi-ethnic group which has stunned audiences through its innovative, syncretic styles of dance.

Prophets of da City is a group of young South African rappers. In their album "Age of Truth"[27] they give violent expression to the rage and desperation of South African township kids, their anger, hopelessness and confusion. In a "no-holds-barred multilingual attack,"[28] they merge languages and musical styles (American rap, raggamuffin and hiphop[29]) with innumerable "four-letter words" to "scream and shout at everything they hate."[30] "Everybody out there is singing love songs and shit," says one member of the group. "And we've heard that for 100 years. We are saying: put your foot down and say fuck this and fuck that."[31] One of their songs was banned by the South African Broadcasting Corporation: it has a "choir singing Nkosi Sikel'iAfrica set against a cacophony of hiphop beats and gunshots."[32] Even in the liberalised climate of South Africa in the Nineties, such unrestrained iconoclasm goes beyond limits. The following quotation from their song "Township dweller" shows their explicitly syncretic approach:

> I'm merchandisin' pay the bill and feel the afrocentricity its on like electricity I'm action packed like a gangsta movie I'm not a butty man so don't try 2 do me guni gugu. i come with an african voodoo that'll go right through you bishop tutu, like mandela I'm packed with a mela-nin I'm the township dwela in effect I gotta get thru wit this verse I'm audi like a corpse in a hearse oh I'm african, but I don't wear leopard skin so let the record spin while ethnic back beats gets mixed with hip hop technique so feel the rhythm of africa and get trapped in a hip hop massacre.[33]

---

24 From "Jo'burg. *Some* **thoughts**" by Adrian Bailey, unpublished.

25 Examples are poems by Seitlhamo Motsapi which can be found in *Staffrider* 10.4 (1992): 44–45 and in *New Coin* 28.2 (1992): 6–7.

26 An important syncretic practice developing in the urban centres of South Africa is township theatre, for which I refer to Balme's article in this volume.

27 Tusc Music Co. (South Africa, 1993).

28 Fred de Vries, in his review of the album in the *Weekly Mail* (19–25 November 1993).

29 One of their songs is called "Zulu Muffin."

30 Fred de Vries, *Weekly Mail* (19–25 November 1993).

31 Quoted in Fred de Vries, *Weekly Mail* (19–25 November 1993).

32 Fred de Vries, *Weekly Mail* (19–25 November 1993).

33 From the sleeve of "Age of Truth."

Dub poetry: Lesego Rampolokeng

Anger paired with laughter, sarcastic humour paired with the pleasure of playing
with words, the enjoyment of trespassing on forbidden territory – these make up a
common element in South Africa's current syncretic culture. In a more individualised style than the Prophets of da City, the dub poet Lesego Rampolokeng
expresses his disillusionment and cynicism about what is happening in his country.
Like the Prophets, his art arises out of the multi-ethnic melting-pot of the big city,
Johannesburg.

Rampolokeng's life embodies syncretism. Asked about his mother tongue, he
replied: "My mother gave me a Tswana name but I don't speak Tswana. I speak
English and the Johannesburg slang, a mix of mainly Xhosa, Zulu, Afrikaans and
English."[34] Born in the Sixties, he participated as a young boy in the 1976
schoolchildren's uprising in Soweto. Initially influenced by Black Consciousness,
he soon tried to counteract the restrictive scope of Bantu education by looking for
literature not taught at school; he discovered, amongst others, Kerouac, Beckett,
Burroughs, Ginsberg and, in Africa, the Zimbabwean Dambudzo Marechera.
"Dambudzo was trying to fight rules set by old men. He was the most free spirit on
this continent. The liberation we really need is from anything that oppresses the
imagination."[35]

Rampolokeng belongs to a scene of young writers from various ethnic origins
who experiment with literary themes and forms. His performance poems – which he
often calls raps – fuse influences from Jamaican dub poetry[36] with American ghetto
rap, jazz[37] and contemporary popular music as well as some indigenous sounds and
rhythms. He is "putting dub and rap together and adding a touch of the European
with the use of rhyming couplets."[38]

His poetry – performed with music – is an angry lamentation about politics of
oppression worldwide, about hypocrisy and the violation and denigration of the
human. Individualistic and anarchic in his outlook, he was sceptical about using
literature as propaganda even before the Albie Sachs debate.[39] He rejects anything
close to a "struggle bonus" and includes the ANC in his sarcastic iconoclasm and the
"black on black black attacks."

---

[34] Personal conversation with R.L., Johannesburg, January 1993. See also Christoph Plate, "Lesego
Rampolokeng (Südafrika)," *Literaturnachrichten* 35 (October–December 1992): 11–13.

[35] Rampolokeng, quoted in Shaun De Waal, "A Melange of Rap and Dub; a Mixture of Blood and
Roses," *Weekly Mail* (26 April–2 May, 1991).

[36] He names Linton Kwesi Johnson, Michael Smith and Mutabaruka as important influences on his
work, see De Waal, "A Melange of Rap and Dub."

[37] In a recent show (early 1994) in Johannesburg by Rampolokeng, called "Rough Words, Sweet
Music," he mixed performance poetry with jazz.

[38] De Waal, "A Melange of Rap and Dub."

[39] ANC activist Albie Sachs   and before him writer Njabulo Ndebele   has stressed the need to
develop more imaginative forms in South African literature, to get away from culture as a "weapon in the
political struggle."

> my struggle is international
> the radar of my conscience is universal
> [...]
> my fire is unfanned by race
> nor does race hasten my marching pace
> there's nothing black about my action
> for no fog clouds my vision[40]

Rampolokeng uses language to cut, analyse, and disrupt. A "doctor of rap," he calls himself, a "rap-surgeon come to operate" (raps 31 and 41). And in a typically post-colonial way, he rhymes "to shoot the british with the bullets that are english":[41] he writes back, subverting the English language. Hence, as in all post-colonial literatures, we find two levels of language: english is parodying English, and the parody is intrinsically hybrid.[42]

Rampolokeng's lyrics are also a good example of the carnivalisation of language: "The subversive force of this hybridising tendency is most apparent at the level of language itself where creoles, patois and black English decentre, destabilise and carnivalise the linguistic domination of 'English' – the nation-language of master-discourse – through strategic inflections, re-accentuations and other perform-ative moves in semantic, syntactic and lexical codes."[43] Rampolokeng uses the traditional English rhymed couplet, but in an ironic way; he plays with sound, makes jokes by bringing the English language into collision with the African accent (in his pronunciation "ship" rhymes with "sheep," for example) and creates unusual, comic, often absurd and dissonant rhymes. Thus his lyrics have a mocking tone; much as a parrot mocks the visitor, he mocks the reader's/listener's expectation of "good poetry" and "proper rhyming." The result is a constant undermining of his own words and their usual meanings, of authorities and ideologies – Marx rhymed with "ducks," Lenin with "adrenaline," as in the following excerpt from "rap 31":

> when i'm rapmaster supreme
> word-bomber in the extreme
> i'm called subversive
> when i'm only creative
> i write to fight
> to make a dark land bright
> they say i'm kinky
> when i'm only inky

---

40 "rap 12" in Lesego Rampolokeng, *Horns for Hondo* (Johannesburg: COSAW, 1990): 21.

41 From Rampolokeng's album "End Beginnings," Shifty Records, Johannesburg, 1992.

42 Cf Mikhail Bakhtin's elaborations on parody in Latin and medieval literature in "From the Prehistory of Novelistic Discourse" in *Modern Criticism and Theory: A Reader*, ed. David Lodge, (London: Longman, 1988): "Thus it is that in parody two languages are crossed with each other, as well as two styles, two linguistic points of view, and in the final analysis two speaking subjects. It is true that only one of these languages (the one that is parodied) is present in its own right; the other is present invisibly, as an actualising background for creating and perceiving. Parody is an intentional hybrid, but usually it is an intra-linguistic one, one that nourishes itself on the stratification of the literary language into generic languages and languages of various specific tendencies" (150).

43 Kobena Mercer, "Diaspora Culture and the Dialogic Imagination: The Aesthetics of Black Independent Film in Britain," in *Blackframes: Critical Perspectives on Black Independent Cinema*, ed. M. Cham & C. Watkins (Cambridge MA: MIT Press, 1988): 57.

> [...]
> but they came sailing in a ship
> to make me bleat like a sheep
> now they drive up in a van
> to silence me with a ban
> for i sing of engels
> when i should sing with angels
> i rap karl marx
> turn them literal ducks
> i unleash vladimir lenin
> & flood them with adrenaline[44]

At the same time, he subverts the Christian values of his colonial masters:

> in a six & nine jesus bled wine
> made vampires of holy believers
> still the preachers say
> there's a heaven up above
> coming down your way with biblical love
> love as sweet as shit that stalks & stinks up the street
> from the bowels of a christian law
> the present is time of war[45]

In a subtle act of iconoclasm, the sexual symbol "six and nine" is used to unmask the reversal of Christian morals: wine becomes blood, believers rhyme with vampires, law with war.

The emergence of syncretism in Zimbabwe

In Zimbabwe, syncretic literary forms as expressions of a hybrid consciousness are less developed than in South Africa. This is due partly to cultural nationalism, which was particularly strong in the years after Independence in 1980, but also to the nature of Zimbabwean society; diglossic, it has had fewer foreign influences; and it has a less developed urban culture. An urban slang, a new syncretic language, has started to emerge but has not yet impacted much on literature. Although some younger writers are starting to experiment, language-purists try to keep the vernacular "clean."[46] Open, innovative, syncretic approaches are mainly found among the newcomers to literature, the "budding writers" or the women writers – again, those who write against the dominant, prescribed culture.[47]

---

[44] From "rap 31," Rampolokeng, *Horns for Hondo*, 53–54.

[45] From "Sebokeng Siege" in Rampolokeng, *Talking Rain* (Johannesburg: COSAW, 1993): 5–6.

[46] Cf Flora Veit–Wild, "The Elusive Truth: Literary Development in Zimbabwe since 1980," *Matatu* 10 (1993): 109–10.

[47] An example of a seemingly syncretic text is Chenjerai Hove's much acclaimed novel *Bones* (Harare: Baobab, 1988), where Hove translates the idiom and rhythm of the vernacular into English; however, by embedding his cross-cultural text in the communal voice of a collective national conscience, he re-creates a monist myth of national identity. Thus his text negates its own hybridity and the hybridised nature of post-colonial society (cf Ashcroft et al., *The Empire Writes Back*, 52–53 and 74–75). For a detailed critique of *Bones*, see Veit–Wild, "Dances with Bones: Hove's Romanticised Africa," *Research in African Literatures* 24.3 (Fall 1993): 5–12.

The Zimbabwe Women Writers is a grass-roots organisation founded in 1990. Their workshops and public readings are forums for the exposure and mingling of different styles, themes, traditions – and are thus birthplaces of syncretism. One of their public readings in Harare in February 1993 embraced a broad variety of ages, races and liberties, in styles ranging from introverted love-poetry by an American expatriate to a Shona story told by a township woman with many gestures and audience participation. The women writers break through the narrow classifications of "literariness" defined by the mostly male guardians of Zimbabwean literature.[48] As their writing is part of a broader process of self-discovery, of redefining women's role in society, it again fosters the individual voice and questions the monocultural status quo of mainstream Independence literature.

In Zimbabwe as in other areas of Africa, modern urban drama is probably the most interesting area for syncretic developments in the arts. This is all the more important as most community theatre in Zimbabwe so far has reinforced the dominant political discourse rather than challenging it through either content or form. One exception, and an outstanding example of inventive syncretism, is the Bulawayo-based Amakhosi Theatre. In their productions they freely mix languages and styles, drawing on traditional dance and song as well as on modern urban culture, using "Ndenglish," a mélange of English and street Ndebele. In 1986 they established themselves as the avant-garde of oppositional arts in Zimbabwe with their controversial play *Workshop Negative*, which exposes and ridicules the socialist rhetoric of the Shona-dominated government and ruling party in Harare. Amakhosi's satirical plays are truly carnivalesque – with wit, humour and aggressive liberty of form they present travesties of post-colonial African reality.

Hybrid and metaphoric: Dambudzo Marechera

The most influential proponent of cultural freedom, Dambudzo Marechera, was also a role-model for the younger generation of writers in Zimbabwe, and a very conscious syncretist. "From early in my life I have viewed literature as a unique universe that has no internal divisions. I do not pigeon-hole it by race or language or nation [...] There is a healthy interchange of technique and themes. That Europe had, to say the least, a head start in written literature is an advantage for the African writer: he does not have to solve many problems of structure – they have already been solved. I do not consider influences pernicious."[49] And, of himself he says with his usual frankness: "I would question anyone calling me an African writer. Either you are a writer or you are not. If you are a writer for a specific nation or a

---

[48] For instance, in the Literature Bureau, the Ministry of Arts and Culture but also among the ranks of the Zimbabwe Writers Union.

[49] Dambudzo Marechera, "The African Writer's Experience of European Literature," in Flora Veit–Wild, *Dambudzo Marechera. A Source Book on his Life and Work* (London: Hans Zell, 1992): 362–63. See also Marechera, *Cemetery of Mind* (Harare: Baobab, 1992): 212.

specific race, then fuck you. In other words, the direct international experience of every single living entity is, for me, the inspiration to write."[50]

Such views inevitably clashed with the cultural nationalism prevalent in Zimbabwe in the early Eighties. Marechera remained an outsider, his work denigrated as "un-African, westernised." His response: "When politicians talk about culture, one had better pack one's rucksack and run, because it means the beginning of unofficial censorship."[51]

In the same vein, Marechera was always wary of his mother-tongue, Shona. It embodied for him the poverty and spiritual starvation of his childhood and youth in the ghetto and a cultural nationalism which he abhorred as outdated and politically dangerous. He saw such nationalism as a mere reversal of colonial policies of keeping literature "native" – and that meant: retarded. In a lecture at the University of Zimbabwe in 1982 he declared: "In Zimbabwe we have these two great indigenous languages, ChiShona and Sindebele [...] Who wants us to keep writing these Shit-Shona and ShitNdebele languages, this missionary chickenshit? Who else but the imperialists?"[52] Hence Marechera chose to appropriate English as his language of writing by abusing and subverting it and creating his own lexical and syntactic idiom.[53] In an astute, consciously post-colonial way, and based on a profound knowledge of world literature, he re-masters the colonial language and writes back to the British canon. His writing is full of explicit and implicit parodies of English language and literature.

Like Wole Soyinka, to whom he felt very close, Marechera's syncretism implies a universalist outlook:"I discovered that the best of the works I read from all these different societies had a common base, which was their supreme humanity."[54] However, unlike Soyinka, Marechera does not marry two traditions of thought so much as he goes beyond them to create something new. This kind of hybridity in Bhabha's sense is particularly reflected in his use of metaphor and myth, which is born from his – to use Wilson Harris's term –"cross-cultural imagination." I shall

---

[50] "Interview and Discussion with Dambudzo Marechera about *Black Sunlight*," in Veit–Wild, *Dambudzo Marechera*, 221.

[51] "'Slow Brain Death Can Only Be Cured by a Literary Shock Treatment': Dambudzo Marechera interviewed by Alle Lansu," in Veit–Wild, *Dambudzo Marechera*, 5–48; 39. The quotation continues: "Zimbabwean writers – my own contemporaries – will never dare to write something like *Mindblast*, precisely because there is this heavy emphasis on developing our traditional values." And in the story "Description of the Universe" in his posthumously published *Scrapiron Blues* (Harare: Baobab, 1994) he writes: "Meanwhile, all and sundry are talking loudly about the need to invigorate the national culture. Which seems to mean a lot of fat women dressed in the Leader's colours and a crowd of half-naked traditional dancers leaping in clouds of dust."

[52] This is part of David Caute's recapitulation of Marechera's famous "Farewell Lecture" in Caute, *The Espionage of the Saints: Two Essays on Silence and the State* (London: Hamish Hamilton, 1986): 11.

[53] There are a number of references where Marechera elaborates on the subversion of English language. See, for instance, documents 1 and 99 in Veit–Wild, *Dambudzo Marechera*. Only in *Scrapiron Blues* are there examples of his rare use of Shona: "The Servant's Ball," a play which mixes Shona and English to reflect the vibes of urban African backyard life; and inserted in his recording of beerhall stories, urban legends are bawdy jokes playing with the di-glossic situation (cf the story "Snakes in Track Suits").

[54] Marechera, *Cemetery of Mind*, 212.

illustrate this briefly by examples of his poetry, which is generally less well known than his prose.

> *Oracle of the Povo*
>
> Her vision's scrubland
> Of out-of-work heroes
> Who yesterday a country won
> And today poverty tasted
>
> And some to the hills hurried their thirst
> and others to arson and blasphemy
> Waving down tourists and buses
>
> Unleashing havoc no tongue can tell –
> Her vision's Droughtstricken acres
> Of lean harried squatters
> And fat pompous overlords
> Touching to torch the makeshift shelters
> Heading to magistrate and village court
> The most vulnerable and hungry of citizens –
> Her vision's Drought Relief graintrucks
> Vanished into thin air between departure point
> And expectant destination –
> In despair, she is found in beerhalls
> And shebeens, by the roadside
> And in brothels: selling the last
> Bits and pieces of her soured vision.[55]

"Oracle of the Povo" was written in 1983, when independent Zimbabwe faced a severe drought and its first political crisis. There were rumours that drought-relief consignments had got into the wrong hands. At the same time, squatter-camps were bulldozed and burnt down by the government; young veterans of the liberation war were unemployed; some turned to acts of terrorism directed against the government. In "Oracle of the Povo," Marechera applies foreign images to an African context. He does this in a subversive way by juxtaposing the figure of the noble "Oracle" (from Greek mythology) with the low-class "povo," a Portuguese expression used in Southern Africa for the poor, the people, the masses. The Oracle has been degraded into a prostitute seen among the poor, in cheap places. Her vision – which has certain resonances of nationalist rhetoric – is "soured" and "sold-out." The "Oracle of the Povo" thus not only symbolises degradation but also the reversal of the vision: it is now the povo's vision of the nation's welfare, which through bitter experience is opposed to that of the leaders. The overall metaphoric and allegorical image of the poem serves to deconstruct the national myth of prosperity and equality for all. This is underlined by other images and metaphors of drought, hunger and thirst, all expressing the same disillusionment, the reversal of hopes and aspirations: "vision's scrubland," "poverty tasted," "to the hills hurried their thirst."

While most Zimbabwean writing shows a metonymic sensibility, a preference for the concrete over the abstract, Marechera's writing is mostly metaphoric.[56]

---

55 In *Mindblast* (Harare: College Press, 1984): 106–107; and *Cemetery of Mind*, 67.

Metonymy is based on contiguity between different signifiers, on a reference-system between words and what they stand for. This – metonymic – coherence of a referential system has been lost in an alienated existence such as Marechera's. His preference for metaphor thus expresses the disjunction – rather, re-connection – between language and meaning.[57] Instead of referring to a known set of signifiers, Marechera creates his own new system of signs and symbols. Thus his writing is close to what Jacques Lacan has said about dream-language. Expanding Freud's theory of the unconscious, especially his *Traumdeutung*, Lacan makes a parallel between poetic language and dream-language, both signifiers of the unconscious.[58] Marechera's writing is indeed related to dream; for him, metaphors, like myth – his poetry is full of allusions to classical Greek mythology – serve to forge a connection with universal human experience: "And it is in dream that we discover our mythical self. The ghosts which hover over Great Zimbabwe are the same as those which tormented Troy, those which overwhelmed Carthage, those which watched over Aeneas."[59]

At the same time, Marechera's preference for metaphor reflects the hybrid nature of his thinking and his carnivalesque attitude.[60] Metaphor – and here I follow Patricia Parker in her exploration of "The Metaphorical Plot"[61] – tends to be close to hyperbole, it implies a trespassing, an overstepping of bounds, a *hubris*. "The 'plot' of metaphor, in these terms, recalls that 'dialogical' space which Bakhtin opposes to 'monologic' and its 'ready-made truth,' a ludic or 'carnival' space."[62] Metaphor as "exile from 'Identity'"[63] links up with Bhabha's view that "metaphor produces hybrid realities by yoking together unlikely traditions of thought."[64] Bhabha's view is that we can no longer speak of any originary, "authentic" culture – all cultural expressions are "translations," all forms of culture hybrid.

It is striking to observe how closely Marechera's views resemble this concept. Central to his understanding is the conviction that all words are translations, imitations, replacements of what remains hidden. One can never know what is

---

[56] I follow here Tim McLoughlin's argument in his article "Cultural Authenticity in Black Zimbabwean Literature in English: A Case for Metonymy," in *Nouvelles du Sud: littératures et anthropologie*, ed. D. Rochay and P. Dakeyo (Paris, 1986): 79–88.

[57] I shall undertake a closer exploration of the distinction of metaphor and metonymy based on textual analysis of Marechera's poetry in a forthcoming publication.

[58] Jacques Lacan, "The Insistence of the Letter in the Unconscious," in *Modern Criticism and Theory: A Reader*, ed. David Lodge (London: Longman, 1988): 91–101. Cf Dirk Klopper's review of *Cemetery of Mind*: "His poems have a hallucinatory clarity about them, and resonate powerfully with the unconscious" (*Southern African Review of Books*, March–April 1993: 16).

[59] *Cemetery of Mind*, 168.

[60] Marechera explicitly placed himself into the subversive, carnivalesque stream in world literature and often cited Bakhtin as an important theoretical reference, cf particularly "The African Writer's Experience of European Literature," 363–64.

[61] In *Metaphor: Problems and Perspectives*, ed. D.S. Miall (Brighton: Harvester, 1982): 133–67.

[62] Parker, "The Metaphorical Plot," 148–49.

[63] Parker, "The Metaphorical Plot," 143.

[64] Bhabha, "The Third Space," 212.

original, what is imitation – an idea he expresses in the mythological image of the short poem "Cassandra's Ball (a fragment)":

> time's fingers on the piano
> play emotion into motion
>
> the dancers through the looking glass
> never recognise us as their originals[65]

The personification of time lends the poem a mythic feeling: Time appears as an allegorical figure similar to Death in religious or metaphysical poetry, implying human temporality. The play with words in "emotion into motion" suggests the close link between psychological and physical movement. Finally, the image of the dancers in the looking glass conveys Marechera's view that it is the reflection, the illusion, which becomes real; the original remains hidden, unrecognised. Ultimately, such a concept leads to a split in personality between imagined and real self, the doppelgänger, which permeates Marechera's work. This again is similar to Lacan's idea of the "mirror phase" assuming a fundamental fictionality of the "I": the sense of identity of the human subject remains always imaginary, there is nothing beyond the infinite reflections in the mirror.[66]

Thus one can conclude: hybridity implies a general – postmodern – scepticism towards any positions of identifiable truth. It challenges all notions of cultural purity or essentialism, since "the meaning and symbols of culture have no primordial unity or fixity; [...] even the same signs can be appropriated, translated, rehistoricised, and read anew."[67] Here lies the immense importance of Festivals of Laughter in times of transition; the importance of figures like Dambudzo Marechera, Lesego Rampo-lokeng and other Southern African artists who have used the "third space" at the margin of society, of sanity, to denounce the mechanisms of power-structures and hegemonic discourses. It is in this sense that their syncretic and prophetic voices should be heard.

WORKS CITED

ARITTI, Michael. "Bribe Talking," *Evening Standard* (London), 21 April 1992: 44.

CLARK, Ebun & Hubert OGUNDE. *The Making of Nigerian Theatre* (Oxford: Oxford UP, 1979).

ASHCROFT, Bill, Gareth GRIFFITHS & Helen TIFFIN. *The Empire Writes Back: Theory and Practice in Post-Colonial Literatures* (London: Routledge, 1989).

BAKHTIN, Mikhail. "From the Prehistory of Novelistic Discourse" in *Modern Criticism and Theory: A Reader*, ed. David Lodge (London: Longman, 1988): 125–56.

——. *Rabelais and His World*, tr. H. Iswolsky (Cambridge MA: MIT Press, 1968).

BARNARD, Ian. Review of *Out of Exile: South African Writers Speak*, ed. Kevin Goddard & Charles Wessels (1992), *Research in African Literatures* 24.3 (Fall 1993): 131–33.

BHABHA, Homi, "The Commitment to Theory," *New Formations* 5 (Summer 1988): 5–23.

——. "The Third Space," in *Identity: Community, Culture, Difference*, ed. Jonathan Rutherford (London: Lawrence & Wishart, 1990): 207–21.

---

[65] *Cemetery of Mind*, 180.

[66] Cf Lacan, "The Insistence of the Letter."

[67] Bhabha, "The Commitment to Theory," 21.

CAUTE, David. *The Espionage of the Saints: Two Essays on Silence and the State* (London: Hamish Hamilton, 1986).

DE WAAL, Shaun. "A Melange of Rap and Dub; A Mixture of Blood and Roses," *Weekly Mail* (26 April–2 May, 1991).

HOVE, Chenjerai. *Bones* (Harare: Baobab, 1988).

JENSMA, Wopko. *i must show you my clippings* (Johannesburg: Ravan, 1977).

KLOPPER, Dirk. Review of Dambudzo Marechera's *Cemetery of Mind*, *Southern African Review of Books* (March–April 1993): 16.

KROUSE, Matthew, ed. *The Invisible Ghetto. Lesbian and Gay Writing from South Africa* (Johannesburg: COSAW, 1993).

LACAN, Jacques. "The Insistence of the Letter in the Unconscious," in *Modern Criticism and Theory: A Reader*, ed. David Lodge (London: Longman, 1988): 80–106.

LLOYD, Fiona. "Images of the Changing City: Painting Pain, Memory and Music with the words of Six Languages," *Africa South and East* (November, 1993): 36.

MARECHERA, Dambudzo. "The African Writer's Experience of European Literature," in VEIT–WILD, *Dambudzo Marechera*, 361–68.

———. *Cemetery of Mind* (Harare: Baobab, 1992).

———. "Interview and Discussion with Dambudzo Marechera about *Black Sunlight*," in VEIT–WILD, *Dambudzo Marechera*, 217–21.

———. *Mindblast* (Harare: College Press, 1984).

———. *Scrapiron Blues* (Harare: Baobab, 1994).

———. "'Slow Brain Death Can Only Be Cured by a Literary Shock Treatment': Dambudzo Marechera interviewed by Alle Lansu," in VEIT–WILD, *Dambudzo Marechera*, 5–48.

MCLOUGHLIN, Tim. "Cultural Authenticity in Black Zimbabwean Literature in English: A Case for Metonymy," in *Nouvelles du Sud: Littératures et Anthropologie*, ed. D. Rochay and P. Dakeyo (Paris, 1986): 79–88.

MERCER, Kobena. "Diaspora Culture and the Dialogic Imagination: The Aesthetics of Black Independent Film in Britain," in *Blackframes: Critical Perspectives on Black Independent Cinema*, ed. M. Cham & C. Watkins (Cambridge MA: MIT Press, 1988): 50–61.

PARKER, Patricia. "The Metaphorical Plot," in *Metaphor. Problems and Perspectives*, ed. D.S. Miall (Brighton: Harvester, 1982): 133–67.

PLATE, Christoph. "Lesego Rampolokeng (Südafrika)," *Literaturnachrichten* 35 (October–December 1992): 11–13.

POWELL, Ivor. "The Shape of the Arts to Come," *Weekly Mail* (December 10–16 1993): 41.

RAMPOLOKENG, Lesego. *Horns for Hondo* (Johannesburg: COSAW, 1990).

———. *Talking Rain* (Johannesburg: COSAW, 1993).

SCHULTE, Bernd, *Die Dynamik des Interkulturellen in den postkolonialen Literaturen englischer Sprache* (Heidelberg: Carl Winter, 1993).

STALLYBRASS, Peter & Allon White. *The Politics and Poetics of Transgression* (London: Methuen, 1986).

VEIT–WILD, Flora. *Dambudzo Marechera: A Source Book on his Life and Work* (London: Hans Zell, 1992).

———. "Dances with Bones: Hove's Romanticised Africa," *Research in African Literatures* 24.3 (Fall 1993): 5–12.

———. "The Elusive Truth: Literary Development in Zimbabwe Since 1980," *Matatu* 10 (*African Literatures in the Eighties*, ed. Dieter Riemenschneider & Frank Schulze–Engler, 1993): 107–20.

WILLEMSE, Hein. "Black Afrikaans 'Soubesie Poesie,'" *Southern African Review of Books* (February–May 1990): 27–29.

———. "Die Skrille Sombesies: Emergent Black Afrikaans Poets in Search of Authority," in *Rendering Things Visible*, ed. Martin Trump (Johannesburg: Ravan, 1990): 367–401.

❦ ❖ ❦

UWE SCHÄFER

"both/and" and/or "either/or"
Syncretism and Imagination
in the Novels of Wilson Harris and Bessie Head

WHILE THE MILLENNIUM IS DRAWING TO A CLOSE, fundamental changes are occurring in the political and literary landscape. Not only has the global map been recently redrawn by the struggles of the peoples of Eastern Europe; an even more dramatic and far-reaching transformation of our conception of the world can be traced back to the mass-migration of people all over the world historically caused by the advance of capitalism and colonialism. In its wake, neatly defined concepts of centre and periphery that Europeans have long taken for granted have become permeable and reveal themselves as an illusion. This is especially true for the ideology of cultural homogeneity, nowadays often sold under the term "identity." A world-view based on concepts of invariant identity, however, extrapolates the creative potential that lies at the heart of every cultural contact-situation into an unchanging sanction. In other words: it blocks every individual and collective creative development.

Let me give an example. One of our favourite cognitive notions is that oppressors rule and the oppressed follow suit. Any individual or any society perceiving a given situation within these static parameters automatically confines herself or himself either to the ghetto of privilege or the ghetto of self-righteousness – thus reproducing the tautology of power. Institutions that were once founded for the production of these ideologies, such as the literature departments of European universities, now begin to mirror these global processes. Increasing numbers of scholars, in spite of institutional difficulties, have now dedicated their efforts to the decolonisation of knowledge "as we know it," which is, roughly, the knowledge of the white Western male individual. Instead of welcoming cognitive change as a token of a growing awareness that Europe is no longer the unquestioned and dominant centre of the world, Western academics often feel obliged to retreat either into variations of the old theme of "the decline of the West" or into the postmodern cynicism of the relativity of all concepts, instead of taking an active part in the struggle for a better (academic) future. At the worst, the reaction is structural violence, eg the establishment and maintenance of historically all-too-familiar barriers to admission.

Nevertheless, the fact that these phenomena exist seems to contain a twofold secret confession: On the one hand, they show the efficiency of the unceasing efforts of people and peoples hitherto silenced by colonial discourse and depicted as the Other in a European fantasy designed to deny a voice to their side of her/his/their story. On the other hand, it is easy to sense the degree of frustration caused by a binary, stereotyped perception of the world in terms of good and evil and the exclusion of whatever may be regarded as Other in everyday conversation. The latter problem and paths towards its solution are what I would like to deal with here; I will therefore focus on two writers whose works and lives are dedicated to the fight against fixed stereotypes and cultural stasis.

It is necessary for the West to comprehend exclusions and silences as moral losses and to draw consequences, one of which should be to allow for a broader, syncretic perception of the world. The key to achieving this goal is a re-definition of our individual conception of ourselves, which is still deeply marked by an ideology of invariant identity that assumes the idealising guise of the independent individual. Man in the West usually conceives of himself (and herself) as a closed entity or space, opposed to and different from whatever he or she perceives as Other. This is the fantasy daily fabricated by images produced in ever vaster amounts of media communication and advertising, leaving its mark on all social contexts in which subjects are standardised. At least in those areas of the globe where communication technologies do have a strong impact on social contexts, a consensus about good and evil is manufactured that leads to a compartmentalised, alienated ego structuring its experiences and relations to others in hierarchical dyads of Self and Other, conscious and unconscious, man and woman, white and black, hetero- and homosexual.

The goal of revising these cognitive structures is to create a more balanced global society in which everyone has learnt to ask the question, "Who is the Other?" and to recognise the creative potential and hidden layers of meaning deriving from any syncretic situation. The term "syncretic" in literature refers to commonsense opposites occuring in the same text, a difference within unity that by contradiction opens spaces of creativity. The paradox of phenomena that seem to contradict each other in commonsense knowledge, forcing the reader to go back and read over again, this unbearable discord – exemplified in the title of this paper – is precisely what coincides with true subjectivity: not the exclusion of the Other, but the dialectical tension between Self and Other which sets in motion the process of interpretation. An early example for this tension is the paradoxical Hegelian proposition "the spirit is a bone": the very failure of the first reading gives us meaning.

Bessie Head and Wilson Harris have been chosen for this paper not only because they create syncretic paradoxes of this kind in their texts by drawing on a wide range of different cultural treasures, but also because there lies at the heart of their writing the utopia of a creative and re-creative balance between cultures. First and foremost, their writings provide profound insights into the architecture of the cognitive mechanisms of colonial and neo-colonial power-relations. Furthermore, by reworking the hardened ground of static power relations, they uncover spaces and processes of regaining our creative imagination in the present state of extreme psychic deprivation. For both writers, the unconscious, reflected in the dream-structure of their texts, becomes the key to a syncretic vision beyond finite positions.

Wilson Harris

Wilson Harris was born of mixed heritage in 1921 in Guyana, where he worked as a land surveyor for the colonial government from 1942 to 1959. He led several geomorphological expeditions in the interior. These expeditions completely transformed his perception of nature and history, leading to his career as a poet, which started in 1945. After the break-up of his first marriage, he went to England, where he married a Scottish dramatist and poet. He published the first of his twenty-one novels in 1960. The need for a transformation of our perception of reality and the regeneration of the imagination if civilisation is to survive the conflicts of the twentieth century is one theme that runs through all his writing. Another is the pressing need for cross-culturalism. In Harris's view, the binary biases and limitations governing our everyday perception (which I mentioned above) are produced by narrative modes of commonsense realism and notions of individualism inherited from the nineteenth-century European novel, a thesis he formulated in his 1967 critical essay "Tradition and the West Indian Novel":

> "character" in the novel rests more or less on the self-sufficient individual – on elements of "persuasion" [...] rather than "dialogue" or "dialectic" [....] The novel of persuasion rests on the grounds of apparent common sense [...] on an accepted plane of society we are per-suaded has an inevitable existence.[1]

Harris fights narrative modes of commonsense realism by merging past and present, thus undermining the surface-texture of character and event. He stresses the cross-cultural elements in his work, a project he describes in his 1983 collection of essays, *The Womb of Space*, as follows:

> The paradox of cultural heterogeneity, or cross-cultural capacity, lies in the evolutionary thrust it restores to orders of the imagination, the ceaseless dialogue it inserts between hardened conventions and eclipsed or half-eclipsed otherness, within an intuitive self that moves endlessly into flexible patterns, arcs or bridges of community...[2]

Harris stages his cross-cultural dialogues between African and Amerindian oral traditions and canonised European literature, positivist science and medieval alchemy, science and art. This syncretism of non-exclusive differences forms itself into a deeply moral vision of a balanced society.

This theme also pervades his novel *The Four Banks of the River of Space*, published in 1992. Its protagonist, the Guyanese engineer and sculptor Anselm, sets out to conceive a better future, a city of God, by converting the deprivations arising from

---

[1] Wilson Harris, "Tradition and the West Indian Novel," in Harris, *Tradition, The Writer and Society: Critical Essays* (1967; London/Port of Spain: New Beacon, 1973): 29.

[2] Wilson Harris, *The Womb of Space: The Cross-Cultural Imagination* (Westport CT: Greenwood, 1983): xviii.

dyadic, hierarchical cognitive structures into syncretic visions. At the beginning of the novel he is visited one evening in Essex by Lucius Canaima, a murderer, encountered in Anselm's earlier life in Guyana, whom he allowed to escape. Canaima's presence arouses in Anselm a moral compulsion to retrace his steps into the past, encountering half-real, half-mythical characters representing the colonial powers of positivist science, the army and the Christian church. This confrontation with the powers of the past is the starting-point for a creative revision of the motives and the frustration underlying every act of violence. The metaphorical wound Anselm receives by the knife of the evil spirit Canaima becomes a door to the unconscious and to history. The seed of memory and metamorphosis lies in his confrontation with the past, according to the motto: "the wound can be healed only by the spear which made it." Absence is thus transformed into presence. An example: despite the attempt of the realist, Inspector Robot, to fix colonial history – represented in the image of a row of Amerindian graves – into a finite absolute, Anselm, having received the wound of memory and regained intuition, is able to carve the graves into a moving procession of living, existential sculptures, thus making the victims of colonial history literally come alive.

Harris defines literacy as a perception of a multiplicity of texts, "different texts playing against each other," as opposed to illiteracy, which excludes the presence of other possibilities. One consequence for his texts is that "the tautology of the story-line is fractured in favour of a mysterious continuity that defies absolute models, absolute formula [...]."[3] Harris refuses to be labelled the "author" of his texts, in the sense of being an authority consciously controlling the process of text-production. He has frequently articulated his conviction that vulnerability and intuitive imagination are the driving force behind his writing. A true writer for him is a "medium" gathering "plural forms of profound identity."

Consequently, his texts defy any authoritative or fixed reading: the reader is entangled in an Anancy-web of interpretations which are never complete. The characters in both his early novels and his later texts – even the narrator – become agents of the text, which itself now comes alive, fictionalising its author. For instance, a figure in *The Infinite Rehearsal* bearing the initials W.H. actually steals the autobiography of the main character, Robin Redbreast Glass, and publishes it; and the manuscript of *The Four Banks of the River of Space* is given by Anselm to a figure bearing the name Wilson Harris, before the former disappears into the Macusi heartland of South America.

Harris stages a dialogue between canonised texts of European literature (Goethe's *Faust*, Dante's *Divine Comedy*, Homer's *Odyssey*; the poetry of Donne, Blake, Hopkins, Yeats; the prose of Melville and Faulkner) and vanished pre-Columbian cultural practices (for instance, the music of the Carib bone-flute, the Toltec cosmogony of successive world-ages, the trickster Anancy, the Arawak

---

3 Wilson Harris, "Judgement and Dream," in Harris, *The Radical Imagination*, ed. Alan Riach & Mark Williams (Liège: L3–Liège Language Literature, 1992): 15.

concept of Zemi or play of forces), working on and with Western cultural practices, such as modern quantum physics, modern cosmogony, land-surveying, music, architecture, and literature. In this interplay or dialogue Harris uncovers creative subconscious powers. The subaltern becomes not only visible, but an active part of a dance of inclusivity in which parallel traditions can be shared in an infinite number of potential encounters between individual and collective imagination(s).

Bessie Head

Bessie Head makes us painfully aware of the difficulties involved in the process of overcoming individual and collective traumas deriving from colonial history and neo-colonial power-relations. Although she employs a complex dream-language, she always comes back to the ground of everyday experience. Her novel *A Question of Power* stages power-relations not only in a metaphysical space, but on the basis of the everyday experience of hierarchised gender relations.

Bessie Head was born in 1937 in Pietermaritzburg as the daughter of a wealthy young Johannesburg socialite and her family's Black stable-attendant. Her mother was subsequently entombed in a mental asylum by her family, committing suicide in 1942. By that time Bessie Head had been taken from her and been given successively to a Coloured foster-family, the Child Welfare Society, and the Christian missionary enterprise. She learned about her real mother at the age of thirteen when the principal of her Christian missionary school bluntly told her:

> You must be very careful. If you are not careful you'll get insane just like your mother. Your mother was a white woman. They had to lock her up, as she was having a child by the stable boy, who was a native...[4]

– a biographical fragment which she integrated into the novel. After a period as a primary-school teacher in Durban and the break-up of a disastrous marriage, she was forced to leave South Africa for Botswana in 1964, together with her son, as a consequence of her marginal involvement in the Pan-African Congress. From this life-experience, characterised by Linda Beard as "traumatised by the experience of dispossession as a nonwhite in an albino paradise obsessed with binary oppositions,"[5] she knows only too well about the tyranny of absolutes. But despite her experiences, she chooses not to replace the despotism of absolute evil with that of absolute good. Her fiction bespeaks process, relationship, and ongoing negotiation, staging a chorus of a multiplicity of traditions integrating elements from autobiography, philosophical commentary, classical mythology, English literature, Christian, Buddhist and Hindu symbolism, and San and Zulu folklore. In place of a linear colonialist or neo-colonialist master-narrative, we find a heterodoxical alchemy continually reworking the ground of the text and reconstituting the historical and imaginative landscape.

---

[4] Bessie Head, *A Question of Power* (London: Heinemann, 1992): 16.
[5] Linda Beard, "Bessie Head's Syncretic Fictions: The Reconceptualization of Power and the Recovery of the Ordinary," *Modern Fiction Studies*, 37.3 (Autumn, 1991): 579–80.

In *A Question of Power* we encounter a vast number of fragments generated by that will to power which produces the hierarchical dyads described above. The text mediates them by using the voice of the unconscious, which insists on integrating apparently distinct, contradictory elements. In a situation of extreme frustration arising from her realisation that she exchanged the racism of South Africa for that of Botswana after her flight, Elizabeth finds a way in which to personalise her oppression and her rage in the figures of the paternal Sello and the husband-like Dan, who appear as nightmare ghosts in the dream-like parts of the text, trying to exert power over her. Elizabeth stages the drama of her inner hells in order to "end all hells forever" (12). Dan wants her body; Sello wants her soul; and Elizabeth wants to be free. During these struggles, she gains insight into the hell of desire caused by invariant identities of man and woman, and from these insights discovers the holiness of man and the goddess within herself: "There is only one God and his name is Man. And Elizabeth is his prophet."[6] A further illustration of the common ground shared by Bessie Head and Wilson Harris can be found in a particular motif emerging from both *A Question of Power* and *The Four Banks of the River of Space*: the universal moral language of mankind. In *A Question of Power*, Elizabeth detects that it is

> in the blackest hour of despair, that you stumble on a source of goodness [...] It was the kind of language she understood, that no-one was the be-all and end-all of creation, that no one had the power of assertion and dominance to the exclusion of other life [...] It was almost a suppressed argument she was working with all the time; that people, in their souls, were forces, energies, stars, planets, universes and all kinds of swirling magic and mystery.[7]

That the source of imagination, of moral regeneration, can be found in the abyss of every individual catastrophe is also central to Harris's *Four Banks of the River of Space*. On his journey into the past, Anselm is shown by his Carnival master Proteus that

> The key to carnival [...] is rooted in imperial and colonial disguises. The key to carnival lies in a displacement of time-frames to break a one-track commitment to history. The key to the reformation of the heart breaks the door of blind consciousness into shared dimensions, the dimension of subconscious age and the dimension of childhood. They cross and re-cross each other within levels of dream. The key to the unconscious future lies in shared burdens of intuitive memory, shared volumes written by mutual science and art within the Spirit of age, dual and triple beggars and kingships and queenships.[8]

The question contained in the title of this paper cannot be answered once and for all. It is intended as an illustration of the dialectical tension, the endless negotiation, between a language of inclusivity − "both/and" − and exclusivity − "either/or" − which is the prerequisite for poetic imagination and creativity. This is what Wilson Harris reminds us of when he points to the common source of science and art, and what Bessie Head reminds us of when she blends dream and reality in *A Question of*

---

6 Head, *A Question of Power*, 206.

7 Head, *A Question of Power*, 34 35.

8 Wilson Harris, *The Four Banks of the River of Space* (London: Faber & Faber, 1992): 59.

Power. At the heart of their writing lies the paradox of similarity in difference, difference in similarity.

The task which these writers have set themselves is to overcome the divisions and reductive polarities blocking our imagination. Their writing reconstructs the dome of continuity between past and present, building arches and bridges between peoples and cultures.

WORKS CITED

BEARD, Linda Susan. "Bessie Head's Syncretic Fictions: The Reconceptualization of Power and the Recovery of the Ordinary," *Modern Fiction Studies* 37.3 (Autumn, 1991): 575–89.

HARRIS, Wilson. "Tradition and the West Indian Novel," in Harris, *Tradition, The Writer and Society: Critical Essays* (1967; London/Port of Spain: New Beacon, 1973): 28–47.

————. *The Four Banks of the River of Space* (London: Faber & Faber, 1992).

————. *The Infinite Rehearsal* (London: Faber & Faber, 1987).

————."Judgement and Dream" (1989), in Harris, *The Radical Imagination*, ed. Riach & Williams, 17–31.

————. *The Radical Imagination: Lectures and Talks by Wilson Harris*, ed. Alan Riach & Mark Williams (Liège: L3–Liège Language Literature, 1992).

————. *The Womb of Space: The Cross-Cultural Imagination* (Westport CT: Greenwood, 1983).

HEAD, Bessie. *A Question of Power* (1974; London: Heinemann, 1992).

MAES–JELINEK, Hena. "'Unfinished Genesis': *The Four Banks of the River of Space*," in: *Wilson Harris: The Uncompromising Imagination*, ed. Hena Maes–Jelinek (Sydney/Mundelstrup: Dangaroo, 1991): 230–45.

❧ ❖ ❧

JOSEPH SWANN

The Abstraction of Language
Jayanta Mahapatra and A.K. Mehrotra
as Indian "Postmodernists"

J AYANTA MAHAPATRA AND A.K. MEHROTRA belong in a sense to two different Indias. Mahapatra was born in 1928 into a third-generation Christian family in Cuttack, on the Bay of Bengal, where he still lives. At the university of Patna he studied physics, and for many years he taught that subject in various colleges in Orissa state. He started writing poetry in the late Sixties, and his first published collection of poems appeared in 1971 – the same year, in fact, in which Mehrotra's first major volume was published. But Mehrotra, at that time, was only twenty-four, a Hindu, a graduate of the English faculties of Allahabad and Bombay universities, and something of an *enfant terrible* in the world of Indian-English poetry. Bruce King, however, in his *Modern Indian Poetry in English*, links the two poets aptly together under the heading of "Experimentalists," and I should like to pursue this line of thought as it reflects on the question of cultural fusion, by demonstrating on the one hand the peculiar Indianness of their experimentation and on the other its peculiar closeness to certain aspects of postmodernism in the West. It is a closeness not of origins – for Indian poetry in English underwent neither a Romantic nor a modernist period, so could not strictly be called postmodernist either – but of concern, and of the form generated by concern.

There is, however, another aspect to this question, for just as postmodernism is a Western category, so the aesthetic starting point of this analysis is *prima facie* different from that of the poets it is addressing, even though, writing in English, they share with the European writer at least certain aspects of influence and growth – Mehrotra's early interest in Ezra Pound or in Dadaism, like Nissim Ezekiel's in Yeats, is a case in point. Such influences are clearly aspects of cross-fertilisation, but the present argument is concerned with expressing the perceived cultural difference as well as the relatedness of Mahapatra's and Mehrotra's writing. That it does so in a terminology drawn from the contemporary West reflects the cultural meeting inherent in that perception, for to predicate a meeting of cultures is either to enact one or to fail altogether. The question of the historical validity of a perception – as of its premises – is the question of whether in its own place and time it makes sense; there is no firm point of reference from which it, or indeed any statement, can be judged. It is my hope that in the present instance the meeting takes place.

To read Mahapatra and Mehrotra is to encounter not only individual meanings, but also the aesthetic suppositions on which they are built. The cross-fertilisation is both aesthetic and *of* our (in this case European) aesthetics. For the models of language and of the reading-process implicit in their poetry reflect the Hindu philosophy of knowing and the concept of *eros* which runs through it. Here, too, there may be a link with some categories of post-structuralist thinking in the West; for all our knowing flows from the same source. Reading is meeting, and in a sense that is close to this poetry, meeting is also reading.

Jayanta Mahapatra

Something of this is evident in a poem from Mahapatra's fourth volume, *A Rain of Rites*:

> Children, brown as earth, continue to laugh
> at cripples and mating mongrels.
> Nobody ever bothers about them.
> The temple points to unending rhythm.
> On the dusty street the colour of shorn scalp
> there are things moving all the time
> and yet nothing seems to go away from sight.
> Injuries drowsy with the heat.
> And that sky there,
> claimed by inviolable authority,
> hanging on to its crutches of silence.[1]

The poem moves in a continuous line from observation to reflection, but that reflection is itself couched in concrete images, so that the whole range of experience expressed in the poem is concentrated and particularised on a single street at Puri (a centre of pilgrimage on the Bay of Bengal). The spiritual and the material are here inseparable. The insight into the "unending rhythm" of the temporal as of the eternal, the contingent as of the unbending absolute, does not lessen the force of the poet's criticism but intensifies and actualises it by displacing it to a different plane of experience. No firm single judgement can be made because (and although) "nothing seems to go away from sight": judgement is itself paralysed in this environment because it cannot untie the knot that binds it to what it sees. This is itself linked to the progressive abstraction of the poem, whose concrete imagery of the opening lines – children, cripples, mating mongrels – is attenuated after the third line into mere indications – "the temple points," "there are things moving," And the injuries that are "drowsy with the heat" comprise all injury, including that of the poet's point of view, which holds all in its own rhythm but must therefore forego any claim to "inviolable authority." The very symbol of that authority, the sky, is reduced to another dweller on the temple street, a crippled silence.

The reciprocity of sight and insight, vision and judgement in this poem – indeed, their utter inseparability – means that neither can assert hegemony, for each is

---

[1] Jayanta Mahapatra, "Main Temple Street, Puri," *A Rain of Rites* (Athens: U of Georgia P, 1976): 16.

continually broken on the other. Far from being abdicated, however, judgement enfolds its own premises within its scope, and the poem affirms and criticises the human condition – *this* human condition – at the same time. Where the categories of language are contingent on emotional encounter they lose the sharp edge, and the stability of definition. But it is, in this perspective, *because* man's devotion, man's injury, man's absolutes all return to the particulars of his experience that they exist at all. Meaning dissolved into the particular, like *eros*, becomes more, not less meaningful: becomes not just meaning, but experience. Continuity and brokenness are themselves a seamless whole in this poem, and this is reflected in its language, with various levels of imagery and types of syntax displayed within the single vision of a street. Like the street itself, the poem seems to stand still, to be an entire universe of movement in its stillness. And that movement reaches out beyond itself to comprise an aesthetic of language, a union of the abstract or *meaning* level of language with its particularising function as pointing beyond meaning to the ineffable otherness of the encountered world.

Read in this way, Mahapatra's poems are reflections on language; but that reflection is never discursive, it is embodied in the movement of the text. Other poems from the same volume make the point with unmistakable clarity. Thus:

> Swans sink wordlessly to the carpet
> miles of polished floors
> reach out
> for the glass of voices
> There are gulls crying everywhere
> and glazed green grass
> in the park with the swans
> folding their cold throats.[2]

Where the language of the first poem began at least in a discursive mode, describing a recognisable physical world, this poem, from its title onwards, disrupts and dislocates the expectations we have of such a world, while at the same time suggesting that it fulfils them. I cannot really hear my fingers sadly touching the keys of a piano, nor do swans sink wordlessly to any carpet. Different discursive or descriptive contexts are here overlaid, and again the effect is of unifying disparate dimensions of experience, of sensation and thought. Again the medium is the image, aptly chosen for its associations, but isolated and juxtaposed. To the European ear the poem sounds thoroughly European: one thinks of Tchaikovsky, of *Swan Lake* and marble halls. Nor is the piano an Indian instrument. Mahapatra's disjointed landscape is that of a dream, an inner universe that expresses the brittleness of an alien cultural tradition, but beyond this the brittle alienness of music and of language itself. The word, the image, is bathed in the cold shine of artificiality; the sadness of the poem is the sadness of words, which codify – but only when their negativity is worn outwardly, as here, can words ever really touch to the otherness of the world we experience.

---

[2] Mahapatra, "I Hear My Fingers Sadly Touching An Ivory Key," *A Rain of Rites*, 41.

A poem from Mahapatra's sixth volume, *The False Start*, shows with great conciseness the force of this negativity:

> This thing
> wakes me like a hand.
> Grass waits
> and rock
> takes the wind's place.
> Huge door
> drifting
> with feet of light,
> my eyes
> quietly open
> before the night's.[3]

There is a door opening in this poem, but it opens onto what is not, or not yet – onto grass, rock and wind – as much as onto what is. For a door, in being itself, is also an entrance to the other. Nor is "this thing" just a door: it is a word, and it is that word becoming closer and closer until it is any word, and wakens the mind, as well as the eyes, onto the night of what it cannot express. In the poem's statement, however, "my eyes / quietly open / before the *night's*" (emphasis mine), and this makes the night into a responding, living thing. The darkness and negativity of the poem are not moral, but ontological; they is something natural, easily accepted, something continuous with the positivity of this world. For just as the darkness of the thing, the endless potentiality of matter, is inseparable from the word, so too is nothingness, in this ontology, continuous with being. With all its movement – as we have seen in the first poem – the thought is essentially static; or, rather, the categories of static and dynamic are themselves abrogated in a moment of opening onto the undefined, the erotic encounter with personified night. It is not for nothing that we do not even know if the word "open" here is a verb or an adjective.

Grass, wind, rock, the door: these things are simply there, part of the set of being, but in relation to each other part of the set of non-being, too. For this is a world of juxtaposed but related entities, not conceived in a linear, functional way, in which the parts receive their meaning from their subjection to the purpose of the whole, but in which the parts in their very fragmentation are inseparable from the wholeness they constitute. Hindu philosophy posits the identity between subject and object, knower and known, as the root of being;[4] unlike the post-Socratic Western tradition, it never considered being as a predicate of things divorced from the moment of their knowing – what Heidegger called "being-as-presence," and what he rejected as such. It is for this reason that the Indian tradition is so aware that being and language, word and thing, are inseparable; for the function of language is to articulate and thereby to effect man's relation to the world, and this relation, breaking the world apart, reinstates the wholeness of the energy that underlies it. For

---

[3] Mahapatra, "The Door," *The False Start* (Bombay: Clearing House, 1980): 69.

[4] Cf the *Upanishads*, tr., ed. & intro. K.M. Sen (Harmondsworth: Penguin, 1965): 117–18, and K.M. Sen, *Hinduism* (Harmondsworth: Penguin, 1961): 19.

relation is an encounter with otherness, a breaking of the self on the other; it is a meeting of energies and a realisation in that sense of wholeness. Speaking of the poem as a work of art, Mahapatra in "The Ruins" likens the quizzical frown on the forehead of one who, seeking wholeness, has "failed to understand" to the word that he seeks: "So like a word, its blue wings broken, / palpitating"; and he continues: "Nothing that is whole / speaks of the past. Or lives. / Or can form into a word."[5] It is not that we inherit only fragments, but that all we inherit must be fragmented before it can be properly experienced.

That the world is only present to us in signs; that language must be broken if it is to release its energy; that the metonymic structure of our language-world is primary – these are all commonplaces of Western postmodernism, the fruit of the West's long struggle with its own romantic dichotomies. In Mahapatra's and in Mehrotra's poetry the same insights flow from a very different source. The theme of Mahapatra's poem "Old Palaces"[6] is the need for abstract meanings and values to break in the experience of our inherited language-world, and the pain of this process. Speaking of the monuments of the past, the poet says:

> What can remain to meaning here
> deadens gestures, footfalls, faces of our nature.

But that deadening turns into something more vivid when the things and artefacts are removed from the context they once had and are realized in their present individuality:

> Disused things yield themselves to our
> arrivals and departures, sun and rain, relationships:
> cold reminders of gods I had hoped to escape forever.

The pain of breaking becomes more positive then, for

> In high ceilinged rooms the lofty uncommon light
> rees things from one another, each object
> on its own darkness, definitive, as though charged
> with the voice of a bird no longer there, sucked into the skies.

And the poem ends with the affirmation that negativity, the awareness of pain and loss, is an essential part of any true encounter:

> What brings us face to face, across the palace's
> golden light locked inside that secret lens?
> Not the thought that succeeds in pushing the darkness, evil and ugliness out of my life.

The manner in which a single object can embody history is expressed very effectively in "The Cannon," from the volume *Life Signs*, where the poet's eye moves from the "footprints / of diseased hollow-cheeked children" on a "grieving pout of earth" to the guts of a swift hanging from a crow's claws in the air. The poem continues:

---

5 Mahapatra, *A Rain of Rites*, 36.
6 Mahapatra, "Old Palaces," *A Rain of Rites*, 4–5.

The cold dust
of forgotten graves of British colonials
waits to escape in the wind. And a past
appears without pity, a morning gone by,
holding the ground, riding the defenceless wind
to the horizons of the sea. As slowly
clinging to the heat's haze,
looms up the cannon,
old and rusting and alone,
graceless in the throes of history's nightmare.[7]

Like "Main Temple Street, Puri," this poem keeps largely to the observed present; but "in the dim consciousness that everything / perhaps is a dream," the perspective is repeatedly lengthened to absorb the past. The dream becomes a nightmare which in turn absorbs the present, for the wholeness of Mahapatra's perspective does not preclude a frequently sombre note. It is his closeness to human concerns, and the relevance to these of his awareness of language not just as a medium of expression but as a constitutive process of the world, that most clearly characterizes Mahapatra's work. Thus the poem "Suppose" from *The False Start* shows the identity in his perspective of love and absence, and it also perfectly illustrates the abstract logic of his writing:

Suppose I write a love poem
to the world. Suppose
the world abounds in innocence.
It is not the first time.
The snow has walked out before
into the black earth.
The present is not what I believe.
A blind habit gropes
against the walls,
barely touching your human face
with my outstretched fear.
Silence. Where do all
the branched waters go?[8]

To call this poem abstract does not mean that it deals consistently in abstractions; rather the opposite, for its abstract categories are constantly reduced to unexpectedly concrete terms. Its subject is love and the expression of love, both of which are directed to the unutterably Other; it is, therefore, a poem about knowledge as an encounter with the unknown. Being, in this sense, about the most real of experiences, it chooses the mode of the unreal and casts its opening statements as a twofold hypothesis: a love-poem to a world that abounds in innocence. This is resumed in the contrastive, concrete image of snow melting into black earth. Similarly, in a second movement, the need to find a new language ("The present is not what I believe") is grounded in an image of non-communication, of the crippled habits of language held out in fearful desire towards the unknown. Finally the statement "Silence" – the silence of a meeting that can never be a comprehension –

---

7 Mahapatra, "The Cannon," *Life Signs* (Delhi: Oxford UP, 1983): 9.
8 Mahapatra, "Suppose," *The False Start*, 14.

is countered by the question-image of the waters melting from the snow. They may comprehend fully; but language never can.

In its alternation between the conceptual and the material dimensions of experience the poem is itself highly particular. It is at the same time an abstract comment on the nature of language as a sign-system that can touch reality only when, at its limit, it enacts the process of its own signification – and that is the process, too, of its non-significance. No poet writes all the time at his limit, however, and the poems used here represent only a small excerpt from the seven years of Mahapatra's work between 1976 and 1983. In terms of the fusion of cultures, these poems neither present nor induce any such fusion. What they impart is the possibility and the value of cultural encounter; and they do this by being poems of encounter, poems which raise encounter to the abstract level of an aesthetic. It is the cross-fertilization of this aesthetic with that of the contemporary West that is the subject of this reading.

Arvind Krishna Mehrotra

Mehrotra came to poetry at a much earlier age than Mahapatra, and he seems immediately to have had his own ideas about how to write. As an undergraduate at Allahabad university he edited a short-lived magazine called *damn you*, which saw itself in the tradition of the San Francisco Beat poets, and among many other European and American influences ranging from William Blake to Ezra Pound he also cited the Surrealist *Manifesto* as a principal influence on his work.[9] In P. Lal's 1969 *Anthology*, which was one of the main instruments in putting modern Indian poetry in English onto the cultural map of India, Mehrotra went out of his way to accuse the entire older generation of poets – what he called the "town-men," including such figures as Nissim Ezekiel and Adil Jussawalla – of incompetence. Despite this, he writes clearly in the tradition of modern Indian-English poetry, taking only to a higher level of abstraction the sense of continuity in discontinuity that is present in the poetry of Jayanta Mahapatra, and that characterizes the work of Kamala Das, Gauri Deshpande, A.K. Ramanujan and Nissim Ezekiel before him.

Language, for Mehrotra, is a vast storeroom of disparate energies, the coded agglomerations of life. His well-known poem "The Sale," from *Nine Enclosures*, expresses this in bold surrealistic terms. The second section of the poem runs as follows:

> Would you mind if I showed you
> a few more things now yours?
> Be careful, one river is still wet
> and slippery; its waters continue to
> run like footprints. Well, this is a
> brick and we call that string.
> This microscope contains the margins
> of a poem. I've a map left, drawn

---

[9] See Bruce King, *Modern Indian Poetry in English* (Delhi: Oxford UP, 1987): 184–85.

> by migrating birds.
> Come into the attic.
> That's not a doll – it's the
> photograph of a brain walking
> on sand and in the next one
> it's wearing an oasis-like crown.
> I must also show you a tiger's skin
> which once hid a palace.
> On one roof you'll see
> the antelope's horns
> on another the falling wind. These round
> things are bangles, that long one
> a gun. This cave is the inside
> of a boot. And here
> carved wheels turn through stone.[10]

The poem reads like a gloss, transposed into a different mode, of Ramanujan's "Small-Scale Reflections on a Great House" – itself a major statement of continuity in alterity. William Walsh writes that

> There is an intrinsic logic, the logic of language, of subject, verb, predicate in the progres-sion of the poem, which leads the listener on in his accustomed ways ... But another economy, a wholly different argument is pitched against our expectations. The disconcerting, the utterly unexpected predicates, undermine our comfortable assurance about what is to come and leave us facing strangeness and danger.[11]

This is well put; but by imposing on normal speech patterns the fantastic logic of what speech *might* say, Mehrotra shifts his level of discourse to the abstract context of language in its workings and structure. Language is seen as perceiving, recognizing, naming, and in all these three functions as correcting the assumptions of that other world outside the saleroom in which we customarily live. It is that correction that is the point. Perception is not the abstraction from experience of a form innate in it, as Aristotle maintained; nor is it any Kantian process locked in the mind; rather, it is the giving of a name, of form as the arbitrary icon of encounter. Far from immuring man in the prison-house of words, as the deconstructionists feared, language in this perspective gives man his freedom; and Mehrotra's poetry is remarkably free and fluent. Even in his youthful outbursts he sought freedom of speech. What his poetry achieves is the enactment, and the reflection, of man's inherent relatedness to the world wherever he meets it.

As in Mahapatra's poetry, this is typically a very concrete, everyday moment. The eighth poem from "The Book of Common Places" captures such a moment:

> From the outlying districts
> Visitors arrive.
> Goldsmith
> And tanner
> In a boat.
> We sit around
> Talking of simple

---

[10] A.K. Mehrotra, "The Sale," *Nine Enclosures* (Bombay: Clearing House, 1976): 21.
[11] William Walsh, *Indian Literature in English* (London: Longman, 1990): 149–50.

> Believable things;
> I show them my new pair of ampersands
> And notice they're singing last year's songs.
> The fish
> Wishes it were
> An illustration
> In a book
> Of symbols.[12]

Again, the discursive context of life is continuous with the fantastic: the poet shows the fisherman "simple believable things" like his "new pair of ampersands." But ampersands are a typographical symbol, a written sign; and the fish too wants to be transformed into a word. Thus the poem becomes a sort of bizarre commentary on Wordsworth's wish to be seen as "a man speaking to men" – bizarre, but modern in its understanding that the world of words is on its own terms both simple and believable; but those are not the terms of our common myth of language.

In reaching back to the foundations of language, Mehrotra shows himself to be fully in the Indian tradition, but his writing frequently touches to the roots of the European tradition, too. Thus his "Between Bricks, Madness" and "Songs of the Ganga" echo – albeit without their formal stringency – the riddles or incantations of early medieval verse, as in the fourth of the "Songs":

> From smoke I learn disappearance
> From the ocean unprejudice
> From birds
> How to find a rest-house
> In the storm
> From the leopard
> How to cover the sun
> With spots
> In summer I tend watermelons
> And in flood I stay
> Near the postman's house
> I am a beggar
> I am a clown
> And I am shadowless[13]

The aphoristic, disjunctive quality of this verse is also, however, clearly Indian, and Mehrotra has made his allegiance to Indian tradition explicit in a number of poems written on earlier poetic models. Thus from "After Kabir":

> Show me the unforked road,
> Lead me till there;
> Or between two rivers
> Make me a hut;
> Or engrave your face
> On my body's parchment.
> This arbour of thorns
> Will enclose you,

---

[12] Mehrotra, "From the outlying districts," *Nine Enclosures*, 41.

[13] Mehrotra, *Nine Enclosures*, 19.

> This dry bush will burn.
> A day is three parts sunset, says Kabir.[14]

It would perhaps be easier to argue in Mehrotra's case than in that of many other Indian poets writing in English that his work represents a real fusion of cultures, for its style as well as its sources seem to draw equally from East and West. In terms of the present argument, however, reading his poetry is certainly an experience of aesthetic cross-fertilization: the same experience as in reading Mahapatra, only more pointed, more reliant on humour, and without the dark undertow of the older poet's concern. Language, in Mehrotra's work, is always at the centre of focus, and that focus is regularly sharper and more abstract than it is in Mahapatra's poetry; but again the abstraction lies even more emphatically in a metonymic alliance of disjointed particulars. This is evident, too, when Mehrotra writes about history, as in this poem from *Distance in Statute Miles*:

> They went with the house:
> A pile of letters on which
> The ink had faded; a silver
> Medal won by Ram Prasad
> The best native student
> In 1896; an iron safe
> With two eight-inch keys.
> The new owners see in them
> Unrelated stories; to us
> They are facts entered
> In a daybook, alongside
> Another transaction.[15]

The poem is reminiscent of a whole tradition of Indian-English writing, notably in the work of Kamala Das and Ramanujan. Its sense of injury is less intense than in Mahapatra, its sense of the omnipresence of language greater. But this does not detract from the vivid reality of the letters, the medal, or the safe: to the new owners, the new readers of their story, they are unrelated, but their assumption into the fabric of a written record enhances their identity in the linguistic act of relating it. It would not be far-fetched to see in this an image of deconstructionism itself, contrasted with an Indian tradition of language that overcomes it.

The meeting in Mehrotra's poetry of the East with the postmodernist West is exemplified in the final poem from his 1984 volume *Middle Earth*. Metonymy is elevated here from a stylistic device to the matter of poetry itself:

> The east wind and
>   A lizard rampant
> Spell rain,
>   Pencils
> Stab dictionaries
>   In the dark,
> Frigate-birds
>   Put rings

---

14 Mehrotra, "After Kabir," *Distance in Statute Miles* (Bombay: Clearing House, 1982): 38.
15 Mehrotra, "The Principal Characters," *Distance in Statute Miles*, 21.

Round the moon,
   The smell
Of ink and
   The shape of
Wyoming,
   Colours like
Burma green,
   Words like
Slough, off-rhymes,
   Translations,
Dead metaphors,
   Things,
The flywheels and
   Sprockets,
The gristle
   Of poems,
Tossed in sleep's
   Fountain,
Garnered in nests,
   Recalled
In holograph,
   At places
Smudged, late for
   Assemblage.[16]

The technique is that of "The Sale," although one might say that the logic of that poem is the subject of this, for this poem is explicitly about language and its disjointedness. Bruce King comments on the background of the idea of the poem as a "conscious assemblage," where "surrealist games of chance are assimilated into a constructivist poetic,"[17] and points to the Sixties as the origin of this sort of writing. There is an element of self-consciousness here in the concentration on language, and the poem is perhaps not so strong as "The Sale." But in another sense one might say that Mehrotra has been faithful to his origins, and has retained the awareness of language which, having obsessed the West for so long, finally gave way there to a preoccupation with the world. These two, in the Indian tradition, have never been separated, nor does Mehrotra here separate them: the scattered poetic fragments, whether east wind or lizards, metaphors, ink or frigate-birds, are all on the same level, all grist to the poet's belated mill. For, where the other is only related in the encounter of language, reality lies in the energy contained in and touched by words.

That is the aesthetic that cross-fertilizes these poems with a burden which is alien to the European tradition of English, but one whose consequences are immensely rich. The consequences themselves, however, are not so very strange; for the European mind, having struggled through the crisis of late-Romantic modernism, has emerged into an awareness that one can live with a world that is available only in signs, and with a language that really only speaks itself (Heidegger), for in so speaking it articulates the whole range of reality. "The gaiety

---

[16] Mehrotra, " Disjecti Membra Poetae," *Middle Earth* (Delhi: Oxford UP, 1984): 53.

[17] Bruce King, *Modern Indian Poetry*, 184.

of language," Wallace Stevens has said, "is our seigneur." That more relaxed attitude in the West does not, however, come from any Eastern tradition, although Europeans and Americans have not been lacking in seeking salvation there. It comes, rather, from the limits to which, in science, philosophy and literature, the West has pushed its own logocentric, transcendentalist thought, and from the alternative tradition of European nominalism, which never subscribed to that philosophy. The modern, postwar period of European and American literature has, not least for this reason, been one in which the aesthetic impact of Eastern – and here in particular of Indian – thought and writing has been very fertile. The two cultures may fuse in the work of an individual, as cultures frequently do; but, beyond any such fusion, the reading of Jayanta Mahapatra and A.K. Mehrotra demonstrates the possibility of encounter with the culturally other, and demonstrates the centrality to the Indian tradition of that concern.

❧ ❖ ❧

WORKS CITED

KING, Bruce. *Modern Indian Poetry in English* (Delhi: Oxford UP, 1987).

LAL, Purshotam, ed. *Modern Indian Poetry in English: An Anthology and A Credo* (Calcutta: Writers Workshop, 1969).

MAHAPATRA, Jayanta. *A Rain of Rites* (Athens: U of Georgia P, 1976).

———. *The False Start* (Bombay: Clearing House, 1980).

———. *Life Signs* (Delhi: Oxford UP, 1983).

MEHROTRA, A.K.. *Nine Enclosures* (Bombay: Clearing House, 1976).

———. *Distance in Statute Miles* (Bombay: Clearing House, 1982).

———. *Middle Earth* (Delhi: Oxford UP, 1984).

SEN, K.M. *Hinduism* (Harmondsworth: Penguin, 1961).

———, tr., ed. & intro. *The Upanishads* (Harmondsworth: Penguin, 1965).

WALSH, William. *Indian Literature in English* (London: Longman, 1990).

❧ ❖ ❧

PETER O. STUMMER

Cross-Over Difficulties
Recent Problems in Cross-Cultural/ Trans-National Communication

The ethnics at our door
Malingering with heritage.[1]

ARRUKH DHONDY, IN HIS NOVEL *BOMBAY DUCK*, has a passage with the title "Chop Suey,"[2] where he develops a serious and disillusioned theory of present-day cross-cultural contact. His thoughts are couched in the language of mocking skit and sarcastic playfulness, with the seriousness only beoming apparent in the abrupt leap from culinary matters, dealt with at length, to panic rumour-mongering in Pakistan after the explosion of an ammunition dump in Rawalpindi, which gives rise to the assumption of a pre-emptive strike by the Israelis against a putative Islamic atom bomb. Government denials speak of the American protective umbrella for Pakistan, just as they speak of so many thousand jobs being provided by American investment after the Union Carbide catastrophe near Bhopal, where poisonous gas killed and maimed a great number of people. The point is, just as in the case of the euphemistic naming of rotten fish as "Bombay Mail or Dak" by the British for their navvies when they built the famous railroad, or in the much-publicized incident in Britain recently, where an English clergyman published the "true" story of an Asian girl, the emphasis is on make-believe and on the fact that there is a fair chance that what you are being offered as genuine from another culture is, in reality, one hundred percent fake, blatant counterfeit. Dhondy conveys his message in the following words:

> Chop Suey is when you've bought something to whose authenticity you cannot attest. Usually because you are ignorant. Usually because the vendor has contrived to culturally mug you.[3]

The entire novel is an intricate elaboration of this idea; for it hinges on the concept of ironized cultural exchange. Indians bring a village version of the *Ramayana* to Britain, while a British director makes a big splash by bringing (à la Peter Brook) a European version to India. However, the director finds himself in a predicament when Hindi fanatics object to the hero being impersonated by a Black-British actor (incidentally, also some sort of cross-over when the Dhondy author–narrator tries to

---

[1] Cyril Dabydeen, "Multiculturalism," in *Voices: Canadian Writers of African Descent*, ed. Ayanna Black (Toronto: Harper/Collins, 1992): 29.

[2] Farrukh Dhondy, *Bombay Duck* (London: Jonathan Cape, 1990): 240.

[3] *Bombay Duck*: 242.

get into the skin of a Black Brit from Jamaica; linguistically not entirely convincing). The book reaches its farcical climax when, at the end, one of the main male Indian characters sits in an English prison awaiting deportation back to India, and, in India, one of the female English protagonists faces the reverse fate of being deported back to Britain. Superficially, this might appear as yet another attempt to deconstruct desire for the Other. But there are two features which undercut this reading. First, the set-up is reciprocal, not a colonial writing back as in the case of, say, Austin Clarke's Barbados/Canada nexus; and second, there is a quite reliable political undercurrent which may be most clearly observed in the pronouncements on Parsee history and Zoroastrianism. Jibes such as the blasphemous use of the name Mazda, the lord of light,[4] indirectly raise a serious point about the crime of blasphemy in a secular but nonetheless Christian society.

I have used *Bombay Duck* to introduce my theme: the fortunes or misfortunes of cultural products in their attempt to cross boundaries, within one and the same country or across frontiers. This is the more obvious aspect of the phenomenon, and I shall be referring to some recent examples from Australia: *Boney, Romper Stomper,* and *Yothu Yindi.* The slightly more complex side of the phenomenon can then be seen in the changing history of cross-over as applied to individuals who internalize more than one cultural frame to varying degrees. This latter angle will involve my analysing in greater detail Eddy Harris's *Native Stranger: A Blackamerican's Journey into the Heart of Africa,* with some clarifying glances, hopefully, at Andrew Hacker's *Two Nations: Black and White, Separate, Hostile, Unequal.*[5] What the problem boils down to there is the changing idea of blackness, of Africanness, and the shift in the image African–Americans have of Africa. This last area will highlight a few more or less successful examples of cross-over in the arts, above all in the music of Ian Hall and Apache Indian.

Cross-cultural communication

Let me state in passing that, in the context of problems of cross-cultural communication, the lethal reception of certain *verses* in certain circles would, no doubt, also qualify. But I shall leave this aside here, just as I shall not go into government interference in BBC transmission policy, leading to the banning, under the Prevention of Terrorism Act, of certain programmes dealing with the situation in Northern Ireland; the reason being that these understandings or misunderstandings represent deliberate international actions. This, by the way, also applies to somewhat outworn cases of leg-pulling in respect to well-established national stereotypes, with one of the more recent examples being Howard Jacobson's novel *Redback,*[6] where the British author, much in the vein of the early Kingsley Amis and

---

[4] *Bombay Duck*: 289.

[5] Eddy L. Harris, *Native Stranger: A Blackamerican's Journey into the Heart of Africa* (1992; London: Viking, 1993); Andrew Hacker, *Two Nations, Black and White, Separate, Hostile, Unequal* (New York: Ballantine, 1993).

[6] Howard Jacobson, *Redback* (1987; London: Black Swan, 1988).

the ageing Tom Sharpe, uses a benighted English hero and his triangular relationship with two female Australian synchronized swimmers to bring out "this national aspiration to nursery innocence" in "the will to babydom in Australia."[7]

But let us stay with Australia for a while, and with our view of it. My first example is from the late news on German television,[8] where the envoi or light-relief afterthought to the programme consisted in the anchorperson''s reporting with a smirk that tourists were shamefacedly sending back bits and pieces they had broken off Ayers Rock, after Aboriginal Australians had put out the rumour that this sacrilege against the holy mountain of Uluru would adversely affect their personal well-being. The tenor was half-serious half-joking, as a preface to a compassionate plea for viewers to heed Aboriginal wishes and abstain from climbing the granite block in future. By playing along at least partly with the imperative to holiness, or pretending to, German television was insinuating itself into the fashion, current in our own culture, for flirting with the mythic and the mysterious. In a classic move, the Other was being used to give the Self a boost.

Henri Safran's series built around Cameron Daddo as David "Boney" Bonaparte might serve as another example. The television series is an Australian–German cooperative venture.[9] The orphaned hero, so the story goes, was not only brought up by Uncle Albert, an old Aboriginal, but was also initiated by him in the old ways, so that he can – as one colleague of his pleases himself to phrase it – put unerring intuition before rationality. The films endorse a romantic view of the landscape (a criminal is brought into the desert, "where it is difficult to lie," and, of course, immediately confesses); worse still, they give the representation of things Aboriginal a kitschy twist. True, the actor Burnum Burnum looks awe-inspiring, a mixture of Marx and an Indian guru. However, the effect created is miles away from the authority which the real man can command, as a cultural and political activist in the Aboriginal land-rights movement. For the German audience, alas, he just brings in a bit of wise old shaman appeal, catering for an exotic view of Aboriginal culture miles distant from the image offered in the original Arthur Upward novels.

It is highly probable that academic discourse, too, has difficulty in ridding itself completely of that kind of prejudice. How else could one explain the general awe with which Lionel Fogarty's abuse of the public at the Aratjara Symposium (Düsseldorf, 1993) was pusillanimously met? Of course, the artist has every right to find his audience stupid; but it does not make sense to insist on some kind of insurmountable secret initiation-barrier by asserting that whites are simply unable to understand Aboriginal culture. You cannot, in one breath, complain about the malign exclusiveness of academic jargon and then go and propagate a hermetic concept of art. Why, then, should anyone bother to recite before such an audience if he or she was convinced that this bunch of people would not understand a single

---

[7] *Redback*, 292.

[8] Zweites Deutsches Fernsehen (7 July, 1993), 22.30.

[9] *Boney*, directed by Henri Safran, 13-part Australian–German television co-production (1993).

word anyway? To bow, under the circumstances, to that kind of assumption is a subtle form of condescension in reverse.[10]

Less obviously, something similar also shows in the non-committal reception of David Mowaljarlai's role in the *Yorro Yorro* project (with white photographer Jutta Malnic),[11] when we compare this with the critical appreciation within Australia of, say, Stephen Muecke.[12]

The success of Yothu Yindi belongs, at least partly, in the same mould. To begin with, the band is advertised in Germany under the label "ethno-rock." Quite frankly, I was glad that the lead singer Mandawuy Yunupingu was wearing just a stylized traditional head-band together with an ordinary black shirt and dark trousers, for the dancers and the didgeridoo players appeared in "native costume," which was, to say the least, superfluous. It is a pity that the texts of the songs were lost on the audience, given the usual volume of the music. Yet it must also be granted that, generally speaking, the political impact of the hit "Treaty" can be applauded all too gratuitously outside Australia, far away from the intertwining interests of mining-industry, world-heritage, and wilderness proposals, not to mention graziers' property-interests. Ethnic romanticism holds hands, then, with the political romanticism of supporting a cause whose main attraction consists in the fact that it is far away.

Geoffrey Wright's film *Romper Stomper* (1992), on the other hand, had the misfortune of being released against the background of a neo-Nazis rampage through post-Unification Germany, and came promptly under fire as a glorification of right-wing skinheads. If shown at all, the German version had been subjected to cuts, and the original could only be seen in small fringe cinemas. The few more insightful reviewers saw affiliations with Genet and Kubrick's *Clockwork Orange*, but shied away from the "anti-Asian" element which is also clearly reflected in the film as an obsession of present-day Australian society. Even more remarkable, the latent homosexuality and the fact that it is a rich man's daughter who finally destroys the all-male gang were aspects that practically nobody connected with the mateship tradition and its feminist critique (so much part and parcel of contemporary culture Down Under).

Cross-over phenomena

A recent poem by the African–American writer Mona Lisa Saloy begins with the lines

> I'm about how words
> work up a gumbo of culture
> stamped and certified African
> delivered on southern American soil[13]

---

10 See Dieter Riemenschneider, *Acolit* 32 (June, 1993): 7–9.

11 *Yorro Yorro* (Broome, W.A.: Magabala, 1993).

12 *Australian Book Review* (July, 1993): 21–22.

13 "Word Works," *African American Review* (Spring, 1993): 155.

In its ironical detachment, this is a far cry from the wide-spread attitude for which Ali Mazrui has coined the label "the gloriana drive," and which stands for African–Americans delving deep into African history, searching there for achievements to celebrate and instil pride in their African heritage. But Mazrui also pointed out, some time ago, that "the black population of the United States is a microcosm of Global Africa," where Global Africa stands for all the people of African ancestry – in short, for the African diaspora.[14] His insistence on diversity directly contradicts the claim, made by Andrew Hacker in his *Two Nations*, of a homogeneous blackness or Africanness of black Americans.

But, then, it is Hacker's intention to paint a stark picture of racial inequality. He mainly covers the changes that have taken place during the last thirty years or so since the mid-Sixties and the advent of the civil-rights movement. His principle aim is to put discrimination in structural perspective, demonstrating methodically the lack of opportunity in the areas of income, employment and education. The irony of a movement from inflicted segregation towards self-segregation is not entirely lost on the author. But he does everything to make it look plausible. Part of his achievement lies in his use of statistics, especially when he compares biased reproaches of the black community with similar trends among whites over a longer period, as in the case of single-parent families (women who raise their children alone).[15] The boldest attempt at explaining away negative traits certainly occurs when he tries to plausibilize black crime-rates and prison over-representation. Quite ingeniously, he points out:

> If more black felons end up in prison cells, not the least reason is that they lacked office-based opportunities.[16]

Revealing in our context is his characterization of the "cross-over" black politician. He is middle-class, career-oriented, and, in his eagerness to get white votes as well, will gradually forget what the real plight of his brothers and sisters is, will most surely avoid harsh words in describing it, as this might upset prospective voters, and will demonstratively dissociate himself from those "who speak in a sharper voice." It is interesting to note that the Canadian poet–painter David Woods has a comparable text in his collection *Native Song*.[17] It is entitled "Epitaph – for Kipoch Nojorge," and begins:

> My friend Kipoch
> Kenyan born,
> Black as coal
> From the Akamba tribe,

---

14 "African Factor in the US," *African Events* (July, 1993): 31.

15 Cf *Süddeutsche Zeitung* (11–12 September, 1993): 12. A brief news item under the headline "Almost every third mother in USA raises family singlehandedly" ends with the line: "Den höchsten Anteil an alleinerziehenden Müttern gibt es unter der schwarzen Bevölkerung mit 68 Prozent" (the highest proportion of single mothers can be found among the black population – 68 percent).

16 *Two Nations*: 184.

17 David Woods, *Native Song* (Lawrencetown Beach, Nova Scotia: Pottersfield Press, 1990): 71–72; for the full text of the poem see the end of this volume.

Has won an award –
and is off to New York,
After years of effort
He has begun to fly.

The difference, though, is that, compared with Hacker's stance, the poem's persona – which is after all not that far removed from its author's Trinidadian–Nova Scotian background – does not speak in an accusatory tone. The tenor is much nearer to a sense of sad resignation. And what is being described is not so much a conscious action, as is the case with Hacker's politician, but a culture worker's reluctant giving-in to the pull of the metropolis. We learn that Kipoch, after his success, "no longer writes to his family," "can no longer bear discussion of his country," but brings whites to tears in his speeches. This is a far cry from Hacker who, in naming a "sharper voice," somewhat tellingly refers us to Louis Farrakhan.[18]

Eddy L. Harris's procedure in his travelogue *Native Stranger* of 1992 is notably different. To begin with, he spells "blackamerican," in the subtitle, as one word, which oddly enough makes it somehow reminiscent of "blackamoor." But that is a minor point. His project has to be seen against the backdrop of the complicated relationship between Africa and Black America, against the history of the reciprocal images they have had of each other, as people and as countries. He sees himself trapped between the extremes of Thomas Wolfe and Alex Haley:

> Africa was so long ago the land of my ancestors that it held for me only a symbolic significance. Yet there was enough to remind me that what I carry as a human being has come in part from Africa. I did not feel African, but was beginning to feel not wholly American anymore either. I felt like an orphan, a waif without a home.[19]

The overall impression of the book is one of more or less calculated understatement. He travels light, emphasizes travel, abhors tourism; it is a pilgrimage, a personal quest of self-discovery. He looks for a common bond, not for what makes men different; he is prepared to "walk a mile in another's moccasins,"[20] "to go where they go, to eat what they eat, to walk this mile in their shoes: these are the things a traveler must do."

The diary-aspect is suppressed though. There are no dates. He "travels like a leaf on a breeze" where wind and whim will carry him.[21] So, to place him and his adventures in time, one has to use diverse pointers of political details, like the Mauretanian–Senegalese conflict, to be able to reach the conclusion that the roughly one year he spent in Africa must have been in the late Eighties (presumably 1987–88). He reminds one of Caryl Phillips, since he is a young athlete, well-trained and strongly built, and because we learn that he lost twenty pounds in the venture. Very often, on first sight, people take him for a Senegalese, but in the end he is nonetheless almost always identified as an American.

---

18 Hacker, *Two Nations*, 208.
19 Harris, *Native Stranger*, 137–38.
20 Harris, *Native Stranger*, 43, 143.
21 Harris, *Native Stranger*: 25.

He hitch-hikes, squeezes into buses, and tries not to fall off pick-up trucks. The random itinerary begins in Paris, with the Africans who live there. Then he visits Sicily, Tunisia, Morocco, Mauretania, Senegal, Gambia, Guinea–Bissau, Mali, the Ivory Coast and Liberia. These are the first seven chapters out of ten. The last three, covering Nigeria, Zaire, Zimbabwe and several other countries in a meagre forty pages or so, seem a let-down. And they are, in several ways. For he abandons his overland mode of travel, gets on riverboats and steamers, and eventually even uses planes. This runs parallel to the rather distressing insight which dawns upon him more and more that, try as he may, he remains an American who, in the end, hankers after credit cards, showers, germ-free cold drinks, electricity, and functioning telephones. Of course, his being upset by the lack of food, by the abundance of flies, by parasites, by malaria, by the practice of infibulation – all these come pretty close to being cliché images of Africa. However, he is vindicated by the context in which he places these observations. There is an ever-increasing critical self-analysis with regard to self-flattering assumptions and harsh reality. There are highly critical reflections about black complicity in slavery; parallels are drawn between corrupt leadership in Africa and in the States, black leaders included. There is a disarming remark about the ease with which mothers would hand over their babies to complete strangers for a while to take a nap, with the babies happily conniving in the procedure and not protesting at all. The symbolism is intricate, despite its unobtrusive simplicity. For instance, his most negative experience at the hands of incompetent soldiers is had in Liberia of all places, and that – one should not forget – before the present upheaval there. Thus he stresses yet another historical tie between the States and Africa that has, in the long run, failed to accrue to the advantage of either. Similarly, it is no accident that the depiction of gigantic Nigeria is gotten over with in just a few lines. Very tellingly, the vast country is shrunk to a never-ending sequence of road-blocks with so many soldierly palms waiting to be nicely greased. Even his surface-message – that you must absolutely resist letting yourself be intimidated, that you have to be assertive, that you should shout back – also reads, for all its practical reasonableness, like a parody of the ordinary self-assured Yankee, who can always and everywhere rely on the strength of the dollars in his wallet or on his American Express account. He reprimands the willingness to wait and to endure on the part of the average African. But, then, he also marvels at the limitless patience and the unbattered hope:

> But somehow they endure, as if they truly believe the proverbs. The world has many mornings. Their faith in the gods of Islam and Christianity, their faith in trees and rivers and rocks, is a mighty weapon in their war for survival and endurance. Job, the man of nearly limitless patience, must have been an African.[22]

So the experience of Africa is not a discovery of his roots, but a catalyst for coming to terms with his cross-over existence. In part, this is affiliated with Tariq El Mirghani (alias Tanner), the hero of Jamal Mahjoub's novel *Navigation of a*

---

22 Harris, *Native Stranger*: 267.

Rain-Maker (1989), who, part-Briton part-Sudanese, ultimately gets drawn, Camus-fashion, into the North–South conflict in the Sudan. His African–American counterpart turns out to be some kind of *agent provocateur* in the end, working for an oil multinational, whereas the hero realizes, in a dream-like vision springing from the local tradition, that the way salvation lies is precisely with people of mixed descent:

> "You see," he began again, "You and I are similar in that we are both born out of opposites, the coming together of differences. We are both born of integration. That is the only solution."[23]

Here, the consciously cross-over existence is seen as the only means to end the age-old strife between North and South, Islam and Christianity, city and country, Nuer and Dinka, slaver and slave.

Finally, a fleeting glance at a further three instances of successful personal cross-overs. These are: the Nigerian painter Rufus Ogundele, whose painting "Between the Tree and the Moon" adorned the conference programme; the multi-talented composer Ian Hall, Guyanese-born, with Ghanaian experience, who now heads the Bloomsbury Society in London; and the musician Apache Indian, who today so successfully embodies cross-over pop in England. "Me bring a brand new style apon the island, fe the black a fe white and fe the Indian," he sings in his ragga chat – and certainly does bridge a gap between West Indians and Asians, combining Punjabi Bhangra, Jamaican reggae and English pop.[24] In so doing, he is, in his syncretic eclecticism, not far removed from creating a new unity as revealed in the music of Lesego Rampolokeng, poet–musician from South Africa.

❧ ❖ ❧

---

[23] Jamal Mahjoub, *Navigation of a Rainmaker* (London: Heinemann, 1989): 162.

[24] Island Records (1993); see also Amanda Wittington, *New Statesman and Society* (26 February, 1993): 34–35. His album *No Reservations* contains the hit "Arranged Marriage." It seems that music lends itself most easily to cross-over experimentation. The group Okuta–Percussion would be another case in point, where Tunji Beier, Rabiu Ayandokun and Ron Reeves combine Bata and Dundun drums of Yoruba provenance with elements taken from Indonesian, Australian Aboriginal and South Indian traditions. They actually use the word "Fusionsmusik" in their publicity material, just as Salif Keita's work is talked about nowadays in terms of "Weltmusik," as it fuses African Pop with Western high tech. Similarly, the didgeridoo players Gary Thomas and David Hudson endeavour to get their inspiration from more than just one tradition.

WORKS CITED

ANON. "Fast jede dritte Mutter in den USA alleinerziehend," *Süddeutsche Zeitung* (11–12 September, 1993): 12.

BLACK, Ayanna, ed. *Voices: Canadian Writers of African Descent* (Toronto: Harper/Collins, 1992).

DHONDY, Farrukh. *Bombay Duck* (London: Jonathan Cape, 1990).

HACKER, Andrew. *Two Nations, Black and White, Separate, Hostile, Unequal* (New York: Ballantine, 1993).

HARRIS, Eddy L. *Native Stranger: A Blackamerican's Journey into the Heart of Africa* (1992; London: Viking, 1993).

JACOBSON, Howard. *Redback* (1987; London: Black Swan, 1988).

MAHJOUB, Jamal. *Navigation of a Rain-Maker* (London: Heinemann, 1989).

MAZRUI, Ali. "African Factor in the US," *African Events* (July, 1993): 31–33.

MOWALJARLAI, David & Jutta MALNIC. *Yorro Yorro* (Broome, W.A.: Magabala, 1993).

SALOY, Mona Lisa. "Word Works," *African American Review* (Spring, 1993): 155.

WOODS, David. *Native Song* (Lawrencetown Beach, Nova Scotia: Pottersfield, 1990).

❦ ❖ ❧

BERNHARD MELCHIOR

"Expertise in cross-cultural mediation"
West Indian–American Writing in the Eighties

"S HE WRITES OF BLACKS, very often of West Indians, simply because a writer writes best when [s]he makes use of what [s]he knows best."[1] Thus ends an article on "Dominant Themes and Techniques in Paule Marshall's Fiction" from the early Seventies. The expertise ascribed to the African–American author of West Indian parentage is based on the personal experience that has continued to be an important source of her writing throughout her career. Marshall's oeuvre (like that of other West Indian and West Indian–American writers) thus deviates from Euro-American notions, which, while expecting (and respecting) a *first* novel to have an autobiographical tendency, often consider the continued presence of this characteristic a sign of the artist's lack of maturity.

The autobiographical dimension

Quite to the contrary, I will try to demonstrate the interdependence of an "autobiographical dimension" and cross-cultural encounters and mediation in and of works evolving from a West Indian–American background. Observations concerning the "autobiographical dimension" of these texts will be followed by a brief discussion of their relevance in the cross-cultural context of the Caribbean, before an analysis of two of Paule Marshall's novels illustrating the advantages of such an approach.

The diversification of literary landscapes both nationally, as in the United States in the wake of the civil-rights, women's, and ethnic movements, and globally, following the anti-colonialist and post-independence periods of the Fifties and Sixties in Africa, for example, and later the Caribbean, was the result of *and*, in turn, produced a great number of literary utterances geared towards the emancipatory project of artistic self-definition and participation in official (written) public discourse. The results of this development are mirrored in publishing policies and Nobel Prize awards for African, Caribbean and African–American writers in recent years. The existential urgency of their cultural and political struggles has inseparably interwoven aesthetic ambition and the personal experience of many of

---

[1] In her article on "Dominant Themes and Technique in Paule Marshall's Fiction," published in the *College Language Association Journal* 16 (September 1972): 59, Leela Kapai thus already hints at the subject pursued in the present essay: the interdependence of life experience and writing; the issue of inclusive language had obviously not yet penetrated the academy to any degree at that time.

these writers; thus a context very different from Euro-American postmodern scenarios has taken shape and must be considered, if we intend to understand the thematic and structural strategies employed by the authors of such texts.

The upsurge of interest in autobiography and autobiographical writings in a larger sense has been almost simultaneous in postmodern as well as ethnic and post-colonial contexts, and the various angles taken in the ensuing critical discourses on the history and theory of the genre have generated some of the most significant recent developments in literary criticism. In African–American literature, for example, the recovery and critical analysis of nineteenth-century slave narratives has not only restored to the black community the roots of a separate literary tradition in America, but it has highlighted various discursive dimensions (ontological, anthropological, political) of these early accounts of the experience of Black people in the New World, parameters relevant to cultural efforts at (re)construction and identity-building in other geographical and cultural contexts as well. The findings were often incompatible with Western concepts of the distinctions between individual and collective and their literary representation, and genre-conventions concerning the boundaries between fiction and autobiography proved inappropriate in cultural matrices differing from Western concepts and value-systems. To account for these emerging and divergent patterns, new terminology was proposed, such as "autophylography," "autoethnography," and "biomythography."[2] And while these terms have certainly enriched the critical discourse on autobiographical writing, none of them has gained widespread acceptance or succeeded in ending the hegemony of Western concepts of autobiography in critical circles. In order not to get caught prematurely in the fault-lines of the academy's "universally valid" definitions of autobiography, I shall use the term "autobiographical dimension." This decision allows for a more open approach to the literature, particularly from a different cultural context, by deliberately avoiding the conceptual rigidity and definitiveness of a generic noun and its (often unreflected and unacknowledged) reference to a specific cultural context.

In contrast to often rather narrowly defined concepts of autobiography based on *formal* textual criteria, my use of the term "autobiographical dimension" is meant to account for the socially and culturally diverse dynamics involved in the self-representation of marginalized individuals and groups. One such diverging realm is what Abdul JanMohamed and David Lloyd have referred to as "the collective nature of *all* minority discourse," and the consequent appropriation by writers of "what were once efficacious vehicles for the representation of individually oriented

---

[2] This short list of terms is only a selection from numerous attempts to designate some variants of "autobiographical" writings from marginal(ised) contexts; they are to be found, respectively, in: James Olney, "The Value of Autobiography for Comparative Studies," *Comparative Civilizations Review* 2 (1979): 57/58; Françoise Lionnet, *Autobiographical Voices: Race, Gender, Self-Portraiture* (Ithaca NY: Cornell UP, 1989): 97ff.; Alice A. Deck, "Autoethnography: Zora Neale Hurston, Noni Jabavu, and Cross-Disciplinary Discourse," *Black American Literature Forum* 24.2 (Summer 1990): 237–56; Audre Lorde, *ZAMI: A New Spelling of My Name* (Freedom CA: Crossing Press, 1982).

experiences [and their transformation] into expressions of collective experiences," a strategy Anne Koenen has observed in women's autobiographies.[3] More importantly, however, my use of the circumscriptive term serves to accommodate and emphasize various *functional* aspects of autobiographical writing, such as personal *"ontological affirmation"* – what Elizabeth Bruss has summed up in the term "autobiographical act," and what Craig Werner has referred to as "the need to establish and assert the reality of the self;"[4] secondly, the corresponding public issue of *discursive participation* – what A. Robert Lee calls "the 'making' of the self in the face of that self's historic denial";[5] thirdly, in moving beyond the previous stages, the achievement of a more complex *anthropological (self-)definition*, summed up by Elizabeth Fox–Genovese as the "discourse of origins" and defined by Sandra Paquet as "self-revelation as a way of laying claim to a landscape that is at once geographical, historical and cultural."[6] To decipher such an "autobiographical dimension," the discernible involvement of the writer's personal experience is a particularly important and valuable critical move in the context of literarily processed and critically conducted cross-cultural encounters. And, in view of the paucity of major publishing outlets in Africa or the Caribbean, plus the relatively small readership in most colonial and post-colonial societies (whether on account of continuing preference for oral transmission or lack of education or economic potency to buy books), the literary process of communication, as a *rule* rather than as an exception, tends to cross cultural boundaries anyway, with North American and European audiences constituting the majority of readers.

In the wake of the success and recognition of African–American women's writing in the USA in the Seventies and Eighties, the United States have increasingly become an attractive place of residence again for African–West Indian writers abroad, "offering" them publishing opportunities and public interest as never before. Among these women writers from the "islands" who live in the USA are Rosa Guy, the late Audre Lorde, Lorna Goodison, Jamaica Kincaid, and Michelle Cliff. Paule Marshall, a first-generation American born of Barbadian immigrants, is usually considered an African–American writer rather than one from the Caribbean; but, from her early childhood on, when she grew up in the Bajan community in Brooklyn, and throughout her literary oeuvre, the Caribbean has played a central role and thus warrants that she be considered in the context of other West Indian–American writers.

---

3 Abdul JanMohammed & David Lloyd, "Introduction: Minority Discourse – What Is to Be Done?" *Cultural Critique* 7 (Fall 1987): 9, 10; Anne Koenen, "Democracy and Women's Autobiographies," *Amerikastudien/American Studies* 35.3 (1990): 323.

4 Craig Werner, "On the Ends of Afro-American 'Modernist' Autobiography," *Black American Literature Forum* 24.2 (Summer 1990): 209.

5 A term coined by Elizabeth Bruss in her *Autobiographical Acts: The Changing Situation of a Literary Genre* (Baltimore MD: Johns Hopkins UP, 1976); the quotation is from A. Robert Lee's *First Person Singular: Studies in American Autobiography* (New York: St Martin's Press, 1988): 154.

6 Sandra Pouchet Paquet, "West Indian Autobiography," *Black American Literature Forum* 24.2 (Summer 1990): 359.

Both the remarkable quantity and quality of material published in the past decade direct our critical attention to common characteristics of writings by West Indian–Americans. Despite the diversity of the writers' geographical, racial, and social backgrounds and the range of their literary production, they share the experience of having lived in at least two very different cultural environments, and many transform that "contact experience" into their literary oeuvre.[7] The immediacy and existential relevance of their experiences to their writing figure prominently and empower their texts thematically and structurally.

As Sandra Paquet has demonstrated in her seminal essay on "West Indian Autobiography," West Indian literature has been characterized by a strong presence of what was outlined above as the "autobiographical dimension" in a number of key texts published since the Fifties.[8] In Paquet's reading, the "autobiographical act emerges as a means to an end rather than an end in itself." In her view, the self functions "as an authoritative and reliable way into the collective experience," while at the same time the "autobiographical self as subject is transformed into a cultural archetype, and autobiography becomes both lived historical reality and the myth created out of that experience."[9] In "The West Indian Writer and the Self: Recent 'Fictional Autobiography' by Naipaul and Harris," Mark McWatt confirms "a preoccupation with the autobiographical self as fictional subject or character."[10] Françoise Lionnet, finally, in a recent analysis of Michelle Cliff's first novel *Abeng* (1984), has challenged the individualistic approach to self-consciousness and self-representation that is at the heart of the Western literary and critical tradition, as exemplified in Georges Gusdorf's well-known essay on the "Conditions and Limits of Autobiography."[11] Lionnet, too, defies conventional genre demarcations and refers to Cliff's book as "at once fiction and autobiography in the third person," emphasizing both the autobiographical traits of the protagonist and the apparent

---

[7] The term "contact experience" is modeled after Marie Louise Pratt's "contact zone" which she, in turn, borrows from linguistics; there, the term "contact language" refers to improvised languages that develop among speakers of different native languages who need to communicate with each other consistently, usually in context of trade. Such languages begin as pidgins, and are called creoles when they come to have speakers of their own" Mary Louise Pratt, *Imperial Eyes. Travel Writing and Transculturation* (London/New York: Routledge, 1992): 6. Perhaps the dual experience of and in the "contact zone," to be a stranger *and* at home in *both* places, the US and the West Indies, the balanced "contact experience" at both ends of the spectrum , will gradually come to be accepted as a valuable experience and factor in its own right, and move from initially being considered a chaotic "pidgin" to an accepted and respected "creole."

[8] Paquet discusses George Lamming's *In the Castle of My Skin* (1953), C.L.R. James's *Beyond A Boundary* (1963), Derek Walcott's *Another Life* (1973), and V.S. Naipaul's *Finding the Centre* (1984). For an analysis of two examples of West Indian autobiography from the nineteenth century, see her recent essay on the narratives of Mary Prince and Mrs Seacole, *AAR* 26.4 (1992): 651–63.

[9] Paquet, "West Indian Autobiography," 358, 364, 359.

[10] Mark McWatt, "The West Indian Writer and the Self: Recent 'Fictional Autobiography' by Naipaul and Harris," *Journal of West Indian Literature* 3.1 (January 1989): 16.

[11] Françoise Lionnet, "Of Mangoes and Maroons: Language, History and the Multicultural Subject of Michelle Cliff's *Abeng*," in *De/Colonizing the Subject*, ed. Sidonie Smith & J. Watson (St Paul: U of Minnesota P, 1991): 321–45; Gusdorf's essay is most accessible in *Autobiography: Essays Theoretical and Critical*, ed. James Olney (Princeton NJ: Princeton UP, 1980): 28–48.

(auto)ethnographic function, the cross-cultural communication of the text. The glossary for culturally uninformed or estranged (non-Jamaican) readers as well as the narrator's numerous explanatory interventions as cultural translator point to an underlying ethnographic project reminiscent of Zora Neale Hurston's. The focus in Cliff's first-person, substantially autobiographical narrative, as Lionnet has aptly observed, is, however, "not so much the retrieval of a repressed dimension of the *private* self, but the rewriting of their ethnic history, the re/creation of a *collective* identity through the performance of language."[12] The author herself is both protagonist and narrator, among the folk and an outsider, involved and looking on, an individual and a member of the collective, subject and object, by virtue of her origin and sense of belonging, as well as her education and experience abroad. Cliff's follow-up novel *No Telephone to Heaven* (1987) yields similar examples, but I will now (re)turn to and concentrate on Paule Marshall's oeuvre.

Paule Marshall

A number of biographical incidents and influences can be traced in Marshall's literary works. Rather than listing them here, I want to refer to a case in point, namely her collection *Reena and Other Stories* of 1983. Draped in a decidedly autobiographical pattern, the collection programmatically opens with the autobiographical essay "From the Poets in the Kitchen," and every story is introduced with an "autobiographical headnote." In the novels we can also trace a shifting interest in exploring various phases and strands of her own identity one by one. Her analysis of the situation of Barbadian immigrants in New York in *Brown Girl, Brownstones* (1959), particularly the young protagonist Selina Boyce's story – and here especially her relationship with her mother – sounds not unlike Marshall's own. Inspired by the social, cultural and political developments of the Sixties, Marshall turns to a panoramic depiction of both her West Indian background and inter-American power relations in *The Chosen Place, The Timeless People* (1969); *Praisesong for the Widow* (1983) tells the story of an aging black middle-class widow from New York who, on a cruise in the Caribbean, miraculously recovers lost portions of her life and returns culturally rejuvenated; and, in *Daughters* (1991), Marshall's relationship with her father and the situation of a professional black woman in New York are the central issues.

Privately, Marshall has had to mediate her double identity as African–American and Barbadian from childhood days on: "How does one, out of this kind of mixed bag, come up with a self?";[13] writing seems to have been an enormously helpful tool in that process. But also publicly, her writings have proved artistically and politically instructive to both the black community and a cross-cultural readership.[14]

---

12 Lionnet, "Of Mangoes and Maroons," 322/323, 334.

13 Interview with Sandi Russell, *Wasafiri* 8 (Spring 1988): 15.

14 German readers, unfortunately, are at present excluded from the community of her admirers as none of her works is currently available in translation. In the Eighties, German translations of *The Chosen Place,*

And *while*, or perhaps *because* she has lived in the USA for most of her life, the Caribbean remains an ideal place for the spiritual orientation and rejuvenation of African–Americans, because she believes the culture and spirit of Africa have somehow survived more intact there.

As in her first novel, the character-constellation in *The Chosen Place, The Timeless People* is Marshall's foremost structural device for introducing and juxtaposing the various perspectives and attitudes. Cross-cultural encounters serve to depict obstacles *and* possible solutions in the difficult processes of intercultural understanding and mutual acceptance. The visiting US–American anthropologist Saul Amron's sensitive perceptiveness is contrasted with his wife Harriet's token- ism as well as with the ignorance shown towards the rural culture and the colonial- style paternalism exhibited by a variety of black and white local leaders in town. They blame the stubborn, backward people of Bournehills themselves for their poverty, ridicule their attachment to their land and traditions, fail to understand why these people have no use for electronic entertainment equipment, and cannot imagine why the Bournehills community refuses to get excited about a new pottery factory that is to produce junk souvenirs for tourists (56–58).[15] The indifference of the international (Western) business community to the existential needs of the local farmers is exemplified in the sugar-mill crisis (representative of the colonial legacy) and the economic development plan favouring foreign investors (indicative of the neo-colonial threats to the sovereign but politically powerless post-independence island societies). These historical attitudes are also mirrored in the nature of the protagonists' counterparts: Merle Kinbona's former buddy, the black ex- revolutionary Lyle Hutson, is now a representative of the corrupt, post- independence ruling class, while the anthropologist's wife Harriet is the descendant of a wealthy Philadelphian family who made their fortune through speculative involvement in the West Indies trade and the African slave trade. Lyle's repression of his own personal and the community's collective history precludes sensitive and competent post-colonial social advancement, and Harriet's inability to transcend her rigid, preconceived conceptualizations (which isolate and alienate her, finally driving her into committing suicide) prevent her from developing even the faintest trace of genuine cross-cultural understanding. Much more complex and open- minded by virtue of their past experiences are, on the other hand, Merle and particularly Saul Amron, who in *this* cross-cultural reading becomes the most important character.[16]

The Timeless People (1981), *Praisesong for the Widow* (1987), and *Reena and Other Stories* (1987) were published in the GDR by Aufbau Verlag, but were never available in the FRG.

[15] Marshall, *The Chosen Place, The Timeless People* (1969; New York: Vintage, 1984). All further references appear in the text.

[16] [...] to the great dismay, I'm sure, of all those who are fascinated by Merle Kinbona, whose complex character was aptly characterised in an early review by Robert Bone as "part saint, part revolutionary, part obeahwoman" (*New York Times Book Review*, 30 November, 1969: 54). In the context of the "The Fusion of Cultures?," the implications of "*this* reading" concern not only the cross-cultural encounters within the text, but also those between reader/critic and text/author. The fact that the present article is the critical response

On account of both his personal and his professional experience, Saul Amron is a model for the kind of attitude and behaviour that can generate genuine cross-cultural understanding. While female readers may (or may not) feel closer to Merle, as Americans or Europeans they also share Saul's cultural and political positionality (rather than hers) as the stranger who visits the Caribbean and strives to understand the people's needs and concerns. As readers we all actually gain access to Merle – and through her to the community of Bournehills itself – through Saul's patience and sensitive receptiveness. Merle's room, to which Saul (and, only then, the reader) is admitted after the woman has suffered a nervous breakdown, reveals her

> struggle for coherence, the hope and desire for reconciliation of her conflicting parts, the longing to truly know and accept herself – all the things he sensed in her, which not only brought on her rages but her frightening calm as well. He almost felt as his gaze wandered over the room that he was wandering through the chambers of her mind. (401–402)

It is through Saul's eyes that Marshall expands the readers' own perception of the repercussions of that "other" experience of colonial, post-colonial, racist and sexist social relations; through *him* the private experience is related to the public, the individual fate placed in the larger context of history as the text continues:

> But the room expressed something more, it suddenly seemed to his own overtaxed and exhausted mind, something apart from Merle. It roused in him feelings about Bournehills itself. He thought he suddenly saw the district for what it was at its deepest level, the vague thoughts and impressions of months slowly coming to focus. Like the room it, too, was perhaps a kind of museum, a place in which had been stored the relics and remains of the era recorded in the faded prints on the walls, where one not only felt that other time existing intact, still alive, a palpable presence beneath the everyday reality, but saw it as well at every turn, often without realizing it. (402)

Because it provides the key to one's orientation in – if not understanding of – the surrounding world (and one's being, one's identity in it), the history of both Merle and Bournehills, in the sense of individual and local historical experience, is essential not only for their own, but also for Saul's – and by extension the reader's – understanding of the chosen place and the timeless people. And this understanding across the boundaries of differing cultural contexts and experiences can be achieved through Marshall's thematic and narrative strategies, both of which are unthinkable without her own personal cross-cultural experience.

In her third novel, *Praisesong for the Widow*, Marshall again sends a North American to the Caribbean, but this time an ageing black middle-class woman on a cruise-ship, estranged from her cultural roots: Avey (short for "Avatara") Johnson. A dream and other mysterious circumstances gradually restore to her a sense of belonging, even of the mission that was ingrained in her name.[17]

---

of a white, male, European reader accounts for both the strategic positionality of the critical approach *and* the value of illuminating the "autobiographical dimension" of a text.

[17] Marshall, *Praisesong for the Widow* (1983; New York: Dutton, 1984). All further references appear in the text. An "avatar(a)" is "earthly incarnation of a deity" and "embodiment of a concept or tradition." In the course of the ritual near the end of the novel, Avey embraces the mission she had been entrusted with (42) by pronouncing her full name Avatara (251) as her great-aunt had insisted on long ago.

Two key visual memories from different chronological and cultural frames of reference merge in the dream: one from Avey's childhood days of ritual instruction by her great-aunt Cuney, and another from her later, materialistic middle-class life in North White Plains. In these scenes, the two value-systems which are at the core of her internal battle throughout the novel, and which reduplicate the external cultural spheres of European and African influence and tradition in the Americas, are juxtaposed (40–45), as is the development of her deceased husband Jay's (later, Jerome Johnson's) biography. The early years of their marriage are full of jazz and blues, Jay's poetry recitations, and make-believe dances in the living-room; after the near-fatal Tuesday, a hard-working, professionally ambitious, and transfixed Jerome Johnson renounces his cultural heritage under the destructive lure and pressure of the American Dream (a theme that figured prominently in Marshall's first novel as well as marginally in her second) and dies early on account of a stroke; 130–35).

Upon leaving the cruise-ship *Bianca Pride*, Avey's first genuine encounter with the Caribbean (as opposed to the tourist industry's guided excursions she is used to as a cruise-ship passenger enjoying the protective shield of a package tour) reveals the clash of two worlds. Still under the influence of her disquieting dream and other events, her frame of perception is destabilized subliminally by the entire natural and cultural reality of the islands. These perceptional shifts gradually generate her own as well the readers' receptiveness to the essence of Caribbean reality.

Instead of the usual hustle and bustle of tourist guides, street vendors, beggars, and idlers meeting the cruise tourists upon their disembarkation, the wharf in Grenada is crowded with respectable-looking people, "all neatly dressed" – "not at all the kind of people ordinarily seen on the wharves." Her sense of wonder is, however, overcome again by displacement when she realizes that everybody but her speaks a French-based patois.

> For the first time in the three years that she had been coming to the islands, she experienced that special panic of the traveller who finds himself sealed off, stranded in a sea of incomprehensible sound. (70)

Not only their language, however, but also the islanders' behaviour towards her is puzzling; "there was a familiarity, almost an intimacy to their gestures of greeting and the unintelligible words they called out" (69).

> The problem was, she decided, none of them seemed aware of the fact that she was a stranger, a visitor, a tourist, although this should have been obvious from the way she was dressed and the set of matching luggage at her side. But from the way they were acting she could have been simply one of them. (69)
>
> What was the matter with these people? It was as if the moment they caught sight of her standing there, their eyes immediately stripped her of everything she had on and dressed her in one of the homemade cotton prints the women were wearing [...]. Their eyes also ban-ished the six suitcases at her side, and placing a small overnight bag like the ones they were carrying in her hand, they were all set to take her long wherever it was they were going. (72)

In a later, parallel scene in the rumshop of Lebert Joseph, Avey again desperately tries to convey that she is a tourist rather than part of a local tradition that he seems to be determined to claim her for. Of course, nothing is wrong with either Lebert or the people on the wharf; on the contrary, it is Avey Johnson who does not know her true self any more, as is repeatedly indicated in the novel by her inability to recognize her own reflection in mirrors aboard the cruise-ship. On the small island of Carriacou, however, after the cleansing rituals of mind (on the hotel balcony) and body (during the channel crossing and the ritual bathing in Rosalie Parvay's house), the ceremony for the ancestors, and the nation and creole dances in particular, restore Avey to her innate self. The encounter is initiated and mediated by Lebert Joseph, an incarnation of Eshu Elegba, and the change is announced by her positive reaction to the rather unimpressive bareness of the yard where the ceremony is to take place. But she realizes that the atmosphere of understatement throughout the excursion has its own quality: "It was the essence of something rather than the thing itself she was witnessing" (240).

In *Praisesong*, Marshall chronicles a black American's loss of the African cultural heritage under the double pressures of poverty and racism. The socially whitened black protagonist Avey Johnson is, however, restored to her innate Africanistic identity and cultural heritage. Her encounter with a seemingly alien culture in the Caribbean reconnects her spiritually to all exiled African individuals and communities in the western hemisphere. The perceptional shifts and defamili-arizing perspectives which form part of the novel's pervasive visual imagery and language initiate the protagonist – and, by extension, the reader – into a deeper understanding of both essence and relative difference among the various cultural traditions encountered in the novel.

Through the experience of Avey's encounters with unfamiliar sights, sounds, and behaviour patterns, and the processes of reorientation and cultural and personal rejuvenation engendered by them, Marshall underscores the latent opportunities for cross-cultural encounter. Not only is her protagonist intent on following in the footsteps of Coleridge's Ancient Mariner and determined to direct other people's attention to her story, but Avey's exemplary encounters are designed to encourage readers to open their eyes and seek out such opportunities for new experiences. In *The Chosen Place, The Timeless People*, the open-minded anthropologist Saul Amron in many ways has served as a model within and beyond the world of the text. In both realms he functions as a mediator between white Euro-America and the black post-independence Caribbean societies. Marshall, by virtue of her life between the lines and her personal struggle to reconcile the various strands of her identity, seems to have become an expert not only in bridging the gap privately, but also in mediating those differences in her writing. In the words of the Barbadian critic Kamau Brathwaite: "Had Paule Marshall been a West Indian, she probably would not have written this book [ie *The Chosen Place, The Timeless People*]. Had she not been an African–American of West Indian parentage, she possibly could not have written it either."[18]

---

18 Edward Kamau Brathwaite, "Rehabilitations: West Indian History and Society in the Art of Paule Marshall's Novel" in *Caribbean Studies* 10.2 (June 1970): 126.

WORKS CITED

BONE, Robert. Review of Paule Marshall, *The Chosen Place, The Timeless People*, *New York Times Book Review* (30 November, 1969): 4.

BRATHWAITE, Edward Kamau. "Rehabilitations," *Critical Quarterly* 13.2 (Summer 1971): 175–83.

BRUSS, Elizabeth. *Autobiographical Acts: The Changing Situation of a Literary Genre* (Baltimore MD: Johns Hopkins UP, 1976).

DECK, Alice A. "Autoethnography: Zora Neale Hurston, Noni Jabavu, and Cross-Disciplinary Discourse," *Black American Literature Forum* 24.2 (Summer 1990): 237–56.

GUSDORF, Georges. "Conditions and Limitations of Autobiography," tr. James Olney, in *Autobiography: Essays Theoretical and Critical*, ed. James Olney (Princeton NJ: Princeton UP, 1980): 28–48.

JAMES, C.L.R. *Beyond A Boundary* (London: Hutchinson, 1963).

JANMOHAMED, Abdul R. & David LLOYD, "Introduction: Minority Discourse – What Is to Be Done?" *Cultural Critique* 7 (Fall 1987): 5–17.

KAPAI, Leela. "Dominant Themes and Technique in Paule Marshall's Fiction," *College Language Association Journal* 16 (September 1972): 45–59.

KOENEN, Anne. "Democracy and Women's Autobiographies," *Amerikastudien/American Studies* 35.3 (1990): 321–36.

LAMMING, George. *In the Castle of My Skin* (London: Michael Joseph, 1953).

LEE, A. Robert. *First Person Singular: Studies in American Autobiography* (New York: St Martin's Press, 1988).

LIONNET, Françoise. *Autobiographical Voices: Race, Gender, Self-Portraiture* (Ithaca NY: Cornell UP, 1989).
———. "Of Mangoes and Maroons: Language, History and the Multicultural Subject of Michelle Cliff's *Abeng*," in *De/Colonizing the Subject: The Politics of Gender in Women's Autobiography*, ed. Sidonie Smith & Julia Watson (Minneapolis–St Paul: U of Minnesota P, 1991): 321–45.

LORDE, Audre. *Zami: A New Spelling Of My Name* (Freedom CA: Crossing Press, 1982).

MARSHALL, Paule. *Brown Girl, Brownstones* (1959, Avon, 1970).
———. *The Chosen Place, The Timeless People* (1969; New York: Vintage, 1984).
———. *Daughters* (New York: Atheneum, 1991).
———. "Interview with Paule Marshall," by Sandi Russell, *Wasafiri* 8 (Spring 1988): 14–16.
———. *Praisesong for the Widow* (1983; New York: Dutton, 1984).
———. *Reena and Other Stories* (New York: Feminist Press, 1987).

MCWATT, Mark. "The West Indian Writer and the Self: Recent 'Fictional Autobiography' by Naipaul and Harris," *Journal of West Indian Literature* 3.1 (January 1989): 16–27.

NAIPAUL, V.S. *Finding the Centre* (London: André Deutsch, 1984).

OLNEY, James. "The Value of Autobiography for Comparative Studies: African vs. Western Autobiography," *Comparative Civilizations Review* 2 (Spring 1979): 52–64.

PAQUET, Sandra Pouchet. "The Enigma of Arrival: The Wonderful Adventures of Mrs Seacole in Many Lands," *African–American Review* 26.4 (Winter 1992): 651–63.
———. "West Indian Autobiography," *Black American Literature Forum* 24.2 (Summer 1990): 348–64.

PRATT, Mary Louise. *Imperial Eyes: Travel Writing and Transculturation* (London/New York: Routledge, 1992).

WALCOTT, Derek. *Another Life* (New York: Farrar, Straus & Giroux, 1973).

WERNER, Craig. "On the Ends of Afro-American 'Modernist' Autobiography," *Black American Literature Forum* 24.2 (Summer 1990): 203–20.

∾ ❖ ᷇

MARGARET KEULEN

"Bringing together all the various strands"
Cultural Roots in Paule Marshall's Literary Oeuvre

> [O]ne of the themes which absorbs me so that I find myself returning to it again and again is the question of identity. And as part of this, a concern for the role of the past – both the personal and historical past – plays in this whole question [...] There was always the desire [...] to bring together all the various strands (the word is synthesis) and thus make of that diverse heritage a whole.[1]

WITH REGARD TO THE GAPS AND SILENCES in the narratives of ex-slaves facing white audiences in the nineteenth century, the African–American feminist critic Barbara Christian once stated that

> to acknowledge that slaves had memory would threaten the very ground of slavery, for such memory would take them back to a culture in Africa where they existed [...] "in terms other than the ones" imposed upon them in America.[2]

This dangerous memory of the African slave has been smuggled past the whites via story-telling, rituals, and artefacts. Melville J. Herskovits, the founder of African–American studies in the USA, in his classic work on the African heritage in the New World, *The Myth of the Negro Past* (1941), encountered a "familiar theme" in the literature about Africa and African–Americans of his day:

> the Negro as a naked savage, whose exposure to European patterns destroyed what little endowment of culture he brought with him; the Negro as a cultureless man, with his entire traditional baggage limited to the fragments he has been able to pick up from his white masters.[3]

Herskovits accused US–American scholars of wholly inadequate research on African–Americans, which was never based on first-hand knowledge – especially when referring to Africa. Thus they were responsible for this myth of the "cultureless Negro." He showed that there existed innumerable Africanisms among New-World Africans, but although they survived in many disguises, this survival has at times been precarious in the USA: Never fully acknowledged in,

---

[1] Paule Marshall, "Shaping the World of My Art," *New Letters* 40 (1973): 106.
[2] Barbara Christian, "'Somebody Forgot to Tell Somebody Something': African American Women's Historical Novels," in *Wild Women in the Whirlwind: Afro American Culture and the Contemporary Literary Renaissance*, ed. Joanne M. Braxton & Andrée Nicola McLaughlin (London: Serpent's Tail, 1990): 333. Christian quotes June Jordan, "The Difficult Miracle of Black Poetry or Something Like a Sonnet for Phyllis Wheatley," in *On Call: Political Essays* (Boston MA: South End Press, 1985) and reprinted in Braxton & McLaughlin.
[3] Melville J. Herskovits, *The Myth of the Negro Past* (1941; Boston MA: Beacon Press, 1990): 227 194 .

for example, science, the media etc (the "master-discourse"), it was not fully present in the consciousness of African–Americans themselves. Thus Herskovits could observe in 1941:

> There is still another point of practical importance that should not be overlooked in appraising the implications of proper study of Negro backgrounds and of the retention of Africanisms. And this is the effect of the present-day representatives of this race without a past, of the deprivation they suffer in bearing no pride of tradition. For no group in the population of this country has been more completely convinced of the inferior nature of the African background than have the Negroes.[4]

And, in a quite farsighted comment, he concluded: "A people without a past are a people who lack an anchor in the present."[5] Since 1941 the situation has improved considerably: The "Negroes" call themselves "African–Americans" today. This discovery of the African connection fuelled the activities of the Black liberation movements and the concept of a "Black Aesthetic" in the USA But the link with Caribbean and South American Black cultures, who share with African Americans the African cultural heritage as well as the history of the Middle Passage and slavery, has for a long time been neglected because of the vast differences between these two groups, which have long overshadowed the similarities. Whereas the Caribbean islands, for instance, are Third-World nations that are economically dominated – not to say exploited – by the USA, African–Americans are citizens of the world's leading political, industrial, economic and military power who exercise cultural and political impact and enjoy more international "visibility" than their Caribbean pendants. The latter came to regard them with suspicion as an "integral part of the American capitalist–imperialist–military complex."[6] However, African–Americans constitute a minority group within a nation, whereas, in the island nations of the Caribbean, the descendants of the African slaves form the "dominant power blocks," thus having achieved "nationhood" in the conventional sense.[7]

Nevertheless, the similarities are important. Herskovits exhorted US scholars to look beyond national borders because Africanisms in the US cannot be studied in isolation. Only a view of all New-World African cultures in comparison with the African cultures from which they derive would truly shed light on the extent of African cultural heritage in the New World and on forms of cultural synthesis. This is due to the different living conditions of slaves in the Caribbean and in North America; and to the degree and kind of cultural exposure to whites, which, as a rule, was greater for North American slaves and allowed them less opportunity for cultural retention. The same cultural dilution can be observed from the South to the North in the USA.

However, as Edward Kamau Brathwaite showed in his talk at the Aachen–Liège conference in 1988, the eurocentric educational system in the Caribbean colonies –

---

4 Herskovits, *The Myth of the Negro Past*, 31.

5 Herskovits, *The Myth of the Negro Past*, 185.

6 Emmanuel S. Nelson, "Black America and the Anglophone Afro-Caribbean Literary Consciousness," *Journal of American Culture* 12.4 (1989): 53 58; 57.

7 Nelson, "Black America and the Anglophone Afro-Caribbean Literary Consciousness," 54.

even after independence – almost managed to obliterate consciousness of the African heritage. Having been immersed in European/English culture, Brathwaite found that he lacked the language to deal with the "geo-psychic aspect of the Caribbean" and the fragmentation of its culture. The historian Brathwaite found this language as a poet when he realized that African history had always been with him in the Caribbean in the form of folklore: rituals, stories, dances, songs, vernacular. Realizing, for instance, that the limbo actually re-enacts the Middle Passage, Brathwaite recognizes

> a wordless kind of history based upon our rituals and upon our instincts. But when one becomes conscious of these things a whole new world begins to open, whole centuries of history rip open like paper because they have always been there, enclosed in this capsule, in this notion of something which is preserved like a kernel.

So Brathwaite, too, can discard the myth of the naked, helpless, and hopeless slave without memory and culture, because "that capsule was the kernel of the beginning [...] of a whole new reconstruction of history and possibility."[8]

↩ ❖ ↪

Like Brathwaite, the American writer Paule Marshall has roots in Barbados: Born in 1929 in Brooklyn, she is the daughter of Barbadian immigrants and spent part of her childhood in Barbados. She has inherited various cultures: Afro-Caribbean, African–American and thus African. On top of these, the larger Euro-American culture also makes its claims. During her childhood this was a strain:

> And for a period I went through quite a rejection of the Afro-West Indian part of myself, because I so desperately wanted to be like my [African–American] peers [...]. And it wasn't until I was grown that I began to see the marvellous gift and the great benefit of that experience. I act as a kind of bridge. I do bring together in my person, and hopefully in my work, these two cultures [African–American and West Indian].[9]

In her autobiographically tinged first novel, *Brown Girl, Brownstones* (1959), the young protagonist Selina, daughter of Barbadian immigrants like Marshall herself, has to struggle hard for a sense of self between her mother Silla, bent on making it in "this man country,"[10] and her irresponsible father Deighton, who dreams of returning to Barbados. The murderous battle between them literally ends in Deighton's death, and Selina, after a shattering encounter with American racism, finally rejects her mother's ambitions and Western ideals. The novel ends with her about to leave for the Caribbean in a blind search for an identity[11] but also making peace with her people, whom she accepts at the very moment she leaves them:

---

8 Edward Kamau Brathwaite, "History, the Caribbean Writer, and *X/Self,*" in *Crisis and Creativity in the New Literatures in English*, ed. Geoffrey V. Davis & Hena Maes–Jelinek (Cross/Cultures 1; Amsterdam/ Atlanta GA: Rodopi, 1990): 23 45, quotes from 26, 32, 33. Although the situation for the Franco-Caribbean islands may be similar, all the material I cite in this context mainly refers to the Anglo-Caribbean islands.

9 "Interview with Paule Marshall," by Sandi Russell, *Wasafiri* 8 (Spring 1988): 15.

10 Paule Marshall, *Brown Girl, Brownstones* (1959; New York: Feminist Press, 1981): 103 and passim. Subsequent page references to this edition are included in the text.

11 Blind, because "I don't know," Selina's reply to her mother's question ("What it is you want?") is "a frail lost sound" (306; anticipating the last sentence of the novel: "A frail sound in that utter silence," 310).

> She wanted, suddenly, to leave something with them. But she had nothing. She had left the
> mother and the meeting hall wearing only the gown and her spring coat. Then she remembered
> the two silver bangles she had always worn. She pushed up her coat sleeve and stretched one
> until it passed over her wrist, and, without turning, hurled it high over her shoulder. The bangle
> rose behind her, a bit of silver against the moon, then curved swiftly downward and struck a
> stone. A frail sound in that utter silence. (310)

Selina's bangles identify her as West Indian. In keeping one and leaving the
other with her people in America, its half-circle in the air behind her building a
metaphorical bridge, Selina is shown poised between a past she finally acknowledges and an open future.

Whereas Selina's story is one of struggle with a personal past, Marshall's
second novel, *The Chosen Place, the Timeless People* (1969), adds the dimension of
historical past to the personal struggle of the protagonist Merle Kinbona. This novel
continues the final movement of *Brown Girl, Brownstones* towards the Caribbean. Set
on Bourne Island, a fictitious "mythical Caribbean island,"[12] the novel revolves
around Merle, who, in Marshall's own words, "embodies the history"[13] of the West
Indies. The daughter of a white man and a coloured woman who was murdered
when she was two, educated in England, where she also had a disastrous lesbian
affair with a rich white benefactress, and married to and divorced from an African
husband who took her daughter to his home, Merle returns to Bourne Island a
psychological cripple. In the opening pages of the novel her outward appearance
constitutes a metaphor for the fragmented culture of the Caribbean. She wears a
dress of African print cloth, earrings in the shape of European saints, and the typical
West Indian silver bangles:

> She had donned this somewhat bizzare outfit, each item of which stood opposed to, at war
> even, with the other, to express rather a diversity and disunity within herself, and her attempt,
> unconsciously probably, to reconcile these opposing parts, to make of them a whole.[14]

Merle's task, "to make of them a whole," relates directly to Paule Marshall's
theory about cultural synthesis and the condition of African–Americans "from
Brazil to Brooklyn":[15]

> How does one, out of this kind of mixed bag, come up with a self? [...] I mean we are, as black
> people, in a kind of existential situation where we, in a sense, can create ourselves. Look, this
> is all that's been given. Some of it has been terribly negative, and we're going to try [...] to
> throw that off. But we're going to look at the whole thing and take from it what is useful, what
> we can use to create a self, and we're going to try to bring together some of those forces into a
> kind of harmonious whole. This is really what I've been trying to do in terms of my life and in
> terms of the work. To say, "This is good from my Afro–American experience; o.k., let's take
> that. This is positive from my Afro-Caribbean experience, I'm going to take that. This is good
> from America or Western civilisation, and to try to bring them together."[16]

---

12 Marshall, "Shaping the World of My Art," 106.

13 "Interview with Paule Marshall," 16.

14 Paule Marshall, *The Chosen Place, the Timeless People* (1969; New York: Vintage, 1984): 5.

15 "Interview with Paule Marshall," 15. Marshall's view that all New World African cultures are one
can also be read off the titles of her short-story collection *Soul Clap Hands and Sing* (1961; Washington DC:
Howard UP, 1988): "Barbados", "Brooklyn", "British Guiana", and "Brazil."

16 "Interview with Paule Marshall," 15.

For Marshall's characters, this cultural synthesis can only be achieved by a long struggle which involves confronting their personal past and recognizing its relation to the larger political issue of liberation for all African–Americans. Merle, at the end of *The Chosen Place, the Timeless People*, attempts this symbolically by departing for Africa – after discarding her earrings and bangles in a way reminiscent of Selina. Although she is much clearer than Selina about the aim of her journey – namely, to seek reconciliation with her African husband – her future is equally open.

These endings, with the heroines poised on the brink of a departure into something new, seem to suggest the ongoing process of the "creation of self." This pattern is continued in Marshall's third novel, which she announced in 1973:

> The third and yet to be written novel will in some way be concerned with Africa. Taken together, the three books will constitute a trilogy describing, in reverse, the slave trade's triangular route back to the motherland, the source [ie Africa ...] The physical return described in the novels is a metaphor for the psychological and spiritual return back over history, which I am convinced Black people in this part of the world must undertake if we are to have a sense of our total experience and to mold for ourselves a more truthful identity. Moreover, I believe this exploration of the past is vital in the work of constructing our future.[17]

As it turned out, this third novel, *Praisesong for the Widow* (1984), is not set in Africa. The protagonist, a widow in her sixties, leaves New York for a cruise in the Caribbean and then returns to the USA rather than completing Merle's journey to Africa. But, as one critic noted, "Thematically, [... *Praisesong for the Widow*] is set in Africa, in that it examines the continuations of African culture in the New World and their connection to the parent."[18]

Brathwaite's praise of Marshall's writing as "literature of reconnection" with Africa[19] would especially apply to *Praisesong for the Widow*. This novel offers a wealth of African imagery and cultural heritage as its heroine, Avey Johnson, is gradually led towards a recognition of her African roots. During her journey on the luxury cruise ship with the telling name *Bianca Pride*, Avey dreams of her great-aunt Cuney, a *griotte*, who impressed the tale of the Ibos on her mind. These, upon their arrival in America, took one good look around and into the future, and walked straight back to Africa. Her dream upsets Avey severely. She breaks off the cruise in Grenada and is initiated into a veritable *rite de passage* which for the first time confronts her with her past.[20]

---

17 Marshall, "Shaping the World of My Art," 106 107.

18 Carol Boyce Davies, "Black Woman's Journey into Self: A Womanist Reading of Paule Marshall's *Praisesong for the Widow*," *Matatu* 1.1 (1987): 21.

19 See Edward Kamau Brathwaite's appraisal of Marshall's *The Chosen Place, the Timeless People* in his essay "The African Presence in Caribbean Literature," in *Slavery, Colonialism, and Racism*, ed. Sidney Mintz (New York: Norton, 1974): 73 109. "Literature of reconnection" is the highest development of "written African literature in the Caribbean" (80). The other three are: rhetorical literature, literature of African survival, and literature of African expression.

20 See, for instance, Barbara Christian, "Ritualistic Process and the Structure of Paule Marshall's *Praisesong for the Widow*," in *Black Feminist Criticism: Perspectives on Black Women Writers* (1983; Oxford/New York: Pergamon, 1985): 149 158.

The memories of Avey's husband Jay and their marriage make up a significant part of the novel. Avey and her husband Jay had gone through hard times during the early years of their marriage in a cramped apartment in Brooklyn, during which they were sustained by Black culture in the form of music (blues, gospel, jazz), poetry, and the like. This was in the Fifties, and, although the list of black cultural elements is massive, Avey and Jay seem to be unaware of the true source and power of their nourishment. In keeping with Herskovits's assessment of these times, their lack of awareness of a cultural past has given them no real anchorage in the present. As a consequence, they all too easily relinquished their Black culture when Jay's dual struggle for professional success and against racist discrimination is finally successful and they leave Brooklyn for "White Plains": There, Jay becomes Jerome Johnson, a burnt-out man who dies an early death, presumably because of the drain on him and the lack of black cultural sustenance; Avey turns into the stiff Mrs Johnson who has trouble recognizing herself in mirrors.

Forced to face this alienation and the despair of total subjection to white America's values, Avey is led to Lebert Joseph, the novel's impersonation of the Yoruban deity Eshu–Elegbara (or Legba in the New World), the messenger of the gods and the chief communicator between them and their devotees.[21] He is gifted with clairvoyance like the Ibos in great-aunt Cuney's tale, and senses Avey's dilemma. She can neither answer his question: "What is your nation"? nor recognize any of the West African tribes that Lebert reels off for her orientation. True to his trickster role, Lebert/Legba cons Avey into attending the Carriacou fete called "Big Drum." On the journey to Carriacou, a small island off Grenada, on a rickety boat with another telling name, "Emmanuel C." (Christ's name), Avey becomes violently seasick and symbolically re-lives the Middle Passage:

> She was alone in the deckhouse. That much she was certain of. Yet she had the impression as her mind flickered on briefly of other bodies lying crowded in with her in the hot, airless dark. A multitude it felt lay packed around her in the filth and stench of themselves, just as she was. Their moans, rising and falling with each rise and plunge of the schooner, enlarged upon the one filling her head. Their suffering – the depth of it, the weight of it in the cramped space – made hers of no consequence.[22]

However, the journey is reversed, as Avey is taken back to Africa, represented by the fete which she is now ready to attend. As Abena P.A. Busia points out, this

---

21 On Eshu Elegbara, see Robert Farris Thompson, *Flash of the Spirit: African and Afro American Art and Philosophy* (New York: Random House, 1984): 18 33. For discussions of Lebert/Legba in this novel, see Abena P.A. Busia, "What Is Your Nation? Reconnecting Africa and Her Diaspora through Paule Marshall's *Praisesong for the Widow*," in *Changing Our Own Words: Essays on Criticism, Theory, and Writing by Black Women*, ed. Cheryl A. Walker (London: Routledge, 1990): 196 211, esp. 204, and Angelita Reyes, "Politics and Metaphors of Materialism in Paule Marshall's *Praisesong for the Widow* and Toni Morrison's *Tar Baby*," in *Politics and the Muse: Studies in the Politics of Recent American Literature*, ed. Adam Sorkin (Bowling Green OH: Bowling Green State U Popular P, 1989): 179 205, esp. 199.

22 Paule Marshall, *Praisesong for the Widow* (New York: Dutton, 1984): 209. Subsequent page references to this edition are included in the text.

reverses the location of the promised land (or utopia): It is Africa, rather than the USA.[23]

The novel reaches its climax in Avey's epiphany as she is drawn into the dance called the "Carriacou Tramp": originating in West Africa,[24] it is the same as the "ring shouts" she used to watch as a child with her great-aunt Cuney on Tatem Island, a "Gullah" island off the coast of Georgia, ie one of the US areas with the highest degree of cultural retention. Avey is stunned by this revelation – a surprise similar to Brathwaite's at the Carifesta in 1972, where it became obvious that the same African rituals had been preserved all over the Caribbean.[25] The link between the cultures of Africa, the Caribbean and African–Americans is finally established, and Avey finds further similarities – to burial rites in the USA, for example, such as the Carriacou custom of honoring dead ancestors, the "Old Parents", by feeding them. Religion provides an interesting insight into cultural synthesis and dilution: On Carriacou, Catholicism and West African religious beliefs mix easily, whereby Catholicism renders the formal frame for a spiritual essence that is predominantly African.[26] Avey's memories of African–American Baptist services also reveal a similar mixture, this time leaning towards Christianity.

≈ ❖ ❧

Much more can be said about this final vision of cultural unity from Africa to the Americas, a vision which claims Avey, too. On account of the way she dances, Lebert remarks: "I can't say for sure but I feels you's an Arada, oui" (252). She is united with African culture and history in time and space,[27] and given back her true name, Avatara (the return of the divine to earth). In the end she is ready to return to the USA, with the firm resolve to become a *griotte* and keep the story of the Ibos alive, thus contributing to the survival of the true history of African–Americans in

---

23 Busia, "What is Your Nation?," 207. This may account for the mythic quality of Carriacou in the novel, although it is a real place and the Big Drum is also authentic (cf 254: "The island more a mirage rather than an actual place. Something conjured up perhaps to satisfy a longing and need"). Incidentally, Carriacou features in a similar way in Audre Lorde's *Zami: A New Spelling of My Name* (Freedom CA: Crossing Press, 1982). Lorde is the daughter of Grenadian immigrants to the US "Zami" is translated as " a Carriacou name for women who work together as friends and lovers" (255). The island itself is introduced in the following way: "*Carriacou*, a magic name like cinnamon [...] which was not listed in the index of the *Goode's School Atlas* nor in the *Junior Americana World Gazette* nor appeared on any map I could find [...] I never found it, and came to believe my mother's geography was fantasy or crazy [...] and in reality maybe she was talking about the place other people called Curacao, a Dutch possession on the other side of the Antilles" (14).

24 See Busia, "What is Your Nation?," 211.

25 Brathwaite, "History, the Caribbean Writer, and *X/Self*," 31.

26 For a description of the Carriacou Big Drum and religious beliefs and practices, see Donald Hill, "More on Truth, Fact, and Tradition in Carriacou," *Caribbean Quarterly* 20.1 (1974): 45 59. See also Thompson, *Flash of the Spirit*, and Herskovits, *The Myth of the Negro Past*, on this issue of Africanisms in the practice of African American Christians.

27 Carriacou is thus a true chronotope in the Bakhtinian sense: "the intrinsic connectedness of temporal and spatial relationships that are artistically expressed in literature" (Mikhail Bakhtin, "Forms of Time and the Chronotope in the Novel," in *The Dialogic Imagination: Four Essays* [Austin: U of Texas P, 1984]: 84).

the way the songs and dances in Carriacou hand down history from generation to generation (176–77).

However, I am left with a few questions. Although *Praisesong for the Widow* seems to be more assertive in its message than its predecessors – for example, Carriacou is a real place, in contrast to the fictitious Bourne Island, and Avey, as opposed to Selina and Merle, has a clear vision of her future task – Avey's final development is not really a question of choosing from among the various cultural strands in the way Marshall outlined earlier. Her epiphany comes closer to Brathwaite's experience of the ripping-open of history, changing consciousness in a flash. This is not choice, this is necessity, inevitable once it has happened.[28]

Although the novel apparently rejects Western values, one aspect seems to offer a more positive view: The spirit of the Big Drum evokes the presence of the Yoruban and Haitian deity Ogun – Avey joins the dance when she senses this presence. Ogun – a divinity of war – is associated with iron and its products as well as with creativity and art.[29] He thus refers to the metafictional level: As Avey tells the story of the Ibos, Marshall tells Avey's story, and Marshall's style of novel-writing illustrates the kind of cultural fusion which Petronella Breinburg describes as available to the artist:[30] The kind of full-blown, richly detailed novel she creates is influenced by writers like Thomas Mann and Thomas Hardy; the language she has inherited from her Barbadian mother and her women friends, and much of her imagery, is African, a result of the influence of Black Aesthetics.[31] But although the page may be a blank before it is written upon, a human being is never a cultural blank, entirely free to choose the parts of his/her cultural makeup; Marshall's own thematic emphasis on African cultural retention seems to be making this point. So Herskovits' dictum still seems to be true: First all Africanisms have to be re-discovered before we will be able to evaluate the true extent of cultural synthesis.

∾ ❖ ৯

---

28 Avey is actually forced through this *rite de passage*, which is essential to her physical and spiritual well-being. Reyes has criticised this whole view as too simplistic and absolute. She regards it as "a romantic approach to history, myth, and socio-political issues," which ultimately compromises Marshall's vision of the interrelation of history and the present (193).

29 On Ogun, see Thompson, *Flash of the Spirit*, 52 57, esp. 53: "Lord of the cutting edge, he is present even in the speeding bullet or a railway locomotive."

30 Petronella Breinburg, in the present volume.

31 See her "Shaping the World of My Art," and the interview with Sandi Russell. See also her "The Making of a Writer: From the Poets in the Kitchen," in *Reena and Other Stories* (New York: Feminist Press, 1981): 3–12; and Omolara Ogundipe–Leslie, "'Re-Creating Ourselves All Over the World': Interview with Paule Marshall," *Matatu* 63 (1989): 25–38.

WORKS CITED

BAKHTIN, Mikhail. "Forms of Time and of the Chronotope in the Novel," in *The Dialogic Imagination: Four Essays*, ed. Michael Holquist, tr. Caryl Emerson & Michael Holquist (Austin: U of Texas P, 1984) : 84–258.

BRATHWAITE, Edward Kamau, "The African Presence in Caribbean Literature," in *Slavery, Colonialism, and Racism*, ed. Sidney Mintz (New York: Norton, 1974): 73–109.

——. "History, the Caribbean Writer, and *X/Self*," in *Crisis and Creativity in the New Literatures in English*, ed. Geoffrey V. Davis & Hena Maes–Jelinek (Cross/Cultures 1; Amsterdam/Atlanta GA: Rodopi, 1990): 23–45.

BUSIA, Abena P.A. "What Is Your Nation? Reconnecting Africa and Her Diaspora through Paule Marshall's *Praisesong for the Widow*," in *Changing Our Own Words: Essays on Criticism, Theory, and Writing by Black Women*, ed. Cheryl A. Wall (New Brunswick NJ: Rutgers UP, 1989): 196–211.

CHRISTIAN, Barbara. "Ritualistic Process and the Structure of Paule Marshall's *Praisesong for the Widow*," in *Black Feminist Criticism: Perspectives on Black Women Writers* (1983; Oxford/New York: Pergamon, 1985): 149–58.

——. "'Somebody Forgot to Tell Somebody Something': African–American Women's Historical Novels," in *Wild Women in the Whirlwind: Afro-American Culture and the Contemporary Literary Renaissance*, ed. Joanne M. Braxton & Andrée Nicola McLaughlin (London: Serpent's Tail, 1990)

DAVIES, Carol Boyce. "Black Woman's Journey into Self: A Womanist Reading of Paule Marshall's *Praisesong for the Widow*," *Matatu* 1.1 (1987): 19–34.

HERSKOVITS, Melville J. *The Myth of the Negro Past* (1941; Boston: Beacon Press, 1990).

HILL, Donald. "More on Truth, Fact, and Tradition in Carriacou," *Caribbean Quarterly* 20.1 (1974): 45–59.

JORDAN, June. "The Difficult Miracle of Black Poetry in America: or, Something Like a Sonnet for Phyllis Wheatley," *Massachusetts Review* 27.2 (Summer 1986): 252–62.

LORDE, Audre. *Zami: A New Spelling of My Name* (Freedom CA: Crossing Press, 1982).

MARSHALL, Paule. *Brown Girl, Brownstones* (1959; New York: Feminist Press, 1981).

——. *The Chosen Place, The Timeless People* (1969; New York: Vintage, 1984).

——. "Interview with Paule Marshall," by Sandi Russell, *Wasafiri* 8 (Spring 1988): 14–16.

——. "The Making of a Writer: From the Poets in the Kitchen," in *Reena and Other Stories* (New York: Feminist Press, 1981): 3–12

——. "'Re-Creating Ourselves All Over the World': Interview with Paule Marshall," by Omolara Ogundipe–Leslie. *Matatu: Journal for African Culture and Society* 6.3 (1989): 25–38.

——. "Shaping the World of My Art," *New Letters* 40 (October 1973): 97–112.

NELSON, Emmanuel S. "Black America and the Anglophone Afro-Caribbean Literary Consciousness," *Journal of American Culture* 12.4 (1989): 53–58.

REYES, Angelita. "Politics and Metaphors of Materialism in Paule Marshall's *Praisesong for the Widow* and Toni Morrison's *Tar Baby*," in *Politics and the Muse: Studies in the Politics of Recent American Literature*, ed. Adam J. Sorkin (Bowling Green OH: Bowling Green Popular P, 1989): 179–205.

THOMPSON, Robert Farris. *Flash of the Spirit: African and Afro American Art and Philosophy* (New York: Random House, 1984).

≈ ❖ ❧

S hirley Geok–lin Lim
(Munich, September 1993; photo Peter Stummer)

SHIRLEY GEOK–LIN LIM

Race, National Identity, and the Subject
in the Novels of Timothy Mo

P ART OF THE APPEAL OF THE CONCEPT of "diaspora" lies in the way it is able to wedge an interrogation of given unequal positions between a hegemonic state authority and individual "selves." Homi Bhabha, valorizing the counter-hegemonic, anti-colonialist, postmodern intellectual, inserts the notion of the diaspora in the idea of the marginal:

> it is the disjunctive, fragmented, displaced agency of those who have suffered the sentence of history – subjugation, diaspora, displacement – that forces one to think outside the certainty of the sententious. It is from the affective experience of social marginality that we must conceive of a political strategy of empowerment and articulation, a strategy outside the liberatory rhetoric of idealism and beyond the sovereign subject that haunts the "civil" sentence of the law.[1]

In addressing the issue of "cultural incommensurability," Bhabha argues that the liberal ethic of tolerance and the pluralistic frame of multiculturalism are no longer adequate perspectives. Instead, because the historical moment is "caught in an aporetic, contingent position, in-between a plurality of practices that are different and yet must occupy the same space of adjudication and articulation," intellectuals must begin to speak from the perspective of the "edge," a "liminal form of cultural identification" for "non-ethnocentric, transcultural judgments."[2]

Bhabha's position is problematical for a variety of reasons. First, the cultural moment he speaks of is not so much a postmodern moment as a historical repetition. The history of humans at a macro- and micro-level is the history of "a plurality of practices that are different and yet must occupy the same space for adjudication and articulation." That is the history of colonialism, of religious and national wars, of race, class, and gender struggles. Moreover, the non-ethnocentric and transcultural judgements he appeals to have for the last century been formulated as the social values possessed by an international and cosmopolitan élite, a formulation that has been persuasively critiqued as eliding the class and metropolitan bases that support such an élite and whose political economies it lives off and supports.[3]

---

[1] Homi Bhabha, "Postcolonial Authority and Postmodern Guilt," in *Cultural Studies,* ed. Lawrence Grossberg, Cary Nelson & Paula Treichler (New York: Routledge, 1992): 56.

[2] Bhabha, "Postcolonial Authority and Postmodern Guilt," 57.

[3] See Timothy Brennan, "Cosmopolitans and Celebrities," *Race and Class* 13.1 (July–September 1989): 1–19. Brennan reads in the postwar Western sociologists and historians' criticism of nationalism an attack on the project of decolonisation in the Third World. While Brennan's term, "cosmopolitanism," and Bhabha's term, "transnational," are different, Brennan's deployment of "cosmopolitanism" suggests an

In inserting the experience of "diaspora" into his reinscription of the cosmopolitan argument, Bhabha's statements can be taken to suggest an idealization of race on a global basis as an empowering strategy to move beyond the ideology of the "freedom" of the "sovereign subject" at exactly the moment when more and more totalitarian systems are forced to take account of this "sovereign subject."[4] My paper will contest Bhabha's construction of "diaspora" – as a social phenomenon in which the "sovereign subject" and the legislated secured borders of a nation-state are irrelevant – with reference to three novels by Timothy Mo, a writer born in Hong Kong and now living in Britain.

Mo can be considered an immigrant, but of a special kind. As a child of Hong Kong, Mo was already a British subject before coming to London in his teens and working as a newspaper man in the Eighties.[5] His novels, *The Monkey King* (1978), *Sour Sweet* (short-listed for the prestigious Booker Prize in 1982), and *The Redundancy of Courage* (1991), set in Hong Kong, Britain, Portuguese Timor and the Americas, range the Chinese diasporic subject as a geographically unrooted individual.[6] The diasporic individual's ambiguity of national identity catalyses the fictions' dramatic conflicts. This ambiguity provides the materials for ironic and dystopic interrogations of Sino culture, colonialist structures, neo-colonialist depredations, and the position of the individual to maintain an autonomous dignity among these hegemonic powers. Ien Ang reads the overseas Chinese double-bind toward China as producing a "continuous ambivalence" which "highlights the fundamental precariousness of diasporic identity construction, its positive indeterminacy."[7] I argue, instead, that the diasporic subject in Mo's novels is already systemically overdetermined. The conditions of these overdeterminations constrain and locate the subject in a life-and-death struggle with and against the diasporic collectivity of race and culture – and within and against the host society: the subject's identity is configured and reconfigured under these conditions.

---

analogue to Bhabha's notion of the intellectual who speaks from a "liminal form of cultural identification": "spokespersons for a kind of perennial immigration, valorised by a rhetoric of wander-ing, and rife with allusions to the all-seeing eye of the nomadic sensibility" (2).

[4] Bhabha's ideas on the transnational are more complex and contradictory than are expressed in this one particular essay. In " "DissemiNation: Time, Narrative, and the Margins of the Modern Nation" (in *Nation and Narration,* ed. Homi K. Bhabha; London/New York: Routledge, 1990), he argues that the established "liminality of the nation-state" transforms the threat of cultural difference from "outside" to "within," and quotes approvingly Foucault's description of "the marginalistic integration of the individual in the social totality" (301–302). Minority discourse, however, "contests genealogies of 'origin' that lead to claims of cultural supremacy and historical priority" (307). It is only by "living on the borderline of history and language, on the limits of race and gender, that we are in a position to translate the differences between them into a kind of solidarity" (320). In arguing for "culture's transnational dissemination," Bhabha appears to assume a depoliticised/demilitarised transnational cultural dynamic which Mo's novel *The Redundancy of Courage* demonstrates (in the historical decolonising moment, albeit through fiction) as impossible.

[5] Mo was born in 1953 in Hong Kong and attended Oxford University; he is over a decade younger than Kingston (*Contemporary Authors,* vol. 117; Detroit: Gale, 1986: 301).

[6] This essay does not discuss Mo's third novel, *An Insular Possession* (1986), as it offers other challenges not within the scope of the essay.

[7] Ien Ang, "Migrations of Chineseness," *SPAN* 34–35 (October 1992–May 1993): 4.

Mo's novels demonstrate a collapsing of the boundaries of fiction and non-fiction, toward a greater transgression of the novel as a discourse of the imaginary, to repoliticize it as a vehicle for sociopolitical critiques on the ways in which non-secured individuals are threatened, manipulated, swallowed up, colonized, erased, and extinguished by powers of the collective, whether of family, race, or state.

The imagined homeland is never simple territoriality, a geopolitical space or original home. His novels show no trace of the kind of diasporic nostalgia and yearning, inseparable from the myth of pure race and resulting in ethnocentrism, that is found in what Lyn Pan has called the Overseas Chinese cultures.[8] Mo's protagonists do not participate in an overseas Chinese community so much as they resist being subsumed by it. A transnational writer owing loyalty to neither China nor Britain, the two nations that can be said to have biographical contingency for him, Mo treats a diasporic Chineseness disarticulated from nationality or territory,[9] but tied to a collectivity whose power encompasses race and culture. The subject in relation to this diasporic collectivity never gets to leave this homeland, which operates like ideology to ironize, eviscerate, and cannibalize the individual who presumes to escape it. In order to preserve the tatters of a sovereign subject-condition, even to preserve his physical life, the subject must abandon his home-land, must unbecome Chinese.

The failed resistance to the homeland/culture of Chinese collectivism forms the major thematic in *The Monkey King*. In *Sour Sweet*, the collectivity in the form of the criminal Triad society destroys Chen. In the form of the more benevolent matriarchal family of Lily, it survives in the future represented in the person of Son. In *The Redundancy of Courage*, Chineseness remains as a trace that overdetermines Ng's positionality in the nation-state of Danu. As social construct and category, it operates as a sensitized, double-layered perspective of multiple diasporas, producing in the diasporic Chinese the marked status of the refugee/witness to the horrors of genocide. Now euphemized as "ethnic cleansing," genocide denotes the extermination of subjects under the rule of territoriality, occurring when the ideology of a homeland erases the human rights of individuals.

Confucianist collectivity

The Monkey King's examination of this thematic is perhaps the lightest among Mo's novels. A domestic novel set in the Hong Kong of the Seventies, it scrutinizes Sino culture by situating the novel's point of view in a putative non-Chinese character. Wallace Nolasco's "Portuguese" Macao ethnicity serves to bracket "Chinese" as a

---

8 Lyn Pan defines the pioneering Overseas Chinese community unproblematically as synonymous with the Chinese diaspora: all those people who can trace their origins to Chinese ancestry and who maintain the speech and customs of the provinces from which their forefathers had come; see Pan's *Sons of the Yellow Emperor: A History of the Chinese Diaspora* (Boston MA: Little, Brown, 1990): 1–22.

9 As a British subject originally from Hong Kong, Mo's diplomatic status may be said to figure the trans-national condition. "Transnational" is a currently preferred term that underlines the mobility, destability, and porous national borders that characterise the movements of global populations.

race. The novel's opening passage deconstructs both "Portuguese" and "Chinese" race as unstable identities – "Centuries of mixed marriages with the Cantonese had obliterated whatever had been distinctive about their shadowy buccaneer ancestors"[10] – while the conclusion ironically represents the syncretic power of the Sino familial community as so monster-like that it absorbs the resisting individual into its undifferentiated collective maw. Wallace enters into an arranged marriage with May Ling, who, as daughter of Mr Poon and his second concubine, "was lucky not to have been sold into a brothel" (7). The match testifies to *Mr* Poon's genius in negotiating the values of Sino civil society to achieve a very Sino goal: "What Mr Poon wanted was posterity, the more the better [...] Even a concubine's grandchildren could venerate an ancestor" (8). Wallace enters the Poon family not as an individual but as a commodified object whose value lies in his position in the Sino collectivity:[11] "It would be possible to economise on the initial capital outlay of the dowry to balance out defrayments on an additional mouth [...] And while not a celestial, Wallace was not a real *faan gwai lo*, a foreign devil. Compromise was at the centre of Mr Poon's political system, and in securing Wallace he had achieved such a balance" (8).

The novel's comedy lies in tracing Wallace's resistance to the Poon political system, whose eccentric economies coupled with hidden wealth are lambasted: "The quantities of food served would have been sufficient for three hungry adults. Eight, and in the school vacations the adolescent grandsons as well, sat down to the round wooden table" (13). Wallace's outsider-position in the family, dramatized as domestic battles over food and minor privileges, affects his marital relationship: "Mr Poon had not exactly welched on his obligations but Wallace had voluntarily turned his back on the dowry; he would not give something for nothing. Mr Poon could expect no grandsons from him in the future" (58). Wallace resists the political economy of the Confucianist state. Rejecting the dowry, and therefore getting nothing, he also ethically could give nothing. Male sexuality, necessary for the continuance of the patrilocal and patrilineal system, is reduced to a commodity; but Wallace's refusal to sell it asserts his dignity as an individual over and against the collective.

However, as the novel proceeds to demonstrate, the autonomy of the subject cannot withstand the hegemonic appetite of the Sino collectivity. Exiled to a village in the New Territories after being manipulated into a civil act of corruption by his father-in-law, Wallace falls into the community burial grave, an accident that sets in motion a series of incidents and stirs up trouble between the Cantonese villagers and British authorities. Averting a bloody war between the Cantonese and their Hakka neighbours, Wallace causes a lake to form, then persuades the villagers to exploit

---

10 Mo, *The Monkey King* (London: Sphere, 1978): 3. Further page references are in the text.

11 The novel's construction of an insider/outsider liminal position through Wallace's resistance to and eventual absorption into the syncretic Confucianist familial unit can be read as an analogue to Hong Kong's position vis-à-vis China and Mo's satirical stance on post-1997 when Hong Kong will revert to the People's Republic of China.

the lake as a weekend resort for Hong-Kong urbanites. His rejection of May's early suggestion – "You thought I could make myself boss of your father house just like you were saying? Things just didn't ever happen like that" (116) – proves incorrect. As the eponymous Monkey King, he is led, thanks to his intelligence, wit, and audacity, to assume the patriarchal authority of the Poon household after Mr Poon's death, displacing Ah Lung, the spendthrift legal son.[12] Mr Poon's will, representing the Confucianist ideal of the "supreme man," "kept [Ah Lung] in perpetual tutelage [...]. a concrete, persistent reminder of his unevolved condition" (199). Forming a partnership with Fong, his sister-in-law, Wallace becomes the economic manager for Mrs Poon, and has a son, whose "wrinkled, simian features" suggest the patrilineal continuance of the Monkey King, a signifier of the triumph of the Chinese family: "If anything, it looked like Mr Poon, reincarnated" (210).

The conclusion subverts the plot of resistance: Wallace's rebellion against the Confucianist patriarch, which concludes in his becoming "boss of your father [sic] house," is thoroughly ironized. The successful revolt of the subject concludes with the absorption of that subject into the Confucianist structure. Wallace's dream of a banquet where diners feast on the brains of a living monkey symbolizes his unconscious recognition that his ascendancy to monkey king itself marks the loss of the subject, whose intelligence becomes a commodity to be consumed by the Chinese family. The image of cannibalistic sacrifice of the individual to the Chinese socius shades *The Monkey King* as a darker novel that its comic texture would intimate.

This critique is further developed in *Sour Sweet*, a novel which continues to be misread as a comedy.[13] In *Sour Sweet*, Mo charges the world of the English novel, set in London, with a diasporic perspective that unsettles the traditional notion of British nationality and polity. Paul Gilroy's remarks on the concept of the African diaspora are enlightening in relation to the horizon of intercultural expectations in which *Sour Sweet* operates. Speaking of "some new intermediate concepts, between the local and the global," Gilroy points out that these concepts "break the dogmatic focus on national cultures and traditions which has characterized so much Euro-American cultural thought. Getting beyond this national and nationalistic perspective is essential," he adds, because of "the postmodern eclipse of the modern nation-state as a political, economic, and cultural unit."[14] Moreover, these concepts

---

12 The novel's title and metaplay refer to the Chinese classic, *Monkey,* in which the protagonist, Monkey, creates havoc among the hierarchical levels of gods and goddesses. An epic comedy as well as a religious text, *Monkey* underlines Buddhist valuation of cosmic harmony and right living at the same time that it valorises the energy and subversive transgressiveness of its lowly hero.

13 *Sour Sweet* has chiefly been constructed as a comedy by its Anglo-American reviewers and publishers; the paperback version of the novel carries a blurb from *The Listener* praising Mo's "delicious gingery sense of humour." Overlooking the lurid psychological and physical violence enacted within the diasporic Chinese cultural system, Peter Lewis in the *Times Literary Supplement* misses the level of Mo's expose of the Chinese Triadic global crime network in *Sour Sweet* and focuses on the text as a late-twentieth-century Austen social comedy: "He has a very sharp eye indeed for the nuances of behaviour in close-knit social units" (cited in *Contemporary Authors,* vol. 117: 302).

14 Paul Gilroy, "Cultural Studies and Ethnic Absolutism," in *Cultural Studies,* ed. Grossberg et al., 188.

of a diasporic perspective question the integrity of cultures and the relationship between nationality and ethnicity. Following on Gilroy's diasporic framing of the Afro-American experience, I would argue that the Chinese–British experience constructed in *Sour Sweet* must be read as "continuous with a hemispheric order that is [...] explicitly anti-ethnic." The identities of Chinese in Mo's novels must be read as "a matter of politics rather than a purely cultural condition."[15]

Just as there are two civil societies in the novel, the British and the Chinese, so the novel treats two families, Chen's extended family – composed of his wife Lily, her sister Mui, their child Mun Kee, and later his father – and the Triad "family" of the Hung, whose international network and knitting of diverse individuals into an economic collectivity offers a criminal mirroring of the Confucianist family. The novel's structure interpellates one family with the other,[16] a device that shadows, juxtaposes, and imprisons the domestic family within the criminal family. This second family is not strictly an imagined one. Based on research that Mo, as journalist, carried out, the information on how Triad society is structured hierarchically, on its initiation rituals, its global criminal network and so forth, is taken from works on the Triad societies in Hong Kong.[17]

John Rothfork argues that *Sour Sweet* dramatizes "the rectification or renewal of an authentic Confucianism leading to [an] authoritatively human life."[18] But, as the critique of the loss of the individual subject to the Confucianist family in *The Monkey King* intimates, Mo's criticism of Confucianist forms of social control in *Sour Sweet* abjures a recuperation of "authentic Confucianism."[19] Chen, the diasporic male subject, in his immigration from original cultural space to the United Kingdom, has been emptied of cultural and social significance. As an immigrant, "Chen had lost his claim to clan land in his ancestral village," but he has gained no identity in the United Kingdom except as "an interloper," "a foreigner," "a gate-crasher who had stayed too long and been identified."[20] His life is calculated as "seventy-two hours in the restaurant, slept fifty-six, spent forty hours with his wife," and so forth. His marriage further serves to strip him of any subject autonomy. Lily, a watchful, controlling wife whose actions are ruled by Chinese cultural beliefs in "dualistic male and female principles of harmony" (2), permits him no space for his individual responses.

---

15 Gilroy, "Cultural Studies and Ethnic Absolutism," 196.

16 Chapters 2, 4, 6, 8, 13, 16, 18, 20, 24, 30, 33, and 35 specifically treat the Triad family.

17 For example, William Stanton, *The Triad Society: or, Heaven and Earth Association of Hong-Kong* (Hong Kong: Kelly & Walsh, 1900) and W.P. Morgan, *Triad Societies in Hong Kong* (Hong Kong: Govt. of Hong Kong, Miscellaneous Official Publications, repr. 1958). Similarly, Mo tells us that he "supplemented personal knowledge with sociological and anthropological studies" in his representation of the rural community in *The Monkey King*.

18 Rothfork, "Confucianism in Timothy Mo's *Sour Sweet*," *Journal of Commonwealth Literature* 14.1 (1989): 64.

19 A notion that indicates Rothfork's essentialising move as coming out of a Western tradition of "orientalising" Chinese society.

20 Mo, *Sour Sweet* (1982; New York: Vintage, 1985): 1. Further page references are in the text.

Lily's character is associated significantly with the Triad society that finally kills Chen. Her "masterful" personality comes from her childhood training in Chinese boxing with her father, a famous practitioner of *sui lum* temple-boxing (11). The leader of the Hung Triad society in London is Red Cudgel, who, we learn in the conclusion, had been a fellow-fighter of Lily's father. Thus, even as he was manipulated out of his leadership position in the triad, he "was most insistent that reparation should be made to [Chen's] widow and family [...] Community of feeling between fighters" (264). This "community of feeling," a Confucianist construction of social dutifulness along a hierarchy, is ironically produced on the death of the individual subject. More clearly, the Triad society's use of the family structure as its principal form of organization (the officers call each other "Elder Brother" or "younger sister" to signify hierarchical status and power) is yet another reproduction of a Confucianist society in which the individual is subordinated to the group. The doubling narrative device, between Lily's control of her husband and sister and the Triad's ringleaders' control of their criminal organization, underlines the commonality between the domestic and public spheres in Confucianist-ruled communities. Chen's eventual entrapment in the Triad's machinations and his physical death is a fate only a degree more extreme than his entrapment in Lily's machinations and his psychological withering.

To Lily, Chen is only "Husband," without an individual name – a husband, moreover, in whom she is disappointed. She finds him "uninspired" (7), but maintains towards him a properly ritualized attitude: "Whatever her well-stifled misgivings, she intended to be a good wife to him. All these new characteristics she incorporated into a revised assessment of Husband – one which remained loyally high" (198). In Lily's construction of Chen, his humanity as subject is erased in his role as "Husband." In contrast, Lily's relationship with her sister Mui comes from an emotional intimacy that humanizes the two women. As Chen noticed, "those two sisters were ather obviously good friends. Life had been going on behind his back; life of a gay, irresponsible, female kind" (108). The women on this Confucianist stage are presented as full of life, their intimacy affording them a vitality that is denied to Chen, whose only escape is in gardening, an expression not only of his peasant roots but of his immigrant condition: the flourishing garden showed "Chen's skills as a farmer were not lost. At home in the New Territories vegetable growing was an ignominious mode of agriculture, practised by refugees and immigrants. It was fitting he should grow them here in alien soil" (168).

Chinese diasporic culture, in reproducing those Confucianist state and social controls that arguably form the core of Chinese culture,[21] is represented as a socio-economic system in which the individual subject is violently consumed (as in

---

21 See Perry Link's "China's 'Core' Problem," *Daedalus* 122.2 (Spring 1993): 189–205, for a sympathetic summary of the hegemony of Confucianism ruling "most of China's imperial history of the last thousand years" (192). As Link notes, the "answer" to the fundamental question of how society in China should be organised was "originally a Confucian one, but after centuries of custom now so deeply rooted in Chinese culture that it tends to appear almost reflexively" (191).

Wallace's dream in *The Monkey King*) or violently exterminated (as with Chen in *Sour Sweet*). Chen's death, therefore, leaves no emotional aftermath for Lily, as long as "The remittances kept coming" (278). In fact, Lily forgives his supposed abandonment of the family, the ultimate Confucianist sin, in the light of the assumption that he has cared for the family economically. The novel's conclusion goes further, to suggest that the patriarchal construction of the Chinese family is, ironically, a matriarchal conspiracy to preserve what is of primary importance to women, the future of their offspring. Far from being devastated by the loss of the male, Lily is set free by his disappearance: "it was as if a stone had been taken off her and she had sprung to what her height should have been " (278). "Husband" is, after all, an expendable object once he has fulfilled his function in the Confucianist matriarchy: "She might have lost Husband for a while but she still had Son. Who could take him away from her?" (278).

Chinese pragmatism

Mo's second-latest novel, *The Redundancy of Courage* (1991),[22] treats the Chinese diasporic subject in a different political world. Mo turns away from the critique of colonialism and Confucianist social organization to a representation of the place of the diasporic subject in post- and neo-colonial contexts. The narrator–protagonist, Adolph Ng, is a citizen of Danu, a state which is a thinly disguised version of Portuguese Timor. Adolph is self-consciously reflexive of his multiple identities, but, counter to postmodernist constructs that play on ambiguity and instability, Adolph, like Chen, is imagined as a stolid or solid personality: he possesses a recognizable core of psychological features, among them worldly intelligence, sensitivity to his problematical identity as Chinese diasporic and citizen of a non-Chinese state, loyalty and affection to friends, and a strong will to survive. In naming himself "Ng," he names his identity as Chinese: "You know I am of the Chinese race."[23] Race, he suggests, is not the most important feature of his character. He is "a citizen of the great world," a cosmopolitan, and his "modernity" makes him, like Wallace and Chen, an outsider in his home country, which is "a desolate place" (24). Adolph's race, nationality, and subject are three different constructs straddled by the force of one cultural value: "Chinese pragmatism" (24).

The novel demonstrates the operation of Chinese pragmatism as a survival-mode, first when Adolph's security is threatened by a civil war between contending Danuese nationalist forces that are racially based, then by the neo-colonialist depredations of the "malai." Mo does not valorize Chinese pragmatism; in fact, he establishes a critical distance from this cultural mode, which he constructs as simultaneously producing, and produced by, an economic rationality to which all political systems are subordinate:

---

[22] He has more recently published *Brownout on Breadfruit Boulevard* (London: Paddleless, 1995).

[23] Mo, *The Redundancy of Courage* (London: Chatto & Windus, 1991): 24. Further page references are in the text.

> Most Chinese didn't give a damn about politics, independence or dependency, it was all one
> and the same to them [...] Exploitation was the name of the game. We'd always done it and were
> cheerfully continuing the tradition of our ancestors. Rip-off didn't begin to describe it. (7)

The novel does not begin with these modern interrogations of the subject's identity
within the competing categories of nation, race, and world. Instead, it opens with a
chapter describing the malai invasion of Danu, "parachutes dropping" (3), the
massacre of women, children, and civilians, and the brutal murder of an Australian
journalist. The malais,[24] we are told, have a history of massacres: "They'd killed
hundreds of thousands in their own country: communists, socialists, liberals even"
(20). The neo-colonialist moment presented as a genocidal fascist scene is almost
unbearably particular in its reportorial strategy while verging on the lyrically
macabre: at the conclusion of the litany of mayhem, Mo contrasts the corpse of the
Australian journalist, "shrinking into a semi-foetal position and quite black now in
the middle of the flames," with "the shoals of giant white jelly fish" that "hung in
the clear water like ghostly canopies, suspended [...] in a fall they suggest but would
never make" (23). The novel moves through these two extreme visions, of humans'
hateful destruction and nature's indifferent beauty.

As narrator and protagonist, Adolph distinguishes himself from the "'blind'
Chinaman with his eyes in the trough along with his snout" (54). He is a politicized,
articulate consciousness serving as commentator on decolonizing and neo-
colonizing dynamics of new and collapsing empires (55). Tracing the course of
rising nationalism, Adolph follows the Danuese "autonomists" as they are drawn
into civil war through greed and power-politics (56). Adolph understands that in this
nativist/nationalist drama, he "didn't have a piece of the action," "that [he] was
Chinese and treated as such" (58).

But it is the non-nationalist who is entrusted with telling the story of the
Danuese, with keeping alive the political memory of an incipient nation. Adolph
begins the narrative: "I didn't want them forgotten: Rosa, Osvaldo, Raoul, Maria,
Martinho, Arsenio" (3). Ironically, the diasporic subject who is constructed by
nationalists as non-national must carry the weight of moral authority and national
history, both threatened by the supranational history of the malais, whose assault on
central human moral tenets – the value of individual lives, respect for the freedom
of others' – demonstrates the evils of neo-colonialist ideology.

Adolph flees into the jungle with the Danuese resistance forces, and, when he is
captured by the malais, survives by serving as a domestic slave to the malai general's wife. When finally he is able to buy his freedom, he leaves for "the Home
Country" in Europe – evidently Portugal – thence to Brazil. Adolph is three times
denied a community; first, by China, the country of his ancestors; then, in Danu,
among his nationalist friends, who deny him a national identity; and last, by the

---

[24] A fictional term to suggest the Indonesian forces that invaded the island nation of Timor in 1975.
Declaring Timor to be Indonesia's 27th province, the Indonesian state has put down the Timorese
resistance; between 100,000 and 200,000 people have been killed. The national language of Indonesia is
Malay, coincidentally the national language of Malaysia.

malais, who reduce him to the final subjectless condition, that of a slave. As the survivor of colonialist and neo-colonialist history, Adolph is eager to leave the dead past behind and begin a future someplace else: "I didn't care if [...] the pangs of birth were ugly; I wanted to be somewhere I wouldn't be defined by what I'd been, where I could fashion a new notion of myself and impose it on others as the truth" (402). The diasporic desire carries the empty subject toward the hope of an imagined subjecthood.

The novel doesn't however conclude on this birth of a new subject. The old subject persists and cannot be rewritten. In this way, Mo's novel is unambiguously modernist rather than postmodern, asserting the existence of the individual subject as the valuation on which history, civilization, and morality are measured. As Adolph recognizes,

> I could not terminate Adolph Ng so conveniently. I was trying to accomplish within my own small person what the malais hadn't been able to do to a nation. An identity and a history cannot be obliterated. I arrived in the vastness of a new country as what I thought a *tabula rasa* but there was writing underneath, the coded determinants of what I was and always would be inscribed. (406)

The inextinguishable condition of the subject resists the evils of totalitarianism. "One woodchuck" is always left in the torched field – a trope for the weak, innocent creature of nature, the unprotected human, that will continue to defeat the fascists' project of genocide. The diasporic subject, stripped of the protective group-status of race and nation, receives this saving illumination.

In *The Redundancy of Courage*, the identity of the subject is no "regnant cliché" of race and identity politics[25] but the very ground on which the totalizing obliteration of genocide is combatted. While his novels do not privilege the subject as sovereign (in fact, they represent this subject condition as historically contingent, entrapped, threatened by erasure, and fragile), they nonetheless speak for the preservation of the subject as a necessary defence against the violence of the collectivity, whether this is the collectivity of the Confucianist family, the Triad society, or the totalitarian state.

❧ ❖ ☙

---

[25] A phrase used by Gates and Appiah in their editorial introduction to the special issue of *Critical Inquiry* devoted to identities (Kwame Anthony Appiah & Henry Louis Gates, Jr. "Editors' Introduction: Multiplying Identities," *Critical Inquiry* 18 [Summer 1992]: 625–29).

WORKS CITED

ANG, Ien. "Migrations of Chineseness," *SPAN* 34–35 (October 1992–May 1993): 3–15.

APPIAH, Kwame Anthony & Henry Louis Gates, Jr. "Editors' Introduction: Multiplying Identities," *Critical Inquiry* 18 (Summer 1992): 625–29.

BHABHA, Homi K. "DissemiNation: Time, Narrative, and the Margins of the Modern Nation," in *Nation and Narration*, ed. Homi K. Bhabha (London/New York: Routledge, 1990): 291–322.

———. "Postcolonial Authority and Postmodern Guilt," in *Cultural Studies*, ed. Lawrence Grossberg, Cary Nelson & Paula Treichler (New York: Routledge, 1992): 56–68.

BRENNAN, Timothy. "Cosmopolitans and Celebrities," *Race and Class* 13.1 (July–September 1989): 1–19.

Contemporary Authors, vol. 117 (Detroit: Gale, 1986): 301–302.

GILROY, Paul. "Cultural Studies and Ethnic Absolutism," in *Cultural Studies*, ed. Grossberg et al., 187–98.

LINK, Perry. "China's 'Core' Problem," *Daedalus* 122.2 (Spring 1993): 189–205.

MO, Timothy. *Brownout on Breadfruit Boulevard* (London: Paddleless, 1995).

———. *An Insular Possession* (London: Chatto & Windus, 1986).

———. *The Monkey King* (London: Sphere, 1978).

———. *The Redundancy of Courage* (London: Chatto & Windus, 1991).

———. *Sour Sweet* (1982; New York: Vintage, 1985).

MORGAN, W.P. *Triad Societies in Hong Kong* (Hong Kong: Govt. of Hong Kong, Miscellaneous Official Publications, repr. 1958).

PAN, Lynn. *Sons of the Yellow Emperor: A History of the Chinese Diaspora* (Boston MA: Little, Brown, 1990).

ROTHFORK, John. "Confucianism in Timothy Mo's *Sour Sweet*," *Journal of Commonwealth Literature* 14.1 (1989): 49–64.

STANTON, William. *The Triad Society: or, Heaven and Earth Association of Hong-Kong* (Hong Kong: Kelly & Walsh, 1900).

WU CH'ENG–EN (c.1500–c.1582). *The Monkey King* (London: Paul Hamlyn, 1965).

❧ ❖ ❧

$\mathcal{B}$ harati Mukherjee
(photo Peter Stummer)

SÄMI LUDWIG

Cultural Identity as "Spouse"
Limitations and Possibilities of a Metaphor in Maxine Hong Kingston's The Woman Warrior and Bharati Mukherjee's Jasmine

C ATHOLIC NUNS WEAR A RING, which symbolises that they are married to Jesus; they are the brides of Christ. In Christianity the notion of being married to a personified metaphysical system of values is common. You attach yourself to this spouse, as a signified is attached to a signifier, and let yourself be defined by it. The divine – and patriarchal – power is not only conceptualised as the father but also as the bridegroom or the husband. Actually, in English there is even the phrase "to espouse a cause."

Thus it is surprising to find allegorical male partners as powerful metaphors in Maxine Hong Kingston, a Chinese–American author, and in Bharati Mukherjee, a writer who was born in India and who now is an American. I wish to show how, in *The Woman Warrior* and in *Jasmine*, these two authors treat the issue of cultural attachment as a relationship with the male Other, and how, in doing so, they define certain attitudes towards ideology and identity. The spouse-metaphor allows for strategies which go beyond simple patriarchal subjugation, and raises interesting questions, such as: Do you attach yourself to a single theory in a take-it-or-leave-it fashion? Or can you choose, can you combine? What happens to the marriage-metaphor if we introduce sexual equality, or divorce, or bigamy, promiscuity? Will we have to redefine the notion of marriage itself? Furthermore, is there something specifically female about this kind of objectivation of ideology and conceptualisation of the self? If so, what would be its male counterpart? Moreover, can the notion of identity-as-spouse be applied to all cultures? Is it multiculturally useful? And finally, does it also imply that identity is outside ourselves – that we attach ourselves, or are attached, to it? Where and what, then, in that case, is our "true core" of being? What kind of control over one's identity does such a strategy of exteriorisation offer? Let me first present examples from Kingston and Mukherjee and then try to formulate some – very tentative – conclusions.

❧ ❖ ❧

Maxine Hong Kingston

Prominent male figures in Maxine Hong Kingston's *The Woman Warrior* are the rapist of the No Name aunt, the Chinese husband of Moon Orchid (who is another aunt), and the prospective spouses for little Maxine in the autobiography, especially the "mentally retarded boy." The first section of *The Woman Warrior*, called "No Name Woman," is about Maxine's aunt in China, who gets pregnant while her husband is away working in the United States. Kingston first presents the inseminator as a rapist,[1] as a male Chinese figure who brutally appropriates the nameless woman. Later, however, Kingston turns the aunt from a victim into an active seductress who wants to attract a lover.[2] She projects and gets her male object of desire:

> Fear at the enormities of the forbidden kept her desires delicate, wire and bone. She looked at a man because she liked the way his hair was tucked behind his ears, or she liked the question-mark line of a long torso curving at the shoulder and straight at the hip [...] Why, the wrong lighting could erase the dearest thing about him. (8)

This male figure, who gets her "pregnant," thus not only stands for a force which subjugates the aunt, but also signifies her ability to project an individual "male" question – a wished-for identity – for herself.

There is another aunt in *The Woman Warrior*, called Moon Orchid, whose husband lives in the USA and supports her financially. He sends her money but wants her to stay in China because he has another, Chinese–American, wife in Los Angeles. The problem starts when Moon Orchid is brought to California to claim her husband back. "You want a husband, don't you?" her sister Brave Orchid asks her provocatively. The main problem with this unreliable male figure is that, when the two Orchids finally track him down, the Chinese husband turns out to have gone native and become an American: "The two old ladies saw a man, authoritative in his dark western suit, start to fill the front of the car. He had black hair and no wrinkles. He looked and smelled like an American" (151–52). He tells them: "'I don't know. [....] It's as if I had turned into a different person. The new life around me was so complete; it pulled me away. You became people in a book I had read a long time ago'" (154). This is, of course, the very reason why he became a bigamist in the first place and did not send for his Chinese wife. Instead he married an American (ie, Chinese–American) woman, a "modern, heartless girl" (149). Having emigrated, the husband is no longer "Chinese," thus he can no longer provide his old wife with a Chinese identity. But Moon Orchid, who has merely a reflexive personality, as her name indicates, and who depends on a powerful, cosmocentric force to provide her with the light of identity, cannot survive this shock and rejection. There is no other notion of self for her; she goes mad and eventually dies.

---

[1] Maxine Hong Kingston, *The Woman Warrior: Memoirs of a Girlhood Among Ghosts* (New York: Alfred A. Knopf, 1975): 6. Further page references are in the text.

[2] Kingston writes: "I hope that the man my aunt loved appreciated a smooth brow, that he wasn't just a tits-and-ass man" (9). Hence, this attraction is not just an affair of the flesh, but also one of the mind: ie, of "brows."

In the last part of the book, Chinese male partners are described in yet another way: Maxine, who has always had a problem with attracting the right boys,[3] is afraid that her parents will marry her off to a "FOB," a *Chinese* Chinese, one who is "Fresh-off-the-Boat."[4] Thus she misbehaves and tries to make herself unattractive – not "sellable, marriageable" (190). The symbol of Maxine's cultural predicament is the mentally retarded boy: "At Chinese school there was a mentally retarded boy who followed me around, probably believing that we were two of a kind" (194). As the most prominent prospective Chinese mate in the book he represents marriage and Maxine's being forced to adhere to the alienated Chinese culture of her mother's memory. Though he is very stupid, this boy is "very rich" (197): ie, powerful.[5] When he starts "sitting at [their] laundry" (194), haunting her, like a "Sitting Ghost," Maxine worries, but the "parents allowed this. They did not chase him out or comment about how strange he was. I stopped placing orders for toys. I didn't limp anymore; my parents would only figure that this zombie and I were a match" (195). He sits on cartons which are full of nudie pictures, as they later find out. Maxine does not want to be "framed" by this person's pornographic "gaze." Moreover, she is afraid that her own, *different* kind of American intelligence (she gets straight A's at the American high school) will be perceived as *no* intelligence at all within the Chinese cultural framework. She protests with a screaming fit, repeatedly referring to her own intelligence, to being "smart," "not retarded," "A's," "scholarships," "brain," and the like (201).

I believe that Kingston's description of Chinese men as rapists, bigamists, and mentally retarded boys may be one of the reasons why she has received so much criticism from her Chinese–American male colleagues, many of whom claim that she puts them down. What a literal reading of these figures overlooks is that in *The Woman Warrior* men mainly play the discursive role of *allegorical husbands*. They are appropriated as cognitive entities, as a figurative means for Kingston to reason about her own identity between two cultures.[6] Men are treated more like real men in her second autobiography, *China Men*, which is devoted to the Chinese–American male perspective. Thus I believe the problem in Kingston's case is mainly that her

---

3 Cf how she describes the dilemma of attraction: "But of course I hexed myself also – no dates. I should have stood up, both arms waving, and shouted out across libraries, 'Hey, you! Love me back!' I had no idea, though, how to make attraction selective, how to control its direction and magnitude. If I made myself American-pretty so that the five or six Chinese boys in class fell in love with me, everyone else – the Caucasian, Negro, and Japanese boys – would too. Sisterliness, dignified and honorable, made much more sense" (12). If, in order to be attractive, she has to make herself "American-pretty," this implies that the Chinese boys in her class are likewise attracted by American culture, an exogamic attitude, which makes cultural closure impossible.

4 This is how FOB's appear to Chinese American girls: "They were all funny-looking FOB's, Fresh-off-the-Boat's, as the Chinese–American kids at school called the young immigrants. FOB's wear high-riding gray slacks and white shirts with sleeves rolled up. Their eyes do not focus correctly – shifty-eyed – and they hold their mouths slack, not tight-jawed masculine. They shave off their sideburns. The girls said they'd never date an FOB" (193–94). These bearers of Chinese cultural qualities obviously do not look like the attractive Elvis Presley, a hero of American popular culture.

5 This grown boy is described as a "Frankenstein's monster, like a mummy dragging its foot; growling; laughing–crying" (195). He is emotionally and cognitively incoherent: "I ... own ... stores" (195). Like a demonic piper he gives away "bags of toys" to the children (195).

6 The question of Kingston's positive or negative presentation of Chinese culture in *The Woman Warrior* is, however, an issue that goes beyond the scope of this paper.

first book was such a great commercial success that, on the level of critical reception, the issue of gender-representation was never adequately addressed.

Bharati Mukherjee

In her novel *Jasmine*, Bharati Mukherjee moves even more freely among men. Actually, enumerating Jasmine's male partners gives away the story. She defines herself very much in terms of her male counterparts. Each one stands for a new life of hers, a fact which can be related to the Hindu notion of rebirth; and in each relationship she defines herself with a new name to indicate a new identity: "I had a husband for each of the women I have been, Prakash for Jasmine, Taylor for Jase, Bud for Jane, Half-Face for Kali."[7]

The protagonist grows up as Jyoti among her family in the Indian village, which she remembers as follows: "It's as though Hasnapur is an old husband or lover" (231). One day, her brothers bring a visitor to their house; she overhears their conversation: "I fell in love with that voice. It was low, gravely, unfooled. I was prepared to marry that voice" (66). Notice that Jyoti falls in love with something abstract; later she calls it a "phantom, a voice without a body" (69). Yet this voice is not just "The Word" given by an authoritative kind of God, but a specific voice of her own choice. It belongs to Prakash, who soon marries her and gives her a new name, "Jasmine." Like a Professor Higgins, he forms the flowergirl into a new person (77). But we should also consider the fact that, when they had their first date, it was Jyoti herself who put a jasmine flower into her hair in the first place in order to make herself attractive and manipulate her own destiny. Notice that Prakash, too, says: "I want to be surprised when I hear your voice" (74); they are partners who are attracted by each other's voices. He is a modern man, a husband who does not just control: "For Prakash, love was letting go" (76); moreover, he has a vision about leaving behind the superstitions and social injustices of his home country, an attitude which of course also defines Jasmine's consciousness.

Unfortunately, religious fanatics kill him, and Jasmine becomes "a widow in the war of feudalisms" (97). At this point she is about to lose her identity – her prospective husband now is "Lord Yama," the God of death (117, 120). However, clinging to the memory of her late husband, she can escape him. In order to fulfil Prakash's mission and bury his "light blue Teriwool" wedding suit in Florida, where he had received a scholarship, she travels to America. This middle passage is brutal. On her arrival to the States she is raped by the trawler's captain, a man called "Half-Face," and then kills him, turning the gender-role around and comparing herself in this situation to the goddess Kali: "I was walking death. Death incarnate" (119).

Destitute, she is picked up by the proverbial good Quaker woman and makes it to New York, where she turns into "Jazzy" (133), "Jassy" (59), or adventurous "Jase" (176, 186), as the "caregiver" (175) of the adopted child of Taylor, a

---

[7] Bharati Mukherjee, *Jasmine* (New York: Grove Weidenfeld, 1989): 197. Further page references are in the text.

Columbia University professor, and his wife. Jazz is a typical phenomenon of American culture and thus defines American identity. Moreover, identity is something that can be appropriated. "'Now remember'," the Quaker lady tells Jasmine, "'if you walk and talk American, they'll think you were born here. Most Americans can't imagine anything else'" (135). It seems that in America you are what you act.

Her next mate is Bud Ripplemeyer, the Iowa banker. He calls her Jane: "Me Bud, you Jane" (26). At this point Jasmine actually lives together with the incarnation of Western culture, with the wounded Fisher King himself: there is a drought in Iowa, and the farmers cannot pay their mortgages. One neighbouring farmer says: "'tell him to bring rain if he's God'" (24). Another farmer shoots Bud in the back; now he is in a wheelchair, cut down to size, a "wounded god" (215). Jasmine writes: "I wish I'd known America before it got perverted" (201). She is pregnant with the crippled banker's baby; and he wants to naturalise this union: "'Marry me, Jane', the pillar of Baden begs [...] 'Marry me before the baby comes. Put this old bull out of his pain'" (213). Yet their relationship is jeopardised by exotic projections. Jasmine is not satisfied with her definition as "Jane." We read that "Bud courts me because I'm alien. I am darkness, mystery, inscrutability [...] I rejuvenate him simply by being who I am" (200). Moreover, there is Karin, Bud's ex-wife, who happens to be a good person and who suffers from Jasmine's presence, which has put things out of balance. By taking away Karin's husband, Jasmine disrupts a given marital order. Thus the logic of the tale also has social consequences; ideological attachments of this kind have an impact on reality.

Fortunately, in this predicament, Taylor and Wylie in New York get a divorce. The young physics professor now has a new job at Berkeley. He and the child Duffy pick up Jasmine on their trip west. Thus Jasmine leaves Bud for yet another man. She comments on the breakup of relationships:

> In America nothing lasts, I can say that now and it doesn't shock me, but I think it was the hardest lesson of all for me to learn. We arrive so eager to learn, to adjust, to participate, only to find the monuments are plastic, agreements are annulled. Nothing is forever, nothing is so terrible, or so wonderful, that it won't disintegrate. (181)

Taylor, her last mate in the book (the one who calls her Jase, we recall), is a male figure who defines the following qualities:

> He smiled his crooked-toothed smile, and I began to fall in love. I mean, I fell in love with what he represented to me, a professor who served bisquits to a servant, smiled at her, and admitted her to the broad democracy of his joking, even when she didn't understand it. It seemed entirely American. I was curious about his life, not repulsed. I wanted to know the way such a man lives in this country. (167)

Taylor is not physically attractive. However, he is intelligent and has a sense of irony (172). He is "a giant" (238) compared to the short Fisher King in the wheelchair, and may even symbolically take the place of the monumental petrified "Colossus" who disintegrated in Sylvia Plath's world. Taylor has overcome the infertility of his own "low sperm count" through adoption, by accepting a "non-genetic child," a notion which Jasmine immediately associates with the "spouse"-

metaphor: "as foreign to me as widow remarriage" (170). Also notice his name: "Taylor" actually replaces Prakash's "husband"-imagery and the notion of the self as one's clothes, one's container or outsize wedding-suit, which Jasmine has buried in Florida.[8] This male Other constitutes surface. Symbolically, Taylor is the maker of custom-made suits. The kind of cut-and-paste identity he provides is different from the traditional organic world of farming in Iowa – a way of life, associated with the old Fisher King, that is going bankrupt and "coming to an end" (229). Taylor suggests a new definition of relationships and identity; he maintains that they will be an "'unorthodox family'" (238). Thus Jasmine wonders about her own future: "How many more shapes are in me, how many more selves, how many more husbands?" (215).

Tentative Conclusions

After this cursory listing of some examples of "husband"-metaphors in Kingston and Mukherjee, let me make a few suggestions and raise some questions which relate to gender, to multicultural applicability, and to the notion of exteriorised identity.

First, because this metaphoric approach indicates a gendered mode of conceptualising, what would be the corresponding notion from a male perspective? Kingston and Mukherjee can express a broad array of very sophisticated attitudes with this metaphor. Is this also possible in the case of the father-figure, as the Bible suggests? Or with the oedipal mother? What makes such comparisons difficult are mainly notions of hierarchy. For example, the female Other is traditionally considered a treasure or possession, an object to be controlled rather than a symbol to attach oneself to. In that sense, "male gaze" and "female gaze" are probably different. Yet, on a level of symmetrical partnership, as we have it with Prakash and Jasmine, and in their voices, such mutual inversion may be possible.

Moreover, how do we deal with the necessary allegorisation of gender, the fact that (male or female) people are used as figures of ideology? Allegorisation, as we know, automatically distorts referential representation. It reifies human beings into mere symbolic objects. Following Kingston, I would suggest that, rather than avoiding this issue of discursive appropriation, we should balance out gendered representation and write books from both perspectives. We should let the sexes represent each other, yet remain aware of the fact that discursive notions never coincide with the real referents, be they male or female.

Secondly, I believe that there is an amazing multicultural potential in the metaphor of cultural identity as "spouse." Men and women exist in all human societies. In all cultures, they get together and organise themselves in some kind of families. Thus there are many different stories of "marriage," which can be compared. This would indicate that there are also useful facets in the view that this metaphor has always got one leg firmly planted in reality. Because of this referent-

---

8 Cf the label on the wedding-suit: "BABUR ALI/MASTER TAILOR/JULLUNDHAR, on the sleeve" (92).

iality, it will never wander too far off into useless abstraction. Moreover, the very nature of the marriage-metaphor will be changed by the increasing number of actual multiracial and multicultural marriages all over the world. In *Tripmaster Monkey*, Kingston's protagonist Wittman believes in "champion kissers,"[9] and claims: "Our foreign policy will be: We want to marry you. Propose to every nation. Leaflet them with picture brides. We'll go anywhere and marry anybody! How do unrelated people get together? They get married" (143).

My third and last point relates to the exteriorisation aspect of the "spouse as identity" approach. This notion of the metonymic self, which is defined by its attachment to an Other, may well demarcate a patriarchal kind of imposition and indicate dependence. Such a limitation is not just symbolic or cognitive, but is often experienced in actual reality as sexual discrimination. However, Kingston and Mukherjee suggest that the person who has defined herself in a relationship also has her own means of manipulating the defining element – that attraction can to a certain extent be controlled, that choice can be selective, that one can actively change lovers and possible identities, have different ones at the same time, or (something that is at least symbolically possible) tailor their different qualities into a new projective entity.

I would even suggest that this exteriorised view of identity, because it allows for metaphoric objectivation, may offer considerable control over one's identity. Let me emphasise that such an approach is wholly different from any kind of depth-psychology, from the notion that our "true self" (whatever that may be!) is buried somewhere deep inside and has to be uncovered. Inward identity does not necessarily mean more control. Note especially, in Mukherjee, the fact that Jasmine does not want to dig up the traumatic experiences of her past: "I wanted to become the person they thought they saw: humorous, intelligent, refined, affectionate. Not illegal, not murderer, not widowed, raped, destitute, fearful" (171). Rather than wishing for psychoanalysis, she even wants to be like the pictures that other people make of her (160). "For me," she writes, "experience must be forgotton, or else it will kill" (33). The only kind of penetration we find in *Jasmine* is when she is raped by Half-Face – an act of violence which Jasmine survives only because she keeps her eyes on Ganpati, the elephant-headed Hindu god (also called Ganesha), who personifies surface as such. The *Encyclopedia Britannica* renders an account of his birth in which the female goddess "Parvati formed him from the rubbings of her body to stand guard at the door while she bathed." Thus Ganpati stands for clothing and respect, for the kind of privacy or distance which means control over your own appearance, over what you want to be.

I hope these examples show that the notion of identity as "spouse," the concept of the self as defined by this metaphor of complementation, is extremely rich – that it can integrate many different kinds of relationships and thus make the self negotiable. As a metaphor of exteriorisation, it offers a certain degree of control in

---

[9] Maxine Hong Kingston, *Tripmaster Monkey: His Fake Book* (New York: Alfred A. Knopf, 1989): 330. Further page references are in the text.

terms of objectivation. It can actively reach beyond given definitions and include aspects of domination as well as attraction. Moreover, it may be applied to all cultures and may, because it is a metaphor rooted in social reality, even offer an experiential field of theoretical discussion.

WORKS CITED

KINGSTON, Maxine Hong. *The Woman Warrior: Memoirs of a Girlhood Among Ghosts* (New York: Alfred A. Knopf, 1975).
———. *Chinamen* (New York: Alfred A. Knopf, 1980).
———. *Tripmaster Monkey: His Fake Book* (New York: Alfred A. Knopf, 1989).
MUKHERJEE, Bharati, *Jasmine* (New York: Grove Weidenfeld, 1989).

❦ ❖ ❦

WALTER GÖBEL

Bharati Mukherjee
Expatriation, Americanality, and Literary Form

B HARATI MUKHERJEE HAS IN HER WORKS continually questioned the binding nature of cultural heritages. Estrangement and loss of the home are themes of her stories and part of her lived experience. Though born in India in a middle-class neighbourhood of Calcutta into a Bengali Brahmin family, she was for some time schooled in England and Switzerland, then again in an élite school run by Irish nuns in Calcutta. She finally left India for America in 1961 and became first a Canadian, then an American citizen, after marrying the Canadian author Clark Blaise. Patterns of migration recur in her novels, in which the theme of estrangement and belonging dominates. Mukherjee's outsiders move beyond traditional ties and their home country towards a global life. Her art aims at the transgression of cultural boundaries; it does not pursue the formation of a post-colonial national identity and a communal memory, as does Salman Rushdie's or Rohinton Mistry's (eg, *Such a Long Journey*, 1991); the latter writer is an Indo-Canadian, as Mukherjee was up to 1981.

My central thesis is that a significant development of the major theme of belonging can be perceived in Mukherjee's works and that it has a structural correlative in their aesthetic form.

The main theme of Mukherjee's first novel, *The Tiger's Daughter* (1971), is the failure of homecoming. Tara, an Indian émigrée, returns home full of nostalgic dreams to find a chaotic Calcutta in which political unrest and explosions of violence are common and in which even relatives see her as an out-caste because she has married a foreigner. Like Mukherjee herself, she has been educated in a nun's school in Calcutta under British supervision, to which fact she traces her endemic foreignness of spirit. Homelessness begins here in the mother country when Irish nuns teach her how to "inject the right degree of venom into words like 'common' or 'vulgar'."[1] Although the novel has an omniscient narrator, Tara's dissociated viewpoint dominates, focusing on grotesquerie, madness and chaos. She is doubly estranged – as an individual by her upper-class education and as a member of the Brahmin caste. It is symbolically evocative that she and her friends like to sit, surrounded below by milling crowds, on top of the Catelli Hotel, a site formerly

---

[1] Mukherjee, *The Tiger's Daughter* (1971; New York: Fawcett, 1992): 45.

favoured by the British colonists. Tara is, furthermore and thirdly, estranged even from her own clique, by her Western self-dependence and especially by her self-arranged marriage. Like Adela Quested in *A Passage to India*, Tara sets out again and again to understand and to discover, but Calcutta will predictably burst into chaos like a pent-up geyser. She panics periodically: for example, when a Tantric wants to read her palm; when at a picnic she observes a snake in the pool; when on an outing a little girl with leprosy demands her sari. Finally, because of her failure to comply with Hindu norms of behaviour, she is assaulted and raped. In the end, all of Calcutta seems to erupt in political rioting.

The structure of the novel is marked by a series of adventures and encounters, all of which lead to violence and chaos. The circle of hope and disillusion is broken only in a very few scenes of understanding with her mother, but finally and inevitably leads towards re-emigration. The cyclical structure is similar to the rhythm of invitation and failure to meet, of adventure and accident, in *A Passage to India*. In *The Tiger's Daughter*, however, an émigrée heroine is the outsider; homelessness is largely acquired, not pre-defined by geographical or cultural borderlines. The dialectic of *us* and *them* is re-defined if Tara experiences her own people, though not members of her own caste, as the threatening Other. Homecoming, which in Forster's novel clarifies and orders the muddle experienced in mysterious India, brings about confusion and estrangement here. The circular structure is the formal correlative of the futility of homecoming, which questions Forster's ordered universe. Calcutta appears to Tara to be chaotic and disordered; in her defamiliarised eyes, Western stereotypes of India as confused and disorderly, which are common in the tradition of the Anglo-Indian novel, are to some extent reproduced.

❧ ❖ ❧

Wife (1975), Mukherjee's second novel, can be regarded as a narrative of initiation, however tragic in nature. *Wife* recounts Dimple Dasgupta's journey to the blessed land, America. In India, Dimple, the daughter of middle-class parents, lives in a state of emotional hibernation and of expectation until she can at last emigrate, a purpose she achieves first by marrying an engineer who has already applied for immigration to Canada and the USA, and secondly by performing an abortion when the visa arrives. In the country of her dreams, however, she becomes more and more isolated and a media-addict, finally unable to distinguish fact from the screen-world of her television. She withdraws into herself, feeling endangered by the models of emancipation she is offered, while at the same time longing for a life of glitter and entertainment. Her husband's neglect leads to emotional starvation in a birdcage existence and to a furtive love-affair with an American, during which she experiences an emotional liberation that leads to a further loss of her sense of reality. Inspired by the violence presented in the media, Dimple kills her staid and unimaginative husband in a traumatic scene in which screenplay and life interpenetrate.

Wife is an impressive psychological study of the disintegration of a personality by fear and by the destabilisation of internalised norms and values. Dimple is able to perceive the protean possibilities of self-realisation and of free choice the new world can offer ("If you plan your moves right, she thought, you could become anything you wanted to"[2]), but when she wants to switch codes of behaviour like television channels she wrecks her marriage and her own prospects in a misunderstood attempt at violent liberation. The structure of the novel is linear, from emigration and expatriation towards an attempt at personal liberation and initiation into sensual self-awareness. Although the ending is ambivalent, the overall theme of emancipation places the final murder in the light of an act of somewhat perverse self-assertion.[3] Between the lines, however, the deconstruction of patriarchal systems of oppression tends to affirm superficial Western constructions of India, here not so much a chaotic culture as an oppressive and backward one. The conflation of emigration and emancipation forms the linear structural principle of the novel, which couples geographical movement with inner liberation. Only with her American lover Milt Glasser does Dimple experience a loosening-up, a breaking-down of inhibitions, and the development of actual love.[4] His world stands for fun, adventure, play and laughter. The paradoxical tension liberation/murder, however, remains finally unresolved and seems to remind the reader of the need for a dialogic mediation of cultural transformations.

≈ ❖ ≈

The oppression of women in a traditional Indian environment and the possibility of emancipation in the USA are juxtaposed in a similar way in Mukherjee's third novel, *Jasmine* (1989). The heroine and first-person narrator comes from the lower classes of the Punjab and knows about female suffering: "All over our district, bad luck dogged dowryless wives, rebellious wives, barren wives. They fell into wells, they got run over by trains, they burned to death beating milk on kerosene stoves."[5] Again it is the husband who is to lead the heroine to freedom, an anglophone background being the prime marriage-condition:

> I couldn't marry a man who didn't speak English, or at least who didn't want to speak English. To want English was to want more than you had been given at birth, it was to want the world. (68)

The heroine's husband, Prakash, an engineer who wants to emigrate, renames the maidenly Jyoti as Jasmine in an attempt to make a modern city-woman of her and to cut off the past. But Prakash is killed by a Sikh fanatic, and Jasmine must emigrate on her own to the United States.

The structure of the entire novel is episodic – Jasmine calls her journey abroad an odyssey, and the closest genre-model would be the picaresque. Like Defoe's Moll Flanders or Dreiser's Carrie Meeber, Jasmine has a succession of lovers, each of whom gives her a new name and a new model to live up to. The demure and

2 Mukherjee, *Wife* (1975; New York: Fawcett, 1992): 198.
3 Mukherjee, "An Interview with Bharati Mukherjee," by Michael Connell, Jessie Grearson & Tom Grimes, *Iowa Review* 20 (1990): 7–32.
4 Cf *Wife*, 202.
5 Mukherjee, *Jasmine* (New York: Grove Weidenfeld, 1989): 41. Further page references are in the text.

obedient girl Jyoti is transformed into the city-woman Jasmine, briefly becomes Kali, the goddess of destruction, for her violator Half-Face, Jase for Taylor the university professor, Jane for Bud, the Iowan banker, and finally Jase again. This serial name-changing, however, goes beyond the picaresque formula, symbolising the complete obliteration of the former identity and producing an uncompromising episodic discontinuity. Integration into the new culture is represented as undoubtedly more successful than in *Wife*. Jasmine has moved away "from the aloofness of expatriation to the exuberance of immigration," a development which Mukherjee herself experienced, describing it in her introduction to *Darkness*.[6] In the end, however, the protean heroine moves beyond the various identities she is offered, towards new frontiers, "greedy with wants and reckless from hope" (240), calling easy solutions into question. But the ending of the novel discloses a formal paradox: on the one hand, we have a move towards new frontiers of experience, on the other, the hope of finding a permanent home with a new family. Besides the formal principle of closure, a psychological need for a core of identity asserts itself and cuts off the episodic structure and the picaresque journey: The heroine, while finally setting out for new boundaries, doubles back at the same time, inscribing a circle. Jane returns to her former lover, Taylor, becoming Jase again and entering academia, the sphere that seems most free. Here she had formerly wanted to belong, had felt at home and beloved:

> I felt lucky [..] Taylor, Wylie and Duff were family. America may be fluid [...] but I was a dense object, I had landed and was getting rooted. I had controlled my spending and sat on an account that was rapidly growing. Every day I was being paid for something new. (179)

The blunt association of the concept of home with money foregrounds the economic subtext and places emancipation in a doubtful light, pairing Jane with Moll Flanders and making her a match for Bud the banker. This subtext surfaces, but rarely – for example, when Karin, Bud's ex-wife, calls Jane a "gold-digger"; generally it is hidden and difficult to decipher, while what is foregrounded is the *exuberance of immigration* which Jane feels in her sudden proclamation of a new identity. The quest seems at an end – when Jane–Jase does finally set out for new frontiers she no longer travels alone, but with her new-found family. They head for California in search of Jase's adopted Vietnamese son Du, in order to add him to her family – the journey is not completed in the novel, however; the multiracial family beyond blood-lines remains an ideal to be achieved. Circularity and episodic progression are finally not reconciled. The author's difficulties with this ambiguous ending can be seen in her attempts to re-plot the novel.[7]

❧ ❖ ❧

---

[6] Mukherjee, *Darkness and Other Stories* (1985; New York: Fawcett, 1992): xv.

[7] For the re-plotting, during which Du was "put out there in California," in order to justify Jasmine's departure from Bud towards "the frontier [...] out there," see Mukherjee, "An Interview with Bharati Mukherjee," 31.

A similar ambiguity is to be found in Mukherjee's concept of "Americanality," which she has defined as a "quality of spirit" born from a "longing to discard what fate, class, gender has given you."[8] Immigrants are for Mukherjee "heroic pioneers" with a marked ability to survive and adapt. On the one hand, Americanality seems to be a cosmopolitan, international quality of spirit directed at the establishment of a multiracial family and at the fusion of cultures. On the other, the term Americanality is linguistically rooted in a specific geographic area, in a culture which today exerts global hegemony and which Mukherjee has in many an interview regarded as her new home:

> Mine is a clear-eyed but definite love of America. I'm aware of the brutalities, the violences here, but in the long run my characters are survivors; they've been helped, as I have, by good strong people of conviction. Like Jasmine, I feel there are people born to be Americans. By American I mean an intensity of spirit and a quality of desire. I feel American in a very fundamental way.[9]

Criticism of American violence is presented between the lines in *Jasmine*: the figure of the Iowan banker Bud, who, with his loans and credits, is finally responsible for the suicide of two farmers and indirectly provokes his own maiming, can be seen as a critique of the very basis of the American economy. This critique, however, is balanced by the heroine's homecoming and by a fundamental reliance on American myths, such as that of the American Adam (Eve) starting anew again and again, and that of the inevitable discovery of ever-new frontiers of the mind, ever-new constructions of the self, which Mukherjee herself has acknowledged in an interview: "I didn't want anyone to know where I fit in, so I could be whoever I wanted to be, anywhere, and I could keep moving."[10] For minorities like the African–Americans, who have for centuries been marginalised, Mukherjee's idea of Americanality may well seem a return to the age-old ideology of the melting-pot: that is, of cultural homogenisation through assimilation. They may well read *Jasmine* as a re-gendered retelling of the story of Esau, who sold his birthright for a mess of pottage, and may discover intertextual messages from *The Autobiography of an Ex-Colored Man*.[11] Though ethnicity may be largely an invention,[12] the effortlessness with which stable cultural constructions are transcended, identities effaced, and assimilation achieved will appear utopian to traditionally marginalised groups.[13]

Bharati Mukherjee and her writings prove how difficult it is to live up to the ideal of cultural fusion – how subversively power-structures and ideologies operate upon strivings for a marriage of cultures. Caught in a patriarchal order and doubly estranged from her native society by a foreign education and by caste-boundaries,

---

[8] Lecture held at Stuttgart University on 19 May, 1992.

[9] Sybil Steinberg, "Bharati Mukherjee," *Publishers Weekly* (August 25, 1989): 47.

[10] Mukherjee, "An Interview with Bharati Mukherjee," 11.

[11] James Weldon Johnson, *The Autobiography of an Ex-Colored Man* (1912; New York: Alfred A. Knopf, 1976): 211.

[12] See Werner Sollors, Introduction to *The Invention of Ethnicity*, ed. Sollors (New York: Oxford UP, 1989).

[13] Sollors, *The Invention of Ethnicity*, ed. Sollors, xiv.

the author and her heroines see flight as the only solution (and this perhaps applies also to many Brahmins in a modern India in which traditional securities and privileges are at stake, and which Naipaul has described as a "shattering world"[14]). Instead of a fusion of cultures we have the attempt to annihilate the past, as Jasmine programmatically declares: "We murder who we were so we can rebirth ourselves in the images of dreams" (34). In murdering the past, however, there is the danger of blackening the image of the native country, in dreaming *within* a hegemonic culture the danger of affirming its ideology – here specifically: of freedom, possibility, adaptability, and continued renewal.[15]

One of Mukherjee's short stories grapples with the paradox of the outcast attempting to stabilise her identity without becoming narrowly limited by national norms and prejudices. In "The World According to Hsü," the Indo-Czech heroine Ratna Clayton feels more at home on an island off the coast of Africa in the middle of a revolution than in her husband's home country of Canada. At her hotel, all the guests seem to be homeless and multiracial: "At the table to her right a German communications expert was teaching an English folksong to three Ismaili–Indian children."[16] "She poured herself another glass, feeling for the moment at home in that collection of Indians and Europeans babbling in English and remembered dialects" (48). The concept of being at home is here transformed into a shared homelessness within a heteroglot community situated on an island of the mind which is not precisely located or named. Shared homelessness in the midst of a chaotic revolutionary scene becomes home for Ratna, while the indefinite location implicitly denies that any existing national entity could qualify for Mukherjee's utopia of Americanality. In another story in the collection *Darkness*, "home" is consequently defined as a "territory of the mind" (78).

❧ ❖ ❧

Three structures have shown the progression of ideas within Mukherjee's novels, from the circularity of estrangement, through the linearity of immigration and initiation, to the complex episodic structure of *Jasmine* with its paradoxical ending, which lingers between circular homecoming and episodic, open-ended adaptation to new names and new identities without a stable core of selfhood, much like Ralph Ellison's hero in *Invisible Man*. The short-story collections, finally, add another structural pattern, which may be described as a colourful mosaic or assemblage. Especially in *The Middleman*, Mukherjee goes far beyond the scope of the novels, in at least two directions: she introduces male first person-narrators, and heroes and heroines from a number of races and nations: that is to say, she quite obviously transcends boundaries of gender and culture, acquainting the reader, for example, with the mind of the Middle-Eastern Jew Alfie Judah, who is "an Arab to some, an

14 V.S. Naipaul, *India: A Wounded Civilization* (New York: Viking Penguin, 1977): 37.

15 Mukherjee, "An Interview with Bharati Mukherjee," 18. Mukherjee has, however, also referred this structure to the Hindu concept of reincarnation.

16 Mukherjee, *Darkness*, 44. Further page references are in the text.

Indian to others"[17] and survives in guerrilla territory in Nicaragua, or, in "Orbiting," with the mind of Renata Marcos, the daughter of an Italian and a Spanish immigrant, and the girlfriend of a refugee from Kabul. Projecting the reader into human minds of any national, religious or cultural background, Bharati Mukherjee manages, albeit sketchily, to achieve a global ubiquity of perspective that outlines her ideal of homelessness, while the artistic form of the short-story collection, a complex unity full of surprises, dissonances and tensions, is a formal correlative to the fragile ideal of the tolerant multi-ethnic community.[18]

Such ventriloquial versatility, however, does not often present fully embodied characters; ethnic designations often seem little more than labels for exchangeable figures, lightly sketched and reduced to a common humanity of feeling. The narrative technique of shifting, multicultural perspectives tends to appear somewhat haphazard and sketchy, in spite of neo-realistic exactitude in the description of everyday life. Whitmanesque catalogues of cultural and ethnic designations – in "Orbiting" alone we find a bricolage of North Italy, Calabria, Sicily, Korea, Sweden, Salvador, Iowa, New Jersey, Florida, Pakistan, Soho, Kabul/Afghanistan and Brooklyn, with mentions of Russia, St Moritz, Beirut, Bombay, Geneva, Frankfurt etc – seem to focus on the duty-free spheres of the airport lounges which the hero, Roasham, describes or on the cosmopolitan off-duty atmosphere of the Club Med, in which the heroine's sister meets her husband. Such bricolage invites postmodern confusion and is uncannily poised between multicultural utopia and satire of the superficiality of everyday jet-set encounters, in which identities seem as exchangeable as partners or TV channels (in the story "Fighting for the Rebound," the protagonist, another Club Med enthusiast called Griffith, even differentiates his multiple exotic girlfriends according to the way in which they switch TV channels!). Facile fusion and confusion merge as the text – perhaps unwittingly – deconstructs any possible utopian message.

Universalism, for Mukherjee, means the transgression of boundaries and an escape from traditions, while multiculturalism, on the other hand, is attacked – most strongly in *Wife* – because it promotes the formation of a ghetto-mentality,[19] an attack which anticipates such recent cultural theoreticians as John Higham.[20] The artistic form reveals the programmatic cultural theory, from expatriation via immigration and emancipation to transnational orbiting and the universalist utopia – this in accordance with a thesis of Theodor W. Adorno, to the effect that the hermeneutics of art is the translation of formal properties into meaning.[21]

---

[17] Mukherjee, *The Middleman and Other Stories* (1988; New York: Fawcett, 1991): 4.

[18] For "Orbiting" and the "Americanization process," see Liew–Geok Leong, "Bharati Mukherjee," in *International Literature in English: Essays on the Major Writers*, ed. Robert L. Ross (New York: Garland, 1991): 498.

[19] Cf Mukherjee, "An Interview with Bharati Mukherjee," 26.

[20] John Higham, "Multiculturalism and Universalism: A History and Critique," *American Quarterly* 45 (1993): 195–219. Higham believes in a rebirth of American universalism through the expansion of our flexible identities. Otherness is for him merely relative (214).

[21] Theodor W. Adorno, *Ästhetische Theorie* (*Gesammelte Schriften*, vol. 7; Frankfurt: Suhrkamp, 1970): 210; my translation.

I shall close on a sceptical note: does the fusion of cultures depend on dislocation, loss of communal memories, and individual alienation – that is, must national or tribal designations become devoid of meaning? Is perhaps even existential fear in a struggle for survival conducive to the forming of cross-cultural bonds, as Mukherjee's pioneer-ethos indicates? Do loss of identity and degradation necessarily precede intercultural fusion? Does such fusion via cultural effacement not ignore what Edward Said has described as the battleground of culture and domination?[22] It seems that the flight from an oppressive culture can endanger the successful mediation or creolisation of cultures and remove ideals of fusion to an utopian sphere. Perhaps you can have your identity and lose it while exploring and negotiating in border-territory;[23] but can you discard your identity and escape unscathed in a world of transnational hegemonic influences and ideologies?

WORKS CITED

ADORNO, Theodor W. *Ästhetische Theorie* (*Gesammelte Schriften*, vol. 7; Frankfurt: Suhrkamp, 1970).

CARB, Alison B., "An Interview with Bharati Mukherjee," *Massachusetts Review* 29 (1988): 647–54.

HIGHAM, John. "Multiculturalism and Universalism: A History and Critique," *American* Quarterly 45 (1993): 195–219.

JOHNSON, James Weldon. *The Autobiography of an Ex-Colored Man* (1912; New York: Alfred A. Knopf, 1976).

LEONG, Liew–Geok. "Bharati Mukherjee," *International Literature in English: Essays on the Major Writers*, ed. Robert L. Ross (New York: Garland, 1991): 487–503.

MISTRY, Rohinton. *Such a Long Journey* (Toronto: McClelland & Stewart, 1991).

MUKHERJEE, Bharati. *Darkness and Other Stories* (1985; New York: Fawcett, 1992).

———. "An Interview with Bharati Mukherjee," by Michael Connell, Jessie Grearson & Tom Grimes, *Iowa Review* 20 (1990): 7–32.

———. *The Tiger's Daughter* (1971; New York: Fawcett, 1992).

———. *Jasmine* (New York: Grove Weidenfeld, 1989).

———. *The Middleman and Other Stories* (1988; New York: Fawcett, 1991).

———. *Wife* (1975; New York: Fawcett, 1992).

NAIPAUL, V.S. *India: A Wounded Civilization* (New York: Viking Penguin, 1977).

SAID, Edward. *Culture and Imperialism* (London: Chatto & Windus, 1993).

SOLLORS, Werner, ed. *The Invention of Ethnicity* (New York: Oxford UP, 1989).

STEINBERG, Sybil. "Bharati Mukherjee," *Publishers Weekly* (August 25, 1989): 47.

WELZ, Gisela. "Anthropology, Minority Discourse, and the 'Creolization' of Cultures," in *Mediating Cultures: Probleme des Kulturtransfers*, ed. Norbert H. Platz (Essen: Die blaue Eule, 1991): 22–28.

❧ ❖ ❧

---

22 Edward Said, *Culture and Imperialism* (London: Chatto & Windus, 1993): xiv–xx. It also excludes cultural creolisation; cf Gisela Welz, "Anthropology, Minority Discourse, and the 'Creolization' of Cultures," in *Mediating Cultures: Probleme des Kulturtransfers*, ed. Norbert H. Platz (Essen: Die blaue Eule, 1991).

23 See Joseph Swann's closing reflection in the present volume.

Roman Kurtz

All the Polarities[1]
A Golden Age Revisited

T HE LITERARY PRODUCTION OF CANADA during the Sixties has been called, by Ronald Sutherland, "Canada's Elizabethan Age."[2] This historical reference implies a qualitative and quantitative boom in the production and publication of fiction, poetry and drama. Readers and audiences in Canada grew more and more aware of and interested in this development while its creative protagonists displayed an increased self-confidence, or, at least, self-consciousness. All these factors have contributed to what a quarter of a century later may still be regarded as the creative explosion of what had been an inter-nationally insignificant post-colonial literature that deserved the prefix "post-" only on paper. Until that time Canada's literary output had reflected the situation of a nation economically and intellectually dominated by other countries. After the Sixties there was no return within the intellectual domain. The "post-" prefix had been earned, literally, on paper.

This essay investigates three Canadian novels of this period that has been compared with England's most glorious literary past. Taking up an important tradition of criticism applied to Elizabethan literature, the focus is on what is usually called imagery.[3] The texts under investigation are *Une saison dans la vie d'Emmanuel* by Marie–Claire Blais, first published in 1965, *La guerre, yes sir!* by Roch Carrier (1968) and *Surfacing* by Margaret Atwood (published in 1972).[4]

≈ ❖ ๑

---

[1] The phrase "all the polarities" is borrowed from Philip Stratford, *All the Polarities: Comparative Studies in Contemporary Canadian Novels in English and French* (Toronto: ECW, 1986).

[2] Ronald Sutherland, "Canada's Elizabethan Age?" *Times Literary Supplement* (26 October , 1973): 1295–96.

[3] Cf Caroline Spurgeon, *Shakespeare's Imagery and What It Tells Us* (Cambridge: Cambridge UP, 1935), or Wolfgang Clemen, *The Development of Shakespeare's Imagery* (London: Methuen, 1951). This artlicle was very much inspired by the work of Philip Stratford, especially his comparative studies *All the Polarities* and "Canada's Two Literatures: A Search for Emblems," *Canadian Review of Comparative Studies* (Spring 1979): 131–38.

[4] The sample is part of a larger research project. The three novels are examined for the same reason Elizabethan texts are still studied today, namely because they are, and are acknowledged by critics and readers to be, great works of literature. Any page references, unless otherwise stated, are to the untranslated editions listed in the bibliography. Translations, unless otherwise stated, are my own.

Canada's Elizabethan Age

Canadian comparative studies themselves abound in images describing the relationship between the Canadian literatures written in English and French.[5] The parallel development of Canada's two main literatures has, for example, been compared to a double staircase designed by Leonardo, which two people can ascend simultaneously without ever meeting,[6] and with the double helix of the DNA which contains "the secret of life."[7] Both analogies suggest a parallel coexistence of "two solitudes" rather than a fusion of the two literatures and their cultures in Canada.[8] Such an emphasis on differences has been opposed by a school of comparatist critics who postulate a common mainstream in which the English and French "twin solitudes" show more similarities than disparities.[9] By contrast, I would suggest that we take into account all the polarities, including similarities, that can be established by comparing the reference-structures of two Canadian novels in French and one in English.

Yet, since the critical term "image" is rather ambiguous, I shall substitute for it the more precise concept "reference." To prevent this critical term from remaining as ambiguous as the one it replaces, we need a definition of what is considered in the following to be a reference.

Sutherland's reference, cited at the beginning, may serve as an illustration. It can be segmented into three components. The first, Canada in the Sixties, is connected to the second, Renaissance England, while a third element consists of a set of features postulated by the selfsame reference as being common to both the Sixties in Canada and the later sixteenth century in England. Sutherland himself names those common features: "dynamic activity, excitement, experimentation, even spirit of discovery and chauvinistic pride."[10]

References are defined here as any defamiliarising relationship between elements of a fictional discourse that has the three-part structure described.[11] I

---

5 For a concise survey, see Stratford, "Canada's Two Literatures."

6 See P.–J.–O. Chauveau, "Mouvement intellectuel." In *L'Instruction publique au Canada: précis historique et statistique* (Québec: Augustin Côté, 1876): 335.

7 James D. Watson, *The Double Helix* (1970; rev. ed. London: Weidenfeld & Nicolson, 1981) quoted in Stratford, *All the Polarities*, 8.

8 This particular image refers to Hugh MacLennan's novel *Two Solitudes* (1945), the title of which is taken from a poem by Rainer Maria Rilke and denotes a strong emotional bond: "Love consists in this,/that two solitudes protect,/ and touch, and greet each other." MacLennan's novel promotes such a closeness for Canada's two *charter groups*. Literary criticism stating the separateness of the two literatures in Canada, however, sees no love lost between them.

9 See, for example, the chapter called "Twin Solitudes" in Ronald Sutherland, *Second Image: Comparative Studies in Québec/Canadian Literature*. Toronto: New Press, 197)1. This paper does not ignore the tendency in Canadian literary criticism and intellectual awareness away from a binary focus on the two traditional literatures of Canada toward an investigation of the literature produced by writers of all the different ethnic groups which constitute the multicultural Canadian society of today (described again by the "solitudes" image in the anthology *Other Solitudes*: : *Canadian Multicultural Fictions*, ed. Linda Hutcheon & Marion Richmond (Toronto: Oxford UP, 1990).

10 Sutherland, "Canada's Elizabethan Age?," 1295.

11 This is by no means the only possible definition. For a survey of current theories of and approaches to literary reference, see Anna Whiteside's conclusion in *On Referring in Literature*, ed. Anna Whiteside & Michael Issacharoff (Bloomington/Indianapolis: Indiana UP, 1987): 175–204. The limitation to an

propose the Latin terms *primum comparandum* (PC) for the first element, the one being compared to something (the Sixties in Canada in our example), *secundum comparatum* (SC) for the second element, the one the first refers to (England's Elizabethan period), and *tertium comparationis* (TC) for the third element, the common ground on which the first two are placed by the reference.[12]

References can have different degrees of complexity. While Sutherland names all three components quite explicitly, this need not be the case. Had his article appeared in the *Globe and Mail* or the *Sun* instead of the *Times Literary Supplement*, it might easily have been headed "Our Elizabethan Age" or "Back in the Roaring Fifteen-Nineties." In the first of the alternatives proposed, the PC (Canada) appears implicitly in the pronoun, yet it would be easily decoded by a reader of the *Globe and Mail*; the second alternative is more complex, in that it omits the explicit reference to the 1590s in England as opposed to (roaring as it may have been at the time) Canada.

References as they are defined here can thus take the form of similes and metaphors. Another frequent form which references take is the quasi-simile, where PC's and SC's are linked by "as if, "as though" etc (eg, "Living in Canada during the Sixties you felt as if you had been transported right back to Elizabethan England").

Two more premises about references have to be made explicit before we turn to concrete textual examples from "Canada's Elizabethan Age." The first concerns our definition of the PC as the textual element described, and thereby foregrounded, through the SC. It is important to note that one can thus say that the PC of a given text belong to the content of a given text, representing part of "*what* is described." The SC are the textual elements by which the PC are described, representing "*how* things are described" in a text: ie, a text's form or expression. Expression in this sense means the interpretation, through the SC, of the fictional world represented by the PC on the plot-level.[13] The second premise concerns the TC which, albeit an

---

identifiable (three-part) structure ensures the identifiability and quantifiability of the references of a given text. The necessary exclusion of larger metaphoric structures, eg metaphors emerging from a text as a whole, such as "surfacing" as finding one's lost past and identity, is at first sight lamentable but in part compensated for by the *interpretative* results of the reference analysis, which are, and must be, included in a study of this kind.

[12] These three components of a reference correspond respectively to what I.A. Richards called the *tenor*, *vehicle*, and *ground* of a metaphor. See Richards, *The Meaning of Meaning* (New York: Oxford UP, 1936): 100. Richards' terms, however, lack in semantic transparency in comparison to the more motivated Latin terms. In the following, the abbreviations will be used for singular and plural (*prima comparanda* etc), which can easily be distinguished within a context.

[13] It should also be noted that PC's and SC's function as signifiers, while the TC constitutes their common signified. In terms of the traditional Saussurean dichotomy, the signifier–signified binarism is extended and semantically enriched by the addition of the SC-level.

The contiguity of these concepts with the field of stylistics in general, and with what is called "mind-style" in particular, is an aspect that has to be passed over here. On "mind-style," see Roger Fowler, *Linguistics and the Novel* (New Accents; London: Methuen, 1977) and *Linguistic Criticism* (Oxford/New York: Oxford UP, 1986), esp ch. 10; Geoffrey Leech with Michael H. Short, *Style in Fiction: A Linguistic Introduction to English Fictional Prose* (London/New York: Longman, 1981), esp ch. 6; and Reingard M. Nischik, *Mentalstilistik: Ein Beitrag zur Stiltheorie und Narrativik* (Tübingen: Narr, 1991). An extremely brief but equally informative article is Michael H. Short's "Mind-Style," *The English European Messenger* 1.3 (Autumn 1992): 31–34.

integral part – even the motivation – of a reference, cannot be considered here statistically, since it is impossible to classify any one so precisely and objectively that a large number of members of the same cultural community would agree on the classification. It is much easier, to remain with our example, to classify both Canada during the Sixties and Elizabethan England as historical periods characterised by certain socio-cultural phenomena than to come up with Sutherland's "dynamic activity, excitement, experimentation," etc as their common features.[14]

With the aid of our concept of reference we can now move to the following questions:

    I. What are the PC's of a given text: ie, which elements of a literary text are foregrounded by a reference?

    II. What are the SC's of a given text: ie, which elements of a literary text are used, or referred to, in order to foreground the PC?

    III. Can consistent correspondences be observed between particular PC's and SC's?

    IV. What other patterns can be observed in the reference structure: ie, in the totality of all references in a given text? For example, do certain PC's tend to occur explicitly or implicitly: ie, are certain elements of the text foregrounded by references although they remain implicit?

The findings

I present here some of the findings of an empirical analysis of three modern Canadian classics – three novels, written in Canada during the Sixties by three Canadian authors who can be regarded as having been at the forefront of the "creative explosion" referred to above.

First, we may analyse the semantic areas where the PC's and SC's of the three novels can be classified as belonging, in order to determine what insights result concerning their plots and the interpretative devices used to foreground certain plot-elements.[15]

Nature, an element considered essential in Canadian fiction and reality,[16] is represented by 45 percent of the PC's in *Emmanuel*, 50 percent in *Surfacing* and 58 percent in *La Guerre*. But when a textual element is foregrounded through an SC, the novels recur conspicuously less frequently to this semantic field: 33 percent of *Surfacing*'s SC's, 37 percent of *La Guerre*'s and 38 percent of *Emmanuel*'s. These statistics offer interesting insights – for example, that a novel taking place almost entirely indoors, Carrier's *La Guerre*, is concerned to a considerable extent with

---

14 Helmut Bonheim, "Teaching Katherine Mansfield's 'The Voyage': Metaphor Boxes." *Literatur in Wissenschaft und Unterricht* 20 (1987): 102, points to the fact that "when we find an unambiguous ground [ie TC] for a metaphor, we prove it to be "dead" the aesthetic use of language [...] usually resides in its ambiguity." The overall reference patterns of a text, however, yield much less ambiguous insights which help to specify the underlying common ground, ie the TC, of references in a text's deep structure, as this paper shall demonstrate.

15 The phenomena described in the following are some of the more conspicuous ones; other, more complex, though not less significant findings have to be neglected here for the sake of brevity.

16 See, for example, Northrop Frye, *The Bush Garden: Essays on the Canadian Imagination* (Toronto: Anansi, 1971), Margaret Atwood, *Survival: A Thematic Guide to Canadian Literature* (Toronto: Anansi, 1972), and Gayle McGregor, *The Wacousta Syndrome: Explorations in the Canadian Landscape* (Toronto: U of Toronto P, 1985).

nature. Indeed, the winter landscape with its masses of snow permeates the events up to the very last sentence of the novel: "La guerre avait sali la neige" (the war had stained the snow). This final reference in the text offers a clue to the overall significance of weather and landscape in the novel. An implicit SC is contained in "la neige": it is the village, or, more precisely still, the villagers' innocence, that has been stained by the war. Hence the implicit reference reads "snow equals (the villagers') innocence." The symbolic significance of snow becomes apparent: its whiteness covers up the dirty reality of war until it is brought home to the Québécois village in the shape of the dead body of one of its young men, Corriveau, escorted by a guard of English-speaking soldiers. This interpretation is supported by other references: for instance, when the soldiers approach the village with the coffin, the snow suddenly stops being alive – it becomes white, silent plaster (34).[17] The coming home to the little village of death is thus reflected in the landscape that had surrounded and protected it from the reality of war, preserving innocence as well as ignorance.

The mere quantity of references in a text, however, does not necessarily correlate with their interpretative significance. Although "only" about one-third of *Surfacing*'s SC's belong to "Nature," they are most essential to the novel's concerns. It is thus necessary always and only to interpret the reference-structure of a text with attention to the meanings represented in its overall structure, themes, symbols etc Although the analysis of references yields interesting and important insights into the meanings and workings of a literary text, it cannot replace, merely enhance, what has traditionally been called interpretation.

As a consequence of the observation that the importance of references, or their elements PC and SC, need not correspond to their overall quantity in a text, the third of the questions formulated above comes into focus: what are the patterns in the relations between PC and SC? In *Surfacing*, the linking of female PC's, especially the intra- and homodiegetic narrator, with nature, is a consistent pattern. The narrator's quest for her past and her identity culminates in her becoming one with nature. She says, or rather, feels, "I am a tree leaning [...] I am a place" (195). The novel's climactic passage abounds with references equating the female narrator with nature and the people searching for her on the island with unfeeling metallic robots (198ff.). For instance, she refers to herself as having "rabbit's choices" in the face of her "hunters": "freeze, take the chance they won't see you; then bolt" (199). The searchers are consistently presented as unfeeling creatures "halfway to machine" (198), "clank[ing] heavy with weapons and iron plating" (199). The female is associated throughout the novel with nature – furthermore. with the body, instinct, and the rejection of language. The male, by contrast. correlates with the head, reason, and culture, reason being represented mainly by science and language. Civilisation or culture, labelled in the novel "Americanism," is identified with war, destruction and disease, whereas nature is victimised by these forces and associated

---

17 "la neige s'arrêtait soudain de vivre, elle était un plâtre blanc et muet."

with sanctity and truth. Relationships between man and woman, husband and wife, are described as warfare; sexuality in general is portrayed as violence and mutilation. This last reference-pattern is not only consistent with the protagonist's traumatic experience and subsequent repression of an abortion (which she eventually refers to as "murder"); it also offers clues to the narrator's psychological state long before she herself realises and verbalises it. The character's schizophrenia, resulting from her traumatic experience, is also reflected in her perception of her surroundings in fragments, her fixation on anatomical parts (fifteen percent of the PC's).

Anatomical parts represent an equally high proportion of the PC's in *Emmanuel* (also fifteen percent), the referential pattern in Blais's novel being related to its focalisation. For the most part, the world of the novel is focalised through children. The novel opens with a lengthy description of the grandmother's feet by the eponymous hero, who is just a few hours old. The feet dominate the room, being referred to as

> animals [...] noble and pious [...] brimming with life, and etching forever in the memory of those who saw them, even only once, their sombre image of authority and patience.[18]

The newborn child perceives the world as distorted and in fragments which acquire synecdochic status, much like the fragments referred to by the psychotic narrator of *Surfacing*. "Authority" and "patience" are indeed the essential qualities of Emmanuel's grandmother. Her authority is expressed by numerous SC's denoting her queenlike appearance: majestically (16, 155) she reigns over the household (28), which resonates with her imperial voice (122).[19] Her patience with the children of the family, who bury themselves in her skirts for comfort and protection, is expressed by the constant equation of her with the landscape,[20] again evoking the distorted perception of the world by small children while at the same time depicting a character larger than life. The number of PC's foregrounding anatomical parts in *La Guerre* (a novel built around a corpse in a coffin and relating the aggression that escalates during a wake) is very close to those of the other two novels (fourteen percent). Whereas the anatomical PC's in *Surfacing* indicate one of the main themes

---

[18] See the English translation by Derek Coltman, *A Season in the Life of Emmanuel* (Toronto: McGraw–Hill Ryerson, 1980): 3–4; the original reads as follows: "Les pieds de Grand-Mère Antoinette dominaient la chambre [...] tranquilles et sournois comme deux bêtes couchées [...] des pieds nobles et pieux [...] des pieds vivants qui gravaient pour toujours dans la mémoire de ceux qui les voyaient une seule fois – l'image sombre de l'autorité et de la patience" (*Une saison dans la vie d'Emmanuel*, 1965; Québec: Stanké, 1980: 7).

[19] It is interesting to note that these very attributes are also assigned to the bawd in *Emmanuel*, thereby ironically undercutting the positive associations related to the grandmother; in *La Guerre*, we have a similar irony: a whore married to the Catholic soldier she first professionally seduced is described by the same SC from the reference area "cultural symbols/icons: monarchy."

[20] "Pour Emmanuel, le paysage de Grand-Mère Antoinette s'agrandissait de plus en plus chaque jour. Le nez de sa grand-mère avait la majesté d'une colline, ses joues, la blancheur de la neige, et de sa bouche coulait une haleine froide comme le vent d'hiver [...] la crête blanche et noire de ses cheveux herissés sur le sommet du front (135ff.). In English: "For Emmanuel, the landscape represented by Grand-Mère Antoinette was growing daily. His grandmother's nose had the majesty of a hill, her cheeks the whiteness of snow, and from her mouth there blew a breath as cold as winter winds [...] the black and white crest of hair that sprang up bristling from the summit of her forehead."

of the novel, the psychic mutilation of the protagonist resulting from her physical mutilation by the abortion, while in *Emmanuel* they support a synecdochic world-view transported by the juvenile focalisers, in *La Guerre* they are mainly motivated by the events of the novel. It starts with a man chopping off his hand with an axe to avoid being drafted and possibly suffering the fate of Corriveau, who was blown to pieces by a mine. Apart from foregrounding the violence, many anatomical references in *La Guerre* are prompted by an overt obsession of the villagers with, especially female, genitalia. This pattern contrasts the crudeness of the rural Québécois with the arrogant coolness of the English guards. Explicit though the obsession with sexual organs is in the novel, when it comes to sexuality as a bodily function or impulse, PC's are almost always implicit.

This brings us to our fourth question pertaining to reference-structures, turning from a semantic focus on the PC and SC to more stylistic considerations. The two Québécois novels depict a society under the strict rule of Catholicism. It is not surprising that sexuality is a taboo topic in such a society. Yet, as is usually the case with taboos, they tend to fascinate. Both these aspects are reflected in the novels' reference-structures. The obsession with sex, combined with the proscription against speaking about it openly, underlies the fact that sexual PC's in *Emmanuel* and *La Guerre* tend to be covert.[21] One character in *La Guerre* will associate anything just to cope with his sexual arousal, his "tender obsession" – a cow, an airplane, a shipwreck, the Satanic, Hitler's moustache, the lavatories he had to clean in the army.[22] The absurdity and irony expressed in such references is paralleled in *Emmanuel* by the persistent equation of a brothel with a nunnery (144ff.).[23] However, sex is not always the object of irony or euphemisation; it is regularly associated with violence as well, both in *La Guerre* and *Emmanuel*.[24] This field of reference supplies considerable portions of the novels' SC's: eighteen percent in *Emmanuel*, seventeen percent in *La Guerre*, and fifteen percent in *Surfacing*, thereby linking Atwood's novel once again to its two Québécois counterparts. This striking similarity is illustrated, for example, by the equation in all three novels of sexual intercourse with extreme physical abuse, such as torture and rape. In *Emmanuel*, the

---

[21] Very significantly, sexual PC in *Emmanuel* are explicit only in dreams, ie in the most securely private of situations (eg 153).

[22] "... sa douce obsession. Bérubé s'efforça de penser à une vache, à un avion, au naufrage d'un grand bateau, le Satanique dont on lui avait raconté l'histoire, à la moustache d'Hitler, aux toilettes qu'il avait nettoyées et lavées ..." (*La Guerre*, 40).

[23] Eg "Mme Octavie [la patronne du bordel est] ... aussi économe que la Mère Supérieure du couvent, comptant les sous, ... craignant la famine pour ses enfants ... Mme Octavie aime trop le vin, elle mange trop de fromage. Mère Supérieure aimait bie le fromage, elle aussi. Mais elle n'en mangeait jamais pendant le carême. Peut-être que Mme Octavie devrait jeûner elle aussi, faire pénitence comme Mère Supérieure" (*Emmanuel*, 144–45). In translation (by Coltman): "Mme Octavie [the madame of the brothel] ... is so thrifty, as thrifty as Mother Superior in the convent, counting her pennies, ... trembling at the thought of her children going hungry ... Mme Octavie is too fond of wine, and she eats too much cheese. Mother Superior was very fond of cheese too. Perhaps Mme Octavie ought to fast also, perhaps she ought to do penance like Mother Superior."

[24] For an intensive study of this thematic complex in Canadian fiction, see John Moss, *Sex and Violence in the Canadian Novel: The Ancestral Present* (Toronto: McClelland & Stewart, 1977).

young Héloïse's sexual phantasies are a "calme torture," her joy "horrible" (103),
her body an "épave" (wreck), and making love is "le travail d'un brutal ravisseur"
(the work of a brutal rapist; 105, see also 153ff.). As a result of her obsession, the
young woman turns from a nun into a whore in the course of the novel. In *La Guerre*
the villagers, aroused by the above-mentioned anatomical parts of their womenfolk,
imagine the dead Corriveau's sexual ravagings in paradise: "s'il y a de si belles
fesses par terre, qu'est-ce que ça doit être au ciel! Quel ravage Corriveau va faire"
(59).[25] In *Surfacing* the narrator overhears David and Anna making love next door;
the woman is

> breathing, a fast panic sound, as if she was running; then her voice began, not like her real
> voice but twisted, as her face must have been, a desperate beggar's whine, *please, please* [...]
> Then something different, not a word but pure pain, clear as water, an animal's the moment the
> trap closes. It's like death, I thought. (88; italics in the original)[26]

The association of orgasm with death is found in both of the other novels as well.[27]
In *Surfacing* the tendency of sexual PC's to appear implicitly – under cover, so to
speak, as in the example above – is a reflection of the way in which the narrator–
focaliser covers up her traumatic experiences psychologically, rather than of an
ideologically restrictive environment, as in the two Québécois novels. Atwood's
protagonist is nonetheless as fixated on sexuality and sexual organs as are the
villagers in *La Guerre* and the children in *Emmanuel*.

Conclusions

This brief analysis of the reference-stuctures of three Canadian novels reveals that
there are similarities as well as differences pertaining to the plot-elements
foregrounded by SC's and to the semantic fields from which the SC's interpreting
these plot-elements are drawn. It also pinpoints occurrences in the texts of such
similarities and differences. The analysis of reference-structures offers insights into
the implications of the correlative patterns emerging between PC's and SC's for the
novels' themes and concerns as well as for their stylistic idiosyncrasies.[28]

---

25 In Sheila Fishman's translation the passage reads as follows: "If there are nice behinds like that on
earth, what is there going to be in Heaven?" (52).

26 The passage also exemplifies the occurrence of sex as an *implicit* PC related to "pain" and "death."

27 See, for example, *Emmanuel* (154) and *La Guerre* (70).

28 Stratford, in "Canada's Two Literatures" (134), points to the pitfalls of mere statistics in the interpretation of literary texts. Referring to a sample of English vs. French Canadian poetry analysed with some
of his students, he says, "we knew very well, as readers rather than as word counters, that the poetry of the
two languages differed far more than our statistical results showed in impact, emphasis, style, and even in
content. With almost identical ingredients the two groups had made two different kinds of poetry." Yet, as
the empirical results are the basis for, rather than the end of, this study, it is useful to present a synoptic
table of the statistics mentioned:

Reference area	*Emmanuel* (total: 556 references)		*La Guerre* (total: 217 references)		*Surfacing* (total: 853 references)	
	PC	SC	PC	SC	PC	SC
Nature	45%	38%	58%	37%	50%	33%
Body/Anatomy	15%		14%		15%	
Violence		18%		17%		15%

All three novels, it is clear, share a great concern with nature, which assumes symbolic significance in *Surfacing* (victim and the place of truth) and *La Guerre* (innocence and ignorance), while in *Emmanuel* its physical enormousness and protective function are personified in the grandmother. *Surfacing* shares with its two counterparts an obsession with anatomical detail and repressed sexuality, the latter domain being linked to violence in all three novels. Sex is presented in all three novels, by means of implicit PC's, as a social (in *Surfacing*, individual) taboo topic. As for idiosyncrasies, the destructive force of civilisation is a specific concern in *Surfacing*, just as *Emmanuel*'s criticism of Catholic institutions, exemplified in the convent that drives Héloïse into prostitution, is not paralleled in either of the other two novels.

Many more, and much more, detailed results are obtained from the analysis of reference-structures which cannot, of course, be presented here.[29] But it has been shown that these results go beyond mere statistics; they reach right into the core of the texts studied, offering insights into the texts' structure and meaning and revealing some of the means by which these are constructed: namely, the references they contain.

For this kind of study, Sutherland's question of "whether or not a Shakespeare or a Ben Jonson [has surfaced] from the [...] whirl of soul searching and literary outpouring" in "Canada's Elizabethan age" is beside the point. Rather, such a study provides empirical data for Canadian comparative studies, analysing individual works as well as investigating theoretical and factual fusions of literatures and cultures in a multicultural society. It thus transcends the ideological confusions of nationalism and thematicism and investigates all the polarities, idiosyncratic and universal, of one of the world's major new (also English) literatures.

---

[29] For example, the quantitative structure of the references can be accounted for: questions concerning the structural complexity of a given text can be answered more easily when one knows whether there is usually more than one PC related to the same SC in the same reference and vice versa; or the semantic functions of the references can be analysed, thus revealing patterns of irony and paradox as well as of personification, reification, etc Some other fundamental insights gained by the study of references pertain to density of plot (references are ± motivated by the immediate context on the level of plot), temporal structure (references ± function as or ± indicate anachronies), characterisation (SC's related to a character are [in]consistent with other textual information), or point of view ([in]consistencies in a narrator's or focaliser's references indicate [un]reliability).

WORKS CITED

ATWOOD, Margaret. *Surfacing* (1972; Markham, Ontario: Paperjacks, 1973).
———. *Survival: A Thematic Guide to Canadian Literature* (Toronto: Anansi, 1972).

BLAIS, Marie–Claire. *Une saison dans la vie d'Emmanuel* (1965; Québec: Stanké, 1980).
———. *A Season in the Life of Emmanuel*, tr. Derek Coltman (Toronto: McGraw–Hill Ryerson, 1980).

BONHEIM, Helmut. "Teaching Katherine Mansfield's 'The Voyage': Metaphor Boxes." *Literatur in Wissenschaft und Unterricht* 20 (1987): 99–113.

CARRIER, Roch. *La guerre, yes sir!* (1968; Québec: Stanké, 1981).
———. *La Guerre, Yes Sir!*, tr. Sheila Fishman (Toronto: Anansi, 1970).

CHAUVEAU, P.–J.–O. "Mouvement intellectuel." In *L'Instruction publique au Canada: précis historique et statistique* (Québec: Augustin Côté, 1876).

CLEMEN, Wolfgang. *The Development of Shakespeare's Imagery* (1951; London: Methuen, 1966).

FOWLER, Roger. *Linguistics and the Novel* (New Accents; London: Methuen, 1977).
———. *Linguistic Criticism* (Oxford/New York: Oxford UP, 1986).

FRYE, Northrop. *The Bush Garden: Essays on the Canadian Imagination* (Toronto: Anansi, 1971).

HUTCHEON, Linda & Marion RICHMOND, ed. *Other Solitudes: Canadian Multicultural Fictions* (Toronto: Oxford UP, 1990).

LEECH, Geoffrey N. with Michael H. SHORT. *Style in Fiction: A Linguistic Introduction to English Fictional Prose* (London/New York: Longman, 1981).

MACLENNAN, Hugh. *Two Solitudes* (1945; Toronto: Macmillan, 1978).

MCGREGOR, Gayle. *The Wacousta Syndrome: Explorations in the Canadian Landscape* (Toronto: U of Toronto P, 1985).

MOSS, John. *Sex and Violence in the Canadian Novel: The Ancestral Present* (Toronto: McClelland & Stewart, 1977).

NISCHIK, Reingard M. *Mentalstilistik: Ein Beitrag zur Stiltheorie und Narrativik* (Tübingen: Narr, 1991).

RICHARDS, I.A. *The Meaning of Meaning* (New York: Oxford UP, 1936).

SHORT, Michael H. "Mind-Style." *The English European Messenger* 1.3 (Autumn 1992): 31–34.

SPURGEON, Caroline. *Shakespeare's Imagery and What It Tells Us* (Cambridge: Cambridge UP, 1935).

STRATFORD, Philip. "Canada's Two Literatures: A Search for Emblems." *Canadian Review of Comparative Studies* (Spring 1979): 131–38.
———. *All the Polarities: Comparative Studies in Contemporary Canadian Novels in English and French* (Toronto: ECW, 1986).

SUTHERLAND, Ronald. *Second Image: Comparative Studies in Québec/Canadian Literature* (Toronto: New Press, 1971).
———. "Canada's Elizabethan Age?" *Times Literary Supplement* (26 October , 1973): 1295–96.

WATSON, James D. *The Double Helix* (1970; rev. ed. London: Weidenfeld & Nicolson, 1981).

WHITESIDE, Anna & Michael ISSACHAROFF, ed. *On Referring in Literature* (Bloomington/ Indianapolis: Indiana UP, 1987).

≈ ❖ ≈

DETLEV GOHRBANDT

Mapping or Constructing Africa?
Notes on R.M. Ballantyne's Juvenile Fiction

T HE IMAGES OF AFRICA latent in the minds of most contemporaries have a genesis and history which can in part be traced to the reading-matter available to schoolboys since the mid-1850s. Samuel Smiles, that most representative of Victorian moralists, was emphatic about the influence of books on the formation of what he called "individual character":

> While books are among the best companions of old age, they are often the best inspirers of youth. The first book that makes a deep impression on a young man's mind, often constitutes an epoch in his life. It may fire the heart, stimulate the enthusiasm, and by directing his efforts into unexpected channels, permanently influence his character. The new book, in which we form an intimacy with a new friend, whose mind is wiser and riper than our own, may thus form an important starting-point in the history of a life.[1]

In an individual biography, and collectively in the development of socio-political groups, books can be starting-points for the history of an idea.

Facts and impressions

What kind of starting-point did the adventure novels of an author like R.M. Ballantyne provide for the idea of Africa in the minds of youthful readers between the 1850s and the 1930s? Ballantyne certainly endorsed Smiles's moral encomium when, in the prefatory note to the eighteen volumes of his "Miscellany of Entertaining and Instructive Tales" (1863ff), he wrote:

> Truth is stranger than fiction, but fiction is a valuable assistant in the development of truth. Both, therefore, shall be used in these volumes. Care will be taken to ensure, as far as is possible, that the facts stated shall be true, and that the *impressions* given shall be truthful.[2]

The distinction between facts and impressions is important for Ballantyne, who was ridiculed after the publication of *The Coral Island* for "a somewhat humorous blunder in regard to the cocoanut, which he described as growing in the form familiar to the English market."[3] To prevent similar mistakes from recurring, Ballantyne took care to gain first-hand experience to supplement the documentary sources he used. But he was also aware that facts were in themselves insufficient to guarantee his main

---

[1] Samuel Smiles, "Preface" to *Character* (1871; London: John Murray, 1902): vi.
[2] Quoted from Ballantyne's introductory note to *Hunting the Lions, or: The Land of the Negro* (1863; London: Nisbet, nd).
[3] *Dictionary of National Biography*, vol. 22, Supplement, s.v. "Ballantyne". The confusion/ conflation of "cocoa" and "coconut" can be traced to Dr. Johnson's Dictionary, cf OED, s.v."coconut".

purposes: ie, truth, and "the glory of God and the good of man." In writing fiction, the kind of literature best calculated to appeal to juvenile readers, the truth of facts had to be supplemented by the truthfulness of impressions. Ballantyne's use of the distinction suggests that he was aware of how dubious "facts" could be, how susceptible to falsification. We will see that this has two consequences for Ballantyne's representation of Africa: first, he is repeatedly concerned to give a balanced view of matters, to apportion blame and praise fairly, taking into account the particular perspectives and interests of his fictional characters in judging their opinions and behaviour (and in inviting his readers to share such authorial judgments); second, he will, where necessary for his purposes, relegate the facts to secondary importance behind the impressions.

The mapping view of language

The distinction between fact and impression is further important in that it innocently prefigures the theoretical tool I want to apply to Ballantyne's African novels. I am referring to the familiar distinction, popularised by Berger and Luckmann,[4] between "mapping" and "construction" in the social sciences, and now applied to a host of disciplines and topics. As expounded by George W. Grace in *The Linguistic Construction of Reality*, the mapping view of how language represents reality holds that "there is a common world out there and our languages are analogous to maps of this world."[5] Basic to this view is the "intertranslatability postulate," according to which "any content that can be expressed in one language can be expressed in any other language" (7). The logical corollary of such a view is that "each language is an empty code" (8), is entirely separate from the culture it belongs to, and has no formative effect on the content it communicates (or fails to communicate). Second, the intertranslatability postulate implies that there is "a set of sayable things" which is unchanged and unalterable. This in turn leads to the assumption that "there is an objectively given world common to all people which defines for all time what can be talked about" (9). This mapping view of language, traditionally espoused by linguistic science in its structuralist versions, is also a view which nineteenth-century Englishmen held when exploring and reporting hitherto unfamiliar parts of the world: everything one might come across in uncharted territories, in the blank spaces of the map, would either permit an English name to be applied to it, or be rejected as unknowable or not worth knowing. To name something is to know it, and to refuse to name it (in the name of some moral principle) is to cast it out of human culture as corrupted or corrupting. While every explorer is set on increasing his store of knowledge by "thinking clearly, seeing things in their essence and beauty," he is also subject to certain cultural constraints which impel him to be blind and dumb to whatever contradicts his basic consciousness (defined by Matthew

---

4 *The Social Construction of Reality: A Treatise in the Sociology of Knowledge* (1966; Harmondsworth: Penguin, 1979).
5 George W. Grace, *The Linguistic Construction of Reality* (London: Croom Helm, 1987): 6. Further page references are in the text.

Arnold as the consciousness of sin).[6] In the same way, the protagonists of Ballantyne's novels take care to record faithfully and even scientifically as many details of Africa and African life as they can, yet at the same time they explicitly demarcate certain experiences as "savage," "cruel," "ugly" and "fiendish." Here the mapping view of reality is superseded by the "reality-construction" view, in which African experiences are encoded only to the extent that they fit within the particular and exclusive framework of the "language-culture system" of English.

There is a seemingly trivial passage in *The Gorilla Hunters* which reads as a striking confirmation of this unacknowledged principle of reality-construction: after at last reaching "gorilla country," the three protagonists go for days without meeting with a single animal. The narrator remarks:

> "It never rains but it pours," is a true proverb. I have often noticed, in the course of my observations on sublunary affairs, that events seldom come singly. I have often gone out fishing for trout in the rivers of my native land, day after day, and caught nothing, while at other times I have, day after day, returned home with my basket full. As it was in England, so I found it in Africa.[7]

To what extent is this last sentence a programme for the novel? Does it just refer to this particular situation, or is Ballantyne asserting, through his narrator, that "sublunary affairs" are really the same all the world over, that there is only one culture? Is Ballantyne interested in the specific identity and difference of Africa, or is he merely narrating it in order to confirm the unalterable identity of what it means to be English? There is probably a measure of contradictoriness in his purposes and motives, caused to some extent by the particular aims and limitations of writing for a juvenile, male, Victorian audience. Novels like those of Marryat, Kingsley, Henty, and Strang (to name just a few of the other writers of the genre), are reflexive, referring more to England than to Africa. While this limits the value of the novels as sources for what Victorian boys really knew about Africa, it makes them all the more interesting as guides to the attitudes these boys were expected to learn. Before discussing some of these, I want to fill in the definition of the reality-construction view of language sketched above.

The reality-construction view of language and culture

I quote those points from Grace's own summary[8] of the reality-construction view of language which bear on the topic in hand.

1) "A language is shaped by its culture, and a culture is given expression by its language, to such an extent that it is impossible to say where one ends and the other begins, ie what belongs to language and what to culture." When one culture

---

[6] Matthew Arnold, *Culture and Anarchy* (*The Complete Prose Works of Matthew Arnold*, vol. 5, ed. R.H. Super; Ann Arbor: Michigan UP, 1965): 173 (from his discussion of the dichotomy of Hellenism vs. Hebraism) and 168.

[7] R.M. Ballantyne, *The Gorilla Hunters* (1861; London: Thomas Nelson, 1875): 209. Further page references are in the text.

[8] Grace, *The Linguistic Construction of Reality*, 10.

encounters another it will try to give a rendering of it through its home language resources. These are inevitably culture specific. From this follows the second point:

2) "What can be said, and what can be talked about, may be quite different from one language-culture system to another." Explorers may thus encounter features of Africa that they cannot verbalise adequately in their mother tongue. They will not be fully aware of this inadequacy, so they will describe and evaluate Africa as if they were mapping it. Insofar as they realise there are aspects of Africa that escape them, they will be strongly tempted to exclude them as unsayable. This leaves language-gaps, silences, white margins, which will sooner or later be recognised as such, and as calling for new linguistic efforts. Which leads to Grace's third point:

3) "New language culture systems are theoretically possible which will have significantly different views of the world from any existing today – which will talk about things that we cannot dream of now." Grace is here describing the project of literature as an expansion of the sayable, "a raid on the inarticulate," as T.S. Eliot has it. Writers as different as Chinua Achebe and J.M Coetzee can be seen as actively involved in this expansion, in giving a voice to those cross-cultural experiences that were not accessible to the language and culture of earlier writers like Ballantyne. In this sense, such authors stand in the continuity of even those writers of the tradition whom they reject.

The visual construction of Ballantyne's Africa

With just one exception, the novels of R.M. Ballantyne would seem to belong to such a rejected tradition. None of his African novels is still in print, and only *The Coral Island* (1858) has remained popular to this day, partly because it was re-cast in William Golding's *Lord of the Flies* (1954). I shall be referring mainly to two of Ballantyne's books, *The Gorilla Hunters* (1861) and *The Settler and the Savage: A Tale of Peace and War in South Africa* (1877), with a brief glance at *Hunting the Lions, or: The Land of the Negro* (1863). Basically, Ballantyne's Africa is built on a series of antitheses or binary terms. Let me illustrate this through the frontispieces of two of the novels. On the next page is the double-page frontispiece of *The Gorilla Hunters* from an 1875 reprint.

The illustration on the left[9] depicts a scene from the climax of the novel, in which Ralph Rover, Peterkin Gay and Jack Martin, the protagonist trio carried over from *The Coral Island*, encounter their first gorilla. On the right is the visual title-page, a carefully constructed summary of some of the book's main ingredients. The central vignette shows Africa's teeming wildlife in the shape of ambling elephants and grazing giraffes, with a white hunter lurking in the bushes at the bottom left, his rifle at the ready. In a moment a shot will ring out, the giraffes will thunder across the plain, the elephants will bellow, a wounded animal will be writhing on the ground – a trophy for the happy hunter. The medallion is framed right and left by sheaves of rifles and spears, British and African weapons united for a common purpose. Curled

---

9 "Our First Gorilla," referring to page 217.

round these are a peaceful-looking lion and a rather more threatening though misshapen crocodile. The half-naked African balanced precariously on a hippopotamus at the top of the page recalls a circus act, whereas his counterpart, a shaggy gorilla baring its teeth and armed with a stout stick, is doubtless meant to look menacing. The whole array is an uneasy and rather naive blend of adventure and amusement, beauty and terror, exoticism and natural history, elements the reader encounters throughout the book.

Figure 1

My second example is taken from *The Settler and the Savage*:[10]

ATTACKED BY AN OSTRICH. - *Frontispiece.—*PAGE 189.

Figure 2

The formal arrangement of this frontispiece is very similar, with a scenic illustration to the left, again showing the encounter of man and beast, and a medallion framed by a narrative frieze to the right. In conformity with the double antithesis of the book's title, the visual title-page presents a clear contrast between the white settler, in the middle, and the multiple threats to his world of peace and plenty. From the

---

10 Ballantyne, *The Settler and the Savage: A Tale of Peace and War in South Africa* (1877; London: Nisbet, nd) "Attacked by an Ostrich," referring to page 189. Page references are in the text.

periphery, poisonous snakes, screeching apes and naked savages with assegais encroach on the central paradise, actually transgressing its borders. This inverts the historical process of colonial incursion from the coasts to the interior. In a counter-movement, a pile of melons and grapes spills over the edge of the medallion into the surrounding wilderness, suggesting that all could share the fruits of the settlers' industry, if they were only willing to keep the peace. It takes a careful second look to see that this promise of plenty is threatened by a row of locusts crawling over the top of the pile into the fertile land. An elephant, an ostrich and a lion complete the fauna, leaving enough room for historical references, a dimension missing from the earlier book. At the top, we are shown a fort (presumably Fort Willshire) flying an unidentified flag, and at the bottom a boatload of settlers arriving at the coast, welcomed by a soldier and setting off on their trek into the interior. Throughout the composite picture one finds the antithesis of war and peace expressed in such a way that assegais, snakes and locusts stand against the plough and the rifle. Much more clearly than in *The Gorilla Hunters*, one recognises an ideological message. It is expressed frequently, in different versions, in the course of both narratives, as in this passage from *The Gorilla Hunters*:

> It was a beautiful scene – this plain with its clumps of trees scattered over it like islands in a lake, and its profusion of wild flowers. [...] As we walked along for some time in silence, I thought upon the goodness and the provident care of the Creator of our world, for during my brief sojourn in Africa I had observed many instances of the wonderful exactness with which things in nature were suited to the circumstances in which they were placed, and the bountiful provision that was made everywhere for man and beast. (227)

Up to here Ballantyne seems to be echoing the conventional doctrine of "God's in his heaven – all's right with the world" (as Robert Browning put it), but as the narrator's reflections continue, a note of scepticism is sounded, which paradoxically serves as an apology for colonisation and mission:

> Yet I must confess I could not help wondering, and felt very much perplexed, when I thought of the beautiful scenes in the midst of which I moved, being inhabited only by savage men, who seemed scarcely able to appreciate the blessings by which they were surrounded, and who violated constantly all the laws of Him by whom they were created. (227)

Ralph's perplexity does not long continue, but it remains latent throughout the tale as an implicit counter-text to the official programme exemplified by the three heroes. The same holds good for *The Settler and the Savage*, as in a passage commenting on the scene of carnage after a battle between Africans and a party of British and Boer settlers:

> Oh! it was a sad sight, – sad to see men in the vigorous health of early youth and the strong powers of manhood's prime cast lifeless on the ground and left to rot there for the mistaken idea on the Kafirs' part that white men were their natural enemies, when, in truth, they brought to their land the comforts of civilised life; sad to think that they had died for the mistaken notion that their country was being taken from them, when in truth they had much more country than they knew what to do with [...], sad to think of the stern necessity that compelled the white men to lay them low; sadder still to think of the wives and mothers, sisters and little ones, who were left to wail unavailingly for fathers and brothers lost to them for ever; and saddest of all to remember that it is not merely the naked savage in his untutored ignorance,

but the civilised white man in his learned wisdom, who indulges in this silly, costly, murderous, brutal and accursed game of war! (385–86)

Ballantyne's sympathy for the black victims and the force of his climactic rhetoric leads him to an ironic comment on the wisdom of civilisation which he might not otherwise have ventured. Such paradoxes are a clear sign that the constructed view of Africa is not static, but is open to modification in the process of its transmission. This, Grace explains, is true for all "subject-matter views": ie, for "the sets of assumptions made about the subject-matter in question."[11] Africa is such a subject-matter, and Ballantyne's subject-matter view of Africa can be defined by describing his sets of assumptions. I shall conclude by sketching Ballantyne's view of Africa with reference to some of the particular topics he focuses on.

Ballantyne's map of Africa

There is a noticeable difference in the way Ballantyne draws the map of Africa in the two novels we are discussing. In *The Gorilla Hunters* he is extremely vague about geographical details. In the first chapter, the three heroes plan to "get to Africa and see the gorilla" (19), in chapter 2, five weeks later, they have suddenly arrived, are "in the midst of it" (30), with no indication of their route, point of arrival or final destination. From "the wilds of Africa" (31) they move "inland" (49), cross a desert (50) and finally arrive in "a totally new, and in some respects, different country" (375). Fleeting references are made to the "west coast" (369) and to "south-western Africa" (415), from which they return home. This avoidance of mapping contrasts strangely with the striving for accuracy and some form of completeness that is embodied in the figure of Ralph. Whereas Peterkin is the hunter, Ralph is the zoologist and botanist who takes care to keep a detailed and factual diary of the animals and plants they encounter:

> "During this long and hurried but intensely interesting and delightful journey we came upon, at different times, almost every species of animal, plant and tree peculiar to the African continent." (267)

He insists on observation as against speculation, and justifies hunting as a means of gathering information:

> "I was anxious to shoot as many gorillas as possible, in order that I might study the peculiarities of, and differences existing between, the different species – if there should be such, and between the various individuals of the same species in all stages of development. I had made an elaborate examination of our first gorilla, and had taken copious notes in regard to it. (239–40)

So Ballantyne claims that he *is* mapping, in the sense of drawing up a scientific inventory of plants and animals. This makes the absence of any interest in mapping the human inhabitants of the continent in their ethnic and cultural diversity all the more conspicuous.

---

11 Grace, *The Linguistic Construction of Reality*, 17.

In *The Settler and the Savage* Ballantyne's method has changed entirely. While the book still includes no actual map, it is specifically related to a political and historical context. It is full of information about the Albany settlement of the early 1820s, when, in a first attempt at systematic colonisation, the British government brought over 4000 settlers to the Zuurveld. It contains information on and criticism of the colonial policies of Lords Somerset and Glenelg, including the campaign for freedom of the press, gives a version of the story of the Gcaleka leader Hintsa, and shows how the Great Trek began in 1837.[12] Ballantyne had visited the Cape in 1876, had interviewed survivors of the events of fifty years before, and now, in parts, adopted the attitude of a documentarist and historian.

Comparison of the two books shows that Ballantyne must have realised the limited truthfulness of any attempt to map Africa without a sufficient knowledge of the facts. He also seems to have felt that the fictional method, in which characters tended to assume a life and opinions of their own, drawing both the author and his readers into sympathy and speculation beyond his original intention, was in danger of opening up into uncontrollable areas of paradox and implication.[13] A final example of this may be found in the theme of hunting.

A-hunting we will go

Ballantyne's description of the first encounter with a gorilla in *The Gorilla Hunters* reads like a symbolic version of the white conquest of Africa. The victim is seen as savage and fiendish, he overtaxes the linguistic resources of those who try to describe him, his hunting and killing arouse "mingled feelings" (218) of exultation and pity in the heroic trio. Once killed, the victim is measured and described in the interests of science, then skinned as a trophy. All the while, Peterkin is being made fun of for his monkey-like antics, just as Jack is teased for resembling a gorilla. Animal similes are applied equally to blacks and whites, as when Jack becomes commander-in-chief of a native army, and Peterkin comments: "'A glorious campaign, truly, to serve in an army of baboons, led by a white gorilla!'" (330). This tends to undermine all the distinctions that have been constructed in the course of the story, preparing for the kind of disillusioned comment on warfare quoted above. A similarly disruptive effect is achieved in *The Settler and the Savage* when a serio-comic hierarchy of attitudes to elephant-hunting is set up. At the top stands one of the young heroes, who "longed to sit down and sketch the lordly elephant in his native haunts" (298). Lower down are those who want to shoot him, while two "moderate souls [...] said they would be satisfied merely to see him." Lowest down, the Hottentots in the party "wanted to eat him." Such an example shows that Ballantyne has replaced the official single perspective, as expressed by one of the Boers (307), by a contradictory plurality of views which contains considerable

---

[12] See T.R.H. Davenport, *South Africa: A Modern History* (Toronto/Buffalo: Toronto UP, 1987): 43–46 and 126–46; Davenport's account bears out most of Ballantyne's history.

[13] Joseph Bristow, *Empire Boys: Adventures in a Man's World* (London: HarperCollins, 1991): 107, makes the same point with reference to *The Coral Island*.

critical power. A final example, from *Hunting the Lions*, otherwise one of Ballantyne's weaker productions, may help to make the point. The hero of this story, allusively called Tom Brown, is asked by his native companion why he has come to Africa. Tom answers:

> "Well, I came for fun, as the little boys in my country say. I came for change, for variety, for amusement, for relaxation, for sport. Do you understand any of these expressions?"[14]

Not enough that the simple true motive for coming to Africa is dissolved into a plurality of dubious meanings, Tom has to go on to explain to his uncomprehending friend *why* English people need such relaxation:

> "It's not easy to answer that question, Mafuta. We have surrounded ourselves with a lot of wants, some of which are right and some wrong. For instance, we want clothes, and houses, and books, and tobacco, and hundreds of other things, which cost a great deal of money, and in order to make the money we must work late and early, which hurts our health, and many of us must sit all day instead of walk or ride, so that we get ill, and require a change of life, such as a trip to Africa to shoot lions, otherwise we should die too soon. In fact, most of our lives consists in a perpetual struggle between healthy constitutions and false modes of living." (117–18)

Similarly, in *The Settler and the Savage*, the authorial narrator comments that "when people are happy they desire no change" (246). This suggests that at the bottom of Ballantyne's adventure stories there is a deep unhappiness, a sense of insecurity, and a Ruskinian dissatisfaction with the condition of England. Adventures to foreign parts become an escape and a quest for a place to be really happy. South Africa qualifies for this, while equatorial Africa fails. That, too, is an aspect of the construction of Africa for British purposes.

WORKS CITED

ARNOLD, Matthew. *Culture and Anarchy* (*The Complete Prose Works of Matthew Arnold*, vol. 5, ed. R.H. Super; Ann Arbor: U of Michigan P, 1965).

BALLANTYNE, R.M. *The Gorilla Hunters* (1861; London: Thomas Nelson, 1875).

———. *Hunting the Lions, or: The Land of the Negro* (1863; London: Nisbet, nd).

———. *The Settler and the Savage: A Tale of Peace and War in South Africa* (1877; London: Nisbet, nd).

BERGER, Peter & Thomas LUCKMANN. *The Social Construction of Reality: A Treatise in the Sociology of Knowledge* (1966; Harmondsworth: Penguin, 1979).

BRISTOW, Joseph. *Empire Boys: Adventures in a Man's World* (London: HarperCollins, 1991).

DAVENPORT, T.R.H. *South Africa: A Modern History* (Toronto/Buffalo: Toronto UP, 1987).

GRACE, George W. *The Linguistic Construction of Reality* (London: Croom Helm, 1987).

SMILES, Samuel. *Character* (1871; London: John Murray, 1902).

---

14 Ballantyne, *Hunting the Lions, or: The Land of the Negro* (1863; London: Nisbet, nd): 117.

TOBIAS DÖRING

The Fissures of Fusion
Akiki Nyabongo's Africa Answers Back (1936) and What It May Teach Us[1]

W HEN THINKING ABOUT FUSION, we may do well to emphasise the bivalency of the notion, for fusion is an integrative as well as a divisive figure of discourse. Paradoxically bound up with both the acknowledgement of differences and with the construction of greater coherence, fusion may operate subversively to transgress the given categories of control, yet may also function to define broader units of domination. In this latter sense, the figure of fusion or, synonymously, of amalgamation looms large in the rhetoric and practice of imperial powers such as Britain, which at the peak of Empire subsumed an ever larger number of regions under her influence and, if deemed expedient, fused them with one another to form more manageable units in their colonial administration. Thus, for all its inclusive, constructive and syncretic potential, fusion is in cahoots with hegemonic aspirations. It is, as I would like to suggest, just as contentious and, indeed, combative a concept as it may be reconciliatory and harmonising. It can be utilised both as a strategy of resistance and as a means to re-inscribe positions of power. What needs to be investigated, therefore, are the concrete terms of fusion: that is, the political and discursive framework in which the operation is defined, regulated and performed.

Before I proceed to attempt such an investigation with reference to a remarkably early, and somewhat neglected, anglophone African text, let me illustrate briefly the topical appeal of fusion by citing a recent and well-known example. In the final chapter of Chinua Achebe's novel *Anthills of the Savannah* (1987), the traditional name-giving ceremony for a newborn girl is performed in a rather untraditional manner: Disregarding time-honoured male prerogatives, the women decide among themselves what name the child shall have and, as if to question perpetuated gender-roles even more, they choose a boy's name for the girl: "AMAECHINA: May-the-path-never-close."[2] The whole procedure of this "improvised ritual," as the event is paradoxically referred to in the narrative, clearly evokes the attractiveness of syncretism as a liberating force. Puzzling though it first seems to members of the older generation, who expect stricter adherence to cultural authority, the de-ritualised

[1] I would like to thank Martina Michel for ample comments, and Susanne Mühleisen for her invaluable help and support in the preparation of this paper.
[2] Achebe, *Anthills of the Savannah* (1987; London: Picador, 1988): 222.

baptism effects an unprecedented joining of male and female, of old and young, of various religions and creeds, and thus represents a fusion which is directed against the rigid order of the powers that be. "Amaechina," too, would seem to signal hope. Emerging from such resolute revision of petrified patterns, and combining cultural constructs formerly kept apart, the name is a figure of fusion which epitomises the bold vision of cultural heterogeneity that concludes Achebe's novel.

This vision is not without textual precedence in African writing and may even be traced in the heyday of Empire. Without assuming generic influence, it is interesting to note that some fifty years earlier another African author presented a scene of name-giving which, in some respects, is surprisingly similar to Achebe's because it, too, insists on linguistically uniting what is otherwise divided. While attempting conceptual fusion, this name-giving also accepts the inevitable disorder and goes on to interpret the name in all its political potential.

❦ ❖ ❧

Chief Ati, a powerful ruler in the East African kingdom of Buganda, decides on an innovative and rather controversial combination of names for his newborn son and heir. In compliance with local tradition, the child has already received the praise-name Abala; in defiance to custom, however, his father is now determined to give him two names in addition which stem from an alien culture. This is how he explains his rationale to the flabbergasted family:

> A white man came into Uganda about fifteen years ago. He was seeking a friend who had been lost in this country. He was well received by Mutesa, King of Buganda, and the impression he left with him was very favourable. Mutesa asked this white man to send him men who could read from a book he always carried with him, and who could make guns. This man's name was Stanley. He was a very good man, and that is why I want to name my child after him. Of course, the men who came in answer to Stanley's invitation were not all like him. These men called themselves missionaries. They go from one place to another, and never settle down. That is why we call them roamers. And since Stanley was their greatest man, the boy shall be named after him. His family name will be Mujungu, after these people that roam.[3]

The untraditional name-giving contains a programme, if not an incantation. Combining an African sign "Abala" with the name of the Western explorer "Stanley" as well as the indigenised term for Christian missionaries, "Mujungu," the name mediates between the conflicting forces of history that have traversed the country. Ati himself legitimises his choice with a historical narrative about European penetration, and the tripartite signification so constructed legitimises the hope that its African bearer will, in turn, penetrate European knowledge and power. As Ati puts it, "when my son grows up, he will learn all about these people, and will know even more than they do" (54). Naming and learning thus constitute a policy by which the African chief hopes to fuse the indigenous with Western tradition and appropriate it to Buganda's advantage. The tale of his son's progress, however, turns out to be a narrative of fissures rather than of fusion.

---

[3] Akiki Nyabongo, *Africa Answers Back* (1935; London: Routledge, 1936): 54. Further page references are in the text.

This tale forms the centre of Prince Akiki Nyabongo's *Africa Answers Back*, published in London in 1936.[4] The author, himself descended from a long line of Toro kings, was born in Kabalore, Uganda, in 1907. He entered on a long and distinguished career of education, which took him, among other places, to Yale and Oxford, where he completed his philosophical and religious studies in 1940 before taking up teaching positions in the United States. His book is a strange mixture (if not to say fusion) of fact and fiction, of history textbook and ethnography, with novelistic and autobiographical elements. The plot is situated in Buganda during a time of turmoil and transition, roughly spanning fifty years around the turn of the century. At base, it is a subversive African *Bildungsroman* which, as the title has it, answers back to European discourse by reversing a missionary success-story into the narrative of African empowerment and emancipation.

It does so by means of the central protagonist Abala Stanley Mujungu, who, living up to his name, combines the best of both worlds. Just as his father insists on having the son baptised twice – namely, in the traditional as well as in the Christian way – the author goes to great lengths to demonstrate that his hero's education, too, proceeds on a double basis and involves no losses.[5] Instead of supplanting or suppressing indigenous roots, Western culture is added to the African, for, apart from the formal schooling in literacy that Mujungu receives from Reverend Hubert at the mission, he is sent to spent school holidays with his grandmother in order to retain and enlarge his oral wisdom in the form of traditional proverbs, riddles, songs and stories. In this way, his education is presented as a process of continuous gain, resulting in a composite genius well adapted to his country's predicament at the interface of cultures.

His accomplishments are put to the test when a smallpox epidemic breaks out and Chief Ati himself contracts the disease. Mujungu takes charge, sends for a German doctor in Zanzibar, and goes on to tackle the problem on a large and scientific scale. When the doctor suggests vaccinations, Mujungu replies with a grand statement of reform policy:

> it is my intention to do what I can do from the point of view of modern science, and I'm sure my people will agree with me. By gradually changing their old culture, but not by throwing it away entirely, I hope to amalgamate what is good in the old and the new. (246)

The cultural amalgamation which the hero, himself a product of it, is here propagating, presupposes a parity of cultures and techniques so that both sides benefit from the joint effort. And, indeed, having established the usefulness of Western medicine, the text goes on to show the strength and practical wisdom of the

---

[4] A year before, the American edition was published by Scribners in New York under the title *The Story of an African Chief*. The biographical information about the author in my discussion is taken from Janheinz Jahn, Ulla Schild & Almut Nordmann, *Who's Who in African Literature* (Tübingen: Erdmann, 1972): 277. In Dieter Riemenschneider, ed. *Grundlagen zur Literatur in englischer Sprache: West- und Ostafrika* (Munich: Fink, 1983): 13, the year 1904 is given for Nyabongo's birth.

[5] Even if Lalage Bown (in Riemenschneider, *Grundlagen*, 55) claims that the book is "about a child, a chief's son, uprooted from his culture and taken to the missionaries," I cannot see how this may be considered a fair summary of the plot.

indigenous way of life, especially with regard to traditional healing methods and to the efficiency of long-distance communication that it can offer: The urgently needed medical supplies are ordered from Zanzibar by means of drums within a day, far quicker than the Western doctors had expected. The old channels are thus utilised to relay new messages. In this way, African communication-technology combines with European medicine for efficient problem-solving. The German doctor, duly impressed by the result, sums up what surely is implied as the readers' reaction: "We have all of us something to learn" (246).

The notion of learning and teaching would indeed seem to provide a key to the ideological as well as illocutionary strategy pursued by this text. As my brief summary of the main story-line should have made clear, all questions of cultural difference, hegemony and emancipation are here being dealt with within the framework of an educational career, which we are made to believe provides the integrative matrix for even the most conflictual of forces. Yet this frame for fusion ultimately proves unreliable, because the pedagogical venture is altogether more dynamic than always to yield the results expected. This pertains to the educational process narrated in the text no less than to the educational effort in which the book itself engages. Clearly, *Africa Answers Back* sets out to provide answers to the burning issues of its time, and it offers cultural amalgamation as one of them. But, as I hope to make clear, by establishing fusion as its central trope it also defuses the discursive antagonisms that shape the colonial field.

In my subsequent analysis I shall use Richard Terdiman's concept of counter-discourse, which he exemplifies, among others, in novels of education, to explore the ambiguities of Nyabongo's narrative and speculate on their relevance for their contemporary as well as for the current context. Far from being "little more than expositions of African life," as G.D. Killam sees it,[6] this early African script both complies with the prescribed text of English historiography and challenges the prescript by inverting its premises. In this as in other respects, *Africa Answers Back* may be seen as paradigmatic for post-colonial writing in english.[7] My reading will focus on the beginning, the middle and the ending of the book and explore its textual terrain as a contested field, a battleground of superimposed meanings, where different stories vie for domination.

In doing so I shall proceed on the assumption that reading itself is an instrument of power. It is interesting to note at this point that, historically speaking, the early Christian converts in Buganda, whose impatience with the "old way" became so strong that King Mwanga decided in 1888 to curb their influence by force, were locally known as "readers."[8] As this designation makes evident, the hermeneutic act cannot be separated from its political framework, nor from its cultural presup-

---

[6] G.D. Killam, *Africa in English Fiction 1874–1939* (Ibadan: Ibadan UP, 1968): 172.

[7] The lower-case spelling follows the usage suggested by W.A. Ashcroft, Gareth Griffiths & Helen Tiffin, *The Empire Writes Back: Theory and Practice in Post-Colonial Literatures* (London: Routledge, 1989): 8, to whose theoretical framework my discussion is indebted throughout.

[8] Samwiri Rubaraza Karugire, *A Political History of Uganda* (Nairobi/London: Heinemann, 1980): 67.

positions. Not only may a specific reading generate and sustain a specific ideology, the reading-process as such is a highly charged political exercise. Pursuing these implications will offer the cue for investigating the reading strategies in Nyabongo's novel of education.

❦ ❖ ❧

Significantly enough, the text opens with a dramatisation of reading and scriptural interpretation, in which the English Book is installed as the icon of cultural power. As Part I sets out to give an extended narrative of East African history in the latter half of the nineteenth century, it begins – and this is surely a revealing point of departure – with Stanley's oft-cited arrival at the court of Mutesa I.[9] Throughout the first chapters, the narrative perspective hovers uncannily between authorial omniscience and personal restriction; the scenes of the actual encounter, however, are clearly presented from Stanley's – that is, the outsider's – point of view. Restricted though this may be, it forms the basis for the intercultural communication which subsequently develops within the textual framework of the English Bible. As Chief Ati's narrative, quoted above, has already indicated, Stanley impresses his African host not only with the efficiency of his gun, but even more so with his powers of reading. They come to form the major impetus of the story's as well as of history's progress.

At his first audience with the King, Stanley witnesses what seems to him to be the wilful execution of a slave (who is, in fact, used as a guinea-pig to test the new gun) and so proceeds, at his next audience, to read the beginning of St John's Gospel to the King, no doubt intending to offer moral correction to his barbarous cruelty: "In the beginning was the Word, and the Word was with God and the Word was God" (9).

This scene, placed at the beginning of Nyabongo's text, rehearses a pattern deeply engrained in colonial mythology: the revelation of the English Book, aptly described by Homi Bhabha as the triumphant inauguration of imperial literature:

> It is, like all myths of origin, memorable for its balance between epiphany and enunciation. The discovery of the book is, at once, a moment of originality and authority, as well as a process of displacement that, paradoxically, makes the presence of the book wondrous to the extent to which it is repeated, translated, misread, displaced.[10]

It is precisely in the sense of Bhabha's analysis that the book here installs the conditions for a beginning and establishes a mode of civil authority and order. In response to the King's somewhat impious question "'What is that, your mythology?',", Stanley defines the Bible as "'the guiding book of our religion'" (9), which should provide the much-needed guidance for Africans as well.

---

[9] Although, strictly speaking, Stanley was not the first European to visit the powerful kingdom of Buganda (Grant and Speke preceded him by more than a decade), his encounter with the Kabaka has come to be regarded as the pivotal moment in Central Africa's penetration by Western influence. The scene is also dramatised in a well-known poem by David Rubadiri, "Stanley Meets Mutesa," reprinted in numerous anthologies (eg, *Growing Up with Poetry*, ed. David Rubadiri (London: Heinemann 1989): 59.

[10] Homi K. Bhabha, "Signs Taken for Wonders: Questions of Ambivalence and Authority under a Tree Outside Delhi, May 1817," *Critical Inquiry* 12 (1985): 144. Further page references are in the text.

But it does even more than that. Consider the interplay of epiphany and enunciation in the following textual encounter:

> Every day the King sent for Stanley to read the Bible and to tell biblical stories. The King and his chiefs asked many questions. One day he told them the story of the children of Israel crossing the Red Sea.
>
> One of the chiefs said to the King, "Hm, that's just like our story, because when the Gods came from the north they reached the River Kira and the waters stopped flowing, so that they could get across. Isn't it strange that his story and ours should be the same."
>
> Stanley was anxious to know more about their story, but it was too complicated. The interpreter could not give an exact translation to many of the words. So Stanley continued his reading of the Bible to the King and his chiefs. (10)

What at first may seem a contribution to the comparative study of religions, at second reading can be made out as a paradigm of imperial discourse: the construction of an analogy as a means of incorporation. Though the biblical story is said to resemble the indigenous one, they are not on a par, because the English Bible already provides an entry for what cannot, and indeed need not, be recuperated in the European code. Oral knowledge does not enter the text we read and is compensated for by a written version readily supplied from elsewhere. Translation into English fails but, for want of a better alternative, the reading may be continued, since mediating meaning in the other direction does not seem to pose a problem for the interpreter. The figure of simile, equally crucial in colonial rhetoric and in the colonial perception of alien cultures, here turns out to operate asymmetrically: the indigenous tale about the African Gods' crossing of the River Kira may well be similar, yet remains outside the European script.

In this way, Stanley's reading and the chief's response conjoin to establish the English text as a sign of recognition; its codified meanings are "just like ours," that is to say, whatever "we" may have to tell, we recognise it scripted in the European book. The Bible here becomes a master-model of incorporation where the native story finds its place already taken. If, as Bhabha argues, the discovery of the English book functions to impose a measure of mimesis (147), the African recipients of Stanley's instruction have, at this point in the book, no choice but to master the mimesis by means of imitation. The King, accordingly, requests the English explorer to have missionaries sent from his country so that the Word may further be disseminated among Africans.

This is the point where the dynamics of learning and teaching are set in motion, in which the text of the English Bible fares rather differently. Before considering the turning-point in the middle of the story, however, the fact needs emphasising that all this is part of a book by an African author, claiming in its title to answer back to eurocentric discourse. But there is no way of denying that, to some extent, Nyabongo's text initially echoes European voices. It recounts East African history by simply reproducing what must be seen as stereotypes of colonial historiography – for instance, when Captain Lugard is cast in the role of impartial peace-maker between religious factions (ch. I 5), or when the presence of British troops in the region is declared necessary to prevent French and German expansion (ch. I 6), which unmistakably replicates the classic reasoning of British governments.[11] Thus, *Africa Answers Back* begins by repeating rather than resisting the argumentational patterns by which England domesticated Africa into the Grand Narrative of exploration and pacification. Yet, as the narrative continues, repetition of the master-code gives way to its manipulation.

The crucial change takes place in Parts II and III, which tell the story of Abala Stanley Mujungu and describe his development from missionary model pupil to African rebel. Significantly though, he attains this stature within the logocentric field first mapped out by Stanley's Bible reading and subsequently administered by the missionaries following his example. But, as Nyabongo's story proceeds, the examplary text turns out to be treacherous, because the attitude of imitation it demands contributes to undermining its privileged position.

This is what happens. In spite of his father's polygamous life-style, which is severely criticised by the Christian missionaries, Mujungu is admitted into their school, where he rapidly acquires the skills of modernity. Above all, he excels in reading and writing, through which he gains access to the texts used to codify and authorise eurocentric culture – apart from the Bible, these include Gibbon's *Rise and Fall of the Roman Empire* and, most notably, the works of William Shakespeare. Mujungu's initiation into the script of authority, however, does not result in total submission, but prepares the way for emancipation. When on holidays at home, he avails himself of the opportunity to read from the Bible to Chief Ati and all his wives in order to prove what he has learnt in school (203). But, rather than simply affirming missionary power, Mujungu's reading reveals that there are more things to the new religion than Reverend Hubert would tell. The biblical text contains rather different stories and allows for different precedents. What strikes Ati most is the story of King Solomon and his many wives, providing a scriptural example of polygamy, the very custom that is now branded as a shameful sin.[12] How can the Holy Book contain improprieties? Thus, the exclusive and legitimising power of the Bible is crumbling away to the extent that the text is opened up by new readers and their new practice of reading. All of a sudden, Reverend Hubert's interpretation can no longer stand as the one and only, because Mujungu's reading contests the missionary's hermeneutic monopoly. As one of Ati's wives puts it succinctly, "'your son will find him out. He can read his books, too! The Reverend Mr. Hubert can't tell us lies any more'" (207).

Punishment follows suit. When school resumes, Reverend Hubert forbids all further readings at home and tells Mujungu to spend the next holidays under his personal supervision at school. In an attempt to regain control over the channels of communication and keep a check on the dissemination of the Word, the teacher here

---

[11] See Karugire, *A Political History of Uganda*, 85.

[12] The book here contains an illustration (by Eleanor Maroney), depicting Mujungu in his sober school uniform, amiably surrounded by Ati's wives in wide, sumptuous gowns, while Ati lies in front, all listening attentively. The Bible, from which Mujungu reads, is placed exactly in the middle of the picture (205).

imposes authority upon his most zealous pupil, whose progress is threatening to supersede him.

Their decisive confrontation takes place in the classroom, where the battle is fought over biblical terrain, while hermeneutics serve as weaponry. Whatever story Reverend Hubert reads to the class, Mujungu's logical mind and argumentative spirit invariably find fault with it (223–28). He discredits the story of Jonah by wondering how a man could survive inside a whale and come out unharmed; he questions the story of Genesis by pointing out that no woman could ever come from a man's rib; he even ventures to cast doubt on the Gospel when he suggests that the story of the virgin birth would be better seen as a fairy-tale, since it is told by only two of the evangelists and stands, at any rate, in stark contrast to both commonsense and biology.[13] In this way, Mujungu fulfils the title of Nyabongo's book, so that the European teacher can only try to reassert his authority by threats: "'I will not tolerate your talking back to me, as you have just done. I am the master of this school'" (218). Yet finally he must admit that Mujungu has "'read too much'" (228). Cornered by his own pupil in front of the whole class, Reverend Hubert resorts to helplessly reiterating doctrine, desperately trying to preempt further doubts and questions.

It is at this point that Terdiman's analysis of the novel of education may offer a theoretical framework for an appropriate understanding of Nyabongo's discursive strategies. If, as Terdiman argues, the genre's tactic is not to subvert the dominant but rather to seek to recontain it,[14] Nyabongo's hero would seem to be a textual construct for just this purpose. What is at stake in the *roman d'education*, Terdiman writes (96), can be seen as education into an experience of the semiotic, by which the process of signification is internalised and may, in turn, be annexed. If domination functions through veiling all notion of control by declaring meaning fixed and natural, any problematisation of the sign may provide a basis for critique and resistance. Such is the textual function of Abala Stanley Mujungu: as his tripartite name already indicates, he is a figure of multiple signification and, conversely, an interpreter of many meanings.[15] Through his career, he is initiated into the dominant sign-system, and, having procured entry into its code, he proceeds to question its make-up and to disclose its construction. His story of education thus erodes the sense-giving authority.

This pertains first and foremost to the biblical text, the epitome of European power. Defined by Stanley early on as the "guiding book," the Bible constitutes a reliable code of conduct only so long as it is itself guided and guarded by a central hermeneutic authority. Missionary instruction, however, exposes the text to a

---

13 For an assessment of the rationalistic discourse here employed, see below.

14 Richard Terdiman, *Discourse/Counter-Discourse: The Theory and Practice of Symbolic Reistance in Nineteenth-Century France* (Ithaca NY: Cornell UP, 1985): 87. Further page references are in the text.

15 This also becomes particularly evident when Mujungu proves his multi-cultural knowledge through star names, which he does by designating them in three ways, following this pattern: "Venus, *Rumara naku*, The Reliever of Sorrow" (173).

widening audience without being able to ensure all readers' containment within the affiliative order of strict discipleship. The preaching and teaching of biblical lore to the natives, which lies at the heart of the civilising project, therefore consumes its own basis. In its course, the Bible text, initially a model for emulation, must suffer displacement and does, in fact, become a battlefield of conflicting readings. In Bhabha's terms (154), one might say that the assumed purity, coherence and authority of the English book must break and open up for processes of deformation.

What follows in Nyabongo's plot spells out the consequence. Mujungu accompanies Reverend Hubert as his interpreter on a missionary journey, but instead of translating the master's word, the former pupil now uses his superior communicative powers to warn his people of Hubert's influence (233–34). Shortly afterwards, he is dismissed from school, takes charge of his father's duties during the smallpox epidemic, and finally succeeds him as his son and heir, apparently fully endowed with all the prerequisites for the exercise of blissful rule. In the end, however, doubts set in.

After his initiation into both the indigenous and the European code, Abala Stanley Mujungu tries to combine what he considers best in both but fails to implement it in his grandiose scheme of reform. For, at the very ending of Nyabongo's story, "fusion triumphant" is marred by female voices: the women have been left out of the new social culture so constructed, and now demur at its ideas. After he has dismissed all his wives but one, the remaining wife complains:

> "While you were gone, many of the old wives came to visit me, and they cried because you had sent them away. My mother tells me there must be something wrong with a man who has many wives and then sends them away. [...] And my aunt says that you do wrong to let everybody shake hands with you, and that everybody should bow to the chief. Otherwise people may get to think that they are as good as you, and they will not respect you any more, and then chiefs will become like ordinary people, and the country will fall into trouble." (277)

Fusion thus fails, on grounds of hidden fissures in the social texture which now open up and, in retrospect, cast doubt on the whole project of cultural amalgamation. The book therefore ends, not in glorious consummation, but in anxious questioning of its own tenets:

> Mujungu began to worry whether all his innovations had been for the best. [...] He still believed in the value of his reforms, but perhaps it was best to slow them up. [...] Then he might have some peace to carry out his plans. (278)

Even if the final paragraph tries to gloss over the problem by declaring it simply a matter of time, the fissures betray a fundamental difficulty in the straightforward concept of empowerment through double education, so impressively presented in the career of Nyabongo's hero. When he finally assumes power, he sets out to implement fusion by decree from above, thereby reproducing the mechanism of control which he himself successfully opposed. As a strategy of resistance against total conversion, cultural fusion served as a means of emancipation. But as a strategy of social engineering, fusion becomes equally useful in defining marginality and disposing of elements that do not fit. In the terms of Terdiman's analysis, we may regard this ambivalence as the process in which the subversive is being re-enveloped by the dominant. Counter-discourses are always interlocked with the authorities they contest and thus, inevitably, run the risk of re-infection by their own practices. The ending of *Africa Answers Back* would seem to bear this out, since the initiation-pattern of this novel of education first counters and finally contains the power of discourse-control.

∼ ❖ ∽

It remains to gauge the implications of Nyabongo's book. Before finally considering its current relevance, I will now attempt to relate its strategies and ideas to those prevalent in the literary field at the time of publication. Even if this survey can only be brief and sketchy, some contextualisation seems all the more necessary as the rhetoric of learning and teaching, essential to Nyabongo's tale of decolonisation, figures just as prominently in the discourse of colonisation. If, as is well documented, the whole imperial enterprise could euphemistically be propagated as an effort to raise the so-called "lower races" to the standards of culture, an anglophone novel of African education must clearly be situated at the intersection of these ideological fields.

As a matter of fact, by 1930 the classic pattern of justifying conquest as an educational project had become increasingly problematical. The more the effects of successful teaching were seen and known, the less Europeans would feel secure in their assumed superiority. The prominent figure of the "educated African," characterised by Coleman as "the bête noir of the European administrator"[16] and treated with scornful condescension in most of the colonial literature of this time, clearly suggests the extent to which the civilising confidence of Stanley's days had waned.[17] In an effort to reconstruct the terms of power, the pride and virtue of "tribal" Africans were now widely extolled and their purity favourably juxtaposed to the disconcerting products of Western education. Nyabongo's book and its cultural hero must therefore be seen and assessed in the context of this debate.

Three examples, all published in London in the same year that *Africa Answers Back* came out, suffice to indicate what is at stake. In his *Critique of British Colonial Administration*, W.R. Crocker, a former District Officer in Nigeria, warned that a continuation of the educational policy in the colonies and a spread of literacy among colonial subjects would lead to a situation where "the Government will find that it has, like Frankenstein, raised up a monster which will consume it."[18] Reporting from his visit to Freetown, Sierra Leone, in *Journey Without Maps*, the writer Graham Greene describes his encounter with local inhabitants, who occupy offical positions and show the insignia of Western civilisation, in purely histrionic terms: "If they had been slaves they would have had more dignity; there is no shame in

---

16 James S. Coleman, *Nigeria: Background to Nationalism* (Berkeley: U of California P, 1958): 150.

17 According to Patrick Brantlinger, the turning-point lies in late-Victorian times, when the entrepreneurial spirit of earlier explorations yielded to the civilised discontents of the *fin de siècle*, which the English tried, but failed, to overcome by imperial displacement; see Patrick Brantlinger, *Rule of Darkness: British Literature and Imperialism 1830–1914* (Ithaca NY: Cornell UP, 1988).

18 Cited in Coleman, *Nigeria: Background to Nationalism*, 150.

being ruled by a stranger; but these men [...] were expected to play their part like white men and the more they copied white men, the more funny it was to the prefects."[19] And thirdly, Joyce Cary's novel *The African Witch*,[20] a popular success on publication, depicts the career of an African heir to the throne, who has received the very best of European education, but whose pretence to civilisation is eroded from within as soon as he returns to Africa to claim his title. Instead of a story of initiation pertinent to the *Bildungsroman*, Cary writes a story of dissociation in which the hero virtually disintegrates into two parts, the rational European and the irrational African, mutually exclusive and ultimately fatal.

Viewed against this contemporary background, Nyabongo's hero gains in significance. He is constructed as a counter-example to the dominant ideology of his time, which would respect "natives" only so long as they stayed within homo-geneous tribal identities, assumed or invented by anthropologists and colonial administrators[21] for the maintenance of the imperial power structure. The three texts cited, although different in genre and character, all agree in their fundamental strategy to construe cultural transformation as a dangerous deviation from pre-determined positions which, potentially, upsets the ruling order.

Even if Crocker, Greene or Cary write about Western Africa, the merits and perils of formally educating a local élite were equally debated with regard to East and Central Africa, where the fictional career of Nyabongo's hero was not without historic precedence. Already in the nineteenth century, early converts had found in the Bible examples of heroism against oppression; with textual reference to Psalm 68 ("Ethiopia shall stretch out her hands"), they went on to establish Ethiopianism as a broad Pan-African movement, heralding the secession of Black Churches from the white missions.[22] More to the point, Nyabongo's novel of education had a specific political parallel in the life-story of Daudi Chwa, the contemporary Kabaka of Buganda, who succeeded to the throne in 1897 when he was only one year old. Growing up in times of transition under the guidance and guardianship of three senior chiefs, he would seem to provide a topical point of reference for any literary engagement with the question of education. In fact, a year before *Africa Answers Back* came out in London, Daudi Chwa himself contributed to the education debate by publishing a treatise entitled *Education, Civilisation, Foreignisation*, declaring to be broadly in favour of the first two but opposed to the last.[23]

Likewise, Abala Stanley Mujungu is presented as an enlightened ruler, readily accepting his position at the crossroads of cultures as an opportunity rather than a plight. Autocratic though he may be in his single-handed attempt at fusion, seen in the discursive context of his time he emerges as a positively challenging figure.

---

[19] Graham Greene, *Journey Without Maps* (1936; London: Heinemann, 1950): 35.

[20] Joyce Cary, *The African Witch* (1936; London: Michael Joseph, 1951).

[21] For a pertinent discussion of the invention of tradition in colonial Africa, see Ranger 1983.

[22] See Emmanuel A. Ayandele, *The Missionary Impact on Modern Nigeria 1842–1914* (London: Longmans, 1966): 175.

[23] This information is taken from the *Encyclopedia Britannica* (*Macropedia*), article on East Africa: History.

Even the fact that Nyabongo refrains from sending his hero on the classic educational journey to the metropolis, otherwise so prevalent in early African writing,[24] should be understood as a self-assertive negation of European expectation patterns. Nor does Nyabongo align himself with the *négritude* philosophy, widely generated by contemporary African intellectuals in the diaspora. In contrast to commonly held believes of the time, *Africa Answers Back* proclaims no African essentialism, but simply and rather pragmatically claims elements of the traditional heritage as yet the best way to tackle practical problems.

In line with the author's enlightened attitude, the oppositional stance taken against missionary doctrine, too, is less an expression of cultural reassertion than a result of scientific reasoning. When Mujungu answers back to the Bible, his critique echoes the common objections against biblical superstition by which European societies marked their own process of secularisation in the modern age. The way in which the author prompts his African mission pupil to argue against the wondrous element in religion is highly ironical, because the whole missionary enterprise was launched by Europeans as a way of re-evangelising their own people as well. By taking the Gospel into the dark places of the earth, the churches also aspired to re-kindle religious zeal at home. The conflicts between doctrinal and secular readings were thus removed by missionary travels, only to re-emerge in the colonial classroom where the displaced biblical text is now turned against its instructors. Such reversal of the enunciative situation, combined with ironic echoes of the master's voice, are the characteristic strategies of dominated literatures which, as the current catchphrase has it, write back to the centre and which, as the title indicates, are prefigured in *Africa Answers Back*.

However, reading Nyabongo's work more than half a century after publication we must, above all, acknowledge the fundamental ambiguity of its textual strategies. On the one hand, his story shows a great teleological development of individual heroism, not entirely free of utopian traits, claiming to bridge cultural contrasts. It does so by using appropriation instead of conversion as its operational principle, thereby transgressing the rigid categories of separation and control. Whereas the norm of missionary activity, by definition, operates within a matrix of complete substitution,[25] the discourse of African empowerment, as it is here developed, challenges European domination by penetrating its text and mastering its code, without forsaking its own. This takes place within the missionary classroom, so intimately related to deculturation and so prominently portrayed in many African

---

[24] See Ulrich Fleischmann, "Afrikanische 'Reisen' in die Erste Welt," *Komparatistische Hefte* 3 (1981) : 37–51.

[25] In *The Invention of Africa*, Valentin Y. Mudimbe characterises the ideological model of conver-sion as follows: "One might say that missionary speech is always predetermined, preregulated, let us say *colonised*. It depends upon a normative discourse already given, definitely fixed [...]. This means, at least, that the missionary does not enter into dialogue with pagans and 'savages' but must impose the law of God that he incarnates. All of the non-Christian cultures have to undergo a process of reduction to, or – in the missionary language – of regeneration in, the norms that the missionary represents" (Mudimbe, *The Invention of Africa*; Bloomington: Indiana UP, 1988: 47).

texts that Richard Priebe has called it "a microcosm of the colonial structure."[26] Yet here this microcosm becomes the battlefield for emancipation, where the texts of power are not internalised but utilised by the Africans for their own purposes.

On the other hand, the foregoing analysis has shown that Nyabongo's text not only reverses but also rehearses patterns of colonial discourse. With regard to the historiographic narrative as well as to the amount of anthropological information it provides, *Africa Answers Back* readily answers the expectations and needs of English readers of its time.[27] Although the title claims to give Africa a voice of her own, Nyabongo's book at points sounds more like an echo of the European voices to which it claims to respond. This holds true even for the title-phrase itself: "answering back" is an expression most commonly used of disrespectful children defying parental authority, so that Nyabongo's Africa, while trying to assert itself, is inadvertently entrapped in the pervasive metaphors of growth and childhood employed by the colonial powers to rationalise imperial rule.

The puzzling ambiguity, by which a self-assertive statement is caught up in its contrary, finally justifies the conclusion that this book is not merely of historical interest to us. Stemming from the archives of African writing and published two decades before the beginning of anglophone literature from the continent is generally dated, Nyabongo's novel still retains some didactic impact, even though we may be inclined to interpret the message somewhat differently from its first conception. Rather than falling for fusion, we may read it for signs of confusion arising at the interstices of the intertwining codes. While the grand amalgamation of cultures, as the ending proves, comes close to an imperial practice of "fuse and rule," the momentary and haphazard joining of disparate signs, achieved at some points in the narrative, seems an altogether more effective, and more topical, strategy of resistance. *Africa Answers Back* may therefore instruct us to be aware of the multiplicity of potential, and often conflicting, meanings that make up the text.

This process of multivalent reading, though ultimately up to each recipient, is hinted at between the narrative lines of the great educational tale. Most memorably, the incitement to semiotic plurality is voiced in the traditional song of Mother Parrot, which Abala Stanley Mujungu sings at one point and in which paedagogical exhortation combines with a call for playful subversion:

> Never despise the power of speech;
> Learn every word as it comes.
> For this is the pride of the parrot race,
> That it speaks in a hundred tongues. (164)

---

[26] Richard K. Priebe, "The Canonization of Texts: The Childhood and Allegories of Salvage and Change," *Matatu* 7 (1990): 17.

[27] The preface by William Lyon Phelps sets the tone: "Prince Nyabongo is 'a gentleman and a scholar'. I can assure readers that the extraordinary incidents and events and customs that appear in this narrative are not the work of imagination, or of a novelist writing under an assumed name, but come from one who plays an important part in the political and social life of his far-away country, and whose high natural intelligence and charming amenity have enabled him to understand English-speaking people so well that he knows not only what we most wish to know about his own people, but knows how to communicate that knowledge to us" (x).

Speaking in a hundred tongues means penetrating many codes and mastering their meanings. Again, learning is presented as a process of empowerment, transferred here to the practice of parrots and their multilingual capacities. Valorising their power of speech no less than their proverbial powers of imitation, Nyabongo's parrot-song calls for creative confusion and, consciously or not, comes close to the politics of the African trickster.

To sum up, let me briefly return to Achebe's scene of syncretic name-giving, referred to at the outset. Arising through a joining of divided concepts, the name "Amaechina," if taken in its semantic value, could also be understood to voice a warning against fusion as a figure of closure: "May the path never close," or, to appropriate it for the present case, "May the fusion never end" – this hope would seem to express what is required to resist monolithic construction: the ongoing interaction, mutual questioning and constant interplay of codes and cultures.

WORKS CITED

ACHEBE, Chinua. *Anthills of the Savannah* (1987; London: Picador, 1988).

ASHCROFT, Bill, Gareth GRIFFITHS & Helen TIFFIN. *The Empire Writes Back: Theory and Practice in Post-Colonial Literatures* (London: Routledge, 1989).

AYANDELE, Emmanuel A. *The Missionary Impact on Modern Nigeria 1842–1914* (London: Longmans, 1966).

BHABHA, Homi K. "Signs Taken for Wonders: Questions of Ambivalence and Authority under a Tree Outside Delhi, May 1817," *Critical Inquiry* 12 (1985): 144–65.

BRANTLINGER, Patrick. *Rule of Darkness: British Literature and Imperialism 1830–1914* (Ithaca NY: Cornell UP, 1988).

CARY, Joyce. *The African Witch* (1936; London: Michael Joseph, 1951).

COLEMAN, James S. *Nigeria: Background to Nationalism* (Berkeley: U of California P, 1958).

FLEISCHMANN, Ulrich. "Afrikanische 'Reisen' in die Erste Welt," *Komparatistische Hefte* 3 (1981): 37–51.

GREENE, Graham. *Journey Without Maps* (1936; London: Heinemann, 1950).

JAHN, Janzheinz, Ulla SCHILD & Almut NORDMANN. *Who's Who in African Literature* (Tübingen: Erdmann, 1972).

KARUGIRE, Samwiri Rubaraza. *A Political History of Uganda* (Nairobi/London: Heinemann, 1980).

KILLAM, G.D. *Africa in English Fiction 1874–1939* (Ibadan: Ibadan UP, 1968).

MUDIMBE, Valentin Y. *The Invention of Africa* (Bloomington: Indiana UP, 1988).

NYABONGO, Akiki. *Africa Answers Back*, intro. William Lyon Phelps (1935; London: Routledge, 1936).

PRIEBE, Richard K. "The Canonization of Texts: The Childhood and Allegories of Salvage and Change," *Matatu* 7 (1990): 5–23.

RANGER, Terence. "The Invention of Tradition in Colonial Africa," in *The Invention of Tradition*, ed. Eric Hobsbawm & Terence Ranger (Cambridge: Cambridge UP, 1983): 211–62.

RIEMENSCHNEIDER, Dieter, ed. *Grundlagen zur Literatur in englischer Sprache: West- und Ostafrika* (Munich: Fink, 1983).

TERDIMAN, Richard. *Discourse/Counter-Discourse: The Theory and Practice of Symbolic Reistance in Nineteenth-Century France* (Ithaca NY: Cornell UP, 1985).

⇜ ❖ ⇝

THOMAS BRÜCKNER

Across the Borders
Orality Old and New in the African Novel

MANY AN ATTEMPT HAS BEEN MADE to categorise the works of African and other "new" literatures in europhone languages. Roughly, these attempts can be classified into four different groups or realms:

1) patterns concerning the development of regional or national literatures that lay emphasis on the cultural specifity of the region or nation in question;

2) concepts of racially determined literatures that take as their basis of operation seemingly common features among different literatures from various regions;

3) comparatist models whose point of departure consists in the assumption of a basic cultural hybridity in the literatures in question; and

4) comparatist patterns that take up as their field of operation the linguistic, historical or cultural specifica of different literatures from various regions.

In recent years, especially one model or pattern in particular has met with academic interest: that of post-colonialism. I shall begin with a quotation from *The Empire Writes Back*:

> We use the term "post-colonial" [...] to cover all the culture affected by the imperial process from the moment of colonisation to the present day. This is because there is a continuity of preoccupations throughout the historical process initiated by European imperial aggression. We also suggest that it is most appropriate as the term for the new cross-cultural criticism which has emerged in recent years and for the discourse through which this is constituted. [...] So the literatures of African countries, Australia, Bangladesh, Canada, Caribbean countries, India, Malaysia, Malta, New Zealand, Pakistan, Singapore, South Pacific Islands and Sri Lanka are all post-colonial literatures. [...] What each of these literatures has in common beyond their special and distinctive regional characteristics is that they emerged in their present form out of the experience of colonisation and asserted themselves by foregrounding the tension with the imperial power, and by emphasising their differences from the assumptions of the imperial centre. It is this which makes them distinctively post-colonial.[1]

Perhaps unconsciously, and without mentioning it *expressis verbis*, Ashcroft et al. hint at a feature that is characteristic at least for the African literatures in question: These literatures are literatures in a situation of change, of "upheaval," and not only with regard to the tensions resulting from opposition to imperial power and its discourse. Most of all, these are literatures of change with regard to their very own situation and development. In the compendium *European-Language Writing in Sub-*

---

[1] Bill Ashcroft, Gareth Griffiths & Helen Tiffin, *The Empire Writes Back: Theory and Practice in Post-Colonial Literatures* (London: Routledge, 1989): 2

Saharan Africa, Albert Gérard refers to European patterns of interpretation and criticism:

> The early negritude controversy, between Senghor on the one hand and Mphahlele and Soyinka on the other, can be interpreted in a number of ways: it illustrated the conflict between Rousseauistic glorification of past values and the aspirations of future-oriented urbanised intellectuals [imagine Soyinka being the prototype of the Nigerian Yuppie; T.B.]; it was a case of French abstraction versus British pragmatism; it was a generational crisis with the sons seeking to destroy their symbolic father in order to take his place. Above all, it was the first piece of evidence for the real existence of a linguistic barrier cutting across Africa as a result of the arbitrary decisions of blind history.[2]

There seems to be something in this. At least, in what Gérard says about the generational conflict between Senghor on the one hand, and Soyinka, Mphahlele and others on the other. Yet, I admit that I feel rather uncomfortable with the other parts of this statement. And I hasten to add why: I doubt that Senghor ever based his argument on the philosophical and ethnological positions of Jean–Jacques Rousseau; I do not think that he saw himself as a Noble Savage. On the contrary. In 1948, he was part of a commission which went through the pages of the constitution for the Fifth French Republic in order to ensure that the French language was applied according to its rules. And even if Senghor – since 1984 a member of the Académie Française – in some of his poems evokes an idealised past, this evocation of a Golden Age of Africa has nothing to do with the kind of criticism of civilisation that Rousseau had in mind when he wrote his *Discours sur l'inégalité* in 1754. It appears to me that Senghor and others – the Nigerian Amos Tutuola, for example – stand at the eve of change from orature to literature. What makes modern literature possible is, among other aspects, bound to the fact that its creator becomes aware of him- or herself as an individual. And this aspect constitutes one of the major differences between orature and literature.

If we skip excursively through the structure of orature, we very soon find that the production and the reception of a work of oral art are inseparably bound to one another. They only exist together, are not separated, neither in terms of time nor in terms of space. This creates a certain tension between artist and audience, and provides the latter with the chance to intervene actively, to take part in the production-process of oral art. This relates to the functionality of such art, which, if not individualised, requires a very distinctive, very direct social function to fulfil its very meaning. We have to agree with Senghor's postulate that traditional African art has always been collective and never resembled the European concept of *l'art pour l'art*. The "institution" of the individual author – as it came into being at the point of transition from oral art to the written one – provides, roughly speaking, for two options of further development: first, the integration of the indigenous artistic tradition into the new and foreign one; secondly, the integration of the foreign into

---

2 *European-Language Writing in Sub-Saharan Africa*, ed. Albert S. Gèrard (Budapest: Akademiai Iado, 1986), vol. 2: 1014.

the indigenous artistic tradition and development. Both options have been part of literary developments in Africa. The history of the rise and development of literatures in Africa thus proves to be a synthetic or syncretistic process.

Euro-American criticism of African literatures has, first and foremost, and more often than not, tended to judge this syncretistic process to have gone on under conditions of domination. This view was followed by the concept of counter-discourse – African and other "new" literatures were said to be operating against the domination of the imperial centre. I would certainly not deny that this is a valid scenario over quite a long period of time. Yet it neglects the fact that in the course of development something happens to the emerging African writer that is only insufficiently explained by the term "becoming a social and historical subject of its own." This may be illustrated by a closer look at the history of modern (written) Nigerian literature. In 1789, a Nigerian, Olaudah Equiano, published his book *The Interesting Narrative of the Life of Olaudah Equiano, or Gustavus Vassa, the African*. This work appeared at the time Europe was at the peak of the Age of Enlightenment. One would think that, if Equiano proudly presents his life achievement, then this should be seen in the light of his own time. Moreover, Equiano's book may serve as an early example for this process of individualisation and "becoming a social and historical subject of its own."

Traditional Nigerian societies were prevailingly oral. The transition to literary societies is largely bound up with the influence exerted by the various ecclesiastical institutions. We find another example in the historical figure of Samuel Ajayi Crowther, a former slave, who may stand for the process of how Africans were shaped, and shaped themselves, under missionary influence by following European patterns and models. He was born in Yorubaland but received his education in Sierra Leone under the auspices of the British Church Missionary Society, returning to Nigeria in 1840. He participated in the British Niger Expedition and worked in Igboland for a couple of years creating the alphabet of the Igbo language. In 1843 his *Vocabulary of the Yoruba Language* was published in London. Later on, Crowther was appointed the first-ever black Anglican bishop in Nigeria. In 1866, he was one of the founding members of a certain "academy" modelled on the British prototype. Since it saw itself as "a social and cultural centre for public enlightenment," it was the declared aim of this organisation to provide for the "promotion of the arts, science and culture."

The book by Equiano and the "academy" of Crowther are, in the first instance, acts of self-apprehension within a changing environment in which these authors try to prove their equality. What is important for us here is the adaptation of "European" forms of cultural and literary self-expression. This creative adaptation is characteristic for more than one generation of African writers. The necessary presupposition for this is that the writer become a subject for and in his or her own right. At the beginning of the twentieth century and under conditions of colonis-ation, this role within society was no longer immutably shackled to the traditional structures of social organisation. Becoming an individual subject meant tearing oneself out of these structures. It did not necessarily mean being completely integrated into new or "modern" structures, since integration was allowed only to the level suitable to the needs of the respective colonial master.

In 1925 the report of the Phelps Stokes Commission stated, about colonial education:

> The Old Testament, and especially the Mosaic Laws, and the verses from the New Testament may be effectively used to strengthen the interest of the pupil in health. [...] The home and family life have so full a place in literature as to make proper selection difficult. There are descriptions [...]of typical European and American homes; biographies of women who have realised the ideals of motherhood and the home in the full meaning of that wonderful place. [...] Sound ideas of recreation are amply presented in many pamphlets and books. The teacher can obtain [...] reading material from Europe or from America that describes the healthful games and amusements of civilized people. It would be helpful for the teacher to encourage the pupils to describe their own games as compared with those of other lands. Classroom discussions would doubtless result in shifting the desirable from the undesirable elements in the amusements.[3]

If one compares this with early documents in African literatures, it becomes obvious that these literary works are more "African" than the authors and their tutors may have intended. I would mention as examples in this connection Félix Couchouro's novel *L'Esclave* (1929), Ousmane Socé's *Karim* (1935), Richard Obeng's *Eighteen-pence* (1943), and Cyprian Ekwensi's novel *People of the City* (1954). One could easily add other examples – Thomas Mofolo's *Chaka*, Amos Tutuola's *Palm-Wine Drinkard*. This is merely to show the wide range and diversity of a process that led to the establishment of the novel as one of the major epic forms in modern African literatures. What all these examples have in common is what could be seen as the most characteristic feature establishing the uniqueness of African literatures in world literature: their orality.

Of course, the novel is not a genuine African literary genre. Of course, African writers had first of all to adapt this genre when they came into contact with the tradition of the European novel. But, in so doing, they had already started to "afri-canise" and "oralise" this genre. A whole generation of novels is characterised by techniques informed by the process of oral performance, such as:

!) linearity of plot, combined with

2) extensive descriptive momentum;

3) "external" business propelling the novel's action forward. Places, situations, and the actions of the characters are what matters most. The "internal," reflective or introspective momentum seems in comparison to be somewhat attenuated.

Moreover, there are the following features:

4) indigenisation of the English language; and, of central importance,

---

[3] Phelps Stokes Commission Report, *Education in East Africa* (New York, 1925): 1

5) the whole corpus of images, metaphors, proverbs and sayings, myths and legends, values, thought-patterns, modes of behaviour, religious belief-systems and epistemological patterns of the traditional world.

Traditional forms of oral art are consciously woven into the network of literary expression and articulation provided by the novel. This becomes evident if we cast a glance at those early pieces of "modern" literature dating from the nineteenth century. Such early writers who employed the English language – Mofolo or Equiano are cases in point – drew heavily on oral tradition, much more so than they modelled themselves after Dickens and others.

In his essay "Named for Victoria, Queen of England," the Nigerian writer Chinua Achebe once described the uniqueness of the situation:

> We lived at the crossroads of cultures. We still do today; but when I was a boy one could see and sense the peculiar quality and atmosphere of it more clearly. I am not talking about all that rubbish we hear of the spiritual void and mental stresses that Africans are supposed to have, or the evil forces and irrational passions prowling through Africa's heart of darkness. [...] On one arm of the cross we sang hymns and read the Bible night and day. On the other my father's brother and his family, blinded by heathenism, offered food to idols. [...] Those idols and that food had a strange pull on me in spite of my being such a thorough little Christian that often at Sunday services at the height of the grandeur of "Te Deum Laudamus" I would have dreams of a mantle of gold falling on me as the choir of angels drowned our mortal song and the voice of God Himself thundering: This is my beloved son in whom I am well pleased. Yet, despite those delusions of divine destiny I was not past taking my little sister to our neighbour's house when our parents were not looking and partaking of heathen festival meals. I never found their rice and stew to have the flavour of idolatry. [...] What I do remember is a fascination for the ritual and the life on the other arm of the crossroads.[4]

In this cultural context, it has been important for the development of modern African literatures that the new did not organically rise out of the internal processes of social development, as has been the case with the development of European national literatures from the seventeenth to the nineteenth century. New literary forms and genres, as these were shaped within African societies under the influence of colonialism, met a relatively mature and fully developed genre, the novel – or, more abstractly: a canonised literature – and continued to shape themselves in constant argument with this genre or with literature in general by shifting from adoption to creative adaptation in accordance with the needs of their own society. Many features exhibited by African novels during the past three to four decades need to be seen in the light of their Africanness, and not according to canonical Euro-American standards. For example, Nigerian author Cyprian Ekwensi has often been accused of writing in the tradition of what in Great Britain is called "sub-literature." If we take his novel *Burning Grass* (1962), this criticism seems to be true. There we have detailed descriptions of cattle-drives and theft, bolting horses, bar-scuffles and bloody fights that remind us very much of familiar "Wild West" patterns of representation. But there can be no doubt that other features of this novel

---

4 Chinua Achebe, "Named for Victoria, Queen of England," in *Hopes and Impediments: Selected Essays 1965-87* (London: Heinemann, 1988): 22–23 (first published in *New Letters* 40 [October 1973], then in *Morning Yet on Creation Day* [London: Heinemann Eduicational, 1975]).

are deeply rooted in the oral tradition: for instance, the didactic mood characteristic of all Ekwensi's novels, or their often cyclical structure ofdeparture, initiation and return (which can also be found in the works of Amos Tutuola and others). One might argue that Cyprian Ekwensi is not necessarily the representative of "crest-of-the-wave" literature as is his compatriot Wole Soyinka, Nigeria's Nobel laureate, but has his roots in what is known as Onitsha market-literature. On the other hand, from the Fifties to the mid-Seventies the didactic aspect has been one of the most common features of all African literatures. It does not have its roots in "sub-literature" but in traditional orature and, moreover, in the actual social situation of African societies themselves. It is here that the fact that African literatures have been literatures of change is most visible. Didacticism partly reflects these actual social conditions and has got something to do with what the writers themselves termed commitment.

In the colonial phase leading immediately up to political independence, didacticism was directed towards both African and Euro-American readers. It was especially via historical novels that writers endeavoured to inform their readers about the cultural and artistic nature of African peoples. This intention to reach readers both in Africa and in Europe and America was supported by expectations the authors cherished with regard to independence. The best-known protagonist of this kind of literary commitment in Nigeria is Chinua Achebe. The hopes many a writer humbly commited him/herself to were, as we know all too well, shattered by the reality of independence. Social development after independence suddenly confronted writers with an almost completely new social role which, moreover, was in opposition to the role they had originally sought in traditional society and had set up for themselves as their chief function in times of change. The writer as an artist accompanying the struggle for independence became a critic of independence. Linked with this is a change of perspective which began in Nigerian literature in the mid-Sixties and experienced its first peak with Wole Soyinka's first novel, *The Interpreters*. In what became known as the "literature of disillusionment," no longer did a whole generation of authors act out of an understanding of the writer's role that was derived from traditional "resources." They directed their interest towards, and focused their intention on, how their writings should operate within their own societies. The aspect of "*counter-discourse*" disappears almost completely, replaced by an interest in the life and strife of the lowest strata of their own societies. This preoccupation is accompanied by changes in expressive ideology. The most radical example of this in all African literatures is the Kenyan author Ngugi wa Thiong'o, who decided not to write in English any more but took up his native language, Gikuyu, instead. I do not want to argue here whether his attempt was successful in artistic terms. My interest is in other implications, which become obvious in the prologue to Ngugi's more recent novel *Matigari*. Ngugi dedicated his work "To the reader/listener" and closed with the following words: "So, say yes, and I am going to tell you a story! Once upon a time in a land with no name...."[5]

Using Gikuyu and dedicating his work both to readers and to listeners clearly shows which public Ngugi has in mind: the common people of his country, who for the most part have not had sufficient Western education to be able to read a novel written in English; those who are perhaps illiterate and dependent on someone reading the novel to them; those who cannot afford to buy a book. In structuring his novel, Ngugi combines a Gikuyu legend with the biblical myth of the Second Coming of Christ and an abstract image of the post-colonial situation in Kenya and other independent African countries. By doing so, he explicitly refers to the knowledge and experience of the readership he has in mind. Moreover, using elements from different mythologies, he tries to break up the complexity of the actual situation in his society, to present it as something masterable or manageable. Behind this one can detect an effort to relate his fiction once more to actual history in the form of stories, something that is very much a feature of oral legends and the autochthonous epic tradition.

The case of Ngugi wa Thiong'o brings us to the question of language with which we shall conclude. If we take Ngugi as an example, it becomes evident that the hypothesis which Chantal Zabus offers to shed light on the nature of literatures in the new African englishes – namely, that these literatures can be likened to a "palimpsest" – is a not uncomplicated one. It is central to Zabus's considerations that a given African language as used by a particular author has been scraped off the papyrus in order to be replaced by some text scribbled down in the English language.[6] But Ngugi has done the contrary. Others, like the Nigerian Ken Saro–Wiwa or the Ghanaian Kojo Laing, take up "varieties" of the English language. In their literary works of art, they use Pidgin English to a degree that goes beyond what we know from, say, Chinua Achebe, Cyprian Ekwensi, Wole Soyinka and others. West African Pidgin is seen as a variety of English. Yet I feel it to be more of an African language in its own right, although it uses large areas of the English vocabulary. But this is not the point here. The point is that this pidgin is very much a language based on orality, on an oral tradition which lacks a written exquivalent, not to mention an established generic tradition based on the novel.

❧ ❖ ❧

---

5 Ngugi wa Thiong'o, *Matigari* (London: Heinemann, 1989): 5

6 See Chantal Zabus, *The African Palimpsest: Indigenization of Language in the West African Europhone Novel* (Cross/Cultures 4; Amsterdam/Atlanta GA: Rodopi, 1991).

Works Cited

Achebe, Chinua. "Named for Victoria, Queen of England," in *Hopes and Impediments: Selected Essays 1965–87* (London: Heinemann, 1988): 22–23 (first published in *New Letters* 40 [October 1973], then in *Morning Yet on Creation Day* [London: Heinemann Eduicational, 1975]).

Ashcroft, Bill, Gareth Griffiths & Helen Tiffin. *The Empire Writes Back: Theory and Practice in Post-Colonial Literatures* (London: Routledge, 1989):

Gèrard, Albert S., ed. *European-Language Writing in Sub-Saharan Africa* (Budapest: Akademiai Iado, 1986).

Ngugi wa Thiong'o. *Matigari* (London: Heinemann, 1989).

Phelps Stokes Commission Report. *Education in East Africa* (New York, 1925).

Zabus, Chantal. *The African Palimpsest: Indigenization of Language in the West African Europhone Novel* (Cross/Cultures 4; Amsterdam/Atlanta GA: Rodopi, 1991).

WOLFGANG HOCHBRUCK

Armed Conflict and Cultural Encounters
Zimbabwean War Fiction
(For Werner Arens, on the occasion of his sixtieth birthday)

A MONG THE ARMED CONFLICTS OF THIS CENTURY, the Zimbabwean Civil War ranks as one of the minor local conflicts only. However, to quote Paddy Griffith, "small wars [...] grow in the telling."[1] There are several truths in this. The meaning I want to confer on Griffith's statement here is that a relatively minor conflict can trigger a series of new political as well as literary developments. This holds particularly true when the outcome – as in the case of the Second Chimurenga,[2] about fifteen years of low-intensity warfare with an estimated 40,000 killed and hundreds of thousands deprived of their health and their homes – is basically but a shift in power structures entailing an officially declared policy of reconciliation.[3] The interpretative possibilities are many: the Zimbabwean conflict has been interpreted as, for example, a revolutionary civil war, an anti-colonial uprising, as yet another instance of intertribal warfare, and as a mixture of all three.

Not surprisingly, literary revisions of the war from the postwar period have also altered perceptions of what actually happened. The narrative platform for this literature, with its astounding growth-rate,[4] has widened to encompass now a conglomeration of several different African peoples and a Euro-African settler colony, where before there were two separate and unequal literary markets, one in the Shona/Ndebele languages for the black population, the other for whites.[5] Seen from this point of view, the diversity of literary responses to the Second Chimurenga becomes more understandable as a series of attempts from different quarters to orientate inherent memories in a discursive order which makes sense to

---

[1] Paddy Griffith, "Small Wars and How They Grow in the Telling," *Small Wars and Insurgencies* 2 (1991): 216–31.

[2] A Shona term denoting liberation fighter as well as the struggle for liberation itself.

[3] For details, see Victor de Waal, *The Politics of Reconciliation: Zimbabwe's First Decade* (Cape Town/ Trenton NJ: David Philip, 1990): ch. 10 and 12.

[4] "Zimbabwean literature in English [...] boasts one of the highest annual growth rates in Africa" (Dieter Riemenschneider, "Short Fiction From Zimbabwe," *Research in African Literatures* 20 [1989]: 401).

[5] One of the problems of the term "post-colonial society" is that in present usage it encompasses so much – those nation-states left behind by colonial administrations that are conglomerates of formerly independent peoples; European settler-colonies (which usually contain one or more subjugated indigenous populations still under colonial rule); and the few extant combinations of both, such as Zimbabwe or South Africa. See Bill Ashcroft, Gareth Griffiths & Helen Tiffin, *The Empire Writes Back* (London: Routledge, 1989): 137.

the participants.[6] There is, as Flora Veit–Wild has observed in her recent doctoral dissertation, no monolithic story-line determining a unified ideological background for contemporary Zimbabwean fiction.[7]

The term "Zimbabwean fiction" therefore denotes a neither nationally nor ideologically coherent body of literary texts; nor were all texts necessarily published in Zimbabwe. For example, one of the first black literary responses to the war, Stanley Nyamfukudza's sceptical novel *The Non-Believer's Journey*, was originally published in British exile in 1984. Also, most of the texts analysed below conform, as I shall be indicating, to conventional older Northern, Southern, Eastern and Western concepts of war, enemy, victory or defeat. I am using the terms "Northern" and, by analogy, "Southern" here not to represent geographical oppositions (even though that is what they contingently are, as well) but in acknowledgement of the fact that the economic, political, military, and partly also ecological dividing-lines in the present world do not run East–West, as one of the axioms of Cold-War rhetoric has tried for almost fifty years to make us believe, but North–South. The North–South conflict both precedes and survives that between East and West. It was a colonial conflict, and continues to be one in the empires' neo-colonial clothes. Writing back to this Northern discourse, however, often takes on forms of an older and, by the early Nineties, historical "Eastern" discourse, confusing anti-colonialism and anti-capitalism and re-enacting sham battles of the Cold War on what turns out to be still colonial terrain.

However – and this is my main point, and the reason why I have persisted with this investigation – there are some texts which deviate from all of the well-trodden paths at least in some points. My impression is that we may be observing in these texts the development of a new direction in writing about and commemorating war. Much of this novelty has to do with attempts to overcome the difference between North and South, but also ultimately with a belief in the translatability of discourses.

The Old Northern–Western response

The old Northern ideological framework insists on binary oppositions, as in yes/no, hot/cold, or, for that matter, black/white. Under closer scrutiny, any of these binary oppositions usually turns out to be too simple to describe what is a fairly diverse pattern. This, of course, does not preclude the possibility of grossly simplified answers and responses.

The white politics (and poetics) of racist supremacy which ultimately triggered the violent phase of conflict between the Unilateral Declaration of Independence

---

[6] My analysis cannot, for now, move beyond a hermeneutically loaded approach based on a rather subjective reading. At a later time, it will hopefully be possible to support or falsify my interpretations by an analysis based on empirical methods in order to establish whether the cognitive change in writing and commemorating war that I see happening in some of the texts analysed below is my invention or an objective fact.

[7] Despite the fact that some of the Rhodesian censoring institutions have remained in place; cf Flora Veit–Wild, *Teachers, Preachers, Non-Believers* (Harare: Baobab, 1993): 2.

from Britain in 1965 and the elections of 1979 has therefore predictably insisted on determining friend and foe along lines of racial colour, allowing whites to be the enemy only in the form of foreign communists.[8] The texts written from this anti-communist and overtly racist position constitute a "body of propaganda and myth-making aimed at justifying or disguising both the social, political and economic dispensations which had been the causes of the war, and the measures taken to counter it."[9] The indulgence in violence, the obsession with macho imagery, and the general racism of these books – ranging from Robert Early's *A Time of Madness* to George Harding Raubenheimer's *Crossfire*[10] – have been pointed out by A.J. Chennells[11] and David Maugham–Brown. They all display their ideological categories on the surface, or very close to it. The form, range of subject-matter, and ideological positions professed in these books are – not surprisingly – almost identical with what I have tried to subsume under the heading of "settler literature" in a study of North American acculturation processes.[12] Because of his politically incorrect position, the intruding settler cannot be interested in a positive depiction of what he does not perceive as just an "Other," but as his enemy. Literary conventions have, of course, changed over the past century, and sexuality (usually in the form of rape) is depicted more openly in the Rhodesian tales of terror and the imagination than in eighteenth- and nineteenth-century American novels. Still, the slaughter of helpless whites by – literally – bloodlusty savages, the animal-like qualities of the Natives, their treacherousness and essential badness are all there: "She lay naked, her skin white and cold in the moonlight, a red circle around her scalp where they had cut off her hair."[13] Fear and loathing of the indigenous population extends to those actually fighting on the white side: "Katchemu [a black policeman; W.H.], his face bathed in sweat, was kneeling on the edge, swaying in time to the rhythm.

---

[8] The prehistory of UDI, the liberal politics of the Garfield Todd administration and the cooperation of European-educated Black intellectuals at the time indicate that armed conflict might have been neither necessary nor inevitable. Also, the relatively small number of white colonisers would not have been able to maintain and defend their system without the aid of numerous Africans in the system, from cooks and housemaids to policemen and servicemen. See the detailed account given by Peter McLaughlin, "Victims as Defenders: African Troops in the Rhodesian Defence System 1890–1980," *Small Wars and Insurgencies* 2 (1991): 240–75, esp. 265ff.

[9] David Maugham–Brown, "Myths on the March: The Kenyan and Zimbabwean Liberation Struggles in Colonial Fiction," *Journal of Southern African Studies* 9 (1982): 93.

[10] Robert Early, *A Time of Madness* (Salisbury, 1977); George Harding Raubenheimer, *Crossfire* (London: Hutchinson/Arrow, 1980).

[11] A.J. Chennells, "The Treatment of the Rhodesian War in Recent Rhodesian Novels," *Zambezia* 5 (1977): 177–202. Chennells' unpublished doctoral dissertation, "Settler Myths and the Southern Rhodesian Novel" (1982) takes up his argument.

[12] Wolfgang Hochbruck, *"I Have Spoken": Die Darstellung und ideologische Funktion indianischer Mündlichkeit in der nordamerikanischen Literatur* (ScriptOralia 32; Tübingen: Gunter Narr, 1991): 50ff. At best, white settler novels in Zimbabwe display a sense of rugged individualism epigonally modelled on the American spirit of independence, as ambiguously celebrated in the novels of Doris Lessing; see Rino Zhuwarara, *The Growth of Zimbabwean Fiction in English 1950–1980* (Fredericton, New Brunswick: Acadiensis, 1984): 52.

[13] Daniel Carney, *The Whispering Death* (London: Corgi, 1980): 50. Besides Carney, Early and Raubenheimer in particular revel in the gory details and gratuitous violence; see Chennells, "The Treatment of the Rhodesian War," 199; Maugham–Brown, "Myths on the March," 116 and 102.

Another moment and he would have leapt into the arena and joined them [...] I reached for a rock and brought it smashing down on his head."[14]

Most of the books in question are of no more literary value or interest than their predecessors, the nineteenth-century American dime-novels about the "Indian Wars," which they resemble most closely in their attitude towards the enemy. What is more interesting in this context is that the Indian-Wars parallel extends to a genre previously thought to be typically American: ie, the captivity narrative.[15]

Michael (Tom) Wigglesworth was a farmer and a former British army officer who was captured in 1978 by ZANLA guerrillas, carried off into Mozambique, and released six months later. His experiences went into a volume he called *Perhaps Tomorrow*.[16] The title already stresses one of the main aspects of the captivity story, the longing for deliverance, which, when it finally comes, is compared to a second birth (198). The captors are described from a curiously detached point of view, and with an interest reminiscent of that shown for the people they encountered by social scientists or the early travellers. This view diminishes as well as objectifies the present Other.

Captivity for Wigglesworth ended in February 1979, in time for him to witness the March Agreement, and shortly before the war ended. In keeping with a precious few North American captivity narratives, Wigglesworth's commentaries on the political situation and his depiction of Zimbabwean political leaders (see, for example, p.200) indicate a learning process:

> It should have been obvious to all thoughtful people that we were going to finish with an agreement that would be more demanding of the whites than one which had been possible years before; and before the loss of thousands of lives and the immense suffering of blacks and whites alike. Before the March 3 agreement the Rhodesian Front Party had made a complete about-turn with its policy towards majority rule... I sometimes wished that some of them had been abducted. (202)

Note how the initial "people" in the above quotation seems to include whites only, whereas the following instances of "the whites" and "blacks and whites alike" signify an observing, objective position, and how, with the final "them," the author detaches himself from political beliefs he might have shared initially.

The captivity-tale as a narrative genre contains the possibility of a changed outlook on the "Other" the narrator is forcibly confronted with. Interaction is brought about by initial violence, but depends for any sort of continuation on a mutually acceptable basis, a general concept of a translatability of discourses. In effect, one of the possible results of this interaction is an exchange of sympathies and ideas – provided neither captor nor captive is as rigidified ideologically as were, for example, American Puritan captives like Mary Rowlandson.[17] Wigglesworth's pragmatism aided him in coping with the situation, and the result is a deviation from

---

14 Carney, *The Whispering Death*, 82.

15 Cf the definition given by P.D. Carleton, "The Indian Captivity," *American Literature* 15 (1943): 170.

16 Michael (Tom) Wigglesworth, *Perhaps Tomorrow* (Salisbury: Galaxie, [1979?]). Further page references are in the text.

17 Hochbruck, "*I Have Spoken*," 56.

the monolithic garrison-mentality expounded by his countrymen. It has to be taken into account, of course, that the book was prepared for the press and published after the elections which gave the power to Mugabe and ZANU.

However, the postscript to the book (203) already anticipates the above-mentioned new positions in (re-)writing war, in that it indicates an acceptance of the new situation and hopes for reconciliation in the future.

The Old Southern response

For most of the black Zimbabwean participants, it has been (and continues to be) very hard to come to terms with the fact that the outcome of the war was not a restitution of the earlier, "Southern" economy and political system, but a forced reconciliation of "Northern" colonial rule and "Southern" popular majority. The insight that restitution could not conceivably have been the outcome of a war that ended at a conference-table was made more difficult by the fact that ZANU and ZAPU rhetoric had been normative, promising redistribution of jobs, housing, and a land-base.[18] Much of this rhetoric drew on the first war of liberation of 1896–97. The First Chimurenga had been an anti-colonial uprising with a plainly restitutive intent, led by traditional spirit-mediums.[19] The practice by ZANLA guerrillas of drawing support from such spirit-mediums seemed to reassure this restitutive element,[20] and it was also a constitutive presence in many of the *Songs That Won the Liberation War*.[21]

> Nyika yaba Zimbabwe
> Yakapambwa kare kare
> Tinoda kuvarwisa vapambepfumi,
> Tiitore
>
> Zimbabwe, the fatherland, was colonised long back
> We want to fight the invaders and regain our fatherland.22

The ZANU party after independence and the spectacular election victory continued to use the *mhondoro* (mediated spirits of royal ancestry) as rhetorical metaphor[23] and political symbol: "On a specially printed banner that was hung whereever the new

---

[18] Norma J. Kriger, *Zimbabwe's Guerrilla War. Peasant Voices* (African Studies 70; Cambridge/ New York: Cambridge UP, 1992): 98.

[19] "two spirit mediums who allegedly inspired the warriors, the female medium of the spirit Nehanda and the male medium of the spirit Kaguvi." Christine Sylvester, *Zimbabwe: The Terrain of Contradictory Development* (Boulder CO/San Francisco CA: Westview, 1991): 20.

[20] David Lan, *Guns & Rain: Guerillas* [sic] *and Spirit Mediums in Zimbabwe* (Perspectives on Southern Africa 38; Berkeley/Los Angeles: U of California P, 1985): xvii: "Many Shona members of the government forces   soldiers, policemen, local government officers   also relate accounts of timely warnings and miraculous escapes which their ancestors engineered. However, it was only within the guerilla army that this belief in the participation of the ancestors was developed into a system of ritual practices believed to place the combatants under their protection."

[21] *Songs that Won the Liberation War*, ed. Alec J.C. Pongweni (Harare: College Press, 1982).

[22] Second verse of "Ruzhinji Rweafrica," in Pongweni, *Songs that Won the Liberation War*, 59.

[23] "The Prime Minister, Mr Mugabe, swearing by the name of the legendary anti-British spirit medium Ambuya Nehanda, vowed that his government would confiscate white-owned land for peasant resettlement," the *Guardian* (10 October, 1983), quoted in Lan, *Guns & Rain*, 219.

nation state was welcomed, Nehanda's head and shoulders hovered above those of Robert Mugabe."[24]

It is one of the ironies of the new political system that the figurative symbol had to be reprinted from a British military archival photograph showing the spirit-medium of Ambuya Nehanda[25] before her execution. In a similar irony, the songs that may not have won the liberation war (at least, not all by themselves), but which certainly raised a number of expectations, were collected in a book and thus likewise elevated to a pedestal (the front cover of the collection fittingly shows the burning flame in Heroes' Acre, Harare); a wholly European – Old Western as well as (and even more so) Old Eastern – form of commemoration.

Whereas a new political upper/middle class was fast establishing itself, the economic expectations of the black popular majority were at best partly fulfilled,[26] and the quarrel over land-confiscations and land-ownership persists to this day. This quarrel accounts for much of the disappointment with the Mugabe government that is heard and felt throughout Zimbabwe,[27] and which facilitates revisionist political readings of the past.

The Old Eastern response

For a few years after independence, harvests at least were bounteous, poets published victory poetry[28] and occasionally victory novels (the Orwellian overtone is intended). Nationalist histomythographies[29] were written.

One of the victory novels is Garikai Mutasa's *The Contact*.[30] Its outlook of friends versus enemies is binary and oppositional, but not along lines of race – as in the fictional white fascist accounts of the "Old North/West" – rather, along lines prefabricated by the Soviet school of socialist realism. In keeping with Marxist and Maoist axioms (some of which are quoted as chapter-headings) the struggle is

---

[24] From the *Guardian* (10 October, 1983), quoted in Lan, *Guns & Rain*, 218.

[25] One popular source of knowledge about the spirit-medium of Ambuya (Grandmother) Nehanda – one of the leading forces in the Chimurenga of 1896, and an inspiration for songs about the topic – was apparently Solomon Mutswairo's novel *Feso*, originally published in the Shona language in 1957, and banned in Rhodesia as soon as the government realised its subversive impact (see Pongweni, *Songs that Won the Liberation War*, 90–91). Mutswairo is grouped with Lessing among "counter-Rhodesian" writers by John Reed, "The Emergence of English Writing in Zimbabwe," in *European-Language Writing in Sub-Saharan Africa*, ed. Albert S. Gérard (Budapest: Akademiai Iado, 1986): 256.

[26] Cf Wigglesworth, who realised that the black population "was suffering extreme hardship and misery [...] Certainly they would demand more equality of opportunity and an immediate improvement in their standard of living from whoever formed the government" (*Perhaps Tomorrow*, 201).

[27] See Doris Lessing, *African Laughter: Four Visits to Zimbabwe* (New York: Viking, 1992), in which the author describes the successive stages in Mr Mugabe, from naive belief and political rhetoric to disillusionment and disappointment.

[28] G.R.Brown, "Recent Zimbabwean Poetry," *Zambezia* 10 (1982): 65.

[29] A. Chigwedere, *From Mutapa to Rhodes* (Harare 1980). It should be noted, though, that some white novels about the war were published and republished until 1980, and also that critical texts (critical of the war as well as of ZANU and the guerrillas) like Michael Raeburn's *Black Fire!* could be published. *Black Fire!*, originally printed in England in 1978 (London: Julian Friedmann), contains, for example, discussions with a ZANLA deserter encountered in London. Michael Raeburn, *Black Fire!: Accounts of the Guerrilla War in Zimbabwe* (Gwelo: Mambo, 1981).

[30] Garikai Mutasa, *The Contact* (Gweru, 1985).

depicted as one of class, even though the race-aspect comes in with the motif of higher class aspirations/respect:

> it was because of him [a mixed-blood guerrilla, W.H.] the peasants in the area realised that the Chimurenga was not a war against people of an opposite colour, but a war against the wider injustice and oppression caused by what the guerrillas explained as capitalism and imperialism. Whenever Lee talked to the people he got the greatest span of concentration from them. This [...] actually reflected the colonised mentalities of his listeners who still regarded those with white blood as superior to themselves. Observing this, Bruce Lee realised that the political education of the masses was going to be a harder task than he had anticipated.[31]

As a result of this striving for political correctness, the characters remain rather lifeless and typecast (even if they bear somewhat unexpected names like Bruce Lee). The pace is fast and the plot packed with action, but the dialogue is stilted, sounding at times as if it were copied from a handbook for agitators. There is also a tendency in the book to romanticise the liberation from imperialist rule. Preben Kaarsholm has even tried to identify in the book a "yearning for a pre-colonial pastoral [...] strangely reminiscent of the romantic anti-capitalism [...] and the quest for a 'natural' alternative which pervade Rhodesian mythologies."[32]

Mutasa never indulges a complete one-sidedness. One of the guerrillas was a petty criminal before the war, and since he does not, like his comrades, read Mao's red book, he returns to thievery afterwards. On the other hand, the white Rhodesian district officer Turnbull is described as insightful and likeable. His insights are furthered by a direct confrontation with the leading guerrilla, who lectures him on liberty of the masses, democratic rights, etc:

> He looked Turnbull straight in the eyes, "You are going to lose. I think you know this. So what keeps you going?" Turnbull privately acknowledged that he was talking to an equal. "I know that we are not going to win the war," he spoke truthfully, "The regions under your influence are numerous." [...] Gadzirai poured some tea into a cup which Hondoinopisa had just brought in, passed this to Turnbull, and then poured himself a cup as well.[33]

Contrived and slightly ridiculous as this teatime conversation may seem, it is in keeping with the Mugabe government's official policy of reconciliation, and indicates the author's willingness to comply with this policy. District Commissioner Turnbull subsequently becomes instrumental in the Lancaster House talks and buys a farm in Zimbabwe after the ceasefire. He is, and this is unusual in black fiction from Zimbabwe,[34] a viewpoint character, and so are several other white soldiers, including several mercenaries from the USA, Israel, and Great Britain.[35] Of these, the American is allowed to escape after he has acknowledged that the guerrillas are

---

31 Mutasa, *The Contact*, 13.

32 Preben Kaarsholm, "From Decadence to Authenticity and Authenticity and Beyond: Fantasies and Mythologies of War in Rhodesia and Zimbabwe, 1965–1985," in *Cultural Struggle and Development in Southern Africa*, ed. Kaarsholm (London: Heinemann Educational, 1991): 57.

33 Kaarsholm, "From Decadence to Authenticity," 58–59.

34 Colin Style, "The White Man in Black Zimbabwean Literature," *ARIEL: A Review of International English Literature* 16 (1985): 55.

35 See Peter McLaughlin, "The Thin White Line: Rhodesia's Armed Forces Since the Second World War," *Zambezia* 6 (1978): 178.

equal to the Vietcong he encountered in Southeast Asia,[36] whereas the British "Colonel,"[37] is captured and flogged to death by villagers.[38] The same treatment is administered to a group of Rhodesian soldiers, apparently all blacks,[39] under the command of a particularly cruel but also black (sergeant-) major: the author actually seems to fall for the very racist notions he otherwise condemns when pointing out that the NCO is "black as a starless night."[40]

The occasional proximity to the Rhodesian novels which speaks from this passage may have been unavoidable in a novel so closely modelled on the tradition of socialist realism. In *The Contact*, both sides, friend and foe, come in the form of clearly identifiable opposites, with clear motives and behaviour. The guerrillas are unquestionably heroes acting heroically; their women are pure and remain so, to the point that they cannot physically be raped by the enemy;[41] renegades of their class receive what is due to them; yet the repentant class-enemy can become a useful member of society. Except for one, as I noted before, all members of the guerrilla outfit rise to good positions in the military and in the administration after the war. They are model figures in a role-playing game, the rules of which were set down in an imported political ideology.

It is difficult to decide whether Mutasa was aware of the ultimate irony incorporated in the ending. The communist-trained guerrilla commander is last seen working for, of all things, a multinational corporation, while the only one who actually acquires a land-base is the white neo-Zimbabwean, Turnbull.[42] One could indeed be tempted to see this as an ironic commentary on the postwar period and its problems, if only the rest of the novel were not so obviously in conformity with socialist standards. *The Contact* is one of the more readable examples of a group of novels which naively celebrate the war effort, the party, its communist basis, and the new society. Books like *The Contact* and, for example, Edmund Chipamaunga's *A Fighter for Freedom* (1983) led Preben Kaarsholm to assume that "the new moral needs of independence" were adequately represented by the "discourse of official celebrations, in novels and poetry published after independence."[43] From a Nineties perspective, this assumption has taken on a degree of cynicism. Furthermore – and fortunately – Zimbabwean literature did not simply shift from one cultural monomyth to another.

---

[36] Mutasa, *The Contact*, 97.

[37] Naturally, Mutasa refers to the Congo conflict of 1960–63, and the role which white mercenaries played there (cf Mike Hoare, *Congo Mercenary* [London: Robert Hale, 1967]), rather than to the more recent Nigerian conflict, in which white mercenaries fought mostly on the side of the Biafrans trying to gain independence.

[38] Mutasa, *The Contact*, 101. It does not seem to occur to the author that this murder of prisoners could in retrospect justify retaliatory attacks on villages by the Security Forces.

[39] Mutasa, *The Contact*, 51–52.

[40] Mutasa calls him a "Major" (39); probably a mistake since Africans could not rise to this level in the Rhodesian forces; cf McLaughlin, "Victims as Defenders," 267.

[41] Mutasa, *The Contact*, 49.

[42] Mutasa, *The Contact*, 125.

[43] Kaarsholm, "From Decadence to Authenticity," 35.

The New Southern response (I)

All of the above responses drew for their ideological background on political myths and metaphors of the prewar period to impose some sense of order on a war that ended on a note of unexpected irony, with more ironies to develop in the decade after the ceasefire.

Shimmer Chinodya's *Harvest of Thorns*[44] presents an individual and largely non-ideological review of society in the Fifties and Sixties, exploring "the psychological reactions and development of a young man, still a boy really, who suddenly found himself in the situation of war."[45] Chinodya mocks the pretentiousness of social upstarts like the protagonist's father, and criticises the brutalities of war – a criticism directed at both sides. Rhodesian troops and freedom fighters for the most part of the novel still occupy extreme opposite positions, but the ground between them has turned into a trajectory for guesswork, misinterpretations, and possible mistakes. There is never the kind of terminal vocabulary[46] that goes with being ideologically righteous. The main protagonist, Benjamin Tichofa aka Pasi NemaSellout, is a reluctant non-hero, his role signified by his bilingual *nom de guerre*, and he comes across as someone who does what seems the most reasonable and right thing to do, but who finds out in the process that nobody is always right. This, of course, is a typical modernist dilemma, and the gradual switch from omniscient narration to personal-viewpoint narrative reflects a modernist outlook.[47]

In the context of this paper, one scene near the end of the novel is of particular importance. Pasi NemaSellout comes face to face with a dying Rhodesian soldier he has shot. The wounded man has fled into a mission church.

> Under his beret, his close-cropped hair was dyed black. He was a young man and underneath the soot or dye or whatever he had applied to his skin he couldn't have been older than nineteen or twenty. Under the dye his hands were slim and the fingers were long and light like a young man's hands. [...]"So you are a Selous Scout," Pasi said in English, standing astride over the man. "Won't you finish me off?" the man pleaded. Some shudder seized him and he moaned. "So stupid..." he gasped, "so stupid to die..." [...] He [Pasi NemaSellout] took one last long look at the man's face, pulled the cloth off the pulpit and covered as much of the body as he could, then stepped back slowly.[48]

The above scene is reminiscent of the famous one in Remarque's *All Quiet on the Western Front* in which Paul Bäumer, a bewildered youth like the guerrilla here,

---

[44] Shimmer Chinodya, *Harvest of Thorns* (Harare: Baobab, 1989). A detailed interpretation of this novel is found in Veit–Wild, *Teachers*, 321ff.

[45] Veit–Wild, *Teachers*, 321.

[46] I borrow this term from Gerald Vizenor, who used it during his lectures at the 3rd Stuttgart Seminar in Cultural Studies, 3 August 1993.

[47] *Harvest of Thorns* has been translated into several languages, including German, and of the books mentioned in this paper it is probably the most widely read, its reception being almost unanimously positive. Ironically, the only criticism directed against the book maintained that the author hadn't painted his protagonist's disappointment bleakly enough. Of the books about the Zimbabwean War I have read, this is the one that is artistically most convincing – which may of course have to do with my Western reading-habits; but then, *Harvest of Thorns* is very successful in Zimbabwe and has recently been assigned for classroom reading in grade school (Shimmer Chinodya, in a letter to the author, 3 May, 1993).

[48] Chinodya, *Harvest of Thorns*, 254–55.

watches a French soldier he has injured die. Confronted with an individual enemy for the first time, the "Other" loses his inimical qualities. Chinodya's is a modified version, adapted for Zimbabwean conditions.

Almost like a parody of the African, the white settler has turned himself into a black man, and the guerrilla and the Selous Scout now face each other in a grotesque inverted re-enactment of a minstrel-show.[49] There seems to be a kind of mutual recognition which places them simultaneously on opposite sides as enemies, and on the same side as young men. Behind their ironic similitude in age, colour and language lies a possible understanding, a translatability of discourses prevented by circumstances. Leaving the ending open and adding no commentary, Chinodya does not close off the scene like Remarque, whose Bäumer states flatly that "war is war, anyway."[50] If there is a commentary in *Harvest of Thorns*, it is this one: "There were so many ironies in this war."[51]

One irony of Chinodya's book itself is that, as in most Zimbabwean novels by black authors, whites do not feature prominently, usually making only cameo appearances before the final encounter-scene. It is this scene, however, which links Chinodya's novel with – of all things – white South African "grensliteratuur":

> the "enemy" is not only found to have a "human face," as in conventional anti-war novels. In the *grensroman* there is a sudden, shocking recognition that he is a fellow South African. As Elsa Joubert points out, for many young white conscripts their first encounter with black fellow South Africans on an equal footing occurs ironically when they confront each other with guns...[52]

The New Southern response (II)

Whereas the enemy changes colour only symbolically in Chinodya's novel, he changes not only colour but also positions in Bruce Moore–King's *White Man Black War*.[53] The blacks in this text by a white Rhodesian and former sergeant are separated from most of the other white soldiers, employers, and civilian home-

---

[49] Most Selous Scouts were blacks (McLaughlin, "Victims as Defenders," 266).

[50] Erich Maria Remarque, *Im Westen Nichts Neues* (1929; Cologne: Kiepenheuer & Witsch, 1974): 177.

[51] Chinodya, *Harvest of Thorns*, 271.

[52] H.E. Koornhof, "Works of Friction: Current South African War Literature," in *War and Society: The Militarization of South Africa*, ed. Jacklyn Cock & Laurie Nathan (Cape Town: David Philip, 1989): 279. The same statement is made by Christopher S. Wren, "Apartheid's Children: Afrikaner Writers Today," *New York Times Book Review* (11 October, 1992): 30.

[53] Bruce Moore–King, *White Man Black War* (Harare: Baobab, 1988). The book, the first by a white Rhodesian to overtly attack and denounce the old system, received considerable attention: Jane Perlez, "Sergeant's War Story is Shame of the Whites," *New York Times* (13 January, 1989) A7/A4; T.O. McLoughlin, "White Man, Black War," *Zambezia* 15 (1988): 207–208; Andrew Meldrum, "White Man, Black War," *Africa Report* 34.4 (1989): 66–67. A number of publications appeared in the early Eighties in which white Zimbabweans, some of them ex-servicemen, recorded their experiences during the war; see, for example, the poems in *None but Ourselves*, ed. Julie Frederickse (Harare: Zimbabwean Publishing House, 1983; Moore–King quotes from several of the texts in this volume); also Peter Badcock, *Shadows of War*, a collection of drawings of security force soldiers, accompanied by poems, for which see: R.S.R.[oberts], "Patriotism or Profit: Nostalgic Moments or Negotiable Asset?," *Zambezia* 11 (1983): 144–45. Flora Veit–Wild has drawn my attention to the fact that Tim McLoughlin also published a novel, *Karima*, in around 1983.

owners through a cordon of racist stereotypes and an assumed untranslatability of discourses.[54] Africans are, however, never the enemy. The enemy are at first the intangible guerrillas, but increasingly the enemy is identified as the face in the mirror. The language of the book is sparse, economical, and concentrated, the situations described and the tone sometimes reminiscent of tales from the Vietnam war. The Vietnam parallel is also underscored by a certain narcissistic insistence on having been victimised, familiar from the novels of Larry Heinemann, Tim O'Brien and others.

> The horror was that I felt nothing for that boy, his mother, or her grief. The horror was that in order to "reserve the standards," "maintain civilised rule," "stop the evils of communism," in order to do all this, I had to lose my humanity. Totally.[55]

On the other hand, no attempt is made to deny the Rhodesian soldier's role as victimiser, but the blame for this is laid at the door of the "Elders." Throughout the book the "Elders" of the "White tribe" of Zimbabwe, and their "High Priest," the former premier Ian Smith, are pilloried for their subversive, reactionary activities and the fascist mythologies they continue to spread. At such points, the novel turns into a pamphlet, and this mixture of tense prose and counter-Rhodesian rhetoric makes for somewhat uneven reading. The message, however is clear: for one, the personal revision of the horrors of war is deeply moralist, and secondly, reconciliation is seen as a chance, and the author is going to grasp it. Subsequently, it seems quite logical that he should at one point select a passage from another of Remarque's works – *The Road Back* – to speak for him.

> One part of my life was given to the service of destruction. It belonged to hate, to enmity, to killing. But life remained in me. And that in itself is enough, of itself almost a purpose and a way. [...] It is there I mean to look for my place. Then the dead will be silenced...[56]

Outlook

One of the main problems of contemporary Zimbabwean literature on the whole and war fiction in particular is the continuing colonialism of the mind. Literary syn-cretists like the late Dambudzo Marechera[57] are isolated figures, but even though all of the white fascist novels mentioned above are now out of print in Zimbabwe, Wilbur Smith, whose novel *The Sunbird* Chennells calls "one of the most perverse books ever written about Rhodesia,"[58] still ranks among the most popular authors according to a survey conducted among Zimbabwean readers by Flora Veit–Wild. English is still the number-one language.[59] The new black upper class established

---

[54] Moore–King, *White Man Black War*, 6.

[55] Moore–King, *White Man Black War*, 64.

[56] Moore–King, *White Man Black War*, 133. The quotation is from Erich Maria Remarque, *The Road Back*, tr. A.W. Wheen (London: Mayflower, 1979): 207.

[57] Flora Veit–Wild, "Forms of Syncretism in Southern Africa," in the present volume.

[58] Chennells, "The Treatment of the Rhodesian War," 187. Veit–Wild concedes that he is "a white Rhodesian writer of mostly adventure stories" (Veit–Wild, *Teachers*, 354).

[59] Cynthia Mparutsa, Juliet Thondhlana & N. Crawhall, "An Investigation into Language Attitudes of Secondary-School Students in Zimbabwe," *Zambezia* 17 (1990): 88–89.

itself in a lifestyle that was traditionally Zimbabwean in theory only.[60] The continuity of the colonial predicament is also visible in novels like I.V. Mazorodze's *Silent Journey From the East*[61] – another novel about the war, written by a former guerrilla, whose stilted and preposterous English constantly undercuts the intentions of the text. It can be felt in essentially social romantic (re-)visions of histories like Chenjerai Hove's popular novel *Bones*.[62] It is visible in political statements such as the following by George Kahari: "Westernisation diminishes traditions, but these traditions must be abandoned if the people are to continue to survive."[63] The only remaining appeal of simplistic eulogies of the kind to be found in school primers[64] as well as in books like the ones by Chipamaunga or Mutasa is their legibility for unskilled readers of English. This category still encompasses many of the black readers in Zimbabwe today.

By contrast, the post-colonial condition insists on the validity and continuity of traditions, even though they may alter their form, free-floating in time and space. One of the most important texts of contemporary Native American literature is Leslie Silko's novel *Ceremony*,[65] in which a Pueblo Indian veteran of World War II is healed through the inventive traditionalist modes of a Navaho medicine person. There is no reason why the traditional languages, customs, and beliefs of the people of Zimbabwe should not be part of the culture of reconciliation. Chinodya already uses a lot of untranslated Shona in *Harvest of Thorns*, insisting on its comprehensibility for the reader, and even some of the traditional spirit-mediums have taken stock of the new situation:

> To all questions about why what was forbidden is now permitted, the mediums reply that their *mhondoro* were consulted and they approve. The war is over. The hostility between black and white is at an end. It is all one Zimbabwe now. The mediums feel that under their control, the beneficial aspects of white society should now be absorbed.[66]

Chinodya and Moore–King represent the first generation of post-colonial writing from Zimbabwe, and there are signs that they (at least in parts) transcend the categories of "colonial" or "anti-colonial," and move on to what Helen Tiffin and,

---

[60] Doris Lessing, "Die fetten Katzen sahnen ab," interview with Doris Lessing on the decline of Africa, *Der Spiegel* 21 (1993): 152.

[61] Isheunesu V. Mazorodze, *Silent Journey From the East* (Harare: Zimbabwe Publishing House, 1989).

[62] Chenjerai Hove, *Bones* (Harare: Baobab, 1988); see Flora Veit–Wild, "'Dances with Bones': Hove's Romanticized Africa," *Research in African Literatures* 24 (1993): 5–12. Hove's program as designed in his Acceptance Speech for the prestigious Noma Award is reminiscent of Achebe's imagining the author as a teacher. However, his outlook on language is still self-consciously counter-colonial when he speaks of "cleansing the colonial languages to the extent of representing them to our former colonisers as languages which can also be used to depict human dignity" (cited in Veit–Wild, "'Dances with Bones'," 6).

[63] George P. Kahari, "New Literatures in Zimbabwe," in *Imagination and the Creative Impulse in the New Literatures in English*, ed. M.–T. Bindella and G.V. Davis (Cross/Cultures 9; Amsterdam/Atlanta GA: Rodopi, 1993): 22.

[64] Cf the *Dandaro Reader 2: The Chimurenga War* (Gwelo, nd).

[65] Leslie Silko, *Ceremony* (New York: Viking, 1977).

[66] Lan, *Guns & Rain*, 214.

following her, Frank Schulze–Engler, have called "'dis-identification' which seeks to transform and deconstruct the dominant hegemonic discourse."[67]

WORKS CITED

ASHCROFT, Bill, Gareth GRIFFITHS & Helen TIFFIN, *The Empire Writes Back: Theory and Practice in Post-Colonial Literatures* (London: Routledge, 1989).

BROWN, G.R. "Recent Zimbabwean Poetry," *Zambezia* 10 (1982): 63–76.

CARLETON, P.D. "The Indian Captivity," *American Literature* 15 (1943): 169–80.

CARNEY, Daniel. *The Whispering Death* (London: Corgi, 1980).

CHENNELLS, A.J. "Settler Myths and the Southern Rhodesian Novel," unpublished doctoral dissertation (1982).

——. "The Treatment of the Rhodesian War in Recent Rhodesian Novels," *Zambezia* 5 (1977): 177–202.

CHIGWEDERE, A. *From Mutapa to Rhodes* (Harare, 1980).

CHINODYA, Shimmer. *Harvest of Thorns* (Harare: Baobab, 1989).

Dandaro Reader 2: The Chimurenga War (Gwelo, nd).

DE WAAL, Victor. *The Politics of Reconciliation: Zimbabwe's First Decade* (Cape Town: David Philip/Trenton NJ: Africa World Press, 1990)

EARLY, Robert. *A Time of Madness* (Salisbury, 1977).

FREDERICKSE, Julie, ed. *None but Ourselves* (Harare: Zimbabwean Publishing House, 1983).

GRIFFITH, Paddy. "Small Wars and How They Grow in the Telling," *Small Wars and Insurgencies* 2 (1991): 216–31.

HOARE, Mike. *Congo Mercenary* (London: Robert Hale, 1967).

HOCHBRUCK, Wolfgang. *"I Have Spoken". Die Darstellung und ideologische Funktion indianischer Mündlichkeit in der nordamerikanischen Literatur* (ScriptOralia 32; Tübingen: Gunter Narr, 1991).

HOVE, Chenjerai. *Bones* (Harare: Baobab, 1988).

KAARSHOLM, Preben. "From Decadence to Authenticity and Authenticity and Beyond: Fantasies and Mythologies of War in Rhodesia and Zimbabwe, 1965–1985," in *Cultural Struggle and Development in Southern Africa*, ed. Kaarsholm (London: Heinemann Educational, 1991): 33–60.

KAHARI, George P. "New Literatures in Zimbabwe," in *Imagination and the Creative Impulse in the New Literatures in English*, ed. M.–T. Bindella and G.V. Davis (Cross/Cultures 9; Amsterdam/Atlanta GA: Rodopi, 1993): 13–23.

KOORNHOF, H.E. "Works of Friction: Current South African War Literature," in *War and Society: The Militarization of South Africa*, ed. Jacklyn Cock & Laurie Nathan (Cape Town: David Philip, 1989): 275–82.

KRIGER, Norma J. *Zimbabwe's Guerilla War. Peasant Voices* (African Studies 70; Cambridge/New York: Cambridge UP, 1992).

LAN, David. *Guns & Rain: Guerillas [sic] and Spirit Mediums in Zimbabwe* (Perspectives on Southern Africa 38; Berkeley/Los Angeles: U of California P, 1985).

LESSING, Doris. *African Laughter: Four Visits to Zimbabwe* (New York: Viking, 1992).

——. "Die fetten Katzen sahnen ab," interview with Doris Lessing on the decline of Africa, *Der Spiegel* 21 (1993): 152–54.

MAUGHAM–BROWN, David. "Myths on the March: The Kenyan and Zimbabwean Liberation Struggles in Colonial Fiction," *Journal of Southern African Studies* 9 (1982): 93–117.

---

[67] Frank Schulze–Engler, "Beyond Post-Colonialism: Multiple Identities in East African Literature," in *US/THEM: Translation, Transcription and Identity in Post-Colonial Literary Cultures*, ed. Gordon Collier (Cross/Cultures 6; Amsterdam/Atlanta GA: Rodopi, 1992): 321.

MAZORODZE, Isheunesu V. *Silent Journey From the East* (Harare: Zimbabwe Publishing House, 1989).

MCLAUGHLIN, Peter. "The Thin White Line: Rhodesia's Armed Forces Since the Second World War," *Zambezia* 6 (1978): 175–86.

———. "Victims as Defenders: African Troops in the Rhodesian Defence System 1890–1980," *Small Wars and Insurgencies* 2 (1991): 240–75.

MCLOUGHLIN, T.O. "*White Man, Black War*," *Zambezia* 15 (1988): 207–208.

MELDRUM, Andrew. "*White Man, Black War*," *Africa Report* 34.4 (1989): 66–67.

MOORE–KING, Bruce. *White Man, Black War* (Harare: Baobab, 1988).

MPARUTSA, Cynthia, Juliet THONDHLANA & N. CRAWHALL. "An Investigation into Language Attitudes of Secondary-School Students in Zimbabwe," *Zambezia* 17 (1990): 85–100.

MUTASA, Garikai. *The Contact* (Gweru, 1985).

PERLEZ, Jane. "Sergeant's War Story is Shame of the Whites," *New York Times* (13 January, 1989): A7/A4.

PONGWENI, Alec J.C., ed. *Songs that Won the Liberation War* (Harare: College Press, 1982).

RAEBURN, Michael. *Black Fire!: Accounts of the Guerrilla War in Zimbabwe* (London: Julian Friedmann, 1978; Gwelo: Mambo, 1981).

RAUBENHEIMER, George Harding. *Crossfire* (London: Hutchinson/Arrow, 1980).

REED, John. "The Emergence of English Writing in Zimbabwe," in *European-Language Writing in Sub-Saharan Africa*, ed. Albert S. Gérard (Budapest: Akademiai Iado, 1986): 251–62.

REMARQUE, Erich Maria. *Im Westen Nichts Neues* (1929; Cologne: Kiepenheuer & Witsch, 1974).

RIEMENSCHNEIDER, Dieter. "Short Fiction From Zimbabwe," *Research in African Literatures* 20 (1989): 401–11.

R.[OBERTS], R.S. "Patriotism or Profit: Nostalgic Moments or Negotiable Asset?," *Zambezia* 11 (1983): 143–47.

SCHULZE–ENGLER, Frank. "Beyond Post-Colonialism: Multiple Identities in East African Literature," in *US/THEM: Translation, Transcription and Identity in Post-Colonial Literary Cultures*, ed. Gordon Collier (Cross/Cultures 6; Amsterdam/Atlanta GA: Rodopi, 1992): 319–28.

SILKO, Leslie. *Ceremony* (New York: Viking, 1977).

STYLE, Colin. "The White Man in Black Zimbabwean Literature," *ARIEL: A Review of International English Literature* 16 (1985): 55–64.

SYLVESTER, Christine. *Zimbabwe: The Terrain of Contradictory Development* (Boulder CO/San Francisco CA: Westview, 1991).

VEIT–WILD, Flora. "'Dances with Bones': Hove's Romanticized Africa," *Research in African Literatures* 24 (1993): 5–12.

———. *Teachers, Preachers, Non–Believers* (Harare: Baobab, 1993).

WIGGLESWORTH, Michael (Tom). *Perhaps Tomorrow* (Salisbury: Galaxie, [1979?]).

WREN, Christopher S. "Apartheid's Children: Afrikaner Writers Today," *New York Times Book Review* (11 October, 1992): 1, 29–31.

ZHUWARARA, Rino. *The Growth of Zimbabwean Fiction in English 1950-1980* (Fredericton, New Brunswick: Acadiensis, 1984).

❦ ❖ ❦

ARMANDO E. JANNETTA

Dialogic Constructions of the Self
in Métis Life-Histories

> There are a few thousand of us, scattered over the prairies. Our fathers were
> French, our mothers were Indian. We thought we were both, but in fact we are
> neither, and our lives were crunched in the gap between.
> (Gabriel Dumont in George Woodcock's play *Gabriel Dumont and the
> Northwest Rebellion*, 1976)

T HE MÉTIS,[1] CANADA'S "FORGOTTEN PEOPLE," appear to be a unique
instance of the feasible fusion or, more appropriately, *métissage*, of different
cultures. In the early nineteenth century the Métis emerged in Western
Canada as a distinctive (semi-)nomadic people stemming from the intermarriage of
French *voyageurs* and *coureurs de bois*, as well as English and Scottish explorers and
fur traders, with Cree or Ojibway women. "Multilingual and bi-cultural, they
formed an indispensable buffer race"[2] between Indians and whites. Owing to the
multi-faceted ethnic identification of Métism, estimations of the Métis population in
Canada, which was only granted aboriginal status in the Constitution of 1982, vary
between 100,000 and some 700,000 today. Some pockets remain across the
international boundary in the United States.

The forgotten people

The "memoirs" of Métis trappers and traders are among the first written sources to
depict ways in which the Métis perceive themselves, the "white man," and their
Native relatives, the Indians and the Inuit. They must be perceived as "traces" (a re-
current word in these texts) in the construction of a Métis Self in relation to its
Other(s). Thus, questions of difference, mediation and dialogicity are at the centre of
these texts, which grow out of oral performance. As part of a considerable indigenous contribution to the Canadian literature of the western plains which has been
(and is still) wholly neglected, these "memoirs" belong to the genre of *as-told-to life-
history*.[3] Compared with other texts, life-histories as documents of mediation and

---

[1] Donald Purich argues that the word "Métis" had become an English word which embraced mixed race
persons of either French or English ancestry, and therefore chooses to spell it, in his study, without an acute
accent (*The Metis* [Canadian Issues series; Toronto: James Lorimer, 1988]: 5).

[2] See Wallace Stegner, *Wolf Willow: A History, a Story and a Memory of the Last Plains Frontier* (New York:
Viking, 1955): 58–61.

[3] For a concise study of the historical and conceptual development of the life-history method in
anthropology see Lewis L. Langness & Gelya Frank, *Lives: An Anthropological Approach to Biography* (Novato
CA: Chandlers & Sharp, 1988).

cultural hybridity, created in collaboration with and filtered through an Other's consciousness (the anthropologist's, for example) represent an "extra degree of dialogicity"[4] and at times a thinly camouflaged "double autobiography" of both interrogator and interrogatee.[5] In addition to the external dialogue between two (or more) people, life-histories incorporate also an internal historicising dialogue between an "earlier" and a "later" self. In Jurij M. Lotman's words, life-histories are a combination of a "spatial communication act" and a "temporal communication act."[6]

The existing life-histories represent an excellent cross-section of different kinds of Métis origins and definitions. Norbert Walsh (b.1845), subject of *The Last Buffalo Hunter*, is a prominent Red River trader and buffalo hunter in Saskatchewan; *Vanishing Spaces* is the account of Louis Goulet (1859–1936), a French-speaking Métis of Manitoba, of his "vagabond life" and its subsequent loss.[7] The "memoirs" of George William Sanderson (1846–1936) depict the life of an English-speaking Métis of mixed Scots, Orkney, French and Indian ancestry, who was born on the Hudson Bay, neighbouring onto Inuit territory.[8] *Ted Trindell* is the memoir of a Métis–Dene from the Northern Territories.[9] Jock Carpenter has written an account of the life of a Métis woman's grandmother, Marie Rose Smith (1861–1960), researched from her diaries, family letters and other records.[10] The importance of these life-histories lies, on the one hand, in their rejection of the stereotypical uniformity of the Native Other and in their success restoration of the language-system from its apparently "naive absence of conflict"[11] (thereby acknowledging the presence of an "alien" linguistic consciousness within the speaker's discourse), and, on the other, in their constitution of a peripatetic tradition in Métis literature. In contrast to the immobile, sedentary white Other, the travel-trope or the (semi-) nomadic life-style of the Métis is a major factor in the constitution of difference and some kind of ethnic identity. This identity, however, in its dialogic orientation,

---

[4] Owing to its production, the as-told-to life-history is, by its very definition, of a dialogic nature: "In it, the reader is placed inside the dialogue between two voices or perspectives, between the subject (informant) and the interviewer (anthropologist); this is, in the simplest terms, what we refer to as the extra degree of dialogicity that distinguishes the life-history (auto-)biography from the other two – the 'purer' – forms of 'biography'"; Hartwig Isernhagen, "Anthropological Narrative and the Structure of North American Indian (Auto-)Biography," in *The Structure of Texts* (SPELL: Swiss Papers in English Language and Literature 3, ed. Udo Fries; Tübingen: Gunter Narr, 1987): 222.

[5] Lewis L. Langness & Gelya Frank, *Lives: An Anthropological Approach to Biography* (1981; Novato CA: Chandler & Sharp, 1988): 99.

[6] Jurij M. Lotman, *Die Struktur literarischer Texte*, tr. Rolf–Dietrich Keil. Munich: (1972; UTB 103; Wilhelm Fink, 1989): 22.

[7] Mary Weekes, *The Last Buffalo Hunter: As told to her by Norbert Welsh* (1939; Toronto: Macmillan, 1945); Guillaume Charette & Louis Goulet, *Vanishing Spaces: Memoirs of Louis Goulet (Memoirs of a Prairie Métis)*, ed. Elizabeth Magnet, tr. Ray Ellenwood (1976; Winnipeg, Manitoba: Editions Bois-Brûlés, 1980).

[8] See Irene M. Spry, "The Ethnic Voice: The 'Memoirs' of George William Sanderson 1846–1936," *Canadian Ethnic Studies* 17.2 (1985): 115–34.

[9] *Ted Trindell: Métis Witness to the North*, ed. Jean Morriset & Rose–Marie Pelletier (1986; Vancouver: Tillacum Library, 1987).

[10] Jock Carpenter, *Fifty Dollar Bride: Marie Rose Smith; A Chronicle of Métis Life in the Nineteenth Century* (Sidney, B.C.: Gray, 1977).

[11] Mikhail Bakhtin, *The Dialogic Imagination: Four Essays by Mikhail Bakhtin*, ed. Michael Holquist, tr. Caryl Emerson & Michael Holquist (Austin: U of Texas P, 1981): 368.

resists binary closure. Despite occasional tendencies towards monologic discourse, it shifts constantly, contaminated with "traces" of the Other's voice. Shaped by hidden dialogue, Métis memoirs reveal, apart from occasional instances of sameness between Métis and Indians (usually in relation to the perception of nature and cultural change and in opposition to the modernisation implemented by the white Other), a multitude of differences and distinctions between Métis and Indians. Ted Trindell's life-history represents such a text exemplifying the dialogic construction of the Self.

The Shakespeare of the Slavey: Ted Trindell

Ted Trindell: Métis Witness to the North is the memoir of a well-known Métis–Dene who spent thirty-five years as a trapper in the bush of the Liard River country, Northern Territories, and who, when fur-prices dropped in the Fifties, lived for another thirty years in town as a Community Health worker, Métis Association field-worker, and tourist guide. Trindell died in 1981. As the "Shakespeare of the Slavey," he was widely known as a story-teller and Native philosopher. Fluent also in Chippewayan, English and French, Trindell was Pierre Elliott Trudeau's interpreter to his people, whereas the Canadian Broadcasting Corporation (CBC) used him to "represent a Dene image."[12] Terry Cousineau even wrote a ballad about him. Trindell's memoirs were compiled and edited from tapes and correspondence by Jean Morisset, a French-Canadian anthropologist and professor of geography at the Université du Quebec, and Rose–Marie Pelletier, his wife, a political scientist.[13]

In Morisset's eyes, Trindell "spoke the enduring languages of that geography of the mind, which both the education system and the government systems have been fighting against so violently since they have moved up to the North country" (21). His mind – "so subtle, so strong, so seducing, so damn bright and so contradictory," not always reliable, "ambiguous," "shrewd," "fighting, double-edged" (20) – expresses the ambivalent, nomadic Métis universe and the polyphony of voices which often find expression within a single utterance. Code-switching between different languages is a distinctive feature in Goulet's life-history. French or Indian expressions are usually put in italics. In *Ted Trindell*, code-switching/mixing and grammatical idiosyncrasies become the dominant mode and mirror a truly hybrid identity as well as unresolved linguistic tensions and cultural conflict. Repeatedly, there were attempts by various groups of the Canadian north to reclaim him as a cultural icon. He became the official image of the genuine northern Métis. Even the Prince of Wales Museum in Yellowknife has used Ted Trindell as the Métis figure for its display on Northern culture. Code-switching as a textual strategy "explore[s]

---

12 *Ted Trindell*, ed. Morisset & Pelletier, 28. Further page references are in the text.
13 Morisset is also the author of *Les chiens s'entre-dévorent: Indiens, blancs et metis dans le Grand Nord canadien* (Montreal: Nouvelle Optique, 1977), a study of the colonial situation in the North in the context of the 1973–74 pipeline projects.

a borderland between dominating and dominated culture."[14] In Trindell's life-history non-English languages usually receive no additional typographical weight, but are incorporated on equal terms. For example, Trindell opens the chapter on Native and Christian beliefs, and how he came to believe in both, in this way:

> Moi, quand j'étais jeune ma grand-mère connaissait pas le Great Spirit. She didn't know what that was. Rien q'des superstitions, eh? Croyance occulte, animal or whatever. Witchcraft – it's all over the world – les nègres, Africa, Mexico. (48)

Often Trindell likes to start, finish or interrupt a sentence in French or English: "J'ai jamais réussi à avoir my diploma! But I think I can do some carpenter work for myself, eh!" (120). Sometimes the second part of the sentence repeats or translates the first part into the other language: "And if you got into drifts, you had to break trail and then rebreak trail. Quais on dit faire les chemins – making the road" (97). Trindell's hybrid language is both English and French, and, at the same time, neither of them. His peripatetic voice is always on the threshold, between the two. It is double-voiced:

> The language is not entirely French and it is not English. What else could it be? Obviously it is Dene. This book speaks in English but it is not English that speaks through it. There are two languages, Dene and Canadien. C'est le sujet de ce livre. It's so simple.[15]

The authoritative French language Trindell had learnt in school, "Grey Nun's French" or "Missionary French," has been appropriated, subverted, adjusted and stripped of its background of Catholic self-righteousness and condescension and thereafter transformed into a Dene language along with English. This "patois Métis" represents a subversion of the normalising francophone purism and is a critique of the (ab)use the French made of the Métis in their political dealings with English Canada. Nevertheless, it seems to be used reluctantly, "probably because it was "la langue des vaincus," whereas English was the language of the victor. It is considered a sub-language, not official" (23). Out of a sense of survival, taking his imagery as usual from nature and his nomadic life-style as a hunter, Trindell proposes a position of mimicry (note the double-voiced punning) and a sense of humour for Native people: "And as I say, you can learn the ways of different animals, how they act, how to outwit them in order to make a living out of it" (47) or to "counteract everything" by "play[ing] the game" (139); "But otherwise there's nothing you can do, only smile" (135). To him, "dressing up" (ie, playing up) to the image of the archetypal Indian by people who have lost their traditions is "just camouflage," because for Trindell true Indians like his ancestors "never showed off, or sang, 'I'm an Indian'" (41). Trindell's linguistic liminality corresponds to his racial liminality. He is both Métis (his father was a French-speaking Scot with Indian blood) and Dene (his mother was a Slavey Indian). Officially, however, Trindell is a non-Treaty Indian and, as such, treated as a white man without any of

---

14 Wolfgang Klooss, "Multiculturalism, Regionalism and the Search for a Poetics of Disparity in Contemporary Canadian Writing," in *Anglistentag 1991 Düsseldorf*, ed. Wilhelm G. Busse (Tübingen: Max Niemeyer, 1992): 356.

15 See Morisset's introduction to *Ted Trindell*, ed. Morisset & Pelletier, 22.

the privileges of the "citizens plus" Treaty Indians. This much-resented fact is due to the impossibility of his being able to "trace" (40) his ancestry when the 1921 Treaty was signed. The recognition of the Métis as a distinct Native people of Canada in 1982 came too late for him:

> We are stuck in between. Renegades. You know Louis Riel. [...] So we're left in between. But we paid our way. I paid my way, so I don't really care.
>
> Besides, when you're treaty, well, you're not a man with any pride at all. The white man thinks that treaty Indians are just living off tax money, and all that. [...] Sure, when it comes down to paying tax, we are white men, but publicly we are still Indians. We are not ashamed of it. We're proud of what we are. (73)

In this quotation, Trindell's mixed-blood voice sounds with the voices of Métis, Indian and white people alike. According to people who knew him, Trindell was "a man of many cultures," a man with "many personalities amongst which he did not seem to be able to make a definite choice" (25). Ted Trindell's multi-vocal discourse, with its striking emphasis on similes, tends, on the one hand, towards a monologism based on binary oppositions ("that awful big gap," as he calls it, 137) – past versus present, white versus Native epistemes, civilisation versus "primitive" life (33), Native fur-trapping versus white environmentalism, north versus south, victim versus victimiser – but simultaneously he continues to affirm the relativity of cultural values and the fundamental sameness of human existence, although the procedures within cultures might be different:

> I go out in the bush and shoot a moose, three or four hundred pounds, and money-wise, I'm equal to you: you got the cash, and I got the meat.
>
> So you work like an Indian. You are only working for your living. The white man's way, you get the money, you accumulate the money, but you spend it buying grub. It's the same thing, only different ways. That's all. (104)

Eventually, expecting the end of his life, all differences and identity-constituting borders collapse into notions of essential sameness. In his confessional, "salvationist," voice, Trindell maintains that "we're all the same. We see, we smell, we hear, we like, we dislike" (162).

In conclusion, the "memoirs" of the Métis trappers and *voyageurs*, represented here by Ted Trindell's life-history, are collective or collaborative texts of a highly ambivalent nature. In the light of the above inquiry, Bakhtin's theory of the "multiaccentuality" of discourse and his attack on the notion of a separable self, free of external influences, lends itself expansion from the novelistic to the (auto-) biographical genre and becomes especially illuminating for the interpretation of texts written by peoples of mixed ancestry. Despite, at times, pronounced tendencies towards racial stereotyping and a "salvationist" monologism or point of view as a means of border-maintenance, simplistic definitions of identity, which would consistently exclude Otherness, are resisted and diversity within one's own voice (being, after all, racially and culturally both "them" and "us") acknowledged. Within a single sentence the disparate voices of both oppressor and oppressed, coloniser and colonised may be incorporated, with contrary meaning being resisted and inscribed simultaneously. A double consciousness, shifting loyalities, ambivalent socialisation-patterns, "novelistic" qualities and an ironic vision are the ontological result of the conflicting forces behind the experience of Métis ethnic liminality. In agreement with the finding that notions of "them" and "us" belong to a complex continuum, attempts at simplistic cultural mediation or transcendence which would collapse differences between competing voices and argue for a fundamental sameness (a position Ted Trindell seems to adhere to in his later stage of spiritual re-awakening) are just as much rejected by the double-voiced discourse as models of the self that are uniquely based on an exclusion of all other voices. The Métis Self is clearly an ideological construct, a location of uncertainty and shifting alliances in race-relationships. In Derrida's terminology, the dialogic discourse of Métis trappers and traders "opposes itself, passes into its other(s)"; it "cannot be assigned a fixed spot in the play of differences."[16]

WORKS CITED

BAKHTIN, Mikhail. *The Dialogic Imagination: Four Essays by Mikhail Bakhtin*, ed. Michael Holquist, tr. Caryl Emerson & Michael Holquist (Austin: U of Texas P, 1981).
——— *Rabelais and His World*, tr. Helene Iswolsky (1965; Bloomington: Indiana UP, 1984).
CARPENTER, Jock. *Fifty Dollar Bride: Marie Rose Smith; A Chronicle of Métis Life in the Nineteenth Century* (Sidney, B.C.: Gray, 1977).
CHARETTE, Guillaume & Louis GOULET. *Vanishing Spaces: Memoirs of Louis Goulet (Memoirs of a Prairie Métis)*, ed. Elizabeth Magnet, tr. Ray Ellenwood (1976; Winnipeg, Manitoba: Editions Bois-Brûlés, 1980).
DELEUZE, Gilles & Félix GUATTARI. *Kafka: Toward a Minor Literature*, tr. Dana Polan, intro. Réda Bensmaia (1975; Minneapolis: U of Minnesota P, 1986).
DERRIDA, Jacques. *Dissemination*, tr. Barbara Johnson (London: Athlone, 1981).
HOCHBRUCK, Wolfgang. *"I Have Spoken": Die Darstellung und ideologische Funktion indianischer Mündlichkeit in der nordamerikanischen Literatur* (ScriptOralia 32; Tübingen: Gunter Narr, 1991).
ISERNHAGEN, Hartwig. "Anthropological Narrative and the Structure of North American Indian (Auto-)Biography," in *The Structure of Texts* (SPELL: Swiss Papers in English Language and Literature 3, ed. Udo Fries; Tübingen: Gunter Narr, 1987): 221–33.
KLOOSS, Wolfgang. "Multiculturalism, Regionalism and the Search for a Poetics of Disparity in Contemporary Canadian Writing," in *Anglistentag 1991 Düsseldorf*, ed. Wilhelm G. Busse (Tübingen: Max Niemeyer, 1992): 346–60.
KRUPAT, Arnold. *For Those Who Come After: A Study of Native American Autobiography*, intro. Paul John Eakin (Berkeley/Los Angeles: U of California P. 1985).
———. *The Voice in the Margin: Native American Literature and the Canon* (Berkeley/Los Angeles: U of California P, 1989).
LANGNESS, Lewis L. & Gelya FRANK. *Lives: An Anthropological Approach to Biography* (1981; Novato CA: Chandler & Sharp, 1988).
LOTMAN, Jurij M. *Die Struktur literarischer Texte*, tr. Rolf–Dietrich Keil. (1972; Munich: Wilhelm Fink, 1989).
MORISSET, Jean. *Les chiens s'entre-dévorent: Indiens, blancs et metis dans le Grand Nord canadien* (Montreal: Nouvelle Optique, 1977).

---

16 Jacques Derrida, *Dissemination*, tr. Barbara Johnson (London: Athlone, 1981): 92.

————— & Rose–Marie PELLETIER, ed. *Ted Trindell: Métis Witness to the North* (1986; Vancouver: Tillacum Library, 1987).

PATTERSON, David. *Literature and Spirit: Essays on Bakhtin and His Contemporaries* (Lexington: UP of Kentucky, 1988).

PURICH, Donald. *The Metis* (Canadian Issues series; Toronto: Lorimer, 1988).

SHEVTSOVA, Maria. "Dialogism in the Novel and Bakhtin's Theory of Culture." *New Literary History* 23.3 (1992): 747–63.

SPRY, Irene M. "The Ethnic Voice: The *Memoirs* of George William Sanderson 1846–1936," *Canadian Ethnic Studies* 17.2 (1985): 115–34.

STEGNER, Wallace. *Wolf Willow: A History, a Story and a Memory of the Last Plains Frontier* (New York: Viking, 1955).

WEEKES, Mary. *The Last Buffalo Hunter: As told to her by Norbert Welsh* (1939; Toronto: Macmillan, 1945).

WERNER SEDLAK

Prison Memoirs by African Writers
(Ngugi, Pheto, Soyinka)
The Cultural Unity and Complexity of Resistance

I N BARBARA HARLOW'S BOOK on resistance literature from "Third World" countries we find a very informative chapter on prison memoirs of political detainees,[1] which contains many pertinent observations on Ngugi wa Thiong'o and Molefe Pheto, but which is surprisingly silent about Wole Soyinka's *The Man Died*.[2] The approach of this paper should be regarded as supplementary to Barbara Harlow's in the following ways: whereas Harlow's interest is in "universals" (such as the power of hegemonic and counter-hegemonic discourse[3] or the women's-liberation factor in prison memoirs written by women), the focus of this paper will be on historical and cultural specificity.

Harlow sees the prison memoirs of political detainees as instances of re-writing the individualistic form of Western autobiography from a collectivist angle, which leads to the political analysis of a larger social body (122). Although this is true on the whole, it should be added that the autobiographical narrative with its formal identity of author, narrator and main character[4] is very effective in the case of the prison memoirs analysed here; it increases the credibility and political impact of prison memoirs written by individuals as testimonies to their personal and common struggle.

Harlow emphasises the collective nature of prisoners' resistance, whereas my interest is in the complex role of the detainee's self within the structure of the text and the flexible and varying relationship between the prisoner and his fellow-detainees, political friends, and people.

---

[1] Barbara Harlow, *Resistance Literature* (New York: Methuen, 1987), ch. 4: 117–53 and 209–12. Further page references are in the text.

[2] Significantly, Harlow also has very little to say about Breyten Breytenbach's *The True Confessions of an Albino Terrorist* (London: Faber & Faber, 1984), the form of which is to a great deal conditioned by the author's inquiry into what the degradation of imprisonment has done to his personal identity. See, however, Erhardt Reckwitz, "'To Break a Structure': Literature and Liberation in Breyten Breytenbach's *The True Confessions of an Albino Terrorist*," in *Crisis and Conflict: Essays on Southern African Literature*, ed. Geoffrey V. Davis (Essen: Die blaue Eule, 1990): 205–14.

[3] Starting from Foucault's observations on the subjection of prisoners by means of various practices of writing – see *Discipline and Punish: The Birth of the Prison*, tr. Alan Sheridan (*Surveiller et punir: La naissance de la prison*; Paris: Gallimard, 1975; London: Allen Lane, 1977), esp. ch. 2 and 4 – Harlow goes on to explore strategies of resistance and analyses writing as a crucial mode of the prisoners' resistance.

[4] See Philippe Lejeune, *Le pacte autobiographique* (Paris: Seuil, 1975): 26.

Ngugi wa Thiong'o, Detained[5]

Ngugi wa Thiong'o, well-established by the mid-Seventies as Kenya's leading novelist and as a professor of literature, was detained for a year during the last phase of Jomo Kenyatta's government, from December 1977 to December 1978. (Daniel Arap Moi was then Kenyatta's Minister for Home Affairs.) The reason for Ngugi's detention was a community theatre project earlier in 1977 near Ngugi's birthplace Limuru, where, together with the local population, Ngugi developed and staged his Gikuyu play *Ngaahika Ndeenda* (later also published in English under the title *I Will Marry When I Want*).

Cultural borrowing: detention as a cultural imitation of colonial rule

In his prison memoirs Ngugi makes a basic distinction between two dialectically opposed traditions of Kenyan culture – between a "reactionary culture of silence and fear" and "a people's revolutionary culture of outspoken courage and patriotic heroism" (28).

The reactionary culture of silence and fear, established by the Kenyan ruling class but ultimately in the service of international capitalist interests (62), is interpreted as a cultural imitation of British colonial rule: in order to curb resistance against imperialist domination and exploitation, "detention without trial was first introduced in Kenya by the colonial authorities" (43). According to Ngugi, the Emergency Powers (Colonial Defence) Order in Council of 1939, itself an enlargement of the 1897 Native Courts Regulations, was repealed at independence in 1963, but was incorporated again in the Preservation of Public Security Act, which granted emergency powers to the new independent government: "By 1966 all the repressive colonial laws were back on the books" (50–51).

In a conversation with one of his prison warders Ngugi sarcastically describes this cultural "borrowing" (72) as a historical chain-reaction: "The British jailed an innocent Kenyatta. Thus Kenyatta learnt to jail innocent Kenyans" (4). In other places this cultural imitation is seen as a resurrection from the dead (61–62, 70): "For a whole year I was to remain in cell 16 [...] They had raised colonial Lazarus from the dead. Who will bury him again?" (80–81). In the biblical allusion to Lazarus a central element of Christian thought is appropriated for Ngugi's satirical purposes: cultural borrowing from the West is seen in terms of a resurrection – but a resurrection both unholy and undesirable.

Resistance-culture: complexity and syncretism of a common tradition

The culture of resistance, of which Ngugi himself is part, is described as a "common national patriotic tradition" (96) which dates back to early Kenyan instances of an indigenous resistance against colonialism and includes the heroic example of the Mau Mau struggle for independence in the Fifties. In spite of the markedly African quality of this tradition (see, for example, the traditional oath taken by the Mau Mau

---

5 Ngugi wa Thiong'o, *Detained: A Writer's Prison Diary* (London: Heinemann, 1981). Page references to this edition are given in the text.

fighters, 96), this resistance-culture is presented as culturally complex. Ngugi's fellow detainees at Kamiti prison belong to different religions: some are practising Christians; others (especially the prisoners of Kenya Somali nationality) are Muslims; Ngugi and one fellow-prisoner belong to neither camp (151–52). Two outstanding names on Ngugi's list of hard-core anti-imperialists who had earlier suffered and resisted detention are Makhan Singh and J.M. Kariuki, the latter author of *"Mau Mau" Detainee*,[6] an earlier book of detention memoirs (93–96). These two figures illustrate the impact on African resistance of the two Western traditions by which Ngugi himself had been influenced – Marxism and nationalist liberalism.[7]

In a memorable passage (64), which echoes through the text of *Detained* (66, 71, 81, 87), Ngugi relates the detainees' lonely struggle against despair to Greek mythology, specifically to Sisyphus: "Were [they] all the children of Sisyphus fated for ever to roll the heavy stone of tyranny up the steep hill of struggle, only to see it roll back to the bottom?" The ancient European myth is, however, accommodated to the specific history of resistance in East Africa, which results in a committed piece of re-writing:

> But wait, I shouted back at the demons of despair. The African Sisyphus had another history [...]. It is the history of Kenyan people ceaselessly struggling against Arab feudalists and slave dealers; against Portuguese marauders who opened up Africa to her four-hundred years of devastating encounter with European domination, and later against British predators trying to embrace Kenya with claws and fangs of blood; yes, a history of Kenyan people waging a protracted guerrilla war against a British imperialist power that used to boast of its invincibility to man or God; the history of Kenyan people creating a resistance culture, a revolutionary culture of courage and patriotic heroism. The culture of the defiant Koitalel and Kimaathi. A fight-back, creative culture, unleashing tremendous energies among the Kenyan people. (64)

Ngugi's concept of resistance culture is syncretic in nature. He also appropriates Christian notions of resistance for his secular stand with allusions to the biblical "wrestling with the demons of despair in the dry wilderness" (80–81) or "Joshua's trumpets bringing down the walls of Jericho" (27, 66),[8] also a Martin Luther quotation ("On this I stand, I can do no other," 172). Highly representative of this fusion of cultures for the purpose of critical social analysis and political resistance is Ngugi's selection of mottos and quotations ranging from Friedrich Engels (91), Karl Marx (1) and such Kenyan politicians as Waruru Kanja (1) or Koigi Wa Wamwere, Wasongo Sijeyo and Martin Shikuku (169–70) to William Blake or Shakespeare (169) and the Palestinian poet Mahmoud Darwish (1).

✧ ✧ ✧

---

[6] Josiah Mwangi Kariuki, *"Mau Mau" Detainee: The Account by a Kenya African of his Experiences in Detention Camps 1953–1960* (London: Oxford UP, 1963).

[7] On the cultural complexity of anti-colonial resistance in Africa, see also Ali Mazrui, *The Africans. A Triple Heritage* (London: BBC, 1986), ch. 14: 281–88.

[8] For a passage in the New Testament which refers to significant examples of the power of faith, see St Paul's Epistle to the Hebrews (11:30 or 36–38).

Molefe Pheto, And Night Fell[9]

Molefe Pheto, a trained musician and teacher of music, director of a Black theatre
group in Soweto, and writer of poetry and prose, was detained for almost ten months
in 1975 because of his active participation in the Black Consciousness Movement
since 1970 and, in particular, after having organised three festivals of the Black Arts
for MDALI (the Music, Drama, Arts and Literature Institute in Soweto, of which
Pheto was a founder-member and spokesman). His detention was based on the 1963
Terrorism Act (49–50, 116–17).

The Black Consciousness Movement and shifting cultural boundaries

Pheto had originally been a member of the ANC (94), but, in response to the
entrenchment of apartheid and enforcement of the colour bar in the Fifties and
Sixties, had finally turned away from the ANC's politics of multiracialism (59). As a
background to his arrest Pheto gives a description of his activities in the Black arts
community:

> [As spokesman of MDALI] I decried apartheid in the arts, demanded that we Blacks determine
> our cause, recommended a dissociation from white artists and impresarios as long as the colour
> bar lasted and I spoke out on the exploitation of the Black artist by the White gallery owners.
> [...] The days when our work aped White productions and people were gone. Gone were White-
> written plays and poems. The same happened in other media such as music. In the short space
> of three years the emphasis had become Black pride and nationhood through the arts, drawing
> on our cultural background: a decided return to our cultural origins. (11–12; see also 215)

Pheto is quite outspoken about the Pan-Africanist sympathies of the Black Arts
movement of MDALI (55, 118–19), and proudly defends the Black Consciousness
Movement against accusations of racism (17).

In Pheto's case, Black self-assertion against white hegemony affects all aspects
of culture: religion, art, and literature, leading to a rejection of Christian
monotheism and a return to indigenous African polytheism (92, 110, 187–89).
When his house is searched by the Security Police, Pheto feels proud of the
paintings, sculpture and musical instruments by Black artists that he has collected
("The tone of the work in the house was Black Consciousness," 33). And he has to
witness how his collection of "Black-written books" is confiscated:

> I saw Wole Soyinka thrown head-first into the pillow slip; the Imamu Barakas that had
> escaped banning by the Publications Board; Chinua Achebe [...] suffered the fate of Soyinka;
> Serote, Mtshali, Senghor, Césaire, Okigbo, the two Diops, Mphahlele, E.K. Brathwaite, Ngugi;
> my own poems and the first manuscript of my novel joining that august company of Black
> writers going to jail in a pillow case and six brown South African government-supply
> envelopes. (37–38)

But in spite of Pheto's commitment to Black art, Black literature and Black cultural
politics, his general concept of resistance to apartheid is inclusive rather than
exclusive: ie, by no means ethnically limited and affected by notions of racial
purity. Thus the list of his political books, which he has kept hidden with the help of

---

[9] Molefe Pheto, *And Night Fell: Memoirs of a Political Prisoner in South Africa* (1983; London: Heinemann,
1985). Page references to this edition are in the text.

his friends ("the Nyereres, Nkrumahs, [...] Fanons and others," 39) includes Mao Tse Tung. He appreciates the Indian contribution to the South African liberation movement (eg, Gandhi's early struggle against the pass laws, 31) or the participation of Coloureds like Don Mattera or James Matthews in the freedom struggle (36; see also 120 and the note "Coloured people are Black," 6). Chapter 21 of his book, which is about his trial and release, is dedicated to supporters and friends in England – Mary Benson, for instance (196). The motto of the book (7) –as in Ngugi's case – is taken from Mahmoud Darwish.

The role of the self in the text: Ngugi and Pheto compared

Ngugi, in *Detained*, says that for him "detention is not a personal affair" (28, also xi). Correspondingly, the comments of the narrating self from chapter 2 onwards develop into critical analyses of Kenyan history and culture in general, and these make up about one-half of the book (see ch. 2–4.i, ch. 5 and 8). These passages, however, are closely linked to the autobiographical narrative, for they lead up to Ngugi's own contributions to the "revolutionary culture of patriotic heroism" (ie, the staging of the play *I Will Marry When I Want*, 71–80, and his writing of a novel in Gikuyu, *Devil on the Cross*, while in prison, 164–67). When twice he refuses to be chained (ch. 6: 105–107 and 112), these crucial acts of resistance inside prison are presented in a heroic light.[10]

In contrast to Ngugi, Pheto concentrates in *And Night Fell* on the auto-biographical narrative and the experiencing self. The focus of the narrative is, at first, on the interrogation-scenes of his first month in prison (ch. 1–14), where the prisoner is repeatedly exposed to very serious physical assault and torture, then on his solitary confinement, survival-strategies, and mental resistance (ch. 15–18). The self remains politically active throughout his imprisonment but is presented as essentially unheroic (eg, "small as a mouse," 15),[11] also as deliberately representative of a Black man from a South African township. Thus, the self's satiric use of nicknames, metaphors and comparisons to identify his interrogators and their assistants[12] is described as "common practice among detainees" (48–49). Charac-

---

10 Similarly, the novel *Devil on the Cross* culminates in a revolutionary act of defiance performed by the heroine. Ngugi's autobiographical text *Detained*, however, because of its formal identity of author, narrator and main character, achieves a much higher degree of credibility and political impact.

11 Cf also Pheto's self-criticism (eg, 153 or 154), or his shedding of tears (191–92).

12 Eg, "Night Pot" (32), "tearful hyena" (43), "Mother Hen" (54), "ox-like" (49), "bull-necked" (51), "as big as Jan Vorster Square," "his neck as thick as Cape Town" (95), "like the monster [in the movie *Frankenstein*]" (109). The frame of reference of Pheto's satirical descriptions is not international but deliberately South African, the nicknaming habit dating back to his and his friends' "boyhood days in the slums of Alexandra Township" (43). For a comparable strategy, see Soyinka, *The Man Died*: "A big slob of a gorilla looked into the office where I sat, eyed me all over as one would an insect destined for pinning and formaldehyde" (29). But in other places Soyinka's references are international (eg, the military, political and economic élite of Nigeria is named the "Mafia," 56–57, the Security Police are usually called the "Gestapo," eg, 39). In Pheto's case the deliberate narrowing of his references to his South African range of experience is conditioned by his emphasis on the representativity of the self. In this context it is remarkable that even a reference later in the text to Hitler's having been "reborn in South Africa" (78) finds a parallel in

teristic of this emphasis on representativity are the self's reflections on "the Black man's lot" in South Africa (eg, 186–87); in passages of this kind even the first-person singular of autobiography may acquire a collective meaning:

> I remembered that [the] ancestors [of these Christian men] had not respected my land [...] and that [...] their government leaders [...] were reserving the most fertile of my ancestral lands for their own use, meanwhile cramming me into only 13 per cent of the most soil-eroded portions. (91)[13]

The greater part of the text of *And Night Fell* centres on the survival of the individual rather than his heroic activism; correspondingly, the role of the self is seen in the following complex manner:

– as deliberatively active (see his defiant attitude towards chaining, 139–40, or the use of collective disobedience, 183);

– as acting spontaneously in response to torture or even favourable opportunities (121–22, 128, 142); these responses may develop into inner drama: ie, sequences of events which take place inside the experiencing self, ranging from fear and frustration to aggression-fantasies or determination and mental resistance (see ch. 8, 10, 12, 13 or 17);

– as victim of circumstances and coincidences (88, 120).

This complex view of the self is also reflected in the role of the author as described by Pheto at the conclusion of the book:

> I have no doubts that the Security Police in South Africa will want to know who really wrote the memoirs. Frankly, I would like to record that they did. Their fists did. Their animalistic hatred of me and my friends, of what we were attempting to achieve for our people, did. Their isolating me, shuttling me from prison to prison and holding me in solitary confinement, wrote the memoirs. Their brutalisation of me and all the other detainees did. I am only a recorder of their deeds, and I am certain that many more books will be written, as long as children can be shot at like wild game by White people. But again, because I know that they are so thick skinned and incapable of understanding how they came to write this book, I carry the burden of saying that I have written it. (218)

Wole Soyinka, The Man Died[14]

Wole Soyinka, who by the late Sixties had already achieved renown as one of Africa's leading authors and in 1986 was to become Africa's first Nobel Prize winner, was arrested soon after the beginning of the Nigerian Civil War in 1967 by General Gowon's military government after his manifold political activities against the genocide raging in Nigeria since 1966 (150) and against the escalating civil war (41), particularly because of his attempt to recruit Nigeria's intellectuals within and outside the country for a pressure-group which would work for a total ban on the

---

actual experience when Bouwer, a white Security Police officer, night after night raises his right hand in the Hitler salute and shouts "Sieg, Heil!," forcing Pheto to imitate him (125).

13 Cf similar observations on Caesarina Kona Makhoere, *No Child's Play: In Prison Under Apartheid* (London: Women's Press, 1988) in Horst Zander, *From Fact to Fiction; From Fiction to "Faction": A Study of Black South African Literature in English* (forthcoming, Tübingen: Gunter Narr, 1996): 415–19.

14 Wole Soyinka, *The Man Died: Prison Notes* (1972; incl. additional preface from 1983 ed.; London: Hutchinson/Arrow, 1985). Page references to this edition are in the text.

supply of arms to all parts of Nigeria, and because of his journey to Enugu, which was directed both against the secession of Biafra and the dictatorship of the Nigerian Army (19).

The role of the self within the structure of *The Man Died*

Soyinka's view of the role of the author differs from Pheto's in that Soyinka is more emphatic about his personal creativity (xiv) and his personal responsibility (to some extent also unrepresentativeness: 13) when he takes an uncompromising stand against the power of Nigeria's military, political and economic élite and against the oppression of the individual by the Security Police. In the two political statements dating from 1971 and 1983 which serve as preface and ch.1 of the 1985 edition, Soyinka makes the following distinction regarding the interaction between the individual author and his people in their struggle against dictatorship: "the true revolution" can only be a collective endeavour (xiv and 13), but the personal testimony of writers and intellectuals and their creation of a forceful, uncompromising language of rejection are an activity preparatory to the liberation of the popular will, as part of a resistance-therapy (xiv–xvi).

In Soyinka's autobiographical narrative, as in Ngugi's or Pheto's, the self is presented as a committed activist (eg, successfully struggling against being chained by starting a hunger-strike, ch. 4, or succeeding in communicating with the outside world, ch. 7–8, and attempting to mobilise fellow-intellectuals in Ibadan against the lawless, corrupt military régime by means of the letter reprinted in ch. 2). In these cases, the external action follows the general pattern "objective defined by the self – steps taken – objective achieved, or failure."[15] But in contrast to Ngugi's presentation of his political activities, Soyinka, like Pheto, avoids heroisation (despite his awareness that he is an internationally renowned figure – eg, 41–42, 53). In several instances his activities lead to self-doubt (eg, 62), even self-irony (92).

After Soyinka's letter to his colleagues in Ibadan is betrayed to a member of the Supreme Military Council, the experiences of the self enter a new phase – detention becomes "a matter of life and death" (72). Ultimately, the self succeeds in preserving his life (ch. 9), his sanity (ch. 26 and 38), and his personal integrity as a committed activist (290), but only after suffering several extreme crises. Correspondingly, from chapter 10 onwards, the narrative is largely devoted to the internal action (ie, to developments within the experiencing self). In these chapters the reader is confronted with an inner drama of Shakespearean dimensions, particularly reminiscent of *King Lear*, when the self struggles to come to terms philosophically with his situation after his moral integrity is called in question by a forged press release from the Security Police (chs. 10–12) or when, in his personal memories, the self reflects on the historical events leading up to the civil war (ch. 22–23), or when the self is near madness in his extreme isolation during solitary confinement (ch. 32–39).

---

15 See Shlomith Rimmon–Kenan, *Narrative Fiction: Contemporary Poetics* (New Accents series; London: Routledge, 1989): 22–28 (on Claude Bremond).

Unity and complexity of resistance: cultural syncretism and fusion

The experiences of the self in *The Man Died* range from profound isolation to deeply felt human solidarity. The latter is experienced when a group of ill-treated Ibo detainees in the Maximum Security Prison of Lagos start singing at night and all the other prisoners including Soyinka are deeply moved by their singing: "Suddenly in the dead of the night the darkness in their hearts had called up sounds from hearth and shrine. It involved us all, strangers to their homes, in one common humanity" (ch. 13: 111).

While this passage may serve as an illustration of the cross-cultural unity of resistance, the immediately preceding chapters (10–12), which deal with the first big crisis of the self, illustrate some of the ways in which the self in Soyinka's narrative draws upon various cultural traditions in order to come to terms with "spiritual isolation" and being imprisoned "in an animal cage" (81).

The inner drama contains a recurring dream (85–86) based on a personal memory of the Dutch lowlands where, years before as a student, Soyinka joined in building new houses for victims of a flood-disaster. This European experience is transferred to the philosophical context of African communalism and mutual aid, and, in Soyinka's dream, becomes the foil of the horrorific experience of suddenly losing one's comrades, of falling into an abyss and being silenced. Thus this dream derives from a fusion of European and African elements.

The feeling of desolation expressed through the recurring dream is next interpreted in terms of Yoruba philosophy (87–88). As a repeated experience of spiritual death it is seen as part of a continuum of life, death and rebirth, as a phase of transition which may lead to something monstrous ("the monstrosity of this birth," 88). Hate may give birth to an evil spirit, an *anjonnu* in Yoruba terminology (90).

This fear and uncertainty about his own future self is next expressed in terms of Western thinking, in this case German philosophy: "Is this then the long-threatened moment for jettisoning, for instance, notions of individual responsibility and the struggle it imposes? Must I now reject Kant? Karl Jaspers?" (88). Jaspers's existentialism with its tragic, ego-centred interpretation of the individual is rejected immediately as "ultimately destructive of the social potential of the self' (88–90).

But even after this emphatic rejection of the "tragic lure," the feeling of desolation remains: "Why even when I have rationally rejected the tragic snare, [am I] still overcome by depressive fumes in my capsule of individualist totality?" (91). This metaphor of the capsule is derived from the concrete experience of the cage in Lagos Maximum Security Prison. Later, in the context of survival and mental resistance against being buried alive in the "Crypt" of Kaduna prison, the capsule will be appropriated semiotically by the detainee so that the régime's instrument for humiliating and isolating the prisoner becomes his own means of self-protection (131–32), though only temporarily (cf also 185 and 290). But here the capsule metaphor refers to the self's continuing feeling of isolation and despair, which stems from the allegation that he has betrayed his ideals (91).[16]

After some mainly European references to fellow-dissidents, Soyinka ends with self-criticism and affirmation of Immanuel Kant's categorical imperative:

> I fault myself now, accepting implicitly that Kantian imperative, recognising that since I had settled within myself all doubts about the bankruptcy of Gowon's moral order [...], it was not enough to send word to a band of emasculated intellectuals. I should have done then what I now stand accused of doing – escaped. For there existed then, and exists even now in spite of its reverses, a truly national, moral *and* revolutionary alternative – Victor Banjo's Third Force. Morality, and therefore actions which come from a moral inspiration, create the only "authentic being," they constitute the continuing personality of the individual. (95–96)[17]

Finally, the inner drama leads to an assertion of human life in the service of humanity and of justice as the first condition of humanity (96).

Conclusion: traditional African thinking and "the social potential of the self"[18]

As we have seen, Soyinka's idea of resistance links concrete experiences and philosophical thinking; it fuses African and European elements, at first sight seeming to reinforce either traditional African notions of mutual aid, communalism and solidarity or characteristic European values such as individual responsibility and personal integrity. But our detailed analysis has actually shown that it is wrong to describe Soyinka's (or Ngugi's and Pheto's) texts and the resistance-culture they represent in terms of the dichotomy between collectivism and individualism, which is a familiar way of Western thinking (cf Soyinka's own criticism of the Western habit of "compartmentalising" in *Myth, Literature and the African World*[19]). The considerable role attributed to individual as well as collective resistance by our three writers has nothing to do with "westernisation." All three texts imply a flexible and variable relationship between self and society, family or political friends which is by no means "un-African" but well within the range of traditional African thinking about the social and communal orientation of the individual. As illustration, let me end my paper by quoting a Yoruba proverb: "*A ò lè b'ára 'ni tan, k'á f'ara wa n'ítan ya.*" In Soyinka's translation: "Kinship does not insist that, because we are entwined, we thereby rip off each other's thigh."[20]

---

16 It would be worthwhile analysing in detail Soyinka's changing responses to the cells which he is confined to (starting from p.46, where he still welcomes his being alone with his thoughts) and comparing these responses with, on the one hand, Albie Sachs's (*The Prison Diary of Albie Sachs* [New York: McGraw–Hill, 1966]: 13ff) or Ruth First's (*117 Days* [1965; London: Bloomsbury, 1988]: 9ff), and, on the other hand, with Ngugi's (*Detention*, 3, 19–22, 128, 131) and Pheto's (*And Night Fell*, 42, 112–13, also 136, 152–55, 190–91) or Caesarina Makhoere's (*No Child's Play*, 9 or 19–20). For further comparison, see Don Foster et al., *Detention and Torture in South Africa* (London: James Currey, 1987), ch. 4: 64ff, and ch. 6: 123–24 and 136–40.

17 For the reference to Victor Banjo, see Soyinka's detailed reflections in *The Man Died*, ch. 23.

18 *The Man Died*, 90.

19 Soyinka, *Myth, Literature and the African World* (1976; Cambridge: Cambridge UP, 1990): 37.

20 *Myth, Literature and the African World*, x–xi. On the role of the individual in African societies see also: J. Solanke, "Traditional Social and Political Institutions," in *African History and Culture*, ed. R. Olaniyan

WORKS CITED

BREYTENBACH, Breyten. *The True Confessions of an Albino Terrorist* (London: Faber & Faber, 1984).

DAVIDSON, Basil. *Africa in History* (1966; London: Paladin, 1984).

FIRST, Ruth. *117 Days* (1965; London: Bloomsbury, 1988).

FOSTER, Don et al., *Detention and Torture in South Africa* (London: James Currey, 1987).

FOUCAULT, Michel. *Discipline and Punish: The Birth of the Prison*, tr. Alan Sheridan (*Surveiller et punir: La naissance de la prison*; Paris: Gallimard, 1975; London: Allen Lane, 1977).

HARLOW, Barbara. *Resistance Literature* (New York: Methuen, 1987).

KARIUKI, Josiah Mwangi. *"Mau Mau" Detainee: The Account by a Kenya African of His Experiences in Detention Camps 1953–1960* (London: Oxford UP, 1963).

LEJEUNE, Philippe. *Le pacte autobiographique* (Paris: Seuil, 1975).

MAKHOERE, Caesarina Kona. *No Child's Play: In Prison Under Apartheid* (London: Women's Press, 1988).

MAZRUI, Ali. *The Africans. A Triple Heritage* (London: BBC, 1986).

NGUGI WA THIONG'O. *Detained: A Writer's Prison Diary* (London: Heinemann, 1981).

PENNINGTON, Dorothy. "Time in African Culture," in *African Culture: The Rhythms of Unity*, ed. M.K. Asante & K.M. Asante (Westport CT: Greenwood, 1985): 123–40.

PHETO, Molefe. *And Night Fell: Memoirs of a Political Prisoner in South Africa* (1983; London: Heinemann, 1985).

RECKWITZ, Erhardt. "'To Break a Structure': Literature and Liberation in Breyten Breytenbach's *The True Confessions of an Albino Terrorist*," in *Crisis and Conflict: Essays on Southern African Literature*, ed. Geoffrey V. Davis (Essen: Die blaue Eule, 1990): 205–14.

RIMMON–KENAN, Shlomith. *Narrative Fiction: Contemporary Poetics* (New Accents series; London: Routledge, 1989).

SACHS, Albie. *The Prison Diary of Albie Sachs* (New York: McGraw–Hill, 1966).

SOLANKE, J. "Traditional Social and Political Institutions," in *African History and Culture*, ed. R. Olaniyan (Lagos: Longman Nigeria, 1982): 27–37.

SOYINKA, Wole. *The Man Died: Prison Notes* (1972; incl. additional preface from 1983 ed.; London: Hutchinson/Arrow, 1985).

———. *Myth, Literature and the African World* (1976; Cambridge: Cambridge UP, 1990).

———. "Theatre in African Traditional Culture: Survival Patterns," in *African History and Culture*, ed. R. Olaniyan (Lagos: Longman Nigeria, 1982): 237ff.

ZANDER, Horst. *From Fact to Fiction; From Fiction to "Faction": A Study of Black South African Literature in English* (forthcoming Tübingen: Gunter Narr, 1996): 415–19.

(Lagos: Longman Nigeria, 1982): 27–37; Wole Soyinka, "Theatre in African Traditional Culture: Survival Patterns," also in Olaniyan: 237ff, esp. 242; Basil Davidson, *Africa in History* (1966; London: Paladin, 1984): 180–82. On the reciprocal functioning of opposites in African thinking, see also Dorothy Pennington, "Time in African Culture," in *African Culture: The Rhythms of Unity*, ed. M.K. Asante & K.M. Asante (Westport CT: Greenwood, 1985): 123–40, esp. 128ff.

FRANK SCHULZE-ENGLER

Riding the Crisis
The Satanic Verses *and the Silences of Literary Theory*

A S MANY COMMENTATORS HAVE NOTED, the literary world has never been the same since the publication of Salman Rushdie's *Satanic Verses* sparked off an international crisis that went beyond anything hitherto experienced in the reception of a single work of literature. With the *fatwa* against Rushdie still in place and Rushdie himself still in hiding, this crisis continues to the present day. Many voices have been raised that see the conflict around *The Satanic Verses* as a conflict between cultures (usually "Islam" and "the West") and Rushdie has time and again been accused of having been responsible for a tremendous step backwards in the process suggested by the theme that has brought about this volume: the fusion of cultures – or at least the improvement of cross-cultural understanding.

Since I am not going to deal with the more general aspects of the Rushdie Affair, I would like to note at this point that for me the most important dimensions of this conflict seem to be political and not cultural or religious. At the core of this political conflict lies what political scientists such as Bassam Tibi have described as the "crisis of modern Islam" which has given rise to "the fundamentalist challenge" – to use the title of Tibi's most recent work.[1] It seems that the implications of the power-politics involved can probably be discussed more competently by sociologists and political scientists than by literary critics.

Yet the conflict clearly has implications that go far beyond simple power-politics or fundamentalist concerns. This paper attempts to highlight some significant, and certainly highly problematical, ways in which "post-colonial" literary theorists and critics have reacted to the Rushdie Affair. The principal argument is that the same post-colonialist discourse theories that have been quite successfully applied to the deconstruction of various discourses of domination have actually retained "essentialist" norms and values which they themselves have not been able to engage critically. The "Rushdie affair" has provided a point of crisis at which these "hidden" norms have re-emerged, and theories bent on subverting "essentialist" notions of culture and society have actually produced a variety of new essentialisms.

---

[1] See Bassam Tibi, *The Crisis of Modern Islam: A Pre-Industrial Culture in the Scientific–Technological Age* (Salt Lake City: U of Utah P, 1988) and Tibi, *Die fundamentalistische Herausforderung: der Islam und die Weltpolitik* [The Fundamentalist Challenge: Islam and World Politics] (Munich: Beck, 1992).

Let us begin, then, with the essay that – owing to some intertextual strong-arm tactics on my part, and quite unwillingly, I am afraid – has provided the title for this paper: Amin Malak's "Reading the Crisis."[2] Following a discussion of the "most offensive part of the novel," ie those sections of *The Satanic Verses* where Gibreel dreams of Jahilia and the Prophet Mahound, Malak's criticism of Rushdie culminates in the following passage:

> Starting with its title, *The Satanic Verses* unearths and copies some of the nastiest claims that a few Orientalists [...] have fabricated about the history and culture of Islam. [...] By copying this reductively edited version of Islamic history, Rushdie, who should have known otherwise, has made his motives seem suspect to Muslims. [...] by doing so, Rushdie, the leftist polemicist, may have qualified himself for what the Marxist–feminist critic Gayatri Spivak calls "the privileged native informant" [...] In other words, Rushdie's narrative, if the hypothesis is valid, becomes in the final analysis alien to the Third World's view of itself. Regrettably, he has, to apply Said's comment on Naipaul, "allowed himself quite consciously to be turned into a witness for the Western prosecution" [...] and has thus rendered himself inoperative within the Third World literary discourse.[3]

I have quoted this passage at length, not only because it seems to me to present the central arguments that have been levelled against Rushdie by a large number of "post-colonialist" critics, but also because it demonstrates in a truly paradigmatic way the underlying tensions, ambivalences and silences in which these arguments are embedded.

The first argument in the above passage centres on the question of "Orientalism," and it is to Edward Said's seminal study, one of the founding texts of post-colonialist theory and one of the most often quoted texts in the critical response to the Rushdie Affair, that we have to turn in order to unravel the tangle of ambivalences from which this argument is constructed.

Methodologically speaking, Said's *Orientalism* is of course itself a thoroughly ambivalent work. In *The Predicament of Culture*, James Clifford has described Said's treatment of his subject in these terms:

> Frequently he suggests that a text or tradition distorts, dominates, or ignores some real or authentic feature of the Orient. Elsewhere, however, he denies the existence of any "real Orient," and in this he is more rigorously faithful to Foucault and the other radical critics of representation whom he cites. [...] Said's concept of a "discourse" [...] vacillates between, on the one hand, the status of an ideological distortion of lives and cultures that are never concretised and, on the other, the condition of a persistent structure of signifiers that, like some extreme example of experimental writing, refers solely and endlessly to itself.[4]

The ambivalence of Said's *Orientalism* thus lies in the fact that it engages in a highly effective deconstruction of "Western" discourses along Foucauldian lines while at the same time suggesting that somehow, somewhere, other, more "truthful" discourses about what is really going on are available. The inevitable result of this ambivalence is a heavy dose of the same "cryptonormativism" that Jürgen Habermas has diagnosed in Foucault's genealogical theory of power: the

---

[2] Amin Malak, "Reading the Crisis: The Polemics of Salman Rushdie's *The Satanic Verses*," *ARIEL: A Review of International English Literature* 20.4 (1989): 176–86.
[3] Malak, "Reading the Crisis," 184.
[4] James Clifford, *The Predicament of Culture* (Cambridge MA: Massachusetts UP, 1988): 260.

continuing, underlying influence of norms and values in a theory that is not geared towards dealing with them.[5] Discourse-theories postulate that the truth-claims of all discourses are simply and squarely constructed and – in the case of post-structuralism – that language itself is self-referential; if you claim (or suggest or imply) that there are some discourses that are truer (rather than just more power-ful) than others, you cannot talk about this claim (or suggestion or implication) in terms of the theoretical framework of discourse-analysis.[6]

Said himself seems to have been quite aware of the ambivalent implications of his stance, since he ended *Orientalism* on the warning note that "the answer to Orientalism is not Occidentalism."[7] Yet he did very little during the Eighties to curb the rise of a veritable army of – may we call them post-Orientalist? – critics who turned the maverick epistemological hybridity of Said's original text into a convenient, mass-produced item of deconstructive machinery to be used for warding off unpleasant criticism of "Third-World" affairs. Arguments classified as "Orientalist," "Imperialist" or "Western" could be taken apart as discursive formations referring to nothing but their own ideological universe, while arguments regarded as "progressive," "Third-World" or "post-colonial" were granted free passage around the deconstructive gristmill.

In the mid-Eighties, in an essay entitled "Intellectuals in the Post-Colonial World," Said deplored the rise of what he referred to as a "rhetoric and politics

---

5 See Jürgen Habermas, *The Philosophical Discourse of Modernity: Twelve Lectures* (1985; Cambridge: Polity, 1990): ch. 10 ("Some Questions Concerning the Theory of Power: Foucault Again"). "Of course, Foucault's dramatic influence and his iconoclastic reputation could hardly be explained if the cool facade of radical historicism did not simply hide the passion of aesthetic modernism. Genealogy is overtaken by a fate similar to that which Foucault had seen in the human sciences: To the extent that it retreats into the reflectionless objectivity of a non-participatory, ascetic description of kaleidoscopically changing practices of power, genealogical historiography emerges from its cocoon as precisely the *presentistic, relativistic, cryptonormative* illusory science that it does not want to be" (275–76; emphasis in the original). "Genealogical historiography is supposed to reach behind discourse totalities (within which alone disputes over norms and values occur) with a strictly descriptive attitude. It brackets normative validity claims as well as claims to propositional truth and abstains from the question of whether some discourse and power formations could be more legitimate than others. Foucault resists the demand to take sides [...] Now this grounding of a second-order value freeness is already by no means value-free. Foucault understands himself as a dissident who offers resistance to modern thought and humanistically disguised disciplinary power. Engagement marks his learned essays right down to the style and choice of words; the critical tenor dominates the theory no less than the self-definition of the entire work. [...] *Foucault's criticism is based more on the postmodern rhetoric of his presentation than on the postmodern assumptions of his theory*" (282, second emphasis mine).

6 See Amanda Anderson, "Cryptonormativism and Double Gestures: The Politics of Post-Structuralism," *Cultural Critique* 21 (1992): 63–95. Anderson characterises the "constitutive tension of post-structuralist thought" as "the incommensurability between its epistemological stance and its political claims, between its descriptions and its prescriptions, between the pessimism of its intellect and, if not the optimism, at least the intrusiveness of its moral and political will" (64). The cryptonormativism underlying this tension is explained in the following terms: "The critiques of power and domination [...] entail implicit normative claims that remain external to the overarching anti-foundationalist epistemology. Ever-encroaching and self-extending power-networks in Foucault, the violence of metaphysics in deconstruction, the painstaking analysis of reified or suppressed otherness in cultural and literary criticism – all of these make appeal at some level to a vision of unalienated relations and undamaged forms of social life" (64).

7 Edward Said, *Orientalism* (1978; Harmondsworth: Penguin, 1987): 328.

of blame," while effectively engaging in the very same rhetoric and politics himself:

> The examples of Lyotard and Foucault [...] describe a striking lack of faith in what Lyotard was to call the great legitimising narratives of emancipation and enlightenment. [...] In both Lyotard and Foucault we find precisely the same trope employed to explain their disappointment in the politics of liberation: narrative, which posits an enabling *arché* and a vindicating *telos*, is no longer an adequate figure for plotting the human trajectory in society. There is nothing to look forward to: we are stuck within our circle. The line is now enclosed by a circle. After years of support for the anti-colonial struggles in places like Algeria, Cuba, Vietnam, Palestine, Iran, that came to represent for the Western Left their deepest engagement in the politics and philosophy of decolonisation, a moment of exhaustion and disappointment was reached. This is when one began to hear and read accounts of how futile it was to support revolutions [...][8]

The discursive strategy of these and similar passages is clear: if you want to find out about how people's views on what goes on in the world change, look at the discourses in which they are trapped – and not at the historical fate, at the concrete history of "anti-colonial struggles in places like Algeria, Cuba, Vietnam, Palestine, Iran." The cryptonormative appeal takes precedence over the analytical exertions of critical practice, and apology is just round the corner.[9] Although it would clearly be futile to associate Said with fundamentalism, it is nevertheless significant that Islamic fundamentalists such as Ziauddin Sardar have found *Orientalism* a most congenial work – undoubtedly very much against Said's own intentions. Thus, in Sardar's and Davies's *Distorted Imagination*, Said is turned into

---

[8] Edward Said, "Intellectuals in the Post-Colonial World," *Salmagundi* 70–71 (1986): 50/51 (emphasis in the original).

[9] The extracts from a panel discussion on Said's "Intellectuals in the Post-Colonial World" published in the same issue of *Salmagundi* that featured his original essay ("The Intellectual in the Post-Colonial World: Response and Discussion," *Salmagundi* 70–71 [1986]: 65–81) provide a very instructive example of the intricate political problems thrown up by Said's epistemological assumption that "one way of getting hold of the commonest post-colonial debate is to analyse not its content, but its form, not what is said so much as how it is said, by whom, where, and for whom" ("Intellectuals in the Post-Colonial World," 46). Faced with criticisms such as Connor Cruise O'Brien's ("if we tell the people [in the post-colonial world] that there's nothing wrong, if we fail even to hint that there are dictatorships, that there are tyrannies, if we fail to assert that those are wrong, we are then letting down the people who live under those undemocratic regimes, the very people whom it is our duty to support, and who are, in the main, silenced," 67), Said manoeuvres himself into an apologetic stance characterised by an instant withdrawal to safer discursive territory: "[...] 'telling the truth' will seem to some people very easy if the truth but no others" (78). Said illustrates his argument by a sustained attack on V.S. Naipaul which prefigures almost verbatim the "Third-Worldist" criticism that was to be levied against Rushdie a few years later: "Naipaul's constituency is not the world of truth seekers everywhere. He writes to the Western liberal [...] on the basis of his being an Indian Trinidadian, he has ascribed to him the credentials of a man who can serve as witness for the third world; and he is a very convenient witness. He is a third worlder denouncing his own people [...] The moment Naipaul defines and crystallises for the Western audience is the moment of *our* disappointment with the prospects of other peoples" (78/79/80, emphasis in the original). This epistemological shift from "what is said" to "how it is said, by whom, where, and for whom" necessarily leads to unending cryptonormative entanglements, since "content" is presumably taken for granted (or implicitly treated as common ground or shared insight), while theory preoccupies itself with "form." It can hardly come as a surprise that the cryptonormative potential inherent in Said's arguments has been put to good use by critics of Rushdie – while, ironically enough, Said himself has, of course, strongly defended Rushdie in his most recent writings.

the principal witness for the thesis that *The Satanic Verses* is part of a long-standing conspiracy of Western secularism aganinst Islamic faith.[10]

By now it has become clear, I hope, why the appeal to "Orientalism" as a critical category in many post-colonialist reactions to the Rushdie Affair is inevitably entangled in a web of cryptonormative values. The texts that unravel the complexities of Rushdie's alleged "Orientalist discourse" have to remain silent about these values, because they cannot treat them with the same kind of analytical rigour that they can muster against "unfriendly" essentialisms. It is this silence, I would suggest, that lies beneath the defensive rhetoric of blame that assigns to Rushdie the role of a latter-day "Orientalist."

Interestingly enough, Said himself has reacted quite differently to the Rushdie Affair and has combined his defence of Rushdie and *The Satanic Verses* with a critical re-assessment of various "Third-World" discourses of power. In *Culture and Imperialism*, Said notes "the stunning acquiescence of the Islamic world to the prohibitions, proscriptions and threats pronounced by Islam's clerical and secular authorities against Salman Rushdie because of his novel *The Satanic Verses*" and continues his assessment of the "Rushdie Affair" in the following terms:

> I do not mean that the entire Islamic world acquiesced, but that its official agencies, spokespeople, secular as well as religious, either blindly rejected or vehemently refused to engage with a book which the enormous majority of people never read. [...] That it dealt with Islam in English for what was believed to be a largely Western audience was its main offense. [...] Few people during the exhilarating heyday of decolonisation and early Third World nationalism were watching or paying close attention to how a carefully nurtured nativism in the anti-colonial ranks grew and grew to inordinately large proportions. All those nationalist appeals to pure or authentic Islam, or to Afrocentrism, *négritude*, or Arabism, had a strong response, without sufficient consciousness that those ethnicities and spiritual essences would come back to exact a very high price from their successful adherents.[11]

Said's insistence on the need to critically engage not only "Western" but also "Third-World" forms of authoritarian cultural and ideological essentialisms clears some space for a fresh look at the normative assumptions concealed within critical discourse analysis. It also provides a perspective on the second major argument that underlies various post-colonialist critiques of *The Satanic Verses*: ie, that Rushdie has left the folds of "Third-World" culture and politics and that *The Satanic Verses* is a novel which, in Malak's phrase quoted above, "becomes in the final analysis alien to the Third World's view of itself."

This second argument is not only closely related to the initial charge of "Orientalism," but is also in many ways even more ambivalent and diffuse than the

---

[10] See Ziauddin Sardar & Merryl Wyn Davies, *Distorted Imagination: Lessons from the Rushdie Affair* (London: Grey Seal, 1990), especially ch. 2 ("The Images of Ignorance"): 34–75.

[11] Edward Said, *Culture and Imperialism* (London: Chatto & Windus, 1993): 370/371 (emphasis in the original). A large part of chapter 4, Part 2 ("Challenging Orthodoxy and Authority"), from which the passages quoted are taken, is based on Said's keynote address to the 1989 "Silver Jubilee Conference" of the Association for Commonwealth Literature and Language Studies (ACLALS) at Canterbury; see Edward Said, "Figures, Configurations, Transfigur-ations," in *From Commonwealth to Post-Colonial*, ed. Anna Rutherford (Sydney/Mundelstrup: Dangaroo, 1992): 3–17.

first one. An excellent example of the epistemological problems involved in the invocation of "the Third World's view of itself" is to be found in Timothy Brennan's *Salman Rushdie and the Third World*. In his preface to this book-length study of Rushdie's major novels (including *The Satanic Verses*), Brennan has the following to say about the epistemological function of the concept "Third World":

> I share the view of Aijaz Ahmad and others who argue that it has no theoretical content whatsoever. As he says, "we do not live in three worlds but in one," mutually affected and affecting.[12]

While this sentence is bound to baffle at least some prospective readers of a book which advertises its concern with the "Third World" in its very title, the sentence that follows it announces a pleasant surprise: this concept with "no theoretical content whatsoever" has managed, by way of a truly amazing act of epistemological parthenogenesis, to give birth to a little "political meaning" of its own:

> Obviously, the term has less to do with what a country essentially *is* – what colour its natives' skin, what longitude or latitude it occupies, what size its GNP – than what it *does*. From the first meetings of Nehru and Nasser in the 1950s until the era of the "Non-aligned Nations," "Third World" has meant simply those countries decolonising from what E.P. Thompson once calles "Natopolis." It has a political not a sociological meaning. To use the title *Salman Rushdie and the Third World* for this book is then not only to place Rushdie in it but to suggest his antagonistic relationship to it.[13]

This passage is remarkable in several respects. Above all, it is the site of a complete breakdown of intertextual communication: Aijaz Ahmad has criticised the term "Third World" precisely for its "political meaning," and there is thus no conceivable way in which one could agree with his criticism and yet uphold the political (or any other) meaning of this term. Ahmad writes:

> The difficulty with deploying this term, "Third World," as a *theoretical category*, however, is that its career has been so contradictory, so riven with detailed contention, that one would first have to specify, with *some* degree of theoretical rigour, the very grid – Nehruvian, or Maoist, or Soviet, or some other – which underlies one's own deployment of it. Meanwhile, the fact that *all* the theoretical variants emphasise the nationalist character of the term's politics should necessarily mean that it is really not possible to adopt the category itself, as the basis of one's theoretical work, and simultaneously break away from that originary underlying presupposition. In order to think of the world differently, one would have to forgo the theoretical category itself.[14]

A political clarification of what exactly should be understood by the term "Third World" is of course neither to be found in Brennan's introductory statement nor in any other part of his book. The "Third World" in which he wishes to place Rushdie in his study thus becomes a place that can be used at will to hint at some progressive or revolutionary essence. Thus Brennan can end his discussion of *The Satanic Verses* by pointing out Rushdie's "responsibility [...] to the decolonisation struggles he interprets (and translates) for a Western reading public," a responsibility that Rushdie has somehow failed to live up to: "The

---

12 See Timothy Brennan, *Salman Rushdie and the Third World: Myths of the Nation* (Basingstoke: Macmillan, 1989): xiv.

13 Brennan, *Salman Rushdie and the Third World*, xiv (emphasis in the original).

14 Aijaz Ahmad, *In Theory: Classes, Nations, Literatures* (London: Verso, 1992): 308.

fullness and complexity of their collective visions are often foreshortened in the personal filter of Rushdie's fiction." The reader is then provided, not with information, but again with allusions, hints and gestures as to what this fullness and complexity that Rushdie has neglected in *Satanic Verses* might actually be: Fanon and Cabral knew and insisted on the necessity of national struggle, "a point of view Rushdie shares in theory, but which he cannot bring himself to fictionalise." A further hint at Bakhtin and a cryptic statement by Gramsci on "a new conformism from below [permitting] new possibilities of self-discipline, or perhaps of liberty that is also individual" round off the picture of the fullness and complexity of the decolonising struggles and their collective visions that Rushdie has allegedly failed to align himself with.[15] What is problematical about the vagueness of these allusions is certainly not the fact that Brennan fails to come up with a full-blown theory of the Third-World revolutionary subject, but that he signals to his readers that this subject might be available somewhere – and that Rushdie has failed to give expression to it. While "upstairs" in the lofty realms of discourse-analysis the Third World has no theoretical content whatsoever, "downstairs," in the dimly lit cryptonormative basement where discourse-analysis cannot be bothered to rummage, it makes all the difference in the world.

Other authors have grappled with the "essential" Third-Worldliness that Rushdie is supposed to have given up (or sold away) in similar, though often much more polemical ways. A truly astonishing example of the strains that emerge in texts where the attraction to prediscursive identities is combined with the critical toolkit of post-colonial discourse-analysis can be found in Uma Parameswaran's "The We/They Paradigm in Rushdie's *The Satanic Verses*."[16] The essay consists of two parts, one dealing with the question whether Rushdie has become "one of them," the other with "his delineation of the status and ethos of Indians-in-Britain and of British racism."[17] The concerns of these two parts are so different that the author actually introduces a persona to present the first one: an Indian in India addressing Rushdie in colloquial Indian English. Here is the core of her critique:

> I don't say you are one of them, not yet, but you are not here I am saying, you are more there than here, more with them than with us. Everyone knows all human beings are samesame, bhaibhai, but everyone also knows that there's always two sides to a wall with us on one side and them on the other, and that who we and they are depends on who's speaking. Confusion comes when the one who's speaking doesn't know which side he is on. And you, Salman Saab, don't know where your good self is standing.[18]

There is an unbridgeable linguistic and stylistic chasm between the chilly mirth of this persona's puzzled reflections on identity and Parameswaran's skilful analysis

---

[15] Brennan, *Salman Rushdie and the Third World*, 166 (all quotations).
[16] See Uma Parameswaran, "The We/They Paradigm in Rushdie's *Satanic Verses*," in *US/THEM: Translation, Transcription and Identity in Post-Colonial Literary Cultures*, ed. Gordon Collier (Cross/Cultures 6; Amsterdam/Atlanta GA: Rodopi, 1992): 189–99.
[17] Parameswaran, "The We/They Paradigm," 193.
[18] Parameswaran, "The We/They Paradigm," 191.

of the discursive strategies developed by Rushdie to deal with the immigrant experience and with racism in Britain. The Indian grappling for a collective identity literally cannot speak to the discourse-analyst unravelling the problems of racism and migration; in the final paragraphs, the two are brought together not through discursive means, through argument or criticism, but in an authorial "fantasy" that starts from the (ironic) image of the immigrant woman turned childbearing-machine in *Satanic Verses* and ends in a vision of irresistible collective identity on the march:

> In my fantasy, the conquering armies marching from immigrant and Asian wombs will outnumber, out-think and outshine the others and take over. Not an unfit retribution for the races that have annihilated aboriginal cultures and peoples in five continents over the past five hundred years.[19]

Gayatri Spivak's "Reading *The Satanic Verses*"[20] offers another striking example of the intricate problems that arise when post-colonial discourse theories based on post-structuralist epistemologies are confronted by political conflicts such as the Rushdie Affair. On one level, Spivak's essay is based on a deconstructive reading of this conflict, which shows that both "sides" are really differently constructed discourses whose truth-claims are equally false. Thus "Khomeini's 'anti-democratic, anti-Enlightenment' behaviour was not only not direct and unmediated evidence of the immutable essence of Islam, but it was a deliberate cultural–political self-representation and an unmediated testifier for the immutable essence of Islam,"[21] while, on the "other" side, "the Rushdie affair has been coded as Freedom of Speech versus Terrorism and even as 'a triumph of the written word',"[22] and "has been domesticated into a possible 'Western' (why?) 'martyrship' for literature, or rather for the book trade!"[23] In *political* terms, this even-handed deconstruction is, of course, highly unsatisfactory. A purely *systemic* view of cultural, political – or any other – interactions or conflicts cannot possibly enter into a *dialogue* with the "subject positions" it analyses; it typically approaches the actors in the discursive field from "behind" or "above." While this methodological consequence may not seem particularly infelicitous in the rarified milieu of Yale deconstruction, it is rather more problematical in the thoroughly politicised arena of post-colonialism, where criticism and theory are expected (and often claim) to be of particular political relevance.

This is probably the reason why "Reading *The Satanic Verses*," like so many of Spivak's more recent texts, is at pains to negotiate a dialogue, or at least some sort of communication, with the protagonists in the discursive conflicts "out there," a

---

[19] Parameswaran, "The We/They Paradigm," 199.
[20] Gayatri Chakravorty Spivak, "Reading *The Satanic Verses*," *Third Text* 11 (special issue: "Beyond the Rushdie Affair," 1990): 41–60.
[21] Spivak, "Reading *The Satanic Verses*," 58.
[22] Spivak, "Reading *The Satanic Verses*," 57.
[23] Spivak, "Reading *The Satanic Verses*," 57

move which Spivak herself has described as "strategic essentialism." [24] One way in which this dialogue is achieved in "Reading *The Satanic Verses*" consists of a series of cryptonormative references to unspecified "activists" or "militants" whose views are referred to positively, and of an appeal to a diffuse (presumably "Third-World") identity (the United States versus "we on the other side"). [25] While these references and allusions provide an important rhetorical framework in the text, Spivak's epistemological strategy for resolving the conflict between "theory" and "agency" lies elsewhere. Like other of her essays (most importantly "Can the Subaltern Speak?" [26]) the text foregrounds the predicament of the "muted ventriloquists," ie, those silenced women whose voices cannot be heard – in this instance, beneath the clamorous voices locked in a conflict that Spivak "recodes" as "Racism versus Fundamentalism." [27] The example Spivak uses to illustrate her thesis (the case of the Indian Muslim woman Shabano, whose – juridically successful – struggle for self-determination became embroiled in an ideologically charged conflict between Muslim and Hindu men) is undoubtedly convincing enough; the problem, however, is that this *particular* constellation eventually *displaces* the very conflict that her text initially set out to explain. Theory may be able to account for the mute subaltern, but how does it assess the discourses of those who raise their voice? Spivak quotes from the statement of the "Southall Black Sisters" and others who deplored the fact that "women's voices have been largely silent in the debate where battle lines have been drawn between liberalism and fundamentalism." [28] What she does *not* quote is their clear and unequivocal solidarity with Salman Rushdie and their outspoken and unwavering attack on fundamentalism:

> "As a group of women of many religions and none, we would like to express our solidarity with Salman Rushdie. [...] Often it's been assumed that the views of vocal community leaders are our views and their demands our demands.
>
> We regret this absolutely. We have struggled for many years in this country and across the world to express ourselves as we choose within and outside our communities.
>
> We will not be dictated to by fundamentalists. Our lives will not be defined by community leaders.
>
> We will take up our right to determine our own destinies, not limited by religion, culture or nationality. [...]
>
> We call on the government to abolish the outdated blasphemy law and to defend, without reservation, freedom of speech." [29]

---

24 See "Criticism, Feminism and the Institution" and "Strategy, Identity, Writing," in Spivak, *The Post-Colonial Critic: Interviews, Strategies, Dialogues*, ed. Sarah Harasym (New York/London: Routledge, 1990): 1–16 and 35–49. For a more detailed analysis and critique of Spivak's "strategic essentialism," see Amanda Anderson, "Cryptonormativism and Double Gestures," 68–71.

25 Spivak, "Reading *The Satanic Verses*," 57.

26 See Gayatri Chakravorty Spivak, "Can the Subaltern Speak?," in *Marxism and the Interpretation of Cultures*, ed. Cary Nelson & Lawrence Grossberg (Basingstoke: Macmillan, 1988): 271–313.

27 Spivak, "Reading *The Satanic Verses*," 57.

28 Spivak, "Reading *The Satanic Verses*," 57, quoting Southall Black Sisters, "Women Against Fundamentalism," in *The Rushdie File*, ed. Lisa Appignanesi & Sara Maitland (London: Fourth Estate, 1989): 241–42.

29 Southall Black Sisters, "Women Against Fundamentalism," 241–42.

That Spivak effectively silences these women at the point where they decide to *act,* *speak out* and *take sides* can hardly come as a surprise. Once the Rushdie Affair is "recoded" as "Racism versus Fundamentalism," the speaking voices of these women are an acute embarrassment for the theoretician: they are obviously not "fundamentalists" but it really wouldn't do to subsume them under "racism" either. Thus the dialogue between "theory" and "agency" fails, and theory once more returns to its vantage-point above the subject-positions trapped in (well-meant but nevertheless deficient) discursive formations: "*In place of mere secularism,* the Southall Black Sisters might propose an instrumental universalism [...].*"*[30] Theory turns out to be structurally dependent on silence, the text becomes an exploration of the conditions for its own possibility and in a rather ironical way there is indeed "nothing outside the text": where women who have chosen to speak, to demand a politics of anti-fundamentalist engagement, literary theory offers silence and a politics of textual displacement.

To conclude, then, it would be foolish to blame Rushdie's predicament on the inadequacies of literary theory. Yet the Rushdie Affair has shown clearly that cryptonormative essentialisms are in so many ways present within literary theory itself and that, in times of strain, they emerge right in the middle of deconstructive sophistication. Faced with a political issue that deeply disturbs convential "West"/"South" perceptions, and entangled in a web of political, social and cultural presuppositions that – for methodological reasons – are not allowed into the discursive open, many post-colonialist critics seem to have opted for the safe havens of renewed collective ("Third-World," "Indian" or "Muslim") identities, thus effectively silencing the critical faculties of literary theory. Whether this response is more questionable than that of "Western" intellectuals who hide away behind a comfortable cultural relativism and paternalistic notions of "respect for 'other' cultures" or who combine their defence of Rushdie, the outstanding international writer, with a pronounced distaste for "messy" Third-World politics and a profound ignorance of the predicament of innumerable intellectuals in non-"Western" parts of the world is, of course, quite a different matter.

Yet the fact remains that the Rushdie affair presents a lost opportunity for many branches of post-colonialist theorising. There may be good reasons for doubting whether literary theory or criticism really make that much political difference, but if they do, one of their prime tasks surely must lie in an unflinching confrontation with authoritarian "collective identities" wherever they seek to model hybrid realities on purist ideals. "No one can deny the persisting continuities of long traditions, sustained habitations, national languages, and cultural geographies," Edward Said concludes in *Culture and Imperialism,* "but there seems no reason except fear and prejudice to keep insisting on their

---

30 Spivak, "Reading *The Satanic Verses*": 60 (my emphasis).

separation and distinctiveness, as if that was all human life was about."[31] And James Clifford reminds us that "intervening in an interconnected world, one is always, to varying degrees, 'inauthentic': caught between cultures, implicated in others. [...] Identity is conjunctural, not essential."[32] Literary (and other) theories that remain silent in the face of clamorous authenticities do so at their own peril.

WORKS CITED

AHMAD, Aijaz. *In Theory: Classes, Nations, Literatures* (London: Verso, 1992).

ANDERSON, Amanda. "Cryptonormativism and Double Gestures: The Politics of Post-Structuralism," *Cultural Critique* 21 (1992): 63–95.

APPIGNANESI, Lisa & Sara MAITLAND, ed. *The Rushdie File* (London: Fourth Estate, 1989)

BRENNAN, Timothy. *Salman Rushdie and the Third World: Myths of the Nation* (Basingstoke: Macmillan, 1989).

CLIFFORD, James. *The Predicament of Culture* (Cambridge MA: Massachusetts UP, 1988).

HABERMAS, Jürgen. *The Philosophical Discourse of Modernity: Twelve Lectures* (1985; Cambridge: Polity, 1990).

"The Intellectual in the Post-Colonial World: Response and Discussion," *Salmagundi* 70–71 (1986): 65–81.

MALAK, Amin. "Reading the Crisis: The Polemics of Salman Rushdie's *The Satanic Verses*," *ARIEL: A Review of International English Literature* 20.4 (1989): 176–86.

PARAMESWARAN, Uma. "The We/They Paradigm in Rushdie's *Satanic Verses*," in *US/THEM: Translation, Transcription and Identity in Post-Colonial Literary Cultures*, ed. Gordon Collier (Cross/Cultures 6; Amsterdam/Atlanta GA: Rodopi, 1992): 189–99.

SAID, Edward. *Culture and Imperialism* (London: Chatto & Windus, 1993).

——. "Figures, Configurations, Transfigurations," in *From Commonwealth to Post-Colonial*, ed. Anna Rutherford (Sydney/Mundelstrup: Dangaroo, 1992): 3–17.

——. "Intellectuals in the Post-Colonial World," *Salmagundi* 70–71 (1986): 44–64.

——. *Orientalism* (1978; Harmondsworth: Penguin, 1987).

SARDAR, Ziauddin & Merryl Wyn DAVIES. *Distorted Imagination: Lessons from the Rushdie Affair* (London: Grey Seal, 1990).

SPIVAK, Gayatri Chakravorty. "Can the Subaltern Speak?," in *Marxism and the Interpretation of Cultures*, ed. Cary Nelson & Lawrence Grossberg (Basingstoke: Macmillan, 1988): 271–313.

——. "Criticism, Feminism and the Institution," in SPIVAK, *The Post-Colonial Critic*: 1–16.

——. *The Post-Colonial Critic: Interviews, Strategies, Dialogues*, ed. Sarah Harasym (New York/London: Routledge, 1990).

——. "Reading *The Satanic Verses*," *Third Text* 11 (special issue: "Beyond the Rushdie Affair," 1990): 41–60.

——. "Strategy, Identity, Writing," in SPIVAK, *The Post-Colonial Critic*, 35–49.

TIBI, Bassam. *The Crisis of Modern Islam: A Pre-Industrial Culture in the Scientific–Technological Age* (Salt Lake City: U of Utah P, 1988).

——. *Die fundamentalistische Herausforderung: der Islam und die Weltpolitik* [The Fundamentalist Challenge: Islam and World Politics] (Munich: Beck, 1992).

❧ ❖ ☙

---

[31] Said, *Culture and Imperialism*, 408.
[32] Clifford, *The Predicament of Culture*, 11.

BERNDT OSTENDORF

Inclusion, Exclusion
and the Politics of Cultural Difference

"Daddy, what are we?"
"What do you mean?"
"You know, where are we from? Are we Italian, Irish, Jewish;
you know like that?"
"Well, we're from here; we're Americans."
"Daddy!!! What am I going to say in school?" [1]

WHENEVER I ARGUE AS I SHALL IN THIS PAPER, my liberal friends ask with shock and hurt (as if I had come out of a neo-conservative closet) "why are you against multiculturalism?" Let me state categorically that I am not against multiculturalism. In fact, I travel around in Germany with Claus Leggewie, Jürgen Miksch, Uli Bielefeld and Dany Cohn Bendit to convince our political class that Germany has become a multicultural society, and that we had better do something about it by adjusting our naturalisation and immigration laws.[2] In the American context I am in sympathy with a multi-cultural, trans-national, trans-ethnic politics that tries to leave behind the pseudo-anthropological category of race and embraces a post-national, post-colonial perspective. I approve of Mary Louise Pratt's or Gerald Graff's notion of education in a contact zone; indeed, my own research at the moment is focused on "creolisa-tion": ie, on the processes of culture-formation in a culture-contact situation.

What I am concerned with is the hiatus that has emerged between educational theory and social practice. Faulkner said in *As I Lay Dying*: How easy words fly up in the air, and hard doing goes along the ground. Indeed, I worry more about the state of politics, both national and international, than about whether the New American Studies have a legitimate theory, or which version of multiculturalism fits the canon better. Has not the whole enterprise that we are involved in become "ideological?" While we, as members of the professional middle class, are talking about entitlement, empowerment and the need for a politics of difference, we watch (from a safe distance) the reconstruction of boundaries in the street. We are witness-ing the realignment of a new global economic order while we debate the merits or demerits of *differance* or the effects of deep structural violence on our habits of the

---

[1] John Garvey, "My Problem with Multi-Cultural Education," *Race Traitor* 1.2 (Winter, 1993): 18–25.
[2] Berndt Ostendorf, "Einwanderungspolitik der USA," in *Politik der Migration*, ed. Konrad Schacht & Elisabeth Kiderlen (Wiesbaden: Schriftenreihe der Hessischen Landeszentrale für politische Bildung, 1993): 25–38.

heart. My question is, what are the chances and long-range costs of multicultural agendas today   all agendas, not only those which with we happen to agree?[3]

The question

In 1903 the black sociologist W.E.B. DuBois wrote: "The problem of the twentieth century is the color line." Today this prophetic sentence might have to be modified to read: "the problem of the twenty-first century will be multiculturalism *on top of the colour line.*" Lebanon, Yugoslavia, the former USSR, Africa, South Africa, India, Belgium, France, England, Spain, Germany – the problems of states with populations of mixed backgrounds are glaringly visible. The three most basic questions in all cases are: 1) How much self-determination of culturally different groups must a state allow in order to conform to universally established standards of human and civil rights? 2) How much fragmentation or separation into cultural lobbies (or political interest-groups) can a state take before it becomes unmanageable or, at worst, disintegrates? 3) Should the three branches of government allow politics to be designed along the lines of racial, cultural or ethnic difference? Or, all three questions in a nutshell, how valid is the eighteenth-century political universalism on which the invention of the American Republic is based, in a fragmented, postmodern, post-fordist and post-national USA?

Universalism versus particularism

On the most fundamental level we are witnessing an old battle over the meaning of culture. The tension in the motto on every dollar bill – *e pluribus unum* – describes the federal compromise, but it also runs between one universal *political* culture (protected by the constitution and the amendments) and many *different, particularistic* cultures.[4] On the one hand, there is the unifying concept of one *culture* of "mankind" (the word itself gives rise to some doubt). It is defined as the glorious project of enlightenment, a liberating project designed to lead humanity out of fear, darkness and discrimination, to free people from tribalistic, primordial or ancestral bondage and to accept each individual on his/her own merits. This is the essence of an older liberal humanism, which inspired what Gunnar Myrdal called the American Creed.[5] On the other hand, we find a differentiating concept

3 A longer version of this paper is available from the John F. Kennedy Institute: *The Costs of Multiculturalism* (Working Paper 50; Berlin: John F. Kennedy Institute, 1992). A collection of essays on the topic has appeared: *Multikulturelle Gesellschaft: Modell Amerika?*, ed. Berndt Ostendorf (Munich: Wilhelm Fink, 1994).

4 Nathan Gardels, "Two Concepts of Nationalism: An Interview with Isaiah Berlin," *New York Review of Books* (21 November 1991): 19–23; Berndt Ostendorf, "Kulturanthropologie und Amerikastudien oder das Reden über Kultur," *Amerikastudien* 29.1 (1984): 5–18; Immanuel Wallerstein, "The Ideological Tensions of Capitalism: Universalism Versus Racism and Sexism," in *Racism, Sexism, and the World-System: Studies in the Political Economy of the World-System*, ed. Joan Smith et al. (Contributions in Economics and Economic History 84; Westport CT: Greenwood, 1988): 3–9.

5 Myrdal's position is brought up to date by Samuel Huntington in "The American Creed and National Identity," in *American Politics: The Promise of Disharmony* (Cambridge MA: Harvard UP, 1981). See also V.S. Naipaul, "Our Universal Civilization," *New York Times* (5 November, 1990): A21, or Leszek Kolakowski,

of *cultures*, groups and aggregates that are distinctly separate, but are all entitled to mutual recognition and respect.[6] This understanding of culture interprets the difference between, say, Chicanos and blacks as an entitlement not only to be unique in cultural matters, but also to differential treatment in politics. And such differential treatment would not be accorded on the basis of individual merit, but to individuals as members of "racial" or ethnic groups. The idea of "ethnic or cultural difference," which under the univeralist credo was considered to belong to the private sphere, has since the Sixties become thoroughly politicised, encouraged by the slogan that the personal is political.

The two concepts (one political culture versus many ethnic cultures) also mark the two extreme positions in a political conflict between two frames of justice.[7] In the words of Michael Walzer, the first "is committed in the strongest possible way to individual rights and, almost as a deduction from this, to a rigorously neutral state, that is, a state without cultural or religious projects or, indeed, any sort of collective goals beyond the personal freedom and the physical security, welfare, and safety of its citizens." The second "allows for a state committed to the survival and flourishing of a particular nation, culture, or religion, or of a (limited) set of nations, cultures, and religions – so long as the basic rights of citizens who have different commitments or no such commitments at all are protected."[8]

The Anglo-American norm

In the first phase of immigration, between 1830 and 1920, when ethnic difference was associated with cultural inferiority, poverty and bad working-conditions, there was a powerful motive to assimilate to the Anglo-American norm of the good life. Many well-meaning progressive reformers quite cheerfully took this norm for granted. Even the ethnic groups themselves contributed to the demise of their own traditions if these stood in the way of economic betterment. The resulting "melting pot" of former immigrants, however, remained white, eurocentric and therefore "encapsulated in white ethnocentrism."[9] Whereas the allegedly "colour-blind"

"Wo sind die Barbaren? Ein Lob des Eurozentrismus oder Die Illusion des kulturellen Universalismus," *Der Monat* 2 (October–December, 1980): 70–83.

6 Axel Honneth deconstructs the ambivalence in the liberal or communitarian discourse of a particularism-within-universalism: "Eine Rhetorik des Partikularismus verhindert die Artikulation der universalistischen Restmotive, auf die gerade derjenige sich heute zu stützen hat, dem die Verteidigung des kulturellen Pluralismus entschieden am Herzen liegt" ("Universalismus und kulturelle Differenz: Zu Michael Walzers Modell der Gesellschaftskritik," *Merkur: Deutsche Zeitschrift für europäisches Denken* 512 [November, 1991]: 1054).

7 Berndt Ostendorf, "Die amerikanische Definition von Kultur und die Definition der amerikanischen Kultur," in *Die Vereinigten Staaten von Amerika*, ed. Willi P. Adams, E.–O. Czempiel, Berndt Ostendorf, K.L. Shell, P.B. Spahn & Michael Zöller (Frankfurt: Campus, 1990), vol. 2: 449–68. See also Hannah Arendt, *The Human Condition* (Chicago: U of Chicago P, 1958) on "The Public and the Private Realm."

8 Walzer writes this in response to Charles Taylor, *Multiculturalism and "The Politics of Recognition"* (Princeton NJ: Princeton UP, 1992).

9 John Higham, quoted in Stephen Steinberg, *The Ethnic Myth: Race, Ethnicity and Class in America* (1981; New York: Beacon, rev. ed. 1989): 255.

American Creed swept some white ethnic groups into its fold, there remained the problem of racism and its baneful social consequences of open or tacit discrimination.[10] Alexis de Tocqueville was prophetic when he wrote in the 1840s that racism when it is removed from the laws withdraws into customs. How does one overcome racist institutional structures and racist habits of the heart, and how does one compensate adequately for the damages of historical discrimination?

Civil rights and the rise of ethnic culture

It is important to remember that the rise of ethnicity began as a fight to stop (racist) sins against the universalism of the American Creed.[11] After the 1954 Supreme Court decision Brown vs. Board of Education Topeka, Kansas established that separate facilities for blacks were "inherently unequal," the notion of racial or cultural difference itself was removed from all legal consideration. To "make a difference" was considered unconstitutional, on the grounds that historical experience showed such difference to lead to separate and *unequal* conditions.[12] Federal institutions were called upon to undo differential treatment and to ensure that blacks were given an "equal opportunity" as members of a colour-blind political culture. Yet we should not underestimate the impact of the experience of exclusion on the collective consciousness of African–Americans. Few blacks could forget that it took America's eighteenth-century political universalism 178 years to recognise them as political equals. By the late Sixties, the accumulated experience of that exclusion from mainstream universalism had nurtured a specific African–American culture which was being recognised and appreciated for the first time on a national level.[13] Indeed, patterns of cultural nationalism and of a defensive black ethnocentrism were deeply inscribed in that

---

10 Well into the twentieth century the census-takers did not consider blacks and Native Americans proper to be "Americans," despite the allegedly universalist definition of an American "citizen."

11 Indeed, during World War II W. Lloyd Warner introduced the term "ethnicity" to diplace the scientifically questionable concept of race; see Warner, Buford H. Junker & Walter A. Adams, *Color and Human Nature: Negro Personality Development in a Northern City* (Washington DC: American Council on Education, 1941) and Warner & Leo Srole, *The Social Systems of American Ethnic Groups* (New Haven CT: Yale UP, 1945). Literature functioned as a sensitive barometer of these changes. See Berndt Ostendorf, "Einleitung" to *Amerikanische Ghettoliteratur: Zur Literatur ethnischer, marginaler und unterdrückter Gruppen in Amerika*, ed. Ostendorf (Darmstadt: Wissenschaftliche Buchgesellschaft, 1983). Cf also *The Invention of Ethnicity*, ed. Werner Sollors (New York: Oxford UP, 1989) and *Beyond Ethnicity: Consent and Descent in American Culture*, ed. Werner Sollors (New York: Oxford UP, 1986).

12 See William M. Wiecek, *Liberty under Law: The Supreme Court in American Life* (Baltimore MD: Johns Hopkins UP, 1988). The German historian Reinhart Koselleck charts the history of asymmetry between groups in "Zur historisch-politischen Semantik asymmetrischer Gegenbegriffe," in *Positionen der Negativität*, ed. Harald Weinrich (Munich: Fink, 1975): 65–104.

13 Berndt Ostendorf, "Black Poetry, Blues, and Folklore: Double Consciousness in Afro-Américan Oral Culture," *Amerikastudien* 20.2 (1975) and "Rediscovering an Invisible Culture," in Ostendorf, *Understanding Black Literature in White America* (Studies in Contemporary Literature and Culture; Brighton: Harvester, 1982).

culture as a consequence of previous exclusion.[14] Here, then, was a cultural tradition in the process of being recognised that would become the breeding-ground for a differential identity.

The Vietnam trauma

It was the Civil Rights movement of black Americans that also set in motion a rethinking of ethnic difference, hence of the relationship between (private) culture and (public) politics. The success of new ideologies of black cultural nationalism or of white ethnicity at this particular time has a lot to do with the failure of the American Creed, with the decline of a broad middle-class ideology after the Vietnam War and Watergate and concurrently with the demise of inter-ethnic "class consciousness" as a factor in social and political orientation. The decline of the older ideological belief in universalist principles that would make Americans into *one people* – indeed, that would turn all mankind into the *Family of Man* [sic], as a much-visited exhibition of photography was called in the Fifties – had much to do with the loss of faith in America subsequent to the Vietnam War. The Vietnam trauma gave rise to a radical rejection of mainstream values and speeded the rise of a counterculture which fed on the riches of a hitherto repressed black culture. Then radical feminism defined power as masculine and white, and the Watergate scandal reduced executive authority. "AmeriKKKa," it seemed, was a construct of pure repression, the American Creed was a sham, the American Dream a nightmare. Add to this growing criticism of the urban capitalist Moloch which – with the help of the military–industrial complex – was set upon the destruction of our natural world. At the same time, a post-fordist mode of production led to a massive de-industrialisation which broke the older class solidarity of workers across racial and ethnic lines, created a split labour market, and, as Richard Rorty and others have claimed, led to a deepening "secession" between the successful and the down-and-out during the Reagan era.[15] In this situation of American self-doubt and declining class-options, the older ethnic memories acquired the glow of a pastoral alternative. Not only ethnic *gemeinschaft* against a burnt-out anonymous *gesellschaft*, but feminine, ethnic culture against phallocratic, logocentric, patriarchal power, small-is-beautiful against centralist

---

14 Isaiah Berlin: "a wounded *Volksgeist*, so to speak, is like a bent twig, forced down so severely that when released, it lashes back with fury. Nationalism, at least in the West, is created by wounds inflicted by stress," in Gardels, "Two Concepts of Nationalism," 19. See also E.J. Hobsbawm, *Nations and Nationalism Since 1870: Programme, Myth, Reality* (Cambridge: Cambridge UP, 1990).

15 Richard Rorty, "Intellectuals in Politics," *Dissent* (Fall 1991): 483–90 and his exchange with Andrew Ross in *Dissent* (Spring 1992): 263–67: "the big problem is that white people whose family income is over $20,000 a year have come to think of themselves as having nothing in common with the weak and the poor (especially the black and brown poor)." This belief is reflected in the "two-nations" theory of Andrew Hacker: *Two Nations: Black and White, Separate, Hostile, Unequal* (New York: Scribner's, 1992). The black–white, rich–poor separation is reflected in the suburban–inner city divide; see Daniel Lazare, "Collapse of a City: Growth and Decay of Camden, New Jersey," *Dissent* (Spring 1991): 267–75.

homogeneity.[16] The Sixties saw a general flowering of non-hegemonic sub-communities into which the "new" ethnicity with its liberationist Herderian ethos fitted hand in glove. In many ways the most victimised group, first African–Americans, then Native Americans and Hispanics, now had the strongest credentials for a differential identity.

The valorisation of difference

Radical anthropologists had been first in fighting the tacit racist and hierarchical assumptions of universalism within evolutionary paradigms ("blacks are not ready yet") by insisting on a decentered, non-hierarchical or decolonialised view of cultures. A new set of scholars in the tradition of Melville Herskovits[17] pointed out that so-called "primitive" cultures were not pathological or inferior, but both "beautiful on their own terms" and "historically different." To undo the "marks of oppression" the battle cry "black is beautiful" of black cultural nationalists called for a reversal of attitudes, and indeed certain black ways of dressing, talking and dancing set a new agenda in the, appropriately named, counterculture of white students. This new appreciation of post-colonial cultural forms set the stage for a critique of enlightenment philosophy and ushered in a wave of European discontent with Western civilisation. Though this critique had old roots (Las Casas, Montaigne) its last wave was inspired by Horkheimer & Adorno's *Dialectic of Enlightenment* or Marcuse's *One-Dimensional Man*,[18] but subsequently owed more to the work of French deconstructionists. These took their inspiration from Nietzsche and Heidegger, both critics of the enlightenment project, and the latter a *bête noire* of the Frankfurt School. What the fighters for Civil Rights had identified as *sins against* eighteenth-century enlightenment turned out, enlarged by the lenses of French theory, to be the *sin of* enlightenment. The sin, its original core, amounted to the exclusion of the colonial Other from "universalistic" world-views. White male hegemony was inscribed in the entire system, and differential identity-politics of hitherto marginalised groups were the answer.

Ethnicity and the dilemma of difference

Most Americans would probably embrace some form of differential political treatment if they could be sure that its implementation would distribute chances more evenly and make the country more tolerant.[19] This explains why the introduction of affirmative action programs was initially uncontroversial. Most Americans accepted Lyndon B. Johnson's metaphor that a runner who had been

---

16 Count Gobineau and Robert E. Park used to refer to Africa as the "Lady of the races."

17 Melville J. Herskovits, *The Myth of the Negro Past* (1941; New York: Beacon, 1958).

18 Theodor Adorno & Max Horkheimer, *The Dialectic of Enlightenment*, tr. John Cumming (New York: Harper, 1945); Herbert Marcuse, *One-Dimensional Man* (New York: Beacon, 1964).

19 Nathan Glazer, author of *Affirmative Discrimination: Ethnic Inequality and Public Policy* (Cambridge MA: Harvard UP,) and opponent of multicultural agendas, takes a less sanguine view of the problem after helping to forge a compromise on a multicultural canon for New York State; see Glazer, "In Defense of Multiculturalism," *New Republic* (September 2, 1991): 18–22.

chained for three centuries could not compete in the rat-race without a "head start." Hence *affirmative* steps were taken to compensate for the many visible and invisible obstacles which, despite the removal of all legal barriers and the introduction of equal opportunity, kept blacks out of certain schools and jobs. Gertrude Ezorsky expresses a sentiment which was widespread in the Sixties and Seventies, but has since been losing support: "We need formal discrimination in favor of blacks to offset the effects of persistent informal discrimination against them."[20]

The combination of factors – first the new appreciation for the legitimacy of black culture, then the policy of affirmative action – did much good; today there is a solid black upper-middle and middle class which has penetrated many professions that were classically white domains. Many blacks from all social strata have embraced their own traditions with new appreciation, as evidenced in the flowering of African–American Studies programs in education and of black film and music. Yet there have been unintentional and unforeseen repercussions. In order to achieve the promise of the colour-blind creed of one universal culture which would treat all Americans, regardless of race, religion and national origin, as equals, the new social policy had to define, on the basis of anthropological criteria of cultural difference, who was entitled to "affirmative action," to set-asides, and to preferential treatment. The question of "who is a minority" became a thoroughly confusing and confused legal issue.[21] Although affirmative action was intended as a short-range remedy for long-range social and economic difference, it actually hardened the ideological and political structures of difference. First, it encouraged what Freud has called "the narcissism of minor difference" and refined the cult of ethnic sensitivity.[22] The second dilemma was that this desire to implement Civil-Rights justice and social equality required a code of legislative "hard" criteria of racial difference to establish who was "black," thus revitalising the anthropological code of "difference" that had buttressed the old racist system of the South along the colour-line.[23] The North

---

[20] Gertrude Ezorsky, *Racism and Justice: The Case for Affirmative Action* (Ithaca NY: Cornell UP, 1992), reviewed by Andrew Hacker, "The New Civil War," *New York Review of Books* 34.8 (April 23, 1992): 30. Stephen Carter, author of *Reflections of an Affirmative Action Baby* (New York: Basic Books, 1992), weighs the pros and cons in "Racism's Victims," *The World & I* (February, 1992): 467–79, but comes out in its defence.

[21] Philip Gleason, "Minorities (Almost) All: The Minority Concept in American Social Thought," *The World & I* (February, 1992): 414.

[22] Freud writes in *Civilization and its Discontents* (1930): "The advantage which a comparatively small cultural group offers of allowing this instinct [the inclination to aggression] an outlet in the form of hostility against intruders is not to be despised. It is always possible to bind together a considerable number of people in love, so long as there are other people left over to receive the manifestations of their aggressiveness. I once discussed the phenomenon that it is precisely communities with adjoining territories, and related to each other in other ways as well, who are engaged in constant feuds and in ridiculing each other – like the Spaniards and Portuguese, for instance, the North Germans and South Germans, the English and Scotch, and so on. I gave this phenomenon the name of 'the narcissism of minor differences,' a name which does not much to explain it" (*Standard Edition of the Complete Psychological Works of Sigmund Freud*, vol. 21, ed. James Strachey (London, 1927–1931).

[23] Bette Novit–Evans & Ashton Wesley Welch, "Racial and Ethnic Definition as Reflection of Public Policy," *Journal of American Studies* 17 (1983): 3, 417–35 remark on the arbitrariness of the colour-line.

American colour-line, as Papa Doc Duvalier has noted, marks a somatic "difference" imposed by the racial paranoia of white Anglo-Saxon men. The shrewd
former ruler of Haiti was once asked by an American journalist how many people of
white blood were still left in Haiti. Papa Doc replied: "About 95 percent." When the
journalist expressed disbelief in view of the nearly all-black population of Haiti,
Papa Doc asked how the Americans defined who was black. The journalist replied
"Anyone with a drop of black blood" – to which Papa Doc responded: "Anyone
with a drop of white blood: that's exactly how we define whites."[24] Papa Doc makes
visible the fact that the colour-line is a line of pathological white fear, and that any
"affirmative action" based on its somatic norms therefore stabilises that older
somatic divide first institutionalised by Dead White Male racists.[25]

The new valorisation of ethnic difference and its attendant wave of ethnic pride
clearly served to build a better sense of self. But defensive identity-politics also
encourages a new ethnocentrism which in turn strengthens ethnic boundaries as a
defence not only against the dominant culture, but also against *other* groups. The
current black antisemitism and white ethnic racism are indications that identity-
politics sets in motion an ugly dialectic of "my otherness is more legitimate than
your otherness."[26] The right to an ethnocentric view is sometimes justified by the
experience of historical or personal social and political discrimination. The argument runs that people who have suffered under racism cannot be racists themselves
– in other words, black antisemitism is, in the larger context of American race
relations, politically legitimate and ought to be accepted by the Jews.[27] Proof of
suffering, then, legitimates ethno-chauvinism, according to the motto: Do unto
others what has been done to you. This leaves us with a troubling question: is the
ethno-chauvinism of victims better than the ethno-chauvinism of oppressors? Prima
facie, yes; in terms of short-range goals for the group vis-à-vis the alleged
oppressor, yes; but it does not solve the problem of inter-ethnic coexistence in the
same political culture. And which universal agency is going to decide whose
suffering outweighs that of others? It therefore comes as no surprise that the anti-
hegemonic discourse of many ethnic groups reads like a public competition in
relative victimisation.[28] The *grand récit* of America used to narrate the success of the

---

[24] The idea of an either–or racial purity is deeply rooted in Northern European popular mythologies.
Papa Doc's parable tells us that somatic norms vary from hard to soft to blurred. Immigrants from South
and Central America arrive in the US with blurred somatic norms which harden as they assimilate.

[25] The current stabilisation of the colour-line has given the fine art of race-detection a new lease of life.
One of the oldest racist games down South was to identify people who had passed. Today there is a renewed
search for the "touch of the tarbrush" in the creation of what is often dismissed as Western Civilisation. A
black musicologist assured me: "You know of course that Beethoven was black," to which I wished I had
replied: "How about Hitler?"

[26] See Jeffrey Alexander, Chaim Seidler–Feller & Cornel West. "Blacks and Jews," *Tikkun* (January–
February, 1992): 12–16.

[27] A position defended by Stanley Fish on William Buckley's *Firing Line* (August 28, 1991); transcript,
Southern Educational Communications Organisation, 1991: 31.

[28] In an American version of the "*Historikerstreit*," Ali A. Mazrui argues that African–Americans and
Native Americans have claims on the term "holocaust"; see Paul Gray, "Whose America?" *Time* (July 8,

melting pot; now a number of *petits récits* of the victims of hegemony are competing for attention. Whose attention? Usually that of the media. (This opens another can of worms: the role of the media and of the new public sphere defined and dominated by specific constraints and hegemonic desires. People have alleged that the current debate on multiculturalism was in large part created by "media hype.")

Difference and social justice

Martha Minow, legal scholar and former assistant to Thurgood Marshall, writes:

> How can historical discrimination on the basis of race and gender be overcome if the remedies themselves use the forbidden categories of race and gender? Yet without such remedies, how can historical discrimination and its legacies of segregation and exclusion be transcended?[29]

This is indeed the dilemma of valorising ethnic difference and of institutionalising such difference by politics and law. She warns: "Solutions to the dilemma of difference cannot work if they redeposit the responsibility for redressing negative meanings of difference on the person who is treated as different." That may well be, but the problem gets infinitely more complicated when negative differences are recoded as positive differences and former ascriptions are claimed as a new ethnic strength. Negative ascriptions then turn into positive identity-politics, thus stabilising the difference, but usually without shedding their negative social consequences within the larger political culture.[30]

As the attitude towards ethnic difference became more positive in certain quarters during the Seventies and Eighties, the older grounds for a "negative discrimination" became new grounds for "positive discrimination" by administrative fiat.[31] Consequently, ethnic difference acquired a dual significance in the political culture: as a positive political marker, it creates group pride and solidarity and calls for affirmative action to make up for previous discrimination. As a negative political marker, it identifies cases of current discrimination of marginal groups by the dominant culture or of one group by another. The problem is that two systems of justice must coexist. Iris Marion Young makes a strong case for a "politics of difference" to combat "sexism, racism, heterosexism, ageism and

---

1991): 23. At the EAAS convention in Seville, Toni Morrison's use of the term "holocaust" was criticised by an Israeli literary scholar.

[29] Martha Minow, *Making all the Difference: Inclusion, Exclusion, and American Law* (Ithaca NY: Cornell UP, 1990): 47. See also Iris Marion Young, *Justice and the Politics of Difference* (Princeton NJ: Princeton UP, 1990).

[30] Minow, *Making all the Difference*, 93. In many nineteenth-century minstrel tunes we find the sentiment that "those niggers sure can sing and dance," which implied a negative slur that blacks are not good at much else. Does the positive recoding of this slur into a special gift as part of a comprehensive and different black aesthetic really succeed in shedding the older social implication? Or do not identity-politics that build on the basis of older discriminatory tropes strengthen those patterns? This may be the psychological trauma at the bottom of the "Rage of the Black Middle Class" which *Newsweek* talks about (November 2, 1993).

[31] Nathan Glazer, "Affirmative Discrimination: For and Against," *Ethnic Dilemmas* (Cambridge MA: Harvard UP, 1983): 159–81.

ableism," but she is vague about how the contradiction between "group specific rights" and "general civic rights" should be worked out:

> A democratic cultural pluralism thus requires a dual system of rights: a general system or rights which are the same for all, and a more specific system of group-conscious policies and rights.[32]

This is a tall order, as the Bakke case has demonstrated. But one thing is clear: thus redefined (and protected), ethnic differences has moved from the realm of private culture or folklore to that of public politics. With this move the problems began to multiply. When other ethnic groups saw that "ethnicity" could be transformed from a cultural liability into a political advantage, they cried "Me too!" Native Americans and Chicanos could also make strong claims on the basis of previous exclusion, hence Red and Brown Power movements followed in the wake of the Black Power movement on the basis of very similar political agendas. A particularly bitter reaction came from a white ethnic working class that had – between 1830 and 1960 – been socialised into the American racialist system, and who were puzzled that their understanding of how the American system worked (including its racial advantages) no longer held. The extreme swing of classical Democratic voters to the conservative independents (George Wallace) and to Nixon, or the success of David Duke in Louisiana where 55 percent of white ethnic workers voted for him, has a lot to do with this feeling of being ignored. The recent Congressional swing towards a fundamentalist right has a lot to do with this. Why were white ethnic workers after 1968 no longer recognised as victims of the system? The ensuing revival of white ethnicity (Italian–Americans, Polish–Americans etc) was interpreted by liberal critics as a knee-jerk reaction of these white groups to Civil Rights and to the new ethnic politics favouring blacks and Native Americans. But it also involves a subtle realignment of political culture: it can be seen as a successful attempt to depolarise the racialist black–white conflict by multilateralising ethnicity.[33] By taking white ethnic entitlements seriously, government could deflect anger over the preferential treatment of blacks (and soon also of Indians and Hispanics). Soon grants were showered on regional ethnic studies programs and white ethnic museums. All this led to a surprising revitalisation, if not reconstruction, of white ethnic consciousness and ethnic affirmation along with black, Hispanic and Native-American ethnic affirmation.

Does this mark a survival of the repressed or primordial ethnicity? Were the American ethnics really "unmeltable" as the conservative scholar Michael Novak had claimed? Are Italian–Americans really closet Italians? Are African–Americans really Africans? Glazer's and Moynihan's claim that "the melting pot

---

32 Young, *Justice and the Politics of Difference*, 174.
33 See Pierre L. van den Berghe, *The Ethnic Phenomenon* (New York: Elsevier/Westport CT: Greenwood, 1981): 212.

did not happen"[34] was often misunderstood to mean that the traditional or original cultures had survived immigration. What they meant, however, was that the American ethnic group was not a "survival from the age of mass immigration, but a new social form."[35] What we have, then, is not the old "primordial" difference, but a new "ethnic" quality. (The charge by black or Hispanic groups that the dominant American culture is "eurocentric" strikes European observers as somewhat short of the mark; American culture is "americocentric.") We should focus on "the ethnic boundary that defines the group, not the cultural stuff that it encloses"[36] – in other words, the cultural stuff need not be "genuine" or "primordial" in order to shape an American ethnic group. For this is their point: in a polity which gives high priority to voluntarism it is as American as apple pie for people to congregate in "americanised" ethnic groups. "Ethnicity," then, is an American quality, all too often characterised by a nostalgia without memory or by what linguists call "structural amnesia," a quality which emerges when several groups of different national origin arrange themselves in the same political system or several ethnic cultures find their slot in the same economic structure and thereby assimilate "to each other" in myriad ways.[37]

The voluntaristic quality of (white) ethnicity is nowhere more evident than in the revised instructions for census-takers. The 1980 census ancestry questionnaire instructs the census-takers: "Print the ancestry group with which the person *identifies*."[38] Ethnic self-identification – as the Census Bureau officers warned – allows for a greater degree of flux and choice. Ethnicity is no longer decided on the basis of "hard" historical data of genealogical descent, but of cultural consent, which invites a good deal of fantasy.[39] A black would have a hard time to pass

---

34 Nathan Glazer & Daniel P. Moynihan, *Beyond the Melting Pot: The Negroes, Puerto Ricans, Jews, Italians, and Irish of New York City* (Cambridge MA: MIT Press, 2nd ed. 1970) and *Ethnicity: Theory and Experience*, ed. Nathan Glazer & Daniel P. Moynihan (Cambridge MA: Harvard UP, 1975).

35 Milton Gordon, "Models of Pluralism: The New American Dilemma," in "America as a Multicultural Society," *Annals of the American Academy of Political And Social Sciences* (Special Issue, vol. 454; March 1981): 178–88.

36 Fredrik Barth, *Ethnic Groups and Boundaries: The Social Organization of Culture Difference* (New York: Little, Brown, 1969).

37 See also Berndt Ostendorf, "What Makes Ethnic Literature 'Ethnic'?," in *Le facteur ethnique aux Etats Unis et au Canada*, ed. Monique Lecomte & Claudine Thomas (Travaux et recherches 12: Etats-Unis, Canada; Lille: Université de Lille III, 1983) and Ostendorf, "Einleitung" to *Amerikanische Ghettoliteratur*, ed. Ostendorf.

38 Mary C. Waters, *Ethnic Options: Choosing Identities in America* (Berkeley: U of California P, 1990): 9: The Census Bureaus introduced this question on pressure from white ethnic organisations. Waters' research among white ethnics concluded that "ethnicity is increasingly a personal choice of whether to be ethnic at all [...] it matters only in voluntary ways [...] First, I believe it stems from two contradictory desires in the American character: a quest for community on the one hand and a desire for individuality on the other. Second, symbolic ethnicity persists because of its ideological 'fit' with racist beliefs" (Waters, *Ethnic Options*, 147). William A. Schambra, ghostwriter for Republican Secretary Louis Sullivan, proposes a Republican platform on the basis of a politics of small communities; see "The Quest for Community in Twentieth-Century America," *The World and I* 5.10 (October, 1990): 489–99.

39 What linguists have called "structural amnesia," a process of selective forgetting, is strongly evident in oral and genealogical memory. See Ostendorf, "Black Poetry." Ernest Renan's dictum "getting its history

before the eyes of the census-taker,.[40] whereas a Greek–American could conceivably be born again ethnically as an Italian–American or vice versa. Even people of mixed background may thus cleanse themselves of bastardisation and reinvent themselves as pure ethnics, choosing the ethnic group they would like to be identified with.[41] In the event of too much confusion of ethnic backgrounds, the first two groups mentioned by the head of the household will be taken for identification. (The Louisiana census for the first time lists about 150 people who self-identify as Aleuts – no doubt citizens with a keen sense of humour.) What these flight-patterns from the melting-pot, now encouraged by the census, express may simply be a reaction to that suburban, melting-pot anonymity so compellingly described by David Riesman.[42] But it also signals a deep phobia against mixing which used to be a WASP or nativist obsession, but which has now gone ethnic. Perhaps it also marks a negative reaction to the real historical cultural mixing that has gone on in American society. In one branch of Western philosophy there is a tacit background assumption which ranks "urity" higher than "ixture"; the notion of biological blending ("miscegenation") or cultural mixture (bastardisation), which has traditionally outraged the nationalist right wing, thus now begins to have a bad press even among Americans whose family trees are hopelessly mixed. The *Harvard Encyclopedia of American Ethnic Groups* (with impeccable credentials as an opponent of ethnic chauvinism) nonetheless treats 106 ethnic groups as if they were discrete and separate (thus loyal enough to the notion of biological and cultural purity to please a Le Pen).[43] And the Harvard encyclopedia obliges: any mixture between the groups, which, unmeltable ethnics notwithstanding, has been rampant in American history, does not receive much attention from the authors of national entries. But mixture or, more elegantly, creolisation is the stuff of American culture. And some of the most significant "merican" contributions to world culture have been such creolised hybrid formations: jazz, pop & youth culture, dance, architecture, everyday consumer culture.[44] Ironically, much of the public acknowledgement of ethnic cultures today

---

wrong is part of being a nation" might be expanded to include ethnicity (see Renan, *Qu'est que c'est une nation?*; Paris, 1882: 7–8). See also *The Invention of Ethnicity*, ed. Sollors, and *Beyond Ethnicity*, ed. Sollors.

[40] George Frederickson and Dale Knobel write: "If history is any guide, one might be inclined to predict that strong prejudice will survive so long as the black community remains an involuntary racial group rather than a voluntary ethnic community."

[41] Dan Foot, "American Indians in the 1990s," *American Demographics* (December, 1991): 26–34. "Today, for reasons of ethnic pride part Indians may tell the Census Bureau they are Indian" (34). One of the deepest impulses of nationalism is that of cleansing the ethnic body politic.

[42] David Riesman, *The Lonely Crowd: A Study of the Changing American Character* (New Haven CT: Yale UP, 1950).

[43] *Harvard Encyclopedia of American Ethnic Groups*, ed. Stephan Thernstrom et al. (Cambridge MA: Harvard UP, 1980). "We radically reject the idea of a global melting pot both for humans and for dogs or horses. The purpose of each culture is to maintain, increase and refine the diversity of the species" (Jean–Marie Le Pen, *Les Français d'abord* [Paris: Carrère–Lafon, 1984]; my translation).

[44] Reed Way Dasenbrock, "The Multicultural West," *Dissent* (Fall, 1991): 550–55: "Our current models of culture all seem to be either/or (eurocentric vs. afrocentric, Western vs. non-Western, monocultural vs. multicultural), but culture itself is both/and, not either/or. Multiculturalism is simply the standard human condition" (553). Dasenbrock takes both sides to task and attacks the Bennetts and Blooms for their "clean"

serves as a symbolic reparation for the damage allegedly done to them by the very cultural melting-pot that ethnic Americans helped to create. Many American ethnic ideologues work on the assumption that their true heritage was destroyed by the hegemonic melting pot and that their revived ethnicity should restore the real older article. They fail to realise how much ethnic groups have changed or influenced what they fight against as "the mainstream," how hopelessly American they have themselves become in exercising their rights, and that even their revitalised new ethnicity is an American cultural creation patterned on that national religious sport called "awakening."

Most Americans would probably opt for some sort of soft, messy pluralism under the auspices of a reformed *eighteenth*-century universalism watched over by the Supreme Court: ie, for some version of what they had before. But the actual political and social implementation of ethnic policies which has emerged in recent years has given rise to some alarm. There seems to be an internal dynamic in ethnic discourse and politics to aim for "pure" or "radical" ethnicity, which in turn would require a corporate or con-sociationalist multiculturalism.[45] In other words, what emerges in political practice is the exact opposite of what most multicultural theorists aim at: namely, a penchant for ethnic cleansing, group territorialisation, and paranoid boundary-maintenance.[46] Few people (except unreconstructed conservatives such as Allan Bloom, William J. Bennett and the aged heads of English departments) would want to resurrect the hypocritical and narrow universalism of the slave-holding Founding Fathers. Clearly, the uncritical acceptance of the older eurocentric American Creed as outlined by Gunnar Myrdal and resurrected by neoconservative critics is not, and has never been, a realistic option in a multi-ethnic America.[47] Nor is the critique of enlightenment universalism advanced by Heidegger

---

idea of European culture: "we need to adopt a good deal of the multiculturalist agenda precisely because it is in keeping with the best and most important aspects of Western and American culture [...] Neither side perceives the world in which we live" (554–55). On creolisation, see Berndt Ostendorf, "Creolization and Creoles: The Concepts and their History," in *La Louisiane française/French Louisiana*, ed. Wolfgang Binder (Würzburg, 1992).

[45] Racial gerrymandering has been an effective strategy to keep minorities away from power by distributing them over several voting districts. The opposite tendency, affirmative gerrymandering, is not much better; for it envisages the redrawing of voting districts along racial lines which would immobilise the racial power differential. See David C. Saffell, "Affirmative Gerrymandering: Rationale and Application," *State Government* 56:4 (1983). See also Jim Sleeper, *The Closest of Strangers: Liberalism and the Politics of Race in New York* (New York: Norton, 1990), reviewed by John Alt in *Telos* 87 (Summer 1991): 173–85 and in his "Cultural Conflict in New York City," *Reconstruction* 1.4 (1992): 142–46. A current case of redistricting involves the 12th district in New York, which favors Hispanics: see "Scrambling Solarz," *Economist* (July 25, 1992): 51.

[46] The affluent American middle class is adjusting to the new climate of difference by withdrawing into "walled cities" or community-independent developments with their own taxes and services, private guards, identity-tags and strict membership rules. These citizens will most likely not vote to increase public spending for services they do not use, "ignoring the needs of people who cannot afford to go private"; see "Government by the nice, for the nice," *Economist* (July 25, 1992): 47–48.

[47] See Gunnar Myrdal, *An American Dilemma: The Negro Problem and Modern Democracy* (New York: Harper & Row, rev. ed. 1962). Werner Sollors writes: "Once America thinks of itself as the only place of grace, once true human universalism is narrowly compacted into the American Dream, it becomes an

and filtered through French sources into the American academic discourse without merit. If, as Stanley Fish, Iris Marion Young and others have argued, a new meta-universalism of constant hermeneutic and critical debate could be guaranteed that would establish inter-ethnic culture as an unending conversation (Kenneth Burke), then all the better.[48] This would require an enormous capacity for self-criticism and sophistication which I do not see emerging from ethnic group or inter-ethnic discourse. Iris Marion Young admits that she is at a loss to say, how "interest group pluralism" plus "meta-universalism" could work: "There is no model to follow."[49] As Isaiah Berlin, a staunch defender of a non-hegemonic pluralism in the tradition of Herder and Vico, admits, any hope for such a meta-universalism is dim: "I admit that, at the end of the twentieth century, there is little historical evidence for the realisability of such a vision," and he ends on a chilling (and somewhat unfair) note: "I am glad to be as old as I am."[50] Although one is tempted at this point to trot out once more the idea of an American exceptionalism, the question remains: would such a tolerant meta-universalist debating society work in the political arena, given its current economic structures and imperatives? Would it work in the judicial arena or would it end in a series of both-either-and-or-Bakke decisions? Would it save the constitutional "progress" made since the age of Jefferson? Not without a major effort in general education for which there is at the moment no recognisable political will, and as little concrete evidence.[51] In fact, the division between well-paid, enlightened, academically trained America and underpaid populist America is today wider than in the *Sixties*.

Displacement of class discourse

Of the foursome "gender–race–ethnicity–class" (GREC) that graces many titles of articles and workshops in American Studies, the term "class" has become devoid of its older significance and punch. It is particularly alarming that the problem of class divisions within and beyond ethnic groups no longer plays a decisive role and has disappeared from most discourse on ethnicity.[52] However, while the discourse of

---

obstacle to its own selfdeclared transcendent ends" (*Beyond Ethnicity*, 261). See also Alan Trachtenberg, *Between Quarrel and Gratitude: Culture, Democracy, America* (Working Paper 44; Berlin: John F. Kennedy Institute, 1992) and Sacvan Bercovitch, *Discovering "America": A Cross-Cultural Perspective* (Working Paper 36; Berlin: John F. Kennedy Institute, 1991).

48 Iris Marion Young presents a forceful argument for a relational rather than substantive politics of difference in *Justice and the Politics of Difference*. However, it is not quite clear to me how one would implement such a politics of difference in the political arena.

49 Young, *Justice and the Politics of Difference*, 190–91.

50 Young, *Justice and the Politics of Difference*, 21–23. Ironically, the "Austro-Hungarian model of political and economic uniformity and cultural variety" is an object of nostalgia for Isaiah Berlin and other proponents of the ideal multicultural society.

51 Christopher Jencks shares that doubt in *Rethinking Social Policy: Race, Poverty, and the Underclass* (Cambridge MA: Harvard UP, 1992). Michael Geyer and Miriam Hansen make an impassioned plea for the reform of general education in "Varieties of Multiculturalism and the Politics of the Curriculum," lecture delivered at the Continuing Education Conference, University of Chicago (November, 1991).

52 See also Benjamin DeMott, *The Imperial Middle: Why Americans Can't Think Straight about Class* (New Haven CT: Yale UP, 1991).

class lacks conviction, there is a growing recognition that America, despite the absence of a European class "consciousness," is moving towards a dichotomised stratification that is geared to education and cuts through the new ethnic fragmentation.[53] Call it what you will, the gap between rich and poor is widening and the American left is not paying much attention to this fact.

The rise of ethnicity has been a boon for the new ethnic élites; we are witnessing the consociational coexistence of these élites as ethnic spokesmen and -women in the public sphere. It is the strengthening of these new élites and of élite ethnic discourses that will in the long run encourage the development of a consociational or corporate multiculturalism. This tendency is reinforced by the convergence of the interests of these élites and the people they speak for; the former desire ethnic empowerment, the latter populist radicalism. Do we not have here a resurgence of the old problem along the racial fault-line that W.E.B. DuBois diagnosed in 1903 as America's most persistent problem? A division is returning between what James Madison in the *Federalist* 10 called the realm of low passion and the realm of high principle, this time compounded by race, class, poverty and a decrepit educational system in the cities. The realm of high principles on which America was founded is abstract, universal, high-cultural, and *was* – until 1954 – under white, male, middle-class control. The deconstruction of Dead White Male power may have expanded this realm to include "all people," but the enjoyment and entertainment of these principles is still tied to class: ie, to the academically trained strata. The realm of popular passions, of warm ethnic feelings, may be of a lower order in the evolution of the philosophy of government, but it is simpler, more affective, more low-down, and it often constitutes the only bond blacks in the inner city have left, short of what Cornel West identifies as an explosive black nihilism.[54] Moreover, political universalism – so claim its black detractors – was mainly observed in the breach and had a hypocritical history until the Civil Rights legislation of the *Sixties* made blacks full citizens. Is there not a class/ cultural difference between the political cultures, between the unenlightened desires and circumscribed aspirations of black populist groups versus the high universal feelings and experiences of the middle and upper classes, most of whom are white? And the new black middle class is often perceived by inner-city blacks as being too close to white.[55] This widening dichotomy between a well-educated upper-middle class that can afford to have principles and an undereducated underclass that is not able to cope with material survival translates the soft multiculturalism of enlightened educational theory into a hard political multiculturalism of the streets. Could it be that the new and largely academic

---

53 One of the most intriguing publications on the realignment of an American class structure comes from an unexpected quarter: target-group research and advertising; see Michael J. Weiss, *The Clustering of America* (New York: HarperCollins, 1988).

54 Cornel West, "Nihilism in Black America," *Dissent* (Spring, 1991): 221–26. See also the influential book by William Julius Wilson, *The Truly Disadvantaged: The Inner City, the Underclass, and Public Policy* (Chicago: U of Chicago P, 1987).

55 See "Race On Campus," *New Republic* (February 18, 1991): 29.

discourse of "gender–race–ethnicity" serves to repress a consideration of the more difficult issues of class and poverty which to many Americans, even to some liberals, seem so intractable (and boring)? Could it be that multiculturalism avoids a serious consideration of poverty by favouring a discourse of difference along the lines of race, ethnicity and gender – in short, that it represents an overdetermination of "cultural" discourses and a repression of class divisions at the very moment when these begin to hurt?[56] The American liberal conscience is today more allergic to injustice based on race than to injustice based on class. Compassion for the economically disadvantaged is held in check by a deep-seated belief in achievement-oriented individualism and the attendant anarchism (of doing your own thing) of which even the hardiest leftist is not quite immune.[57] It is thus much easier to rally the bad consciences around the issue of racism than around class oppression. Yet the hurts of town and the discourse of gown are farther than ever apart within my own memory. It is indicative of the current ethnic fragmentation of a liberal agenda and of the academisation of leftist political culture in the USA that it takes a conservative, Kevin Phillips, to point out the new class divisions,[58] and that, for a critique of the new global realignment of capitalism, we find more in the conservative *Economist* than in most radical American journals.[59]

The education of America's ethnics

While the nation was trying to overcome the trauma of Vietnam and Watergate, the student bodies and faculties of American universities did in fact become more "multicultural." But as the universities expanded numerically and ethnically, they also went into a recession, and the battle over scarce resources and shrinking opportunities became more intense. It is no accident that the debate over multiculturalism should have arisen in the universities, for it is a battle over access to the educational resources that are required for the only well-paying career tracks left in a post-fordist economy. In the split labour market of the post-fordist American economy, a university degree marks the difference between badly paid unskilled and highly paid skilled jobs, between lucrative work and minimum-wage McWork. In sum, as long as there is no political will for social reform that would benefit not only the "coping strata" of ethnic groups (as did affirmative action) but also the poor across the entire ethnic spectrum, little will change, and multiculturalism will remain a highly ideological issue with conflicting agendas. One thing is clear: there is a complex of motives at work in the current confusing and confused debate, and, despite all the

56 Immanuel Wallerstein argues that identity-politics along lines of "racial" and "ethnic difference" serve to stabilise the class system; see Wallerstein, "The Ideological Tensions of Capitalism." In Marx's words, America's poor form a "*Klasse an sich,*" not a "*Klasse für sich.*"

57 Martin Trow, "Class, Race, and Higher Education in America," *American Behavioral Scientist* 35.4–5 (March–June 1992): 599ff.

58 Kevin Phillips, *The Politics of Rich and Poor: Wealth and the American Electorate in the Reagan Aftermath* (New York: Random House, 1990).

59 For example, the special-issue leaders, "Rich North, hungry South" (October 1, 1994): 15–16, and "Slicing the cake" and "For richer, for poorer" (November 5, 1994): esp. 13–14 and 19–21.

culturological rhetoric, most of these motives have a sound economic base.[60] The corporate world has discovered multiculturalism as yet another strategy to fragment its customers into docile units of a global consumption society. Benetton, Disney and McDonald's know that the ethnic and cultural clustering of their customers into target-groups of specific desire works well for their purposes.

WORKS CITED

ADORNO, Theodor & Max Horkheimer, *The Dialectic of Enlightenment*, tr. John Cumming (New York: Harper, 1945).

ALEXANDER, Jeffrey, Chaim SEIDLER–FELLER & Cornel WEST. "Blacks and Jews," *Tikkun* (January–February, 1992): 12–16.

ALT, John. "Cultural Conflict in New York City," *Reconstruction* 1.4 (1992): 142–46.

———. Review of Jim Sleeper, *The Closest of Strangers, Telos* 87 (Summer 1991): 173–85.

ANON. "For richer, for poorer," *Economist* (November 5–11, 1994): 19–21.

———."Government by the nice, for the nice," *Economist* (July 25, 1992): 47–48.

———. "Race On Campus," *New Republic* (February 18, 1991): 29.

———. "Rage of the Black Middle Class," *Newsweek* (November 2, 1993).

———. "Rich North, hungry South" *Economist* (October 1–7, 1994): 15–16.

———. "Scrambling Solarz," *Economist* (July 25, 1992): 51.

———. "Slicing the cake," *Economist* (November 5–11, 1994): 13–14.

———. "Special Focus: PC In Our Time," *Tikkun* 6.4 (July–August 1991): 35–62.

ARENDT, Hannah. *The Human Condition* (Chicago: U of Chicago P, 1958).

BARTH, Fredrik. *Ethnic Groups and Boundaries: The Social Organization of Culture Difference* (New York: Little, Brown, 1969).

BERCOVITCH, Sacvan. *Discovering "America": A Cross-Cultural Perspective* (Working Paper 36; Berlin: John F. Kennedy Institute, 1991).

CARTER, Stephen. "Racism's Victims," *The World & I* (February, 1992): 467–79.

———. *Reflections of an Affirmative Action Baby* (New York: Basic Books, 1992).

DASENBROCK, Reed Way. "The Multicultural West," *Dissent* (Fall, 1991): 550–55.

DeMOTT, Benjamin. *The Imperial Middle: Why Americans Can't Think Straight about Class* (New Haven CT: Yale UP, 1991).

EZORSKY, Gertrude. *Racism and Justice: The Case for Affirmative Action* (Ithaca NY: Cornell UP, 1992).

FOOT, Dan. "American Indians in the 1990s," *American Demographics* (December, 1991): 26–34.

FREUD, Sigmund. *Civilization and its Discontents* (1930) (*Standard Edition of the Complete Psychological Works of Sigmund Freud*, ed. James Strachey; London, 1927–1931), vol. 21.

GARDELS, Nathan. "Two Concepts of Nationalism: An Interview with Isaiah Berlin," *New York Review of Books* (21 November 1991): 19–23.

GARVEY, John. "My Problem with Multi-Cultural Education," *Race Traitor* 1.2 (Winter, 1993): 18–25.

GEYER, Michael & Miriam HANSEN. "Varieties of Multiculturalism and the Politics of the Curriculum," lecture delivered at the Continuing Education Conference, University of Chicago (November, 1991).

GLAZER, Nathan. "Affirmative Discrimination: For and Against," in *Ethnic Dilemmas* (Cambridge MA: Harvard UP, 1983): 159–81.

———. *Affirmative Discrimination: Ethnic Inequality and Public Policy* (Cambridge MA: Harvard UP,)

---

[60] See the furore over it in "Special Focus: PC In Our Time," *Tikkun* 6.4 (July–August 1991): 35–62. Both the opponents and the defenders of PC or multiculturalism seem confused, save for the pointed response by Elizabeth Fox–Genovese, "The Self-Interest of Multiculturalism." Cf also Wallerstein, "The Ideological Tensions of Capitalism."

————. "In Defense of Multiculturalism," *New Republic* (September 2, 1991): 18–22.

———— & Daniel P. Moynihan, *Beyond the Melting Pot: The Negroes, Puerto Ricans, Jews, Italians, and Irish of New York City* (Cambridge MA: MIT Press, 2nd rev. ed. 1970).

———— & Daniel P. Moynihan, ed. *Ethnicity: Theory and Experience* (Cambridge MA: Harvard UP, 1975).

GLEASON, Philip. "Minorities (Almost) All: The Minority Concept in American Social Thought," *The World & I* (February, 1992): 414.

GORDON, Milton. "Models of Pluralism: The New American Dilemma," in "America as a Multicultural Society," *Annals of the American Academy of Political And Social Sciences* (Special Issue, vol. 454; March 1981): 178–88.

GRAY, Paul. "Whose America?" *Time* (July 8, 1991): 23.

HACKER, Andrew. "The New Civil War," *New York Review of Books* 34.8 (April 23, 1992): 30–34.

————. *Two Nations: Black and White, Separate, Hostile, Unequal* (New York: Scribner's, 1992).

HERSKOVITS, Melville J. *The Myth of the Negro Past* (1941; New York: Beacon, 1958).

HOBSBAWM, E.J. *Nations and Nationalism Since 1870: Programme, Myth, Reality* (Cambridge: Cambridge UP, 1990).

HONNETH, Axel. "Universalismus und kulturelle Differenz: Zu Michael Walzers Modell der Gesellschaftskritik," *Merkur: Deutsche Zeitschrift für europäisches Denken* 512 (November, 1991): 1049–54.

HUNTINGTON, Samuel P. *American Politics: The Promise of Disharmony* (Cambridge MA: Belknap/Harvard UP, 1981).

JENCKS, Christopher. *Rethinking Social Policy: Race, Poverty, and the Underclass* (Cambridge MA: Harvard UP, 1992).

KOLAKOWSKI, Leszek. "Wo sind die Barbaren? Ein Lob des Eurozentrismus oder Die Illusion des kulturellen Universalismus," *Der Monat* 2 (October–December, 1980): 70–83.

KOSELLECK, Reinhart. "Zur historisch-politischen Semantik asymmetrischer Gegenbegriffe," in *Positionen der Negativität*, ed. Harald Weinrich (Munich: Fink, 1975): 65–104.

LAZARE, Daniel. "Collapse of a City: Growth and Decay of Camden, New Jersey," *Dissent* (Spring 1991): 267–75.

LE PEN, Jean–Marie. *Les Français d'abord* (Paris: Carrère–Lafon, 1984).

MARCUSE, Herbert. *One-Dimensional Man* (New York: Beacon, 1964).

MINOW, Martha. *Making all the Difference: Inclusion, Exclusion, and American Law* (Ithaca NY: Cornell UP, 1990).

MYRDAL, Gunnar. *An American Dilemma: The Negro Problem and Modern Democracy* (New York: Harper & Row, rev. ed. 1962).

NAIPAUL, V.S. "Our Universal Civilization," *New York Times* (5 November, 1990): A21.

NOVIT–EVANS, Bette & Ashton Wesley WELCH. "Racial and Ethnic Definition as Reflection of Public Policy," *Journal of American Studies* 17 (1983): 3, 417–35.

OSTENDORF, Berndt. "Die amerikanische Definition von Kultur und die Definition der amerikanischen Kultur," in *Die Vereinigten Staaten von Amerika*, ed. Willi P. Adams, E.–O. Czempiel, Berndt Ostendorf, K.L. Shell, P.B. Spahn & Michael Zöller (Frankfurt: Campus, 1990), vol. 2: 449–68.

————. "Black Poetry, Blues, and Folklore: Double Consciousness in Afro-American Oral Culture," *Amerikastudien* 20.2 (1975): 209–59.

————. *The Costs of Multiculturalism* (Working Paper 50; Berlin: John F. Kennedy Institute, 1992).

————. "Creolization and Creoles: The Concepts and their History," in *La Louisiane française/ French Louisiana*, ed. Wolfgang Binder (Würzburg, 1992).

————. "Einleitung," in *Amerikanische Ghettoliteratur: Zur Literatur ethnischer, marginaler und unterdrückter Gruppen in Amerika*, ed. Ostendorf (Darmstadt: Wissenschaftliche Buchgesellschaft, 1983).

————. "Einwanderungspolitik der USA," in *Politik der Migration*, ed. Konrad Schacht & Elisabeth Kiderlen (Wiesbaden: Schriftenreihe der Hessischen Landeszentrale für politische Bildung, 1993): 25–38.

————. "Kulturanthropologie und Amerikastudien oder das Reden über Kultur," *Amerikastudien* 29.1 (1984): 5–18.

————. "Rediscovering an Invisible Culture," in Ostendorf, *Understanding Black Literature in White America* (Studies in Contemporary Literature and Culture; Brighton: Harvester, 1982).

————. "What Makes Ethnic Literature 'Ethnic'?," in *Le facteur ethnique aux Etats Unis et au Canada*, ed. Monique Lecomte & Claudine Thomas (Travaux et recherches 12: Etats-Uni, Canada; Lille: Université de Lille III, 1983).

————, ed. *Multikulturelle Gesellschaft: Modell Amerika?* (Munich: Wilhelm Fink, 1994).

PHILLIPS, Kevin. *The Politics of Rich and Poor: Wealth and the American Electorate in the Reagan Aftermath* (New York: Random House, 1990).

RENAN, Ernest. *Qu'est que c'est une nation?* (Paris, 1882).

RIESMAN, David. *The Lonely Crowd: A Study of the Changing American Character* (New Haven CT: Yale UP, 1950).

RORTY, Richard. "Intellectuals in Politics," *Dissent* (Fall 1991): 483–90.

———— & Andrew Ross. "Intellectuals in Politics," *Dissent* (Spring 1992): 263–67.

SAFFELL, David C. "Affirmative Gerrymandering: Rationale and Application," *State Government* 56:4 (1983).

SCHAMBRA, William A. "The Quest for Community in Twentieth-Century America," *The World and I* 5.10 (October, 1990): 489–99.

SLEEPER, Jim. *The Closest of Strangers: Liberalism and the Politics of Race in New York* (New York: Norton, 1990).

SOLLORS, Werner, ed. *Beyond Ethnicity: Consent and Descent in American Culture*, (New York: Oxford UP, 1986).

————, ed. *The Invention of Ethnicity* (New York: Oxford UP, 1989).

STEINBERG, Stephen. *The Ethnic Myth: Race, Ethnicity and Class in America* (1981; New York: Beacon, rev. ed. 1989).

THERNSTROM, Stephan et al., ed. *Harvard Encyclopedia of American Ethnic Groups* (Cambridge MA: Harvard UP, 1980).

TRACHTENBERG, Alan. *Between Quarrel and Gratitude: Culture, Democracy, America* (Working Paper 44; Berlin: John F. Kennedy Institute, 1992).

TROW, Martin. "Class, Race, and Higher Education in America," *American Behavioral Scientist* 35.4–5 (March–June 1992): 599–613.

VAN DEN BERGHE, Pierre L. *The Ethnic Phenomenon* (New York: Elsevier/Westport CT: Greenwood, 1981).

WALLERSTEIN, Immanuel. "The Ideological Tensions of Capitalism: Universalism Versus Racism and Sexism," in *Racism, Sexism, and the World-System: Studies in the Political Economy of the World-System Economy*, ed. Joan Smith et al. (Contributions in Economics and Economic History 84; Westport CT: Greenwood, 1988): 3–9.

WALZER, Michael. *Multiculturalism and "The Politics of Recognition"* (Princeton NJ: Princeton UP, 1992).

WARNER, W. Lloyd, Buford H. JUNKER & Walter A. ADAMS. *Color and Human Nature: Negro Personality Development in a Northern City* (Washington DC: American Council on Education, 1941).

———— & Leo SROLE. *The Social Systems of American Ethnic Groups* (New Haven CT: Yale UP, 1945).

WATERS, Mary C. *Ethnic Options: Choosing Identities in America* (Berkeley: U of California P, 1990).

WEISS, Michael J. *The Clustering of America* (New York: HarperCollins, 1988).

WEST, Cornel. "Nihilism in Black America," *Dissent* (Spring, 1991): 221–26.

WIECEK, William M. *Liberty under Law: The Supreme Court in American Life* (Baltimore MD: Johns Hopkins UP, 1988).

WILSON, William Julius. *The Truly Disadvantaged: The Inner City, the Underclass, and Public Policy* (Chicago: U of Chicago P, 1987).

YOUNG, Iris Marion. *Justice and the Politics of Difference* (Princeton NJ: Princeton UP, 1990).

❧ ❖ ❧

PETRONELLA BREINBURG

Culture, Fusion, and Language
The Case of Surinam

W HEN ANTHROPOLOGISTS OR SOCIOLOGISTS (usually white or black using Western theory and research methods) studied cultural fusion in the former colonies, their emphasis was usually on the influence of the so-called perceived "superior culture" of the white missionaries and colonial powers on the "inferior culture" of the colonised. It is only in recent years, as African–Caribbean scholars have begun to make their own studies of cultural influence and to reject the criteria of white anthropologists and Western theories, that the African influence on Caribbean cultures has been seriously discussed.

Factors often ignored

What is now being increasingly recognised is the cultural fusion generated by contact between African culture and white missionary and other Western influences. Indo-Caribbean people have also begun studying their roots in Asia – among them such scholars as Cita Krishna, who has studied the linguistic roots of the language of the Caribbean people in Surinam in particular, where about fifty percent of the population is of Asian descent.

What must also be noted is the fusion between the aboriginal peoples (descendants of the Arawaks, and known as the Indianen in Dutch and as Amerindians in Guyanese English) and other cultural groups whom the Europeans encountered upon their arrival, and the former slaves of African descent. These Africans, referred to by white sociologists and anthropologists as "runaways," removed themselves from the plantations to set up a new life in the dense rainforest. There the Africans were often befriended by Indians who were also in hiding from the pistols and ropes of the Europeans. It would be surprising if cultural mixing did not take place in such a setting.

Before we enter further into the debate over whether what we have is a fusion of cultures or similarities between cultures, we need to clarify the notion of "cultural fusion." For my present purposes, I take culture to mean a state of manners, behaviour, religious or other spiritual beliefs, and language. Fusion would simply mean that two or more cultures have merged into a third. For instance, a painter may mix black and white paint on a palette. S/he then gets grey, a third colour. The shade of grey would depend on the proportion of white into black or black into white. We then get degrees of darkness within the grey. If, in addition, the artist should add some red or green paint when mixing black and white, the grey would change accordingly. Using this analogy we can say that Surinam people are a mixture not only of two cultures, but often of many, given the many races and cultures which were thrown together during colonialism.

As cultural linguists often point out, when cultures meet there is never a complete fusion of one culture with another; nor is there total elimination of one or the other. Often features of the dominated cultures survive. Admittedly, cultural influence does tend to be in one direction – particularly under conditions of colonialism and conquest, the culture of the dominant group generally exercises a greater influence on the dominated group than is conversely the case. But the culture of the dominant group may also exists in a parallel relationship to that of the dominated, making the latter bicultural. Two areas where this cultural parallelism is evident are language and religion.

Language and religion

Throughout the past centuries, the religion of the original inhabitants of Surinam would appear to have become intertwined with the religious beliefs of the African, in a mixture that is sometimes referred to as "tribal religion" (ie, non-Christian). This mixture arose particularly among the Arawaks, as H. Stephens has indicated, remarking that when the Africans ran away from slavery and set up lives along the river banks where there were Indians, it was easy for two groups of fugitives to watch or even join in each other's form of worship.[1]

If we look, for example, at religious practices among the Creoles, we find that they call on the same deities as the Arawak cultures, but under different names. There are bush spirits and gods in Arawak culture, just as there are in Winti (Creole) culture. Among the latter there is a bush deity called "Boesi Inji" (Bush Indian) which Creoles are known to worship. At the Baramske (a type of masked ball without masks), people dress up as their inner spirit. If this is a Boesi Inji, they dress up in navy-blue clothes and feathered headdresses; if it is a "blauw Inji" (blue Indian), they dress in blue. There is also a "blaka Inji" (black Indian) spirit, whose Winti devotees similarly imitate. At Winti religious ceremonies, people become possessed by their deity or spirits.

The Arawaks have a water-spirit known as "Konokuya," while the Creoles have the "Watra Inji" (water Indian) – not to be confused with "watra mama," which is a folklore entity similar to a mermaid but older (thus cannot be called a "maid").[2] According to the Indians many illnesses are caused by a spirit taking hold of the person's body, a belief also held by the Creoles in Winti culture. In both cases the medicine person known to the Indians as the "Plaiman" and as the "Bonoe man" by the Creoles, enters into a dialogue with the spirit and asks what it wants. Often the "Plaiman" or "Bonoe man" demands that the spirits clear off. As

---

[1] Henri J.M. Stephen, *Lexicon van de Surinaamse Winti kultuur* (Amsterdam: De West, 1988).

[2] Stephen, *Lexicon van de Winti kultuur*, 17.

it can be argued that European culture also chases out evil spirits (by means of exorcism), what we are dealing with here may well be, not a parallel, but rather the fusion or adaptation of aspects of one culture by another culture group.

In both Amerindian and Winti culture, language plays a central role. Just as the Indians used a type of language which even the missionaries who worked with them could not understand, so too is the language used in Winti ceremonies secret or esoteric. There is a European analogy in the use of Latin in the Catholic mass, which was recited during church services without being exactly understood by the majority of the congregation.

The Dutch, unlike the British, made a serious effort to learn Sranan, the mother-tongue of the Creoles, even during the colonial period. The language is the object of scholarly attention in Dutch universities scholars study Sranan, as are Djoeka (spelt Ndjuka by white scholars) and Saramaccan. Nevertheless, the Sranan Tongo used by the Winti culture for its ceremonies and dialogue with its gods is not understood by people outside of that culture. Even when the words are clear, the meaning may not be, since Surinamese Creoles are well-known for the use of *odo*'s (idiomatic expressions and the use of satire). For example, even linguists who have studied Sranan would have difficulty in deciphering the following:

> *fowroe wiwiri n'ab foetoe ma a krin na sodro*
> [the fowl feather has no legs but climbs stairs]

or:

> *San Boeriki Skrefi, Asi no kan Lesi*
> [What donkey has written, horse cannot read][3]

In the case of the second *odo*, it would be difficult to understand for anyone outside of the group to which the *odo* belongs. Misunderstanding would arise from the difference underlying the concepts of donkey and horse: a donkey in many other cultures is stupid, while a horse is powerful, whereas in Creole Sranan culture a donkey is clever and stubborn: you cannot beat it, for if it does not wish to go somewhere it simply will not. A Western parallel would be the difference between a dog (which can be trained) and a cat (which cannot). Is a dog cleverer, because it can take orders and the cat cannot, or is the cat too clever and more independent in not doing so? To understand *odo*'s and everyday expressions, one has to understand the norms and concepts of the culture.

Stephen has pointed out that much of what is considered sacred language may well be comprehensible to people in Africa. For instance, the *Kromanti* (a "Winti" to the Creole) is a bush spirit, but it is also an ethnic group living in West Africa. It has also been revealed by black Jamaican scholars that many of the lexical items found in non-Christian religions in Jamaica and Surinam are of African origin. Stephen lists some of the languages which African peoples could have taken to Surinam with them; even if they were not allowed to speak their mother-tongue, they could have

---

3 The first is an *odo* universally familiar in Surinam; the second is cited from Henri J.M. Stephen, *Winti: Afro-Surinaamse Religie en magische Rituelen in Suriname en Nederland* (1983; Amsterdam: Karnak, 1985).

retained a number of words and phrases for clandestine use in religious ceremonies. He lists, for instance, among the Bantu group of languages, Ewe, Yoruba, Fon and Twi, pointing out that "Kromanti" is a word derived from Twi.

European culture

Surinam is one of the most culturally complex societies in the Caribbean. This area of the Guianas was inhabited by various Indian tribes and ethnic groups, then colonised by the Spanish and then the French; once part of Brazil and under Portuguese rule, it was subsequently colonised by the British, followed by the Dutch, who waged war against the British, were defeated, and then recaptured Surinam again from the British. Each time a group assumed power, it enforced its own culture – religion, language, behaviour, system of education.

The various colonial powers responded very differently to the presence of the indigenous cultures. The Dutch, for example, were less restrictive about the use of vernaculars, whereas the British, using a carrot-and-stick approach, banned and severely punished anyone who dared speak anything but English.

The religious denominations of the colonisers varied. Some Europeans were strict Catholics, so the people they ruled adopted elements of the Catholic religion. Others were strict Protestants – known in Surinam as the Evangelise Broeder or Gemeente Broeder. The earlier missionaries in Surinam, who encouraged the use of Creole, were members of the Moravian mission, which was of German origin. This mission also encouraged early writing in creole in the Danish West Indies during the early eighteenth century.

The encounter between the European colonisers and indigenes produced what could be termed a "fusion of cultures." Although the Surinam peoples were made to believe that anything European was superior to anything African, they did not want to reject their own culture entirely, so mixed the two. In some cases they lived and still live in two parallel cultures, for it is not unusual for Creoles to be both staunch Christians and worshippers of Winti deities as well.

A "fusion of cultures" reveals itself as soon as one examines Winti ceremony and Catholicism comparatively. For example, the Creole Winti's *Kra* corresponds to the *Soul* of Catholicism. The Catholic faith has what is known in Dutch theological parlance as an *Angel bewarder* or guardian angel; this is similarly the function fulfilled by the *Jeje* of the Winti religion. A good person in the Catholic faith goes to heaven (the land of god), while a good person in the Winti culture goes in spirit to the fatherland (which is Africa). Winti has an *Aisa* (goddess of the earth), but one who often liaises with other gods on behalf of the Creole supplicant; by the same token, *Mary*, Mother of Christ, liaises with God on behalf of the Catholic supplicant. In Creole Winti culture, one prays to *Mma Aisa* (Mother Aisa):

Mma Aisa
Ma Aisa
Mi de begi alen
Mi de begi alen
be kasi nja njanna gro
a mo gro...
fisi na ini liba watra o...
Kaw an in boeroe we...
No moe dede mama,
No moe dede mama.

The *Aisa* prayer is sung at the beginning of a ceremony, and there are other *Aisa* equivalents to Christian psalms.

The *Nenedofi* or high priestess of the Lakoe society would chant at the beginning of all ceremonies or Lakoe performances:

Gado na fesi ala trawan na baka [God first, all others after]

The above can be explained as a placatory formula uttered as a sop to the missionaries by a group who stood to be punished by law if caught practising Winti. The missionaries in turn noticed that, no matter what they preached, they could not suppress the culture and religion of the people.

Early Creole texts, such as those of Johanis King, a Matuary Maroon who wrote in Sranan, were the product of the activity of the Moravian Brothers, who ran missions in both Surinam and the Danish West Indies (now the Virgin Islands).[4] The translation of the New Testament into Sranan by Johanis King, who also wrote a number of prayer and story books, was the direct result of encouragement by these German missionaries. The style of King and his contemporaries is typical of "biblical preaching," and it would be interesting to investigate the extent to which these texts were influenced by nineteenth-century German language and philosophy. Even though Sranan is identified as an anglophone Creole, which developed while the British were in power in Surinam, there may well be Moravian influences.

Asian influence

The Asians were the last group to arrive in Surinam in large numbers. Their arrival followed the abolition of slavery, which in Surinam was not until the middle of the nineteenth century. They came as indentured labourers – often enough another form of slavery.[5] Influence from this group on Winti culture – and, to a lesser extent, conversely – manifests itself in the language and in Creole cuisine. As is the case with the aboriginal peoples, Hindu spirits can also be found in Winti worship. It is not unusual for a Creole, while performing a Winti ceremony, to invoke a Hindu spiritual guide and to speak in Hindi, the language (now called Sarnami)

---

4 See Neville A. Hall, *Slave Society in the Danish West Indies: St Thomas, St John, and St Croix*, ed. B.W. Higman (Atlantic History and Culture series; Baltimore MD: Johns Hopkins UP, 1992).

5 On cultural, religious and linguistic aspects generally, see esp. David Dabydeen & Brinsley Samaroo, *India in the Caribbean* (London: Hansib, 1987).

of the indentured labourers from the Indian subcontinent; it follows that many other Creole speakers present will not be able to understand what is being said.

Another aspect is the Creole presence at such Hindu festivals as *Ramlila*, although one is not sure how much of this display of "Good triumphing over Evil" is actually understood by the Creoles. To them it may just be an open-air dramatic spectacle. Similarly, for two weeks every year Creoles can be seen attending the making of the *Tadjan*, which will be carried high up in the air along the roads of the villages. Although the Creoles enjoy Hindu festivals, one cannot say that they have taken them over into their own culture. In this case we have a reciprocal sharing of culture without actual adoption.

Language is the most obvious influence. Sranan speakers, especially the younger people, use Sarnami words and phrases in their everyday speech just as often as they use Dutch. It is not uncommon for a Sranan speaker or writer to use Dutch, Sranan and a sprinkling of Sarnami words in one sentence. Here we have a blending of three languages into one; hence the difficulties for non-Surinamese researchers, who may know Dutch but not the other two languages. A typical example of Sranan/Sarnami mixing would be the phrase "*mi n'abi pisa* [I have no money]," the elements of which are derived from "*mi n'abi*" (spoken Sranan) or "*mi no abi*" (written Sranan) and "*pisa*" (Sarnami). If a Surinamese youth living in Holland or an urban location in Surinam wants to tell a friend jokingly that he is mad, he might say, "*Man, joe pagla*" (Man, you are mad), where syntactically reduced Dutch is combined with "*pagla*," the Sarnami word for "mad."

Hindu cuisine has also been adopted in Surinam, though not to the same extent as in neighbouring Guyana, despite the similarly high percentage of inhabitants of South-East Asian origin. While Surinam Creoles might frequent Hindu restaurants, one would not necessarily find Hindu cuisine at a Creole party, although this is a very common occurrence in Guyana.

Summary

I have touched briefly in this paper on the question of "cultural fusion" in Surinam, where many races and cultures have been thrown together in not altogether pleasant historical circumstances. The initial European invasion resulted in the almost complete annihilation of the original inhabitants. There were battles between the European powers for control of the territory, each imposing its own culture and religion on the local population. Africans of different cultural and ethnic backgrounds were brought in chains. These were followed by Asians (Indians, Indonesians, Javanese) bringing with them various religions. The Europeans introduced a variety of faiths, all competing for the souls of the people and influencing their culture in the process.

It is difficult to decide whether Surinamese practices constitute instances of cultural fusion or perhaps a situation of cultural parallelism between two or more cultures. More study needs to be done on the biculturalism of Surinamese who are both devout Christians and members of the Winti culture, just as they are speakers of both Dutch and Sranan. Any researcher is thus faced with the problem of having to be familiar with many languages and cultures when studying cultural fusion in Surinam.

WORKS CITED

DABYDEEN, David & Brinsley SAMAROO. *India in the Caribbean* (London: Hansib, 1987).

HALL, Neville A. *Slave Society in the Danish West Indies: St Thomas, St John, and St Croix*, ed. B.W. Higman (Atlantic History and Culture series; Baltimore MD: Johns Hopkins UP, 1992).

STEPHEN, Henri J.M. *Winti: Afro-Surinaamse Religie en magische Rituelen in Suriname en Nederland* (1983; Amsterdam: Karnak, 1985).

────── *Lexicon van de Surinaamse Winti kultuur* (Amsterdam: De West, 1988).

DAVID WOODS

Epitaph

(for Kipoch Nojorge)

My friend Kipoch
Kenyan born,
Black as coal
From the Akamba tribe,
Has won an award –
and is off to New York,
After years of effort
He has begun to fly.

He is a riser in our
little town,
He is on the board of this
He is on the board of that,
He has appeared on local
television,
He is known by politicians.

Kipoch has a vision
And it disturbs him day by day,
He must succeed!
He must succeed!
He is strict in his manner
He works slavishly,
He has improved his English
He has earned two degrees.

He is from Ikutha village
In Kenya's east,
His people are diseased and
strife-torn,
But he will not talk of that
now

He no longer writes to his
family,
He can no longer bear discussion
of his country.

Kipoch makes speeches
Whenever given a chance,
Among whites – he is known
to produce tears,
He does his native dance
For their amusement,
At night he is restless
and possessed by fear.

When black people in
the North-end began to
uprise,
Kipoch was quick to reproach:
"The world is ruled by a new
order of men:
The educated, the diligent,
One should not be fooled
by these lazy people
Or cloud the mind with
racial sympathies."

When a group of refugees
washed up along the shore,
Kipoch was even more
severe:
"These men are the flotsam
of troubled spots,
To allow them in the country
is to inherit their lowly woes,
And corrupt all we have achieved here."

I see him in a halo
of gold,
Standing in a brightened
ceremony,
Receiving applause from those
Who consider him extraordinary.

He will be standing there.
("Tucked" in tuxedo
Fixed in smile)
Standing there trembling and alone.

Once slavery took 15 million
men and women,
Raped and tortured their souls,
Kipoch is a modern type
He goes and serves willingly.

M argaret Atwood
(Grainau, February 1992; photo Peter Stummer)

HEIKE HÄRTING

The Profusion of Meanings
and the Female Experience of Colonisation
Inscriptions of the Body as Site of Difference in
Tsitsi Dangarembga's Nervous Conditions
and Margaret Atwood's The Edible Woman

T HE READER MIGHT WONDER why two novels have been chosen which
at first sight appear to be difficult to compare, since one originates in a
settler-colony and the other in Zimbabwe (formerly Rhodesia).

Obviously, there is clearly a danger of universalising interpretations –
where, for example, the specific experiences of black women are subsumed under
white feminist discourse in which, as black feminist critics have remarked, the
image of the Third-World Woman is constructed. One can nevertheless detect and
justify a common ground upon which both novels move, if one keeps in mind, on
the one hand, the fact that the frequently marginalised psychological effects of
colonisation – such as schizophrenia, anorexia nervosa, or heteronomy generally –
designate a specific experience of women and colonised people; and, on the other,
that female writing, particularly when perceived as what Jane Gallop describes as
the image of "The Bodily Enigma,"[1] denotes a signifying process, engendering
infinite meanings and desires, in which the reader's modes of reception co-create.
In both novels, *Nervous Conditions* and *The Edible Woman*, taken as medical
histories of colonialism, the symptoms of psychological disease, especially
anorexia nervosa, surface in a similar fashion; but the causes, their definitions and
development are, owing to their specific historical, regional and cultural contexts,
fundamentally different.

By theorising the female body, once exoticised and mystified as a dark
continent as well as abused as an ideological battlefield in an exclusive system of
hierarchically ordered binary oppositions, this paper attempts to describe the
painful process of dissociation and reappropriation of the body as a means of self-
determination and cultural production. I will therefore focus on possibilities of
redefining patterns of female subjectivity within a literary and theoretical framework of what I will call a female aesthetic of anticipation.

---

[1] Jane Gallop, *Thinking through the Body* (New York, 1988): 11–20.

The main difference between the novels discussed here concerns their notion of subjectivity. To begin with, the body takes on the role of mediator in a historio-graphical process of subject-constitution, as it is linked to communal life and to the search for infinite beginnings in *Nervous Conditions*. Secondly, Atwood's novel, though equally concerned with the psychological effects of patriarchal rule, delineates the process of subject-loss and transformation by means of intertextual mimeticism.

In a recent reading, Tsitsi Dangarembga explained that one "cannot develop a stable identity out of unstable conditions" (Berlin, November 1992) and that society would therefore need a completely new "psychological make-up." The words unfold in her novel *Nervous Conditions*. But even before the reader opens the book she or he is disturbed by its title, which turns out to be adapted from an observation in Fanon's *The Wretched of the Earth*:

> Our enemy betrays his brothers and becomes our accomplice: his brothers do the same thing. The status of "native" is a nervous condition introduced and maintained by the settler among colonised people with their consent.2

As such, nervous conditions, taken as a result of a generally violent social and political environment, represent internalised strategies of hegemonic rule and colonial or patriarchal strategies of containment. The experience of open, vertical violence is transformed into horizontal violence: a kind of violence that is rooted in displaced aggression against the oppressor, and which eventually takes self-destructive directions or is transferred to equally oppressed people, by no means vanishing with official independence. As a matter of course, coercive systems of heteronomy, distorted self-perception resulting from the ambivalent situation of being subject and object at the same time, repressed rage and violence are decisive aspects of the psychological experience inflicted by colonialism.

The impact of the body, particularly the female body, on patriarchal and colonial discourse seems to be imperative, not only providing as it does the physical matrix of subject-constitution, but also functioning as one pole of the mind/body opposition.

During colonialism, as Dangarembga points out in *Nervous Conditions*, the Shona people were generally represented as mere material for physical labour; they were perceived in terms of an undifferentiated plurality allegedly lacking individual personality:

> The authorities thought Babamukuru was a good African. And it was generally believed that good Africans bred good African children who also thought about nothing except serving their communities.3

---

2 Frantz Fanon, *The Wretched of the Earth*, tr. Constance Farrington (1961, tr. 1963; Harmondsworth, 1967): 16–17.

3 Tsitsi Dangarembga, *Nervous Conditions* (London: Women's Press, 1988): 107. Further page references to this edition are in the text.

The extent to which the biological and genetic reduction of colonised people has affected their self-perception and cultural representation becomes evident when Nyasha, suffering from acute schizophrenia and anorexia, cannot get psychological treatment, and Babamukuru accedes to the white psychiatrist's view that Nyasha cannot be ill, because Africans did not suffer in that way; apparently Nyasha is making a scene. Even today it is not unusual to come across such racist assertions, as in Lilli Gast's feminist study on anorexia, *Magersucht*, where the author writes: "The syndrome of anorexia is exclusively a feature of Western industrial societies."[4]

From a dualistic (mind/body) point of view, the coloniser is very often identified as an incorporeal, rational being whose physical existence is subordinated to the maintenance of colonial rule, whereas the colonised remain at best variants of either the "wild man" or the Noble Savage. Consequently, psychological liberation from slave-status involves the subject's transforming corporeal regression into equilibrium of body and mind and transmuting into universal imperatives of civilisation the internalised normative values of British rule. Tambu, who has grown up in a rural environment among an extended family that is not characterised by symbiotic relationships, perceives her uncle's house as the English House and finally anticipates the truth in her mother's warnings and the causes of Nyasha's anorexia: "It's the Englishness [...] It'll kill them all if they aren't careful" (202).

The antiseptic sterility of the whole house – its English furniture and white bathroom – also account for Tambu's own alienating physical experiences at the mission:

> The onset of my menses, then, should have been placid, but when it came to washing those rags in Maiguru's white bathroom ... the business became nasty and nauseating. I became morose and moody about it. (95)

But, as the whole structure of the novel makes clear, the body cannot be separated from the soul. The female body opens up a deconstructive reading-space and thereby mediates the space in between rigid oppositions, as Tambu's process of subject-constitution and Nyasha's loss of subjecthood may be regarded as demonstrating. In a social environment which deprives the characters of their language and autonomy, physical presence becomes a signifying text, materialising what both women and men are thinking. Although Nyasha's sparkling personality once radiated with alternatives and possibilities, the loss of her mother-tongue increases her schizophrenic entanglement in conflicting social and emotional power-systems and reaches its peak in a self-effacing act of anorexic starvation. Anorexia here can thus be seen as the "embodiment" of the devastating psychic effects of colonial and patriarchal rule. Babamukuru is frequently characterised as a man with "bad nerves" and an "elusive identity" (102). This points to the fact that his

---

4 Lilli Gast, *Magersucht: Der Gang durch den Spiegel* (Anorexia: The Pathway Through the Mirror; Pfaffenweiler: Centaurus, 1989): 6; my translation.

body, too, is inscribed with the impotent violence and constant fear embedded in an economy of "returns" in the colonial "Realm of the Proper,"[5] which, considered as a whole, represents the schizophrenic outcome of the colonial experience.

Looking at the body from a more positive angle, we see that Lucia, whose beauty and roundness are coextensive with her wild, bold personality, provides a self-determined female role-model in the text. Tambu's position, however, is more complex. She is involved in a reverse process of subject-constitution exploring the space in between, which also is a nervous one. Trusting to her unambiguous set of moral values and universal truths and her conviction of being integrated in the Symbolic Order, Tambu initially perceives herself as a "wholesome and earthy" being (39) – which, in fact, reflects a form of self-deception rooted in the pre-oedipal mirror-stage. She is fascinated by Nyasha's adventurous personality but also feels threatened by her:

> Most of me sought order. Most of me was concrete and categorical. These parts disapproved of Nyasha very strongly and were wary of her. (75)

However, the relationship between the two girls constitutes Tambu's first love-affair: It was "the first time that she grew to be fond of someone whom she did not wholeheartedly approve" (78). In that sense their relation may be depicted in terms of what Hélène Cixous has called the "other bisexuality":

> that is, each one's location in self of the presence [...] of both sexes, non-exclusion either of the difference or of one sex [...] it doesn't annul differences but stirs them up, pursues them, increases their number.[6]

This "other bisexuality," consequently, is clearly differentiable from androgynous concepts like the hermaphrodite, where two sexual entities are incorporated in a platonic and exclusive fashion.[7] Cixous' demand for the "other bisexuality" runs counter to what has often been criticised: namely, a positive re-evaluation of an established catalogue of exclusive oppositions by mere inversion. Critics seem to have neglected the fact that Cixous has availed herself here of a binary code to retrace a discourse of male meaning-production which is primarily founded on the marginalisation of women and the representation of what female subjectivity ought to be in relation to patriarchal presentation of self. The "other bisexuality," however, strives to transcend fundamental oppositions of male and female in a mimetic and transpositional process incorporating both aspects in a non-hegemonial scheme which allows for self-realisation and clears a space for an imaginary language to stride through the vacuum of linguistic mutilation. The female subject, though, is set in the Symbolic Order; but, since she cannot fully

---

[5] These terms were coined by Hélène Cixous in her seminal study *The Newly Born Woman* (tr. Betsy Wing; Minneapolis: U of Minnesota P, 1986), and have since become an integral part of the terminology of feminist psychoanalysis.

[6] Hélène Cixous, "The Laugh of the Medusa," *Journal of Women in Culture and Society* 4 (1976): 884.

[7] Apart from a lack of conflicting fusion, the metamorphosis of the hermaphrodite resulted from an unrequited love followed by a self-effacing act by the woman involved. The hermaphrodite generally symbolises the implementation of patriarchal structures into a prior matriarchal society.

identify with that Order, she also remains in a different, semiotic place, from where she speaks.

While Tambu gradually discovers the possibilities of her own "other bisexuality" she is able to anticipate her own situation. She moves in a constantly shifting space of fore- and backshadowings, doubts, dreams, and desires: She is on the verge of "reincarnation" (92), able to strike out in unpredictable and multiple directions, and is therefore literally the bearer of female vision. In order to maintain the patriarchal family-structure, Babamukuru announces the Christian wedding of her parents. But she does not want to participate in that shameful event, which poses a vital threat to her own subjectivity. Her rejection, though, can only be expressed in both ways: first physically, as her body leaves her in a state of paralysis, then verbally, as she tentatively regains her own language. Tambu, in contrast to Nyasha, does not disintegrate, because she can gain support from her mother's heritage: On the one hand, she moves within the patriarchal system in order to transcend it from within; on the other, she stems from a female community which is based on difference, solidarity, and the open resolution of conflict, and which relies on principles of collective, dissipative self-organisation.[8]

Her mother's heritage of self-assertion and subversion constitutes a second Symbolic Order of collective tradition occupying a space of its own. The kitchen, the traditional Western site of discrimination against the female, is transformed into a place of resistance where women struggle to attain their very own place in society, thereby fashioning bonds of solidarity that pose a vital threat to a patriarchal society which, under colonial rule, was even more deformed and now arbitrarily manipulates women's roles to its own end. The kitchen is a trope for the site of self-definition, subversively undermining the restrictions of male and colonial heteronomy. Thus it is not surprising that Tambu should enter the mission through the back door of the kitchen, just as the reader is invited to construe Dangarembga's text backwards, as the final sentences of the novel suggest. The text apparently has been written and is constantly rewritten in a re-reading process that once more enters history through an allegedly closed exit-door.

The process of expansion which Tambu undergoes is carved out of her mother's voice while the novel re-inscribes the body as signifying system into history. Therefore her refusal to be "brainwashed" (204) opens up the field of potential beginnings. Nyasha's and Tambu's physical and mental (re)actions to a colonial and patriarchal system turn into what various post-colonial critics and writers (Michael Gilkes and Wilson Harris, for instance) call the experience of colonialism as creative schizophrenia. Furthermore, however, the process of subject-constitution and meaning-production can never be complete, since reader and writer create both from without and from within, re-writing the future as it modifies history.

---

[8] Tambu describes moving into the mission as her "transplantation" (59), which points to the fact that she is uprooted but also takes her roots with her.

To summarise, in Dangarembga's text the constitution of subjectivity is interwoven both with the historiographical process of collective writing, determined by the pre-independent state of anticipatory nervousness, and with the double employment of the colonised body as a mirror of colonial schizophrenia and a linguistic and deconstructive mediator.

Compared to Dangarembga's text, Atwood's novel is clearly concerned with the experience of subject-loss, in which the body assumes the role of a subject in its own right. Of course, in *The Edible Woman* the female body remains a crucial site of male ideological struggle but also serves as a mimetic matrix to elude its complete domination. In Atwood's novel the colonial experience of Canada features as a sub-text and metaphorically depicts the two pillars on which female heteronomy rests. There is, first, Canada's split identity, which is epitomised by the competing existence of francophone and anglophone culture and which, intensified by the presence of various other ethnic communities, resembles the inner contradiction of female self-determination and assimilation or fragmentation; moreover, the Canadian political and geographical landscape suggests that the notion of a holistic identity is inapplicable – instead, Canada's cultural policies have developed along the lines of a mosaic of differences. Secondly, the threat of neo-colonisation via US-American consumer society designates the inner female colonisation, characterised by artificially produced lacks and desires camouflaged as individual, self-generated needs. As a result, women and men engage in a self-denying complicity which integrates women into a hegemonic scheme of divide and conquer. This, as frequently emphasised in Atwood's text, leads to self-inflicted female inertia and stasis, as well as a quasi-anxiety neurosis about turning hysterical and actually being stigmatised as a social drop-out. Furthermore, women consent to their existence in passive Immanence, as Simone de Beauvoir has termed it – which in turn leads to horizontal psychological violence among women causing constant division and lack of solidarity, as exemplified in the "three office virgins"[9] and the landlady in Atwood's novel.

As Sherrill Grace has pointed out, these aspects generate the "violent dualities" which provide the structural framework of Atwood's text: product and process, fix and fluidity, control and escape, essentialism and transgression, enclosure and anticipation, to mention but a few. Yet the "potential acts of creation"[10] do not arise *out of* the unpredictable tension of these dualities, as Linda Hutcheon argues in *The Canadian Postmodern*,[11] though that clearly is a vital part, but dwell in between the erogenous space within those dualities. More specifically: being closest to the drives of lover or oppressor enables one to make use of the Semiotic as anticipation and to explore creatively the ever-shifting and

9 Margaret Atwood, *The Edible Woman* (1969; New York/Toronto: Bantam, 1970): 15. Further references to this edition are in the text.

10 Sherrill E. Grace, *Violent Dualities: A Study of Margaret Atwood* (Montreal: Véhicule, 1980): 170.

11 Linda Hutcheon, *The Canadian Postmodern* (Toronto: Oxford UP, 1988): passim.

indefinable drives and desires of beloved and lover, oppressed and oppressor. The creative potential is thus generated within the erogenous space of anticipated tension within and beyond the binary code, making boundaries superfluous but not dissolving them.

Atwood's novel, then, exemplifies the effects of what I shall call the contradictions of symbiosis. Marian, the novel's protagonist, an emotional cannibal, "manipulator of words" (109) and hunted animal trapped in the viewfinder of her future husband's camera, gradually experiences loss of subjectivity: instead of acting herself, she can only react. Most of the time her reactions occur in an eruptive and to her incomprehensible way. The use of an unreliable first-person narrator in the first part of the novel indicates that these fissures and disruptions may be a surfacing residue of Marian's semiotic subconscious, which to her, as to Tambu, is threatening but also full of anticipation:

> I had broken out; from what, or into what, I didn't know. Though I wasn't at all certain why I had been acting this way, I had at least acted. (75)

> It was my subconscious getting ahead of my conscious self, and the subconscious has its own logic. (100)

But quickly she adds that life is governed by adjustment, and quotes one of Peter's pieces of advice. It is therefore not surprising that the first part of the novel should end with her resolution: "I must get organised. I have a lot to do" (102). Subsequently, her increased self-alienation, coinciding with the first signs of anorexia, is made blatant when, in the second part of the novel, the narrative voice changes into the third-person singular. Interestingly enough, the story – now clearly set in the Symbolic Order – unfolds Marian's "blank of ego, like amnesia" (102), and loss of subjecthood in a twofold way. On the one hand, she consents to being absorbed by what Cixous has termed the "Realm of the Proper," stressing the proper – appropriate/property – and characterised by the monstrous, authoritarian normality of Peter and the pseudo-feminism of Marian's flatmate, Ainsley, based on sexist essentialism. On the other hand, she starts an emotionally and socially ambiguous relationship with Duncan in which she first thinks herself to be in control but which in fact exacerbates the process of subject-loss.

Although her body corresponds to rejection and dissociation, Marian isn't able to abandon her mutilating journey of self-deception. On the contrary: she feels repelled by the grotesque and commercialised femininity displayed by her female colleagues at the office party. She doesn't, however, notice that it is precisely this attitude that brings her dangerously close to the metamorphosis she so utterly dreads:

> She was one of them, her body the same, identical, merged with that other flesh that choked the air in the flowered room with its sweet organic scent; she felt suffocated by this thick

sargasso-sea of femininity. She drew a deep breath, clenching her body and her mind back
into her self like some tactile sea-creature withdrawing its tentacles. (171)[12]

Apart from being stuck in slow dissolution, she conversely embarks on a relationship with Duncan, a student of English literature currently working on pre-
Raphaelite pornography. As he informs her, he is not at all human; he comes from
underground, and in fact functions as her excluded and abused other. His warning to
Marian, that "hunger is more basic than love" (98), makes this clear: Marian's desire
to rescue and protect him is intended to disguise her blind escape from herself and
her desire for symbiosis in order to be relieved of taking decisions on her own. She
is Florence Nightingale – and the novel a grotesque parody of the romantic-love
theme. Eventually, however, annihilated after labouring in the beauty-mines in order
to "fit" herself out for Peter's impending party, she lies naked in the bath and for the
first time perceives the hidden possibilities her body offers:

> It was a moment before she recognised, in the bulging and distorted forms, her own
> waterlogged body. She moved, and all three of the images moved also. They were not quite
> identical: the two on the outside were slanted inwards towards the third. How peculiar it was
> to see three reflections of yourself at the same time, she thought. (227)

Her "amnesia" turns into loss – which in turn provides the source for a mimetic
process of self-determination, as demonstrated in the final part of the narrative.
Being now able to respond to her body, Marian transforms male fantasies and the
commercialised female body into the image of an edible cake-woman. With
respect to mimetic and carnivalesque strategies of re-writing binary codes, it is
interesting to note that baking a cake is both a traditional female activity and
physically sensous work. Finally Marian delightedly consumes what has virtually
eaten her up. Significantly enough, the medical symptoms and causes of anorexia
nervosa combine idiosyncratic and social features, such as symbiotic individual
relationships, in a monolithic and simultaneously decaying social order. However,
anorexia is a painful illness which can seldom account for a strategy of resistance
but involves a transgressively and actively emancipating analysis of those aspects
which primarily carve out the anorexic physiognomy. As a corollary, anorexia
nervosa provides a fertile metaphor in post-colonial and feminist discourse, and
thereby establishes its own signifying system.[13]

---

[12] The profusion of femininity and its simultaneuous reduction of women to a physical commodity
echoes the fearful alienation of Antoinette's husband in Jean Rhys's *Wide Sargasso Sea*, who, feeling
threatened by the exuberant and yet unconquerable landscape of the island, eventually escapes his own
anticipated madness in a sardonic and self-destructive manner.

[13] For detailed information on anorexia nervosa as a female mode of non verbal communication and
resistance, see: Hilde Bruch, *Eating Disorders: Obsessity, Anorexia Nervosa, and the Person Within* (New York:
Basic Books, 1973); Phyllis Chesler, *Women and Madness* (Harmondsworth: Penguin, 1972); Sheila
MacLeod, *The Art of Starvation* (London: Virago, 1981); R.L. Palmer, *Anorexia Nervosa* (Harmondsworth:
Penguin, 1980); Elaine Showalter, *The Female Malady: Women, Madness and English Culture 1830 1980*
(London: Virago, 1987); and Joan J. Brumberg, *Fasting Girls: The Emergence of Anorexia Nervosa as a Modern
Disease* (Cambridge MA: Harvard UP, 1988).

By the end of these two novels, we begin to grasp what David Dabydeen was driving at in a lecture he delivered in Berlin:

> The experience of loss and violence could be the very engine of your need for transformation. Transfiguration is about doing something else and being something else. The ground of our originality is our experience of nothingness.[14]

Taking into consideration, however, the fact that the voice of erotogeneity has left hidden trails on the semiotic and mental map of both the individual and the collective subconsciousness, we cannot regard the experience of loss as complete – rather, as mirroring the constant historical experience of violence and schizophrenia in a Colonial and Patriarchal Order.

To conclude, I would like to stress the fact that both novels are deeply engaged in the process of historiographical metafiction within which the individual is often balanced by the collective; history itself, in all its forms, turns out to be the ultimate intertext. The reader is challenged to take up the task of re-reading the future and of re-writing history. One way of doing so is through the reappropriation of the female body as erogenous reading- and writing-space reflecting the individual's indissoluble heterogeneity.

Instead of symbiosis we may stress the multiple experience of the "other bisexuality" and reappropriate Beauvoir's notion of Othering. She states that the boundaries of self are re-defined by the affirmation of division, as this enables one to perceive the Other as Other. One becomes the Other's Other without abandoning the Self. In the spirit of the moment, this closeness overcomes the finality and division of time and enables us to communicate. In this respect, Cixous' comment on female literary production opens up the discourse of what I have been discussing as a female aesthetic of anticipation:

> I throw death out, it comes back, we begin again. I am pregnant with beginnings.[15]

---

[14] David Dabydeen, "The Empire Knives Back. A Reading of *Disappearance*," Berlin 1993.

[15] Hélène Cixous, quoted in Toril Moi, *Sexual/Textual Politics: Feminist Literary Theory* (London/New York: Routledge, 1985): 116.

WORKS CITED

ATWOOD, Margaret. *The Edible Woman* (1969; New York/Toronto: Bantam, 1970).

BRUCH, Hilde. *Eating Disorders: Obsessity, Anorexia Nervosa, and the Person Within* (New York: Basic Books, 1973).

BRUMBERG, Joan J. *Fasting Girls: The Emergence of Anorexia Nervosa as a Modern Disease* (Cambridge MA: Harvard UP, 1988).

CHESLER, Phyllis. *Women and Madness* (Harmondsworth: Penguin, 1972).

CIXOUS, Hélène. "The Laugh of the Medusa," *Signs: Journal of Women in Culture and Society* 4 (1976): 875–93.

———. *The Newly Born Woman*, tr. Betsy Wing (Minneapolis: U of Minnesota P, 1986).

DABYDEEN, David. "The Empire Knives Back: A Reading of *Disappearance*." Berlin: unpublished lecture, 1993.

DANGAREMBGA, Tsitsi. *Nervous Conditions* (London: Women's Press, 1988).

FANON, Frantz. *The Wretched of the Earth*, tr. Constance Farrington (1961, tr. 1963; Harmondsworth: Penguin, 1967).

GALLOP, Jane. *Thinking through the Body* (New York: Columbia UP, 1988).

GAST, Lilli. *Magersucht: Der Gang durch den Spiegel* (Pfaffenweiler: Centaurus, 1989).

GRACE, Sherrill E. *Violent Dualities: A Study of Margaret Atwood* (Montreal: Véhicule, 1980).

HUTCHEON, Linda. *The Canadian Postmodern* (Toronto: Oxford UP, 1988).

MACLEOD, Sheila. *The Art of Starvation* (London: Virago, 1981).

MOI, Toril. *Sexual/Textual Politics: Feminist Literary Theory* (London/New York: Routledge, 1985).

PALMER, R.L. *Anorexia Nervosa* (Harmondsworth: Penguin, 1980).

RHYS, Jean. *Wide Sargasso Sea* (1966; Harmondsworth: Penguin, 1968).

SHOWALTER, Elaine. *The Female Malady: Women, Madness and English Culture 1830–1980* (London: Virago, 1987).

❧ ❖ ❧

CAROLA TORTI
KARIN KILB
MARK STEIN

Groping for Coherence
Patriarchal Constraints and Female Resistance
in Tsitsi Dangarembga's Nervous Conditions

*N*ERVOUS CONDITIONS, PUBLISHED IN 1988, is the first novel by the Zimbabwean writer Tsitsi Dangarembga. This paper is primarily concerned with the conflicting concepts of identity explored on the various levels of the text. Our starting-point will be a critique of Fanon's distinction between horizontal and vertical violence. Taking gender-issues as an example, we will criticise his theory for being one-dimensional. Dangarembga's novel as a whole supports post-structuralist concepts of identity which are characterised by their multi-dimensionality. In these theories, identity is assumed to be constructed within and by a network of discursive power-relations. On another level of the text, one of the main characters of the story, Tambu, represents the concept of identity as essence. In this respect *Nervous Conditions* is a novel which accurately mirrors what Linda Alcoff calls the current "Identity Crisis in Feminist Theory."[1] In an attempt to reconcile the two positions which characterise today's feminisms, she outlines her concept of positionality – one which provides us with the possibility of a coherent interpretation of Dangarembga's novel. We use the above theories to determine whether the novel as a whole endorses the possibility of change. The question of the individual's ability to act is of central importance here.

Nervous Conditions is the story of the young Shona girl Tambu and her struggle to position herself within the changing Rhodesian society of the Sixties and Seventies, which itself is torn between Shona tradition and English cultural influence. In the manner of autobiographical fiction, Dangarembga has the older Tambu reflect on her early youth in a village and her desire for education, which is realised after her

---

[1] Linda Alcoff, "Cultural Feminism versus Poststructuralism: The Identity Crisis in Feminist Theory," *Signs* 13.3 (1988): 405–36.

brother's early death. Her contact with English values in the mission school and her rich uncle's household leads togrowing confusion on her part as she finds herself in the crossfire of conflicting value systems. Especially her cousin Nyasha, who has been educated in England, influences Tambu by constantly questioning traditional Shona *and* English values. Tambu increasingly discovers that patriarchy is a universal structure. After her arrival at the mission she falls into the fairly passive role of an observer, witnessing the conflicts arising in the life of the women in her family. In fact, Tambu's story is inseparable from the fate of the other women portrayed. None of the older women can serve as a positive role model for Tambu or Nyasha; yet Tambu's search for identity is influenced by them. In spite of their individual situations, all of the women seem to be in a "nervous condition," be it Maiguru's overdoing of the "angel in the house," Mainini's retreat into passivity and lethargy, Tambu's initial extreme conformity and later paralysis before her essential decision, or, most extremely, Nyasha's anorexia nervosa and subsequent breakdown.

The title Tsitsi Dangarembga has chosen for her novel alludes to Fanon's *The Wretched of the Earth*. In the preface to Fanon's text, Sartre writes: "The condition of *native* is a nervous condition."[2] It consists in the coloniser's contradictory stance of demanding of the colonised that they be human beings while simultaneously denying that they are. The colonised subscribe to the colonisers' system of values in order to gain the status of human being, but by doing so they subscribe to the system of values which has defined them as inferior. This paradox determines a neurosis, "introduced and maintained by the settler among the colonised people *with their consent*" (16–17). Fanon thus explains the mechanisms of domination which lead to *horizontal violence* among the oppressed themselves rather than to *vertical violence* against the oppressor who has initially induced violence.

The plural "s" which Dangarembga has chosen for her title *Nervous Conditions* implies that the opposition between coloniser and colonised is not the only one governed by these mechanisms of domination. As Sue Thomas rightly points out, Dangarembga qualifies and rewrites Fanon's key concepts, applying them to the domination of women by men.[3] What Thomas does not seem to see is that, by extending Fanon's theory, Dangarembga makes it partly collapse.

Fanon's theory is based on the assumption that existing oppositions such as male/female, young/old, poor/rich, heathen/Christian, etc are dominated by the "master-opposition" coloniser/colonised. Only by establishing a hierarchy of oppositions can he distinguish between *horizontal* and *vertical violence*. If we transfer

---

[2] Jean–Paul Sartre, Preface to Frantz Fanon, *The Wretched of the Earth*, tr. Constance Farrington (Harmondsworth: Penguin, 1967): 17. Further references are in the text.

[3] Sue Thomas, "Killing the Hysteric in the Colonized's House: Tsitsi Dangarembga's *Nervous Conditions*," *Journal of Commonwealth Literature* 27.1 (1992): 26–36. Further references are in the text.

Fanon's theory of colonial domination to patriarchal domination, violence among women could be explained as *horizontal violence*. But a combination of the power-relations between men/women and coloniser/colonised makes it difficult to be consistent in giving a name to the violence that occurs. The following may serve as an example.

Babamukuru, headmaster of a mission school and one of the first members of the black élite to study in England, disapproves greatly of his daughter's behaviour. Nyasha, having grown up partly in England, finds it hard to adapt to Shona morals, which serve as a standard of decency for her father. When Nyasha is found, unchaperoned and dressed in a mini-skirt, talking to a white boy late at night, Babamukuru reproaches her with indecency, and, in the heated argument that follows, is driven to calling her a "whore."[4] This situation can be interpreted in various ways. Thomas calls it "an act of horizontal psychological violence" (30–31), because, as she argues, the source of the conflict is the dual acculturation of Nyasha brought about by colonialism. In other words: had it not been for colonialism, her father would never have gone to England, Nyasha would never have come to question paternal authority; instead, she would have behaved as her father demanded and no conflict would have arisen. Obviously, in this line of argument the colonial conflict dominates gender and generational conflicts.

However, from those points of view which stress generational or gender conflict, the violence directed by Babamukuru against his daughter would have to be called *vertical*. We would hold that in the above case more than one set of conflicting oppositions are causing the tension between father and daughter. Reducing the conflict to only one set of oppositions amounts to an oversimplification of their complex relationship. Although *Nervous Conditions* clearly emphasises the issue of patriarchal domination, monocausal interpretations of the main source of violence do not do justice to Dangarembga's novel.

The point we want to make here is, that in order to distinguish between *horizontal* and *vertical violence* it is imperative to define a person's identity within the terms of a single or at least a dominant opposition. We neither think that this is possible or desirable, nor that Dangarembga's novel actually depicts these conflicts in such a clear-cut manner. Quite the contrary: it is the complexity of the characters' conflicts that impresses and makes unambiguous judgements impossible.

Dangarembga's characters bear witness to Teresa de Lauretis's post-structuralist concept of identity:

> The female subject is a site of differences, differences that are not only sexual or only racial,
> economic or (sub)cultural, but all of these together, and often enough at odds with one another

---

[4] Tsitsi Dangarembga, *Nervous Conditions* (London: Women's Press, 1988): 114. Further references are in the text.

[...] these differences, then, cannot be again collapsed into a fixed identity, a sameness of all
women as Woman, or a representation of Feminism as a coherent and available image.[5]

Although the characters in *Nervous Conditions* exemplify de Lauretis's explanation
of identity, the terminology and the plot of the novel are based on essentialist
assumptions about subjectivity. This is evident from the very first page, when
Tambu, the narrator, introduces us to the characters of the novel: "my story is not
after all about death, but about my escape and Lucia's; about my mother's and
Maiguru's entrapment" (1). The notion of "escape" is incompatible with the concept
of identity as constructed by and within oppositional power-relations. How can a
subject escape the very things that determine his/her subjectivity? Especially
Tambu's thoughts and actions are dominated by the aim of "freeing" herself. With
every step she takes "upwards in the direction of [her] freedom" (183), she
encounters a "new self," or, rather, grows into her "true" self.

> The self I expected to find on the mission would take some time to appear. Besides, it was not
> to be such a radical transformation that people would have to behave differently towards me. It
> was to be an extension and improvement of what I really was. (85)

At times when circumstances make it difficult for Tambu to maintain this
idealised image of her self, she resorts to housework. Thus Tambu regains a feeling
of being needed, and the praise of the other women includes her in their community:
"It was comfortable to recognise myself as solid, utilitarian me" (40).

Nervous Conditions is marked by a contradiction central to our argument. On the
one hand, the novel conveys a post-structuralist notion of subjectivity by showing
the complexity of what determines the character's positions. Their identity is
constructed on and through a diversity of conflicting oppositions. On the other hand,
the reader is confronted with the essentialist concept of a humanist subject, capable
of taking those decisions that presumably lead to freedom.

Linda Alcoff's theory of positionality mediates between these two conceptions
characterising contemporary feminist debates. She discusses the drawbacks and
advantages of post-structuralist and essentialist constructions of women's identity,
endeavouring to avoid the pitfalls of a post-structuralist approach to the construction
of identity which paralyses the *humanist subject* and threatens to deprive feminism of
its subject: woman. At the same time she is careful not to posit *woman* as an
essentialist category. She argues "that the innateness of gender differences in
personality and character is [...] factually and philosophically indefensible" (413);
moreover, this view would be all too limiting to both feminist theory and women.
Alcoff conceives of the subject as "nonessentialised and emergent from a historical
experience." Her concept thus involves two characteristics: first, *woman* is seen as a
"relational term identifiable only within a (constantly moving) context"; secondly,

---

[5] Teresa de Lauretis, *Alice Doesn't: Feminism, Semiotics, Cinema* (Bloomington: Indiana UP, 1984): 103.

"the position that women find themselves in can be actively utilised (rather than transcended)" (434).

Alcoff's *concept of positionality* can be applied to the novel by comparing the coping strategies of the two main characters, Tambu and Nyasha. Despite their different life stories, the women face a similar struggle. Nyasha is well aware of the different oppositions by which her position is determined, but it is impossible for her to accept her situation. "Far-minded" Nyasha, who can be seen as the psychological double of Tambudzai, is "isolated" (1) from the others because of the insights she gains into the positionality of her identity. The young woman realises that she is torn between the values she was exposed to in Britain at an early age, and those of her more traditional Shona society. She is critical of the former colonisers of Rhodesia/Zimbabwe, yet her conception of her role as a woman is clearly influenced by Western thought and stands in contradiction to that of her conservative father. She aspires to education and knowledge while at the same time despising much of what she has to learn. Her schooling directs her towards a position in the black élite of her society, a role which she denounces as playing the "good kaffir" (200).

Does Nyasha's knowledge empower her to decisive action? It definitely threatens the status and role of the other family members, especially of the patriarch Babamukuru, who informs her that "there can only be one man in this house" (115). Confronted with his daughter's non-acceptance of his supremacy and infallibility, he resorts to helpless violence. Her critique also undermines the role and status of her mother, who has chosen to be the "angel in the house" caring for her "daddy-sweet" husband while belittling the scope of her education and forsaking the fruit of her labour, her salary, so that her husband Baba can play his traditional role. However, in the end Nyasha initiates her own destruction rather than changing the power-structures she analyses and attacks.

Is it in keeping with Alcoff's theory that Nyasha's subversive power, based on her awareness of the positionality of her identity, not only undermines the status of her family members but causes severe problems for the adolescent herself? Let us turn to Alcoff again:

> [...] When women become feminists the crucial thing that has occurred is not that they have learned any new facts about the world but that they come to view those facts from a different position, from their own position as subjects. When colonial subjects begin to be critical of the formerly imitative attitude they had toward the colonists, what is happening is that they begin to identify with the colonised rather than the colonisers. (434)

Nyasha seems to fail to take the crucial step required in the light of Alcoff's thinking: although she sees the "habits, practices, and discourses" (431) constructing her position, she has problems with laying claim to any position she can call her own. She is too aware and too critical of the conflicting discourses which position her as a determined daughter, a black woman, an African with a European education, a rich girl with socialist ideas. Consequently, she is without a basis from which to start modifying herself and her social environment. Her rebellion is not directed: rather, it is global – therefore self-destructive, not effective. Alcoff would probably say that Nyasha tries to "transcend" her position and the factors determining it, rather than to "utilise" it.

Nyasha's cousin Tambu also rebels against circumstances she dislikes; she convinces her parents to let her go to school, earns money for the fees, and eventually attends Babamukuru's mission school and later Sacred Heart College. How does Tambu achieve this career while Nyasha suffers from a nervous breakdown?

First of all, Tambu lacks Nyasha's perceptivity and is never entirely sure of what determines her situation. But she is pragmatic enough to decide on what she wants and to act accordingly. The subtler contradictions discerned by and harmful to Nyasha are overlooked by Tambu. Secondly, Tambu does not attempt to think things through as Nyasha would do whenever her thoughts revealed conflicts which she felt she was unable to resolve. Instead, she suppresses what she can't handle at the moment, and puts off dealing with it.

One example should suffice to demonstrate this. When Babamukuru, Maiguru and their children come back to the homestead straight after their return from England, Tambu is startled by the change that has taken place in her cousins, and she reflects on why she is no longer able to like them:

> These were complex, dangerous thoughts that I was stirring up, not the kind that you can ponder safely but the kind that become autonomous and malignant if you let them. [...] Sensing how unwise it was to think too deeply about these things in case I manoeuvred myself into a blind alley at the end of which I would have to confront unconfrontable issues, I busied myself with housework. (38)

Her strategy of staving off dangerous thoughts – thoughts that question her own situation – serves as a means of survival. "I thought I was wise to be preserving my energy, unlike my cousin, who was burning herself out" (116).

Throughout the novel these disturbing thoughts keep coming back, and each time she opens her eyes a little wider to their implications, until finally the time comes when Tambu feels she has to take a decision. This is when Babamukuru organises a Christian wedding ceremony for Tambu's parents. He suggests that their "living in sin" is responsible for the bad state the family is in. Tambu finds the whole business of a wedding as a cleansing ceremony highly humiliating and after several days of painful consideration about whether or not she ought to disobey her "divine" uncle, she decides to stay at home; "I had made my decision and the decision at least was mine" (168). She is punished for defying Babamukuru's authority but "went about these chores grimly, with a deep and grateful masochistic delight: to me [Tambu] that punishment was the price of my newly acquired identity" (169).

Identifying with her parents, whose traditional life-style she does not wish to see ridiculed by a Christian ritual, she consciously risks having to leave Baba's house and forsake her education. In grasping her situation and in acting accordingly, Tambu in the end manages to claim her rightful position.

The novel does not only depict positioning as a possibility for the subject to claim an identity as a basis on which to act. The act of positioning is essential for the characters' self-assertion and a necessary step in their groping for coherence. However, the women of whose entrapment Tambu speaks, her mother and Maiguru, are characterised by self-effacement.

Maiguru, who teaches at the mission, accepts the role of inferior appendix to her husband's family, which she supports with her salary; she explains that she has had "to choose between self and security" (101), and has opted for security. Tambu, the narrator, remarks ironically:

> If it was necessary to efface yourself, as Maiguru did so well that you couldn't be sure she didn't enjoy it, if it was necessary to efface yourself in order to preserve [Babamukuru's] sense of identity and value, then, I was sure, Maiguru had taken the correct decisions. (102)

In an effort to position herself, Nyasha's mother Maiguru temporarily leaves her husband. Tambu expects Nyasha to be hurt by Maiguru's leaving her, but Nyasha understands: "She thought there was a difference between people deserting their daughters and people saving themselves" (174).

To summarise, the "entrapped women" (1) do not position themselves but accept the roles designated for them by patriarchy. Although Nyasha refuses to be pigeonholed, she fails to position herself. Tambu, despite her opportunism, manages to lay claim to a position.

Our reading of the novel criticises the one-dimensionality of Fanon's approach, which constructs as a master-opposition the relationship between coloniser and colonised. Thomas's feminist reading inserts a secondary opposition but is equally limiting, for it adheres to the same master-opposition. Post-structuralist theories are criticised for negating the subject's scope of action by assuming an overdetermination of the subject to the extent of paralysis. We make use of the concept of positionality because it mediates between post-structuralist determination and the subject's capability to act. It draws from post-structuralist theories the concept of the individual's constructedness by a plurality of oppositions, while maintaining the individual's scope of action.

In consequence, those readings of *Nervous Conditions* whose argument is based on a hierarchy of oppositions fail to do justice to the novel's complexity. Critics to whom *Nervous Conditions* exemplifies the dissolving subject overlook the subject's capability to act as depicted in the novel.

The characters of the novel are constructed within and by a network of discursive power-relations, yet the strategy of positioning provides them with scope for action. Tambu is the character who makes the best use of these possibilities. Still, the text as a whole judges her actions and success with ambivalence. The older Tambu's narration carries a critical tone which cannot be ignored: it runs through the description of Tambu's life, so that the reader is led to disapprove of her selfish pragmatism, especially when she neglects Nyasha's call for help.

While Nyasha's singlemindedness entails her near self-destruction, Tambu's success is bought at the risk of her integrity. Does this imply that the scope of action Linda Alcoff speaks of is too limited to allow for change? We are of the opinion that Tambu initiates change by bringing herself into a position from which she can make herself heard. In narrating her story, she is writing women's problematics into Rhodesian history. The shifts of meaning thus induced signify change from within; any escape from discursive constraints, however, is depicted as an illusion.

WORKS CITED

A L C O F F , Linda. "Cultural Feminism versus Poststructuralism: The Identity Crisis in Feminist Theory," *Signs* 13.3 (1988): 405–36.

D A N G A R E M B G A , Tsitsi. *Nervous Conditions* (London: Women's Press, 1988).

L A U R E T I S , Teresa de. *Alice Doesn't: Feminism, Semiotics, Cinema* (Bloomington: Indiana UP, 1984): 103.

S A R T R E , Jean–Paul. Preface to Frantz Fanon, *The Wretched of the Earth*, tr. Constance Farrington (Harmondsworth: Penguin, 1967).

T H O M A S , Sue. "Killing the Hysteric in the Colonized's House: Tsitsi Dangarembga's *Nervous Conditions*," *Journal of Commonwealth Literature* 27.1 (1992): 26–36.

See also:

B O S M A N , Brenda. "A Correspondence without Theory: Tsitsi Dangarembga's *Nervous Conditions*," *Current Writing* 2 (1990): 91–100.

M C W I L L I A M S , Sally. "Tsitsi Dangarembga's *Nervous Conditions*: At the Crossroads of Feminism and Post-Colonialism," *World Literature Written in English* 31.1 (1991): 103–12.

F L O C K E L M A N N , Miki. "'Not-Quite Insiders and Not-Quite Outsiders': The 'Process of Womanhood' in *Beka Lamb, Nervous Conditions* and *Daughters of the Twilight*," *Journal of Commonwealth Literature* 27.1 (1992): 37–47.

S T R A T T O N , Florence. "The Shallow Grave: Archetypes of Female Experience in African Fiction," *Research in African Literatures* 19.1 (1988): 143–69.

V E I T – W I L D , Flora. "Creating a New Society: Women's Writing in Zimbabwe," *Journal of Commonwealth Literature* 22.1 (1987): 171–78.

——."Women write about the things that move them," *Matatu* 3.6 (1989): 101–108.

❧ ❖ ❧

AFUA COOPER

I Don't Care If Your Nanny Was Black

I don't care if your nanny was Black
and you ate grits for breakfast every morning
and you knew a Black girl in high school and she
was nice
I don't care, because
Howard Beach is dead
killed by white youths
who got off free, even though witnesses
testified to their crime
I don't care if your nanny was Black, because
six Black youths are in jail charged for raping
a white woman
and Donald Trump takes out a three-page ad
in the New York Times calling for their deaths
calling for the lynching of six Black youths
while the four white cops who raped Black woman
Tawana Brawley
are still on the street
So when you hear Black rage
feel Black anger
you raise your hands in exasperation and
white guilt pours from your mouth
and you start to tell the audience
that you are not a racist, because
your nanny was Black
and you ate grits for breakfast every morning
and you knew a Black girl in high school and she
was nice

I don't care
you hear
I don't care, because
for too long we have held our pain in our very flesh
for too long we have held our wounded hearts
in our chests
for too long our eyes have seen
what they can no longer bear to see
Our anger will rise like a red flood
and spread across this land
tear down monuments built on our blood
cast away false idols
and like Joshua, tear down the walls of this Jericho

❧ ❖ ❧

JOHN J. FIGUEROA

The Sea Still Going On
Derek Walcott's Omeros[1]

I WILL NOT BOTHER THE READER with facts that are no doubt already known, such as: that the poem, first published in 1990, is some 325 pages long, almost entirely in terza rima, which sometimes rhymes and sometimes does not. It is, as so often with Walcott, mosaic in structure, and richly textured by a subtle use of various registers of language – in fact, of various languages. So it starts – and these few lines should be read inwardly aloud, as a reminder that we are dealing with a poem, even if it is a novel-poem, and only the *angustiae* of time forces me to omit those aspects which make it a *poem* – it starts:

> "This is how, one sunrise, we cut down them canoes."
> Philoctete smiles for the tourists, who try taking
> his soul with their cameras. "Once wind bring the news
>
> to the *laurier-cannelles*, their leaves start shaking
> the minute the axe of sunlight hit the cedars,
> because they could see the axes in our own eyes.
>
> Wind lift the ferns. They sound like the sea that feed us
> fishermen all our life"[2]

Here, incidentally, is the first Homeric touch: *polluphloisboio thalassesesie*.[3]

E.V. Rieu, in the Introduction to his English translation of the *Odyssey*, states that while the *Iliad* might be considered a tragedy, the *Odyssey* is really a novel.[4] Walcott's *Omeros* uses as its reference-point both the *Iliad* and the *Odyssey*: Helen and the battle for her, caused by her, are present, but so also is the father-and-son relationship; our author is almost Telemachus, and Maud Plunkett, the Irish woman living in St Lucia with her English husband, shows characteristics not unlike those of the weaving, patient Penelope.

One central aspect and pleasure of the poem is its depiction of the variety of cultures involved in the making of the Caribbean, especially of St Lucia, Walcott's local habitation and place. What brings Homer to many of us in the Caribbean is

---

[1] This address draws on material already published in the essay *"Omeros,"* in *The Art of Derek Walcott*, ed. Stewart Brown (Bridgend, Mid Glamorgan: Seren, 1991): 193–213.

[2] Derek Walcott, *Omeros* (London: Faber & Faber, 1990): 3. Further page references to this edition are in the text.

[3] Homer, *The Iliad*, B, line 209.

[4] E.V. Rieu, "Introduction," Homer, *The Odyssey*, tr. Rieu (1946; Harmondsworth: Penguin, 1963): 10. An early review of *Omeros* which I wrote for the *London Magazine* was in fact entitled "A Novel Poem."

that sound of the sea: "they sound like the sea that feeds us." To wake up to that sound or to watch what Walcott somewhere calls the hexameters of the waves breaking on the beach is to be, if one is from the Caribbean, at home, whether in the Caribbean or in Sitges, in far-away Cataluña, or on the shores of Lake Nyasa.

But to return, as it were, to a more even keel.

Omeros shows certain real developments in Walcott's work, even though some have felt that after *Another Life* little was left to be said. In *Omeros* the author continues his mastery over the use of many registers of language, as can be seen in the passage the beginning of which I have just quoted. This ability with languages can be seen even more clearly in the passages which deal with the attempts at forming a new political party by Professor Statics (107).

Walcott also widens his concerns to take in the Indians of the North American Plains, the people of transatlantic African cultures, and Polish refugees. As he puts it, after the fact, in his Nobel Prize speech (referring to the population of Trinidad and Tobago, but also, by implication, to the whole Caribbean, including those parts about which the other Nobel Laureates, Saint-John Perse and Aimé Césaire, wrote):

> They survived the Middle Passage and the *Fatel Rozack*, the ship that carried the first indentured Indians from the port of Madras to the fields of Felicity, that carried the chained Cromwellian convict and the Sephardic Jew, the Chinese grocer and the Lebanese merchant selling samples on his bicycle.[5]

Those are the ones that Port of Spain reminds him of. But *Omeros* adds many others to these, people who were, and are, all part of European geopolitics and the European outpush throughout the whole of the Americas, an outpush that brought together so many cultures.

Walcott had started his public poetic and caring life with the fire which gutted Castries in his youth:

> After that hot gospeller had levelled all but the churched sky,
> I wrote the tale by tallow of a city's death by fire;
> Under the candle's eye, that smoked in tears, I
> Wanted to tell, in more than wax, of faiths that were snapped like wire.[6]

Then he had stretched out to the countryside and country people of St Lucia because of his painting, under the tutelage of Harry Simmons, with Dunstan St Omer, the Gregorias Apilo of *Another Life*. Then he moved on to Jamaica and Trinindad, and in *The Arkansas Testament* to the ex-slave population of the USA.

So *Omeros*, besides being a good read, shows our author expanding his humane concerns, and making even greater use of his language inheritance. Remember that, mainly because of European plans and domination, St Lucia has French and English, West African, Ameridian and Asian cultures in its history. Walcott grew up speaking at least three languages; many St Lucians control at

---

[5] Derek Walcott, *The Antilles: Fragments of Epic Memory; The Nobel Lecture* (New York: Farrar, Straus & Giroux, 1993): unpaginated.

[6] Derek Walcott, "A City's Death By Fire," *In A Green Night: Poems 1948–1960* (London: Jonathan Cape, 1962): 14.

least two. More and more, Walcott has used these languages in a texture that makes meanings not easily available in any other way.

This can be seen, of course, in his "Schooner *Flight*," where the narrator is a "Shabine," a man of mixed race *and*, more important, of mixed culture, who naturally tells his tale in the creole language of Trinidad. But this language texture is also seen to advantage, and is to be much enjoyed, in *Omeros*, especially, as I mentioned above, in the Political Party meeting which is in more senses than one a *wash out*:

> The night of the Statics Convention Blocko it rained,
> it drenched out his faith in the American-style
> conviction that voters needed to be entertained. (108)

Notice the implications for the fusion of cultures here: added to the St Lucian *mélange du tout* is now the North American conviction that voters need to be entertained. This element has not been brought, like the others, by the sea, but by more up-to-date means of communication.

I wish now to turn my attention especially to two aspects of this poem, using two of Dante's categories of interpretation, the historical and the moral. I am going to put more stress on the latter, which perhaps modern usage would prefer to call social or political, rather than moral.

To start with the historical in the sense of both the story and its meaning as well as the usual sense of historical. The theme is not so much, as had been asserted, *exile*. It is, rather, *where is home?* In our context we could phrase it differently: do modern people really exist in one culture only? And is "man's inhumanity to man" endemic?

The historical movement of people – which is the movement of cultures – is so often forgotten now, even in places like the Caribbean, which has been one of the greatest recipients and results of this movement, whether voluntary or forced. It cannot be by accident that the poem opens with what is to the local fishermen their main means of movement, the making of a canoe:

> "This is how, one sunrise, we cut down them canoes."
> Philoctete smiles for the tourists

And much later in the poem we hear, of Plunkett, that his wanderings are over:

> Despite that morning's near-accident, the old Rover
> sailed under the surf of threshing palms and his heart
> hummed like its old engine, his wanderings over,
>
> like the freighter rusting on its capstans. (259)

And the poem ends with the beach and "the sea still going on."

In between the beginning and the end, Achille has travelled back to Africa, the (subcontinental) Indian diaspora has taken place, the Indians of the Plains have been moved very nearly into extinction. We have been to Holland, where the young midshipman, also called Plunkett, has been spying for Rodney, the English admiral who operated far from home in the Caribbean. We have been in the desert with Plunkett's colleagues fighting against Rommel; we have been in Istanbul, and seen Athens and Atlanta, Georgia. We have, as they say in Nigeria, that country of a variety of cultures, *travelled*.

Although the pivot and focal point is St Lucia, where Maud and Hector, and the father of the narrator, end their lives, and where Omeros appears to show the narrator the way, the general displacement appears to be pervasive – almost a secular version of the Augustinian insight: *our hearts are restless until they rest in Thee*.

As we hear in connection with Seven Seas, who is the islander who has travelled most, and has lived among the "Red Indians":

> Seven Seas sighed. What was the original fault?
> "Plunkett promise me a pig next Christmas. He'll heal
> in time, too"
>   "We shall all heal."
>   The incurable
>
> wound of time pierced them down the long, sharp-shadowed street. (319)

The historical aspects of this remarkable poem, then, are wide-ranging. It is not only Helen of St Lucia who is portrayed and explored, but St Lucia itself – and the displacement of peoples, and people, as an aspect of the human condition, and often with the consequent displacement rather than the fusion of cultures.

For instance, Ma Kilman is referred to as an Obeah-woman, and in a sense she functions as such in modern St Lucia. But in fact she has suffered a displacement: her function as one who cures, as a Myalman, has been displaced into that of Obeah-woman; the Asante healer has been, through the disruption of slavery, and the passage over the seas, been turned into the Asante curser and setter of evil spells. As she puts it:

> "It have a flower somewhere, a medicine, and ways
> my grandmother would boil it. I used to watch ants
> climbing her white flower-pot. But, God, in which place?" (19)

And in the end it is the trail of the ants that leads her eventually to the curing plant that relieves Philoctete of the curse which his namesake in the *Iliad* suffered, the stinking wound which cut him off from his fellows.

The cure that works on Philoctete – the prayerful use of the traditional, of the *native*, which is downgraded by the modern, whether secular or religious – mysteriously works on the narrator's heart-wound of living, and perhaps loving, not wisely but too well. As he exclaims:

>   There was no difference
> between me and Philoctete. (245)

Just as Ma Kilman's search for the proper native, traditional curative herbs begins to succeed with Philoctete, so the narrator, who is also isolated, but by his heart wound, is cured: "There was no difference between them."

So the fictional and poetic power of the poem, and the poet, seem to suggest to us in the heat of reading. But I have to say that on this occasion, when recollected in tranquillity, the sleight of hand does not seem quite to work. You will have to judge for yourself:

> [Ma Kilman] rubbed dirt in her hair, she prayed
> in the language of ants and her grandmother, to lift
>
> the sore from its roots in Philoctete's rotting shin
> [....]
> Philoctete shook himself up from the bed of his grave,
> and felt the pain draining, as surf-flowers sink through sand.
>
> III
>
> See her there, my mother, my grandmother, my great-great-
> grandmother. See the black ants of their sons,
> their coal-carrying mothers. Feel the shame, the self-hate
>
> draining from all our bodies in the exhausted sleeping
> of rumshop closed Sunday. There was no difference
> between me and Philoctete. (244–45)

That Homeric name gives us the opportunity to note that, despite its title, and despite the loving appearance of the blind Bard himself – in St Lucia and on the steps of St Martin's-in-the-Field – this poem is in no way written, as it were, over the template of the *Iliad* or the *Odyssey.* Helen (of St Lucia) appears, and Hector and Achille, also of St Lucia. And there is a fight over Helen and her mysterious beauty. But these St Lucians also bear these names because of the tradition started in slavery of giving slaves such heroic names. Walcott somewhere calls the results of this custom "the shadow of names." Perhaps as a poet he has always exaggerated the power and importance of names, the giving of which, he has more than once reminded us, was Adam's role and privilege.

The Homeric aspect, and context of meaning, in *Omeros* is to be found more in the sea and the struggles with it; in what humans fight for, whether in Homer or elsewhere; in the displacement and dislocation of people: the Wrath of Achilles in the *Iliad* sent the souls of many noblemen to Hades, leaving their bodies as carrion for the dogs and passing birds. Also sent Odysseus wandering through many lands and cultures. But note, as far as the historical aspect goes, that the real heroes in this poem are not nobles, nor *anax androon,* "Kings of Men" as they are called in Homer; or princes. They are noble people, but most without rank. There *are* a few of rank: such as the Comte de Grasse and Rodney; but these are few and unimportant. The real heroes are the St Lucian Hector and Achille and Helen and Philoctete and Seven Seas, some of them fishermen, most of them finding it difficult to make a living in the days of trawling foreign fishnets almost as big as their island home:

> banks robbed by thirty-mile seines,
> their refrigerated scales packed tightly as coins,
>
> and no more lobsters on the seabed. All the signs
> of a hidden devastation under the cones
> of volcanic gorges. Every dawn made his trade
>
> difficult and empty (300)

So that Aristotle's dictum about the hero needing to be a prince or a leader is turned around. This is in fact one of the achievements of this story, this history of this people. A new culture has grown, and is growing, here. And not only with respect to the fishermen: Ma Kilman, who cures Philoctete, is a shopkeeper and a Sybil/Obeah woman; Helen is a maid and waitress; Maud Plunkett, one of the most sympathetic characters in the book, is a gardener from Ireland, who is in St Lucia because her husband is there, looking for a son, and for a connection with History. All these are indeed noble people – but not people of the nobility. They belong to another stage and type of History in which some various cultures are fused, and some merely mixed, nodding at each other from a distance.

This poem, however, is too important, too well constructed, and too *concerned*, not to be interpreted at the moral level, as Dante would have called it. And this I now wish to do. Note, incidentally, that although V.S. Naipaul has the reputation for condemning all things Caribbean, not least the politicians, Derek Walcott has never been quiet about the failings of our leaders. In fact, he has been so critical of parts of the tourist developments in St Lucia that the Minister of Tourism is alleged to have called him a "jumped-up intellectual." Certainly that Minister was not seen at the celebrations for Walcott's Nobel prize in St Lucia. In fact, one St Lucian wag who runs a news sheet announced the award in the following terms: "Jumped-up intellectual wins the Nobel."

We have to think of the serious implications of this poem for human living, and of its echoes, at least, of what Dante called "eternal matters." This poem often depicts or implies the suffering inflicted on whole groups of displaced people. It decries in moving terms the over-fishing of the Caribbean, the changes caused by tourism, and the doubtful decisions made by local, post-independence politicians, whose existence has hardly "made any difference" to Philoctete's burdensome life. Yet in the end it seems to protect some sort of satisfied acceptance on the part of the Narrator – in fact, a sort of celebration:

> "but the right journey
> is motionless; as the sea moves round an island
>
> that appears to be moving, love moves round the heart –
> with encircling salt, and the slowly travelling hand
> knows it returns to the port from which it must start.
>
> Therefore, this is what this island has meant to you,
> why my bust spoke, why the sea-swift was sent to you:
> to circle yourself and your island with this art." (291)

True, these words are spoken in a dream by Seven Seas/Omeros. But some such "resolution" connected with love and care and art does seem in the end to be delineated.

Does this resolution ring true? It is a question which must be asked, because this superbly crafted poem is not the work of some clever dandy showing how well he can handle and vary terza rima, although he certainly can do that. Moreover, in the poem itself moral questions are raised, such as the ineptitude and dishonesty of local politicians: making other people's children waiters, while theirs, no doubt, become lawyers. The narrator also shows clearly how human beings displace other human beings, and therefore their cultures, at will, noting of the Revolutionary Citizens of the USA:

> all colonies inherit their empire's sin,
> and these, who broke free of the net, enmeshed a race. (208)

The question or questions I am raising here are too important to dodge, although it might be easier to do so.

One must remember, however, that a poem, even a long poem which is clearly close to the author and to the major experiences of his life, is not a moral treatise. And it must make its profound effect, and be enjoyed, through the architectonics and music of its structure and its images, rather than by any particular quotable sayings within it. It is evident that *Omeros* marks a humane expansion and development of the author's poetic concerns. We are indeed far beyond his early "You in the castle of your skin, I the swineherd."[7] In fact, we are far beyond even Lamming's variation of those lines: *In the Castle of My Skin*. We are now concerned with the fate of the sea-floor and the stocks of fish as well as with the fishermen who are losing their living and selling their canoes to buy "transports" in which, for a price, they run tourists up and down the pot-holed roads.

As I pointed out above – but it is worth mentioning again in connection with the moral aspects of this poem – the concerns no longer remain with St Lucia or the Caribbean, but spread all over the world to those who suffer, in a special way, displacement, dismay and oppression. One of the clearest implications of this poem, as a whole, is that people who have been relegated by others to being peripheral should not so relegate themselves, and so find it impossible, or improper, to portray, sympathetically or otherwise, any human persons, white, black or brown. The poem also clearly supposes and demonstrates that Homer, and the various cultures his great poems embody, does not belong to one group of people only – Northern Europeans, for instance.

At the moral level this novel poem illustrates what many progressive people, especially nationalists, seem to miss: the difference between environment and immediate physical conditions. Through reading, for instance, one can import into one's enviroment much that does not spring from one's immediate surroundings: Greek or Latin, or Urdu, or Igbo for instance, or Marxism or Christianity. There is however, a further question, at the moral level of interpretation, which one might ask about this poem: to what extent is a certain sort of fatalism and quietism implied in it? And if it is, is that really the way of human history: *que sera, sera*? How deeply has the Salve Regina sent his roots? – *Exules filii Hevae*? This question about fatalism and quietism can be phrased differently: does the denouement of this novel poem seem contrived? Not perhaps in the heat of reading, such is the intensity of the lyrical quality of the poem, and its rhythmic sweep. But in quiet

---

[7] Derek Walcott, *Epitaph for the Young* (Barbados: Advocate Co., 1949), Canto III: 6.

contemplation of the poem as a whole one wonders if one has not too easily acquiesced to the image of the motionless journey ("as the sea moves around an island / that appears to be moving, love moves round the heart"). Of course, the full meaning, even at the moral level and at the level of "eternal verities," must rest in the tension built up between the parts. It is a question of whether the displacement parts – what one might call *the whiteness is everywhere* parts – do not totally outweigh the integrative parts, represented by Achille, for instance, and by the guidance of Omeros himself. It is not a matter easy to settle at this early stage of the public existence of this poem. But it would be cowardly and trivialising not to raise it.

It is connected with what one might call the *Salve Regina* aspect, which might be taken as a wonderful example of the fusion of cultures. Towards the end of the poem one reads:

> Behind lace Christmas bush, the season's red sorrel,
> what seemed a sunstruck stasis concealed a ferment
> of lives behind tin fences, an endless quarrel (310)

Seven Seas, in his penetrating blindness, contemplating the whole situation,

> at his window heard their faint anthem:

> *"Salve Regina"* in the pews of a stone ship,
> which the black priest steered from his pulpit like a helm,
> making the swift's sign from brow to muttering lip. (310)

In whatever way the "the swift's sign" might alter the basic message of the *Salve Regina* – and it might in fact underline it – it is worth looking at the *Salve*'s words, which are usually sung to one of the most haunting of Gregorian plain chants; it is of course addressed to that Star of the Ocean, Star of the Sea, Mary the mother of Jesus:

> Salve Regina, Mater misericordiae, vita, dulcedo et spes nostra,
> salve. Ad te clamamus, exules filii Hevae. Ad te suspiramus,
> gementes et flentes in hac lacrimarum valle...

It is the *clamamus, exules filii Hevae* which particularly interests us: We cry to thee; we are exiles, children of Eve, groaning and weeping in this valley of tears... And the hymn ends: After this exile show unto us the blessed fruit of thy womb, Jesus....

Notice the notion of exile, and of "another life" in which the blessed fruit will be experienced, and notice also the popular hymn-connection between Mary and the sea and the wanderer:

> Star of the Ocean, Star of the Sea
> Pray thou for the wanderer, pray thou for me...

And of course Homer's Odysseus is one of the great wanderers: a fit icon for modern humans, driven from the islands, dragged from Africa, beaten across the snow-floured plains of North America, hastening from Poland and Nazi Germany, consoled only from time to time by birds that are free to leave, to return, either every night, or annually like the cattle bird of Couva. No wonder the people in Homer's poems are so concerned with the birds, and speak of "Wingèd thoughts"!

This displacement of human persons Walcott delineates brilliantly. Have not he himself, his family and his generation suffered – or should one say enjoyed? – displacement? He has gained because he is not afraid of the fusion of cultures!

Despite the *Salve*, however, he goes out his way to say that he has lost his faith in myths and religion; and Omeros seems to persuade him to the view "to love your own above all else." The context of that bit of advice is Omeros asking him:

> "Are they still fighting wars?"
> [...]
> "Not over beauty," I answered. "Or a girl's love." (284)

How does this injunction "to love your own above all else" fit in with Walcott's strong concern for all the other displaced peoples he has so sympathetically portrayed?

And how does the loss of faith square with his real heroes, who are consoled by the *Salve*, cross themselves before most activities, and seek cures in the old traditional, sympathetic medicine? They groan for the coming of justice but, for good or ill, they are consoled by something that is to happen *after this our exile*.

And is not one of the main reasons for the disappearance of the Amerindians – like their smoke signals in the evening – precisely that the paleface ever *loved their own*? And Plunkett learned to accept not only Maud's death but also his real relationship to St Lucia; he had no longer found "his own" all that lovable!

There are other echoes of the eternal in human experience which are worth mentioning, as they go well beyond the usual uses of metaphor, implications that are of more than passing interest. We will note two.

First, when Achille goes back to Africa in his vision, he, who was originally called Afolabe, and had been renamed Achille by his master as a kind of honour, enjoys a interesting encounter with his father. One of the things his father has to say to him is cruelly moving, and relates to human experience at a deep level indeed:

> Why did I never miss you until you returned?
> Why haven't I missed you, my son, until you were lost?
> Are you the smoke from a fire that never burned? (139)

What lives, what loves, what faith, we do not miss until they are lost? And what sons and daughters did Africa not miss until they returned, hundreds of years after disappearing?

Second, an epigram from the Interlude which contains pithily one of the antinomies in this poem so concerned with displacement and the location of home:

> House where I look down the scorched street
> but feel its ice ascend my feet
>
> I do not live in you, I bear
> my house inside me, everywhere (174)

Is there an unresolved confusion here? How does this view of bearing my house inside me everywhere – with which I certainly sympathise – fit in with the special place St Lucia is to have, and with the notion of being displaced when not being in one's original home?

Simone Weil has claimed that the main drift of Homer in the *Iliad* – one of the poems which overshadows Walcott's poem – is against violence, which she describes as any force, or idea, or action which turns people into things.

One stresses again the realisation that, in a poem like this, one is dealing with a tension and structure of images and ideas, but there can be a point at which parts seem to be hauling again away from the overall design. Do we have examples of this in the two cases cited above?

Where is our home? Is there any everlasting rest? When do we turn people, on the periphery, or in the centre, into things? These might well be questions which cannot be answered in entirely here-and-now, historical, terrestrial terms, any more than the fate of the Native Americans should have been decided entirely by where it suited the railroad companies to drive in the iron spike that linked the East to the West of the United States by rail.

But there is one thing that moves and remains in all this; one majestic thing that brings Homer near to the Caribbean person who has read him, one thing that leads to the defusion, isolation and fusion of cultures: the sea, the loud-sounding sea. The ancient method by which one left home, and searched and explored, and by which one returned home – in fact, by which one lived. *The sea that feed us/fishermen all our life.*

The fishermen will always know the sea and its challenge, and its way of bringing us face to face with reality, and with our true status and abilities.

But I wonder how many modern people, even islanders, know now, and will know in future, the sea. Perhaps Walcott's poem will be the last so to depend upon the sea. The aeroplane, even in small islands, is taking over; and intercontinental travel by boat is a rare event for the rich, who are likely to be kept away from the sea by the large hotels in which they cross the wine-dark ocean. They will hardly ever be up early enough to see *rhoda dadaktylos Era* coming up out of the ocean to paint the skies with a wash of rose.[8] Yet the poem ends:

> When he left the beach the sea was still going on.

The Homeric fight for Helen was over; the travelling had been done. Philoctete's cure had been wrought; people had tried to find their selves as their homes, but brought with them their various cultures. And the sea was still going on.

This is what we of the Caribbean, especially in the smaller islands, share with Ulysses and Telemachus, and with people from the cape coast of West Africa and the Mediterranean shores. As Paul Valéry, who used to look out to that central sea

---

8 Homer, *The Odyssey*, II.1, tr. E.V. Rieu: "Dawn with her rose-tinted hands."

from the hill cemetery in which he is now buried at Sète, said in his wonderful poem, "*La mer, la mer, toujours recommencée!*"[9]

When he left the beach, the sea was still going on. The sea was still going on.

WORKS CITED

F I G U E R O A , John. "*Omeros,*" in *The Art of Derek Walcott,* ed. Stewart Brown (Bridgend, Mid Glamorgan: Seren, 1991): 193–213.

H O M E R , *The Odyssey,* tr. & intro. E.V. Rieu (1946; Harmondsworth: Penguin, 1963).

V A L É R Y , Paul. *Le cimitière marin / The Graveyard by the Sea,* ed. & tr. Graham Dunstan Martin (Edinburgh Bilingual Library 1; Edinburgh: Edinburgh UP, 1971).

W A L C O T T , Derek. *The Antilles: Fragments of Epic Memory; The Nobel Lecture* (New York: Farrar, Straus & Giroux, 1993).

———. *Epitaph for the Young* (Barbados: Advocate Co., 1949).

———. *In A Green Night: Poems 1948–1960* (London: Jonathan Cape, 1962).

———. *Omeros* (London: Faber & Faber, 1990).

---

[9] Paul Valéry, *Le cimitière marin* (stanza 1, 1.4; "The sea, the sea, forever recommencing!"); *Le Cimitière Marin/The Graveyard by the Sea,* ed. & tr. Graham Dunstan Martin (Edinburgh Bilingual Library 1; Edinburgh: Edinburgh UP, 1971): 12.

J ohn Figueroa
(Munich, September 1993; photo Peter Stummer)

GORDON COLLIER

The "Noble Ruins" of Art and the Haitian Revolution
Carpentier, Césaire, Glissant, James, O'Neill, Walcott and Others

I N THE EIGHTEENTH CENTURY, the Caribbean island territory of Saint-Domingue was the most prosperous colony in the New World. Its plantations were cultivated by the labour of half a million West African slaves, chiefly from the kingdom of Ouidah in Dahomey. On the eve of the French Revolution in 1789, Saint-Domingue accounted for nearly two-thirds of France's foreign investments. While the Revolution was raging, the colony was liberated from slavery and servitude to the white Europeans. Thenceforth known as Haiti, it was the first country in the Americas, after the United States, to win freedom from colonial rule, and counts (albeit temporarily, under Dessalines) as the first socialist state in independent America; Napoleon, "the Corsican bandit," received his first military defeat here; and what came to be known as the "Black Terror" was the first successful insurrection of a non-white people against European domination.[1] Haiti is the only francophone republic in the Western Hemisphere, and is the most densely populated country in Latin America. In 1789, there were some 32,000 whites ruling over those half-million mostly illiterate blacks and about 30,000 mostly literate *gens de couleur* or mulatto freedmen. In the whole of Haiti today, there are fewer than 1200 white inhabitants (0.1 percent of the population). About 95 percent are Afro-Caribbeans, most of whom still adhere to West African cultural patterns, including the syncretistic religion of Voodoo, where a pantheon of African nature gods is merged nominally with the attributes of Catholic saints and the Christian godhead; 80 percent of the population are Roman Catholic, of whom some 80 percent also practise Voodoo. The dominant minority (4.5 percent) is made up of mulattoes, who had always formed a favoured class, aspiring to the privileges of the whites in the eighteenth century (indeed, less that one percent of "black blood" could disqualify one as a *Blanc*), and clinging to the French cultural tradition ever since. The seeds of the Haitian revolution lay in the resistance of Creole planters to the proposal that mulattoes be represented in metropolitan France's republican National Assembly. The subsequent rebellion of blacks and mulattoes, sometimes united, sometimes in disarray, usually at logger-heads with each other and in cahoots with one or other European power, destroyed the

---

[1] Subsequent rebellions in the first half of the nineteenth century (Ceylon 1818, Java 1825–30, the Indian Mutiny 1857) all failed, as did black revolts elsewhere in the Caribbean – where, however, Saint-Domingue served as the signal-beacon of hope, as it also did in the American North. See esp. Alfred Hunt, *Haiti's Influence on Antebellum America: Slumbering Volcano in the Caribbean* (Baton Rouge: Louisiana State UP, 1988).

entire structure of Haitian society. The mulatto–black hostility has persisted to the present day, and has been a major factor in ensuring that Haiti has remained in a condition of economic and political anarchy. Sugar, which formed the backbone of the economy in the eighteenth century, now accounts for only 3 percent of export earnings. The country now has the lowest per capita income in the Caribbean; in the rest of the Americas, only Guyana and Nicaragua are worse off. Haiti also has the lowest literacy rate and the highest rate of infant mortality in the New World. Lines of historical causality are always dangerous hypotheses; but at the very least one can say that the aftermath of the revolution has been characterised by almost unrelieved hardship, poverty, inertia, cruelty, and by new forms of tyranny and neocolonial servitude matching the horrors of the age of plantation slavery.[2]

This waking societal nightmare has known no parallel in the Americas in terms of its persistence, and not even Peru is a close present-day rival for Haiti's crown of thorns. Nevertheless, Haiti was not born in baseness but in high ideals and a modicum of intellectual rigour, characteristics also of the besieged literary and intellectual élite throughout the country's history. The question which exercises both Haitian thinkers and outsiders alike is a psychologically fascinating one: How could the broad and shining path of black revolution, which had been so auspiciously embarked upon by Toussaint L'Ouverture, darken and narrow to a blood-drenched jungle trail after the advent of Toussaint's lieutenants, first Jean–Jacques Dessalines, and then Henri Christophe, Emperor and King respectively of a country that mocked all such European pretensions to dignity?[3] Yet, Haiti's revolutionary figures remain heroes to even

---

[2] The course of the revolution and the ideological motivation and policies of the participants are profoundly complex and ambiguous in their dynamic. Two of many books in English which shed some systematic light (as well as processing a mass of francophone research and primary documentation) are Carolyn E. Fick, *The Making of Haiti: The Saint Domingue Revolution from Below* (Knoxville: U of Tennessee P, 1990) and David Nicholls, *From Dessalines to Duvalier: Race, Colour and National Independence in Haiti* (1979; Warwick University Caribbean Studies; Basingstoke: Macmillan Caribbean, 1988). A lucid brief overview is offered by David Geggus, "The Haitian Revolution," in Beckles & Shepherd, *Caribbean Slave Society and Economy*, 402–18, and a useful economic–strategic account is Mats Lundahl, "Toussaint L'Ouverture and the War Economy of Saint-Domingue 1796–1802," in Beckles & Shepherd, *Caribbean Freedom*, 2–11. Still one of the most accessible book-length studies – historical and social – is James G. Leyburn, *The Haitian People* (Caribbean Series 9; 1941; New Haven CT: Yale UP, rev. 1966). The demographic uniqueness of the African heritage in Haiti, and the revolutionary roots of its chronic *macoutiste* régimes and their relevance to the rest of the Caribbean are aspects explored by Lloyd Best in a lecture initiating celebration of the Bicentennial of the 1791 revolt: "Two Hundred Years After Bois Caiman: Freedom and Responsibility in the Caribbean," *Trinidad and Tobago Review* 13.7 (July 1991): 11–18. As the historiography of the revolution is itself characterised by ideological fixations and strategies, one can hardly expect more from dramatic or poetic representations than crystallisations of universal human motives; this only by way of caveat to the *literary* critic.

[3] The "anthropological eurocentrism" exhibited by much creative and factual writing about the Haitian revolution, which was viewed by many (in the throes of, and well after, the French Revolution) as "la Vendée de Saint-Domingue," is succinctly charted by Hans–Jürgen Lüsebrink, "Mise en fiction et conceptualisation de la révolution haïtienne: La génèse d'un discours littéraire (1789–1848)," in *Proceedings of the Xth Congress of the International Comparative Literature Association, New York 1982*, ed. Anna Balakian (New York: Garland, 1985): 228–33. The postwar shift towards an autochthonous view of the revolution as a New-World Genesis in its own right is summarised by Wolfgang Bader, "Tradition et décolonisation:

the present-day population, especially Henri Christophe, whose brilliant military campaigns and subsequent reign were characterised by his deep-seated, paranoid suspicions and the deliberate horrors he unleashed.[4]

There is a vast literature on aspects of the Haitian revolution, its connection with the French Revolution, and its various guiding personalities. The actions and psychology of the revolutionary leaders have captured the imagination of numerous writers, poets, essayists, dramatists and novelists, including (from the very beginning) that of Haitian writers, and have been responsible also for some of the finest historiographical writing in the francophone world. Representations of the Saint-Domingue rebellion must wrestle to clarify or simplify massive complexities of interrelationship and protean motivation. Gordon Lewis puts the situation succinctly:

> The revolutionary leadership had, of course, its differences; most notably, Toussaint and Henri Christophe and Dessalines have been put in the black camp, Pétion and Rigaud in the mulatto camp. Toussaint had imagined a place for the whites in the new society, a misplaced faith that finally led to his fatal acceptance of Napoleon's good intentions and his death in the Jura mountain prison, while Dessalines, with his obdurate distrust of all whites, could never have made that mistake. Henri Christophe, again, had a complete grasp of the detail of statecraft, while Pétion was impatient with it. Yet all of them shared a common passion for a new Haiti governed by the newly emancipated race.[5]

My survey proceeds according to genre and in roughly chronological sequence (Toussaint – Dessalines – Christophe), and pays due attention to both Old-World and New-World representations. It is, however, Derek Walcott's involvement with the theme that has yielded among the richest and most interesting results – an involvement spanning practically the whole of Walcott's creative life so far. The latter part of this conspectus therefore examines Walcott's dramas in loose chronological relation to a number of other key works from the anglophone, francophone and hispanophone Caribbean; the long "build-up" to this closing discussion is meant to indicate by quantitative illustration that these key works, albeit each original in its approach, have a long genealogy. It is not merely the inherent dramatism of the material which has prompted artistic treatment of the Haitian revolution; Caribbean perspectives in particular indicate that this unique nexus of race, culture, and historical process constitutes a topos of permanent relevance to current theoretical debates concerning the nature of the pan-Caribbean experience.

Fonction et image de la révolution haïtienne dans la littérature des Caraïbes après la seconde guerre mondiale," *Proceedings*, ed. Balakian, 234–39.

[4] Indeed, for the whole of the Caribbean region and beyond, Haiti has supplied "les seuls vrais héros légitimes"; Vere W. Knight, quoted in Keith Q. Warner, "De l'écrivain devenu leader politique" (see Works Cited): 423, within the context of an essay arguing that Aimé Césaire's dramatic portrayal of Christophe as an expressly tragic figure is an indirect extension of Césaire's own political responsibility towards the Afro-Caribbean societies of the Caribbean. Hunt Hawkins ("Aimé Césaire's Lesson About Decolonization," 146) has pointed out how often critics have misunderstood Césaire's Christophe as a positive portrait of a misunderstood personage, instead of as a tragic instance of "bad decolonisation" – and it is this "bad decolonisation" which has most exercised the imagination of modern treatments of the revolution.

[5] Gordon K. Lewis, *Main Currents in Caribbean Thought* (Baltimore MD: Johns Hopkins UP, 1983): 229. Lewis's mastery of a mass of documentation is shown in his analysis of views on the Haitian revolution, which, however, does not draw on literary or dramatic representations (see esp. 252–64).

Poetry

It goes without saying that there were countless celebratory anthems composed during the period of the revolution itself. In this and succeeding periods, much of the focus was understandably on Toussaint and his liberationist precursors, as in such celebrated poetic side-glances as those of Wordsworth.[6] Among the poets of the Romantic period, mention should be made of Alcibiade Fleury–Battier (1841–83), who wrote a considerable amount of patriotic verse commemorating Haiti's early revolutionary figures, including "Le Défenseur de La Crête-à-Pierrot."[7] The more Whitmanic verse of Oswald Durand (1840–1906), who became president of the Haitian National Assembly, encompasses celebrations of early liberators like Ogé, Dessalines and Pétion, but especially Toussaint (eg, in the closing lines of such nationalistic lyrics as "Les Forts" from *Rires et Pleures*, 1869, or in the national anthem beginning "Quand nos aïeux brisèrent leurs entraves"), depicted as languishing in his French dungeon, and as a Sphinx which Napoleon could not un-riddle. The volume *Patrie: espérances et souvenirs* (1885) by Tertullien Marcelin Guilbaud (1856–1937) includes reflections on Haiti's political forefathers.[8] Book One of Massillon Coicou's (1867–1908) nobly conceived but indifferently executed *Poésies nationales* (1892) in particular treats relevant themes: "Complaintes d'esclave" rehearses, from the lyrical standpoint of racial identity, the pre-revolutionary situation of Saint-Domingue, while "Toussaint Messie" is a salute to the revolutionary leader in a patriotic cavalcade of early revolutionaries, while the best-remembered poem of Louis Arnold Laroche (1869–90), published in *Les bluettes* (1887), is "Les plaintes de Louverture au Fort de Joux." Of the pre-First World War "*La Ronde*" generation (named after a literary review 1898–1902), Alcibiade Pommeyrac (1844–1908) composed a long monologue entitled *La Dernier Nuit de Toussaint Louverture: monologue en vers* (1877). Part of the long poem *Le Flibustier* (written 1895–96, published 1902) by Etzer Vilaire (1872–1951) consists of an evocative scene in which the protagonist sails into the colonial harbour of Port-Républicain and, amid reflections on the history of the striving for liberty, hears the cries of the slaves, of "la maternelle Afrique." In the modern period, the lyric impulse associated with Toussaint has ebbed somewhat,[9] but Aimé Césaire's

---

6 William Wordsworth, "To Toussaint L'Ouverture," in *The Poems*, ed. John O. Hayden (Penguin English Poets; Harmondsworth: Penguin, 1977), vol. 1: 577; composed August 1802 while Toussaint was in Fort-de-Joux prison. See Bernard Hickey, "Wordsworth's Sonnet 'Toussaint L'Ouverture'," *Caribana* 2 (1991): 37–43.

7 Unless otherwise indicated (or self-evidently "metropolitan"), francophone writers mentioned are Haitian. The handiest current overview of the literature of Haiti is offered by Léon–François Hoffmann, *Littérature d'Haïti* (Universités francophones: Histoire littéraire de la francophonie; Paris: EDICEF, 1995); Hoffmann briefly treats historians of the revolution (111–14); his discussion of literary representations of the theme (119) is cursory.

8 As in "Le Premier Janvier" (1885), where, amidst the bloody rebirth of the African people, Dessalines is depicted as a sternly intolerant Mosaic leader; "Dix-huit cent quatre" (1881) summarises the defeat of the invincible French, the "sublime despair" of the dynamic Christophe, the meteoric fall of Rochambeau, and Toussaint's inspired resignation to his imprisonment by the French. "Les Fils de Louverture" and "Toussaint Louverture à l'aspect de la flotte française (1802)" (1883) contain similar commemorations.

Cahier, half-way through, in taking stock of the islands of the Caribbean archipelago, details "Haiti where negritude rose for the first time and stated that it believed in its humanity" before a brief, intense passage dwelling on Toussaint in "a little / cell in the Jura," "imprisoned in / whiteness."[10]

Less lyric attention has been paid to Toussaint's successor, Dessalines.[11] As managing editor of the Port-au-Prince journal *L'Union* in the 1830s, Ignace Nau (1808–45) pioneered the nationalist movement; his poem "Dessalines" (1837) celebrates the contribution of "cet aigle africain" to Haitian independence from colonial slavery. "Pétion" by Gustave Léonard Coriolan Ardouin (1812–35) is a brief, lyrical character-study of the general, while "Le Pont rouge" excuses the destructive grandeur of Dessalines. Massillon Coicou's "A Dessalines" is a eulogy, which was followed by "Vertières," a dramatically grandiose celebration of the eagle-eyed general's victory over Rochambeau; his epyllion-like poem "L'alarme" evokes the atmosphere of civil war and the bloody conflict at Crête-à-Pierrot. Ernest Douyon (1885–1950) wrote a poem on "La statue de Dessalines," recalling the "monstrous fury" of this "god of vengeance" in massacring the whites. Haiti's national anthem, "La Dessalinienne" (1903) was composed by the Parnassian poet and novelist Justin Lhérisson (1873–1907). Luc Grimard, in such poems as "Et la flûte gronde" and "Aux pistolets de Saint-Domingue," evokes the revolutionary battles to warn off the neo-colonial designs of the USA, and calls upon Ogé, Chavannes, Christophe, Dessalines and Toussaint to rise again.[12] René Depestre, in his *Un arc-en-ciel pour l'Occident chrétien* (1967), explores the soul of Haiti by rejecting Christianity in favour of a detailed celebration of the Voodoo *loas*; it includes as its fifth of seven sections a group of seven ode-like songs entitled "Les Sept Piliers de l'Innocence," which treat

---

9 Charles Moravia (1875–1938) composed an ode "A la mémoire de Toussaint Louverture" (published in *Roses et camélias*, 1903), while Edmond Laforest's (1876–1915) collection of 95 *Sonnets-Médaillons* (1909) devotes its sixth section to celebrations of the great liberators of recent history, including Toussaint and Pétion. J. Dieudonné Lubin's sonnet-sequence *Héros et héroïnes de la liberté d'Haïti* (1953) covers much the same ground. In his first collection, *Le psalmiste dans l'ouragan* (1933), Christian Werleigh (1895–1947) includes several odes and anthems on Haiti's historical forefathers: "Dix-huit cent quatre," "La Crête-à-Pierrot," and "Dessalines et Défilée (Le Miracle)." Duraciné Vaval (1879–1937) wrote a poem "A la mémoire de Toussaint Louverture" (in *Stances haïtiennes*, 1912), while Luc Grimard (1886–1954) commemorated the early phase of Haitian liberty in "La Légende du premier drapeau," "Aux pistolets de Saint-Domingue" and "Au roy Christophe" (all published 1927). One of the most celebrated pieces in the *Poèmes d'Haïti et de France* (1925) by Emile Roumer (born 1903) is the "Chanson de lambis," which celebrates the beginnings of the Revolution.

10 Aimé Césaire, *Cahier d'un retour au pays natal* (1939/1949; definitive edition 1956), in *The Collected Poetry* [bilingual edition], tr. Clayton Eshleman & Annette Smith (Berkeley: U of California P, 1983): 46/47 ("Haïti où la négritude se mit debout pour la première fois et dit qu'elle croyait à son humanité"; "une petite / cellule dans le Jura"; "emprisonné de / blanc"); see Bernard Mouralis, "L'Image de l'indépendance haïtienne dans la littérature négro-africaine," *Revue de Littérature Comparée* 48 (1974): 513–16.

11 Cf, however, Régis Antoine, "Poéticité de la révolution haïtienne: Dessalines," in *La Deriva delle francofonie: Atti dei Seminari Annuali di Letterature Francofone: Figures et fantasmes de la violence dans les littératures francophones de l'Afrique subsaharienne et des Antilles*, vol. 2: *Les Antilles*, ed. Carla Fratta, M.R. Baldi & M. Mengoli (Bologna: Cooperativa Libreria Universitaria Editrice, 1992): 39–62.

12 Luc Grimard, *Sur ma flûte de bambou: poèmes* (Paris: Nouvelle Revue Française, 1927).

the female deities, the first three pairing Makandal with Ayizan, Toussaint with Aida Wedo, and Dessalines with Erzulie.[13]

Henri Christophe stimulated little lyric creativity, perhaps understandably; but the revolutionary spirit of the aftermath years was kept simmering in poetry. The patriotic songs of Antoine Dupré (?1782–1816) fuelled resistance to Christophe's siege of Port-au-Prince in 1812. Dupré continued to issue verses harrassing Christophe until his death in a duel; he wrote a pseudo-classical, periphrastic paean to Haiti titled "Hymne à la liberté," and a six-line epitaph titled "Vers pour être gravés au bas d'un buste de Pétion." As a young poet, Hérard Dumesle (1784–1858) was with Dupré at Môle; he supported Pétion and attacked Christophe 1819–20 in his journal *L'Observateur*, became an opposition deputy in Boyer's government, and led the revolution deposing the latter. A long narrative by him, in prose and verse, *Voyage dans le Nord d'Haïti ou Révélation des lieux et des monuments historiques* (1821/24), celebrates Haiti's landscape and attacks the memory of Christophe. Juste Chanlatte (1766–1828), who features in Aimé Césaire's play about Henri Christophe, collaborated with the English during the Revolution, returned from the USA to become Dessalines' press officer, and was later editor of *La Gazette du Cap* during the reign of Christophe. Chanlatt's "Chant inaugural" (1814) celebrates the coronation of Christophe. His undated "Ode à l'Indépendance" includes twenty-two characters, from a watchman to the shade of Pétion, who commemorate Haiti's independence; his "Cantate à l'Indépendance" (1821) recalls the accession of Boyer after the death of Christophe; the long poem "La Triple Palme: Ode à Boyer" (1822) depicts, in the epic manner of the French dithyramb, the martial exploits of Boyer, including the crushing of the insurrection led by Christophe's maroon ally, Goman, Count of Jérémie, against Pétion at La Grand' Anse in the South, the death of Christophe, the reunion of the North with the East, and the conquest of the East. Jean–Fernand Brierre (born 1909) composed a patriotic dramatic poem in traditional forms, "Au coeur de la Citadelle" (1930; published in *Dessalines nous parle*, 1953), in which Christophe is brought together with other heroic personages and victims of Haiti's bloody past in order to swear allegiance to the nation.[14] The works mentioned are, of course, devoted entirely to revolutionary

---

13 This last evoking the power of fire, as the slaves cut off the heads of their masters and torch their houses. Depestre views these three as an "indissoluble entity" in revolt against the state of slavery, restoring both an African, "telluric," life-giving connection with the soil and the attachment to Africa that is intimately bound up with *marronnage*; Christophe's entry into historical reality induces rupture, inversion and incoherence into this scheme; see Mouralis, "L'Image de l'indépendance haïtienne," 524–25.

14 One of many later, equally sanguinary invocations of the Haitian past occurs in a creole poem by Félix Morisseau–Leroy: "One of these days Dessalines will rise [...] All Negroes cut off heads and burn houses / You will then hear them crying all over America: 'Stop him!' The voice of Dessalines can already be heard on the radio" ("Oun jou Dessalines va lévé [...] Toute nèg coupez tête boulez caille / Ous tendez n'an toute l'Amérique / Ya pé rélé: rétez'l / Voix Dessalines déjà nan radio") and, for a still-vital nationalistic view, "Thank you, Dessalines, Dessalines, sir, thank you / Every time I realise who I am / Every time I hear a black who has been colonised speak / A black who is [still] not free / I say: thank you, Dessalines" ("Mèsi, Desalin / Papa Desalin, mèsi / Chak fwa m-santi sa m-ye / Chak fwa m-tande yon nèg kolini / Nèg ki poko lib pale / M-di: Desalin, mèsi"), in Morisseau–LeRoy, *Diakout 1, 2, 3* (1953; Miami: Jaden Kreyòl, 1983): 19–20/24.

themes; but there are residual echoes and allusions in countless poetic works not centrally concerned with this historic and historical moment.[15]

Fiction

Two Frenchwomen who experienced the "Black Terror" from afar place the insurrectionist period and early phase of Toussaint within the broader context of slavery: Claire Duras' novel *Ourika* (1823) deals with the massacres of 1791 from the viewpoint of a freed female slave, while Sophie Doin's *La Famille noire* (1825) explicitly condones the reign of terror, at the same time showing the dissolution and destruction of the family of the slave hero Phénor at the hands of a white colonist.[16] Jean Baptiste Picquenard, who witnessed the rise of Toussaint at first hand, wrote a pair of novels about the revolution (practically contemporaneously with the events described), *Adonis ou Le bon nègre* and *Zoflora ou la bonne négresse*.[17] One work is worth mentioning for the curiosity value of its dramatis personae. Exiled to St Thomas after the 1848 rebellion in Port-au-Prince, Émeric Bergeaud (1818–58) wrote *Stella* (1850, published 1859), the very first novel to be written by a Haitian.[18] Although it is a historical romance chronicling the early phase of the revolution in Saint-Domingue from 1791 to 1804, including the arrival of the French expeditionary forces, the plague of yellow

---

[15] To cite only two examples, one radically hermetic, the other openly emblematic: Césaire's line about "the breathing of slaves dilating under their Christophoric steps the great sea of misery" in his first play, *And the Dogs Were Silent* (*Lyric and Dramatic Poetry 1946–82*, ed. Eshleman & Smith: 14–15), overlays historical personages to characterise the Caribbean plantation economy based on slave labour by melding Christ, the eighth-century Roman prince Christophorus, and Henri Christophe; the Cuban Nicolás Guillén places his "Elegy for Jacques Roumain" within a fabric of historical references to revolutionary figures from "that tremendous, open book: that very bloody Haitian page" – Toussaint, Leclerc, Rochambeau, Dessalines and Christophe (*Man-making Words*, tr. Márquez & McMurray: 90–101, esp. 94–97).

[16] Claire Duras, duchesse de Durfort, *Ourika*, ed. Claudine Hermann (1823; Paris: Editions des Femmes, 1979) and Sophie Doin, *La Famille noire* (Paris: Henry Servier, 1825). See Doris Y. Kadish, "The Black Terror: Women's Responses to Slave Revolts in Haiti," *French Review* 68.4 (March 1995): 668–80. A gentlewoman in Césaire's *Christophe* mentions that the novel is all the rage in Paris, and a child sings a song about the heroine, prompting Vastey to the thought that Christophe would not have much time for Ourika, who is ashamed of her complexion (II.2; 81–82). The earlier phase of maroon insurrection after Mackandal was treated in a favourable light by Jean Saint–Lambert in his novel *Ziméo* (1769; in *Œuvres complètes*; Clermont: Laudriot, 1814).

[17] Jean Baptiste Picquenard, *Adonis, ou Le bon nègre* (Paris: Didot, 1798), *Zoflora, ou La bonne négresse* (Paris: Didot, 1799). Régis Antoine notes that these narratives feature role-reversal: "whites escaping into the woods like runaways; white women forced to disguise themselves as black. Military initiative and literary focus now belong to the rebels"; "The Caribbean in Metropolitan French Writing," in *A History of Literature in the Caribbean*, vol. 1: *Hispanic and Francophone Regions*, ed. A. James Arnold (Amsterdam/ Philadelphia PA: John Benjamins, 1994): 357. There are several other novels dealing with various aspects of revolutionary incipience up to and including Toussaint or Dessalines; among these are Honoré de Balzac's *Zébédée Marcas* (1840), on Toussaint, and Robert Gaillard's *La volupté et la haine* (1971), covering the revolutionary period up to Dessaline's self-election as Emperor. Marie Vieux Chauvet (1917–75) wrote a historical novel called *La Danse sur le volcan* (1957) which concerns a young free mulatta woman called Minette who enjoys success as an actress at the playhouse in the capital of Saint-Domingue on the eve of the French Revolution, spurns a white suitor, abandons her lover, a freed mulatto landowner who treats his slaves as badly as the whites, and goes underground to work for the liberation of the blacks on the island.

[18] On *Stella*, see esp. Léon–François Hoffmann, *Haïti: Lettres et l'être* (Toronto: GREF, 1992).

fever, and the terrorist atrocities of General Rochambeau, the revolutionary leaders such as Toussaint are never designated, and the two chief polar protagonists, pure African and Creole mulatto respectively, are given the typologically "genetic" names Romulus and Remus, sons of Marie l'Africaine. The sons are aided by Stella, a Frenchwoman brought to Saint-Domingue and betrayed by a French planter; she fights alongside the revolutionaries and, when victory is proclaimed, is revealed to be the personification of Liberty. Marie had already turned up in a novel, *Bug–Jargal*, written by Victor Hugo when he was still in his teens. This work barely mentions Toussaint, who is still a background figure at the time of the action, which centres on the initiating insurrections of 1791. Hugo, who (like Theodor Körner and others) shares the subliminal sentiments of the *ancien régime* suprematists, maintains a firmly white – at times racist–colonialist – perspective on a narrative which nevertheless includes much meticulous depiction of African folkways (including Voodoo) and focuses on black and mulatto insurgents: Ogé, Georges Biassou, Boukman, Rigaud, and Burg–Jargal, a West-African prince (better-known historically as Pierrot) and hero of the battle of Morne-Rouge, who is killed by the French at the close.[19]

A curiosity is the adventure-novella *Les trésors du roi Christophe* (1954) by Gérard Duc; set in 1820 just after Christophe's death, this fantasy features one Margof, a son of the Haitian king, the plans to send a new expeditionary naval force to recapture the island for France, and the (partly successful) hunt for gold bullion which Christophe had seized from the whites and hidden in his citadel at La Ferrière. Heiner Müller's play *Der Auftrag* (1988) takes an oblique fix on the historical phase involved, by having three French commissioners trying to further the goals of the Haitian revolution in Jamaica, rather than in Saint-Domingue. A similarly oblique line appears in a novella by the socialist-realist writer Anna Seghers, "Das Licht auf dem Galgen" (1960), which is largely set in Jamaica at the time of the maroon uprising under Cuffee, but which carefully establishes the genesis of that uprising in the Haitian revolution at the time of Toussaint a couple of years earlier. Seghers' story "Die Hochzeit von Haiti" (1949) relates the events in the revolutionary phase, from Ogé's rebellion to the capture and transportation of Toussaint, from the point of view of Michael Nathan, a Jewish merchant, who dies (at the same time as Toussaint) when he is no longer needed by the African revolutionaries. A later story by Seghers, "Der

---

19 Victor Hugo, *Bug–Jargal*, in *Œuvres complètes*, ed. Jean Massin (Paris: Club français du livre, 1967), vol. 2.1: 577–704. This edition collates the mature text of 1826 with the teenage version written in late 1818 which appeared in the *Conservateur littéraire* (1820). Hugo adds to the second version the love-interest with Marie (personifying liberation), who is held captive by the rebelling slaves. On the novel, see entries in Works Cited for Pierre LaForgue, Bernard Mouralis and Pompilus Pradel. As Régis Antoine points out, metropolitan conservatism and horror pull against a sense of conflict and "the justified perception of a black ideology and a nation taking shape" ("The Caribbean in Metropolitan French Writing," in Arnold, 358) – a grasp of the contradictory forces of history that was to characterise most of the later, mature representations of the Haitian revolution. If Toussaint seldom features prominently in early francophone prose fiction, what works there are receive mention inter alia in J.A. Ferguson's discussion of prose devoted to the leader, "*Le Premier des noirs*: The Nineteenth-Century Image of Toussaint Louverture," *Nineteenth Century French Studies* 15.4 (Summer 1987): 394–406.

Schlüssel" (1980), centres on a young slave, Claudine, who is incarcerated in a room until she is freed by her lover, Amédée, a devoted follower of Toussaint, in the early stages of the revolution.[20] Two magic-realist novels by Hans Christoph Buch, of German–Haitian ancestry and the originator of the post-colonial theory of the *"kolonialer Blick"* or colonial gaze, involve aspects of the Haitian revolution. *Haïti Chérie* (1990) takes the Voodoo goddess Erzulie on a picaresque jaunt through history from Toussaint to Hitler's *Reichsbunker* before slipping over into the age of Papa Doc. *Die Hochzeit von Port-au-Prince* (1984)[21] is in part a "faction"-history of Buch's own family; its first book (narrated by a caiman or crocodile) concerns Vincent, the French emissary who took Toussaint prisoner and later died in the service of Dessalines.[22]

Among novels in English on Haitian revolutionary topics, Harriet Martineau's historical romance about Toussaint, *The Hour and the Man* (published in 1841) is particularly interesting because of the writer's relative closeness to the period dealt with. Armand Fresnau from the Dominican Republic wrote a novel on the revolutionary period which was translated into English as *Theresa at Santo Domingo* (1889). Edward Gilliam's *1791: A Tale of San Domingo* (1890) deals with the same inceptive phase. Other fictional treatments include Henry Bedford–Jones's *Drums of Dambala* (1933) and Guy Endore's *Babouk* (1934), while Eleanor Heckert's *The Little Saint of St. Domingue* (1973) provides a sweeter portrait of Toussaint than Martineau's. The most recent treatment of Toussaint's rise to power is *All Souls' Rising* (1996) by the American Madison Smartt Bell;[23] this novel is an action-packed quality blockbuster, whose central character, a young French doctor, is swayed (like the Guinea slave and

---

[20] The stories by Seghers mentioned here were collected as follows: "Die Hochzeit von Haiti [The wedding in Haiti]" and "Das Licht auf dem Galgen [The light on the gallows]" in *Karibische Geschichten* (1962); "Der Schlüssel [The key]" in *Drei Frauen aus Haiti: Drei Erzählungen* (1980). "Das Licht auf dem Galgen" was made into a film (East Germany, 1976, director Helmut Nitzschke). For discussion of these stories, see esp. entries in Works Cited for Sima Kappeler and Vibeke Rutzou.

[21] This is an intertextuality with Heinrich von Kleist's story "Die Verlobung in St. Domingo" (1811), set in Saint-Domingue in 1803, which treats the passion of Gustav, a Swiss officer in the French army, for Toni, the beautiful daughter of a mestiza working on the estate of Congo Hoango, an uncompromising freed slave. Gustav is sheltered by the women against pursuit by Dessalines' troops, but Gustav's father and brothers arrive and capture Hoango. Through a tragic misunderstanding, Gustav kills Toni, then commits suicide (a closing scene which parallels the equally senseless revenge-motif in the opening scene, where Hoango blows his generous master's brains out). See "Die Verlobung in St. Domingo," in Kleist, *Sämtliche Werke und Briefe*, vol. 3: *Erzählungen, Anekdoten, Gedichte, Schriften*, ed. Klaus Müller–Salger (Bibliothek deutscher Klassiker 51; Frankfurt am Main: Deutscher Klassiker Verlag, 1990): 222–60. Part of Kleist's concern was transcendence of inhumane race-laws through "miscegenation." The story was turned into a blank-verse drama (derived from an early printing of Kleist's story in the Viennese journal *Der Sammler*, July 1811) by Karl Theodor Körner in his *Toni* (1812). Körner stuffs the play full of sensationalist effects and removes Kleist's complexity of geographical and cultural specificity, as well as erasing both the story's profound biracial sexuality and its tragic absurdity by simply having Toni spurned by her mother, whereupon the two lovebirds, hand-in-hand, leave the island for "that white land" in Europe.

[22] For German-language treatments generally, see esp. Thomas E. Bourke, "Toussaint L'Ouverture and the Black Revolution of St Domingue as Reflected in German Literature from Kleist to Buch," *History of European Ideas* 11 (1989): 121–30.

[23] Madison Smartt Bell, *All Souls' Rising* (London: Granta, 1996). The book is the first novel in a projected trilogy on the Haitian revolution, the second part of which ("The War of the Knives") is to deal with the reign of Dessalines, the third ("The Stone That the Builder Refused") with that of Christophe.

Voodoo adept, Riau) by the enigma of Toussaint on the one hand and enlisted by the planter class on the other.

Drama

The world-historical significance and psychological complexity of the leading figures in the Haitian revolution are factors, among others, that lend themselves readily to stage dramatisation involving the dialectical interplay of individual and social forces. Indeed, a continuing fascination is the extent to which these materials lend themselves to ideological projection and historical reinterpretation.[24] One of the plays closest to the events depicted is *L'Esclavage des noirs* (1789) by Olympe de Gouges, a pronouncedly abolitionist Frenchwoman who had followed the "Black Terror" with great engagement and depicted the phase of insurrection immediately before the rise of Toussaint.[25] Pierre Faubert (1806–68) was secretary to Boyer before fleeing to France in 1843. Faubert attacked the dissension between blacks and mulattoes; as director of the national Lycée Pétion, he wrote a play for his pupils, designed to instruct them in the evils of racial prejudice, called *Ogé ou Le préjugé de couleur* (1841; staged 1844).[26] The play centres on the efforts of Vincent Ogé and other mulattoes and free coloureds such as Jean–Baptiste Chavannes to secure equal rights with the whites, and concentrates on the build-up to the slave rebellion of August 1791 which touched off the revolution. A central characterological opposition is set up between the courage and magnanimity of the mulattoes and free coloureds and the pridefulness and cruelty of the white colonists who are taken prisoner and tried.

An early metropolitan attempt, in the 1820s, to come to terms with the significance of Toussaint is the play *L'habitation de Saint Domingue ou l'insurrection* by the politician Charles François Marie, Comte de Rémusat.[27] But the most significant of nineteenth-century French writers to dramatise aspects of the revolution was Alphonse de Lamartine, whose colossal five-act "poème dramatique" in hexameter couplets, *Toussaint Louverture*, opens a narrow window on the liberator's career.[28] Act

---

24 A broad overview is provided by Vèvè A. Clark, "Haiti's Tragic Overture: (Mis)Representations of the Haitian Revolution in World Drama (1796–1975)," in *Representing the French Revolution: Literature, Historiography, and Art*, ed. James A. Heffernan (Hanover NH: UP of New England/Dartmouth College, 1992): 237–60. Clark estimates that some 63 plays on the Haitian revolution were published and/or performed in the period which she discusses.

25 Olympe de Gouges, *L'Esclavage des noirs, ou L'Heureux naufrage* (1789/1792; in *Œuvres*, ed. Benoîte Groult; Paris: Mercure de France, 1986). On this play, see Kadish, "The Black Terror."

26 Pierre Faubert, *Ogé, ou Le préjugé de couleur* (Paris: C. Mailet–Schmitz, 1856).

27 Charles François Marie, Comte de Rémusat, *L'habitation de Saint Domingue ou l'insurrection*, ed. Jean René Derré (Paris: CNRS, 1978).

28 The play, written 1839–40, was intended for performance at the Théâtre Française in 1840 under the title *Haïti ou les Noirs*, but had to wait until April 6 1850 for its first performance at the Porte-Saint-Martin playhouse in Paris. The play was moderately well received by audiences but was panned by the critics. Intellectual responsiveness to the relative delicacy of Lamartine's treatment was somewhat dampened by the disillusionment following the 1848 revolution; see René de Planhal, "La Première de *Toussaint Louverture*," *Minerve Française* 5 (1 April 1920): 37–51 and Rodney E. Harris, "*Toussaint Louverture*: Paris, 1850,"

I plays in an insurgent camp near Gonaïves as Leclerc's naval expedition approaches, against the background presence of Toussaint working in a candle-lit tower – "l'étoile de l'île / Sa clarté nous conduit à la gloire!" (1276); black and mulatto children are being taught the Black Marseillaise, but accents of discord are set – by Adrienne, the mulatta niece and ward of Toussaint, recalling her guardian's civility towards the French and the ethnic conflict within her breast; and Toussaint's nephew Moïse, who sees his uncle's pride and ambition as "l'esclavage encore!" (1277); how bow to a new master who is mulatto, not black? Act II presents variations on the theme of the ambiguity of allegiance. Toussaint mentions the irony of praying to the Christian god for victory, while noting that divine justice is colour-blind; Moïse ironically renews his loyalty to Toussaint's God-fearing faith; Antoine, a disguised monk, serves neither whites nor blacks, and confirms that God is on the leader's side. Letters brought from Napoleon by Dessalines offer diplomatic assistance, but disturb Toussaint by their superior tone. Pétion and Dessalines blame Toussaint for vacillating while the French land to take Port-au-Prince. Toussaint rallies the people, but enjoins them to feign amity towards the French and to wait for the yellow fever to decimate them (1303); on his command, they are to put the land to the torch, and Haiti will be free, led by the bellwether of the blacks ("bélisaire des noirs", 1309). Adrienne's mulatta faith in him serves as a metonym for Toussaint's people. Act III resumes the theme of inner division by initiating a battle of souls between Toussaint's sons – Albert the mulatto, loyal to his French heritage, and Isaac the black, conscious of the brutalities of slavery. Leclerc enters with his wife Pauline, who sees herself as a second Cleopatra enchanted by the rural scene, just as Albert is smitten by her beauty. The remainder of this act piles up unhistorical improbabilities: soldiers arrive to demolish the hut of an old blind peasant (Toussaint in disguise); Adrienne casts herself at the feet of Pauline, who is impressed by the old man's noble speech and persuades her husband to spare the dwelling. Leclerc later introduces himself as the Governor over a country in a state of uneasy peace, asking the old man to take a message to Toussaint, "votre maître" (1342). Leclerc, Rochambeau and other generals, this time, are astounded by the philosophical depth exhibited by the blind man, who, in introducing his two sons, is so overcome by emotion that Albert and Isaac almost give the game away. In the closing scene, Moïse introduces himself to Leclerc as Toussaint's nephew (not seeing who the old man really is); offering his services to the French, Moïse promises to reveal how Toussaint's military plans are for self-aggrandisement, not liberty. Revealing himself, Toussaint plunges a dagger in his nephew's throat before leaping into the sea, while soldiers take Adrienne prisoner. In Act IV, Adrienne, in shackles, is visited by her two brothers; Père Antoine is instructed to take her to safety on a ship bound for France, but this plan is thwarted when black insurgents rescue Antoine and Adrienne. Act V reunites Adrienne with Toussaint in his fortified camp at Crête-à-Pierrot. Accompanied by Pétion and Dessalines, Toussaint swears death to the French.

Nineteenth Century French Studies 5 (1977): 206–11. Analysis of the play since the Sixties has been sparse: see esp. the entries in Works Cited for E. Freeman, Gianni Iotti, Charles Joatton and Roger Mercier.

Rochambeau enters blindfolded, and now sees who the blind old man really is. French troops arrive with Toussaint's sons as hostages, in order to persuade the rebels peace under French governance. Torn between loyalty to his father and to the French, Albert is led off, causing Toussaint to fainting, whereupon Adrienne seizes the bicolore and is shot down by the advancing French. Reviving to weep at the death of this "ange de la victoire" (1400), Toussaint grabs the flag and thunders "Aux armes!!!" as the curtain falls.

The play, which treats a tiny slice of revolutionary history, is vitiated to a great degree as an exploration of complex political dialectic by incredible excesses of pathos and sentimentality, by sensationalist, near-farcical colportage and distortion of fact, and – though the idea is plausible if structured successfully – by the wholesale "domestication" of political, cultural and ethnic conflict into an externalisation of Toussaint's own psychomachia via his various blood-bonds. Although Lamartine drew on documentary sources for Toussaint's thought, he dilutes its power, and never allows the presence of Leclerc, Rochambeau or Dessalines to act as counterweights of clarifying motivation. The only part of the play that really stands up to closer scrutiny is Act II with its covert and overt ironies of juxtaposition.

Vendenesse Ducasse (1872–1902) wrote a verse play in four acts entitled *Quatre cent et quatre* while he was still a pupil at the Lycée Pétion. His unpublished play *Noirs et Jaunes* deals with the plot hatched by the advisors of the mulatto Rigaud to cause the downfall of Toussaint by dividing the blacks from the mulattoes, and culminates in the schismatic war in the South of 1802 and an armistice with Toussaint, which is objected to by Dessalines. Toussaint points out to the assembled generals how they have plunged the country into a fratricidal war, and Rigaud decides, against Toussaint's entreaties, to leave the country. Written in collaboration with Placide David, the three-act play *Le torrent* (1939) by Dominique Hippolyte (1889–1967) was premiered in 1940, when it won the Haitian President's Prize. It has as its subject the popular resistance to the French expeditionary force of General Leclerc. The fictional plot-line concerns the love of a mulatto for Emilie, a young white woman, and her father's resistance to this liaison. The historical plot has two main strands: one concerns the black insurrectionist Ti-Noël and his hatred for the white planter-class and, later, for the French soldiers; the other involves Dessalines (who enters the play half-way through), his pretence of accepting Leclerc's plan to exterminate the mulattoes and thereby gain arms and money, and his confiding this plan to Pétion, thereby securing the union of blacks and mulattoes. The revolt against Leclerc is released like a flood upon the land.

Jean–Fernand Brierre has dealt with the career of Toussaint in his three-act verse play *L'Adieu à la Marseillaise* (1934), in which he selects three turning-points for dramatisation. Act 1, "Le première houle," treats a moment in 1773 during the "fallow" period of intermittent maroon uprisings after the fall of Mackandal and four years before Toussaint, coachman and stall-master on the Bréda plantation, is granted his freedom. Plantation slaves from all parts of West Africa discuss with Toussaint and among themselves the meaning of "liberté" and "propriété," a discussion joined by the owner of the plantation, the Comte de Noé, and its manager, Bayon–Libertat; discussion centres on the anti-slavery teachings of the Abbé Raynal. Act 2, "L'ambassade tragique," is set on Toussaint's plantation at Ennery, as he awaits arrest by General Leclerc's emissary after the betrayal by Dessalines and Christophe. Act 3, with the Passion-play heading "Au sommet du Calvaire," features Toussaint imprisoned in Fort-de-Joux immediately before his death in 1803, pining for home and recalling the spirit of liberation that produced the revolution. Jeanne Pérez (?1918–57) wrote *Sanite Belair* (1942) as a study in the tragic fate of General Charles Belair, who is enjoined by his wife Sanite to continue the work of Toussaint, exiled in France. The general and then his wife are arrested and imprisoned at Le Cap; sentenced to death by Boyer, they are executed by firing squad. René Philoctète (born 1932) has written a play in collaboration with Gérard Rézil, on the beginnings of the revolution, *Boukman ou Le rejeté des enfers* (performed 1964), and another on the Christophe period, *Monsieur de Vastey* (1975), while the sole play to be written by the novelist, poet and essayist Edouard Glissant is *Monsieur Toussaint* (1961; see below).[29]

Liautaud Ethéart (1826–88) wrote a play, *La Fille de l'Empereur* (1860, which is set during the reign of Dessalines and treats the love-affair between the young Captain Chancy and Célimène, the daughter of the Emperor. Dessalines has gone back on his promise to allow his daughter to marry Chancy, wanting instead to wed her to Pétion. Harassed by Dessalines, Chancy blows his brains out in the Emperor's presence (this scene takes historical liberties: Chancy actually committed suicide after being consigned to a dungeon at Port-au-Prince). A firm and convincing portrait is given of Dessalines' imperious (rather than imperial) manner and tactics, and the play is peopled with such historical personages as Pétion, Vernet and Boisrond–Tonnerre. Massillon Coicou (1867–1908) wrote two plays worth noting, *Les fils de Toussaint* (1895) and *L'Empereur Dessalines* (1906). The latter work, a two-acter in verse, is set in the National Palace. Dessalines and his generals, including Pétion and Christophe, figure, but the central action concerns a brutal captain called Cangé, who incurs the Emperor's wrath for denying that he has stolen an old peasant's land. The wrath mounts to fury at the news that an insurrection is taking place in the South. There follows a phase of calm deliberation, during which Dessalines resolves to put the

---

[29] Other dramatic works worthy of mention: Ducasse was also the author of *Fort de Joux ou Les derniers moments de Toussaint Louverture: drame historique en un acte* (performed in 1896). Isnardin Vieux (1865–1941) wrote several plays on revolutionary themes, among them *La mort d'Ogé et Chavannes* (1921), *La Marche à l'Indépendance* (1923), and *Mackendal* (1925), on the legendary black maroon. Marcel Dauphin (born 1910) wrote a three-act play called *Boisrond-Tonnerre* (1954). There has even been a four-act Danish dramatisation of Toussaint's career, *Borger Toussaint* (1962), by Charles Haugbøll. Claude Vixamar (born 1930) wrote a historically superficial five-act drama, *Les briseurs de chaînes* (1961), which covers the initial response in Saint-Domingue to the French Revolution, with discord between *grands Blancs* and *petits Blancs* and the stirrings of slave rebellion, Toussaint and Christophe trying to prevent the Voodoo leader Boukman from over-precipitate action, the secret gathering of August 1791 at Bois-Caïman to plan the insurrection (this scene done in creole), the death of Boukman and the rise of Toussaint to leadership, the arrival of Leclerc's expeditionary force and its decimation by yellow fever, and, in closing, Leclerc's plan to capture Toussaint and thus put a brake on the revolution.

South to the sword. Charles Moravia wrote a static historical verse drama in two acts entitled *La Crête-à-Pierrot* (1908) centred on events in 1802 and composed in a series of tableaux held together by the presence of Dessalines. A white colonist is captured and dispatched to a dungeon by Lamartinière, who is surprised in the arms of his wife Marie–Jeanne. Dessalines enters, commenting disapprovingly that a woman in the fort will weaken the morale of the troops, then, impressed, like Boisrond–Tonnerre, by her courage, invites her to join their forces. Marie–Jeanne is troubled to discover a white among Dessaline's advisors, and is informed that he is the music-master and a friend of the blacks. The first act ends with the imprisoned planter being led out of his dungeon and with a tirade by Dessalines against the whites. In Act Two, the crimes of the whites and those of the blacks are discussed in turn, along with Napoleon and the French Revolution. A captured white officer is brought before Dessalines, and Boisrond–Tonnerre counters a choir's singing of the Marseillaise with a Black Marseillaise that he has composed. This pleases Dessalines so much that he commands the soldier–poet to draw up the Act of Independence. All that is lacking is the bicolor; Marie–Jeanne appears draped in the blue and red, all gather round the flag, and Dessalines commands his forces into battle. (The creation of the bicolor and the presence of Boisrond–Tonnerre and the music-master are historical liberties taken by Moravia.)

The play *Dessalines ou Le sang du Pont–Rouge* (1967) by Hénock Trouillot (born 1923) is a historical drama in five tableaux. The Emperor Dessalines reflects on ways to remedy the financial situation in the South and decides to return to Port-au-Prince. Though he has traitors in his midst (Pétion is so depicted), he will not listen to those who warn him of this. Tableau 5 presents the preparations for the ambush; Dessalines is captured and assassinated. The closing tableau includes a cavalcade of Dessalines' disciples and re-enacts the legend of Défilée the Madwoman. Jean–Fernand Brierre (born 1909) has dealt with the period around 1816 in his one-act verse-play *Pétion et Bolivar* (1932), in which the two liberators discuss the bloody rule of Dessalines and share the vision of a continental federation of brotherhood. Brierre's two-act verse-drama *Le drapeau de demain* (1931) represents a play-within-a-play: some young people from Plaisance meet an old man (the incarnation of Haiti's past) on his way to l'Arcahaie to help stage the Festival of the Flag. They accompany him, and help re-create the origins of the *Bicolore* and the evils of slavery, the most patriotic young man playing the part of Dessalines, the others acting as Pétion and Christophe. "Dessalines is the only Black Jacobin who has been divinised," commented René Depestre recently;[30] even recent plays (perhaps by comparison with the age of Duvalier) show him in an enlightened perspective. Vincent Placoly's *Dessalines ou La passion de l'indépendance* (1983) depicts Dessalines as the victim of his self-aggrandisement but as submissive to his mortal destiny. To relativise this image, Placoly juxtaposes Dessalines' grim idealism and high rhetoric (a contrast to the frequent inarticulacy or brutal directness of some earlier renderings, and a reflection of the influence of

---

30 In Joan Dayan, "France Reads Haiti: An Interview with René Depestre," *Yale French Studies* 83 (1993): 140.

Edouard Glissant) with a realistic, ironic, mythic and folkloric mode conveyed in the creole registers of soldiers and servants.[31]

As early as 1823, a play by Jean–Baptiste Romane (?1807–1858), *La Mort de Christophe*, was performed before Boyer, and extracts published. Antoine Dupré's (?1782–1816) *La Mort du général Lamarre* celebrated the heroic death of Lamarre at the battle of Môle against Christophe in July of 1810, when the latter awarded the dead general full military honours. The play was hissed during its premiere in England in 1813, but was well-received when it was performed at Port-au-Prince in 1815, where some of the parts were played by soldiers who had survived the battle. Juste Chanlatte is remembered for his unpublished play *Nehri* (an anagram for Henri [Christophe]), which praised Christophe's victory over the French military expedition of General Leclerc, and for *L'Entrée du roi en sa capitale en janvier 1818* (1818), which takes the occasion of the celebration of Christophe to sketch the various social classes of Le Cap; the first scene, a dialogue between a servant and a tinsmith, is one of the few early instances in Haitian literature of creole being employed in a literary text. A lawyer, Vergniaud Leconte (1866–1932), as well as writing a scholarly work entitled *Henri Christophe dans l'histoire d'Haïti* (1931), composed a play on the same subject, *Le roi Christophe* (performed in 1901, printed 1926). On the dawn of Christophe's birthday celebrations, the King imprisons the Comte de Varron for high treason and disbands the Household Cavalry. Meanwhile, the chief plotter, the Duc de Marmelade, fearing for his life, resolves to take defensive action. Dramatically disguised by a mask, he manages to induce the cavalry to march on Sans-Souci. In a parallel scene, Varron's wife, whom Christophe loves passionately, manages to stay the execution of her husband. The whole court of Sans-Souci is celebrating the King's birthday when news of the insurrection and approaching troops leads to Christophe's suicide. Leconte (especially by focusing on the King's passion for the Countess of Varron) succeeds in depicting Christophe with considerable psychological depth; the play is more of a realistic study of political action than, say, Aimé Césaire's *La Tragédie du roi Christophe*, where Christophe is a quasi-metaphysical philosopher-king.

English-language dramatisations of the revolution are discussed below; worth mentioning at this juncture, however, are a small number of African–American contributions to the literature. William Edgar Easton wrote two plays between 1893 and 1911, each concentrating on one of the key historical figures, Dessalines and Christophe, while Leslie Pinckney Hill's historical play from about 1928 deals with Toussaint.[32] Theatre chronicles record two radio dramas, on Toussaint and

---

31 Vincent Placoly, *Dessalines ou La passion de l'inépendance* (Havana: Casa de las Américas, 1983); see Juris Silenieks, "Toward *créolité*: Postnegritude Developments," in Arnold, 520–21.

32 William Edgar Easton, *Dessalines: A Dramatic Tale; a single chapter from Haiti's history* (Galveston TX: J.W. Burson, 1893) and *Christophe: A Tragedy in Prose of Imperial Haiti* (Los Angeles CA: Press Grafton, 1911); Leslie Pinckney Hill, *Toussaint L'Ouverture: A Dramatic History* (Boston MA: Christopher Publishing House, [1928]). See also Robert J. Fehrenbach, "William Edgar Easton's Dessalines: A Nineteenth-Century Drama of Black Pride," *College Language Association Journal* 19 (1975): 75–89, and Edward O. Ako, "Leslie Pinckney Hill's *Toussaint L'Ouverture,*" *Phylon: A Review of Race and Culture* 48.3 (Fall 1987): 190–95.

Christophe, that were broadcast from Chicago, primarily for the edification of the city's African–American citizens, in 1948–49.[33] An interesting phenomenon is Lorraine Hansberry's engagement with the enigma of Toussaint; her play, extant in fragments (1958–65), opens in 1780 on the plantation managed by Bayon–Libertat and would have been a multilayered drama ending with Toussaint's death in Fort-de-Joux. From the few scenes that can be consulted, it is clear that Hansberry saw Toussaint as a complex and sophisticated personality within a constellation of enslavement and oppression which did not exempt the mulatto class and the white Creoles themselves from entrapment in human and historical circumstance.[34]

Eugene O'Neill, *The Emperor Jones* (1920)

Among anglophone dramatic treatments of the revolution, a significant North American precursor of West Indian versions is Eugene O'Neill's *The Emperor Jones*. This play was first produced by the Provincetown Players on 1 November 1920 at New York's Playwright's Theatre. It features a black American Pullman-car porter, Brutus Jones, who becomes Emperor of an anglophone island in the Caribbean. The lead role – perhaps the first truly significant part fashioned for an African–American – was played by Charles Gilpin in the play's first run and its extension on Broadway, where it ran for 204 performances to great acclaim.[35] O'Neill's stage direction in scene 1 delineates Jones as a "full-blooded negro [...] underlying strength of will [...] eyes alive with a keen, cunning intelligence [...] shrewd, suspicious, evasive [...] something not altogether ridiculous about his grandeur."[36] O'Neill confirmed that the figure of Jones was suggested by "the character of a bartender he had known, but other acquaintances and the figures of Henri Christophe and Haiti's President [Vilbrun Guillaume] Sam, who, like Jones, had a silver bullet, contributed elements to the portrait," as did a visit by O'Neill to the jungles of Honduras.[37] Jones is aware that his rise from "stowaway to Emperor in two years" has been meteoric, and sees his function as offering the people of his island "de big circus show" in exchange for

---

33 *Destination Freedom: Citizen Toussaint* (1948) and *Destination Freedom: The Black Hamlet* (1949; on Christophe); audiotapes C-318 and C-329, New York Public Library.

34 The most useful account is by Steven R. Carter, *Hansberry's Drama: Commitment amid Complexity* (Urbana/Chicago: U of Illinois P, 1991): 173–83; a slightly misinformed view is provided by Anne Cheney, *Lorraine Hansberry* (Boston: Twayne, 1984): 146–48. For the text, see "*Toussaint*: Excerpt from Act I of a Work in Progress," in *Nine Plays by Black Women*, ed. Margaret B. Wilkerson (New York: New American Library, 1986: 53–67) and Hansberry, *To Be Young, Gifted and Black: Lorraine Hansberry in Her Own Words*, adapt. Howard Nemiroff, intro. James Baldwin (1969; New York: New American Library, 1970): 138–43.

35 Gilpin was replaced for the London productions in 1924, 1925 and 1933 by the young actor Paul Robeson. The text of the play, which originally bore the working title "The Silver Bullet," was first published in *Theatre Arts Magazine* (January 1920), then in book form by Boni & Liveright (New York, 1921).

36 O'Neill, *The Emperor Jones*, in *Complete Plays 1913–1920*, sel. Travis Bogard (New York: Library of America, 1988): 1029–61; here 1033.

37 Travis Bogard, *Contour in Time: The Plays of Eugene O'Neill* (1972; New York: Oxford UP, rev. ed. 1988): 135. The conjunction of bartender and Christophe as sources here is felicitous. Jones has also been taken – erroneously – to be modelled on Toussaint L'Ouverture, as by Margaret Loftus Ranald, *The Eugene O'Neill Companion* (Westport CT: Greenwood, 1984): 207.

money, which he obtains by levying high taxes and by conniving in and himself practising corruption (1035). To cow the people, he invents a story (which is actually the stuff of European Romantic legend) about having fashioned a silver bullet so that "when de time comes I kills myself wid it," as he is otherwise unassailable;[38] Jones is no idealist, nor is he so power-hungry that he won't drop the job and leave if the going gets too hot – but this cynicism is counteracted by the fact that he is also "strangely fascinated" by his bullet (1036–37).

Apart from the opening and closing scenes (which also feature a white Cockney mercenary advisor), Jones, whose life is now threatened by conspirators, is lost in the dark forest of the soul, and the play is an expressionist monodrama, its scenes timed (like a Western shoot-out) by the number of times he fires a shot in panic from his revolver – after the five normal bullets, the only projectile left is his lucky rabbit's foot, the silver bullet. By the penultimate scene, Jones, spirit-haunted, is reduced by the machinations of a "Congo witch-doctor" (1057) to preverbal, hysterical near-nakedness. A great green crocodile (symbol both of his own self and of the atavistic divinity he has forsworn) crawls out of a river and Jones squirms like a reptile across the ground towards it. Instead of giving himself up to the crocodile's maw, Jones, filled with Christian repentance, fires his silver bullet at it and lapses into unconsciousness.

We can infer, from the discovery of his corpse in the closing scene, that Jones, in the forest's heart of darkness beyond the plain and "civilisation," has brought about his own death as well. There is no political configuration to the play, no sense of rebellion within a social and ethnic context; O'Neill is interested in the Euripidean hubris of a black man which prevents him from fulfilling his human nature. Jung's theories of the archetype and the instinctual are applied to uncover the psychological valency of the dramatic images (night, forest etc) employed. Rather than revealing the dramatist's consciousness (as in Strindberg), O'Neill's expressionism dramatises the psychological condition of the protagonist (as in Ibsen). There is clearly a "stage-business" text of Voodoo atavism – a feature central or peripheral to most depictions of the Haitian revolution, too, but for historical reasons.[39] Through this text, Jones is

---

[38] It is Robert Hamner, in his interesting interpretative summary and survey of "politically correct" reservations afflicting reception of O'Neill's play ("O'Neill, Walcott and Césaire on Christophe," *Journal of West Indian Literature* 5.1–2 [August 1992]: 30–47) who mentions in passing that Sam also had a silver bullet. But the primary historical source for the motif (allied, incidentally, to the silver button of Ibsen's *Peer Gynt*) is surely more likely to be the golden (some say silver) bullet with which Henri Christophe is said to have shot himself (from a golden pistol) in Sans Souci palace. (Legends can easily get confused; one commentator, imperfectly recollecting a heroic *sauteur*-topos originally connected with Toussaint and used thus by Victor Hugo and Lamartine, claims of Christophe that the "conquered emperor leaped to death from his Citadel"; Germán Arciniegas, *Latin America: A Cultural History* [New York: Knopf, 1977]: 457.)

[39] The classic study of Voodoo in Haitian society is by Alfred Métraux, *Voodoo in Haiti*, tr. Hugo Charteris, intro. Sidney W. Mintz (*Le vaudou haïtien*, Paris 1958; tr. 1959; New York: Schocken, 1972). Métraux's treatment is highly complicated at times, gappy at others. More accessible is Maya Deren's *Divine Horsemen: The Living Gods of Haiti* (1953; Kingston NY: McPherson, 1970). Of contemporary relevance is Luc de Heusch, "Kongo in Haiti: A New Approach to Religious Syncretism," in *Slavery and Beyond: The African Impact on Latin America and the Caribbean*, ed. Darién J. Davis (Jaguar Books on Latin America 5;

represented as a victim of inscrutable life-forces, incapable of rebellion against the
dread, guilt and despair deriving from the absence of God and from the harsh reality
of the modern world. The play is strongly tempered by realistic elements such as the
materiality of Black-American vernacular speech. Jones's African–American dialect
in scene 1 is credibly realised; in subsequent scenes, it is subjected to a process of
gradual syntactic and phonological regression (though not towards anything one
might call "back-to-Africa pidgin"). This manifestation of the archetype of return is
matched by O'Neill's manipulation of grotesque exaggeration, including the overt use
of African drumming and dancing, to function as a vehicle for the transition from
comedic realism to demonic irrationality.

O'Neill's portrayal is essentialist, and has been called racist, in that Brutus (the
brutish) is inwardly "savage" or uncivilised not because all human beings are so, but
because he is a Negro. Jones's will, pride and individuality as Emperor are false
(Fanonesque) masks of "whiteness," denying his connection with a primordial God of
communalism to whom he must try and return in the failed "salvation" at the end of
the play.[40] What provides an anticipatory affinity with Walcott's view at the
"historical" level is the notion that Jones's imperial rule, which has inherited white
processes of manipulation and corruption, is no better than that of his erstwhile
oppressors. But this thesis is only imperfectly present, given that Jones is a "US
import" to the West Indies. Nevertheless, the representation of Jones in O'Neill's play
aligns itself with a central uncomfortable feature of Christophe's self-awareness in
Walcott's *Henri Christophe*:

> I am not a civilised man [...]
> I am at heart very primitive; there is that urge –
> A beast in the jungle among primitive angers
> Clawing down opposition; what is the expression –
> The instinct? (scene 6)

C.L.R. James: *Toussaint L'Ouverture/The Black Jacobins* (1936)

Among the few anglophone-Caribbean treatments of the revolution, the classic among
historical investigations is, of course, C.L.R. James's *The Black Jacobins*, first published
in 1938; the centrality of this Marxist treatment to all subsequent endeavours to
delineate Black identity in the Caribbean is undisputed.[41] James himself wrote a play,

---

Wilmington DE: SR Books, 1995): 103–19 (tr. Noal Mellott; originally published in *Man* 24.2 [1989]: 290–
303).

[40] Bogard, *Contour in Time*, 141–42.

[41] *The Black Jacobins: Toussaint L'Ouverture and the San Domingo Revolution* (London: Secker &
Warburg/New York: Dial, 1938; rev. ed. with 1962 preface and appendix "From Toussaint L'Ouverture to
Fidel Castro" New York: Random House, 1963 and London: Allison & Busby, 1980). The book has been
translated into French (1949), Italian (1968), and German (1984). The libretto of David Blake's opera
Toussaint (produced by the English National Opera in 1979 and 1983) is based on James's narrative. Other
anglophone treatments include a play (in manuscript) by McDonald Dixon (born 1945 in St Lucia) titled
Toussaint: A History of the Haitian Revolution, and a dramatic treatment, *Toussaint L'Ouverture* (1968), by
Denis Martin Benn. There has even been a choreographed presentation, with drumming, by Astor John-
ston's Repertory Dance Theatre, under the title *The Defiant Era*, centering on the spiritual liberation, triumph

Toussaint L'Ouverture, which was based on the historical material he was currently researching in the Thirties and which was intended by him as an intervention in the debates surrounding the Ethiopian crisis; it was produced in London in 1936, with – an interesting connection with O'Neill's play – Paul Robeson as Toussaint.[42] Reinhard Sander has written a thoroughly contextualised interpretation of James's play, concentrating on the documentary realism underlying its constellation of historical figures according to ideological standpoint and its intertextual relation to the nationalist and anti-imperialist debates of the Thirties.[43] I would simply like here to indicate a few of the accents which James sets, in a play that is ostensibly about its eponymous protagonist. It is indicative that the Prologue introduces the historical figures in reverse order in terms of their active role in the course of the revolution: first, the silent Christophe, still a hotel waiter, witnessing whites agreeing that "animals are worth more than blacks" (70); then Dessalines, vowing to kill all whites after a mulatto speaker is shot dead at a clandestine gathering of slaves; last, "the Leader," Toussaint, absorbing the Abbé Raynal's statement that "A courageous chief only is wanted" (71). In Act I, scene 1, James has Toussaint and Dessalines together on the same plantation, with the former interceding against Dessalines' intention to murder their white master, Bullet. The two positions are dramatised via Dessalines' primitive syntax and Toussaint's command of language, encoding two distinct forms of ethical decisiveness, and by Toussaint's residual courtesy towards the whites (though this courtesy later turns out to be partly a form of self-interest, on account of his erotic and spiritual involvement with Mme Bullet[44]).

---

and betrayal of Toussaint. This dance-production, under the auspices of Walcott's Trinidad Theatre Workshop, formed the first part of an overall presentation called *Pieces Two* (the second part being a dramatisation of Edward Brathwaite's "Wings of a Dove"), to which Walcott contributed scene designs. The performances took place in the auditorium of Bishop Anstey High School, Port of Spain, 25–29 April 1973. See Syl Lowhar, "Drums and Colours: Review of *Pieces Two*," *Tapia* 3.18 (Sunday, 6 May 1973): 9–10.

[42] Peter Godfrey directed the Stage Society production of the play at the Westminster Theatre in March 1936. James later revised the play under the title *The Black Jacobins*; this version was first performed under the direction of Dexter Lyndersay by the Arts Theatre Group at the University of Ibadan in 1967; a London production was staged by Yvonne Brewster at the Riverside Studios in 1986, and a radio adaptation was transmitted in the Monday Play series by the BBC in 1971. The text of the later *Black Jacobins* version is included in *A Time ... and a Season: Eight Caribbean Plays*, ed. Errol Hill (Trinidad & Tobago: Extra-Mural Department, U.W.I., 1976) and has been republished in *The C.L.R. James Reader*, ed. & intro. Anna Grimshaw (Oxford: Basil Blackwell, 1992): 67–111. For background information, see Errol Hill, "The Emergence of a National Drama in the West Indies," *Caribbean Quarterly* 18.4 (December 1972): 20–21, Judy S.J. Stone, *Theatre* (Studies in West Indian Literature, ed. Kenneth Ramchand; Basingstoke: Macmillan Caribbean, 1994): 19–20, and Grimshaw, 5–7, 423–24. Page references are to Grimshaw. Mouralis, "L'image de l'indépendance haïtienne," although discussing James's historical study and showing its relevance to the drama of Césaire and Glissant (506, 511–13), does not even register James's own dramatic treatment of the same material.

[43] Reinhard W. Sander, "C.L.R. James and the Haitian Revolution," *World Literature Written in English* 26.2 (1986): 277–90.

[44] Paralleled later by Walcott in the mulatto Anton Calixte's infatuation with Pauline Leclerc (in *Drums and Colours*) and in the same character's love for the Baroness de Wimpffen (in *The Haytian Earth*); see below.

The central dilemma of Toussaint's rule is established subtly in a comic dialect scene where ex-slaves, aides to Dessalines, Christophe and Moïse, parrot the French Republican motto, which they can grasp and explain except for the notion of "Fraternity" (75). Toussaint's wish to have both a Constitution and independence of action from France on the one hand (what Sander likens to Dominion status), and good relations with – or ultimate loyalty to – France on the other (which explains his rejection of American and British manipulations to introduce, variously, independent monarchy and independent republicanism) is the political expression of this impossible ideal of Fraternity – a theme resumed bitterly by Moïse when Dessalines and Toussaint have him arrested for treason (96). Constant reversion to the topic of the black conquest of mulatto forces, and to the question of the future status of the mulattoes, is a further aspect of the problematic of Fraternity. The belated recognition by Toussaint of his dilemma – that he is actually protecting whites, by 1802, against blacks, even though the whites want to restore slavery – elicits a choice irony from his erstwhile mistress (in both senses): "What are you saying? How could half a million blacks be masters and twenty thousand whites be slaves?" (97). Hesitating to sign Moïse's death-warrant, Toussaint contemplates exiling him to avert internecine disarray; instead, the news that Leclerc's expeditionary force has arrived makes him, under the urging of Dessalines, take the first fatal step away from Fraternity as international humanity and towards Fraternity as partisan national interest: he signs the death-warrant of the man he has raised as a son (99).

Act III is concerned with further binaries and symmetries – among them, the male/female parallel of Dessalines and the spiritual influence of the mulatta, Marie–Jeanne, and an ironic juxtaposition of a passage from Racine on blood-flecked love (106)[45] with the rebels' song of vengeance against the whites, "*Ça ira*," and an altercation between Christophe and Dessalines on Voodoo (102), where we are aware that "Africanism" and blood-revenge will gradually overtake Toussaint's Rousseauesque meliorism. As Dessalines proclaims himself Emperor, the news comes of Toussaint's death in a French prison – and the last stage-direction has Christophe moving ominously "to the right of Dessalines' throne" (111). That James's play still has contemporary relevance was indicated in the fact that a highly successful three-week revival (starting 23 April 1993) was directed by Rawle Gibbons at the Curepe Scherzando Cultural Centre of the University of the West Indies at St Augustine, Trinidad, under the auspices of the Theatre Arts Faculty. The aim of the production was to combat the "tremendous apathy and even aversion to the discussion of the problems in Haiti," and it framed James's text with an Immediate Theatre involvement of

---

45 This ethnocultural juxtaposition occurs later in Carpentier's *Kingdom*: while Henri Christophe, the master chef at the Auberge de la Couronne, fashions magical dishes, the mistress of a plantation recites to herself lines from Racine's *Phèdre* about incest, "murderous hands" and "guiltless blood" – lines taken by the black servants for admissions of real crimes (41–45); this is followed closely by Voodoo chanting at Boukman's conspiratorial gathering (48–49).

Haitian villagers waving slogans such as "Bring back Aristide" and "Down with the Ton Ton Macoutes" and being clubbed down by Haitian secret police thugs.[46]

Alejo Carpentier: *El reino de este mundo* (1949)

The best treatment in the novel-genre of the Haitian revolution and its implications is the Cuban writer Alejo Carpentier's *El reino de este mundo*,[47] which was begun as a result of the author's visit to Haiti in 1943. The novel is a *relato* – indicating Carpentier's intention to stylise historical action archetypally to capture what he calls, in the introduction to the Spanish edition, *lo real maravilloso* (or magic realism). It is divided into four parts: 1) the early slave rebellion led by the mystic named Mackandal; 2) the massacre led by Boukman in 1791, and the yellow fever epidemic that afflicted the French troops in 1803; 3) the tyrannical rule and suicide of Henri Christophe; 4) the rise of the mulattoes under Boyer (1820–1843), a period of reunification which perpetuated many of the old abuses against the blacks. The whole is held together by the observing presence of the black slave Ti Noël.

Part I begins with a description of the rudimentary colonial "present" of Haiti, before shifting in chapters 2–8, via Ti Noël's recollections, to the 1750s. The initial chapter is chiefly noteworthy, by hindsight, for two features which serve to bind the whole novel into the figure of Henri Christophe. There is, first, Christophe's proleptic presence in Ti Noël's vision of "some experienced, macabre cook" (5) preparing the heads of white men for a banquet (a motif repeated on page 9). Secondly, the Conradian overtones of this motif (European cuisine/African headhunters) can be associated with the first stirrings of the themes of kingship, the colonial status of Saint-Domingue, and African belief-systems, when Ti Noël – in a significant shift of hierarchy from the earthly to the transcendent – contrasts the insipidity of European monarchies with the strength of the African gods, who are identified by his mentor Mackandal with African princes. This contrast is continued into the flashback phase, when Ti Noël, labouring with Mackandal in de Mézy's sugar mill, contrasts the rudimentariness of the European presence in Cap Français with the wealth of the African kingdoms (ch. 2; 11–12). His arm crushed in the mill and amputated, Mackandal is relegated to cattle-watching, and close observation of nature reawakens a gift for identifying plants and fungi that can poison invisibly; he is aided (ch. 3) by the *obi* Maman Loi (her hut protected from the Voodoo graveyard *loas*). Now an escaped Voodoo priest, he persuades plantation slaves (including Ti Noël) to poison first the livestock, then the white planters. Voodoo references start to accumulate (ch. 4–6): Mackandal is said to be hiding near Jacmel, where the living dead (zombies) till the soil (27); nocturnal drumming spreads word of Mackandal's supernatural powers, predicting that Damballa and Ogun will rise to crush the whites (29).

---

[46] Raymond Ramcharitar, "A Change of Form; Invocation of Immediacy," *Trinidad and Tobago Review* (May 1993): 23–24.

[47] Mexico, 1949; tr. as *The Kingdom of This World* (New York: Knopf, 1957; page references are to the translation).

Toussaint is introduced casually as a cabinetmaker on de Mézy's estate, carving Christmas decorations (ch. 7). Four years after the hunt for him began, Mackandal appears at a nocturnal Voodoo festival, and is seized by armed planters, who stage an un-Christmassy and decidedly exorcistic festival of their own at Le Cap. Slaves brought in as witnesses already know that Mackandal, master of metamorphosis, will escape from being burned at the stake by turning into a mosquito. This they then witness – not seeing the soldiers ensuring that their prisoner actually burns; for the slaves, their deliverer has escaped death to stay in the "Kingdom of This World" (37).

In Part II, twenty years have elapsed since the death of Mackandal, whose memory is still cherished. The Cap has progressed in European amenities – including the culinary arts of one Henri Christophe. White heads must roll: it is time for a new Mackandal. At Bois Caïman on Morne-Rouge, the Jamaican Bouckman speaks of far-away events in France, and of the colonists' refusal to grant the blacks freedom. Bouckman's Voodoo priestess of the Rada cult sings to Ogun, god of war (49); the Christians' god must be replaced. Ti Noël and other slaves take over de Mézy's plantation and rape his wife. Bouckman is executed, de Mézy's wife dies. De Mézy nevertheless saves his rebel slaves from execution (the Governor wants to execute all those of Negro blood), as he needs his workers. He realises for the first time the pervasive presence of Voodoo – and complains that he cannot dine out decently now that the cook Henri Christophe has joined the French-colonial artillery (ch. 4; 59). The narrative shifts to Santiago de Cuba, and to the libertine excesses of the refugee planters, who have brought French manners to the primitive Spaniards. Ti Noël finds "a Voodoo warmth" in the Catholic cathedral – an Afro-Christian syncretism also made plain in the merging of Santiago with Voodoo's Ogoun Faï (ch. 5; 65–66). Rochambeau's plan to massacre the Saint-Domingue rebels is foreshadowed in dogs being loaded on board ship in Cuba (ch. 6). With no temporal transition, this merges with Leclerc and Pauline Bonaparte on board ship and on Tortuga; the narrative sets up a contrast between Pauline's lightheaded eroticism and her teasing of her black manservant Soliman and the onset of the yellow fever, with Pauline engaging in Voodoo practices (including spirit-possession, 77) to keep at bay the plague which kills Leclerc. With the departure for France of Pauline, who takes with her a fetish of Papa Legba, her "common sense" is replaced by licentiousness (78) and the eruption of Rochambeau's horrors; here the time-zones intersect with the ordering of the dogs from Cuba. Part II ends with a new syncretism – the black Fathers of the Savanna combining Latin ritual with African inflections (80).

In Part III, Ti Noël returns from Cuba after being sold by his master in a card-game; Haiti's landscape is leached, "a grim, silent plain" (84) filled with Voodoo symbols and sacrifices. It is a land between this world and the next, symbolised by an evil tree harbouring Legba, *loa* of the crossroads (85); Ti Noël recalls that the Voodoo gods caused Dessalines' victory. In III.2, the wasteland of the old de Mézy plantation is contrasted with another landscape, green and orderly, but with black soldiers dressed "in the pomp of Napoleonic fashion" (88) guarding black field-workers like prisoners. Ti Noël sees the splendour of Sans Souci palace, a European vision of a black court, before he is taken prisoner and forced to labour, in a new slavery, alongside "children, pregnant girls, women, and old men," carrying bricks up a mountain to build Christophe's Citadel, La Ferrière. Bulls are sacrificed for blood, added to the mortar to make the Citadel impregnable. In the twelfth year of Christophe's reign, the king is described visiting his Citadel, a labyrinthine hell out of Piranesi (ch. 3; 94. 97). Ti Noël escapes to the old estate, and then to Le Cap, where he hears the dying screams of Archbishop Breille (Brelle), buried alive by the king for wanting to take his secrets to France.

Christophe is aware of Voodoo signs all about him, indicating the people's animosity. Ignoring all advice, he commands the Mass of the Assumption to be sung at Limonade; the dead Archbishop appears, and Christophe is struck down. The paralyzed king is attended in his palace, whose Hall of Mirrors reflects him only (113); as he sits on his throne, drums advance, the burning land reflected now in all the mirrors as Christophe shoots himself (III.6). His African pages, wife, children, and Soliman take the king's corpse to the Citadel, from which all have fled save the Governor, who sinks the body in fresh mortar, "one with the stone that imprisoned it" (III.7; 124). After the king's son, Victor, is executed, the Queen and her daughters are taken by English merchants to the familiar warmth of Rome, whose citizens are fascinated at the sight of Soliman (passing himself off as Christophe's nephew). In a drunken frenzy, he sees a naked odalisque as Pauline Bonaparte (not knowing it is the *Venus* of Canova) and, recalling Leclerc's death of yellow fever, himself succumbs in Voodoo terror to the Roman miasma.

Part IV opens with Ti Noël living on in the ruins of the de Mézy estate, surrounded in his solitary court of peace by the débris of Europe looted from Sans Souci, dressed in Christophe's frock coat, and filled with mad visions of a mission intimated to him years before by Mackandal. Boyer's mulatto surveyors appear to supervise reconstruction of Haiti by black prisoners (IV.3). All that is left of Christophe's vision is "in Rome, a finger floating in a rock-crystal bottle filled with brandy" (142–43). To escape Boyer's "rebirth of shackles," Ti Noël, like Mackandal before him, metamorphoses into successive creatures, but is ignored by the geese he tries to live among. Realising he is being punished for his passivity, for not trying to be better than he is within "the Kingdom of This World," Ti Noël declares war on the new mulatto masters before disappearing in a whirlwind.

The historical figures whom Carpentier focuses on are Mackandal/Boukman (the phase of revolt) and Christophe (the phase of political power), with Pauline Bonaparte as an ironising reminder of European epistemology and one of the chief incarnations of the "white" world of theatrical illusion and illusory desire. Carpentier trims his cast for thematic emphasis: Toussaint is (as in Hugo) mentioned only once, Rigaud barely makes an appearance, and Dessalines and Rochambeau, though instrumental to the historical action recounted, are present only beneath the narrative surface. The antithetical historicity of the narrative is then both undermined and unified by the presence throughout of the bystander-figure Ti Noël; at the end of the novel, Ti Noël, depicted as having the transformative Voodoo powers of Mackandal, unleashes another cycle of rebellion. His deconstructive presence is meant to convey the sense that for the characters "lo mágico es real," whereas, for Carpentier, "lo mágico es maravilloso."[48] Via Ti Noël's viewpoint, Christophe's construction of Sans-Souci and La Ferrière (imitations of European culture) assumes the aspect of Voodoo conjuration (thus illustrating a central aspect of Carpentier's theory of contamination or syncretism); at this point of perception, Christophe's magical vision is also that of his people. But dissolution sets in when Christophe abandons his "primitive" beliefs (his "not-knowing," like the people) to adopt Christian mythology (his "knowing," like the engineers of his citadel). White magic replaces black – as a consequence of which, the *loas* of Voodoo rise up and destroy Christophe. It is up to Ti Noël to close the circle of Afro-Caribbean consciousness first inscribed by Mackandal; far from constituting merely the picaro/trickster figure of Caribbean folklore, he embodies the rebirth of revolutionary awareness (albeit in an aged and powerless *houngan*) within a whirlwind blowing away the last remains of colonialism.[49]

Derek Walcott: *Henri Christophe: A Chronicle in Seven Scenes* (1949)

Both Alejo Carpentier's novel and Aimé Césaire's play later were prompted into existence by their authors' direct experience of Haiti, whereas Walcott, who must have been aware of the common yet divergent French-colonial heritage of Haiti and his native St Lucia, had been encouraged to write about the Haitian revolution by his brother Roderick. The brothers had written and acted playlets together since early boyhood, and Walcott wrote at least six plays of substance himself between the ages of sixteen and nineteen years. *Henri Christophe: A Chronicle in Seven Scenes* is the play Walcott regards as his first, and it is such in terms of being extant and complete. It was written between April and September 1949, when Walcott was eighteen years old. The year before, Walcott had already had his first book, *25 Poems*, privately printed. The play, which runs for some two-and-a-half hours in the full version, was first staged at St Joseph's Convent, Castries, on 18 May 1950, by the St Lucia Arts Guild (a theatre group which Walcott had co-founded with Maurice Mason, and which he here directed in the company's first full-length production).[50] An edited version was then broadcast in two half-hour instalments on the BBC's *Caribbean Voices* programme under the direction of Errol Hill in February 1951.[51] A full version with the same line-up of actors had its first international staging at the Hans Crescent

---

48 Emir Rodríguez Monegal, "Lo real y la maravilloso en *El reino de este mundo*" (1971), in *Asedios a Carpentier*, ed. Klaus Müller–Bergh (Santiago de Chile: Editorial Universitaria/Cormoran, 1972): 125.

49 For relevant political and cultural interpretations of the novel's action, see esp. entries in Works Cited for Jeannette Allsopp, Jai Jebodhsingh, and Barbara Webb (27–40).

50 Bruce King, *Derek Walcott and West Indian Drama* (Oxford: Clarendon, 1995): 10. Henceforth cited as "King 1995".

51 Not the first piece of Walcott's to be thus broadcast – his *Senza Alcun Sospetto* (later staged as *Paolo and Francesca*) was transmitted by the BBC in London on 28 May 1950 (King 1995: 10).

House in London early in 1952 (25–27 January), with Hill once again directing and with Errol John in the lead role.[52] It is perhaps indicative of a prevalent view of the play that Henry Swanzy should have been struck by the fact that this "story of ideas" seems to evince a "lack of characterisation, of direction," on paper which falls away on stage, where "a powerful and unified theme appears, the struggle for power and its inevitable aftermath." In 1954, his last year at the University College of the West Indies in Kingston, Jamaica, Walcott designed and directed a further production of *Henri Christophe* by the student drama society, the University Players,[53] and a production in Trinidad followed in November, with Hill directing and John once again in the lead role.[54] There have even been productions of the play by secondary-school pupils.[55] The dental student Ruby Atwell, of San Juan in Trinidad, directed performances of the play by the West Indian Drama Group at the Edinburgh University Adam House Theatre in late 1961, which were well received by reviewers

---

[52] The play, which had been cut for the BBC broadcasts, was evidently further pruned for this production, which was sponsored by the West Indian Student Association, and involved the participation of George Lamming (reading a prologue), erstwhile actors from the St Lucia Arts Guild, Hill himself as Vastey, the historian Roy Augier, and the Trinidadian painter Carlisle Chang (costumes and scenery) (King 1995: 12). "The cast included even a future Prime Minister of Trinidad and Tobago, Arthur Robinson. The reviews were among the best the play was ever to receive" (Judy Stone, *Theatre*, 25). Reviews included the following anonymous pieces, "Errol Hill Overcomes Obstacles in the Way of *Henri Christophe*," *Evening News* (Port of Spain; 11 January 1952) and "West Indians Score Success with West Indian Play in London," *Port of Spain Gazette* (January 1952), as well as Henry Swanzy's "*Henri Christophe*," *Public Opinion* (Kingston; 29 March 1952): 6.

[53] The cast of the production, which opened on Friday 12 March at the UCWI Dramatic Theatre, included the poet Slade Hopkinson as Dessalines and the dancer, choreographer, and theatre and cultural historian Rex Nettleford playing both Sylla and the witch-doctor (King 1995: 13; Harry Milner, see below). See the preview by E.N., "*Henri Christophe* to be staged by UCWI," *Daily Gleaner* (Thursday, 11 March 1954): 4. For reviews, see: Dorothy Duperly, "University Drama: *Henri Christophe*," *Jamaica Times* (20 March 1954) and Harry Milner, "*Henri Christophe*: 'Courageous Effort' by University Players," *Daily Gleaner* (15 March 1954). It was, interestingly, noted by E.N. that Walcott would be graduated B.A. three days after the final production. The occasion of the first performance was taken by the Governor of Jamaica, Sir Hugh Foot, to praise the achievements of the Haitian revolution: "It was an astonishing thing that in that comparatively short period four such great figures should emerge, the figures of Toussaint and Dessalines and Christophe and Pétion [...] Christophe, a most complex character [...] is remembered particularly for the building of his magnificent Palace and Citadel, but he was also a great agriculturist [...] constantly thinking how the moral standards of the Haitian people could be raised"; it was tactful of the Governor – and not irrelevant to the Caribbean at large – to concentrate on matters pastoral; but it is unlikely that he would suggest that agricultural and other policies should be implemented today in quite the manner depicted by Walcott. See "Governor draws lessons from Haitian history," *Daily Gleaner* (Monday, 15 March 1954): 6. As Walcott does not neglect reference in his play to the crucial aspect of land ownership and management – which later assumes thematic preeminence in Walcott's *Haytian Earth* – background reading is recommended; see esp. Robert K. LaCerte, "The Evolution of Land and Labour in the Haitian Revolution 1791–1820," in Beckles & Shepherd, ed. *Caribbean Freedom*, 42–47.

[54] Reviewed by Olive Walke, "*Henri Christophe*: Successful Production," *Port of Spain Gazette* (30 November 1954). Eric Williams, historian and future prime minister of Trinidad, wrote the prologue for this Port of Spain production (New Company & Whitehall Players, 27 November–1 December) at the Government Training College; the cast also included Errol Jones and Neville La Bastide (King 1995: 13, 28).

[55] Along with *Malcochon* and *Dream on Monkey Mountain*, it was also a set text for the Trinidad secondary schools' CXC (General Certificate) examinations in 1981 (King 1995: 307).

in the Scottish press.[56] *Henri Christophe* was one of the major attractions of the Trinidad and Tobago Festival of 1968, with Walcott himself directing the Trinidad Theatre Workshop in three performances at Queen's Hall in Port of Spain (26–28 April) and later at Naparima Bowl in San Fernando (9–11 May), all with Albert Laveau as Christophe;[57] this production, which was the first to receive proper financial sponsorship, had, in Walcott's judgement, both the best cast and a much more realistic and concentrated approach to performance.[58] Along with Walcott's *The Sea at Dauphin*, the play was recorded in 1971, in two forty-five-minute segments, and broadcast under Walcott's direction in late August on the Sunday-evening "Theatre Ten" program sponsored by Texaco for Trinidad's 610 Radio station.[59] Again under Walcott's direction, it was recorded subsequently in a half-hour production in 1972 along with *Jourmard* for 610's up-dated Sunday series, "Theatre Fifteen," and broadcast in July.[60] The play was privately printed in 1950, and there is also a later, defective typescript version.[61]

In order to place *Henri Christophe* impressionistically in terms of its contribution to West Indian theatre history, I should like to offer two quotations relating to early reactions. In the first, the painter, critic, actor and dancer Geoffrey Holder, who responded favourably to the "grandeur, passion and beauty" of the radio play's verse

---

[56] Edinburgh had a flourishing West Indian Students' Association, and members from Trinidad, Jamaica and Barbados took part in the production. The play was regarded by theatre critics as both unusual and exciting. See summary of a British Information Services report in the *Trinidad Guardian*, "Scots rave over Henri Christophe" (Friday, January 19, 1962): 5.

[57] This was one of the main productions which followed on from the round of hectic activity (including the premiere of *Dream on Monkey Mountain*) at Canada's Centennial Celebrations in Toronto (August 1967); Walcott noted, in early November 1967, that he was rehearsing *Henri Christophe* with the Workshop – alongside three other plays (by Pinter and John Pepper Clark); King 1995: 85–86.

[58] A Jamaican venue at Kingston's Creative Arts Centre had originally been planned; the Festival venue was an afterthought. The idea of putting on *Henri Christophe* in Kingston was also entertained for October, when the Workshop undertook a tour of the islands, but the Jamaican part of the tour was cancelled for lack of funding (King 1995: 104) and the company toured only with *Dream* and Eric Roach's *Belle Fanto*. See the anonymous notice, "Walcott's *Henri Christophe* to run for three nights," *Trinidad Guardian* (Thursday 11 April 1968): 6, and, with substantially the same content, Agnes Sydney–Smith: "*Henri Christophe*: Poet Walcott's first major play on Haitian revolution," *Sunday Guardian* (21 April 1968, Trinidad and Tobago Festival Supplement): 3; also published under the same headline on the same day in the Port of Spain *Evening News*. A quarter-column preliminary notice was printed in the *Trinidad Guardian* on Friday 26 April ("Tonight: Walcott's *Henri Christophe*": 6), but this was not followed up in the *Guardian* with a performance review – only by a letter of complaint from Winston Smart on 14 May, after the San Fernando performance, though there was a favourable report by Earl Lovelace in the *Express* on 30 April ("*Christophe*: Image Packed Essay Mouthed By Actors": 12) and by Brunell Jones in the *Evening News* on 3 May ("Walcott's Play: A Success at Festival").

[59] King 1995: 155, 366.

[60] King 1995: 168, 367.

[61] Walcott, *Henri Christophe: A Chronicle in Seven Scenes* ([Bridgetown,] Barbados: Advocate Company, 1950), 59pp.; the later – defective – transcription in italic type (39pp foolscap) is on deposit at the Mona Campus of the University of the West Indies, and was produced in the series of Caribbean Plays supervised by Errol Hill for the university's Extra-Mural Department (a series dating from 1954 "which for many years provided the only available texts of West Indian drama for the new acting groups [and which at first were] cyclostyled like acting scripts"; King 1995: 13).

lines and congratulated Errol Hill on his production of an "ambitious and satisfying play," recounted a down-home West Indian response as follows:

> I was listening at a wayside loudspeaker when the rain began to drizzle and three or four people took shelter. Two men, barefooted, were talking when Christophe momentarily flared up; then his voice grew quieter.
>
> > Anyway, he died, broken, grey and quiet
> > White-haired as the moon and stumbling just as lost
> > Through peace-fleeced colonies of clouds, a foolish, mad old man.
>
> The two men stopped talking and even when the rain had ceased, they remained listening to the end of the play. At that late stage they could not have followed the events; they were held by the poetry, striking in its vividness and beauty and spoken with sympathy and sincerity. I thought of the Elizabethans.[62]

A useful encapsulation of the play's significance is offered by Rhonda Cobham in an essay on the background to West Indian literature:

> The occasion which best epitomised the spirit of the time was the production in January 1952 in London of Walcott's verse play, *Henri Christophe*. The play's cast included the whole spectrum of West Indian talent then in Britain. The prologue was written by George Lamming whose first novel, *In the Castle of My Skin*, received a critical ovation when it appeared the following year. The play was directed by Errol Hill, now a successful West Indian dramatist in his own right, who later wrote the first major dissertation on the Trinidad Carnival. Another Trinidadian playwright, Errol John, played the lead role. His own script, *Moon on A Rainbow Shawl*, won first prize in the *Observer* drama competition in 1957 and was later published by Faber. The rest of the cast and production team reads like a roll of honour of leading West Indian artists and intellectuals of the next two decades, many of whom were students in Britain at the time. Reviewing the production for *The West India Committee Circular*, one critic underlined its significance:
>
> > In the development of an indigenous culture in the Caribbean (and no West Indian Federation can be really without it) no element is of greater potential importance than a West Indian theatre, for the theatre is the meeting place and the nursery of the arts. At the same time the initial obstacles are formidable. The three essential elements in the theatre – the playwright, the actor and the audience – must exist together if the theatre is to be a living reality in the life of the people. This condition has not hitherto existed in the West Indies. [...] There have certainly been writers, actors and audiences in the West Indies in the past, but not West Indian writers of West Indian plays for West Indian actors to perform to West Indian audiences. [...] In this critical stage of development of a West Indian theatre, the recent production of *Henri Christophe* [...] is an event of the first importance. It was in every way a West Indian production. [63]

A psychological pattern relating to political liberation in general is discerned by Syl Lowhar in a comparison between Walcott's *In A Fine Castle* and *Henri Christophe*, both of which involve "distinctions of complexion" (the French Creole plantocracy versus black insurrectionists in colonial Trinidad in *Fine Castle*; the gradation French Creole plantocracy versus mulattoes versus blacks in the revolutionary and counter-revolutionary Haiti of *Henri Christophe*). Violence, rage and resentment against domination ebb over time, and are at their most intense when required at the moment of revolution; however, the dynamic (as in falling out of love) breeds its own

---

[62] G[eoffrey].A. Holder, "BBC's Broadcast of *Henri Christophe*," *Bim* 4.14 (January–June 1951): 141–42.

[63] Quoted in Rhonda Cobham, "The Background," in *West Indian Literature*, ed. Bruce King (London: Macmillan, 1979): 21–22; rev. ed. (1995): 18–19. Cobham attributes the review, "A West Indian Play," *West Indian Committee Circular* (February 1952): 38, to "A Special Correspondent"; it was written by Hugh Paget.

irrational inhumanity and injustice: "the poet is wary of black leaders whose motive force is an intense hatred of the whites. They often end up enslaving the very people in whose name they shouted power."[64]

At the beginning of *Henri Christophe*, Dessalines is with his generals in the Government Palace at Cap Haytien on the north coast, waiting for news of the death of Toussaint. A lot of historical data is taken for granted, and is not even mediated via pseudo-expository allusion. The stage directions provide no indication of chronology in the form, say, of the year in which the action of a given scene takes place. Ideally, the playgoer needs to be aware of the fact that Dessalines had colluded with Leclerc, the French commanding general, in removing Toussaint from the scene of power. Despite the fact that Toussaint had been defeated in 1802 and that a peace treaty had been drawn up, and despite Toussaint's being allowed to retire with honour to his plantation at Ennery, he was seized by trickery and sent to France, where he was imprisoned in a dungeon at Fort-de-Joux in the Jura. He died in April 1803 after exposure to the cold of a European winter (this motif of the black man of the tropics surrounded by the whiteness of snow is a topos which crops up in a large number of literary renderings of Toussaint's last days). When Rochambeau took over the French forces after the death of General Leclerc and embarked upon mass extermination of the black population, and when it became known that Napoleon intended to reintroduce slavery, Dessalines, as temporary commander-in-chief of the revolutionary forces, revolted against the French, and used guerrilla tactics to raze the whole country, being aided in this by the British.

The action of Scene One – or, rather, the dialogue of what is essentially a conversation-piece, conveying opinions and sentiments rather than recounting actions – takes place in early 1804, after Dessalines has been chosen governor for life of the newly independent state now called Haiti. It must be assumed that the ship from France that is anchored in the harbour has brought its messenger to Haiti many months after Toussaint's death.

Scene One may serve to indicate Walcott's structuring of verbal action. The epigraph to Part I is taken from *Hamlet* – a speech by Rosencrantz just before Claudius sends him and Guildenstern to England as messengers in the company of the prince, with the intention of getting rid of him.[65] The content of the passage has to do with the stock image of the Wheel of Fortune, and with the fact that the fall of a king drags his subjects with him. Walcott will also have been drawn to the physical image of "boisterous ruin," and to the notions bracketing the speech quoted, to the effect that

---

64 Syl Lowhar, "Another Station of the Cross," *Tapia* 23 (26 December 1971): 19, reviewing a production (October–November 1971) of *In A Fine Castle* at Queen's Hall and Town Hall in Port of Spain.

65 III.iii.15–22, "The cess of majesty / Dies not alone, but like a gulf doth draw / What's near it with it; or 'tis a massy wheel / Fixed on the summit of the highest mount, / To whose huge spokes ten thousand lesser things / Are mortised and adjoined, which when it falls, / Each small annexment, petty consequence, / Attends the boist'rous ruin," *Hamlet Prince of Denmark*, ed. & intro. Willard Farnham, in William Shakespeare, *The Complete Works*, gen. ed. Alfred Harbage (The Complete Pelican Shakespeare; New York: Viking, 1969): 956.

the uncontrolled individual (imaged as "fear" itself) must be fettered, just as the "many bodies [...] that live and feed upon" a ruler must be controlled by "holy and religious fear."[66] In terms of the turn of the wheel in *Henri Christophe*, Toussaint is fettered by Dessalines, the latter in turn by Christophe; and the rule of Dessalines and Christophe is by fear (in Dessalines' case, a fear that cynically exploits Catholic religiosity before destroying it; and in Christophe's case, a fear that is the atavistic "holy" fear instilled by Voodoo). The mulatto general Pétion talks of Dessalines' vanity, dissimulation and dreams of kingship, and intimates that the death of Toussaint would lead to Dessalines' cutting the throat of Haiti's hopeful historical ascendancy, like a cock at sunrise: the tragic cycle of history, fuelled by insane desires, is already encoded in the infant state. Dessalines enters, followed by a messenger who delivers an affecting account of Toussaint's imprisonment and death. Dessalines is unmoved, and is interested only in gauging public reaction to his death and working it to his advantage. In counterpoint to the heartfelt sentiments of loss expressed by the Abbé Brelle, Dessalines utters terse statements of intent, action and policy. His assumption of control must be broken carefully to the impetuous Christophe, who is fighting in the south. His advisers talk among themselves about the country's problems: the long war has depleted the treasury, the peasants are not working the fields, African cult religion is displacing the church, partisan resentments prevent unity. Dessalines cuts through all this scornfully, asserting the need for draconian decisions and punishment, not mercy. Sylla and Pétion speak resentfully of the treacherous white aristocracy, Brelle protests at the generals' intention to exact bloody revenge on the whites, this protest is countered by a reminder of the whites' collusion with the clergy, and Dessalines interrupts again to paint a contemptuous picture of the white rabble and the church tyrannising the black slaves. His stated intention is to massacre the whites, and he places the rule of his own conscience "and the memory / Of a red past" before the laws of Brelle's church. Now it is Brelle's turn to take the offensive, accusing Dessalines of obeying no principles but those of violence, cruelty and treachery. Despite Dessalines' warning that the priest is tolerated only because he is a priest, Brelle persists: he hopes that Christophe will oppose Dessalines' rule. He exits angrily, and Dessalines, maintaining his cool equilibrium, enlists his generals in a plan to delay notification of Christophe while he works secretly to be made king of "a black nobility, the white flower destroyed." Matching the Messenger's long descriptive speech about Toussaint's demise, Sylla recounts his monitory dreams of military *virtù* being sapped by the "corrupted purposes" of politics in a wasteland. For Dessalines, this is merely "bloody rubbish." In the closing words of the scene, General Pétion allows himself the irony of addressing his boss as "Your Majesty." The unfolding, tension-generating theme of unspoken and distrusted motives is clinched in the final stage direction: "Dessalines looks at him cautiously, then smiles, then bursts into laughter, as the bell sounds and the lights fade out."

---

66 *Hamlet* III.iii.8–11, 25–26, in *Complete Works*, ed. Harbage, 956.

There's a lot going on here, both on and under the verbal surface, and Walcott engineers masterfully the systole and diastole of contrasting, oppositional and complementary moods and attitudes. A considerable complexity of dialectic is being worked out on stage. The subsequent course and architecture of the dramatic action build on this. Scene Two, at Christophe's camp in the south, provides an inverse image of Scene One. The soldiers on their own and in the company of Christophe dwell lovingly on the fame and stature of Toussaint, the news of whose death they have received. They are aware of the dangerous duplicity of Dessalines and his aspiration to be king. Christophe deflects the advice of his secretary, Vastey, to work towards kingship himself, by asserting that his very behaviour is naturally kingly. But after Christophe exits, his advisers describe his love for Haiti as destructively well-intentioned, his personality that of "a two-sided mirror" hiding both a Toussaint and a Dessalines. Scene Three brings Dessalines and Christophe together. Christophe has returned to the north as King Dessalines' Commissioner, his illiteracy sitting uneasily with the paperwork he is supposed to do. Christophe mocks the imperial pretensions of his erstwhile comrade-in-arms, who is also angered by Christophe's accusations that he is conducting a bloodthirsty racial war against the whites, threatening to attack the mulattoes, and enslaving his people. Christophe and the mulatto Pétion decide to split the country between them and plot Dessalines' overthrow and death. A Messenger enters with a vivid description of the massacring excesses of Dessalines' soldiers. When Dessalines himself enters to justify his actions to Christophe, the latter launches the most duplicitous action of the play by proving his true friendship in confessing that he had been plotting to assassinate Dessalines. Solicitously, he comforts the distracted Emperor: "Tonight I will see the light in your / Room is put out."

Which is what happens in the brief Scene Four, where two Murderers wait in a wood at night for Dessalines, who has been advised by Christophe to travel south to check Pétion's insurrection. At the close of the scene and Part One of the play, Dessalines confronts his killers. The interesting thing about this scene, which was cut from the radio broadcast version,[67] is that it represents Walcott's attempt to introduce a doubly demotic or dialect flavour into a play otherwise rendered in Standard (West Indian) English. The opening speeches have dialect shading in terms of accidence and syntax, as well as quotations in French creole. This then gives way to non-dialect yet simple and prosaic statements, before the murderers, just before the moment of truth, ascend to the higher rhetoric of the poetic mode. This movement is clearly designed, and the tonal function of the scene as a kind of inter-text also becomes clearer when

---

[67] John Figueroa, who was teaching in England in the early Fifties, has pointed out to me that the BBC people responsible for producing the play were put under considerable pressure by "cultural vigilantes" in the Caribbean to ensure that dialect was avoided – such folk expressiveness would spoil the image of cultural aspiration, might create the "wrong impression." This instance of "upwardly mobile" linguistic politics is made all the more ironical in view of the fact that the BBC Overseas Service was transmitting to listeners in the West Indies, not to listeners in Great Britain. Judy Stone (*Theatre*, 95–96) mentions that the murderers' scene was omitted from the St Lucia premiere at the request of the nuns of St Joseph's Convent (thus on moral grounds), its restoration in the 1954 Trinidad production coming "as welcome relief" to audiences and critics no longer accustomed to a non-realist "Elizabethan throwback."

one notes the quotation from Shakespeare's *Richard III* which immediately follows as an epigraph to Part Two of the play.[68] These words of the Duke of Clarence, with their mention of perjury, faction, and "dark monarchy," echo ironically the situation in Haiti; of further contextual import is the fact that Clarence's premonitory nightmare comes after a scene in which his two murderers are given their instructions by Richard, Duke of Gloucester, and that the murderers are shown conversing colloquially after Clarence's speech.

Scene Five jumps forward to 1811. Christophe, elected President of the northern republic after the assassination of Dessalines in 1806, here declares himself King. His private secretary, Vastey, and Brelle, now Archbishop of a schismatic Haiti, reflect on Christophe's consolidation of power in the north and his plotting against Pétion, who is president of a separate republic in the south. Christophe enters, his moody presence framed by the surging and receding pulse of the crowd. With the guarded help of Brelle and the rhetorical manipulations of a soldier planted in the crowd, Christophe, after one botched trial run, is finally confirmed as King amidst general confusion. Before, Christophe's mood was downcast – he is disillusioned about the efficacy of politics, haunted by memories of bloodshed, in two minds about the value of monarchy and what he calls "this nigger search for fame." Now, his spirits rise – "I who was a slave am now a king." At the close of the scene, he presents his expansive vision of a flourishing Haitian kingdom. On its heights are "cathedrals" of power, opulent châteaux and "white-pointed citadels / Crusted with white perfections over / This epilogue of Eden."

In Scenes Six and Seven, Walcott exercises some Shakespearean licence with historical chronology. The action has shifted to the second half of 1820, at the very end of Christophe's reign, but Pétion is still president in the south, although he actually died in 1818 and was succeeded by Jean–Pierre Boyer. This is a dramatic necessity in order to retain the figure who has been a background presence throughout the play as a counterweight of power and responsible mulatto government. In Scene Six, Vastey, exploiting Christophe's inability to read, concocts letters purporting to incriminate Brelle in a conspiracy with Pétion. The scene proceeds to Christophe wrangling with Brelle, who openly criticises him for the bloody traduction of Toussaint's ideals; Brelle is then stabbed to death in the King's presence.[69] Christophe's increasingly death-teasing thoughts, paranoid suspicions of lurking treachery, and desperate clinging to the empty symbol of a bloody crown all concentrate to produce in him attacks of physical paralysis. In Scene Seven, the action takes the form of inaction, the basic stage setting being a visual representation of

68 I.iv.48–51: "The first that there did greet my stranger soul / Was my great father-in-law, renownèd Warwick, / Who spake aloud, 'What scourge for perjury / Can this dark monarchy afford false Clarence?'," *The Tragedy of King Richard the Third*, ed. & intro. G. Blakemore Evans, in *Complete Works*, ed. Harbage, 564. There must have been an extra piquancy here in the mention of "Warwick," which was also the name of Walcott's father (later introduced as a revenant in the autobiographical *Another Life*).

69 These circumstances and motivations differ from the historical record and other literary treatments, which usually have Brelle walled up and starved to death for declaring his wish to return to France.

vanitas. Vastey urges Christophe to leave the citadel of La Ferrière, in which he has sequestered himself as his last refuge against the approaching troops of Pétion and the counter-revolution. But Christophe sprawls paralyzed and crownless on his throne, wearing instead his general's garments from the long-gone days of military accomplishment. Although Christophe has no faith in either Christ or Damballa, a Voodoo priest uses a skull and incense to try and activate him; but what Christophe wants is for the herbs to consign him to oblivion.[70] As the drums of the troops sound, and Christophe puts a pistol to his head, he pitilessly sums up his place in the history he has created, as "this dark anarchy / The graves of children, and years of silence."

Derek Walcott: *Drums and Colours* (1958)

The material concerning Henri Christophe upon which Walcott concentrates was also given dramatic treatment by the same writer in his fifth play, *Drums and Colours*. Part One ("Conquest") of this commissioned historical pageant centres, in successive scenes, on such figures as Christopher Columbus and Sir Walter Raleigh. Part Two ("Rebellion") depicts nineteenth-century insurrection in Jamaica; preceded by a treatment of the Haitian revolution. The play, directed by Noel Vaz at the Royal Botanical Gardens in Port of Spain (25 April–1 May 1958), was the first production by Walcott's Trinidad Theatre Workshop and a colossal four hours long.[71]

The initial scene of Part II is a soirée of generals and their wives held for Napoleon's emissary, General Leclerc, at Malmaison, the Saint-Domingue home of the planter Calixte.[72] The opening perspective is thus French-colonial (aristocratic pretensions plus muted republicanism). The General predicts "democratic despotism" and "mere patterns of revenge" if the incipient revolution succeeds, and mentions "the most efficient generals [...] Boukman, Dessalines, and ... the other ... what's his name? Christophe."[73] A brooding presence is the illegitimate mulatto son (or "nephew") of

---

[70] Voodoo functions here as a powerful litmus test for the depth of Christophe's negative psychic entrapment, whereas at earlier points in the play (as in Césaire's, O'Neill's and James's, as well as in Carpentier's novel and in the figure of Basil in Walcott's later *Dream on Monkey Mountain*) its tacit or overt presence was an index to the possibility of liberation. On the place of Voodoo as a liberationist medium in Caribbean literature, see, for example, Patrick Taylor, *The Narrative of Liberation: Perspectives on Afro-Caribbean Literature, Popular Culture, and Politics* (Ithaca NY: Cornell UP, 1989): esp. 95–128, 208–14.

[71] The scenes under discussion involved Errol Hill as Dessalines, Errol Jones as Mano, Jean Herbert as Yette, and James King as Pompey. For comment, see Adrian Espinet, "*Drums and Colours* Seeks to Trace Evolution of West Indian Consciousness," *Sunday Guardian* (27 April 1958): 7; Tony Swann, "Federal Arts Festival: *Drums and Colours*: Guts at Least," *Public Opinion* (10 May 1958): 7; Veronica Jenkin, "*Drums and Colours*," *Bim* 7.27 (July–December 1958): 183–84; Stone, *Theatre*, 103–106; King 1995: 19–23.

[72] "Malmaison" is a satiric touch, withdrawn in Walcott's later *Haytian Earth*, where Calixte's home is called "Belle Maison."

[73] Derek Walcott, "Drums and Colours: An Epic Drama Commissioned for the Opening of the First Federal Parliament of The West Indies, April 23rd 1958," *Caribbean Quarterly* 38.4 (special issue: "*Caribbean Quarterly*'s Derek Walcott"; December, 1992): 22–135; here 90–91. The play was first published as the *Caribbean Quarterly* Special Issue 7.1–2 (March–June 1961): 1–105, with illustrations. I provide page references to the more easily accessible 1992 reissue, but use the full subtitle as provided in the 1958 issue, as well as the earlier text. The later publication was re-set, not necessarily to the advantage of the layout, and there are a large number of typos (including "Slave Regina" for "Salve Regina").

Calixte, Anton, who recounts with angry sarcasm how, "both spectator and victim" (94), he witnessed the spectacle of Dessalines' public tortures. Both Anton and the coachman on his father's estate, one Toussaint, are "tormented with division" of loyalty between family and people (95). Anton is also erotically involved with Leclerc's wife, Pauline, "white and lovely as the moon, and equally remote" (95).[74] In the ensuing night-scene, against the backdrop of burning canefields, the black servants of the estate murder Anton because of his father's white blood (98).[75] The Bois-Caïman Voodoo-conspiracy scene follows, in which the Jamaican obeah-man Boukman smashes the white cross of the Christians (implicitly in favour of the *vèvè* of the crossroads-god Legba), sacrifices a white rooster to Damballa, and calls for the burning of the cane (99–100). Toussaint, on finding Anton's body, takes up the "heavy burden": "My other life is finished. Love is dead" (100).

The centrepiece, the long scene 12 (101–10), features Dessalines and Christophe (both under strain, self-protectively exultant, and drunk) and, later, Toussaint, in the autumn of 1801 and the "new century," and telescopes via dialogic rehearsal a multitude of historical events treated at more leisure in *Henri Christophe*: the black republic; the defeat of Napoleon's mulatto general Rigaud; the slaughter of thousands of mulattoes by various forces led by Toussaint and Boukman; the sacking of Les Cayes; the unharvested canefields burning; the decimation of Leclerc's forces by yellow fever; the plotting by Dessalines to hand Toussaint over to Napoleon because of his "monarchic aims" (103). The image of Toussaint presented differs from that of *Henri Christophe*: here, he is reluctantly but actively complicitous in massive brutality and inhumanity, directly responsible for "Those leaves of yellow bodies whirled in [the] wind" of revolution (105). There is a suggestion that both Dessalines and Christophe are using him as a justificatory model for their own planned excesses, rather than constituting figures in historical, negative contrast to him. The characters are differentiated, however, in terms of their emotional–ethical relation to the *raison d'état* – when Calixte, who believes mistakenly that the General has killed Anton (rather than trying to save him) accuses Toussaint, only the latter is able to retort in anguish (while defending Calixte against, then surrendering him to, Dessalines' rough justice): "When we tried to love you, / Where, O chaos, where was your heart?" (107). The tensions among the three generals are expertly sketched in small compass, as are their covert intentions. The scene ends with Christophe assuring Dessalines that, after selling Toussaint, "we will share our power to restore the peace" (110); which is met with justified mistrust by Dessalines. No more need be said.

The thematic point of the Haitian episodes is saved up for a summary within the first of the later scenes of rebellion in Jamaica, when Deacon Sale (standing for Sam Sharp during the Baptist War of 1831–33) recounts the aftermath of the Haitian revolution. The generals' "cause was corrupted by greed," and they "caught the

---

74 This moon/woman-image anticipates the dramatic enactment of Makak's fixation in Walcott's *Dream on Monkey Mountain*; and a lunar sublimation can also be found in the imagery of his *Henri Christophe*.

75 In Walcott's *Haytian Earth*, Anton dies of yellow fever.

contagion of hate" – even Toussaint – while Dessalines and Christophe turned "from free slaves [...] to insane emperors [...] / Revenge is easier than love" (113).

Edouard Glissant: *Monsieur Toussaint* (1960)

Monsieur Toussaint, the sole play to be written by the Martinican philosopher, post-colonial theoretician, poet and novelist Edouard Glissant, was intended as a "thought-piece" working through some of the author's central cultural theses relating to theatre in Martinique (it should make the past present in the collective consciousness and should assume that popular audiences can absorb intricate, complex art without excessive, folkloric use of creole).[76] The primary acting space of the play is the Fort-de-Joux prison, scene 1 being set in February 1803, two months before Toussaint's death. As at the end of Brierre's and James's plays, the Corsican gaolers play their taunting role throughout. Although specific accents are set in the various acts – titled "The Gods," "The Dead," "The People," and "The Heroes" – and although both the present, prison-bound dramatic movement and the invocations of the past are ordered chronologically, every scene is structured upon visionary intercalations of time and space. The historical past is visited upon Toussaint alone through the apparitions of the dead (even when Toussaint's gaolers are present, these figures are invisible to them; but their presence is "real" to the audience, as Toussaint's "mad" responses are real to his gaolers). Among the revenants who appear singly or together are Mackandal, the maroon and one-armed obeah-man who massacred whites in the 1750s; the black rebel leader Macaïa; Toussaint's adopted nephew, General Moïse; Delgrès, leader of the slave revolt in Guadeloupe in 1802 (who also features in Hugo's novel); and Mama Dio, a Voodoo priestess or *mambo* resembling the one who assisted Boukman at the Bois-Caïman conspiracy of 1791 which launched the revolution. In prose or verse rhythms distinct from the cadences of the other figures, these recall historical phases of liberation before and during Toussaint's rule, criticising or praising his philosophy, policies, character, and ethics. Interwoven with this apparitional level are sub-scenes featuring historical figures living on Saint-Domingue concurrently with Toussaint in the French Jura: he is visited spectrally in his cell by his wife, tormented by thoughts about his well-being, by his mulatto general Rigaud, by white colonists, and by his lieutenants Christophe and Dessalines.

The scenes successively invoked (by way of allusive evaluation more than by re-tellings) include: the mutilation of Mackandal; Bois-Caïman; Toussaint on the Bréda

---

76 The play was published in 1961 (Paris: Seuil), broadcast complete in 1971, and republished in revised form (as *Monsieur Toussaint: version scénique*) in 1978 (Fort-de-France: Acoma) after being staged (in Paris) for the first time on 21 October 1977 by the Théâtre Noir. An English translation by Joseph G. Foster and Barbara A. Franklin appeared in 1981 (intro. & notes Juris Silenieks; Washington DC: Three Continents); page references are to this edition. On the relation of the play to its historical material and its performative function, see esp. the relevant entries in Works Cited for Marcel Oddom, Bernard Mouralis, 525–29, and J. Michael Dash, 100–106. Some critics also specifically address the connections and discontinuities between Glissant's play on Toussaint and Aimé Césaire's on Christophe within the broader framework of Antillean theatre: see entries in Works Cited for Thomas Bremer, Bridget Jones (40–43), and Juris Silenieks (1968).

plantation; the concessions of the Constituent Assembly of 1789–91 to the mulattoes; Mama Dio's Voodoo prayers for improvisatory victory versus Toussaint's advocacy of methodical warfare and the banning of Voodoo; the conquest of Santo Domingo by Biassou and Toussaint's defection to the Republican French; his governorship and protection of the Bréda manager, Libertat. Mama Dio accuses Toussaint of relinquishing worship of Ogun the warrior in favour of the Catholic god, fraternity in favour of rule from on high (I.8, 39–41). The whites predict that Toussaint will ultimately be destroyed by his own love of order, which the blacks (unlike the mulattoes) will never accept (I.9, 42–43). Dessalines' suspicious presence (II.2), vengeful military determination and scorched-earth policies are contrasted with Toussaint's need to feed the armies via agricultural reconstruction. Amidst Dessalines' victories, bloody dissension spreads between blacks and mulattoes as Toussaint, in monologues (eg, II.3, II.5, III.1), exhorts the living and the dead to practise solidarity. By Act IV, Toussaint is awaiting the arrival of Napoleon's emissary Brunet, come to arrest him. As Mackandal reads from the list of honours bestowed on him by the French, his gaolers replace his military uniform with rough peasant's clothing. With Toussaint in France, Dessalines uses the magic of his former leader's name to incite his troops to victory, and defends his sanguinary savagery and betrayal of Toussaint. By the last two scenes, it is early April: "Spring pokes about endlessly in the snow without finding the way through. It's there, the opening [l'ouverture]. But, at the moment, it's the closing for Toussaint" (94). Mackandal appears, recalling the scene of his own death at the stake, and invites Toussaint out of the Northern cold to share the flames of death. Fading fast, Toussaint resists with a lyrical litany of the island's burgeoning, hopeful verdancy: "It's hot. I'm burning up ... The snow of the pyre, all the heat sleeping in the depths of their winter" (97) – and, slumped in his chair, attended by Mackandal from the beginnings of revolutionary time, he dies, the name of the African war-god Ogun on his lips (98). Glissant gradually makes it clear that Toussaint's whole value-system, too much bound to a eurocentric/universal understanding of revolution and freedom, paying too little heed to the cultural differentiae underpinning the radical break with Europe implied by the experience of *marronnage* – until, that is, Toussaint's imprisonment, where the dialect gradually reverses direction.

A more detailed example of the interflowing of temporal and spatial planes is provided by III.2, where Dessalines discusses with Toussaint the approaching French warships, and they review the lietenants of resistance: the ambitious Christophe, the fanatical Moïse, the honest but white-loving Belair, the vain yet brilliant Clairvaux. Toussaint whispers that Dessalines will remain – but he is too fond of wars, and Christophe of palaces. The popular Moïse, says Toussaint, "is the man of my choice" (64). Mackandal and Macaïa enter after Dessalines exists, in anger, to remind Toussaint that he executed Moïse (who is also present on stage). The "live" figures reenter, replaying the tribunal that sentenced Moïse, and Madame Toussaint pleads for their nephew's life. The spectre of Moïse then defends itself before the unrepentant Toussaint before melting away. Time beyond Toussaint's death is also intimated, as when Christophe later appears alone (III.6) to defend his bloody tactics and negotiating strategy alongside Dessalines "through fifteen years of war" (76). The simultaneity of time frames (in what Glissant in his preface calls "a prophetic vision of the past," 17) is not simply a dramaturgical device but aligns itself with Afro-Caribbean concepts of temporal coexistence, as well as with communion with ancestral spirits. (Although Glissant intimates that this structuring principle is new to Caribbean theatre, there is an earlier instance in Brierre.[77]) The arguments and counter-arguments of the many characters are braided with such rapidity that an inescapable sense of ethical complexity, ambiguity and irresolvability is created, along with a powerful sense of contradictions that are experienced as being part of present-day Antillean existence as well. Glissant's play is arguably the one most apposite as a complex image of the "basic insecurity of being" (Glissant, 17) of the Caribbean, its history-bound, perpetually cyclical and mythically potentiated realities and future. Complaints about the high rhetoric of Walcott's *Henri Christophe* (such as the letter by Smart to the effect that blacks don't speak like that) were later voiced with regard to Glissant's *Monsieur Toussaint*. Both plays are highly "textual," logocentric displays of scenic rather than actional oppositions. Glissant points out in his foreword that the play "tried to reproduce [...] the rhetoric of the revolutionaries of 1789 which so strongly influenced the speech of the leaders of the Haitian revolution" (19); the sprinkling of various creoles introduced into the 1978 production version are, Glissant emphasises, no replacement for the opportunities a director and cast possess at any time "to complete by improvisation what the author has intended." And the same applies to productions of Walcott's *Henri Christophe*.

Aimé Césaire: *La Tragédie du roi Christophe* (1964)

Césaire's second play[78] is certainly the finest dramatic treatment of the Haitian revolution. Since its premiere at the Salzburg Festival in 1964, it has been performed at many important venues, and has been a formative influence on subsequent drama.[79]

---

77 There are two central scenes in Act III of *L'Adieu à la Marseillaise*, one of which dramatises the import of the title, the other the long persistence of colonialism and resistance: in III.4, Toussaint is visited in Fort-de-Joux by Casnabo, an Amerindian chief of the time of Columbus; Casnabo reminds the prisoner that they are both blind victims of Destiny (115–16); the play's closing scene, III.9, has the dying Toussaint conversing with La Marseillaise, the spectral female figure of liberty (126–31).

78 After the dramatic poem *Et les chiens se taisaient* (1946). *La Tragédie du roi Christophe* was premiered at the Salzburg Festival in 1964 under the direction of Jean–Marie Serreau. There were subsequent performances in Venice, Berlin and Brussels. The Paris premiere was at the Odéon theatre in 1965. Further important early performances by the Serreau company were given at the Premier Festival Mondial des Arts Nègres in Dakar, 1966; at Expo 67 in Montreal; and at the Cultural Festival of Fort-de-France in Martinique, 1978. The second play in the trilogy, *Une Saison au Congo* (1965), takes the fate of Patrice Lumumba as an illustration of the difficulty of achieving any real independence under neo-colonialist conditions, and the third and most famous play, *Une Tempête* (1968), is familiar to all researchers in the new literatures as a paradigmatic, intertextual encoding of the colonial process.

79 Not only in the Caribbean – as witness the treatment of Henri Christophe in the play *Îles de tempête* (1973) by Bernard B. Dadie from the Ivory Coast. A Brazilian study which compares Dadie's play with

Like Walcott's *Henri Christophe*, the play is ambitious in scope and execution. It was the first in a projected anti-colonial trilogy, and covers the nine years (from 1811 to 1820) of Christophe's imperial reign. It is a portrait of a slave turned king, but is above all an essay on the real problems besetting African and Afro-Caribbean countries at the dawn of independence.[80] (It was in the same spirit that Césaire wrote a sympathetic historical study of Toussaint L'Ouverture in 1961.)

After Dessalines' death, Christophe is named President of the Republic of Haiti. He abandons Port-au-Prince (held by the mulattoes under Pétion) and sets up his headquarters in the North. The conflict between the two leaders pre-dates the action of the tragedy, and is such a secondary consideration that it is scarcely referred to in Act I. Indeed, the Prologue takes the form of a comic–parodic cockfight (an – illegal – Haitian national passion), in which the roosters are called Christophe and Pétion. It is then indicated by the Présentateur–Commentateur, as he reviews the course of the revolution, from Toussaint through Dessalines to Christophe the black king in the North and Pétion the mulatto president in the South, that the external political conflict is reducible to a mere cockfight or "combat emplumé."[81]

Christophe's preoccupation is with how to appease his own hunger for power. The tragedy is born out of his isolation. To show the French, who "have no respect for republics," that blacks are not lacking in dignity, he decides to create a monarchy – on the surface of it, a caricature of a European monarchy. He thus invests his power, through visual symbolism, in those surrounding him. There are farcical scenes which are nevertheless fundamentally serious, such as the ridiculing of the Counts of Trou-Bonbon or Sale-Trou, the lords of Limonade or Marmelade, where the grotesque titles out-do superbly their European models, and where the ridicule is only on the surface. Vastey and the other mulatto generals make fun of Christophe's energetic desire to be different, and of his fear of white ridicule.

> HUGONIN: It's the King's way of baptising anyone he pleases and of being godfather to everyone! It's true that if the husbands were to let him do what he liked, then he would not be the godfather of all Haitians, but their father! [...]
> CHRISTOPHE: Our names – as we cannot snatch them from the past, then may we snatch them from the future! *(Tenderly)* I wish to cover over your slave-names with names of glory, our names

---

Césaire's and with Alejo Carpentier's novel is Maria Nazareth Soares Fonseca, "Henri Christophe: Mito e Historia," *Cadernos de Linguistica e Teoria da Literatura* (Belo Horizonte) 7.14 (December 1985): 179–92.

[80] There is an extensive critical literature on the play; of particular value are the relevant studies listed in Works Cited under the following names: Régis Antoine, Christian Armbruster, A. James Arnold, Hunt Hawkins, Lilyan Kesteloot, Maximilien Laroche, Bernard Mouralis (516–19), Juris Silenieks, Keith Q. Warner, Marianne Wichmann Bailey, and Hal Wylie.

[81] At one level. Yet the cockpit scene is bivalent: within the Afro-Caribbean scheme of latencies in the play, the ecstatic possession of the participants, and the fact that the cocks fight to the death, hints at a supernatural realm of conflict between the play's historical personages, leading to the death of Christophe. Even the Présentateur's (historical) reference to Christophe as a cook has been construed as implicitly identifiable with the function of the holy man or priest of the Voodoo *loa*, the *houngan macoute* (see Marianne Wichmann Bailey, in Works Cited, 34–35, 76–77) of the body politic.

of infamy with names of pride, our orphans' names with names of redemption! What we're dealing with, gentlemen. is a new birth![82]

An interesting parallel with O'Neill's play, where Jones has a Cockney advisor, is the white Master of Ceremonies who puts the court monkeys through their paces: in keeping with a stage direction that Act I should be parodic, Césaire has this figure dressed like a delegate of a development-aid organisation called TESCO. After putting down a rebellion and executing his commander-in-chief, Métellus, who has made the mistake of reminding the king that the glorious fellowship of liberation under Toussaint has merely brought to Haiti "la double tyrannie / celle de la brute / celle du sceptique hautain" (43), Christophe, in Act I.6, contemplates re-taking Port-au-Prince and suppressing Pétion. But he rejects the risk of civil war that this would entail, and, to general astonishment, proposes a ceasefire and entente, with a view to "rebuilding this country and uniting its people." In a parody of parliamentary procedure in the republican Senate, Pétion rejects the proposal amid fears that a reconciliation would mean that the whole island would come under Christophe's control.

Christophe then sets about reshaping the "human material" of his subjects in the North and proclaims his opposition to "servile imitation." The first anniversary of his coronation is accompanied by a change in national policy: in order to lend the wings of eloquence to the genius of the nation, he is encouraged by the poet Chanlatte to make rum the national drink in place of champagne (I.7; 53–54). Congratulated by William Wilberforce on his coronation, he rejects the abolitionist's views on slow change. Madame Christophe draws her husband's attention to the hellish conditions he has imposed on his people: "Christophe, don't demand too much of the people and of yourself, don't demand too much!"

> I ask too much of people! But not enough from the negroes, madam! [...] All men have the same rights; that I can subscribe to. But it is the common lot of man that some have more duties than others – that's inequality; an inequality of debts, you see? Who could ever be made to believe that all men – I mean all – without privilege, with no special dispensation, have known the experience of transportation, the Middle Passage, enslavement, collective reduction to the state of animals, total dishonour, unlimited insult; who believes that all their bodies and faces have been spattered with this all-denying spittle! Only us, madam, you hear? – only us, the negroes! Right at the bottom of the pile! [...] And it's there that we raise our cry, longing for air, light, sun. And if we try to climb upwards again, see how certain things force themselves on us, the braced foot, the tensed muscle, the clenched teeth, a head, oh! a head, so broad and cold! That is why more must be demanded of negroes than from others – more labour, more faith, more enthusiasm, one step, another step, yet another step, holding fast to each step gained! It is a wholly new ascent I am speaking of, gentlemen, and woe to him whose step falters![83]

---

[82] I.3: HUGONIN: "C'est pour le roi une manière de baptiser qui il veut et d'être le parrain de tout le monde! Il est vrai que si les maris le laissaient faire, de tous les Haïtiens, il eût été non le parrain, mais le père" (33). CHRISTOPHE: "Nous, nos noms, puisque nous ne pouvons les arracher au passé, que ce soit à l'avenir! *(Tendre)*. / de noms de gloire je veux couvrir vos noms d'esclaves, / de noms d'orgueil nos noms d'infamie, / de noms de rachat nos noms d'orphelins! / C'est d'une nouvelle naissance, Messieurs, qui'il s'agit...!" (37).

Page references are to the revised Présence Africaine edition (1970); English translations are my own.

[83] I.7: "Christophe, ne demande pas trop aux hommes et à toi-mme, pas trop!"; "Je demande trop aux hommes! Mais pas assez aux nègres, Madame! [...] Tous les hommes ont mêmes droits. J'y souscris. Mais du commun lot, il en est qui ont plus de devoirs que d'autres. Là est l'inégalité. Une inégalité de

He thus ignores her, and, grimly mindful of the Voodoo drumming and dancing in the night, takes it into his head to make the Haitian achievement literally tangible (in what was to become, for Walcott, less than noble ruins). Christophe's vision is of a fortress – an edifying edifice – built for the people, by the people, whose cannon would fire from the battlements in a vast black shout that would shake the foundations of the old world of the whites. In his fancy, Christophe sees his citadel rising up:

> Look, its head is in the clouds, its feet dig into the abyss, its mouths spit cannon-shot far out to sea, to the bottom of the valleys, it is a town, a fortress, a massive stone battleship... [...] Look... But look! It is alive. It sounds in the fog. It flares in the night. Annullment of the slave-ship/slave-trader! A tremendous cavalcade! My friends, having drunk the pungent salt, the black wine of the sand, I, we, tumbled about in the great sea-swell, I have seen the enigmatic prow, foam and blood in its nostrils, smashing through the wave of shame![84]

The entr'acte, inverting the sequence prologue/commentary, has the Présentateur describing the massive waterways of the Artibonite and the radayeurs who guide huge rafts of logs down to the coast on the dangerous flood; the raftsmen enter, chanting to the Afro-Caribbean sea-god Agwé. The scene is emblematic of the perils of statecraft (however consecrated in Act I.4 by the choral litany of Voodoo gods that is intercalated between the Latin prayers of Archbishop Brelle as he crowns Christophe). The peasants, however, soon become suspicious of their leader. At siesta-time in Act II.1, the weather is good, but the times are bad; is Christophe's brutality more educative than Pétion's laxness? If they had fought against the whites, it was in order that the land would belong to them, and not to "work themselves half to death on someone else's property, even that of blacks [pour peiner sur la terre des autres, même noirs]" (II.1; 74). Can liberty be served by employing the means of servitude? To build his Citadel by transporting bricks, he first puts the women to work, then the children: "C'est leur avenir que nous construisons! [it is their future that we are building!]" (II.3; 83), says the King, and issues a scathing reprimand to both the populace and his officers: "It is time to make these blacks see reason – those who believe that the Revolution consists in taking the place of the whites and continuing to

---

sommations, comprenez-vous? A qui fera-t-on croire que tous les hommes, je dis tous, sans privilège, sans particulière exonération, ont connu la déportation, la traite, l'esclavage, le collectif ravalement à la bête, le total outrage, la vaste insulte, que tous, ils ont reçu plaqué sur le corps, au visage, l'omni-niant crachat! Nous seuls, Madame, vous m'entendez, nous seuls, les nègres! Alors au fond de la fosse! [...] C'est là que nous crions; de là que nous aspirons à l'air, à la lumière, au soleil. Et si nous voulons remonter, voyez comme s'imposent à nous, le pied qui s'arc-boute, le muscle qui se tend, les dents qui se serrent, la tête, oh! la tête, large et froide! Et voilà pourquoi il faut en demander aux nègres plus qu'aux autres: plus de travail, plus de foi, plus d'enthousiasme, un pas, un autre pas, encore un autre pas et tenir gagné chaque pas! C'est d'un remontée jamais vue que je parle, Messieurs, et malheur à celui dont le pied flanche!" (58/59).

[84] I.7: "Voyez, sa tête est dans les nuages, ses pieds creusent l'abîme, ses bouches crachent la mitraille jusqu'au large des mers, jusqu'au fond des vallées, c'est une ville, une forteresse, un lourd cuirassé de pierre... [...] Regardez... Mais regardez donc! Il vit. Il corne dans le brouillard. Il s'allume dans la nuit. Annulation du négrier! La formidable chevauchée! Mes amis, l'âcre sel bu et le vin noir du sable, moi, nous, les culbutés de la grosse houle, j'ai vu l'énigmatique étrasse, écume et sang aux naseaux, défoncer la vague de la honte!" (63).

live like they did: on the backs of the Negro, so to speak."[85] Inconsistencies are presented in starkly ironic juxtapositions: an indolent labourer is shot like a military deserter (II.2); a black estate-manager is quartered alive for flogging a worker like a slave (II.3); he places a higher value on his horses (and, as one of his subliminal Afro-Caribbean emblems, proclaims them immortal) than on his stallmaster (II.3); to uphold public morality, he has his court jester enforce "Christian marriage" upon peasant couples (II.4); he rejects Napoleon's olive-branch, ordering the emissary to be executed (II.5); because the Pope has failed to endorse Brelle as a proper archbishop, and because the latter has requested to return to France to retire from his labours, he orders his engineer to immure him in the cathedral (II.7). Christophe's answer to a storm that demolishes part of the Citadel, killing those labouring there under terrible conditions, is to shake his sword at the sky (II.8).[86]

In the second entr'acte, the peasants reappear, expressing their fear that the land they love will be given to Christophe's soldiers rather than to "l'armée souffrante" (111) of the workers. Scarcely is the Citadel completed than Christophe commands a new construction project, even more gigantic than before, near Crête-à-Pierrot, to house all the sovereigns of the world at an "ecumenical Congress" (118). The people complain. The King compels Gonzales, the new Archbishop, to officiate at the feast of Ascension in the town of Limonade, instead of at Le Cap. While Gonzales reads the Latin service, Christophe intervenes with Voodoo chants, until the ghost of Brelle appears to him and to the Archbishop, and the king, muttering about Voodoo magic being directed against him, is stricken with paralysis (III.2). The King, aged and sick, continues to rule (with the jester Hugonin complaining to Damballa), but Boyer, chief general of Pétion's army, arrives to rally Christophe's generals to the southern cause. The latter, learning that his fields have been put to the torch, hearing his soldiers drumming the Voodoo "mandoucouman" instead of military taps, and knowing that his dream is coming to an end, launches an impassioned appeal to the spirit of Africa: "Africa! Help me to return, carry me in your arms like an aged child and undress me and bathe me. Strip me of all these garments, strip me of them the way one strips away the dreams of night at the coming of the dawn."[87] The King and the Queen invoke Attibon Legba and Damballa, he manages to rise and totter to the balcony to harangue his soldiers, hands over command to the mulatto secretary, Vastey, and

---

85 II.3: "Il est temps de mettre à la raison ces nègres qui croient que la Révolution ça consiste à prendre la place des Blancs et continuer, en lieu et place, je veux dire sur le dos des nègres, à faire le Blanc" (84).

86 Although Christophe rejects Voodoo politically, spiritually he is enmeshed in Afro-Caribbean spirituality, as is the whole play; when he challenges St Peter and the lightning-bolt that explodes the Citadel's arsenal here (107), he is not defying Christianity but is issuing a hubristic challenge to the saint's syncretist mate, Legba – the first of the Voodoo loa, which, as controller of the passage between life and death, here initiates Christophe's downfall. Indeed, the whole play is marked by such omens and curses, indications that Christophe, though resisting the inevitable until the last, is the destined victim of a Voodoo death. See esp. Marianne Wichmann Bailey (passim) in Works Cited.

87 III.7: "Afrique! Aide-moi à rentrer, porte-moi comme un vieil enfant dans tes bras et puis tu me dévêtiras, me laveras. Défais- moi de tous ces vêtements, défais-m'en comme, l'aube venue, on se défait des rêves de la nuit" (147).

prepares to shoot himself (III.7). Hugonin, dressed in a top-hat as Baron Samedi, the *loa* of death, invokes the god Ogun as a pistol-shot rings out (III.8). In the closing scene, Christophe's body is carried to the Citadel and buried upright in fresh mortar; the Queen, his African page, and Vastey take their leave.

Tragedy needs half-mythic characters in which spectators can see themselves, and without the hero ceasing to evoke the whole range of the human condition. Césaire therefore turned from his dashed expectations about the "new Negro" of negritude that the corrupt, hero-less régimes of independent Sixties Africa had half-promised, to the mythology of negritude as embodied in the history of a demi-god from Haiti. Why the choice of Christophe? Césaire's visit to the citadel at La Ferrière in 1944 made a deep impression on him. Christophe was held in high esteem in Haiti (even to the point, later, of President "Papa Doc" Duvalier naming him a national political saint), and was the object of massive official pilgrimages. Césaire's interpretation of Christophe owes something to the poet's awareness of the abortive adventure under- taken by the new nations of Africa. Furthermore, Césaire, as the departmental deputy to France for Martinique, will have been aware of his powerlessness to lead his people to independence, yet ultimately sought a solution to the burning question of the inertia that was the Antillean malaise.

The play can hardly be read as just an anti-colonial manifesto and a reminder (however shadowy) of the Manichaeism of Duvalier's torpor-perpetuating tyranny. Césaire treats of the powerlessness of the leader and the moral poverty of the masses, as is clear from the speech of the chorus immediately after the Prologue:

> He is, then, in all his glory, General Christophe, the much-feared and much-respected Com- mander of the Northern Province, a Father of the Nation, as this kind of personality is termed in the Caribbean [...] But I said that he was a cook – which is to say, a clever politician – and, in his capacity as cook, he found that the dish was somewhat lacking in spices, that the magistracy they were offering him was much too sparing of meat.[88]

Césaire's passage from Toussaint to Christophe marks an intensification of pessimism. In his study of Toussaint, he examined the renewed struggle of the Haitian people under the iron rule of Dessalines. Like Christophe, Dessalines was the victim of the bloodthirsty despotism which his patriotic ideals and ethnic pride had led him to. This is the curse haunting all black leaders: the curse of a modern god (colonialism), and a tragic one. The funereal lamentation that closes the play holds out no promise of any words of hope.

The most painful aspect is that Christophe embodies a profound ideal of negri- tude. Paradoxical though it may seem, this king, in seeking to establish in the Caribbean a royal court possessing all the features of European etiquette, opposes the caricature of Western democracy established at Port-au-Prince. Christophe's court is to have no "servile imitation," for "the national genius must be encouraged to express

---

[88] "C'est alors, dans toute sa gloire, le général Christophe, le très craint et très respecté commandant de la province du Nord, un Père de la Patrie, comme on appelle, dans la Caraïbe, ce genre de personnage [...] Mais j'ai dit que c'était un cuisinier, c'est à dire un habile politique, et en sa qualité de cuisinier, il trouva que le plat manquait un peu d'épices, que la magistrature qu'on lui offrait était de viande par trop creuse" (15).

itself' (albeit in rum rather than champagne). Conditioned by his own attendance at the French National Assembly, Césaire shows President Pétion hiding mechanically behind liberal phraseology ("c'est notre fierté de tolérer une opposition! [it is our pride that we can tolerate opposition!]," I.6; 47) in order to push through the unscrupulous policies of the propertied mulatto class. The whole later history of Haiti derives from this republic: the menacing shadows of dictators can already be sensed, all more or less fathers of the nation, from Soulouque to Duvalier by way of Lescot, Vincent and other tyrants. Not for one moment does Césaire side with this false parliamentarianism against the dictatorship of Christophe. The form taken by power is not of interest to him; better to have a black king filled with a sense of mission than a cartoon republic. Better to force men to work than to tolerate bureaucratic mimicry.

In terms of his heart, Christophe is the hero. He instilled affection for his grandiose plans, moved as he was by the recognition that it was his people at work on his construction projects. It was impressive to witness an Antillean monarch reviving, on the other side of the Atlantic, the splendour of the former millennial courts of Africa, restoring a patriarchal royalty based on "respectability" rather than pleasure-seeking. Above all, Christophe is an African resisting the Graeco-Latin bourgeoisie of Port-au-Prince, just as Césaire resisted that of Fort-de-France: "Je ne suis pas un mulâtre à tamiser les phrases [I am not a mulatto who minces his words]" (I.1; 20). Essentially concerned with the working class and unconcerned with privilege, he wants to "correct," "educate" and compel his people to "awaken to themselves and to go beyond themselves"; "People of Haiti, Haiti has less to fear from the French than from herself! The enemy of the people is their indolence, their shamelessness, their hatred of discipline, their torpid, pleasure-obsessed spirit."[89] In having himself crowned in the cathedral at Le Cap, Christophe is crowning the whole of the black race. But his goal is not simply to make princes of slaves, as Napoleon made imperial noblemen of his soldiers. He must build a nation; first as rebel and then as monarch, Christophe draws on his African tradition to achieve this goal. The whole play concerns his determined effort to "regenerate" his race; he wants to reorganise the family, the State, religion, the economy. But reinforcing this by military discipline is part of his undoing, leading to black insurrection and betrayal, and to the blacks running over to Boyer, Piétion's successor.

In contrast to the historical figure, Christophe is not wilfully cruel in this play: his rigour derives from love of country, and from a keen awareness of responsibility. Driven to superhuman efforts by his vision and his desire not to be humiliated by accusations about the inefficiency of his people, he asks the same energy of others:

> I will not have the world ever say, ever suspect, that ten years of black freedom, ten years of black slackness and dereliction, will suffice to squander the treasure amassed by the martyrdom

---

[89] I.1: "... à naître à lui-même et à se dépasser lui-même" (23); I.2: "Peuple haïtien, Haïti a moins à craindre des Français que d'elle-même! L'ennemi de ce peuple, c'est son indolence, son effronterie, sa haine de la discipline, l'esprit de jouissance et de torpeur" (29).

of our people in a hundred years of toil and whiplash. So let's get this clear right away: with me you will have no right to be tired.[90]

He is a martyr rather than a tyrant, ceaselessly confessing his doubts and complaining about the heavy burden of his mission. He is not seduced by any illusions about his people: "Dust! Dust! Dust everywhere! No stone! Dust! Shit and dust!" He sees them as not glimpsing the dangers that lie ahead: "The foul crimes of our persecutors lie at our heels, encircling us, and my people dance!"[91]

But, gradually, he begins to rest on his laurels, seeking refuge in the allure of a desperately quixotic attitude, then immobilised by disillusion. More seriously, he revels in the solitude of his grand mission. He tries to impose his version of truth on others without talking to them. He doesn't really educate his subjects, but imposes himself on them by force, demanding free rein to do whatever he pleases. The most tragic aspect of his character derives from his lack of self-criticism, especially concerning his worst vice, which is the romantic pride of the national leader.

Comparison with the areas of Carpentier's novel that treat Christophe prompts further consideration of the image of the driven tyrant and of the approach taken by the two writers. Both texts have a biographical genesis (Carpentier's visit to Haiti in 1943, Césaire's in 1944), but Carpentier wrote (like Walcott in his early play before the rise of Duvalier and before Senghor assumed political significance within négritude, whereas Césaire wrote amidst the process of African decolonisation and with some awareness of the historical predeterminism (or Caribbean cyclicity) that had helped breed Duvalier. Armbruster, in his study of Carpentier, includes a useful section on the connection between decolonisation and Afro-Caribbean religion (Voodoo) in the two works.[92] In Act I of Césaire's play, the imitation of European models is accompanied by Christophe's renunciation of Voodoo as damaging to national reconstruction; in Carpentier, Christophe shackles his subjects to a new slavery via the introduction of a degenerate form of Voodoo. The intersection between Voodoo and Catholicism is differently handled.[93] In Césaire, Christophe deconstructs the Mass upon his re-encounter with the Abbé Brelle at the Assumption of the Blessed Virgin by superimposing Voodoo invocations (127–28); he is

---

[90] "je ne veux pas qu'il puisse jamais être dit, jamais être soupçonné dans le monde que dix ans de liberté nègre, dix ans de laisser-aller et de démission nègre suffiront pour que soit dilapidé le trésor que le martyr de notre peuple a amassé en cent ans de labeur et de coups de fouet. Aussi bien, qu'on se le dise dès à présent, avec moi vous n'aurez pas le droit d'être fatigués" (I.2; 29).

[91] I.6: "Poussière! Poussière! Partout de la poussière! Pas de pierre! De la poussière! De la merde et de la poussière!" (49); I.7: "le crime de nos persécuteurs nous cerne les talons, et mon peuple dans!" (60).

[92] Claudius Armbruster, *Das Werk Alejo Carpentiers: Chronik der "Wunderbaren Wirklichkeit"* (Editionen der Iberoamericana III.7; Frankfurt am Main: Vervuert, 1982): 277–85. Mouralis, "L'Image de l'indépendance haïtienne" (530–34), is particularly acute in his concise analysis of cultural oppositions in respect to Christophe, while the particular nuances of Afro-Caribbean belief-systems in Carpentier's novel are brought out by Emma Susana Speratti–Piñero, "Creencias afro-antillanas en *El reino de este mundo* de Alejo Carpentier," *Nueva Revista de Filología Hispánica* (Mexico City) 29.2 (1980): 574–96.

[93] This partly syncretist and partly ideologically oppositional intersection forms either a central aspect or a contributory epiphenomenon in many literary treatments of the Haitian revolution – and, of course, in representations of Haiti generally; see esp. Leslie G. Desmangles, *The Faces of the Gods: Voodoo and Roman Catholicism in Haiti* (Chapel Hill: U of North Carolina P, 1992).

possessed by Africa (reunited with the war-god Shango[94]) and heightened towards transfiguration at his death. In Carpentier, Christophe is punished for a factitious reunion with Africa and a concurrent adherence to eurocentric Cartesianism. Both Césaire and Carpentier, however, relativise by sceptical contrasts – Césaire by having the court jester provide an ironic parallel as an incarnation of Baron Samedi; Carpentier by using the *picaro* Ti Noël's perspective to ridicule the Ozymandian grandiosity of Christophe's vision. Walcott and Glissant do not handle the Voodoo element in the way Césaire and Carpentier do: in the former, it is integral, yet causally peripheral to the central action. There is in all, of course, a connection between belief, ethnic awareness and the nature of power. Césaire stresses Christophe's hubristically pure motives, Carpentier his Manichaean racism. Unlike Césaire's, Carpentier's picture of dictatorship is more pronounced (even: archly blissful in ironic acceptance of its systemic, mythic yet everyday nature), anticipating the later tradition of García Márquez and Roa Bastos. In Césaire, grassroots resistance to tyranny is not bound up with Afro-Caribbean religion so much as with the connection between man and the soil; instead, the question of religion is affixed to the personality of Christophe himself, whereas Carpentier connects grassroots resistance to tyranny with Afro-Caribbean religion (and only secondarily with the telluric immanence of the latter) in order to condemn its *abuse* by Christophe.

Derek Walcott: *The Haytian Earth* (1984)

This third foray of Walcott's into the arena of the Haitian revolution apparently had its inception in a proposal made to him in 1977 by Michael Schultz of Universal City Studios in California that he write a television screenplay, with the working title "The Black Napoleon," viewing Toussaint's insurrection from "underneath" rather than from the viewpoint of the generals.[95] The play itself, however, as staged in 1984 under the title *The Haytian Earth*,[96] was a "political" commission, as *Drums and Colours* had been – this time from the St Lucian government, as a celebration of 150 years of emancipation from slavery.

The play is divided into two parts; Part One extends from the execution of Ogé in March 1791 to July 1800 and Dessalines' defeat of the mulattoes under Rigaud at Les Cayes; Part Two opens in about July 1802 and closes in 1820 just before Christophe's

---

[94] Armbruster notes that these details of africanisation were inserted only in the second edition of 1970, at the behest of African actors in the play. Arnold ("D'Haïti à l'Afrique," 144–45) sees the interference between Christian and African cultural codes as an opposing of historical time to mythic time.

[95] The script's title was evidently a reflection of Schultz's intention that Percy Waxman's eponymous historical biography of Toussaint be taken as a material starting-point.

[96] It carries the alternative title *Black Emperors*, indicating a broader historical (plural) reach than that indicated by the title of Waxman's book. Factual details on this play, and references to its public reception, are drawn from King 1995 (esp. 324–29, with a useful résumé of first reviews) and Stone 1994 (137–38), as well as from extra information kindly supplied to me by Bruce King, to whom I am also indebted for generously providing me with a typescript photocopy of the playscript from the West Indian Collection of the University of the West Indies at St Augustine.

suicide.[97] A kind of symbolic prelude features Dessalines as a buccaneer on a lonely beach, tusked by a charging boar, "black like me ... a nigger like myself," before he manages to kill it – thereby fulfilling a "wild dream" of invincibility in which he drives the "French pigs" into the sea and emerges a king. A woman acting as Chorus rehearses (in French creole switching to English creole) the stages of revolutionary consciousness, from Toussaint through Dessalines to Christophe, as Dessalines chains himself to a column of slaves trudging past the Calixte–Bréda plantation with its "Belle Maison," home of Toussaint. The notion of colour and allegiance is then taken up by the planter Calixte's mulatto son, Anton, as he and the Baroness de Wimpffen watch the slaves being taken to witness the execution of Ogé at Le Cap. Anton, a "bastard," abhors his mixed blood, "like the colour of the earth," and feels paralysed between the whiteness of European art and thought (which he espouses but is tired of) and the blackness of action, to which he is attracted despite his view that the rebels' "African nostalgia" is "rubbish." This split of self-hatred between art and action is an image of the younger Walcott himself: "rubbish" was Christophe's word in Walcott's 1949 play, and "nostalgia" was what Walcott attacked in "What the Twilight Says." Anton's father explains the need to execute Ogé: rights for mulattoes may be in order (after all, he has adopted Anton, friend of Ogé, as his son), but rights for blacks are dangerous, like the romantic notions of Robespierre and Rousseau. The female Chorus then comments on the futility of Ogé's having petitioned the French Assembly for the mulattoes' cause. This dialectical phase of the play is reinforced by the contrasting views first of Dessalines, who makes savagely ironic comments from within the column of slaves, then of Henri Christophe, who is serving as a waiter at the Auberge de la Couronne as preparations are being made for the torture and execution. Before he quits his job as waiter, Christophe remarks cynically of the waiting crowd that "the nigger blood will show; they remind me of monkeys," angers the mulatto Baron de Vastey by calling him "a philosophical monkey" using imported ideas, then cows the mulatta whore Yette by taunting her for her desire to have white children. For Christophe, there is no split, no halfway house of allegiance: one is either black or white.

Basic ideological stances are subsequently underlined. Calixte witnesses with satisfaction the torture of Ogé and Chavannes and the end of mulatto rebellion; the mulatto Anton expresses his love for the white Baroness de Wimpffen; her husband (an influential French documentarist of pre-revolutionary Saint-Domingue) declares the planter/slave régime as immutable. When the escaped Dessalines encounters Christophe, he pours contempt on him for believing that Ogé (himself a slaveholder) died for the blacks (rather than, out of self-interest, for the mulattoes).

---

97 I should note that the version of the play that I refer to here is a hybrid. It is not a playscript that can be directly staged – the disposition of individual scenes (22 in Part One, 17 with one inserted, compacted re-writing in Part Two) and the presence of perspectival notations such as closeups betray the residual presence of Walcott's original television screenplay.

When the mulattoes sack Le Cap, the city is likened to a too-proud woman destroyed by corruption, and to a Sodom of "fire and ashes." Two emblematic attitudes to this destruction are dramatised: Christophe and his wife, Marie-Louise, ensure a Catholic burial for a child killed in the fire: an intimation of resurrection from ashes through Christophe's residual allegiance to a eurocentric faith. Yette, by contrast, "her skin the same shade as the ground," resolves to plant afresh on a small allotment of land given her by her aunt. This theme of peasant allegiance to the soil is a central anchoring-point in the play.

The next stage of insurrection is initiated through dramatic indirection from within this context of the soil: Pompey, a section-overseer on the Bréda canefields, is attracted to Yette, whom he threatens for taking provisions before learning that Calixte has permitted this; the colour-theme arises again when Yette curses Pompey as a black for whom "all mulattoes is whore." Dessalines is mistaken for a snake when he emerges from concealment in a cornfield and asks the way to Bois-Caiman and Boukman: as co-initiator of revolution, he is a "snake in the grass." Anton finds a decapitated chicken as Voodoo sign; the blame for this is placed not on Toussaint but on his nephew Moise; this scene is followed by Boukman, holding a headless white rooster and a Voodoo fetish, addressing the tribes of his army and invoking Shango and Africa. Dessalines looks on as the "crazy nigger" guerrillas are massacred by the French troops. He joins Boukman and Biassou, who have staggered up (in "resurrection") from beneath their dead soldiers, to exact revenge, he tells them, they must employ the tactic of fear with "an army of shadows," renouncing both African and Christian religion in favour of military rationality. Toussaint, however, is aghast at the resulting "godless brutality" of the blacks and wishes the vengeance to cease – "the soil itself is bleeding," and he needs "soldiers, not animals!"

Another "telluric" interlude (as in Césaire and Depestre) occurs, with Pompey tilling the soil and swearing devotion to Yette; as they reflect on the military victories of old Toussaint, Yette confesses that only the "black part" of her is "in the country." This "split-allegiance" contrasts with an episode in which Dessalines, asserting unconditional supremacy (also over Toussaint), matches a white act of barbarism with a black act of desecration by contemptuously hurling aside the severed head of Boukman. When Christophe discovers that Toussaint and Moïse have gone to fight for Sonthonax and the Spanish in San Domingo, Dessalines expresses disgust at their leader's royalist leanings.

Part One culminates in a long scene in which Dessalines drunkenly celebrates the destruction of Rigaud's mulatto troops at Les Cayes, while Christophe and Toussaint have misgivings at the barbaric excesses of this victory. Calixte appears, searching for his adoptive son Anton, and threatens to shoot his old friend and servant Toussaint for letting "wild pigs" loose on the land. Toussaint defends himself by saying that there had been no help from sympathetic whites when this was still possible; now he must squeeze peace out of an exacerbated situation like "a rag soaked in blood." Toussaint and Dessalines command that Calixte be executed (with a Christian burial). In anguish at having to sacrifice Calixte for reasons of state, Toussaint signs the Bréda plantation over to Pompey's and Yette's safe-keeping – once again, the reactive dialectic between military violence and investment in the soil. This theme of chthonic nurture/nature is then contrasted with the theme of cultural artifice, as Dessalines conveys to Christophe his resentment at Toussaint's superior ways and at the eurocentric hypocrisies of mulatto political functionaries. His hatred for the attitudes concealed within the metropolitan tongue is, significantly, expressed by adversion to the trueness of creole. There is a concentration of animal imagery: Dessalines calls the mulatto parlamentarians "ragged blackbirds"; the peasant blacks furrow their brows "like a marmoset." If they surrender to the language of the mulattoes, Dessalines argues, they will have "won nothing" – "We will remain / one hundred, two hundred years from now, waiters, / maids, servants, parrots and monkeys"; the blacks will be made into mulattoes, "earth-coloured people who produce nothing. / I would slaughter every one of them again." This tragic prescience makes Dessalines' extremism psychologically comprehensible, though still reprehensible.

Part Two opens with Leclerc languishing with yellow fever in a military hospital five months after arrival in Saint-Domingue, dictating a letter to Napoleon as Pauline tends him (unlike Carpentier, Walcott marginalises her, replacing eroticism with loving concern). Although a ceasefire has been arranged between Leclerc and Toussaint, the latter orders a group of his soldiers, including his nephew Moïse, to kill themselves for shooting French troops. This decline into retributive excess is paralleled by Yette's withdrawal to a tawdry existence as a whore in Le Cap: this is where her "white" yearnings have landed her. Pompey initiates a counter-movement by asserting that "you and I, we is Hayti" and persuading her to return with him to till the land peacefully at the plantation. By contrast, the political counter-movement initiated by Christophe and Dessalines (in Leclerc's words, "two black buzzards" circling Toussaint's carcass) is fraught with ethical complications. Selling their leader to the French "for peace" induces a struggle against remorse in the generals: Christophe demands that they grant Toussaint some "honour," whereas Dessalines recalls bitterly how "that smart little monkey" betrayed his nephew, his soldiers, his whole people to the whites. A parallel scene has Toussaint imprisoned on Leclerc's ship bound for France, accusing his generals of being mere "slaves" to the French Empire, "swine, not panthers" in an "African" tradition. For Leclerc, Dessalines and Christophe are "hungry wolves" protected from "tribal genocide" by that very Empire. These ideological collisions are cut through by Toussaint, the colonial speaking back, correcting Leclerc: in the Caribbean there are "wild boars" but no wolves. At any rate, says Leclerc, French culture straightened their spines "from animals to men." But, counters Toussaint, what does this bookish civilisation mean under slavery "to a slave whose back is flayed so raw that, like a book, you can read the spine?"

Amidst ethnic confusions and loyalties, blacks and mulattoes are deserting the countryside. Yette, on the Bréda plantation, is torn between peasant simplicity and dedication to the resilient Pompey on the one hand, and the finer life of the city on the other; but she declines his offer to let her go. Now that Toussaint has died, "shrivelled as a marmoset" in the "cold, white peace" of the Jura winter (*Henri Christophe* is echoed here), while "two jackals fight for his carcass" in Haiti, Dessalines proclaims himself Emperor. For Yette and Pompey, "this, the Haytian earth" will now be different: "now come / the angry kings." After his investiture, and recalling his own nobility over the dead wild boar on the beach, Dessalines appoints Christophe Secretary of Agriculture, "to make our people go back to the earth!" But what looks like rigorous support for the rural aspirations of Yette and Pompey turns out to be a new betrayal. When Dessalines' court is received by Pompey at Belle Maison, Christophe complains to Vastey how the Emperor, "this medalled jackass," rules by undisciplined, base intuition and corruption, dividing up the plantations among his soldiers; "that pig should be butchered."

The *principled* extremism of Christophe revealed in this homicidal urge seems justified by Dessalines' ensuing abuse of power at the personal level, when he forces his sexual attentions on Yette, who submits dully, exciting him to climax by calling him a black pig; this rape is, of course, emblematic of the rape of the land. At dawn, Christophe delivers a long speech recalling Dessalines' past exploits: he once was a "panther," an African welded to his steed "like a black centaur" – an evocation (as in Carpentier) of a magical, amulet-protected past linked with ancestral Africa. Now, however, Dessalines' proud blackness is a shadow over the land. His response to Christophe's urging that he relinquish the crown is to assert his power by ordering a worker punished savagely for indolence. Christophe's plea (like his frank opposition in *Henri Christophe*) is made after he has already resolved to destroy Dessalines: in a laconically cryptic exchange, he confirms with two labourers the arrangements for the Emperor's assassination.[98]

Christophe's chequered reign as king is passed over in *The Haytian Earth* as a given, its aetiology being sufficient illustration, and the closing scenes of the play take place in the year 1820. Instead of providing a dark psychomachia of inner conflict, Walcott "africanises" Christophe's psychosomatic affliction by making it the result of Yette's implementation of *chienbois* (the retributive Voodoo practice of sticking pins in an effigy). The King accepts this as a normal political (rather than supernatural) transgression, connecting it with his accusation that Yette (as a mulatto) is siding with Rigaud and Pétion in the mulatto South; Christophe's belief in Voodoo is thus an assertion of his blackness. In defence of Yette, "silent as the earth self silent," Pompey speaks of Haitian king following French king, the sun of monarchy casting a shadow over slave, then over peasant, making life "one long, long night." Christophe offers no defence, recounting instead his African

---

[98] In the longer version, the scene ends with one labourer donning a boar's head as Christophe says: "the boar will find him [...] on the same beach."

dream of a forest full of *bolom*-spirits, and of the ghosts of past rebels (à la Glissant) standing on the Guinea coast where Toussaint has conveyed the "black hearse" of Haiti before the whiteness of the Northern snow begins to fall. Walcott thus, via dream-poetry, projects the cultural tensions contained within the future of Haiti; ensnared within his own draconian rectitude, Christophe has no dialectical choice but to condemn Yette to death. But this death will have the substance of a dream, as the individual human wins out over polity: granted the last word before the defiant closing Chorus, Yette affirms that she loves "the Haytian earth" even more than she does her husband, "the sweat and salt of the earth," and she is prouder of him "than if he was a king."

≈ ❖ ও

Walcott's Dramatic Styles

Henri Christophe

Surveying Walcott's poetic and dramatic career, we can understand by hindsight that it lay always in his nature – but especially in his earlier, Websterian–Metaphysical years – to avoid treating a figure like Toussaint centrally and to choose instead characters of psychic extremes, inward tensions and paradox like Christophe, who could be a proleptic paradigm of the colonial process as presented in the studies of Frantz Fanon.[99] The selection of historical incidents and the constant evaluative ruminations and argumentation of the characters in *Henri Christophe* ensure that the unresolvable extremes of human psychology are effectively played out. How Walcott packages all this in terms of verbal artistry can only be sketched here.

Already, Walcott, in his late teens, is a master of traditional dramatic verse. There is a judicious mixture of economically dialogic stretches and more expansive, descriptive "set speeches." Occasional rhyme functions, as in Shakespeare, to indicate tropic moments closing a line of argument or a scene, or to bind concepts closer together. Further, however, Walcott often ironises his prosodic model by introducing rhyme to underscore or expose hypocritical or superficial tonalities in political and moral utterances. There are intermittent applications of alliterative clusters, where sound imitates and reinforces extreme moods of contempt, anger, and so forth. At the level of figuration, the texture is both familiar in many of its tropes and astonishing in its command of complex interrelationship. I shall restrict myself here to a simple, contextless listing. There are elaborated metaphors familiar to us from Elizabethan drama, such as planting and harvest, or the unweeded and decaying garden of the body politic, revitalised here by their interlinkage with the wasteland condition of the Haitian pastoral economy. There is the same predilection for reified analogies with

---

[99] It has been acutely observed that "the young Walcott's vision of the world is already divided [in *Henri Christophe*] into an arena composed of sanity and insanity. Personal vanity is the fundamental factor in the tragic and mad psychology of history," a theme that recurs in Walcott's later drama; see Erskine Peters, "The Theme of Madness in the Plays of Derek Walcott," *College Language Association Journal* 32.2 (December 1988): 162–63. Walcott himself acknowledges the centrality of madness, and the introduction of a new colonial paradigm by Fanon and Césaire, in his essay "What the Twilight Says" (10–14).

print culture and language found in Shakespeare, the Metaphysicals, and elsewhere in Walcott: "an anthology of creeds and skins"; "a syntax of the probable"; "the crazy graph of power"; citadels as "brick biographies"; "what is your alphabet, the bullet?"; "my primer is blood"; "your dictionary, only treason"; "the vocabulary of ruin." Untypical of Shakespeare is Walcott's repeated centering on a narrow range of concepts crucial to the obsessions of the main characters: memory, dream, hope; tyranny, authority; light, sun and moon, white and black; pawns and chessboards, history, ruin, martyrdom, fathers and children. Sub-sets of negatively evocative abstracts and concretes, each of which term occurs repeatedly, point in another tonal direction: intrigue, treason, treachery, betrayal, plot; duplicity, suspicion; pride, ambition. Or: physician, sanity, lunatic, madness; rot, infection, corruption, disease; skull, bone, skeleton, dust, grave. These are the obsessive counters of Jacobean revenge tragedy, crowned here by some 36 occurrences of terms relating to blood and bloodshed.

Commentators have seen disjunction between subject matter, scene and character on the one hand, and mode of expression on the other. Illiterate black ex-slaves, it has been maintained, shouldn't speak in Shakespearean verse and high poetic rhetoric.[100] Walcott himself, reflecting back on this play, has been enlisted to support this view. But his references to the cynical fustian of the play's language are not dismissively negative.[101] The cynicism of a young poet's application of Shakespearean models is really a necessary irony; and it is a further irony that we, over-committed to verism, should take high rhetoric to be fustian. And fustian, anyway, is the ideal term for the central disjunction of the play – between the characters' aspirations and their inability to realise these. So John Figueroa's observation that fusion of cultures is confirmed in *Omeros* does hold true for *Henri Christophe* as well, though in reduced measure. A central expressive mode of European provenance and universal validity colonises, as it were, a site of history where "history" – even in the awareness of Dessalines and Christophe – is merely an aspiration, a nascent dream of a new future.

Early West Indian commentators on both the printed version and the radio and stage performances drew attention to their own lack of firm and detailed historical knowledge of the period,[102] without, however, going so far as to state that this lack (or the lack in the text) had seriously impeded their comprehension of the play. *Henri Christophe* is not a historical documentary, but a skein of modal reflections on and refractions of central aspects of Caribbean and human identity in their relation to

---

[100] See, for example, Robert D. Hamner, "Mythological Aspects of Derek Walcott's Drama," *Ariel* 8.3 (July 1977: 35–58), esp. 40–41; revised and expanded in Hamner, *Derek Walcott* (Boston: Twayne, 1981): 52–53.

[101] In his third year of school-teaching after graduating from university, while he was employed at Jamaica College and towards the end of his stint as features reporter on the Kingston weekly *Public Opinion*, he was distanced enough from the play he had himself directed at the university in 1954 that he could write of its 1957 production at a secondary-school drama festival that "Cornwall College's *Henri Christophe* was a well edited version of an overwritten play"; Walcott, "Schools Drama Festival," *Public Opinion* (6 April, 1957): 6.

[102] For example, Aubrey Douglas–Smith, "*Henri Christophe: A Chronicle in Seven Scenes*" (a review of the Advocate Company edition), in *Bim* 3.12 (349–53): 349–50.

power, hope and disappointment, trust and treachery, innocence and guilt, patience and vengeance, political responsibility and racial paranoia, reality and illusion. These are constants of human psychology, even as the gross physicality of the historical cruelties reflected in the play stands in a feedback relationship to the dark distortions of human consciousness under stress. All this is fully in accord with the play's poeticity, for the young Walcott is trying to get behind surfaces to essentials, and the burden of the play's language has an Elizabethan and Jacobean pitch not because Walcott was incapable of crafting his own, new, Haitian or Caribbean mode of representation, but because these great pre-texts and inter-texts cover similar ground.

The play invites a more positive re-evaluation, both in terms of its topic and in terms of its poeticity and the relationship of the latter to the structuring of a specifically dramatic discourse. The sparse criticism of the play has mistaken Walcott's own tone of indulgence towards this piece of highly precocious "juvenilia" and has intimated, in a form of "post-colonialist" aetiological anachronism, that its generic indebtedness to such European dramatic modes as Jacobean tragedy somehow makes it less "original" than unqualified masterpieces like *Dream on Monkey Mountain*. Walcott's own explicit aesthetic disavows all mechanical applications of the principle of "originality" – we must, he maintains, take lessons from our masters. I would argue for the conscious, intertextual necessity for generic "unoriginality" as the critical dynamic underlying *Henri Christophe*, and would emphasise the magisterial appropriateness of Walcott's "traditional" verse-modes and dramatism to his subject-matter, as a necessary evolutionary stage on the road towards the "mature" plays.

Drums and Colours
In *Drums and Colours*, it is astonishing how much Walcott has managed to compress together in the way of thematic implication with regard to the Haitian revolution while still maintaining a balanced, tight relationship with the other episodes. The questions of tone and the pitch of language are important – in regard to the latter, Walcott was already under the spell of what he referred to three years later as the "terrifying" clarity of the plain poetic style, despite his "nostalgia for obscurity."[103] The Haitian scenes correspondingly possess a new, sparse urbanity, so as not to distance them too far from the linguistic and poetic registers employed elsewhere. The Columbus and Raleigh episodes in Part I are mediated in two distinct "Elizabethan" styles: the Spanish scenes (partly as a knowing linguistic joke) use the more archaic "thou/thee" register of formality, with "high" figuration à la Tourneur (in this latter respect, there are echoes of *Henri Christophe* here); the sequent "Anglo-Saxon" scenes dispense with most of this linguistic archaism in favour of a cooler, cleaner, more dispassionate style, with a "Donnean" scrupulousness about the tropes applied. As *Drums and Colours* is a pageant, Walcott also frames it linguistically with two creole contexts.

---

103 Derek Walcott, "Walcott on Walcott," interviewed by Dennis Scott, originally published in *Caribbean Quarterly* 14.1–2 (special issue "The Arts," March–June 1968): 77–82; reprinted in *Caribbean Quarterly* 38.4 (special issue: *"Caribbean Quarterly*'s Derek Walcott"; December, 1992): 136–41; here 137.

The comedic, opening meta-text is a representation of Carnival or Mas' in the present, with characters discussing the selection of players to act appropriate historical roles. These figures recur briefly in choric interludes. The closing phase of the pageant (the Morant Bay Rebellion) moves progressively back towards creole, to the point where the high comedy reached by the close melts away all distinction between the historical event of 1865 and its carnivalesque "historic" commemoration in 1965. One notes the inclusion of "folk-mythic continuity" in the figure of Pompey, who is a supratemporal analogue of Carpentier's Ti Noël. Bound up with this comic presence is a pervasive sense of ironical humour, which recalls the undercutting of pretensions to the grandeur of pure tragedy found in both Carpentier and Césaire (whereby, in the latter's treatment of Christophe, the presence of the jester Hugonin serves specifically this function). There is thus a tonality, common to Walcott, Carpentier and Césaire, that is an ideal means of conveying the cultural complexity of revolutionary processes. In Walcott's first play, bleakly sardonic Jacobean tropes do much of this work, but the only scene that represents an incipient awareness of the folk as a vehicle for the relativisation of history is the "anomalous" assassins' scene embedding the changeover from the old order of Dessalines to the carnivalesque idealism of Christophe.

It might seem that I am straying from my brief, away from the Haitian theme into a general consideration of the play – but the function and valency of the Haitian episode can only be fully appreciated in terms of structural and contextual embedding. This even applies to the area of characterisation – just as the creole expressiveness slips the leash of time, so do the meta-characters of the Mas' prelude, and one of these – by the name of Pompey – constitutes an intertextual absence from the historical Haitian scene as displayed in *Henri Christophe*. The preludial characters are called Mano, Pompey and Yette. It is asked of Mano, when he is inspecting the Mas' participants for likely candidates to play historical roles, how he knows so much about personalities like Raleigh and Columbus (24). A figure with the same name (and an African king) turns up in the *Conquista* tableaux among a fresh shipment of Ashanti slaves being inspected by Spanish brokers in Cádiz before trans-shipment to "the estates of Hispaniola" (46, 50); already here there is a covert Haitian connection. The mulatta, Yette, features later in the Jamaica of 1830 as a housekeeper ejected for theft from a white planter's Great House (110); she then joins the Jamaican Maroons – under the command of a general called Mano (116). Mano and Pompey the shoemaker also feature as a double act (fall guy and straight man) during a couple of the intervals, though the most important commentative role is assumed by a Chorus which announces, after the death of Raleigh in the Tower, how "Time turns now from Europe [...] revolves its gaze and shows [...] Hundreds of battles past the discovery, / To the slaves' suffering and the settlers' wealth, / Until an exiled people finds release, / Through revolutions of despair and love" – and the scene shifts to Haiti: "How shall we live, till these ghosts bid us live?" (86). Pompey, like the general Sylla in Walcott's *Henri Christophe*, is marked by a "Roman" name typical of those imposed upon the African house-slaves (and not uncommon as a historical figure alongside Caesar and Cleopatra in the Carnival masquerade and road-marches); a Pompée was one of many important rebel leaders during the Haitian revolution, but he does not appear in the Haitian scenes of *Drums and Colours*, nor under that name in *Henri Christophe* – he is, however, indeed present in the latter play in the form of the pamphleteer and chief mulatto advisor to Christophe, Baron de Vastey, whose forenames were Pompée Valentin. Pompey the shoemaker turns up in Jamaica during the Baptist Rebellion, "scattering pamphlets / Bout emancipation" (111). The Vastey/ pamphleteer connection is further underpinned by Walcott's re-employment of the name of Vastey's wife, Yette, for a later female insurrectionist. After George William Gordon is hanged during the Morant Bay Rebellion, Pompey is there again, his uncontrollable rage at the white Gordon's execution leading Mano to observe: "He getting like some mad Haitian rebel" (122). Shot by the British soldiers, he preaches peace and togetherness. Most of the closing business of *Drums and Colours* is a general lament for Pompey's death – but he turns out, in true Mas' spirit, to be only wounded, and, as "the most important man in this country" (135), revives to win the day. If, for Walcott, the "most important man" happens to be a mulatto astride two cultures (the European side at least onomastically, and in terms of Christian ethics), then it is also made quite clear that nineteenth-century rebellion is as multicultural an endeavour as Mas' or Port of Spain: by the aftermath of Morant Bay and the collapse of the sugar market, the destitute maroon rebels gathered round the callaloo-pot include General Yu, "a Chinese cook," and Ram the tailor, an indentured "East Indian tactician" (118–19). Indeed, the play represents a dramaturgical multiculturalism unique in West Indian theatre history: it was the first (and, to date, the only) production "to bring together such an extraordinary array of some two hundred of the foremost talents from all around the Caribbean and further afield."[104]

The Haytian Earth

The centrality here of Pompey and Yette differs significantly from their centrality in *Drums and Colours*: in the latter, they are activist archetypes alongside other folk-figures; in *The Haytian Earth*, they constitute a pole of nature-bound equilibrium, of stoic passivity. Pompey (Yette's "Ti-Moune") differs from Carpentier's Ti Noël in not giving himself up to fantasies of post-colonial reinvestiture. Whereas Ti Noël occupies the mansion and surrounds himself with the relicts of the European past, Pompey does not avail himself of the riches of the Big House, as Yette would like him to do; instead, he will wear rags and patiently till his patch of land until it bears fruit. This is an evolutionary, not a revolutionary, position based on a form of radical foundationalism, whereby the only true ethic is a kind of "work ethic." The other characterological features of note are the care with which Walcott employs Christophe as a counterweight of ethical and political moderation to the emotionalised vitality and activism of Dessalines,

104 Stone, *Theatre*, 106.

and the skill with which he enables both Dessalines and Christophe to comment devastatingly on the moral flaws of their respective predecessors. By the same token (as in *Henri Christophe*), Walcott bypasses the task of passing dramatically internal judgement on Christophe as the last fateful link in the revolutionary chain, save through the bald juxtaposition of his physical decline (through unarticulated hubris) with the sentence he passes on Yette; this juxtaposition allows the play to open out at the end towards a mythic perspective, with the dimension of the vacancy of earthly power being overlaid with that of the of the earth's powerless plenitude.

The political insights of the characters are many and varied, and are kept compactly talismanic by being linked reactively to concrete situations; very seldom does Walcott allow political sentiments to be embedded in prolonged rhetorical statements. The argumentational gradation of economy from *Henri Christophe* through *Drums and Colours* to *The Haytian Earth* is at its strongest here, as well as in the deployment of metaphor and imagery. When these elements of expression do occur, they are punctuative and naturalised to the discourse of speaking men. The leitmotivic patterns that are established – the nuances of animal metaphor; the implications of the idea of shadow/light, blood/skin/earth – are thus all the more pregnant for their economy of means. In terms both of clarified verbal texture and of the employment of creole registers to precise effect, Walcott has moved far since *Henri Christophe*; *The Haytian Earth* (given the historically conditioned absence of faith in dialect expression which compelled Césaire, Glissant and others to alternative forms of expressive ingenuity) counts as a successful endeavour on Walcott's part to lead the creole continuum back into the cockpit of politics and history.

≈ ❖ ❧

WORKS CITED

AKO, Edward O. "Leslie Pinckney Hill's *Toussaint L'Ouverture*," *Phylon: A Review of Race and Culture* 48.3 (Fall 1987): 190–95.

ALLSOPP, Jeannette. "History Re-Interpreted in Carpentier's *El reino de este mundo?*," in *History and Time in Caribbean Literature: Proceedings of the XI Conference on Spanish Caribbean Literature, April 1988*, ed. Claudette Williams (Mona, Kingston: Institute of Caribbean Studies, University of the West Indies, 1992): 20–31.

ANON. "Errol Hill Overcomes Obstacles in the Way of *Henri Christophe*," *Evening News* (Port of Spain; 11 January 1952).

——. "Governor draws lessons from Haitian history," *Daily Gleaner* (Monday, 15 March 1954): 6.

——. "Scots rave over *Henri Christophe*," *Trinidad Guardian* (Friday 19 January 1962): 5 (summary of British Information Services report).

——. "Tonight: Walcott's *Henri Christophe*," *Trinidad Guardian* (Friday 26 April 1968): 6.

——. "Walcott's *Henri Christophe* to run for three nights," *Trinidad Guardian* (Thursday 11 April 1968): 6.

——. "West Indians Score Success with West Indian Play in London," *Port of Spain Gazette* (January 1952).

ANTOINE, Régis. "The Caribbean in Metropolitan French Writing," in ARNOLD, 349–62.

——. "Poéticité de la révolution haïtienne: Dessalines," in *La Deriva delle francofonie: Atti dei Seminari Annuali di Letterature Francofone: Figures et fantasmes de la violence dans les littératures francophones de l'Afrique subsaharienne et des Antilles*, vol. 2: *Les Antilles*, ed. Carla Fratta, M.R. Baldi & M. Mengoli (Bologna: Cooperativa Libreria Universitaria Editrice, 1992): 39–62.

————."Transe et régence dans *La Tragédie du roi Christophe*," in *Soleil Eclaté: Mélanges offerts à Aimé Césaire*, ed. Jacqueline Leiner (Tübingen: Gunter Narr, 1984): 13–26.

ARCINIEGAS, Germán. *Latin America: A Cultural History*, tr. Joan MacLean (*El continente de siete colores*, 1965; Borzoi Books; New York: Alfred A. Knopf, 1967).

ARMBRUSTER, Claudius, *Das Werk Alejo Carpentiers: Chronik der "Wunderbaren Wirklichkeit"* (Editionen der Iberoamericana III.7; Frankfurt am Main: Vervuert, 1982).

ARNOLD, A. James. "D'Haïti à l'Afrique: *La Tragédie du roi Christophe* de Césaire," *Revue de Littérature Comparée* 60.2 (April–June 1986): 133–48.

————, ed. *A History of Literature in the Caribbean*, vol. 1: *Hispanic and Francophone Regions* (Amsterdam/Philadelphia PA: John Benjamins, 1994).

BADER, Wolfgang. "Tradition et décolonisation: Fonction et image de la révolution haïtienne dans la littérature des Caraïbes après la seconde guerre mondiale," *Proceedings of the Xth Congress of the International Comparative Literature Association, New York 1982*, ed. Anna Balakian (New York: Garland, 1985): 234–39.

BECKLES, Hilary & Verene SHEPHERD, ed. *Caribbean Freedom: Economy and Society from Emancipation to the Present; A Student Reader* (Kingston: Ian Randle/London: James Currey, 1993).

————. *Caribbean Slave Society and Economy* (Kingston: Ian Randle/London: James Currey, 1991).

BEDFORD–JONES, Henry. *Drums of Dambala* (New York: Covici–Friede/London: J. Long, 1933).

BELL, Madison Smartt. *All Souls' Rising* (London: Granta, 1996).

BERGEAUD, Émeric. *Stella* (Paris: E. Dentu, 1859).

BEST, Lloyd. "Two Hundred Years After Bois Caiman: Freedom and Responsibility in the Caribbean," *Trinidad and Tobago Review* 13.7 (July 1991): 11–18.

BOGARD, Travis. *Contour in Time: The Plays of Eugene O'Neill* (1972; New York: Oxford UP, rev. ed. 1988).

BOURKE, Thomas E. "Toussaint L'Ouverture and the Black Revolution of St Domingue as Reflected in German Literature from Kleist to Buch," *History of European Ideas* 11 (1989): 121–30.

BREMER, Thomas. "Probleme des Theaters der Antillen: Césaire, Glissant, Macouba," *Französisch heute* 17.1 (1986): 202–14.

BRIERRE, Jean–Fernand. *Dessalines nous parle* (Collection du Sesquicentenaire de l'indépendance d'Haïti; Port-au-Prince: Deschamps, 1953).

————. *Le drapeau de demain: poème dramatique en deux actes* (Port-au-Prince: Imprimerie Valcin, 1931).

————. *Petión y Bolívar/Pétion et Bolivar* (1932) with *El Adiós a la Marsellesa/L'Adieu à la Marseillaise* (1934) (Buenos Aires: Ediciones Troquel, 1955); bilingual edition, French and Spanish.

BUCH, Hans Christoph. *Haïti Chérie* (Frankfurt am Main: Suhrkamp, 1990).

————. *Die Hochzeit von Port-au-Prince* (Frankfurt am Main: Suhrkamp, 1984).

CARPENTIER, Alejo. *El reino de este mundo* (Mexico City: Edición y Distribución Iberoamericana de Publicaciones, 1949). Tr. Harriet de Onís, as *The Kingdom of This World* (1957; London: Victor Gollancz, 1967).

CARTER, Steven R. *Hansberry's Drama: Commitment amid Complexity* (Urbana/Chicago: U of Illinois P, 1991).

CÉSAIRE, Aimé. *And the Dogs Were Silent* (*Et les chiens taisent*, 1946), in Césaire, *Lyric and Dramatic Poetry 1946–82*, tr. Clayton Eshleman & Annette Smith, intro. A. James Arnold (Charlottesville: UP of Virginia/CARAF BOOKS, 1990): 3–70.

————. *Cahier d'un retour au pays natal* (1939/1949; definitive edition 1956), in *The Collected Poetry* [bilingual edition], tr. Clayton Eshleman & Annette Smith (Berkeley: U of California P, 1983): 32–85.

————. *La Tragédie du roi Christophe: Théâtre* (1963; Paris: Présence Africaine, rev. ed. 1970).

CHANLATTE, Juste. *L'Entrée du roi en sa capitale en janvier 1818* (1818), repr. With intro. Roger Gaillard, *Le Nouveau Monde* (Port-au-Prince; 19 August 1979): 6–13.

CHAUVET, Marie Vieux. *La Danse sur le volcan* (Paris: Plon, 1957); tr. Salvator Attanasio as *Dance on the Volcano* (New York: Sloan, 1959).

CHENEY, Anne. *Lorraine Hansberry* (Boston: Twayne, 1984).

CLARK, Vèvè A. "Haiti's Tragic Overture: (Mis)Representations of the Haitian Revolution in World Drama (1796–1975)," in *Representing the French Revolution: Literature, Historiography, and Art*, ed. James A. Heffernan (Hanover NH: UP of New England/Dartmouth College, 1992): 237–60.

COBHAM, Rhonda. "The Background," in *West Indian Literature*, ed. Bruce King (London: Macmillan, 1979): 9–29; rev. ed. (Basingstoke: Macmillan Caribbean, 1995): 11–26.

COICOU, Massillon. *L'Empereur Dessalines: drame en deux actes, en vers* (Port-au-Prince: Imprimerie E. Chenet, 1906).

DADIE, Bernard Binlin. *Îles de tempête* (Paris: Présence Africaine, 1973).

DASH, J. Michael. *Edouard Glissant* (Cambridge Studies in African and Caribbean Literature; Cambridge: Cambridge UP, 1995).

DAUPHIN, Marcel. *Boisrond–Tonnerre: pièce en trois actes* (Port-au-Prince: Dorsinville, 1954).

DAYAN, Joan. "France Reads Haiti: An Interview with René Depestre," *Yale French Studies* 83 (1993): 140.

DE HEUSCH, Luc. "Kongo in Haiti: A New Approach to Religious Syncretism," in *Slavery and Beyond: The African Impact on Latin America and the Caribbean*, ed. Darién J. Davis (Jaguar Books on Latin America 5; Wilmington DE: SR Books, 1995): 103–19 (tr. Noal Mellott; originally published in *Man* 24.2 [1989]: 290–303).

DEREN, Maya. *Divine Horsemen: The Living Gods of Haiti*, intro. Joseph Campbell (1953; Kingston NY: McPherson, 1970).

DESMANGLES, Leslie G. *The Faces of the Gods: Voodoo and Roman Catholicism in Haiti* (Chapel Hill: U of North Carolina P, 1992).

DEPESTRE, René. *Un arc-en-ciel pour l'Occident chrétien: Poème-mystère vaudou* (Paris: Présence Africaine, 1967).

DOIN, Sophie. *La Famille noire* (Paris: Henry Servier, 1825).

DOUGLAS–SMITH, Aubrey. "*Henri Christophe: A Chronicle in Seven Scenes*" (a review of the Advocate Company edition), in *Bim* 3.12 (349–53): 349–53.

DUC, Gérard. *Les trésors du roi Christophe* (Port-au-Prince: Les Presses Libres, 1954).

DUPERLY, Dorothy. "University Drama: *Henri Christophe*," *Jamaica Times* (20 March 1954).

DURAND, Oswald. *Rires et pleurs* (1869, 1896), repr. Nendeln: Kraus Reprint, 1970.

DURAS, Claire, duchesse de Durfort. *Ourika*, ed. Claudine Hermann (Paris: Ladvocat, 1823; Paris: Editions des Femmes, 1979).

EASTON, William Edgar. *Christophe: A Tragedy in Prose of Imperial Haiti* (Los Angeles CA: Press Grafton, 1911).

——. *Dessalines: A Dramatic Tale; a single chapter from Haiti's history* (Galveston TX: J.W. Burson, 1893).

ENDORE, S. Guy. *Babouk* (New York: Vanguard, 1934).

ESPINET, Adrian. "*Drums and Colours* Seeks to Trace Evolution of West Indian Consciousness," *Sunday Guardian* (27 April 1958): 7.

ETHÉART, Liautaud. *La Fille de l'Empereur: drame historique en trois actes* [with: *Un duel sous Blanchelande*] (Paris: Moquet, 1860).

FAUBERT, Pierre. *Ogé ou Le préjugé de couleur: drame historique suivi de Poésies fugitives et de Notes* (Paris: C. Maillet–Schmitz, 1856).

FEHRENBACH, Robert J. "William Edgar Easton's *Dessalines*: A Nineteenth-Century Drama of Black Pride," *College Language Association Journal* 19 (1975): 75–89.

FERGUSON, J.A. "*Le Premier des noirs*: The Nineteenth-Century Image of Toussaint Louverture," *Nineteenth Century French Studies* 15.4 (Summer 1987): 394–406.

FICK, Carolyn E. *The Making of Haiti: The Saint Domingue Revolution from Below* (Knoxville: U of Tennessee P, 1990).

FONSECA, Maria Nazareth Soares. "Henri Christophe: Mito e Historia," *Cadernos de Linguistica e Teoria da Literatura* (Belo Horizonte) 7.14 (December 1985): 179–92.

FREEMAN, E. "From Raynal's *New Spartacus* to Lamartine's *Toussaint Louverture*: A Myth of the Black Soul in Rebellion," in *Myth and its Making in the French Theatre*, ed. E. Freeman, H. Mason, M. O'Regan & S.W. Taylor (Cambridge: Cambridge UP, 1988): 136–57.

FRESNAU, Mme Armand. *Theresa at Santo Domingo: A Tale of the Negro Insurrection*, tr. Emma Geiger Magrath (Chicago: McClurg, 1889).

GAILLARD, Robert. *La volupté et la haine* (Paris: Fleuve noir, 1971).

GEGGUS, David. "The Haitian Revolution," in BECKLES & SHEPHERD, ed. *Caribbean Slave Society and Economy*, 402–18.

GILLIAM, Edward Winslow. *1791: A Tale of San Domingo* (1890; Black Heritage Library; Freeport NY: Books for Libraries, 1972).

GLISSANT, Edouard. *Monsieur Toussaint*, tr. Joseph G. Foster & Barbara A. Franklin, intro. Juris Silenieks (1961; Washington DC: Three Continents, 1981).

GOUGES, Olympe de. *L'Esclavage des noirs, ou L'Heureux naufrage* (1789/1792; in *Œuvres*, ed. Benoîte Groult; Paris: Mercure de France, 1986).

GRIMARD, Luc. *Sur ma flûte de bambou: poèmes* (Paris: Nouvelle Revue Française, 1927).

GUILBAUD, Tertullien. *Patrie, espérance et souvenirs* (Paris: Léopold Cerf, 1885).

GUILLÉN, Nicolás. *Man-making Words: Selected poems of Nicolás Guillén*, tr. & intro. Robert Márquez & David Arthur McMurray (Amherst: U of Massachusetts P, 1972).

HAMNER, Robert D. *Derek Walcott* (Boston: Twayne, 1981).

——. "Mythological Aspects of Derek Walcott's Drama," *ARIEL: A Review of International English Literature* 8.3 (July 1977): 35–58.

——. "O'Neill, Walcott and Césaire on Christophe," *Journal of West Indian Literature* 5.1–2 (August 1992): 30–47.

HANSBERRY, Lorraine. *To Be Young, Gifted and Black: Lorraine Hansberry in Her Own Words*, adapt. Howard Nemiroff, intro. James Baldwin (1969; New York: New American Library, 1970).

——. "*Toussaint*: Excerpt from Act I of a Work in Progress," in *Nine Plays by Black Women*, ed. Margaret B. Wilkerson (New York: New American Library, 1986): 53–67.

HARRIS, Rodney E. "*Toussaint Louverture*: Paris, 1850," *Nineteenth Century French Studies* 5 (1977): 206–11.

HAUGBØLL, Charles. *Borger Toussaint: et spil i fire akter* (Copenhagen: Dansk Boghandlers Kommissionsanstalt, 1962).

HAWKINS, Hunt. "Aimé Césaire's Lesson About Decolonization in *La Tragédie du roi Christophe*," *College Language Association Journal* 30.2 (December 1986): 144–53.

HECKERT, Eleanor Louise. *The Little Saint of St. Domingue* (Garden City NY: Doubleday, 1973).

HICKEY, Bernard. "Wordsworth's Sonnet 'Toussaint L'Ouverture'," *Caribana* 2 (1991): 37–43.

HILL, Errol. "The Emergence of a National Drama in the West Indies," *Caribbean Quarterly* 18.4 (December 1972): 9–40.

HILL, Leslie Pinckney. *Toussaint L'Ouverture: A Dramatic History* (Boston MA: Christopher Publishing House, [1928]).

HOFFMANN, Léon–François. *Haiti: Lettres et l'être* (Toronto: GREF, 1992).

——. *Littérature d'Haïti* (Universités francophones: Histoire littéraire de la francophonie; Paris: EDICEF, 1995).

HOLDER, G[eoffrey].A. "B.B.C.'s Broadcast of *Henri Christophe*," *Bim* 4.14 (January–June 1951): 141–42.

HUGO, Victor. *Bug-Jargal* (1818; Paris: Canel, 1826), in *Œuvres complètes*, ed. Jean Massin (Paris: Club français du livre, 1967), vol. 2.1: 577–704. Tr. *The Slave-King* (Philadelphia PA: Carey, Lea & Blanchard, 1833).

HUNT, Alfred. *Haiti's Influence on Antebellum America: Slumbering Volcano in the Caribbean* (Baton Rouge: Louisiana State UP, 1988).

IOTTI, Gianni. "*Toussaint Louverture*: La tragedia e la storia," in *Lamartine, Napoli, l'Italia: Atti di Convegno, Napoli 1–3 ottobre '90*, ed. Georges Vallet (Naples: Guida Editore, 1992): 131–52.

JAMES, C.L.R. *The Black Jacobins*, in *A Time ... and a Season: Eight Caribbean Plays*, ed. Errol Hill (Trinidad & Tobago: Extra-Mural Department, University of the West Indies, 1976).

——. *The Black Jacobins*, in *The C.L.R. James Reader*, ed. & intro. Anna Grimshaw (Oxford: Basil Blackwell, 1992): 67–111.

——. *The Black Jacobins: Toussaint L'Ouverture and the San Domingo Revolution* (London: Secker & Warburg/ New York: Dial, 1938; rev. ed. with 1962 preface and appendix "From Toussaint L'Ouverture to Fidel Castro," New York: Random House, 1963 and London: Allison & Busby, 1980).

JEBODHSINGH, Jai. "The Writer as Historian: Poetic Truth or Factual Truth in *El reino de este mundo?*," in *History and Time in Caribbean Literature: Proceedings of the XI Conference on Spanish Caribbean Literature, April 1988*, ed. Claudette Williams (Mona, Kingston: Institute of Caribbean Studies, University of the West Indies, 1992): 32–42.

JENKIN, Veronica. "*Drums and Colours*," *Bim* 7.27 (July–December 1958): 183–84.

JOATTON, Charles. "L'auteur dramatique: Les avatars du texte de *Toussaint Louverture*," in *Centenaire de la mort d'Alphonse de Lamartine* (Macon: Comité permanent d'études lamartiniennes, 1973): 127–35.

JONES, Bridget. "Theatre in the French West Indies," *Carib No. 4: Caribbean Theatre*, ed. Edward Baugh & Mervyn Morris (Kingston, Jamaica: West Indian Association for Commonwealth Literature and Language Studies, 1986): 35–54.

JONES, Brunell. "Walcott's Play: A Success at Festival," *Evening News* (Port of Spain; 3 May 1968).

KADISH, Doris Y. "The Black Terror: Women's Responses to Slave Revolts in Haiti," *French Review* 68.4 (March 1995): 668–80.

KAPPELER, Sima. "Historical Visions: Anna Seghers on the Revolution in Haiti," in *Insiders and Outsiders: Jewish and Gentile Culture in Germany and Austria*, ed. Gabriele Weinberger & Dagmar C.G. Lorenz (Detroit MI: Wayne State UP, 1994): 66–72.

KESTELOOT, Lilyan. "*La Tragédie du roi Christophe* ou Les indépendances africaines au miroir d'Haïti," *Présence Africaine* 51 (1964): 131–45.

KING, Bruce. *Derek Walcott and West Indian Drama: "Not Only a Playwright But a Company"; The Trinidad Theatre Workshop 1959–1993* (Oxford: Clarendon, 1995).

KLEIST, Heinrich von. "Die Verlobung in St. Domingo" (1811), in Kleist, *Sämtliche Werke und Briefe*, vol. 3: *Erzählungen, Anekdoten, Gedichte, Schriften*, ed. Klaus Müller–Salger (Bibliothek deutscher Klassiker 51; Frankfurt am Main: Deutscher Klassiker Verlag, 1990): 222–60.

KÖRNER, Karl Theodor. *Toni: Ein Drama in drei Aufzügen* (1812), in Körner, *Werke*, ed. Hans Zimmer (Meyers Klassiker-Ausgaben; Leipzig/Vienna: Bibliographisches Institut, 2 vols., 1916), vol. 2: 9–52.

LACERTE, Robert. "The Evolution of Land and Labour in the Haitian Revolution 1791–1820," in BECKLES & SHEPHERD, ed. *Caribbean Freedom*, 42–47 (originally published in *The Americas* 34.4 [Washington DC: Academy of American Franciscan History]: 449–59).

LAFORGUE, Pierre. "*Bug-Jargal* ou De la difficulté d'écrire en « style blanc »," *Romantisme* 69.3 (1990): 29–42.

LAMARTINE, Alphonse de. *Toussaint Louverture* (1850), in *Œuvres poétiques complètes*, ed. Marius–François Guyard (Bibliothèque de la Pléiade 165; Paris: Gallimard, 1965): 1259–1401.

LAROCHE, Maximilien. "*La Tragédie du roi Christophe* du point de vue de l'histoire d'Haïti," *Etudes Littéraires* 6.1 (April 1973): 35–47.

LECONTE, Vergniaud. *El Rey Cristóbal*, intro. & tr. José Villalba Pinyana (*Le roi Christophe*, 1901; Mexico City: Barrios, 1954).

LEYBURN, James G. *The Haitian People*, intro. Sidney W. Mintz (Caribbean Series 9; 1941; New Haven CT: Yale UP, rev. 1966).

LEWIS, Gordon K. *Main Currents in Caribbean Thought: The Historical Evolution of Caribbean Society in Its Ideological Aspects, 1492–1900* (Baltimore MD/London: Johns Hopkins UP, 1983)

LOVELACE, Earl. "*Christophe*: Image Packed Essay Mouthed By Actors," *Express* (Port of Spain; 30 April 1968): 12.

LOWHAR, Syl. "Another Station of the Cross," *Tapia* 23 (26 December 1971): 19.

——. "Drums and Colours: Review of *Pieces Two*," *Tapia* 3.18 (Sunday, 6 May 1973): 9–10.

LUBIN, J. Dieudonné. *Héros et héroïnes de la liberté d'Haïti et du monde: sonnets* (Collection du Tri-Cinquantenaire; Port-au-Prince: Imprimerie de l'Etat, 1953).

LÜSEBRINK, Hans–Jürgen. "Mise en fiction et conceptualisation de la révolution haïtienne: La génèse d'un discours littéraire (1789–1848)," in *Proceedings of the Xth Congress of the International Comparative Literature Association, New York 1982*, ed. Anna Balakian (New York: Garland, 1985): 228–33.

LUNDAHL, Mats. "Toussaint L'Ouverture and the War Economy of Saint-Dominigue [sic] 1796–1802," in BECKLES & SHEPHERD, ed. *Caribbean Freedom*, 2–11 (originally published in *Slavery and Abolition* 6.2).

MARTINEAU, Harriet. *The Hour and the Man: An Historical Romance* (New York: Harper/London: E. Moxon, 1841).

MERCIER, Roger. "Lamartine et le problème noir dans *Toussaint Louverture*," in *Centenaire de la mort d'Alphonse de Lamartine* (Macon: Comité permanent d'études lamartiniennes, 1973): 173–81.

MÉTRAUX, Alfred. *Voodoo in Haiti*, tr. Hugo Charteris, intro. Sidney W. Mintz (*Le vaudou haïtien*, Paris 1958; tr. 1959; New York: Schocken, 1972).

MILNER, Harry. "*Henri Christophe*: 'Courageous Effort' by University Players," *Daily Gleaner* (15 March 1954).

MORAVIA, Charles. *La Crête-à-Pierrot: poème dramatique en trois tableaux et en vers* (Port-au-Prince: Imprimerie J. Verrollot, 1908).

——. *Roses et camélias: poésies* (Port-au-Prince: Imprimerie Madame F. Smith, 1903).

MORISSEAU–LEROY, Félix. *Diakout 1, 2, 3 ak twa lòt poèm* (republ. *Diacoute 1*, Port-au-Prince: Deschamps/ Culture, 1953: Miami: Jaden Kreyòl, 1983).

MOURALIS, Bernard. "Histoire et culture dans *Bug-Jargal*," *Revue des Sciences Humaines* (January–March 1973): 47–68.

——. "L'image de l'indépendance haïtienne dans la littérature négro-africaine," *Revue de Littérature Comparée* 48.4 (1974): 504–35.

MÜLLER, Heiner. *Der Auftrag/Quartett: Zwei Stücke* (Frankfurt am Main: Verlag der Autoren, 1988).

N., E. "*Henri Christophe* to be staged by UCWI," *Daily Gleaner* (Thursday, 11 March 1954): 4.

NICHOLLS, David. *From Dessalines to Duvalier: Race, Colour and National Independence in Haiti* (1979; Warwick University Caribbean Studies; Basingstoke: Macmillan Caribbean, 1988).

ODDOM, Marcel. "Les tragédies de la décolonisation: Aimé Césaire et Edouard Glissant," in *Le théâtre moderne*, vol. 2: *Depuis la deuxième guerre mondiale*, ed. Jean Jacquot (Paris: CNRS, 1967): 85–101.

O'NEILL, Eugene. *The Emperor Jones*, in *Complete Plays 1913–1920*, sel. Travis Bogard (New York: Library of America, 1988): 1029–61.

PAGET, Hugh. "A West Indian Play," *West Indian Committee Circular* (February 1952): 38.

PÉREZ, Jeanne. *Sainite Belair: drame historique en trois tableaux* (Pétionville: La Semeuse, [1942]).

PETERS, Erskine. "The Theme of Madness in the Plays of Derek Walcott," *College Language Association Journal* 32.2 (December 1988): 148–69.

PETERSEN, Vibeke Rutzou. "Revolution or Colonization: Anna Seghers's *Drei Frauen aus Haiti*," *German Quarterly* 65.3–4 (Summer–Fall 1992): 396–406.

PLACOLY, Vincent. *Dessalines ou La passion de l'inépendance* (Havana: Casa de las Américas, 1983).

PLANHAL, René de. "La Première de *Toussaint Louverture*," *Minerve Française* 5 (1 April 1920): 37–51.

PRADEL, Pompilus. "Notre Victor Hugo," *Conjonction* 166 (June 1985): 7–20.

RAMCHARITAR, Raymond. "A Change of Form; Invocation of Immediacy," *Trinidad and Tobago Review* (May 1993): 23–24.

RANALD, Margaret Loftus. *The Eugene O'Neill Companion* (Westport CT: Greenwood, 1984).

RÉMUSAT, Charles François Marie, comte de. *L'habitation de Saint Domingue ou l'insurrection*, ed. Jean René Derré (Paris: CNRS, 1978).

RODRÍGUEZ MONEGAL, Emir. "Lo real y la maravilloso en *El reino de este mundo*," *Revista Iberoamericana* 76–77 (1971): 619–49; repr. in *Asedios a Carpentier: once ensayos críticos sobre el novelista cubano*, ed. Klaus Müller–Bergh (Santiago de Chile: Editorial Universitaria/Cormoran, 1972): 101–33.

ROUMER, Emile. *Poèmes d'Haïti et de France* (Collection haïtienne d'expression française, ed. Louis Morpeau; Paris: Editions de la Revue mondiale, 1925).

SAINT–LAMBERT, Jean. *Ziméo* (1769), in *Œuvres complètes* (Clermont: Laudriot, 1814).

SAMUEL, Kennedy. "The Vision and the Reality," *Weekend Voice* (St Lucia), 18 August 1984: 12.

SANDER, Reinhard W. "C.L.R. James and the Haitian Revolution," *World Literature Written in English* 26.2 (1986): 277–90.

SEGHERS, Anna. *Drei Frauen aus Haiti: Drei Erzählungen* (Munich: Luchterhand, 1980).

——. *Karibische Geschichten* (Berlin: Aufbau-Verlag, 1962).

SHAKESPEARE, William. *The Complete Works*, gen. ed. Alfred Harbage (The Complete Pelican Shakespeare; New York: Viking, 1969).

SILENIEKS, Juris. "Deux pièces antillaises: Du témoignage local vers une tragédie moderne," *Kentucky Romance Quarterly* 15.3 (1968): 245–54.

——. "Toward *créolité*: Postnegritude Developments," in ARNOLD, 517–25.

SMART, Winston. "There Were More Faults Than Virtues," *Trinidad Guardian* (14 May 1968): 6.

SPERATTI–PIÑERO, Emma Susana. "Creencias afro-antillanas en *El reino de este mundo* de Alejo Carpentier," *Nueva Revista de Filología Hispánica* (Mexico City) 29.2 (1980): 574–96.

STONE, Judy S.J. *Theatre* (Studies in West Indian Literature, ed. Kenneth Ramchand; Basingstoke: Macmillan Caribbean, 1994).

SWANN, Tony. "Federal Arts Festival: *Drums and Colours*: Guts at Least," *Public Opinion* (Kingston; 10 May 1958): 7.

SWANZY, Henry. "*Henri Christophe*," *Public Opinion* (Kingston; Saturday, 29 March 1952): 6.

SYDNEY–SMITH, Agnes. "*Henri Christophe*: Poet Walcott's first major play on Haitian revolution," *Sunday Guardian* (21 April 1968, Trinidad and Tobago Festival Supplement): 3; also published under the same headline on the same day in the Port of Spain *Evening News*.

TAYLOR, Patrick. *The Narrative of Liberation: Perspectives on Afro-Caribbean Literature, Popular Culture, and Politics* (Ithaca NY: Cornell UP, 1989).

VIEUX, Isnardin. *Mackendal: drame en trois actes* (Port-au-Prince: Imprimerie V. Pierre–Noël, 1925).

WALCOTT, Derek. "Drums and Colours: An Epic Drama Commissioned for the Opening of the First Federal Parliament of The West Indies, April 23rd 1958," *Caribbean Quarterly* 38.4 (special issue: "*Caribbean Quarterly*'s Derek Walcott"; December, 1992): 22–135. First published as the *Caribbean Quarterly* Special Issue 7.1–2 (March–June 1961): 1–105.

——. *Henri Christophe: A Chronicle in Seven Scenes* ([Bridgetown,] Barbados: Advocate Company, 1950).

——. *Henri Christophe: A Chronicle in Seven Scenes* (Caribbean Plays, ed. Errol Hill; Mona, Kingston: Extra-Mural Department, University of the West Indies, mimeograph, nd).

——. "Schools Drama Festival," *Public Opinion* (6 April, 1957): 6.

——. "Walcott on Walcott," interviewed by Dennis Scott, originally published in *Caribbean Quarterly* 14.1–2 (special issue "The Arts," March–June 1968): 77–82; reprinted in *Caribbean Quarterly* 38.4 (special issue: "*Caribbean Quarterly*'s Derek Walcott"; December, 1992): 136–41.

——. "What the Twilight Says: An Overture," in Walcott, *"Dream On Monkey Mountain" and Other Plays* (1970; London: Jonathan Cape, 1972): 3–40.

WALKE, Olive. "*Henri Christophe*: Successful Production," *Port of Spain Gazette* (30 November 1954).

WARNER, Keith Q. "De l'écrivain devenu leader politique: à la recherche d'un héros antillais," in *Soleil Eclaté: Mélanges offerts à Aimé Césaire*, ed. Jacqueline Leiner (Tübingen: Gunter Narr, 1984): 421–31.

WAXMAN, Percy. *The Black Napoleon: The Story of Toussaint Louverture* (New York: Harcourt, Brace, 1931).

WEBB, Barbara J. *Myth and History in Caribbean Fiction: Alejo Carpentier, Wilson Harris, and Edouard Glissant* (Amherst: U of Massachusetts P, 1992).

WERLEIGH, Christian. *Le psalmiste dans l'ouragon: poèmes* (Cap-Haïtien: Imprimerie du Séminaire, 1933).

WICHMANN BAILEY, Marianne. *The Ritual Theater of Aimé Césaire: Mythic Structures of the Dramatic Imagination* (études littéraires françaises 49; Tübingen: Gunter Narr, 1992).

WORDSWORTH, William. *The Poems*, ed. John O. Hayden (Penguin English Poets; Harmondsworth: Penguin, 2 vols., 1977).

WYLIE, Hal. "Henri Christophe: King of Haiti," in *Crisscrossing Boundaries in African Literatures*, ed. Kenneth Harrow, Jonathan Ngate & Clarisse Zimra (Annual Selected Papers of the African Literature Association; Washington DC: Three Continents, 1991): 99–108.

❧ ❖ ❧

CONTRIBUTORS

CHRISTOPHER BALME is Professor of Theatre Studies at the University of Munich. He has published widely on various aspects of theatre theory and history. He has just published a book-length study on post-colonial drama and theatre, *Das Theater im postkolonialen Zeitalter* (1995).

PETRONELLA BREINBURG is a Senior Lecturer at the University of London. Her main area of interest is linguistics (particularly Caribbean).

THOMAS BRÜCKNER, a specialist in anglophone literature in Africa, works freelance and has held teaching positions at the Universities of Leipzig and Essen.

GORDON COLLIER is Co-General Editor of the series *Cross/Cultures: Readings in the Post/ Colonial Literatures in English*, and Caribbean editor of the journal *Matatu*. He teaches the New Literatures in English and post-colonial cultural studies at Justus Liebig University, Giessen. He has edited *US/THEM: Translation, Transcription and Identity in Post-Colonial Literary Cultures*, and is the author of *The Rocks and Sticks of Words: Style, Discourse and Narrative Structure in the Fiction of Patrick White* as well as of articles on West Indian poetry and on contemporary Australian and New Zealand film and fiction. He is currently completing a study of Jane Campion, as well as editions of the occasional journalism of Derek Walcott and the selected prose of John Figueroa.

AFUA COOPER has long been active in the performing and literary arts. She was born in Jamaica and emigrated to Canada in the early Eighties, obtaining academic degrees at the University of Toronto. She is the author of two books of poetry, *Breaking Chains* and *Memories Have Tongue* and a collection of children's poetry, *Red Caterpillar on College Street*, and has been widely anthologised. Her readings are recorded in such audio-collections as *Woman Talk* and *Poetry Is Not A Luxury*.

TOBIAS DÖRING has an M.A. in Modern Literature from the University of Kent; he read English, German and Philosophy at the Free University, Berlin, where he now teaches anglophone literatures and is working on a doctorate in post-colonial studies. He has published articles, interviews and reviews on Matura, Soyinka, Dabydeen, Randhawa, Warner, Morrissey and Kureishi; a book-length study on Chinua Achebe's rewriting of Joyce Cary's fiction is forthcoming.

JOHN J. FIGUEROA, as a specialist in education and cultural policy, has held professorships at the Universities of the West Indies – the first Jamaican to occupy a chair there – Jos (Nigeria), and Puerto Rico, and has taught at other universities including Indiana, Moscow, Washington and Makerere. He has been President of PEN (Jamaica), and is an Honorary Fellow of the Centre for Caribbean Studies (Warwick University) and a foundation member of ACLALS (the Association for the Study of Language and Literature in the Commonwealth), the Caribbean Studies Association, and the Association for the Study of Caribbean Language. He has published several volumes of poetry, including *Love Leaps Here* (1962), *Ignoring Hurts* (1976) and *The Chase: A Collection of Poems 1941–1989* (1991). The first General Editor of Heinemann's Caribbean Writers Series, he has edited a number of anthologies, among them *Caribbean Voices* (2 volumes, 1966–70) and *An Anthology of African and Caribbean Writing in English* (1982). His *West Indies in England* (1991) reflects his long-standing interest in cricket, and his expertise in educational theory and practice is demonstrated in *Society, Schools and Progress in the West Indies* (1971). Figueroa produced *West Indian Poets Reading Their Own Work*, one of the first sound-recordings of Caribbean literature (Caedmon), and co-produced, with Ed Milner, the Open University/BBC film *St Lucia: Peoples and Celebrations* (1982). He has also co-written, with David Sutcliffe, *System in Black English* (1992).

WALTER GÖBEL is an Assistant Professor at the University of Stuttgart. He has published books on Sherwood Anderson and Edward Bulwer–Lytton and articles on the African–American novel, on literary and cultural theory and on eighteenth-century English literature, focusing on the literature of sensibility. He is currently working on Laurence Sterne and the Enlightenment.

DETLEV GOHRBANDT teaches English and the New Literatures in English at the University of the Saarland, Saarbrücken. He has recently completed a research project on reading ("Textanlässe, Lesetätigkeiten," forthcoming) and has published numerous articles on teaching language and literature, with special reference to questions of genre and intercultural communication. His current research is focused on the construction of moral judgement in narrative texts.

HEIKE HÄRTING lives and works in Berlin, and is at present engaged in a feminist research project at the University of Victoria, British Columbia..

WOLFGANG HOCHBRÜCK is Assistant Professor of North American Studies, University of Stuttgart. He has published on American, Canadian and Native American Studies. His present research focuses on the cultural reproduction and memory of war.

ARMANDO E. JANNETTA is a specialist librarian in English Studies at the University of Berne.

MARGARET KEULEN studied English and American Literature, linguistics, and art history at the Rheinisch-Westfälische Technische Hochschule Aachen and completed her M.A. in 1989. She has written a study of feminist science fiction (*Radical Vision: Feminist Conceptions of the Future in LeGuin, Piercy, and Gearheart*, 1991). Since 1992 she has been a member of the English Department of the Carl von Ossietzky University, Oldenburg. Currently she is completing a doctorate on contemporary African–American women writers.

KARIN KILB studied English and French at the Universities of Frankfurt and Rennes. Since completing her state examinations in 1994, she is training to be a school teacher.

ROMAN KURTZ taught until recently in the English Department of Cologne University.

SHIRLEY GEOK-LIN LIM, winner of the Commonwealth Poetry Prize in 1980, has published four collections of poetry, two books of short stories and two critical studies, *Nationalism and Literature* (1993) and *Writing South/East Asia in English* (1994), and has co-edited four books, one of which, *The Forbidden Stitch*, won the 1990 American Book Award. Her book of memoirs, *Among the White Moon Faces: An Asian American Memoir of Homelands*, is forthcoming with Feminist Press, New York. She is currently Professor of English and Women's Studies at the University of California, Santa Barbara.

SÄMI LUDWIG (University of Berne, Switzerland) is currently employed by the Swiss National Science Foundation to do research on the issue of representation in American literary realism. He has published on Henry James in *Mosaic* and on Ishmael Reed. His book-length study, "Concrete Language: Intercultural Communication in Maxine Hong Kingston's *The Woman Warrior* and Ishmael Reed's *Mumbo Jumbo*," is forthcoming.

BERNHARD MELCHIOR studied at the Universities of Mainz, Harvard, and Bamberg, where he recently earned a doctorate in English and American Literature; he has also taught at the University of Michigan, Ann Arbor. His 1989 M.A. thesis dealt with "Black History and Folklore in Toni Morrison's *Beloved*," and his doctoral dissertation is entitled "'Re/Visiting' the

Self Away From Home: Autobiographical and Cross-Cultural Dimensions in the Works of Paule Marshall."

BERND OSTENDORF is Professor of North American Cultural History in the Amerika Institut, Munich and author of: *Black Literature in White America* 1983; *Ghettoliterature: Zur Litertatur ethnischer, marginaler und unterdrückter Gruppen in Amerika* (1982); *Die Vereinigten Staaten von Amerika* (1992); and *Die multikulturelle Gesellschaft: Model Amerika?* (1994). Current projects include: "'A Perfect Death': Jazz Funerals in New Orleans," "Kunst, Kommerz und bürgerliche Republik: Die Amerikanische Kultur; Kontexte, Spannungen und Widersprüche," and "The Politics of Difference: Theories and Practice in a Comparative U.S.–German Perspective," forthcoming in *Multiculturalism in Transit: A German-American Exchange*, ed. Dieter Dettke, Jeffrey Peck, and Klaus Milich.

UWE SCHÄFER obtained his degree in English Literature from the Free University Berlin and is currently writing a doctorate on the novels of Wilson Harris and Bessie Head. He has published on corpus linguistics and post-colonial literatures.

FRANK SCHULZE-ENGLER studied History and English at the Universities of Freiburg and Frankfurt, and currently teaches the New Literatures in English at Frankfurt University. His chief research interests are sub-Saharan African literature and post-colonial literary theory, on which he has published extensively. He is the author of *Intellektuelle wider Willen* [Reluctant Intellectuals], a study of East African literature and society 1960–89 (1992), and has co-edited, with Dieter Riemenschneider, *African Literatures in the Eighties* (*Matatu* 10, 1993).

WERNER SEDLAK teaches in the English Department of Munich University. He has published on Shakespeare and various aspects of nineteenth- and twentieth-century British literature and culture. More recent research interests include multiculturalism and the new English literatures, with emphasis on Africa and cross-Atlantic relations.

BODE SOWANDE's first publications were in the mid-Sixties. From 1968 to 1971 he was the author of plays for Soyinka's drama group Orisun Theatre. In 1972 he formed his own group, ODU Themes, and in 1977 earned a doctorate in Dramatic Literature from the University of Sheffield, England. In 1987 he won the Drama Award of the Association of Nigerian Authors. Of his many performed plays, *Farewell to Babylon* (1979) and *Tornadoes Full of Dreams* (1989) are at present in print, along with *Flamingo and other plays*. Sowande is also a novelist (*Our Man the President*, 1981; *Without a Home*, 1986; *The Missing Bridesmaid*, 1988). He has been the General Secretary of the Association of Nigerian Authors, and is a Senior Lecturer in Theatre Practice and Dramatic Literature, Department of Theatre Arts, University of Ibadan, Ibadan, Nigeria.

MARK STEIN has studied in Frankfurt, Oxford and Warwick. In 1994 he received his M.A. in Colonial and Post-Colonial Literatures in English from the University of Warwick for his thesis on Dambudzo Marechera's early prose, and is currently a postgraduate student in Frankfurt. He has published an essay entitled "The Perception of Landscape and Architecture in V.S. Naipaul's *The Enigma of Arrival* and David Dabydeen's *Disappearance*."

PETER O. STUMMER is a senior lecturer in the English Department of the University of Munich, and is active there in the postgraduate programme on English-speaking countries. He has taught at the universities of Aberdeen, Cologne, Trento and Passau, and has published widely on contemporary English literature, political discourse, and African, Australian and Indian literature in English. He edited *The Story Must be Told: Short Narrative Prose in the New English Literatures* (1986) and co-edited the two-volume collection *Die industrielle Revolution in England: Literarische Texte und ihre Kontexte* (1991).

JOSEPH SWANN teaches at the University of Wuppertal, and has publishes extensively on African, Indian, Australian and New Zealand literature, with a special focus on poetry.

CAROLA TORTI studied at Frankfurt University and Trinity College Dublin. She received her M.A. in English philology in 1995 in the field of New English Literature, and is currently working as a journalist.

FLORA VEIT-WILD is professor of African literature at the Humboldt University, Berlin. She has published extensively on Zimbabwean literature, including the socioliterary history, *Teachers, Preachers, Non-Believers* (1992), the posthumous works of Dambudzo Marechera, and the documentary biography *Dambudzo Marerechera: A Source Book on his Life and Work* (1992).

DAVID WOODS is a powerful voice from the Canadian Black community. In Nova Scotia he is well-known for his work in theatre, writing, and art. He was born in Trinidad and emigrated to Canada at the age of twelve. Since the late Seventies he has been active in organisations such as Black Youth Organisation, Black United Front, and Black Cultural Centre. He paints, writes for radio and television, and acts on stage and in film. He is the author of the poetry collection *Native Song*, which also contains eight of his paintings.

Cross Cultures
Readings in the Post/Colonial
Literatures in English
Series Editors:
Gordon Collier, Hena Maes-Jelinek, Geoffrey Davis

Laurence's *The Stone Angel* and *The Diviners*. Amsterdam/Atlanta, GA 1994. 212 pp.

Vol. 14: ISBN: 90-5183-616-3   Hfl. 48,-/US-$ 32.-
BERNTH LINDFORS: Comparative Approaches to African Literatures.Amsterdam/Atlanta,GA 1994.160pp.
Vol. 15: ISBN: 90-5183-723-2   Hfl. 55,-/US-$ 36.50
PETER HORN: Writing my Reading. Essays on Literary Politics in South Africa. Amsterdam/Atlanta, GA 1994. XI,172 pp.
Vol. 16: ISBN: 90-5183-742-9   Bound Hfl. 160,-/US-$ 107.-
ISBN: 90-5183-765-8   Paper Hfl. 50,-/US-$ 33.-
READING RUSHDIE. PERSPECTIVES ON THE FICTION OF SALMAN RUSHDIE. Ed. by M.D. Fletcher. Amsterdam/Atlanta, GA 1994. 400 pp.
Vol. 17: ISBN: 90-5183-731-3   Hfl. 120,-/US-$ 80.-
CHRISTIANE FIOUPOU: La Route. Réalité et représentation dans l'œuvre de Wole Soyinka. Amsterdam/Atlanta, GA 1994. 390 pp.
Vol. 18: ISBN: 90-5183-814-X   Hfl. 75,-/US-$ 46.50
DAVID FAUSETT: Images of the Antipodes in the Eighteenth Century. A Study in Stereotyping. Amsterdam/Atlanta, GA 1995. VIII,231 pp.
Vol. 19: ISBN: 90-5183-879-4   Bound Hfl. 140,-/US-$ 93,-
ISBN: 90-5183-863-8   Paper Hfl. 45,-/US-$ 30.-
THE GUISES OF CANADIAN DIVERSITY / LES MASQUES DE LA DIVERSITÉ CANADIENNE. New European Perspectives/Nouvelles perspectives européennes. Ed. by Serge Jaumain & Marc Maufort
Amsterdam/Atlanta, GA 1995. 288 pp.
Vol. 20: ISBN: 90-5183-964-2   Bound Hfl. 250,-/US-$ 165.-
ISBN: 90-5183-953-7   Paper Hfl. 55,-/US-$ 36.50
A TALENT(ED) DIGGER. Creations, Cameos, and Essays in honour of Anna Rutherford. Ed. by Hena Maes-Jelinek, Gordon Collier, Geoffrey V. Davis. Amsterdam/Atlanta, GA 1996. XIX,519 pp.
Vol. 21: ISBN: 90-5183-972-3   Hfl. 60,-/US-$ 40.-
ALBERT GÉRARD: Afrique plurielle. Études de littérature comparée. Amsterdam/Atlanta, GA 1996. 199 pp.
Vol. 22: ISBN: 90-5183-984-7   Bound Hfl. 175,-/US-$ 116.50
ISBN: 90-5183-967-7   Paper Hfl. 45,-/US-$ 30.-
"AND THE BIRDS BEGAN TO SING". Religion and Literature in Post-Colonial Cultures. Ed. by Jamie S. Scott. Amsterdam/Atlanta, GA 1996. XXVII,327 pp.
Vol. 23: ISBN: 90-420-0021-X   Bound Hfl. 150,-/US-$ 100.-
ISBN: 90-420-0013-9   Paper Hfl. 45,-/US-$ 30,-
DEFINING NEW IDIOMS AND ALTERNATIVE FORMS OF EXPRESSION. Ed. by Eckhard Breitinger. Asnel Papers 1
Amsterdam/Atlanta, GA 1996. XXVI,282 pp.

ETHIK UND POLITIK AUS INTERKULTURELLER SICHT

Hrsg. von R.A. Mall und Notker Schneider

Amsterdam/Atlanta, GA 1996. 327 pp.
(Studien zur Interkulturellen Philosophie 5)
ISBN: 90-420-0012-0   Bound Hfl. 160,-/US-$ 107.-
ISBN: 90-420-0003-1   Paper Hfl. 45,-/US-$ 30.-

Inhalt: R.A. MALL: Was heißt 'aus interkultureller Sicht'? Ryosuke OHASHI: Die Zeit der Weltbilder. Wilhelm HALBFASS: Beobachtungen zur Grundlegung einer interkulturellen Ethik. Franz Martin WIMMER: Polylog der Traditionen im philosophischen Denken. Dieter SENGHAAS: Interkulturelle Philosopie angesichts der Fundamentalpolitisierung der Welt. Bernhard WALDENFELS: Der Andere und der Dritte in interkultureller Sicht. Ernst Wolfgang ORTH: Universalität und Individualität der Kultur. Hans Rainer SEPP: Werte und Variabilität. Denkt Scheler über den Gegensatz von Relativismus und Universalismus hinaus? Önay SÖZER: Kultur als Inszenierung. Andreas CESANA: Kulturelle Identität, Inkommensurabilität und Kommunikation. Morteza GHASEMPOUR: Zarathustras Konzeption einer elementaren Ethik und Nietzsches Zarathustra-Rezeption. Yihong MAO: Sein, Wert, Erfahrung des Lebens. Das Verhältnis zwischen Mensch und Natur aus der Sicht des Daoismus. Byung-Chul HAN: Liebe, Gerechtigkeit und Gesetz. Ein interkultureller Streifzug. You-Zheng LI: Ethics and the Present World-Context. Gregor PAUL: Grundprobleme idealistischer und neokonfuzianischer (*Li xue*) Philosophie. Die Ontologisierung der Ethik, Tradition, Moderne und Humanität. Rafael Angel HERRA: Rassismus und Selbstbetrug. Douwe TIEMERSMA: Über ethnisch-narrative und ethische Identität (Senghor und Ricœur). Bina GUPTA: Status and Gender-Ascribed Stereotypes: A Bi-Cultural Comparison. John ERPENBECK: Interkulturalität, sozialer und individueller Wertewandel. Ole DÖRING: Gedanken zur Interkulturellen Philosophie aus praktischer Perspektive. Angela Ales BELLO: Religiosität aus interkultureller Sicht. Heinz KIMMERLE: Das Problem des Todes aus interkultureller Sicht. Frank VIELLART: Phénoménologie et "Non-Dualité". Notker SCHNEIDER: Interkulturalität und Toleranz im Ausgang von John Locke.

USA/Canada: Editions Rodopi B.V., 2015 South Park Place, Atlanta, GA 30339, Tel. (770) 933-0027, *Call toll-free* (U.S. only) 1-800-225- 3998, Fax (770) 933-9644, *E-mail:* F.van.der.Zee@rodopi.nl
All Other Countries: Editions Rodopi B.V., Keizersgracht 302-304, 1016 EX Amsterdam, The Netherlands. Tel. + + 31 (0)20-622-75-07, Fax + + 31 (0)20-638-09-48, *E-mail:* F.van.der.Zee@rodopi.nl

WRITING THE NATION
SELF AND COUNTRY
IN THE POST-COLONIAL IMAGINATION

Ed. by John C. Hawley

Amsterdam/Atlanta, GA 1996. XXVII,217 pp.
(Critical Studies 7)

ISBN: 90-5183-938-3   Bound Hfl. 125,-/US-$ 83.-
ISBN: 90-5183-936-7   Paper Hfl. 40,-/US-$ 27.-

The fourteen essays in this volume contribute significantly to a consideration of the interplay between nation and narration that currently dominates
both literary and cultural studies. With the fervent reassertion of tribal
domains throughout the world, and with the consequent threat to the
stability of a common discourse in putative countries once mapped and
subsequently dominated by colonizing powers, the need for such studies
becomes increasingly obvious. Whose idea of a nation is to prevail
throughout these "postcolonial" territories; whose claims to speak for a
people are to be legitimized by international agreement; amid the demands
of patriotic rhetoric, what role may be allowed for individual expression
that attempts to transcend the immediate political agenda; who may assume
positions of authority in defining an ethnic paradigm — such are the
questions variously addressed in this volume.

The essayists who here contribute to the discussion are students of the
various national literatures that are now becoming more generally available
in the West. The range of topics is broad — moving globally from the
Caribbean and South America, through the African continent, and on to the
Indian subcontinent, and moving temporally through the nineteenth century
and into the closing days of our twentieth. We deal with poetry, fiction,
and theoretical writings, and have two types of reader in mind: We hope to
introduce the uninitiated to the breadth of this expanding field, and we
hope to aid those with a specialized knowledge of one or other of these
literatures in their consideration of the extent to which post-colonial writing
may or may not form a reasonably unified field. We seek to avoid the new
form of colonialism that might impose a theoretical template to these quite
divergent writings, falsely rendering it all accessible and familiar. At the
same time, we do note questions and concerns that cross borders, whether
these imagined lines are spatial, temporal, gendered or racial.

USA/Canada: Editions Rodopi B.V., 2015 South Park Place, Atlanta, GA
30339, Tel. (770) 933-0027, *Call toll-free* (U.S. only) 1-800-225- 3998,
Fax (770) 933-9644, *E-mail:* F.van.der.Zee@rodopi.nl

All Other Countries: Editions Rodopi B.V., Keizersgracht 302-304, 1016 EX
Amsterdam, The Netherlands. Tel. + + 31 (0)20-622-75-07, Fax + + 31
(0)20-638-09-48, *E-mail:* F.van.der.Zee@rodopi.nl

DIFFERENCE AND COMMUNITY
Canadian and European Cultural Perspectives

Ed. by Peter Easingwood, Konrad Gross, Lynette Hunter

Amsterdam/Atlanta, GA 1996. XIII,267 pp.
(Cross/Cultures 25)

ISBN: 90-420-0046-5   Bound Hfl. 140,-/US-$ 93.-
ISBN: 90-420-0050-3   Paper Hfl. 40,-/US-$ 27.-

This volume brings together essays which suggest that the relationship between Canada and Europe is a two-way process, as historically the traffic between them has been: either may have something to offer the other. Europe too acknowledges situations today in which "difference" and "community" are hard terms to reconcile. "Difference" refers to gender, sexuality, race, nationality, or language. "Community" is the collective understanding which must continually be renegotiated and reconstructed among these factors. The Canadian-European connection is one in which it seems especially appropriate to explore such circumstances. The topics covered include pioneer women's writing, transcultural women's fiction, canonical taxonomy of the contemporary novel, the city poem in Confederate Canada, poetry of the Great War, various ethno-cultural perspectives (Jewish, South Asian, Italian; Native reappropriations; Quebec cinema), literature and the media, and small-press publishing. Some of the authors treated: Sandra Birdsell, Nicole Brossard, Jack Hodgins, Henry Kreisel, Robert Kroetsch, Janice Kulyk Keefer, Archibald Lampman, Malcolm Lowry, Lesley Lum, Daphne Marlatt, Susanna Moodie, Bharati Mukherjee, Alice Munro, Frank Paci, and Susan Swan.

USA/Canada: Editions Rodopi B.V., 2015 South Park Place, Atlanta, GA 30339, Tel. (770) 933-0027, *Call toll-free* (U.S. only) 1-800-225- 3998, Fax (770) 933-9644, *E-mail:* F.van.der.Zee@rodopi.nl

All Other Countries: Editions Rodopi B.V., Keizersgracht 302-304, 1016 EX Amsterdam, The Netherlands. Tel. + + 31 (0)20-622-75-07, Fax + + 31 (0)20-638-09-48, *E-mail:* F.van.der.Zee@rodopi.nl

AFRIKAANS LITERATURE RECOLLECTION, REDEFINITION, RESTITUTION

Papers held at the 7th Conference on South African Literature at the Protestant Academy, Bad Boll

Edited by Robert Kriger and Ethel Kriger

Amsterdam/Atlanta, GA 1996. 336 pp.
(Matatu 15-16)

ISBN: 90-420-0053-8   Bound Hfl. 165,-/US-$ 110.50
ISBN: 90-420-0051-1   Paper Hfl. 45,-/US-$ 30.-

Contents: INTRODUCTION. Robert KRIGER: Afrikaans Literature: Recollection, Redefinition, Restitution. ARTICLES. Achmat DAVIDS: Laying the Lie of the "Boer" Language: An Alternative View of the Genesis of Afrikaans. Jean LOMBARD: The Reorientation and Redevelopment of Afrikaans in Namibia. Vernon FEBRUARY: The Many Voices of the Land. Hein WILLEMSE: The Invisible Margins of Afrikaans Literature. Ampie COETZEE: Afrikaans Literature in the Service of Ethnic Politics? Johan van WYK: Afrikaans Poetry and the South African Intertext. Philip van der MERWE: What the Canon Saw: Socio-Political History, Afrikaans Poetry and its "Great Tradition". Marlene van NIEKERK: Afrikaner Woman and Her "Prison": Afrikaner Nationalism and Literature. Etienne van HEERDEN: Answering the Father's Father: Koos Prinsloo's "By die skryf van aantekeninge oor'n reis". Patrick PETERSEN: Publication and Power: Views of the Marginalised. Andries Walter OLIPHANT: COSAW and Publishing for All. MARKETPLACE. Henry CHAKAVA: Publishing Ngugi: The Challenge, the Risk and the Reward. With an Appendix on Useful References on Ngugi's Work. Cristine MATZKE: A Preliminary Checklist of East African Women Writers. CREATIVE WRITING. Louis CHARLES: Friday Night. Louis CHARLES: The Postman. Madeleine LOYSON: Four Poems. Sidwell DESAI: The circus site. Nick HARTEL: For the sake of the cause. Andrina FORBES: Section 29. Mzi MAHOLA: Return to my birthplace. Peter PLÜDDE-MANN: Homecoming (in F). Peter PLÜDDEMANN: One Azania, One Oration. Andries Walter OLIPHANT: Two Love Poems and A Self-Portrait. Andries Walter OLIPHANT: The Splash. A Short Story. Lesego RAMPOLOKENG: Rap 1. Lesego RAMPOLOKENG: dark light, light dark. Interviews. Reviews.

USA/Canada: Editions Rodopi B.V., 2015 South Park Place, Atlanta, GA 30339, Tel. (770) 933-0027, *Call toll-free* (U.S. only) 1-800-225- 3998, Fax (770) 933-9644, *E-mail:* F.van.der.Zee@rodopi.nl

All Other Countries: Editions Rodopi B.V., Keizersgracht 302-304, 1016 EX Amsterdam, The Netherlands. Tel. + + 31 (0)20-622-75-07, Fax + + 31 (0)20-638-09-48, *E-mail:* F.van.der.Zee@rodopi.nl

JANE PLASTOW

African Theatre and Politics
The evolution of theatre in Ethiopia, Tanzania and Zimbabwe
A comparative study

Amsterdam/Atlanta, GA 1996. XIV,286 pp.
(Cross/Cultures 24)

ISBN: 90-420-0042-2   Bound Hfl. 150,-/US-$ 100.-
ISBN: 90-420-0038-4   Paper Hfl. 45,-/US-$ 30.-

This study, the first book-length treatment of its subject, draws on a large base of elusive material and on extensive field research. It is the result of the author's wide experience of teaching and producing theatre in Africa, and of her fascination with the ways in which traditional performance forms have interacted with, or have resisted, non-indigenous modes of dramatic representation in the process of evolving into the vital theatres of the present day. A comparative historical study is offered of the three national cultures of Ethiopia, Tanganyika/Tanzania, and Rhodesia/Zimbabwe. Not only (scripted) drama is treated, but also theatre in the sense of the broader range of performance arts such as dance and song. The development of theatre and drama is seen against the background of centuries of cultural evolution and interaction, from pre-colonial times, through phases of African and European imperialism, to the liberation struggles and newly-won independence of the present. The seminal relationship between theatre, society and politics is thus a central focus. Topics covered include: the function in theatre of vernacular and colonial languages; performance forms under feudal, communalist and socialist régimes; cultural militancy and political critique; the relationship of theatre to social élites and to the peasant class; state control (funding and censorship); racism and "separate development" in the performing arts; contemporary performance structures (amateur, professional, community and university theatre). Due attention is paid to prominent dramatists, theatre groups and theatre directors, and the author offers new insight into African perceptions of the role of the artist in the theatre, as well as dealing with the important subject of gender roles (in drama, in performance ritual, and in theatre practice). The book is illustrated with contemporary photographs.

USA/Canada: Editions Rodopi B.V., 2015 South Park Place, Atlanta, GA 30339, Tel. (770) 933-0027, *Call toll-free* (U.S. only) 1-800-225- 3998, Fax (770) 933-9644, *E-mail:* F.van.der.Zee@rodopi.nl
All Other Countries: Editions Rodopi B.V., Keizersgracht 302-304, 1016 EX Amsterdam, The Netherlands. Tel. + + 31 (0)20-622-75-07, Fax + + 31 (0)20-638-09-48, *E-mail:* F.van.der.Zee@rodopi.nl

NARRATIVE IRONIES

Ed. by Raymond A. Prier and Gerald Gillespie

Amsterdam/Atlanta, GA 1996. 326 pp.
(Textxet 5)

ISBN: 90-5183-918-9   Bound   Hfl. 160,-/US-$ 107.-
ISBN: 90-5183-917-0   Paper   Hfl.   45,-/US-$ 30.-

This volume focuses on the flourishing of irony as a primary characteristic of the great era of European narrative sophistication from the Goethezeit to Modernism. Its eighteenth essays explore varieties of ironic consciousness associated with texts especially of northern Europe, and the ways they established a dialogue with and on literature and culture at large. As the volume shows, this interrogation of Europe's self-awareness of cultural identity bound up in reading and writing habits gained a new post-Cervantine complexity in Romanticism and has been of lasting significance for literary theory down to postmodernism. By its comparativistic framing of the issues raised by ironic consciousness, *Narrative Ironies* duly serves as a Festschrift honoring Lilian R. Furst. Among major writers treated are Sterne, Goethe, Godwin, Schlegel, Hoffmann, Poe, Stendhal, Kierkegaard, Disraeli, Keller, Maupassant, Zola, Huysmans, Wilde, Tolstoi, Hofmannsthal, Strindberg, Proust, Mann, Musil, Kafka, Joyce, Faulkner, and Szczypiorski.

USA/Canada: Editions Rodopi B.V., 2015 South Park Place, Atlanta, GA 30339, Tel. (770) 933-0027, *Call toll-free* (U.S. only) 1-800-225- 3998, Fax (770) 933-9644, *E-mail:* F.van.der.Zee@rodopi.nl

All Other Countries: Editions Rodopi B.V., Keizersgracht 302-304, 1016 EX Amsterdam, The Netherlands. Tel. + + 31 (0)20-622-75-07, Fax + + 31 (0)20-638-09-48, *E-mail:* F.van.der.Zee@rodopi.nl